IMAGINE NO POSSESSIONS

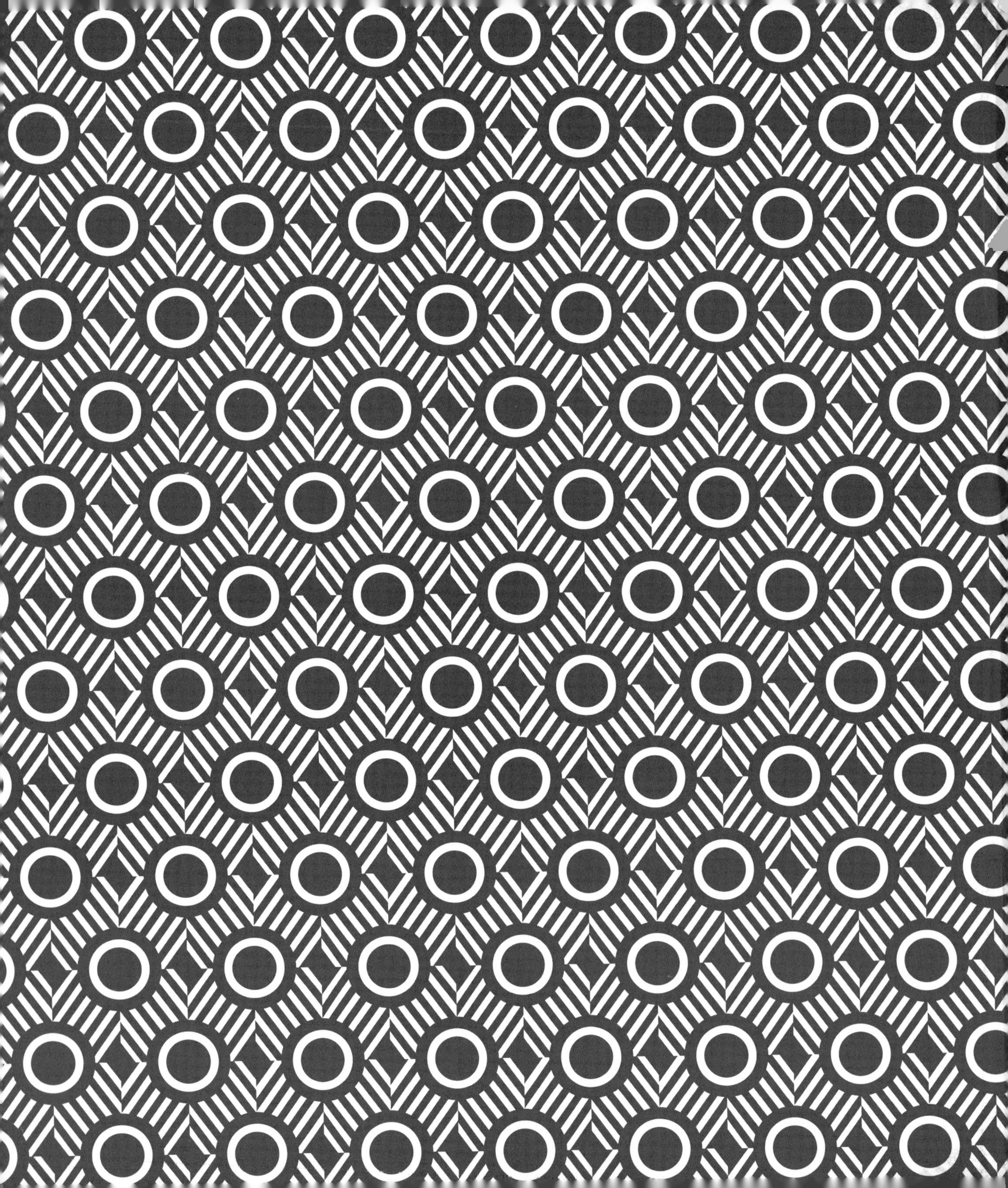

CHRISTINA KIAER

IMAGINE NO POSSESSIONS

THE SOCIALIST OBJECTS OF RUSSIAN CONSTRUCTIVISM

THE MIT PRESS CAMBRIDGE, MASSACHUSETTS LONDON, ENGLAND

MIT Press books may be purchased at special quantity discounts for business or sales promotional use. For information, please email special_sales@mitpress.mit.edu or write to Special Sales Department, The MIT Press, 55 Hayward Street, Cambridge, MA 02142.

This book was set in Adobe Jenson by The MIT Press, and was printed and bound in the United States of America.

Library of Congress Cataloging-in-Publication Data

Kiaer, Christina.
Imagine no possessions : the socialist objects of Russian Constructivism / Christina Kiaer.
p. cm.
Includes bibliographical references and index.
ISBN 0-262-11289-2 (hc : alk. paper)
1. Constructivism (Art)—Russia (Federation). 2. Socialism and art—Russia (Federation). 3. Productivism (Art)—Russia (Federation). 4. Avant-garde (Aesthetics)—Russia (Federation)—History—20th century. 5. INKhUK (Art school). I. Title.

N6988.5.C64K53 2005
709′.47′0904—dc22

2004062533

10 9 8 7 6 5 4 3 2 1

TO THE MEMORY OF MY STEPFATHER, DR. JOSEF VÁŇA

CONTENTS

LIST OF ILLUSTRATIONS

LIST OF COLOR PLATES

ACKNOWLEDGMENTS

I have been fortunate to receive support from a number of institutions for the preparation of this book. Research for the dissertation on which the book builds was supported by an International Research and Exchanges Board (IREX) Individual Advanced Research Grant to the Russian Federation, the American Council of Teachers of Russian (ACTR) Research Scholar Program, the University of California Education Abroad Program Faculty and Young Scholar Exchange to St. Petersburg, and a Humanities Graduate Research Grant from the University of California, Berkeley. The writing of the dissertation was supported by an American Association of University Women Dissertation Fellowship, a Social Science Research Council Dissertation Fellowship, and a Mellon Fellowship in the Humanities. The writing of the book was supported by a J. Paul Getty Postdoctoral Fellowship in the History of Art and the Humanities. My home institution during the writing of this book, Columbia University, has generously provided financial help toward the production of illustrations, in the form of three Publications Grants awarded by The Harriman Institute, and a Council Grant awarded by the Faculty Development Committee. I want to express my thanks to all of these institutions for making this project possible.

It began as a doctoral dissertation at the University of California, Berkeley, under the guidance of an inspiring and exceptionally generous and dedicated committee: my advisor, T. J. Clark, and Anne Wagner in art history and the late Reginald Zelnik in Russian history. Reggie's intellectual generosity was legendary, and I add my voice to that of generations of his students to say that he is much missed. The participants in the art history departmental Mellon dissertation colloquium offered valuable comments on the chapter they read and created a rigorous and collegial atmosphere. I especially want to thank the members of our informal dissertation group, Sarah Fraser, Robin Greeley, and Amy Lyford, as well as my graduate teaching partner Jennifer Shaw, for their close readings of chapters and their friendship and support. During the time I spent in Russia doing dissertation research, Nataliia Borisovna Lebina provided good sense and much wisdom about Soviet history and culture, as well as the warmth of her friendship and a family away from home. My many conversations in Moscow with Maria Gough about Constructivism and Russian culture were inspiring and sustaining; key moments in this book have emerged from them. (Her book *The Artist as Producer: Russian Constructivism in Revolution* [University of California Press, 2005] appeared as this book was going to press, so I was unfortunately unable to draw on it.) Leah Dickerman was also particularly generous in sharing sources and insights with me. My dialogue in Moscow with Susan Buck-Morss about the socialist economy of desire and the socialist object transformed the direction of my project, and she has been a source of intellectual inspiration, as well as friendship and support, ever since that winter of 1993.

I want to thank the people and institutions who have given me an opportunity to present parts of this book as public talks over the years: Janet Wolff, Michael Leja, Leila Kinney, and Nancy Troy at sessions of annual meetings of the College Art Association; Alan Birnholz at the State University of New York at Buffalo; Susan Buck-Morss at Cornell University; Leah Dickerman at symposia organized at Columbia and Harvard Universities; Richard Meyer at the University of Southern California; Alla Efimova at a session of the annual meeting of the American Association for the Advancement of Slavic Studies; the graduate student lecture series at the City University of New York Graduate Center; Steve Kotkin and Hal Foster at Princeton University; George Baker and the Réclame project; the "In the House" lecture series at the Institute for Research on Women and Gender, Columbia University; the Modernist Colloquium at the Department of Art History, Yale University; the organizers of the symposium New Work on the Russian Avant-Garde at the University of California, Berkeley; Maria Gough at the Clark Art Institute; and, most recently, Greta Slobin at Wesleyan College.

Aleksandr Lavrent'ev, grandson of Aleksandr Rodchenko and Varvara Stepanova and director of the Rodchenko–Stepanova Archive, has been extraordinarily generous and helpful over the years; I thank him especially for his assistance in providing illustrations. Svetlana Artamonova, head of the Department of Graphics at the Russian State Library, is a consummate professional; it has been a pleasure working with her. The staff of the State Mayakovsky Museum has been very helpful to me, and I am especially grateful for the unusual permission granted me to publish for the first time the Mayakovsky drawings that appear in chapter 4. The late Vasilii Katanian invited me to tea in his art-filled apartment and shared his knowledge of the avant-garde with me, and also gave me books that proved invaluable to my research. Dmitrii Sarabianov shared his vast knowledge and amazing art collection with me. In the United States, Howard Schickler and Merrill Berman have both been helpful in securing illustrations, and I would also like to thank Randi Cox for her help with the images.

A book that has taken as long as this one to bring out has racked up a giant debt of gratitude to many people. No fewer than six able research assistants have contributed to its final form: Janet Cavallero, Molly Brunson, Robyn Murgio, Bethany Pappalardo, Kevin Lotery, and Masha Chlenova. Bethany especially worked with me for the final two and a half years of its main production, and she was heroic in every way. I would like to thank my colleagues in the Department of Art History and Archaeology at Columbia University for their support over the years, especially Rosalind Krauss, Benjamin Buchloh, and Hilary Ballon. Early on, I benefited from participating in a writing group of junior faculty women organized by the Institute for Research on Women and Gender at Columbia University; I thank Rachel Adams, Sandhya Shukla, Kristina Milnor, and Julie Crawford for their critical responses. I learned a lot from the students in three graduate seminars on various aspects of the Russian avant-garde that I taught at Columbia between 1997 and 2003. I would also like to thank the students in the seminar I taught at the University of California, Berkeley, in spring 2000; their comments helped, in particular, to shape chapter 3.

Anonymous reader reports for two different presses—both positive and less so—helped to make this a better book. I am especially grateful to an anonymous reader for MIT Press who wrote a detailed and generous ten-page critique, replete with bibliographic references: whoever you are, I thank you for taking that sometimes onerous academic responsibility so seriously. I thank my acquiring editor, Roger Conover, for encouraging me to write the book I wanted to write, and for having the patience to let me do it. Also at MIT Press, I wish to thank Judy Feldmann for her keen and meticulous editing of the manuscript, Lisa Reeve for guiding the project through all but the final stage, and Derek George for contributing his brilliant design skills to this book and making the design process so satisfying.

For their responses to various parts of this project, I am indebted to Evgenii Bershtein, Hal Foster, Andrew Hemingway, Steve Kotkin, Rosalind Krauss, Christina Lodder, Annette Michelson, Nadia Michoustina, Peter Nisbet, Greta Slobin, Margarita Tupitsyn, and Chris Wood. Eric Naiman has been not only a critical reader but also an excellent collaborator and a fount of Slavic knowledge since the inception of this project. Alan Birnholz provided encouragement and a bibliographic windfall.

I am happy to have this opportunity to thank T. J. Clark and Anne Wagner for the sustaining friendship as well as hard criticism that they have offered over the years; this project is deeply indebted to their intellectual example. Darcy Grimaldo Grigsby has been a source of warm friendship and professional support as well as, most recently, an astute reader. Robert Gamboa was an imaginative, exacting, and dissatisfied reader; more than anyone else, he left his mark on this book. For that I will always be indebted to him. Richard Meyer has been a constant source of unselfish scholarly criticism, intellectual energy, professional collaboration, close friendship, and fun since long before this project was even conceived.

I want to thank all the friends far from art history who have sustained me in various ways during the long duration of this project, in San Francisco, Moscow, St. Petersburg, Copenhagen, and New York; in particular, Sarah Chester, Amy Greenstadt, Mette Strømfeldt, and Ksenia Voronova have been steadfast in their friendship, and I count myself lucky for it. Closest to home, Whitney Chadwick and Bob Bechtle extended their kindness and interest as well as the inspiring setting where much of the writing of this book took place. Midwife extraordinaire Deborah Simone helped me to integrate the different pieces of my life. My father, Torben Kiær, has always encouraged my interest in art history, despite his hopes that I would go to business school. My stepfather, Dr. Josef Váňa, was the impetus for my decision to learn Russian in high school, because I wanted to be able to talk with his family when we visited Czechoslovakia, and he was the original inspiration for my interest in Marxism. For years I had looked forward to presenting him with a copy of this book, but his death has now made that impossible. I dedicate it to his memory. My mother, Joyce Váňa, has been invariably loving, supportive and enthusiastic. She has been my Rock of Gibraltar—as she would put it—as well as an eagle-eyed proofreader and an intellectual model; she began her doctoral studies the year I started college, and received her Ph.D. four years before I did. I am happiest of all to be able to thank George Kresak, for his forbearance, and for being who he is and being in my life for so many years; he contributed intellectually to this book project at every stage, but he also enchanted my life while I was writing it. And finally, I want to thank our daughter Zora Kresak-Kiaer for delaying the completion of this book with her radiant arrival.

Portions of chapters 2 and 3 appeared, in significantly different form, as "Les objets quotidiens du constructivisme russe," translated by Jacques Mailhos, in *Les Cahiers du Musée national d'art moderne* 64 (summer 1998). A slightly different version of chapter 3 was published as "The Russian Constructivist Flapper Dress" in *Critical Inquiry* 28, no. 1 (fall 2001). A shorter, somewhat different form of chapter 5 was published under the same title in *October* 75 (winter 1996).

Note on Russian transliteration: this book uses the transliteration system of the Library of Congress, with the exception of well-known proper names such as Trotsky and Mayakovsky that are already familiar in their nontransliterated spellings.

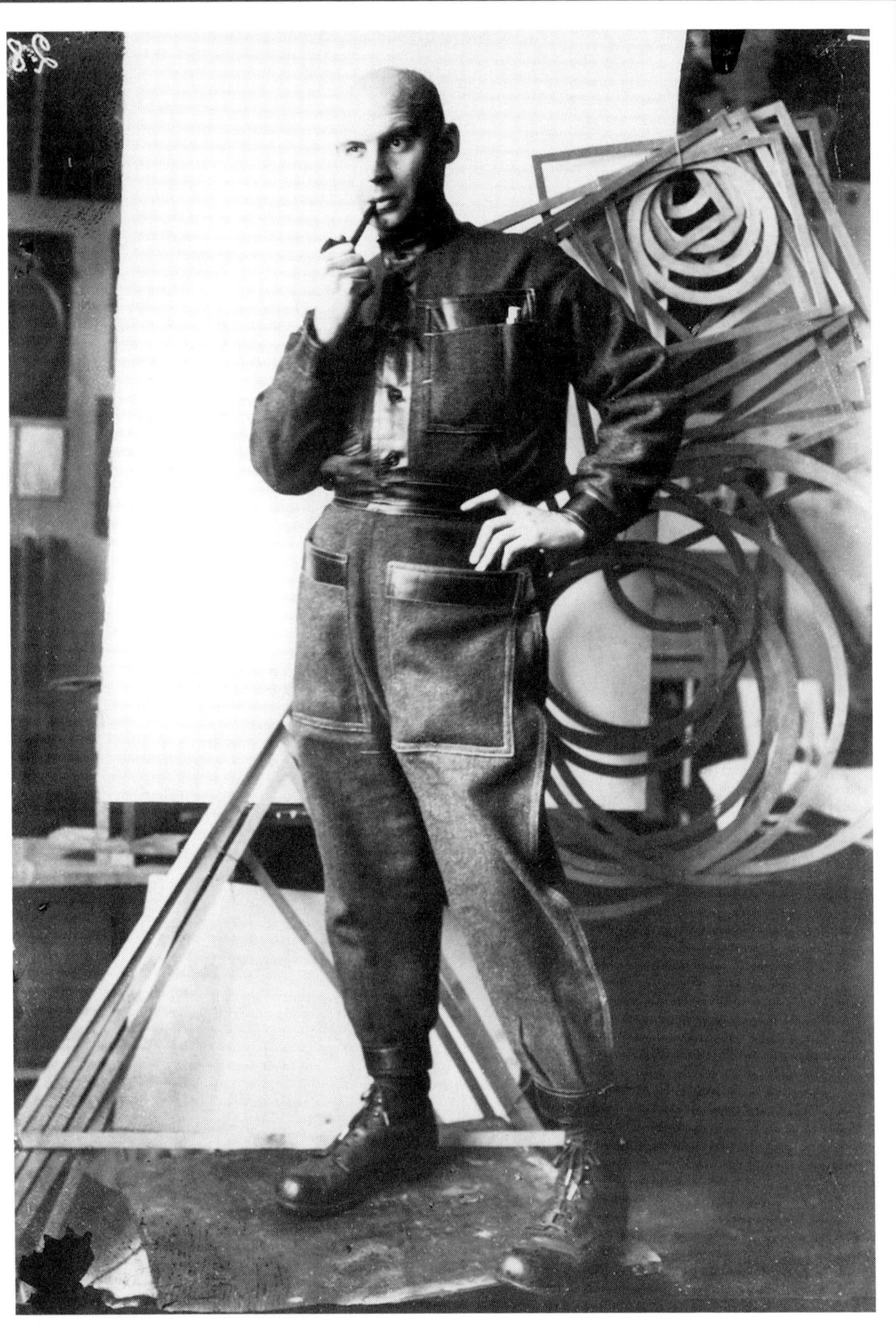

FIGURE I.1
Mikhail Kaufman, photo of Aleksandr Rodchenko, 1922.

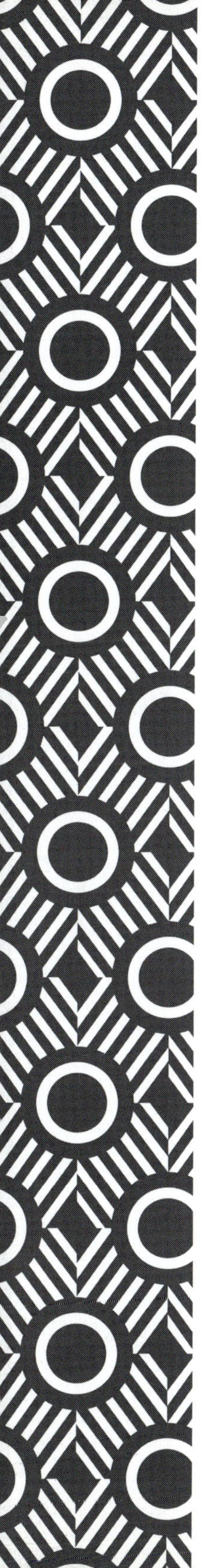

CHAPTER 1

THE SOCIALIST OBJECT

Imagine no possessions
I wonder if you can...
—John Lennon, "Imagine," 1971

"The light from the East is not only the liberation of workers," writes the Russian Constructivist Aleksandr Rodchenko in a letter home from Paris in the spring of 1925, "the light from the East is in the new relation to the person, to woman, to things. Our things in our hands must be equals, comrades, and not these black and mournful slaves, as they are here."[1] In these evocative lines, Rodchenko names a new kind of emotionally affective object: the comradely object of socialist modernity. Unlike the commodities he encounters on his visit to capitalist Paris, which elicit a possessive relation that makes the objects into "slaves," things made in the socialist East will actively promote egalitarian socialist culture. They will replace the pleasure of commodity possession, not with its presumed Communist opposite of material renunciation, but with something far more peculiar and psychologically powerful: the material object as an active, almost animate participant in social life. This book investigates this concept of the "socialist object" as Russian Constructivism's original contribution not only to the history of the political avant-garde art movements of the twentieth century, but also to the theory of a noncapitalist form of modernity. The socialist object addresses a fundamental problem in Marxist thought: what happens to the individual fantasies and desires organized under capitalism by the commodity fetish and the market after the revolution? Capitalism, in its honing of the commodity form that endlessly organizes and gives form to these desires, has a profound weapon that socialism cannot simply cede to it. The Constructivist counterproposal to this weapon is the object-as-comrade.

Rodchenko's "things in our hands" are specifically utilitarian things. A member of the original group of Constructivists to emerge from the debates on "construction" in postrevolutionary art at the Moscow Institute of Artistic Culture (INKhUK), he was a signatory of the first Constructivist program of March 1921. This program called for artists to abandon the nonobjective (*bezpredmetnyi*) paintings and sculptural experiments that the Russian avant-garde had pioneered in the preceding decade, and to enter instead into Soviet industrial production, where they would use their artistic expertise in form and material to produce useful objects for the new socialist collective.[2] The famous photograph of Rodchenko posing for the camera in his heavy work-boots and self-designed "production clothing" (*prozodezhda*) has become an iconic image of this Constructivist turn toward production (figure 1.1).

The mass production of technologically advanced utilitarian objects as the most appropriate form of Constructivist artistic activity was promoted by the so-called Productivist theorists of the INKhUK in the years immediately following the first Constructivist declarations. Not all INKhUK artists were equally enamored of this Productivist utilitarian imperative, and even those who contributed to its formulation and elaboration found its practical implementation difficult: how exactly could an artist enter industrial production as an "artist-engineer," as demanded by the Productivist theorists, rather than as a traditional applied artist? This book examines some of the relatively few examples of objects that implemented the utilitarian Constructivist program, all stemming from the brief, most intense period of Productivist activity of 1923 to 1925: Vladimir Tatlin's prototype designs for everyday objects such as pots, pans, overcoats, and stoves (chapter 2); Liubov' Popova's and Varvara Stepanova's fashion designs and mass-produced textiles (chapter 3); Rodchenko's packaging and advertisements for Soviet state-owned businesses, made in collaboration with the revolutionary poet Vladimir Mayakovsky (figure 1.2; chapter 4); and Rodchenko's most famous Constructivist object, the design for the interior of a workers' club that he displayed in Paris in 1925 (chapter 5). Investigating the motivations and specific historical contexts of these artists as they developed their utilitarian practices demonstrates how they elaborated the Productivist theory of the socialist object-as-comrade in practice, developing it to its greatest social and psychological potential.

In our imaginations the Russian avant-garde seems always to exist in a context of revolutionary upheaval and radical collectivism, but the main years of Constructivist activity coincided with the relatively peaceful and semicapitalist period in Soviet history known as the New Economic Policy, or NEP (1921–c. 1928).[3] The Constructivists were therefore attempting to develop the comradely object of socialist modernity in an economic context that was not yet noncapitalist,

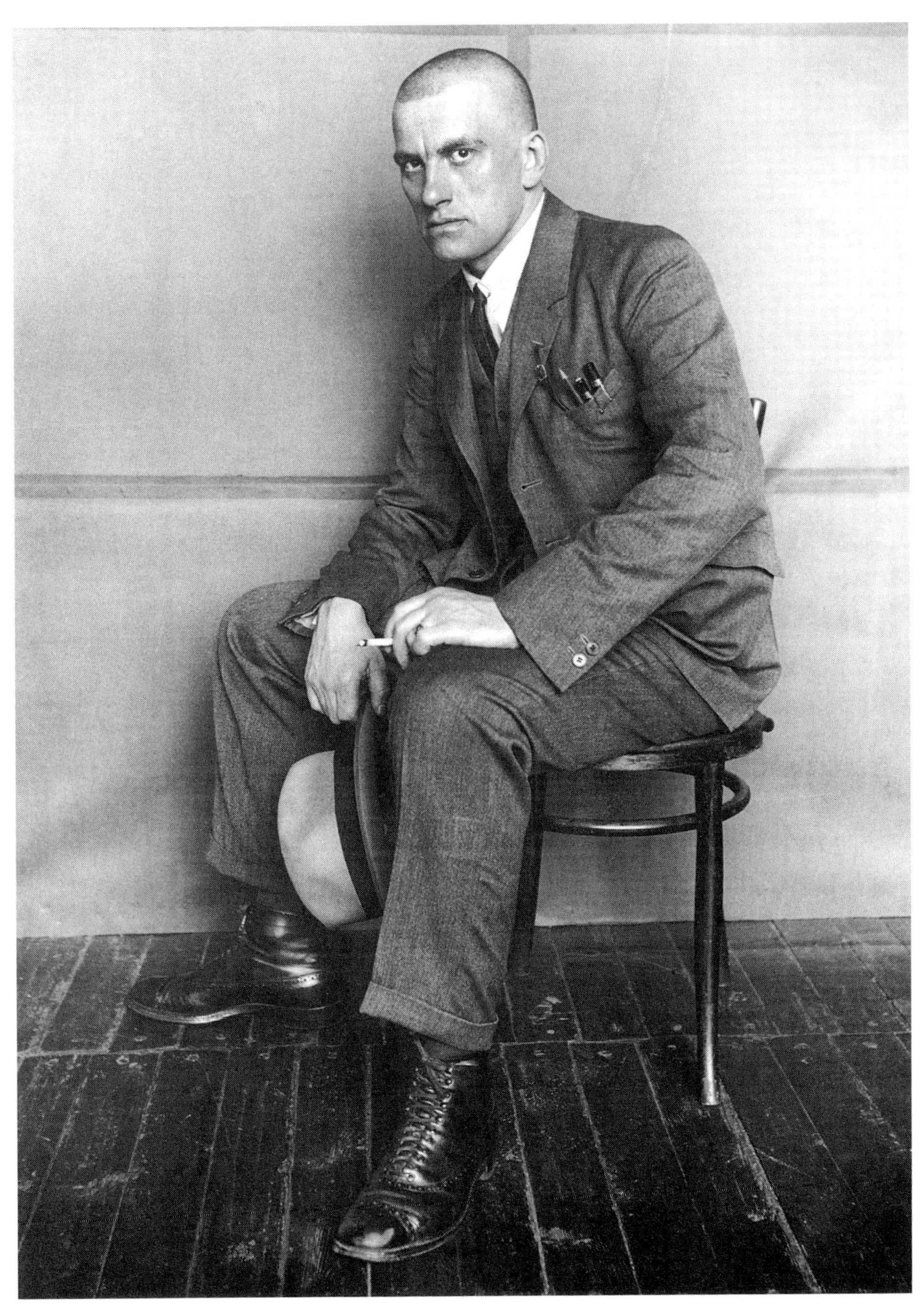

FIGURE I.2
Aleksandr Rodchenko, photo of Vladimir Mayakovsky, 1924. Howard Schickler Fine Art.

let alone socialist. Nor was NEP Russia fully modern; the Russian economy was still predominantly agricultural, and the devastations of World War I, the Bolshevik revolution of 1917, and the civil war (1918–1921) had largely decimated what little modern industry had existed before 1914. Outside the major urban centers—and even to a great extent within them—the everyday life in which utilitarian Constructivist objects would potentially be used was primitive compared with the industrialized commodity economy of Western modernity. The socialist object as it was developed in the early 1920s was therefore of necessity a transitional one, anticipating a future socialist culture that had not yet arrived. Understanding the Constructivist socialist objects as transitional objects helps to explain their often quirky visual forms in comparison both with the earlier artistic achievements of their authors and with the technological ambitions of Productivist engineerism. Demonstrating the self-consciously transitional nature of these objects will also complicate the various historical accounts that have judged these objects as falling short of Constructivist art-into-life ambitions.

The foundational text on the avant-garde strategy of art-into-life, Peter Bürger's *Theory of the Avant-Garde* of 1974, provides a model for understanding the significance, within the history of artistic modernism, of the Constructivist transition from making autonomous art objects to participating in a form of revolutionary mass culture.[4] Bürger distinguishes between the avant-garde as it has typically been defined since the later nineteenth century—a group of artists who critique the conventions of bourgeois art in the form and content of their works—and what he calls the "historical avant-gardes" of the early twentieth century, whose works aim to break down the very institution of bourgeois art—the academy, the museum, the gallery, the dealer, but also the concept of the expressive artist and the organic work of art itself. He distinguishes, in effect, between a more generalized modernism, in which self-reflexive artistic strategies become the means to critique the social forms of modernity, and the more specific examples of artistic groups that self-consciously attempt to use their modernist practices to intervene into social life directly. Bürger names Dada, Surrealism, and Russian Constructivism as the "historical avant-gardes" of the early twentieth century that challenged not only the formal conventions but the institutional structures upholding the autonomy of art in bourgeois society, in an attempt to "reintegrate art into the life process" and so to regain a social use value for art.[5] Bürger's text only alludes to the example of Russian Constructivism, however, because it departed from the formal practices that most interest him—montage, fragmentation, estrangement, the nonorganic work, allegory—precisely at the moment that it could be understood to have become most fully "historical" by radically contesting the institutions of bourgeois art.[6]

Despite their origins in modernist formal experimentation, Constructivist art-into-life objects such as furniture, utensils, fabric, clothing, and advertisements, in their proximity to the commodity, are closer to mass culture than to art. Constructivism broke with the traditional model of the autonomous avant-garde not in order to establish a more effective space for art to resist the dominant institutions of society, but, on the contrary, in order to participate more fully in the political project of the Bolshevik state, including its commodity economy, mass culture, and propaganda. Bürger, however, always sees "popular literature and commodity aesthetics as forms of a false sublation of art as institution." If art enters into life as a form of mass culture, "art becomes practical but it is an art that enthralls"—enthralls and subjugates rather than emancipates.[7] Yet the Bolshevik state was at least nominally committed to instituting a socialist economy in which workers would no longer be exploited and the products of industry would no longer be exchanged as commodities for profit. The Constructivist choice to close the distance between art and life, therefore, could have led to the more radical possibility that Bürger calls the "sublation of autonomous art."[8]

But Bürger does not explore this possibility of a different, emancipatory role for mass culture; he stays firmly allied with the Frankfurt School's modernist critique of it. He concludes this passage on sublation by wondering whether "the distance between art and the praxis of life is not requisite for that free space within which alternatives to what exists become conceivable." In a footnote, however, he muses that "one would have to investigate to what extent, after the October revolution, the Russian avant-gardistes succeeded to a degree, because social conditions had changed, in realizing their intent to reintegrate art into the praxis of life."[9] This book follows the line of investigation suggested by Bürger by analyzing Constructivism's attempt to develop its modernist forms to forge a conscious and socialist—rather than enthralling—relation between human subjects and the mass-produced objects of modernity.

In our post-Soviet world of global consumer culture, older leftist models of asceticism and material renunciation have lost critical force. John Lennon's song "Imagine" from 1971, with its vaguely Communist injunction to "imagine no possessions," has become a fixture of the pop-cultural landscape, a symbol of hippie-dippy, feel-good 1960s sentiment rather than a political rallying cry. But Lennon was actively involved in the New Left movement, and his song caught the spirit of what Herbert Marcuse, the movement's patron philosopher, called

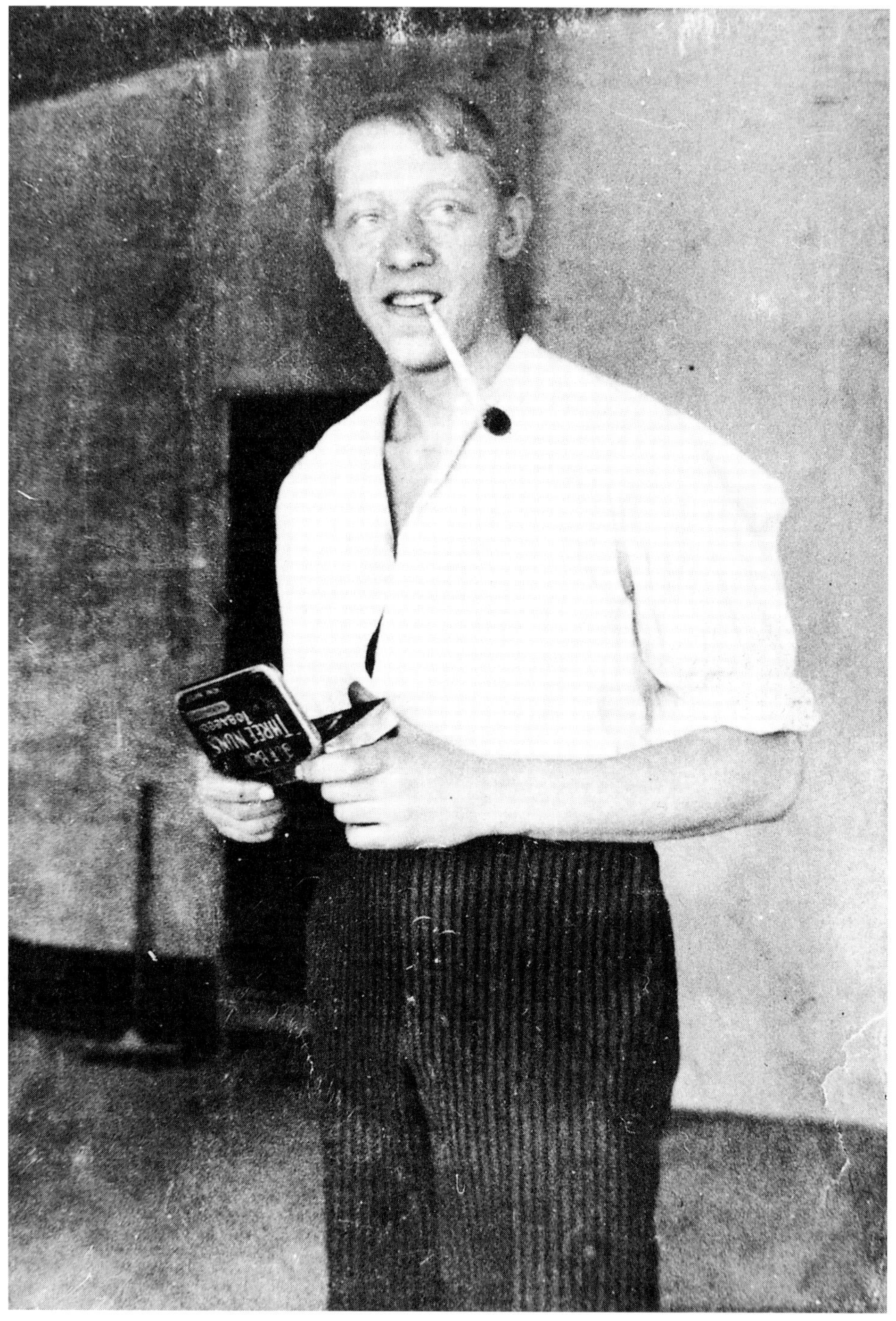

FIGURE 1.3
Aleksandr Rodchenko, photo of Vladimir Tatlin, c. 1917. Private collection.

"the utopian imagination"—even if 1971 was a year of deflation and regrouping for the movement.[10] The Constructivist effort, fifty years earlier, to imagine a world without possessions was far less utopian: in revolutionary Russia the concept of "no possessions" was alarmingly real. (The poet Andrei Belyi famously noted that "the victory of materialism in Russia resulted in the complete disappearance of all matter.")[11] By 1921, state expropriation combined with the famine and upheaval of the civil war had eliminated most prerevolutionary private property, from large estates to pairs of boots. But there was a less literal way in which the Constructivists imagined no possessions: their emphasis was not on the elimination of material objects, but on the elimination of a possessive relation to them. The socialist object of Russian Constructivism offers an alternative model of how commodity desire can become comprehensible to us, and available for social transformation, as we try to imagine a response to our own overloaded object world at the beginning of the twenty-first century.

The Artistic Origins of the Constructivist Object: The INKhUK Debates, 1920–1922

The appropriate form of the postrevolutionary art object was debated in the vigorous discussions that took place at the Moscow Institute of Artistic Culture (INKhUK) in 1920–1922. Although the utilitarian, industrial object would emerge as the dominant model within the INKhUK by the fall of 1921, competing definitions of the art object continued to flourish among avant-garde artists; the Constructivist "socialist object," as defined in this study, would turn out to be one, limited model among many art practices of the early 1920s. Its relation to the modernist practices that preceded it and the specificity of its utilitarian imperative were hammered out in the INKhUK debates, even if its final form would only emerge in practice.

The INKhUK was organized in Moscow in March 1920 by the painter Wassily Kandinsky. It consisted of painters, sculptors, architects, poets, and composers, as well as critics and art historians, who had participated in, or were heir to, prerevolutionary avant-garde movements like the broadly defined Futurism, Kazimir Malevich's Suprematism, the sculptural "culture of materials" invented by Vladimir Tatlin (figure 1.3), and Kandinsky's own spiritual form of painterly abstraction. The INKhUK was an unprecedented institution: a state-sponsored art institute that was set up for the sole purpose of conducting research on the very building blocks of art-making, or, in other words, on artistic modernism itself, in its most standard definition.[12] The INKhUK's brief was to establish "the objective criteria of artistic value in so far as this is defined as a professional value"; the criteria to be investigated were material, facture (*faktura*), color, space, time, form, and technique (*tekhnika*).[13] Kandinsky described his ambitious research program as a "science" for investigating the analytic and synthetic elements of the separate arts, as well as of art as a whole; his program specified that the research should include the effects of art on the psyche, naming in particular the well-known psychological effects of different colors, as well as the spiritual effects of art.[14]

Inspired by the antisubjective materialism of Tatlin's sculptural constructions, as well as by his outspoken stance against individualism and personal taste in art, a number of INKhUK members came to consider Kandinsky's psychological approach to art to be "subjective," and aimed instead to develop an "objective method" for analyzing artworks. Grouped around Rodchenko—Tatlin was at that time based in Petrograd—in November of 1920 they formed the "Working Group for Objective Analysis" (*Rabochaia gruppa ob"ektivnogo analiza*).[15] The main theme of this group would be the analysis of the distinction between the methods of "composition" and "construction" in making works of art. The group followed Kandinsky's research model of holding meetings to analyze particular works of art, even though the new "objective" approach of these discussions resulted in Kandinsky's precipitous departure from the INKhUK already in January 1921. "Construction" rather than "composition" soon emerged as the primary problem to be worked through, with distinctions proposed between construction as a more technical term related to engineering, and construction as an artistic term designating the process of organizing the elements of a given artwork.

Rodchenko immediately disagreed with this distinction between engineering and art, announcing that "there is only one kind of construction, and construction is primarily a goal [*tsel'*]. Composition is tasteful selection, and not a goal." Elaborating on this problem of construction as the goal or purpose of art, he added that "only naked construction is contemporary expediency [*tselesoobraznost'*]" (*INKhUK*, p. 39). *Tselesoobraznost'*, a key term in these debates, can be translated as "expediency" or more literally as "formed in relation to a goal," from *tsel'*, meaning goal or purpose, and *obraz*, meaning form or shape.[16] It was the nature of the "goal" of the expedient (*tselesoobraznyi*) form that would become the major point of contention in these debates.

Rodchenko soon made clear his position that the only appropriate goal of art was utility; he noted that his own nonobjective paintings did not contain pure construction, only "constructive composition," and that "true construction is utilitarian necessity" (*INKhUK*, p. 42). At a later meeting, his fellow artist and life partner Varvara Stepanova (figure 1.4) would state even more bluntly that "true

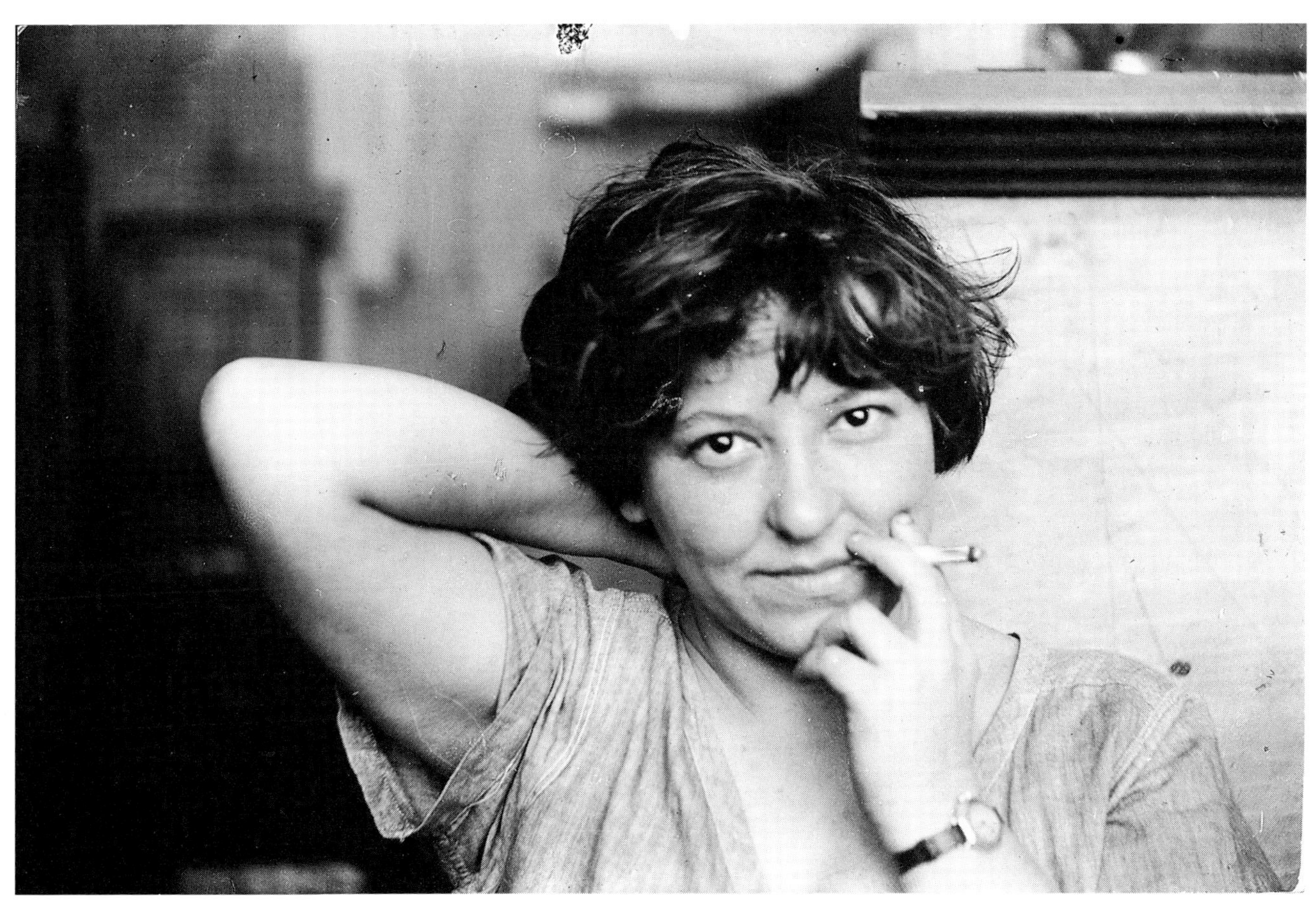

FIGURE 1.4
Aleksandr Rodchenko, photo of Varvara Stepanova with a cigarette, 1924. Private collection.

construction cannot exist in painting . . . true construction appears only in real things, operating in real space" (*INKhUK*, p. 66). For most members of the Working Group for Objective Analysis, however, the goal of construction could be the optimal organization of a painting, sculpture, or other work of art. As the artists Liubov' Popova and Varvara Bubnova put it, construction is "purpose and necessity, the expediency of organization," and could be used toward "aesthetic goals" (*INKhUK*, pp. 40–41). The sculptor Aleksei Babichev differentiated between "mechanical necessity" and "plastic necessity," and warned against collapsing the technical with the artistic in the analysis of works of art (*INKhUK*, p. 43). The rift between members advocating construction as an artistic term, and those who believed that true construction could exist only in utilitarian things, came to a head in March–April 1921 when the former joined together into the Working Group of Objectivists and the latter formed the Working Group of Constructivists.[17]

The main initiators of the Working Group of Constructivists—Rodchenko, Stepanova, and Aleksei Gan, a theorist and organizer of mass revolutionary actions—had held informal meetings since December of 1920, but the group was officially announced on March 18, 1921, and by then included the sculptor Karl Ioganson and three younger art students—Konstantin Medunetskii and the brothers Vladimir and Georgii Stenberg—who were known as the OBMOKhU (Society of Young Artists) group within Constructivism. The group's program, written by Gan, articulated not only the practical or utilitarian direction of its conception of "construction," which Rodchenko and Stepanova had already been advocating in the context of the INKhUK debates, but also a newly explicit political understanding of the term. The well-known opening salvo of the program set the Constructivist task as "the Communistic expression of material structures" and confirmed "the necessity of synthesizing the ideological part with the formal part for the real transference of laboratory work onto the rails of practical activity."[18] Point one of the program identified "scientific Communism" as the ideology in question. The program declared an "uncompromising war against art" and allied artists with industrial production by redefining their activity as "intellectual production" (*INKhUK*, p. 96). The jargon of Soviet Marxism was likely introduced into the Constructivist program by Gan, an experienced agitational writer, but there is no reason to doubt that the program's political goal of cooperating with organs of Soviet power to "create Communist culture" (*INKhUK*, p. 96) was shared by the entire Constructivist group.[19] The romance that attached to the dream of a technologically advanced industrial culture in the early Soviet years gave a particular, urgent coloring to the term "construction," removing it from the more conventionally plastic or artistic meaning of the term that had been emphasized in the discussions of the Group for Objective Analysis.

Despite the artists' enthusiasm for the practical and political aspects of the Constructivist program, they were frustrated by its conspicuous vagueness about the actual nature of artistic work under Constructivism. In the meetings of the Constructivist group that spring, the artists kept trying to turn discussion to the status of their own current experimental works in relation to the newly articulated industrial goals, but ended up spending most of their time discussing Gan's idiosyncratic use of the terms tectonics (*tektonika*), construction (*konstruktsiia*), and facture (*faktura*), which he had defined as the three main elements of the Constructivist program.[20] Several members protested the abstract term "tectonics," which Gan had borrowed from geology and used as a synonym for "the organicity that comes from internal essence" (*INKhUK*, p. 100). In one meeting Rodchenko complained that "there is a lot of talk about geology and other things, but almost nothing is said about the object itself"; Ioganson objected that the concept had "nothing to offer practically"; and Stepanova noted that Gan's ideas were almost entirely based on philosophy, and that it would he helpful if he knew a little more about contemporary art (*INKhUK*, pp. 102–103).

At this time, Rodchenko, Ioganson, Medunetskii, and the Stenberg brothers were all making radical nonobjective constructions that they understood as researches into technological forms in real space; Rodchenko's systematic *Spatial Constructions* series, for example, is visible in collapsed form surrounding him in the photograph in which he models his *prozodezhda* (see figure 1.1). In the view of the artists, their constructions seemed to contribute to the newly defined idea of Constructivism because they resulted from the processing of materials rather than the mysticism of artistic inspiration. Speaking about these works, which were about to be publicly displayed for the first time at the Second Spring Exhibition of the OBMOKhU in Moscow at the end of May, Rodchenko said with some exasperation at a meeting on May 4, "What's important to us is not throwing words around philosophically, but clarifying how our art fits into the program" (*INKhUK*, p. 106). There was only one more meeting of the Working Group of Constructivists that spring, and the question of the status of experimental constructions like those in the OBMOKhU exhibit, or of how to make the transition from experimental works to practical work in industrial production, never did get clarified.

In contrast with the Constructivists, the other major splinter group formed that spring, the Working Group of Objectivists, was formed exclusively by artists—

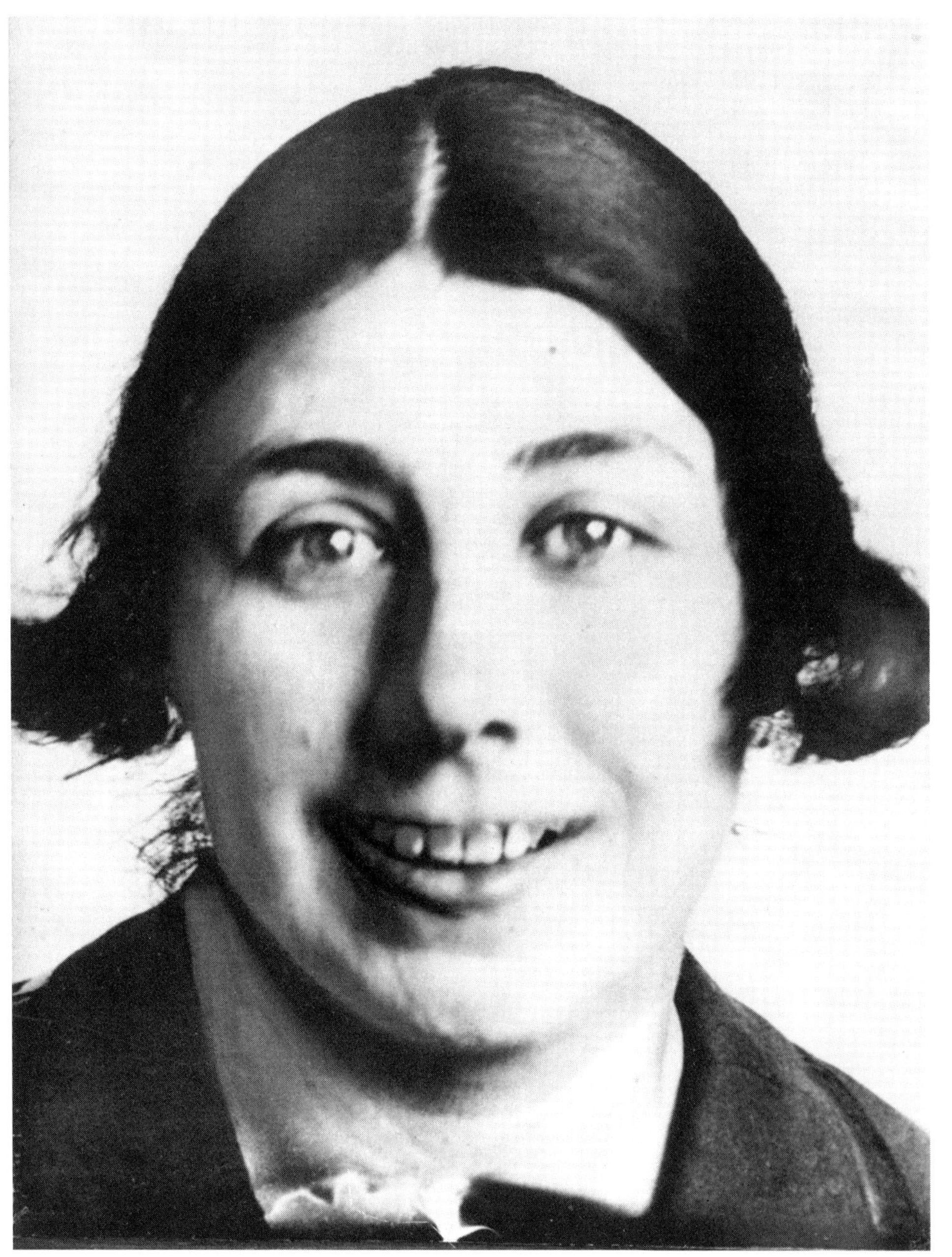

FIGURE 1.5
Aleksandr Rodchenko, photo of Liubov' Popova, 1924.

Liubov' Popova (figure 1.5), Nadezhda Udaltsova, and Aleksandr Drevin—and upheld the idea that a constructive approach to the object did not necessarily entail a rejection of painting. In the view of art historian Selim Khan-Magomedov, the Objectivists were less willing than the Constructivists to relinquish their professional identity and experience as accomplished professional artists (*INKhUK*, pp. 73–74). The Objectivist program called for the "creation of material and concrete structures in space and on the plane," signaling their continuing interest in the picture plane and their difference from the Constructivist insistence on the creation of utilitarian objects in real space.[21] The term "objectivism" (*obzhektivizm*), though related to the term "objective" (*ob"ektivnyi*) from the title of the Working Group for Objective Analysis, was here more closely related to the foreign cognate word *ob"ekt* or *obzhekt*, meaning "object," often used as a synonym for the Russian word *veshch'*, meaning object or thing. The group's goal, like that of the Constructivists, was the creation of a new kind of object, but their conception of this object might be described as more traditionally modernist: "Objectivism [*obzhektivizm*]—from the word object [*veshch'*]—materiality [*veshchestvennost'*]—derives from the negation of the representational, figurative, illustrative, etc. world . . . and proclaims the organization of the concrete properties of its elements into a new material organism."[22] This newly organized material organism could be a painting or a practical, technical object.

A complete hiatus in INKhUK activity over the summer of 1921 was followed, in the fall of that year, by a dramatic shift in the institute's theoretical direction. The various working groups were disbanded, and the leadership of the institute passed to the so-called Productivist theorists—critics and writers who were for the most part more politically educated in Marxism than the artists, such as Osip Brik, Boris Arvatov, Nikolai Tarabukin, and Boris Kushner. Brik replaced Rodchenko as the head of the presidium, and the institute now focused its efforts on developing the theory and practice of Productivism.[23] The Productivists built on the anti-art, proindustrial, and utilitarian imperatives of the Constructivist group, but emphasized more strongly that the only path open to the artist was to abandon form-creation (*formoobrazovanie*) as an autonomous activity and instead participate directly in mass industrial production.[24] The Productivist theorists regarded both the Objectivists' continued interest in painting, and the research into technological forms in real space carried out by the Constructivists in their various sculptural constructions, as useful but already completed phases in the development of Productivism (*INKhUK*, p. 88). Khan-Magomedov emphasizes the violence of this Productivist take-over of INKhUK, which tended to denigrate the artistic experimentation of the artist members in favor of a vaguely formulated engineerism, and which led to a historical perception of artists as passive forces in the development of Productivism in comparison with the active role of the theorists.[25]

There is ample evidence of artists' frustration with the pronouncements of the Productivist theorists to support Khan-Magomedov's contention. At an INKhUK meeting in December 1921, for example, the chairman of the discussion, Boris Arvatov, stated three times in the course of the debate that the most suitable course of action for the artist today was to enter a polytechnical institute in order to learn enough to be useful in industry.[26] The artist Bubnova protested Arvatov's proposal because it demanded "self-denial" on the part of artists and gave "the impression that we have forgotten that people have an organ called the eyes."[27] Stepanova countered Arvatov by stating that there was no need to fear that the artist knew so little about industry that he needed to start over by going to polytechnical school: already "the artist can enter industry and can provide methods of strengthening it in the area of form."[28]

At a later INKhUK discussion in April 1922, Rodchenko similarly suggested that the artist already had something to offer industry precisely by virtue of his artistic skills: "the artist, as we picture him, is different from the mere engineer who makes a given object. The engineer will perhaps . . . carry out a whole series of experiments, but as far as observation and the capacity to see are concerned we are different from him. The difference lies in just this fact that *we know how to see*."[29] Rodchenko was protesting the incompleteness of the theory of production art, which did not adequately address how the particular aesthetic skills of the artist could be put to use. For example, Brik stated that the artist should not sit in his studio and dream up new forms, but instead should develop new "principles" for production, while Boris Kushner emphasized the anachronism of the artist's individual and private relation to the art object, advocating that the artist should enter the factory not within the traditional craft areas of production, but as an advisor in the "technical office."[30] These abstract pronouncements about entering polytechnical institutes, working with "principles" rather than materials, and sitting in offices had the unfortunate effect of seeming to limit the significance and scope of artistic activity in the creation of new kinds of advanced technological objects.

This Moscow conflict between a dogmatic Productivist theory of industrial utility and the more open-ended, experimental approach of artists was introduced to the international avant-garde in the journal *Veshch'/Gegenstand/Objet* in Berlin in early 1922. Organized by the artist El Lissitzky (figure 1.6), a member of INKhUK

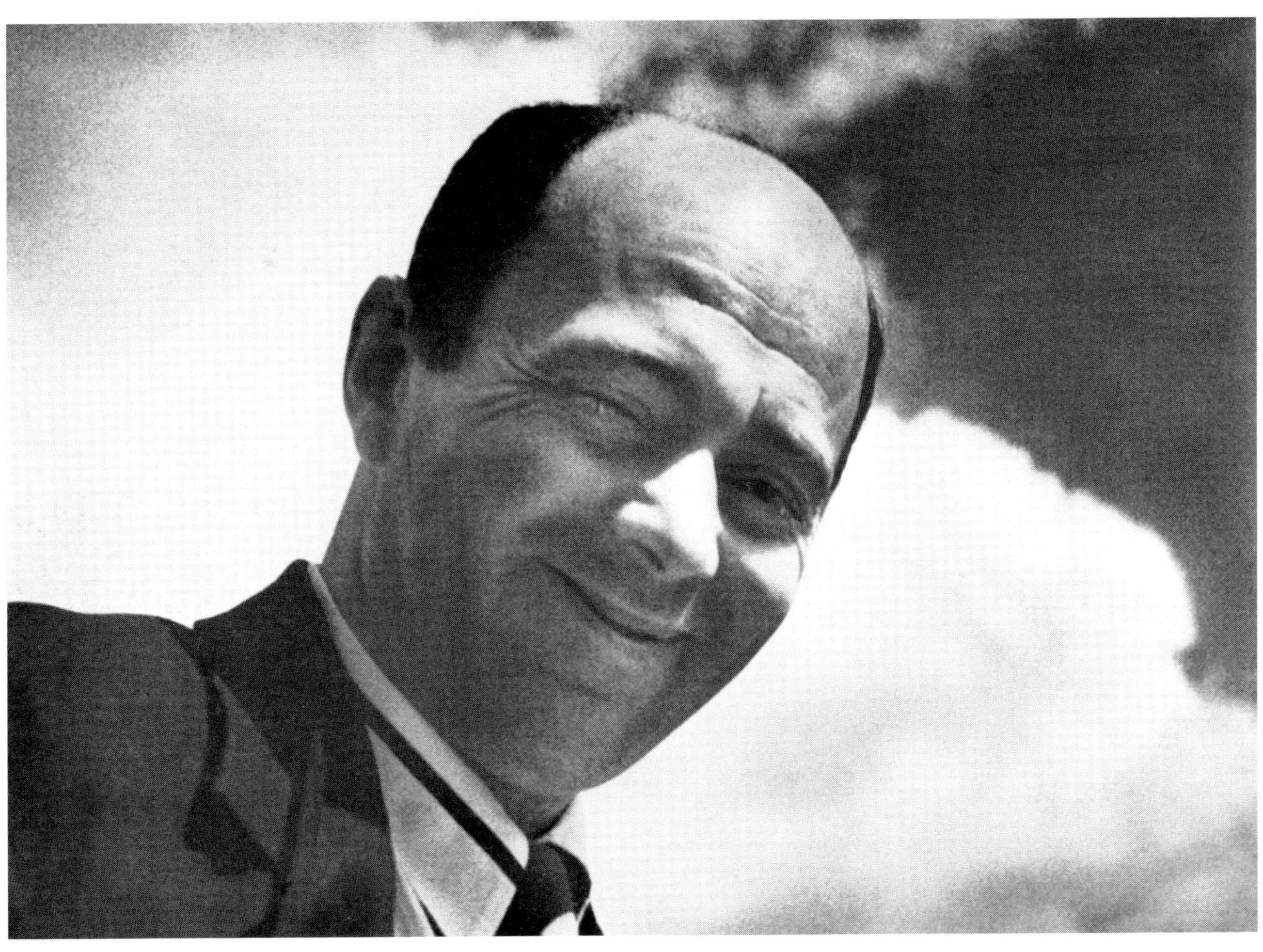

FIGURE 1.6
Mikhail Prekhner, photo of El Lissitzky, Moscow, 1932.

who was closely allied with Malevich's Suprematism but who also acknowledged the significance of Constructivism, and the writer Ilya Ehrenburg, the journal adopted a position that favored the experience and personal inclination of the individual artist. As they famously put it in the opening *Veshch'* editorial:

> We have named our journal *Veshch'* because to us art is the CREATION of new OBJECTS. . . . But it should by no means be supposed that by objects we mean household articles. Of course we see genuine art in utilitarian objects produced in factories, in the airplane or the automobile. But we do not wish to limit the production of artists to utilitarian objects. Any organized work—a HOUSE, a POEM or a PAINTING—is an EXPEDIENT OBJECT [*tselesoobraznaia veshch'*] that does not isolate people from life but helps them to organize it.[31]

Lissitzky's more inclusive view of utility, like that of the aborted Working Group of Objectivists at INKhUK in the spring of 1921, defends artists from what he regarded as the narrow utilitarianism of the Productivists and declares the right of artists themselves to decide on the purpose or goal of the "expedient" (*tselesoobraznyi*) new objects that they would make. Khan-Magomedov takes up Lissitzky's view of the importance of autonomous artistic creativity when he defends the inventiveness of the INKhUK artists in the face of what he sees as the destructive effect of the Productivist theorists, and especially when he devotes close historical attention to the previously neglected work of the Objectivists.

The present study follows Lissitzky and Khan-Magomedov by examining the centrality of the motivations and artistic choices of individual artists to the Productivist goal of inventing "socialist objects." But instead of regarding the utilitarian imperative of the Productivists as an exclusively constraining factor for artists, this book proposes that, at least for some of the artists associated with Constructivism, it initiated a set of productive limits that led to the invention of extraordinary objects. Although Khan-Magomedov and others are right to point out the tensions between theorists and artists at INKhUK around the question of actual artistic practice in production, the reality was that most of the theorists expected that artists themselves would take the lead in figuring out what Productivism would mean in practice. In an April 1922 lecture presented at INKhUK, for example, Brik stated: "theory doesn't show the way to work, but on the contrary practice dictates the laws which are determined by theory. The artist, working practically in production, draws his strength in this work from his ideology."[32] Or Arvatov, in the same INKhUK discussion in which he advocated that the best path for artists was to enter polytechnical institutes, also invokes OBMOKhU and the Constructivists when he declares in ringing tones, "it's Utopia, but we have to say it. . . . It's true that the situation is tragic, like any revolutionary situation, but it isn't a dead-end situation. This is the situation of a man on a riverbank who needs to cross over to the other side. You have to lay a foundation and build a bridge."[33]

In various ways, Tatlin, Rodchenko, Stepanova, and Popova used their experience in artistic experimentation to build a bridge to industry and to the "socialist object." Their activities occasionally intersected with the theoretical proposals of Productivists like Brik and Arvatov, but more often they developed those proposals in unexpected directions. To a great extent they shared the Productivist fascination with engineerism and technology, but as they attempted to put the utopia into practice in the years following the INKhUK debates, they confronted the particular historical moment of the New Economic Policy (NEP), which would significantly alter the picture of Soviet industry with which most Productivist theorists operated. The transitional period of NEP provided another set of productive limits on Constructivist activity, leading to the creation of comradely "socialist objects" that exceeded the theoretical boundaries of Productivism.

The Socialist Object in the Era of NEP

The rhetoric of early Constructivism and INKhUK Productivism envisioned "artist-engineers" participating in advanced, technological industry to produce large-scale, collective environments, but the reality of Soviet industry lagged far behind this vision. With the exception of a few urban areas, Russia had been industrially backward even before the outbreak of World War I in 1914, and by the end of the civil war in 1921, what little heavy industry remained was crippled by shortages of supplies and capital, outdated technology, and the destruction of plants and infrastructure caused by the wars. The Bolshevik government needed to rebuild and expand the industrial base of the country for ideological as well as practical reasons: Russia's peasant economy was a drawback according to Marxist theory, in which industrial production represents the highest form of human economic achievement, and the industrial proletariat is the most advanced social class. The revolution had been fought in the name of the proletariat, despite its relatively small size in Russia, and the new government was committed to strengthening this class as part of the larger attempt to modernize Russia—

to bring its economy and social structure up to the advanced level of modernity of its socialist government, which was the most radical in the world. Productivism was invented in the expectation that artists would participate in this process of socialist industrialization. The unformed, even imaginary nature of Soviet industry in 1921, always a projection into the future, facilitated the invention of the optimistic concept of the "artist-engineer" to an extent that the established industry of Western modernity, with its more ingrained traditions of the division of labor, could not. But the institution of the New Economic Policy in 1921 effectively postponed a large-scale socialist industrialization process for most of the 1920s.

The paradox of NEP was that it retreated dramatically from the most radical Communist policies that had defined the preceding period of War Communism (1918–1921) in order to lay a strong economic foundation for the future Communist industrial state. The economic policies that became known as War Communism did not result from a coherent plan, but comprised a series of emergency measures taken by the new Bolshevik government after the October Revolution of 1917 as it fought the civil war and foreign intervention. All major industries were nationalized, private trade was banned, and grain was forcibly requisitioned from the peasantry to support the Red Army and the urban populations. Private houses and apartments were expropriated by the state and communalized. Most larger stores were nationalized, dispersing trade to outdoor bazaars and individual street sellers. Inflation was so severe that the money economy was virtually eliminated, leading to an informal barter economy as well as simple scavenging for physical survival that affected all citizens, irrespective of their previous class status. By late 1920 the new Bolshevik state was in dire circumstances: the economy was in a state of total collapse; industrial production was at only 20 percent of prewar levels; millions of people had died from starvation and disease epidemics; people abandoned the cities to search for food in the countryside to the point that Moscow had lost half its population, and Petrograd two-thirds; and grain requisitioning resulted in peasant unrest and revolts against the government. Yet to many Bolshevik Party members, the policies of War Communism—chaotic, unenforceable, and catastrophic as they were—seemed to be on the right path to creating a Communist society. This view appears to have been shared by most of the leftist artists and theorists of INKhUK, shivering in the unheated rooms where INKhUK discussions took place, surviving on meager government rations, but exhilarated by the sense that an entirely new form of industrial modernity would be forged under the Bolsheviks, which artists would participate in forming visually and materially to a degree unimaginable under capitalist modernity.[34]

Lenin, however, had little patience for the revolutionary romanticism of War Communism. The new state could not survive without the support of the peasantry, he argued pragmatically: "We must satisfy the middle peasantry economically by going to free exchange. Otherwise it will be impossible—economically impossible—to preserve the power of the proletariat in Russia, given the delay of the international revolution."[35] What began in the spring of 1921 as an attempt to pacify the peasants by allowing them to sell their grain privately in local markets soon ballooned into a series of measures that legalized private wholesale and retail trade. Private manufacture was also legalized as part of Lenin's plan to build up the Soviet proletariat; the state would own most large factories and control large-scale industry, but for the time being, private manufacture would perform a supporting role, as would private trade. By the fall of 1921, these and other measures collectively became known, in the party and the party press, as the New Economic Policy. Many Bolsheviks, bewildered by this ideological retreat that seemed to carry the country backward into capitalism, rather than forward toward socialism along the path set out by War Communism, complained that the new acronym NEP stood for the New Exploitation of the Proletariat.[36] Lenin brusquely dismissed this view, asserting that developing the economic basis for Soviet industry must take precedence over Communist purity: "It may seem a paradox: private capitalism in the role of socialism's accomplice? It is in no way a paradox, but rather a completely incontestable economic fact."[37]

The results of the new NEP policies were incontestably visible on the streets of Moscow and other urban centers, to the well-documented dismay of Bolshevik Party members, committed leftist cultural workers such as the members of INKhUK, and famous leftist foreigners visiting Soviet Russia in the 1920s such as Walter Benjamin. The so-called Nepmen—the speculators, financiers, merchants, middlemen, manufacturers, and so on who could suddenly operate legally—immediately began to make enormous profits in the gold rush economy, even though they were steeply taxed by the government. They also sought ways to spend these profits quickly, given the uncertain future of the capitalist concessions under Bolshevism. Ostentatious public displays of wealth reintroduced the visible class distinctions that had been largely eliminated by the conditions of civil war—distinctions that were exacerbated, especially in the early years of NEP, by the hunger and poverty that still predominated among everyone but the NEP profiteers. After the austerity of the war years, it was a shock to see Nepmen dressed in elegant suits and fur-lined coats, their wives in silks, furs, jewels, perfume, and heavy makeup. Hordes of prostitutes haunted the cities. Luxurious food stores, restaurants, hotels, nightclubs, casinos, and racetracks catered to the new bourgeoisie. Prerevolutionary class distinctions in speech returned: the ubiquitous revolutionary mode of address of "comrade" (*tovarishch'*) was replaced, in the mouths of waiters, drivers, and other servants, by the old-fashioned "sir" or "madam" (*barin* or *barina*).[38]

The main forum for Productivist protests against NEP was the journal *Lef* (from *Levyi Front Iskusstv*, or Left Front of the Arts). Although INKhUK continued to exist as a think tank until 1924, the foundation of the journal in 1923 gave a more public and permanent forum to INKhUK ideas. Founded by the Productivist theorists Osip Brik, Boris Arvatov, Boris Kushner, and Nikolai Chuzhak, along with Sergei Tret'iakov, a writer, critic, and playwright with strong Bolshevik sympathies, and Vladimir Mayakovsky, the famous Futurist poet who served as the editor-in-chief, the journal's orientation was literary as well as artistic and theoretical. A commitment to revolutionary culture and hostility to NEP permeated all aspects of the journal, exemplified in the position piece "*Lef* and NEP" by Tret'iakov (figure 1.7), which appeared in the second issue. The article opens with a vicious description of the typical Nepman's body:

> There are two NEPs. One is fat and insolent, the kind that gets chewed over in all the satirical newspapers. His snout is in the display cases of the extra-gluttonous stores, in the sparkle of jewelry stores, in Cotys and silks, in the cafes and casinos. His bull head is in cozy apartments bought for billions of rubles, made "habitable" with curtains, fichus trees, porcelain elephants and sometimes even plates from the Soviet porcelain factory with the slogan "he who does not work, does not eat." His heart is in the stock market. . . . His very existence is an acrobatic act between trillions of rubles and the black muzzle point of a Soviet rifle.[39]

Tret'iakov's description of "NEP no. 2" begins, conversely, with the simple sentence "The revolution continues." This second NEP consisted of those who continue to work toward the Communist ideals of the revolution, fighting the "toxin" of the first NEP.[40] *Lef* represented this second NEP, resisting the return of the old art of aesthetic illusion and continuing the struggle for productivist art. Ending his article with another image of commercial display, he wrote that *Lef* must remove itself from "the display cases of aesthetic products (magazines, theaters, exhibitions) where, in alien surroundings, its products lose their sense of urgency."[41]

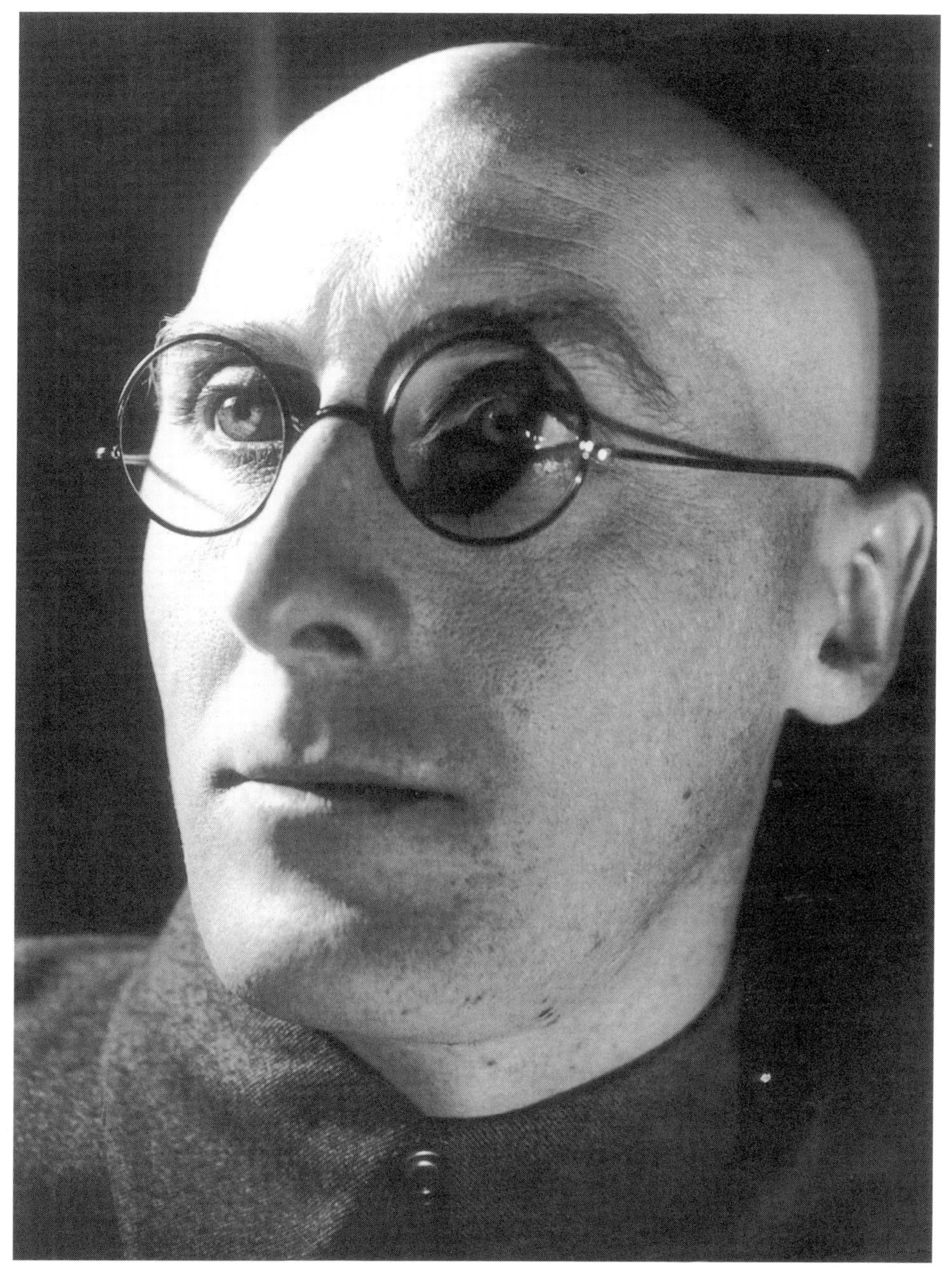

FIGURE 1.7
Aleksandr Rodchenko, photo of Sergei Tret'iakov, 1928.

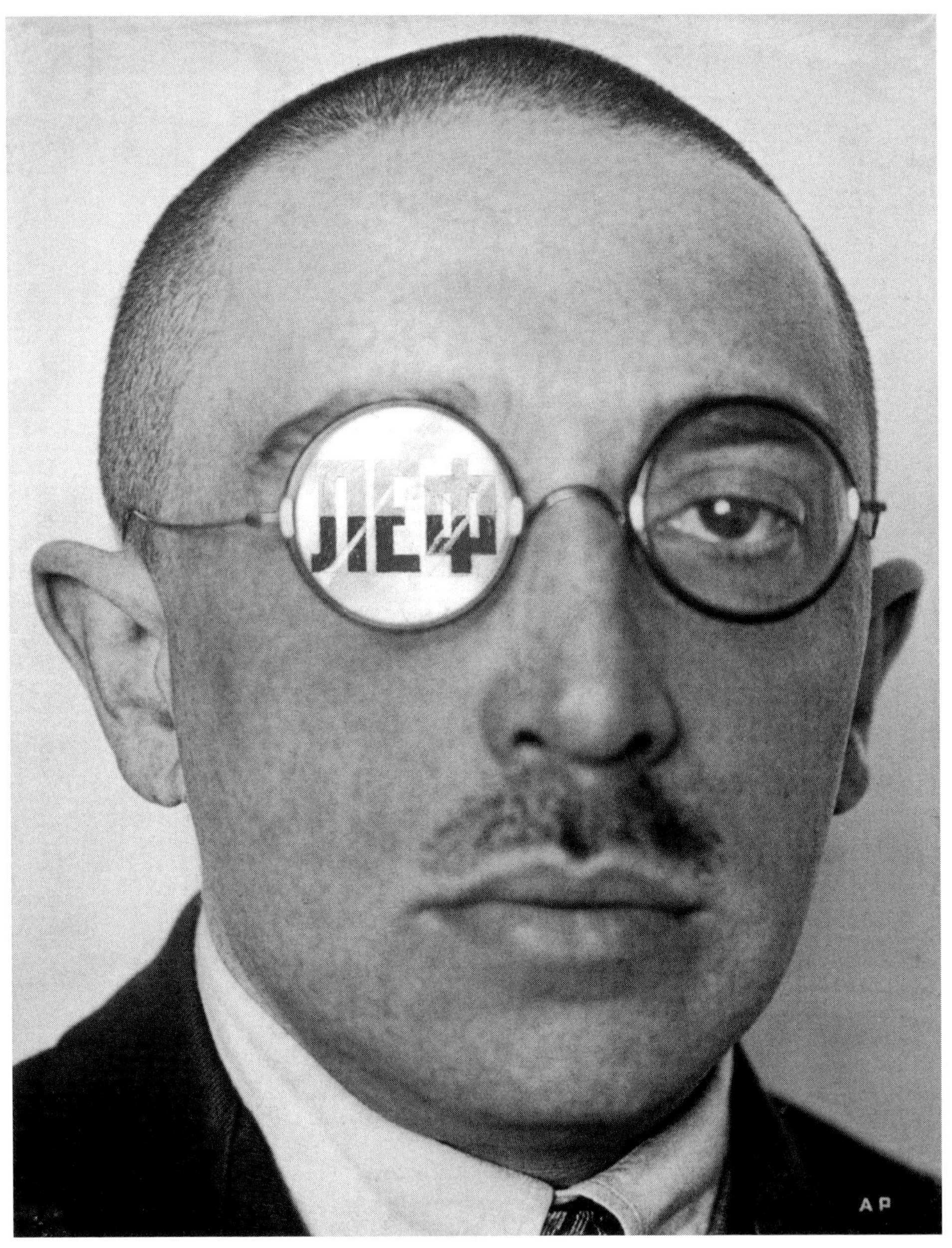

FIGURE 1.8

Aleksandr Rodchenko, photomontage of Osip Brik with *Lef* logo, 1924. Howard Schickler Fine Art.

The complaint that a semblance of the prerevolutionary art world had returned with NEP, jeopardizing the prospects of the Productivist agenda, was common among *Lef* writers. In his article "Into Production!" in the first issue of *Lef*, Osip Brik (figure 1.8) wrote:

> Things are hard right now for the Constructivist-Productivist. Artists turn away from him. Economic planners brush him aside with annoyance. The philistine goggles at him and fearfully whispers: "Futurist!" It takes a lot of endurance and strength of will not to lapse into the peaceful bosom of canonized art, not to start to "create" like the "fair copy" artists, or to concoct ornaments for cups and handkerchiefs, or to paint up pictures for cozy dining rooms and bedrooms.[42]

The NEP bourgeoisie represented a potential new patron class for artists that could make up for the lessening of the government support they had enjoyed during War Communism, but owing to its nouveau riche vulgarity and lack of education in comparison with the prerevolutionary patron classes, its tastes were assumed to be for more conventional, figurative works of art, and for traditional objects of display, such as painting and sculpture—not for the utilitarian, industrially produced objects imagined by Productivism.[43] But in the 1920s, most artists, including young art students, rejected what they saw as the extremism of the *Lef* artists in favor of easel painting of various degrees of realism, from the nineteenth-century genre painting of the Association of Artists of Revolutionary Russia (AKhRR), to the Cézanne-influenced New Society of Painters (NOZh), to the more experimental but still figurative Society of Easel Painters (OST). Most of these painters actively embraced revolutionary subject matter; their difference with the *Lef*ists was not necessarily one of political content, but of method. While *Lef* protested that figurative painting was an inherently bourgeois form of the art object as a commodity, its "enemies" countered with the charge that Constructivism and Productivism had their origins in foreign, bourgeois trends such as Futurism and Cubism, and were therefore even more problematic as revolutionary art. Although the party strongly favored the AKhRR group with its patronage, state support of the arts remained relatively democratic until the later 1920s, with a number of groups and tendencies, including the *Lef*ists, receiving subsidies, commissions, and so on.[44] The private art market, on the other hand, favored only traditional art objects—what Tret'iakov called "aesthetic products"—and provided no patronage at all to Constructivism.

Distasteful and frustrating as it was to the *Lef*ists, the partial return of a system of private art patronage with its more traditional tastes under NEP was not the greatest threat to the Productivist agenda. Rather, government emphasis during NEP on reviving trade and fostering light industry and manufacture, as a necessary step toward the eventual promotion of heavy industry, significantly shifted Soviet state rhetoric and practice away from the War Communist dream of immediate industrialization and collectivism that had fostered Productivism. Under the new policy of *khozraschet* (self-financing), state-owned businesses like factories and cooperative stores were no longer subsidized through the state budget, but were expected to operate on their own, at a profit, in the NEP marketplace. In this form of production, which suspiciously resembled prerevolutionary Russian or Western capitalist industry, traditional relations of production between workers and management, as well as traditional wage differentials, continued. Harried managers charged with turning a profit had little interest in cooperating in experimental ways with "artist-engineers."

Dominant accounts of the history of Constructivism have therefore tended to emphasize that Constructivism failed to achieve its promise owing to historical circumstances. Christina Lodder's authoritative study *Russian Constructivism*, while carefully documenting the theoretical and experimental breakthroughs of early Constructivism, argues that "the Constructivists' attempt at direct engagement in industry was not successful" and that "the principal reason why few projects got beyond the drawing board was the material poverty that dominated all Soviet activity in the 1920s. Material and technological standards of a higher level were required for producing industrial prototypes than for producing drawn designs and traditional artworks."[45] She concludes that "Constructivism had failed in its primary objective of totally transforming the environment," and that the Constructivist artist therefore "lowered his sights to more practical problems such as . . . typographical, poster and exhibition design, which fitted more neatly into traditional artistic categories."[46]

Many of these "limited" Constructivist objects were also more traditionally representational or figurative—particularly in their widespread use of photomontage—signaling, for Lodder, a retreat from the modernist critique of illusionism that had defined Constructivism. She interprets the Constructivist use of the photograph, for example, as a compromise with the various forms of realist painting that gained popularity during NEP, and notes ruefully that Constructivism, "setting out to transform the environment was itself being transformed by that environment, returning to existing reality as a source of inspiration, of imagery. . . . The process of the decline of Constructivism had in fact begun."[47] Although Lodder does not discuss the policies of NEP in any detail, or even stress NEP's significance, her overall argument—that the low level of Soviet industry in the 1920s, combined with the conservatism of the popular and party preference for realist art, led to the "confinement" and "decline" of Constructivism's original program—amounts to an argument that the historical circumstances of NEP were to blame.

Another influential Western account of Constructivism, written by Paul Wood as the opening essay of the major catalog *The Great Utopia: The Russian and Soviet Avant-Garde, 1915–1932,* disagrees with the specific reasons that Lodder offers for the decline of Constructivism, only to propose an even more sweeping argument for the negative effects of NEP on the avant-garde.[48] Wood rightly points out that the material scarcity that Lodder names was not an undifferentiated, blanket condition of the 1920s, but was rather a factor of economic decision making that affected different sectors of the economy in varying ways for varying reasons; some enterprises did get funded and thrived, while others did not. Further, he cautions against accepting the overgeneralized argument about the innate conservatism of the party and the people when it came to art. There is substantial evidence—some of which will be explored in this study—that some of the modernist, geometric, nondecorative objects produced by the Constructivists enjoyed great popularity among various audiences or users. Wood instead locates the reasons for the "failure" of Constructivism firmly in politics. "War Communism," he writes, "framed the project of Constructivism, of 'material culture,' and of 'art into production.'"[49] But as it turned out, NEP, not War Communism, provided the conditions in which the avant-garde would have to operate; with its return to private property and the profit motive, NEP was antithetical to the collectivizing ideals that had spawned the Constructivist idea of the artist-engineer. For Wood, the failure of Constructivism to implement its original, grand program was a consequence not just of material scarcity or visual conservatism, but of the larger Bolshevik betrayal of the ideals of revolution that had been lived only briefly in War Communism: "What is at issue is a far wider 'failure': the failure of the October Revolution itself. The failure of Constructivism or, indeed, of the 'left front' of art in general is best regarded as a symptom of this larger defeat."[50]

But what if we were to understand NEP not as a total defeat of revolutionary ideals and of Productivist goals along with it, but as a circumstance that forced these ideals and goals to take a different, but perhaps still productive, path toward socialism? The trial by fire of War Communism, which had attempted to industrialize and collectivize Russia in one bold gesture, had instead resulted in the precipitous demodernization of the country. NEP brought back visible class difference, but it also brought back the infrastructures of modernity that had been decimated during the civil war. The policies of NEP acknowledged that functioning systems of consumption were the necessary counterparts to modern systems of production, and that a path toward socialism that took consumption into account was more likely to succeed in the conditions that the Bolsheviks faced in 1921.

NEP was, as Wood points out, a temporary defeat of the notion of the planned economy: "the balance of forces shifted from planning to that which is nowadays usually dubbed 'enterprise,' but for which the terms 'greed' and 'self-seeking' often do just as well."[51] The Constructivists clearly agreed with Wood about the greed of the derided Nepmen, but the argument of this book is that they envisioned a future in which a desiring relation to the mass-produced objects of socialist modernity would not necessarily have to be defined as greed. Without being able to rely on a planned economy to impose their objects on consumers, the Constructivists during NEP had to take seriously the problem of consumer desire. In this sense they did have to confront the popular taste of the NEP public, as Lodder argues, but the debatable Constructivist "compromise" with realism is treated here as a side effect of their larger strategies for working toward the creation of future socialist objects in a transitional period. Constructivism is unique among the politically engaged avant-gardes of the twentieth century because it imagined "no possessions" both from the perspective of an achieved socialist revolution that made such imagining more than utopian dreaming and—at the same time—from within the commodity culture of NEP that forced that imagining to contend with the present reality of commodity-desiring human subjects. Where Lodder evaluates Constructivist projects of the mid-1920s as a "confinement" of the original goals of the Constructivist program, this study addresses them as productive developments of an original program whose social context of War Communism had been eliminated.[52] Where Wood posits that War Communism was the necessary "frame" of Constructivism, this study proposes the period of NEP as the crucible of the Constructivist object, because the policies of War Communism had not confronted the power and tenacity of the commodity fetish within modernity.

Perhaps the most widely influential account of the failure of Constructivism as an avant-garde practice, with a notoriety extending beyond art history to the art world and the broader culture, is one that completely discounts the flexibility of Constructivist practice in response to the historical circumstances of NEP. The critic and aesthetic philosopher Boris Groys has famously proposed that the sweeping ambitions of the Russian avant-garde to remake art and life, which had their origins in the radical period of War Communism, were in fact realized—rather than defeated, as is usually argued—in the rise of Stalinist Socialist Realism in the 1930s. Groys charges that the Russian avant-garde was motivated by an undemocratic will-to-power rather than genuine socialist ideals; that it aimed to destroy the past and recreate the world in its own technological image; that it opportunistically collaborated with Soviet power in order to implement its "unitary artistic plan" for subjecting the population to its "total and boundless" aesthetic system; and that in all of this it prepared the way for the eventual triumph of the total art of Stalinism: "Under Stalin the dream of the avant-garde was in fact fulfilled and the life of society was organized in monolithic artistic forms, though of course not those that the avant-garde itself had favored."[53] Despite its pervasive influence, Groys's provocative narrative of avant-garde totalitarianism is not supported by the historical record of what artists and theorists actually made and said in the course of the 1920s—a record that, as a number of art historians have demonstrated, is more varied and contains more shifts and turns than Groys's unitary narrative allows.[54] The examples of Constructivist theory and objects presented in this book are intended to provide further evidence against Groys's thesis, and to demonstrate conversely that Constructivism adapted its original avant-garde "plan" and "system" to respond to the transitional situation of NEP, without sacrificing its commitment to socialism.

Groys singles out the Productivist theorist Boris Arvatov as an "illustrative example" of the avant-garde's dream of "drawing up the unitary plan of the new reality."[55] In contrast, Arvatov figures in this study as the Productivist theorist who developed a theory of the "socialist object" of modernity that specifically responded to the exigencies of NEP, and so can clarify and amplify our understanding of the objects produced by the Constructivists in the mid-1920s. Although mordantly opposed to capitalism and vehemently Marxist in his training and sympathies, Arvatov recognized the affective power of the mass-produced objects of modernity, proposing the idea of a socialist object as a "coworker" as a response to the power of the commodity fetish under capitalism. Arvatov remained true to the original Productivist ideal, born under War Communism, of the artist-engineer as an active participant in collectivized industry, but his texts constructively addressed the present needs of Soviet industry and business under NEP, as well as the need to equal, in socialist forms, the achievements of industry under advanced capitalism in the West.[56] Arvatov was unique among the *Lef* theorists in his reinterpretation of the Marxist commodity fetish as a tool for socialism, just as the examples of Constructivist "socialist objects" that are considered in the following chapters form a particular subgroup of Constructivist objects that were specifically oriented toward the everyday circumstances of NEP Russia at their most mundane and often commercial levels. Arvatov's ideas therefore form an integral part of this story of the Constructivist object.

Boris Arvatov's Socialist Things

Throughout the 1920s, Arvatov (figure 1.9)[57] published extensively on art history, Constructivism, and production art, as well as on literature, poetry, theater, and proletarian culture, gaining a reputation as an uncompromising hard-line Productivist who subordinated artistic creativity to the needs of production.[58] His biography is a textbook case of Bolshevik zeal. It includes a history of radical political activity dating back to his teenage years, and frontline military service in the Red Army during the civil war. Of Russian nationality, Boris Ignat'evich Arvatov was born in 1896 in Kiev, the son of a lawyer. He graduated from the gymnasium in Riga, and from the Faculty of Physics and Mathematics of Petrograd University. He was a member of the Socialist Revolutionary Party before 1917, joining a socialist youth group already in 1911. He became a member of the Communist Party in February of 1920, and served on the Polish front of the civil war as a commissar in the Red Army until he was demobilized in March 1921. He served in the army's revolutionary soviet (*revsovet*). Beginning in 1918 he served as academic secretary in Proletkul't (from *proletarskaia kul'tura* or "proletarian culture"), the mass working-class organization established immediately after the October Revolution in 1917 to promote the formation of an ideologically pure form of proletarian culture. He joined INKhUK in 1921 and became a cofounder of *Lef* in 1923. On the personal questionnaire that he filled out in 1922 as a member of the Russian Academy of Artistic Sciences—the source of much of the foregoing information—he put down his social origins as "intelligentsia" and his profession as "art critic–Marxist."[59] The questionnaire asked him about his theoretical/Marxist preparation, to which he replied that it was "total" (*polnyi*). He was twenty-six years old.

His was the ideal pedigree for a Bolshevik cultural worker: an educated intellectual who had repudiated his class status at a young age and committed

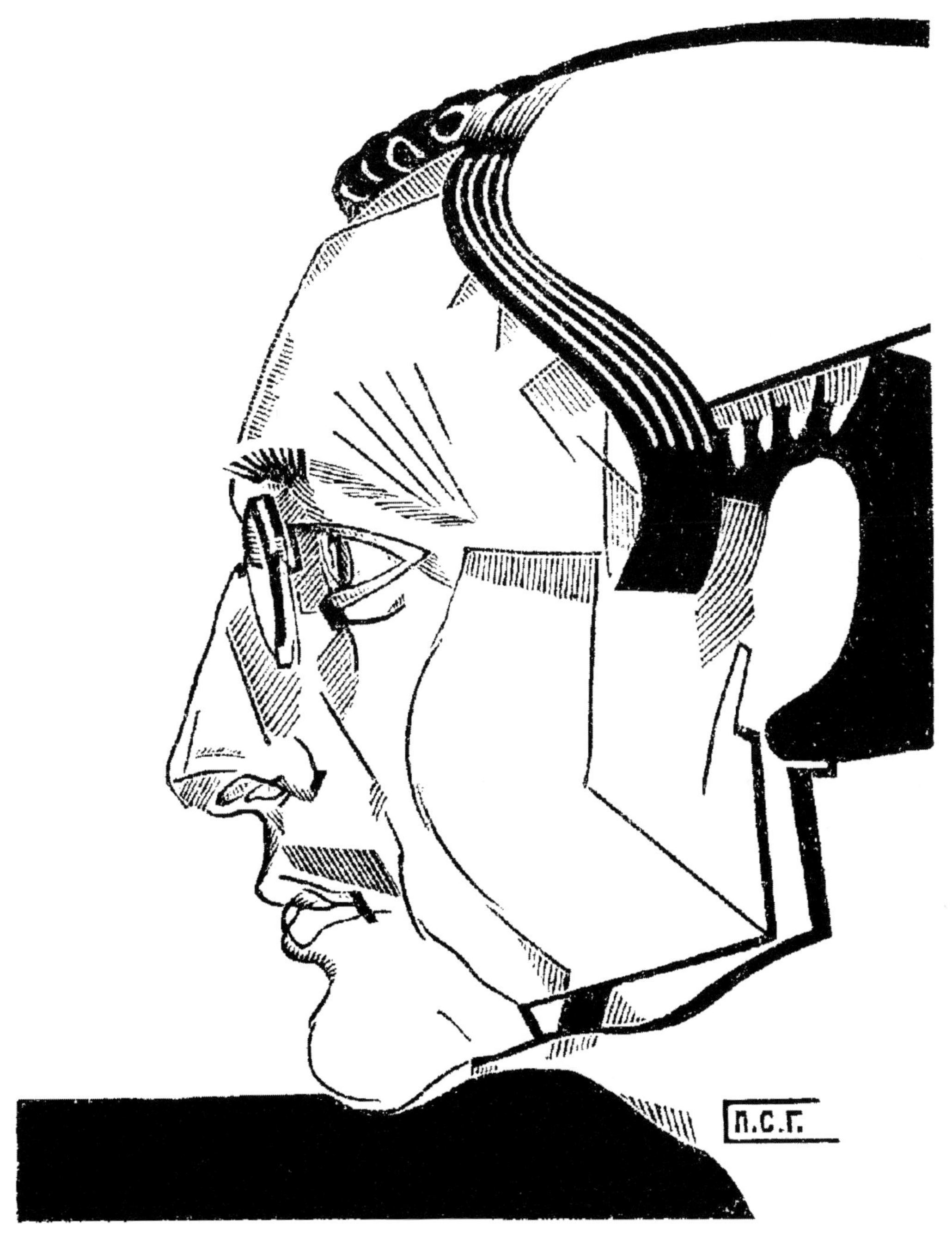

FIGURE 1.9
Petr Galadzhev, drawing of Boris Arvatov, reproduced in the journal *Zrelishcha*, 1922. Private collection.

himself both intellectually and bodily to revolutionary Marxism. These kinds of Bolsheviks were esteemed, at least in the early 1920s, almost as much as Bolsheviks with authentic working-class origins. But this predictable biography was soon turned on its head, as was its power to predict or explain his writing. A half year after he so confidently demonstrated his exemplary pedigree on the questionnaire, in the summer of 1923, he was diagnosed with a severe nervous illness, likely the result of shell shock suffered during the war. He spent the rest of his life in psychiatric sanatoriums.[60] The disease did not affect his mental capacity; he continued to publish regularly until 1930, and continued his historical and theoretical studies until his death in 1940. Most of his important works, including his best-known book, *Art and Production* (1926), were all published after his incarceration.[61] His insights into both Western and Soviet modernity are all the more remarkable when we consider that they were written from inside a mental hospital while socialism was being built on the outside.

Arvatov's pivotal essay "Everyday Life and the Culture of the Thing" (*Byt i kul'tura veshchi*) of 1925 attempts to imagine how socialism will transform passive capitalist commodities into active socialist things.[62] These things, connected like "coworkers" with human practice, will produce new experiences of everyday life, new relations of consumption, and new human subjects of modernity (EL, p. 124). Arvatov's attention to the transformative potential of the material culture of everyday life (*byt*) differentiates him from other early Soviet Marxists who, he claims, approach the question of culture "on a purely ideological level," emphasizing consciousness over material culture (EL, p. 119). If his Marxist colleagues display a "peculiar ideologism" (EL, p. 119) when it comes to material culture, this is because they have known only "the bourgeois world of things," which is disorganized and sharply divided into domains of technical things and everyday things (EL, p. 120). They have not been able to free themselves from the classic dualism in bourgeois philosophy between the material and ideal, matter and spirit. Arvatov responds to their "ideologism" by claiming that the creation of a proletarian culture "will require the elimination of that rupture between things and people that characterized bourgeois society . . . proletarian society will not know this dualism of things" (EL, p. 121).

In order to highlight Arvatov's explicitly materialist criticism of previous Marxist thinking about material culture, I am here translating the key Russian term *veshch'*—which can be translated as thing or object, depending on context—deliberately as "thing," to distinguish Arvatov's use of the term *veshch'* from that of other Marxist writers. In most English-language texts on Marxist theory, the term "object" is used to refer to material artifacts, partly to preserve the sense that the philosophical term "object" always carries within itself of the possible slippage between material and ideal. This standard dual meaning of the term, in artistic as well as Marxist theory, is exemplified in El Lissitzky's opening editorial in his journal *Veshch'/Gegenstand/Objet* that we examined above: "any organized work—a house, a poem or a painting—is an expedient object [*veshch'*]." As Arvatov uses it in his essay, the term *veshch'* cannot refer to something as immaterial as a poem. The English word "thing," on the other hand, is more strictly material when referring to artifacts, and is at the same time more informal and everyday—capturing Arvatov's insistence on the potential cultural significance of everyday things, which Marxists have long ignored as "static and secondary" in comparison with the technical things in production.[63]

Although integral to Arvatov's theory of Soviet production art, "Everyday Life and the Culture of the Thing" does not mention Constructivism or art at all. It takes as its subject matter the industrially produced thing in Western modernity, not in Russia. His homeland is still too industrially backward to provide evidence for his grand thesis, which is that industrial production is a source of human creativity that, when liberated from the oppressive labor and class conditions of capitalism and reinvented in socialist culture, "will directly form all aspects of human activity" (EL, p. 121). Already in America, Arvatov imagines, despite the harmful effects of capitalism, this industrial creativity is beginning to transform human beings through the agency of the innumerable new things that it mass produces: "The new world of things, which gave rise to a new image of a person as a psycho-physiological individual, dictated forms of gesticulation, movement, and activity. It created a particular regimen of physical culture. The psyche also evolved, becoming more and more thinglike in its associative structure" (EL, p. 126). In Arvatov's theory, then, the industrial thing—in Marx's terms, the commodity fetish—has an agency that is potentially beneficial to the human subject, which is itself rendered more "evolved" through interacting with, and even mimicking, this active and creative thing.

But the potentially dynamizing effects of the "new world of things" are stymied by the commodity relation, which prevents things from acting on consciousness. Grounded in exchange value, the commodity form isolates production from consumption and promotes private-property relations to things; it entails "the maximum isolation of the system of production, as a machine-collective system, from the system of consumption, as a system of individual appropriation" (EL, p. 122). The bourgeois has no direct physical contact with the technological creativity of things in production. His interaction with things is limited to his narrow, private-property form of everyday life, which takes place in the spaces of private apartments and offices filled with possessions: "for the bourgeois there exist 'my' things and 'someone else's' things. 'My' things appear . . . as social-ideological categories" (EL, p. 123). The everyday life of the bourgeoisie is a passive sphere of experience diametrically opposed to the active creation associated with production; the thing in bourgeois material culture exists "outside its creative genesis" and therefore as "something completed, fixed, static and, consequently, dead" (EL, p. 122).

Arvatov's emphasis on this passivity of the commodity substantially reformulates Marx's theory of the commodity. For Marx, the commodity is a fetish because people project value onto it, a value that is arbitrary because it exists only as a consequence of practices of exchange on the market.[64] The real value of the thing, its labor value, is constituted by the labor power that produced it, but this is suppressed by the commodity form. The commodity has agency only in the negative sense of leeching that agency away from the human producers to whom it rightly belongs; its agency is negative and antisocial. It "reflects the social relation of the producers to the sum total of labor as a social relation between objects, a relation which exists apart from and outside the producers."[65] This shift in agency from producers to objects renders the human producers passive, while exchange-value confers on commodities the role of active agents of social relations.

For Arvatov, on the other hand, the commodity form renders the things themselves passive—uncreative, fixed, dead. They may serve as substitutes for relations between producers, but this is an inherently static and formal function, governed by the spontaneous forces of the market: "The thing as the fulfillment of the physiological-laboring capacities of the organism, as a social-laboring force, as an instrument and as a co-worker, does not exist in the everyday life of the bourgeoisie" (EL, p. 124). This list of qualities that commodities lack enumerates, of course, precisely what will be desirable in the socialist thing. Whereas Marx laments that the commodity fetish resulted in "material [*dinglich*] relations between persons and social relations between things,"[66] Arvatov wants to recuperate thinglike (*dinglich*) relations between persons and social relations between things for the benefit of proletarian culture. Instead of wishing for Marx's lost set of "direct social relations between persons in their work,"[67] Arvatov claims that industrial society has infinitely more and better things than humanity has ever known, and therefore it makes sense that relations between people should be more thinglike. The problem is not just with the commodity as a social form—

as Marx sees it—but with the actual material qualities of the things produced under the capitalist system of production. What separates Arvatov from Marx is his conviction that the elimination of the "rupture between things and people" will be achieved not only through the socialist transformation of relations of production but by formal transformations of the things themselves—such as those proposed by the Constructivists. This obsessive, even unseemly emphasis on the things themselves characterizes the particular Constructivist version of materialism.

By imagining a material object that is animated differently from the commodity, Arvatov attempts to bestow a different kind of social agency on the thing that is not immediately reducible to the structure of the fetish. Only socialist revolution can achieve this, by freeing the creative forces of production from capitalist structures. But certain conditions that lessen the power of the commodity already exist in embryo, Arvatov contends, in the everyday life of the technical intelligentsia of the industrial city in faraway America.[68] In his vivid imagination from inside the walls of a provincial Russian mental hospital, he imagines that the American city boasts an "everyday life of enormous offices, department stores, factory laboratories, research institutes and so on" (EL, p. 125) as well as "the collectivization of transport and . . . heating, lighting, plumbing" (EL, p. 125). The reactionary financial bourgeoisie may continue, obliviously, to live its commodified everyday life of private consumption, but the everyday life of the technical intelligentsia has been completely penetrated by these collectivizing forces originating in production. The technical intelligentsia is in the unique position of organizing the advanced technological things of industry through its work, without forming an ownership attachment to those things, because it is only "a group of hired organizers" (EL, pp. 125–126). It lives "in a world of things that it organizes but does not possess, things that condition its labor" (EL, p. 125). The technical intelligentsia is structurally less affected by the commodity form.

The less commodified everyday life of the technical intelligentsia leads it to demand new values of activity and flexibility from things—values that will eventually, under socialism, become the values of socialist things. In contrast to the display or status value of bourgeois things, or to the decorative forms of the privately owned home—the weighty furniture, heavy draperies, and endless coverings of the bourgeois interior—the new criteria of value are "convenience, portability, comfort, flexibility, expedience [*tselesoobraznost'*], hygiene, and so on—in a word, everything that they call the adaptability of the thing, its suitability in terms of positioning and assembling for the needs of social practice" (EL, p. 126).[69]

Portable and flexible, ready to be assembled or disassembled on short notice, these things respond formally to the newly collectivized everyday life of the technical intelligentsia by rendering themselves transparent: "Glass, steel, concrete, artificial materials and so on were no longer covered over with a 'decorative' casing, but spoke for themselves. The mechanism of a thing, the connection between the elements of a thing and its purpose, were now transparent, compelling people practically, and thus also psychologically, to reckon with them, and only with them" (EL, p. 126). The newly transparent thing logically embodies and demonstrates the labor power—the technical intelligence—of the technical intelligentsia. Arvatov endows modernism with Marxist credentials; the transparent modernist object that displays its mode of construction and its function is already, it turns out, by virtue of its form, on the way toward engendering socialist culture, because it contests the secrecy of the commodity fetish.

Yet Arvatov's theory is not a simplistic technological one, all breathless wonder at modern machines and contraptions. There is an aspect of that, certainly, but understanding that as the core of his thesis would miss the more interesting claim he is making about people's relation to material objects. In a key passage, he writes that even the most mundane, low-tech, everyday objects can engender socialist culture: "The ability to pick up a cigarette-case, to smoke a cigarette, to put on an overcoat, to wear a cap, to open a door, all these 'trivialities' acquire their qualification, their not unimportant 'culture'" (EL, p. 126). As the forms of such simple, everyday objects of consumption begin to approach the more advanced technical forms that already exist in the objects of production that have entered everyday life—he cites revolving doors and escalators, among other things—they will become better qualified as active agents of a potentially socialist culture. Arvatov's analysis of the thing in Western modernity in this essay lays out the necessary elements for a theory of how Constructivist artists in the Soviet Union, filling the role of the "technical intelligentsia," can use their experience with material and form, and their commitment to industrial techniques, to produce well-qualified, active "socialist objects" that will be "coworkers" in the construction of socialism.

Writing a History of the Comradely Object

Other than his anthropomorphic use of the term "coworker" to describe the potential of the thing in socialist culture, Arvatov's text does not evoke the same kind of emotion as Rodchenko's faith, in his 1925 letter from Paris, in "our things in our hands" that will be "equals, comrades." In another essay from around this time, however, Arvatov does directly address the "emotionality" of things, in language that resonates with Rodchenko's:

> There exists the opinion . . . that the course toward expediency [*tselesoobraznost'*] murders the so-called humanity of things, deprives things of "emotionality" or, what's the same thing, of their harmonious sociality. Such an opinion can only be maintained by those for whom the thing in and of itself, in its rational functioning, cannot be the embodiment of human thought, of the human relation to the object world and to his social existence.[70]

Arvatov's notion of the transparent, expedient (*tselesoobraznyi*) thing should therefore not be interpreted too narrowly in terms of an instrumental utilitarianism or technicism. When he writes that "the mechanism of a thing, the connection between the elements of a thing and its purpose, were now transparent, compelling people practically, and thus also psychologically, to reckon with them" (EL, p. 126), the "purpose" in question is not necessarily only the mechanical purpose of the thing, but can be interpreted as the larger purpose of confronting the phantasmatic power that the commodity wields in capitalism. Addressing consumer fantasy must be a purpose of the comradely object of Constructivism, which elaborates in practice the theoretical ideas that were articulated by Arvatov in print, even if its ultimate, socialist goal is to "compel the consumer psychologically" toward transparent objects that embody the creativity of industrial production.

With his emphasis on the psychological force of objects, as well as on the necessary "material qualification"—or form—of the active socialist object, Arvatov's theory answers the concerns expressed by artists at the INKhUK debates about their role in Productivism. Rodchenko, as we recall, had asked what use would be made in the factory of the artists' main qualification, which was that "*we know how to see.*" The chapters that follow examine Constructivist objects like stoves, flapper dresses, cookie advertisements, and speakers' platforms, to discover how both their formal origins in the previous avant-garde practices of the artists, and their possible psychological significance in the context of the careers of their makers, might endow them with a "comradely" potential in everyday life under socialism. In addition to the social history of art, this study therefore relies on some of the most traditional methods of art history, such as the analysis of the stylistic development and biography of the individual artist. A reading of the anti-authorial strategies of Tatlin's nonobjective sculptural reliefs of the mid-1910s, for example, helps to make sense of the startling anonymity and plainness of his everyday objects in 1923–1924; understanding the form and reception of Popova and Stepanova's experimental paintings from 1918 to 1921 allows for a better understanding of the artists' motivations and procedures, particularly as women, in turning to textile design in 1923–1924; Mayakovsky and Rodchenko's advertisements of 1923–1925 take on their full significance when read in conjunction with Mayakovsky's famous lyric poem of early 1923, *About This*, and Rodchenko's equally famous photomontage illustrations for it; and the full ambition of both Rodchenko's advertisements and his workers' club of 1925 becomes more apparent when these works are placed in dialogue with the systematizing logic of his hanging *Spatial Constructions* series of 1920–1921. Creating such a dialogue between the widely acknowledged avant-garde works of these artists and the quirkier, less appreciated utilitarian objects they made in their Productivist moment, is a central goal of this book.

Approaching the affective or psychological aspects of the socialist object also invites, at various moments in this study, the use of psychoanalytic models of interpretation—not applied to the artists themselves, but rather used as a means to understand their artworks and texts. This is especially the case in the attempt to make sense of the aggressive orality of many of the Rodchenko–Mayakovsky advertisements, for example, or of the intensity of the sexual references that pervade Rodchenko's letters from Paris. Finally, feminist methods of analysis clarify, from different theoretical and historical perspectives, the investigation of the contradictory notion of the "active" as opposed to passive material object and its possible role in bringing about a more egalitarian social order—one that might be egalitarian in terms of gender as well as class. The feminist dimension of the socialist object is articulated directly only by Rodchenko, when he writes from Paris that "the light from the East is in the new relation to the person, to woman, to things"—an idea that will be analyzed in relation to his workers' club in chapter 5. But it arises throughout the other examples of Constructivist practice that we will examine: in Tatlin's deliberate "descent" into the feminized domain of everyday life (*byt*) when he makes his everyday objects; in the work of the women artists Stepanova and Popova within the feminized fields of textile and fashion design; in Rodchenko and Mayakovsky's refusal of stereotyped gender images in their advertisements; and in Tret'iakov's portrayal of an active Bolshevik femininity in his eugenic play *I Want a Child!*, the subject of the epilogue.

The use of art historical methods in this study of utilitarian objects will prompt questions about the objects' artistic status. Are they still art objects, or do they constitute a new category of object, and if so, what kind? One answer might be that utilitarian Constructivist objects are best analyzed within the history of design, rather than art history. But as the design historian Victor Margolin has noted, the Constructivists advanced the model of the artist-constructor "without any accountability or reference to prior forms of design practice."[71] They also consciously disassociated themselves from contemporary design movements such as Le Corbusier's Esprit Nouveau or the Bauhaus, with which they were frequently compared, protesting that these movements simply designed aesthetic versions of capitalist industrial objects in the tradition of applied or decorative art, while they aimed to produce an entirely new order of objects within socialist production.[72] While acknowledging that Constructivist objects form a part of the history of design, this study will follow their self-definition and consider them within the art history of the "historical avant-garde" as defined by Bürger.

Do these "socialist objects" then look different from other objects? The answer offered here is that they do look different from the other mass-produced objects of the time that they were meant to equal and surpass, precisely because they were made self-consciously by artists who were still working individually from a particular set of artistic and personal commitments. They had not yet arrived at the model of the artist-constructor, fully integrated into the industrial mass-production process. But the eventual goal of the Constructivists was to achieve the integration of the artist-constructor into industry, at which point the objects that they made would no longer look different, because all industrial objects would by then be transparent and expedient, and all would be coworkers or comrades.

The Constructivist notion of the industrial object as a coworker, fulfilling or amplifying the sensory capacities of the human organism, is at the core of what could be called the aesthetics of Constructivism—a term that might be more apt than the art history of Constructivism, given the Constructivists' own declaration of a "war against art" in their program. While the category of the aesthetic might seem far removed from the industrial, anti-art ambitions of Constructivism, Terry Eagleton reminds us that "aesthetics is born as a discourse of the body."[73] The meanings of the ancient Greek words from which the term aesthetics derives are "that which is 'perceptive by feeling'" and "the sensory experience of perception."[74] Constructivist aesthetics was an attempt to enrich the body of the socialist subject through the most appropriate forms of modern objects—to have industrial technology amplify sensory experience, rather than sedate or lull it, as it did under capitalism. As Susan Buck-Morss argues in her essay "Aesthetics and Anaesthetics," this lulling was the effect of modernity, either through the deadening of the senses that was the body's natural response to the sensory shock of the factory, the railroad, the metropolis; or through the narcotic of what Walter Benjamin called, following Marx, "the commodity phantasmagoria."[75]

The transparent socialist object as elaborated by Arvatov is aesthetic rather than anaesthetic. It would make the experience of industrial production an extension of the senses, rather than a shock or a narcotic that mystifies the relation to the object. Benjamin wished to awaken people from the "dream sleep" of the commodity phantasmagoria through the "materialist history" that he presented in his unfinished *Arcades Project*, just as the Constructivists wished to do through their materialist practice. In Benjamin's analysis of the revolutionary potential of mass culture, the moments of potential awakening took the form of a dialectical image: "that wherein what has been comes together in a flash with the now to form a constellation."[76] The transitional nature of Constructivist objects, operating within the semicapitalist context of NEP but looking toward the socialist future, make them into material incarnations of Benjamin's dialectical image. The proposal of this book is that the transparency of the Constructivist object was not just material, but also psychological, offering the flash of critical understanding of mass culture under NEP that would be necessary for waking up from the commodity phantasmagoria of capitalism into the future socialist culture.

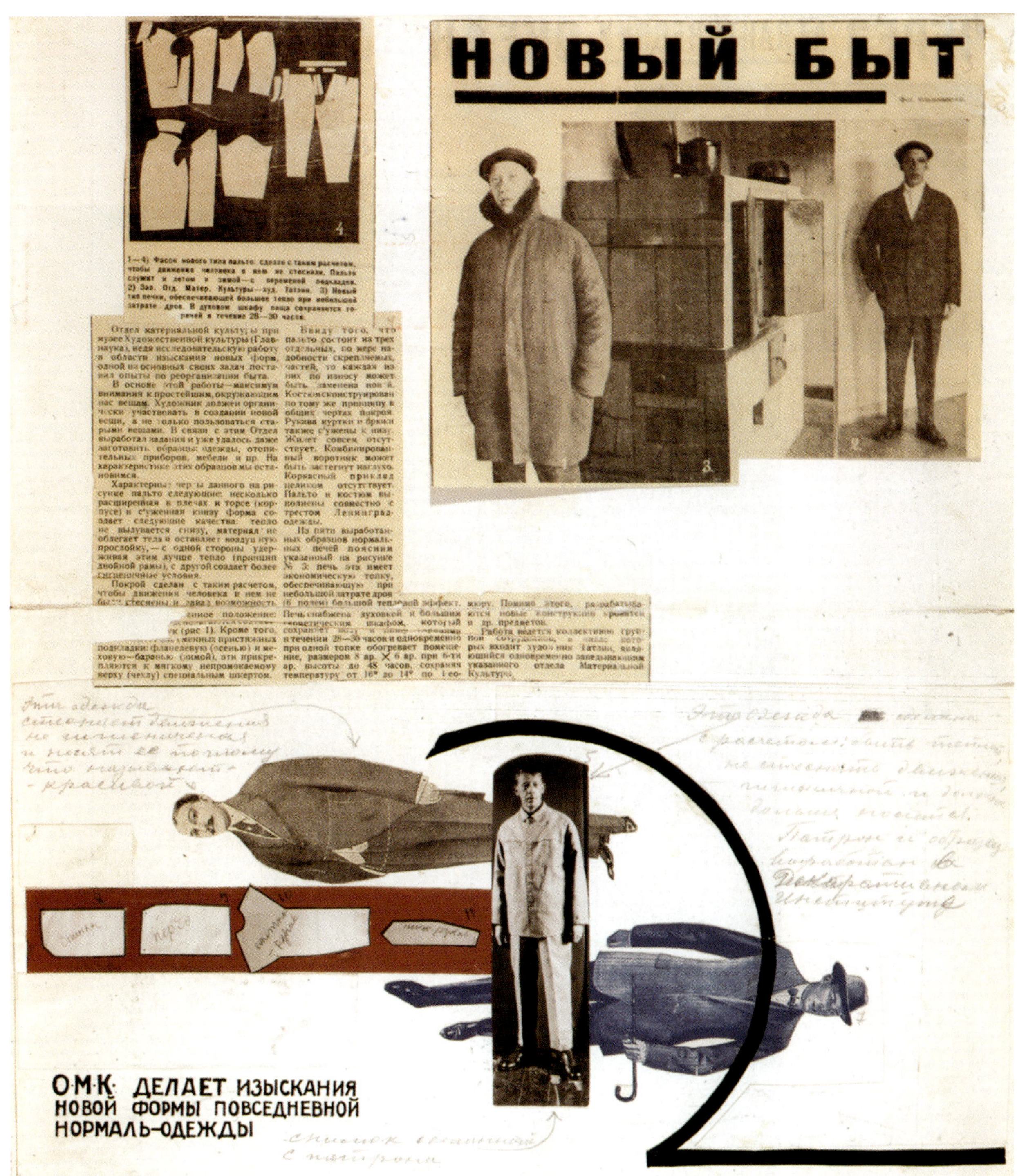

PLATE I

Vladimir Tatlin, montage incorporating the article "The New Everyday Life," 1924–1925. Cut-and-pasted printed papers, photographs, india ink, and pencil on paper.

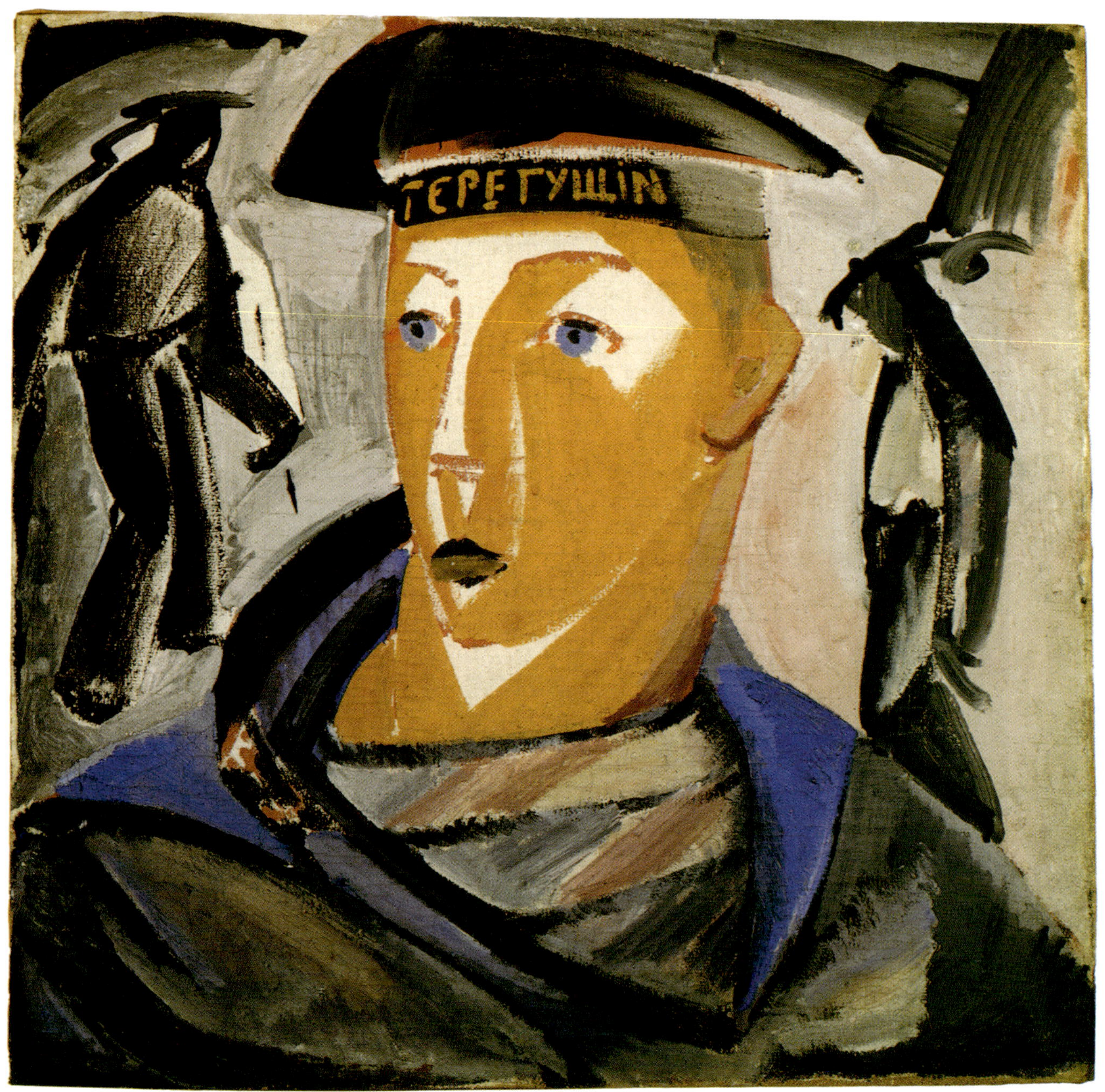

PLATE 2

Vladimir Tatlin, *Sailor (Self-Portrait)*, 1911. Tempera on canvas. Courtesy State Russian Museum, St. Petersburg.

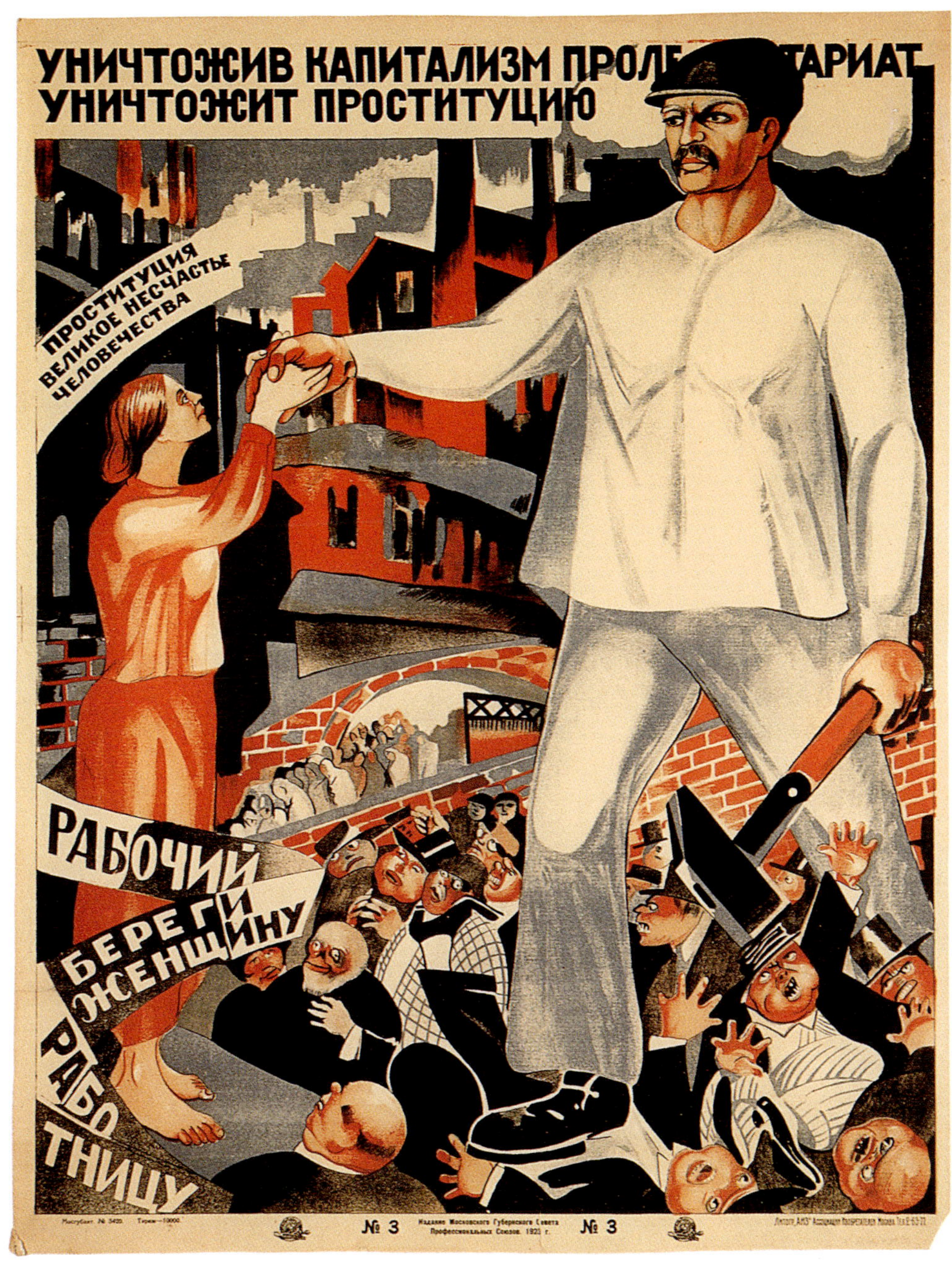

PLATE 3

Poster: "Having wiped out capitalism, the proletariat will wipe out prostitution," 1923.
Courtesy Russian State Library Department of Graphics, Moscow.

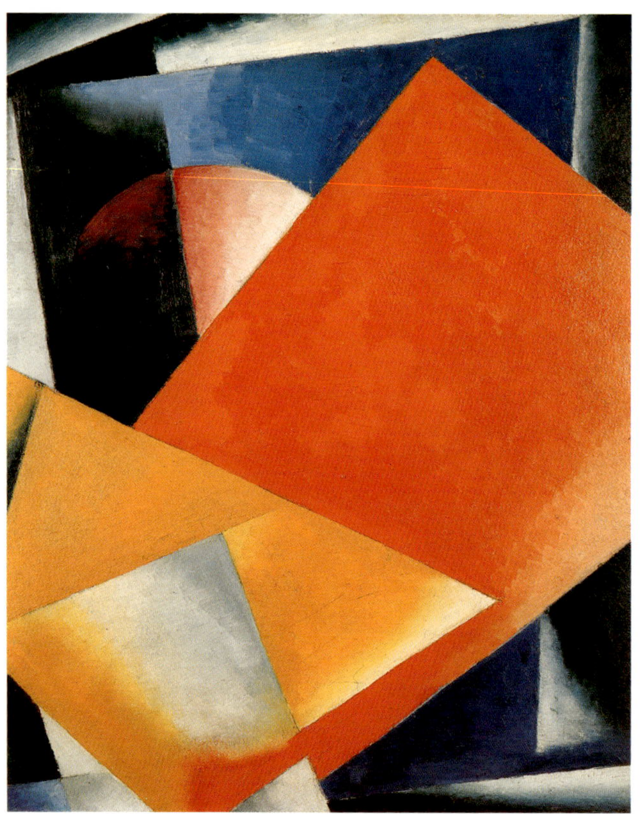

PLATE 4

Liubov' Popova, *Painterly Architectonics with Pink Semicircle*, 1918.
Oil on canvas. State Tret'iakov Gallery, Moscow.

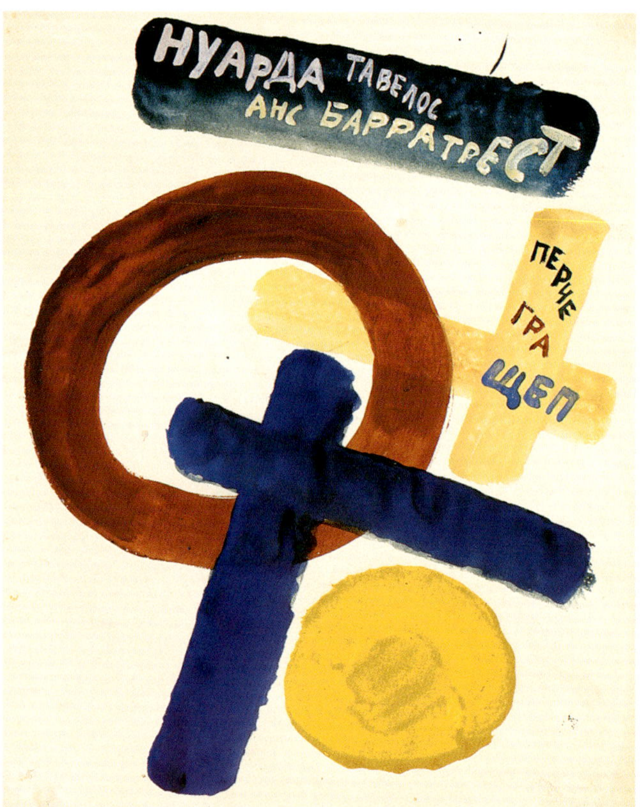

PLATE 5

Varvara Stepanova, illustration for *Rtny Khomle*, 1918.
Tempera on paper. Private collection.

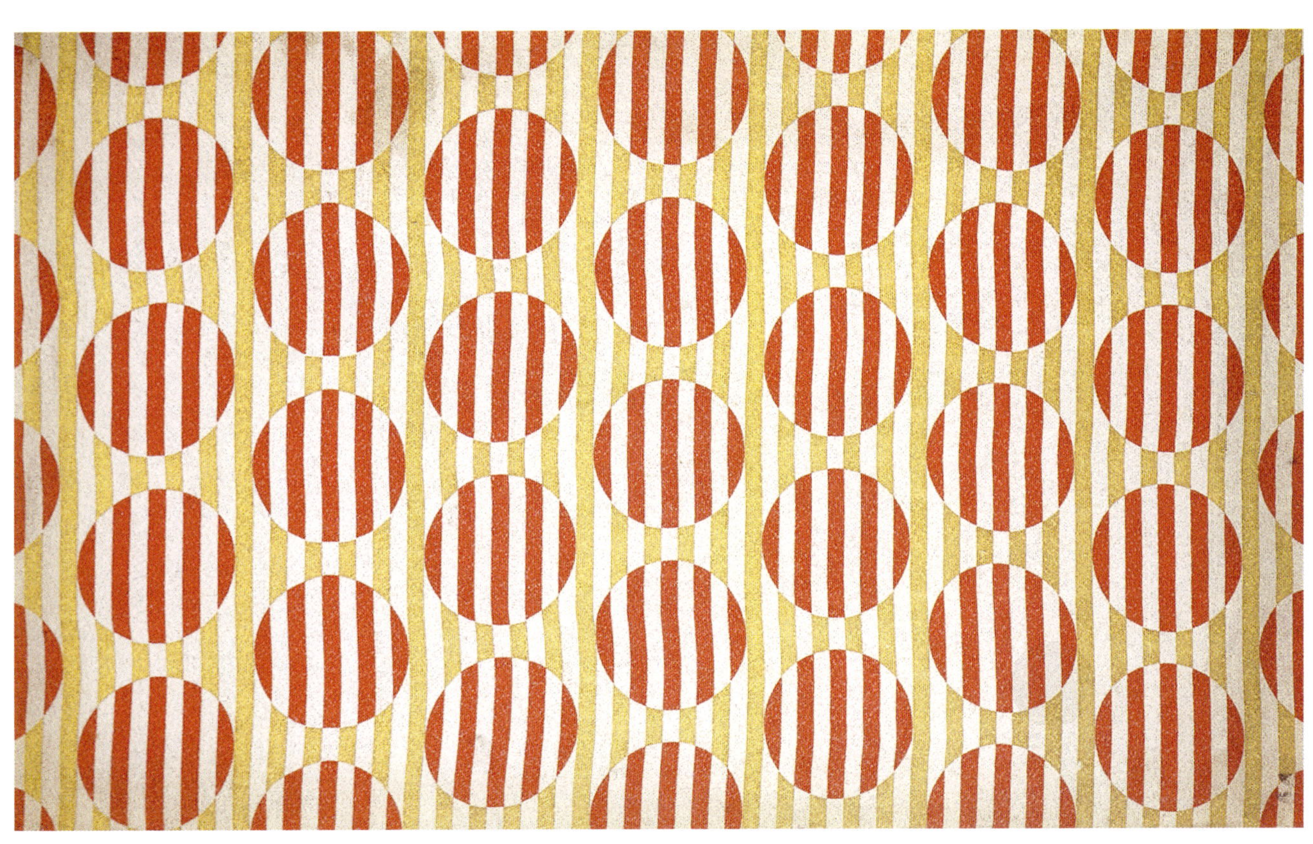

PLATE 6
Varvara Stepanova, weaving sample of fabric, 1923–1924. Private collection.

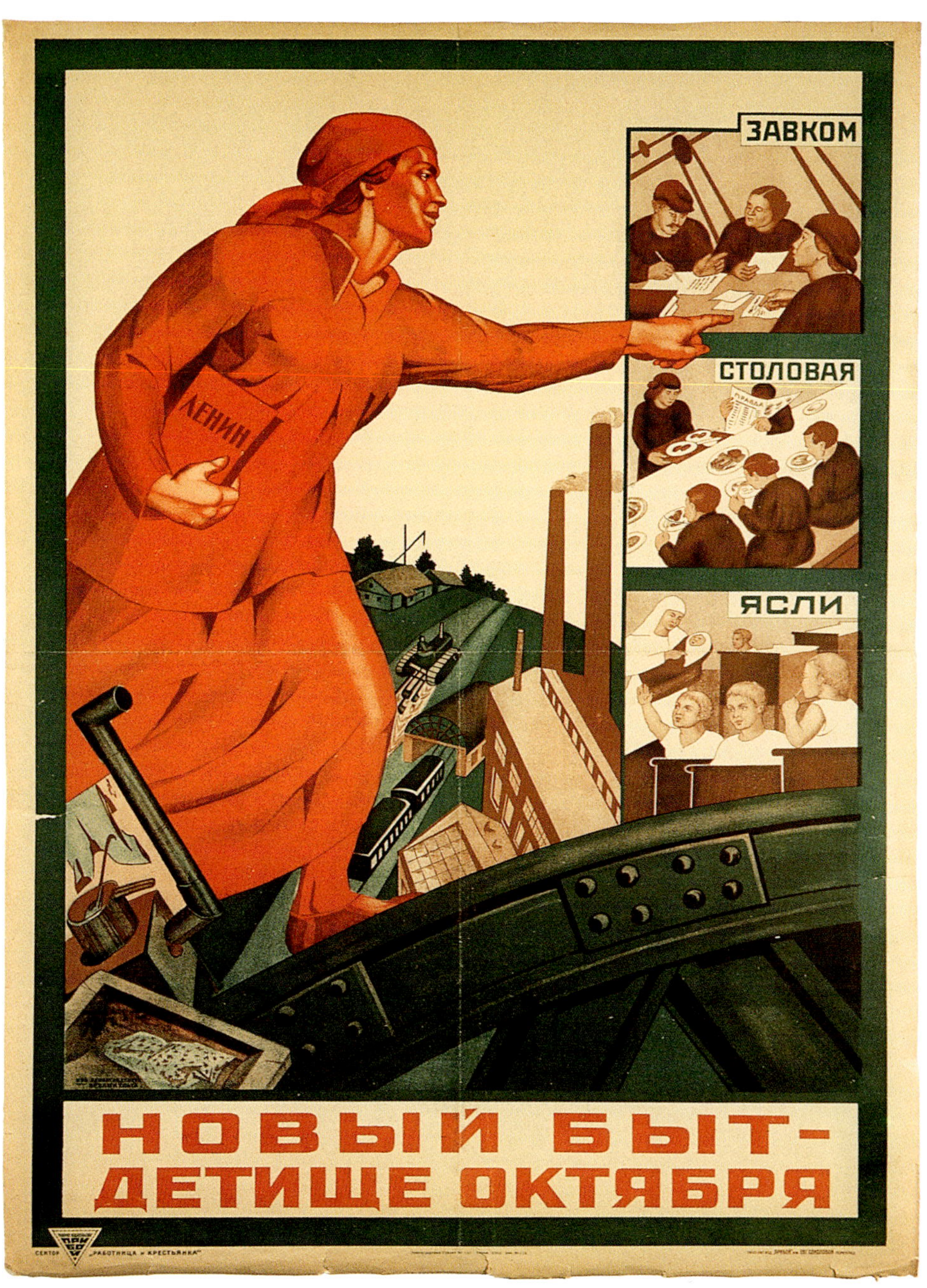

PLATE 7
Poster: "The new everyday life is the child of October," 1923.
Courtesy Russian State Library Department of Graphics, Moscow.

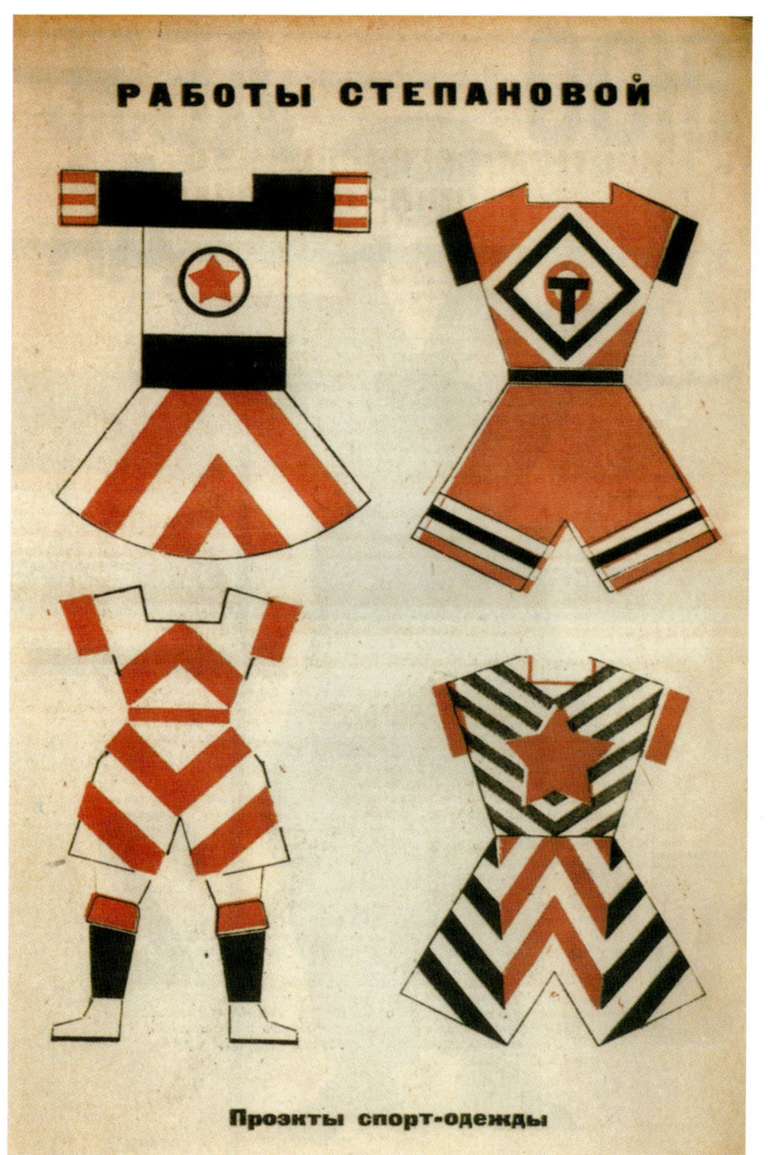

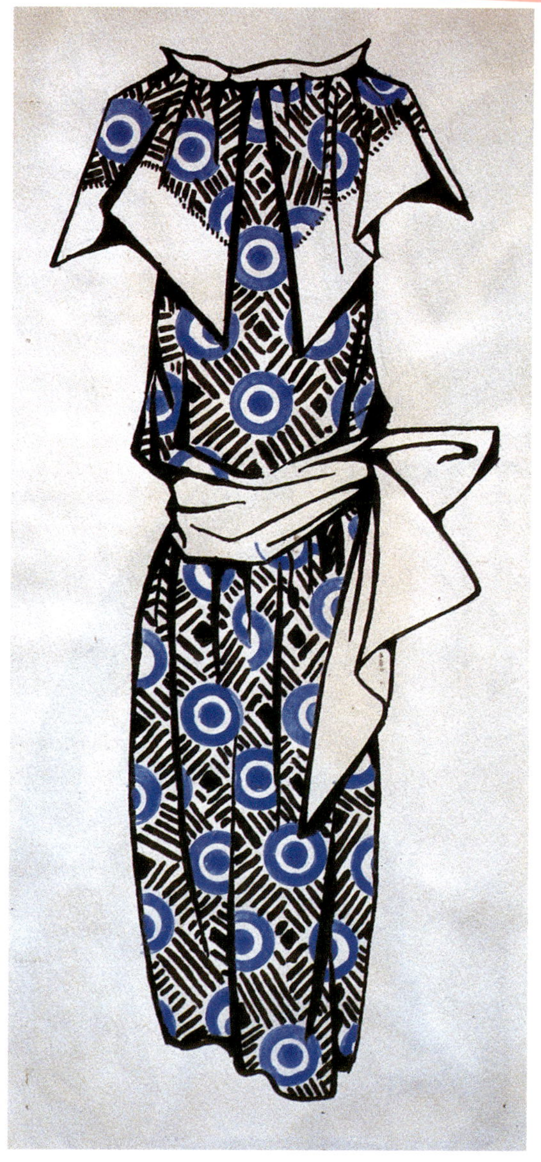

PLATE 8
Varvara Stepanova, designs for sports clothes, 1923.

PLATE 9
Liubov' Popova, design for a dress, 1923–1924.
India ink on paper. Courtesy Dmitrii Sarabianov.

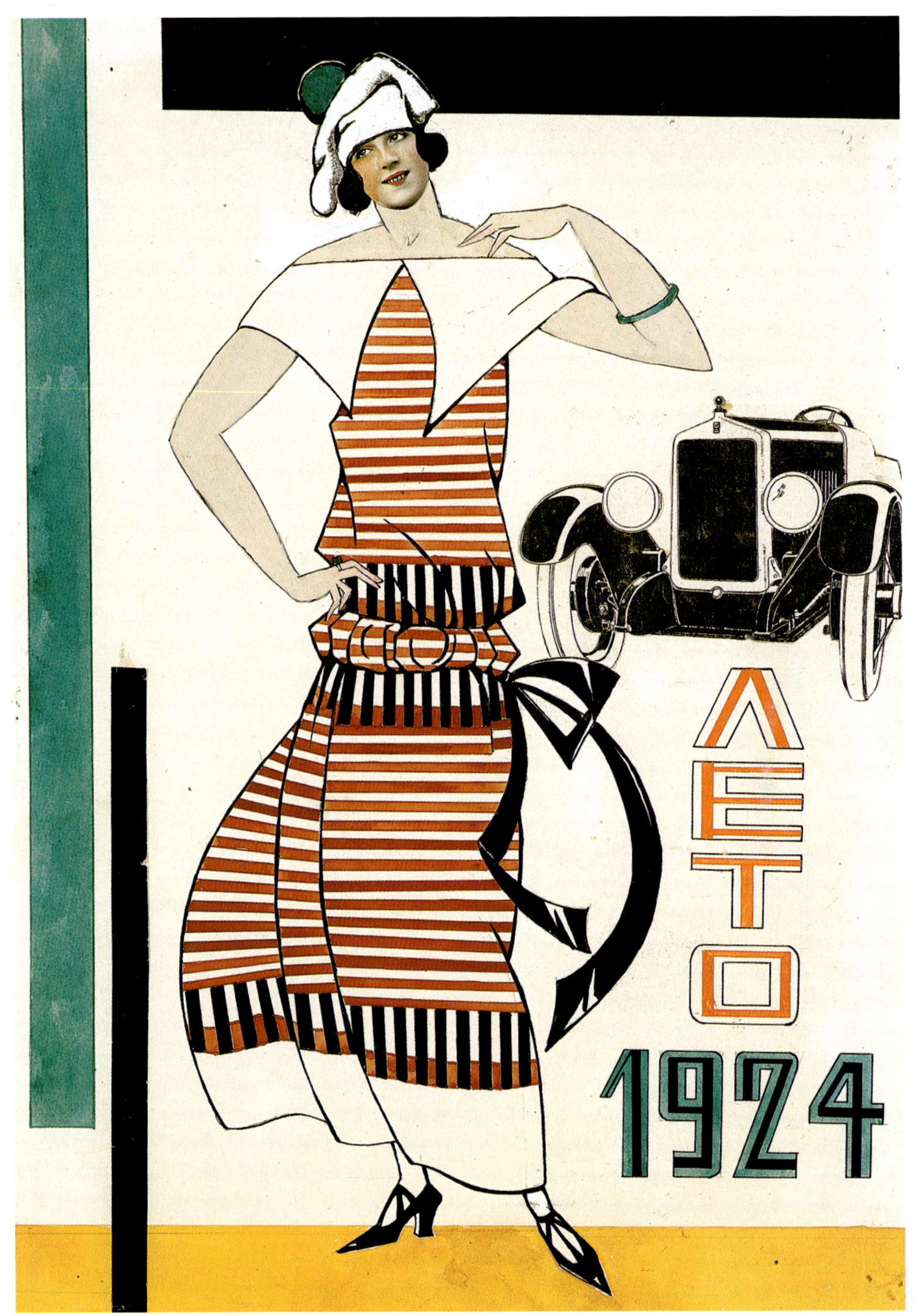

PLATE 10

Liubov' Popova, design for a window display, 1924. India ink, gouache, cut-and-pasted printed papers, varnish on paper. Photo courtesy State Tret'iakov Gallery, Moscow.

НОВЫЙ БЫТ

Фот. Ольшанского.

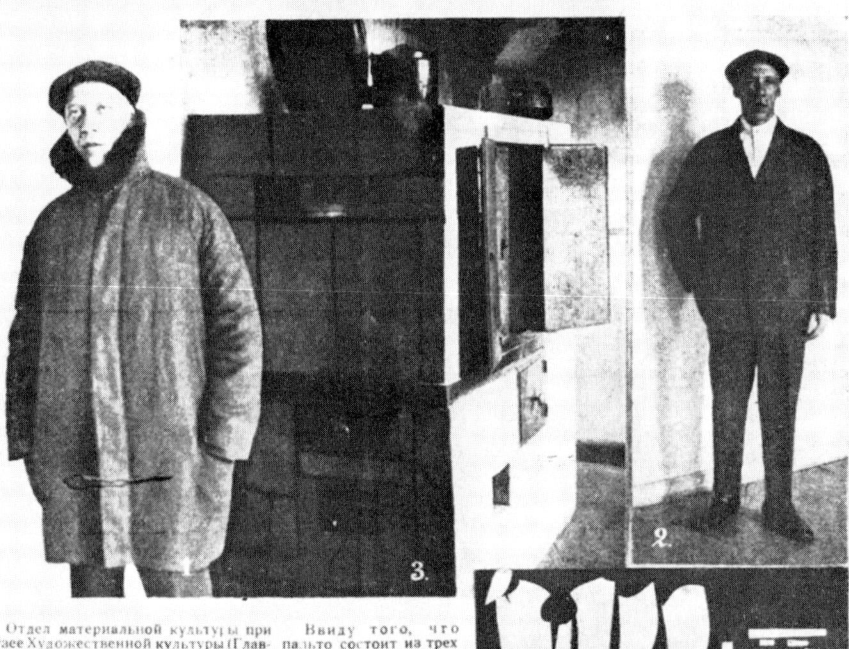

Отдел материальной культуры при музее Художественной культуры (Главнаука), ведя исследовательскую работу в области изыскания новых форм, одной из основных своих задач поставил опыты по реорганизации быта.

В основе этой работы—максимум внимания к простейшим, окружающим нас вещам. Художник должен органически участвовать в создании новой вещи, а не только пользоваться старыми вещами. В связи с этим Отдел выработал задания и уже удалось даже заготовить образцы: одежды, отопительных приборов, мебели и пр. На характеристике этих образцов мы остановимся.

Характерные черты данного на рисунке пальто следующие: несколько расширенная в плечах и торсе (корпусе) и с'уженная книзу форма создает следующие качества: тепло не выдувается снизу, материал не облегает тела и оставляет воздушную прослойку,—с одной стороны удерживая этим лучше тепло (принцип двойной рамы), с другой соадает более гигиеничные условия.

Покрой сделан с таким расчетом, чтобы движения человека в нем не были стеснены и давал возможность сохранять естественное положение: напр., карманы располагаются соответсвенно длине рук (рис 1). Кроме того, пальто имеет две сменных пристяжных подкладки: фланелевую (осенью) и меховую—баранью (зимой), эти прикрепляются к мягкому непромокаемому верху (чехлу) специальным шкертом.

Ввиду того, что пальто состоит из трех отдельных, по мере надобности скрепляемых, частей, то каждая из них по износу может быть заменена новой. Костюмсконструирован по тому же принципу в общих чертах покроя. Рукава куртки и брюки также с'ужены к низу. Жилет совсем отсутствует. Комбинированный воротник может быть застегнут наглухо. Коркасный приклад целиком отсутствует. Пальто и костюм выполнены совместно с трестом Ленинградодежды.

Из пяти выработанных образцов нормальных печей поясним указанный на рисунке № 3: печь эта имеет экономическую топку, обеспечивающую при небольшой затрате дров (6 полен) большой тепловой эффект. Печь снабжена духовкой и большим герметическим шкафом, который сохраняет воду и пищу горячими в течении 28—30 часов и одновременно при одной топке обогревает помещение, размером 8 ар. × 6 ар. при 6-ти ар. высоты до 48 часов, сохраняя температуру от 16° до 14° по Реомюру. Помимо этого, разрабатываются новые конструкции кроватей и др. предметов.

Работа ведется коллективно группой сотрудников, в число которых входит художник Татлин, являющийся одновременно заведывающим указанного отдела Материальной Культуры.

1—4) Фасон нового типа пальто: сделан с таким расчетом, чтобы движения человека в нем не стесняли. Пальто служит и летом и зимой—с переменой подкладки. 2) Зав. Отд. Матер. Культуры—худ. Татлин. 3) Новый тип печки, обеспечивающей большое тепло при небольшой затрате дров. В духовом шкафу пища сохраняется горячей в течение 28—30 часов.

FIGURE 2.1

Vladimir Tatlin, designs for clothing and a stove, illustrated in the article "The New Everyday Life," *Krasnaia panorama* no. 23 (1924).

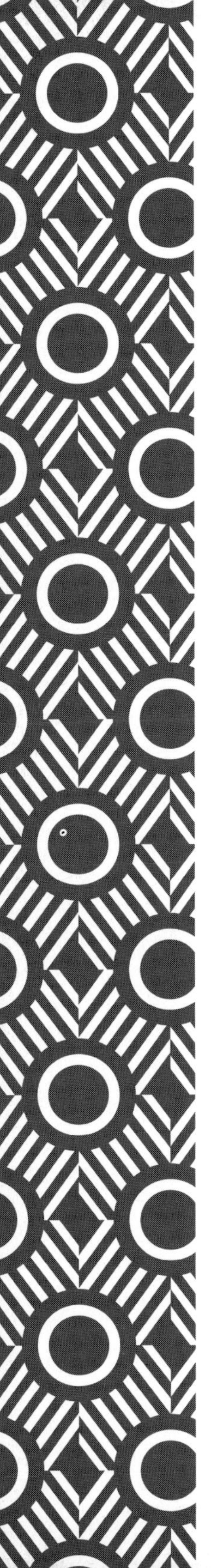

CHAPTER 2

EVERYDAY OBJECTS

In November 1920, the Russian avant-garde artist Vladimir Tatlin was photographed with the wooden model of his *Monument to the Third International*. Projected to spiral almost half a kilometer into the sky, the monument would span the width of the Neva river in Petrograd; the outer latticework frame would be built of iron, while on the inside, four giant buildings made of glass would hang suspended above the river, each rotating at a different speed. Four years later, in December 1924, Tatlin again had himself photographed with his work—this time, an overcoat, a practical men's suit, pattern pieces, and a wood-burning stove, all prototypes for industrial mass production—which illustrated a brief article in the popular magazine *Krasnaia panorama* (Red Panorama) under the boldface title "The New Everyday Life" (*Novyi byt*; figure 2.1).[1] The towering, tilted, open-framework spiral forms of the monument (figure 2.2) have given way, in the intervening four years, to the heavy, rooted boxlike shape of the undecorated and human-scale tile stove. The two photographs also present vastly different versions of the convention of "the artist with his work": Tatlin the leader of the left avant-garde, casually posed at the base of his spectacular tower in proletarian jacket and cap, pipe in hand, has given way to these stiff, even dour photographs of Tatlin the Constructivist, modeling his sensible overcoat and practical suit.

In a statement issued about his *Monument* in late 1920, Tatlin had famously declared "Distrusting the eye, we place it under the control of touch,"[2] yet this declaration seems to apply at least as much to the everyday material objects he would go on to make in 1923–1924. The declaration also forms an instructive counterpoint to Aleksandr Rodchenko's assertion during the debates on

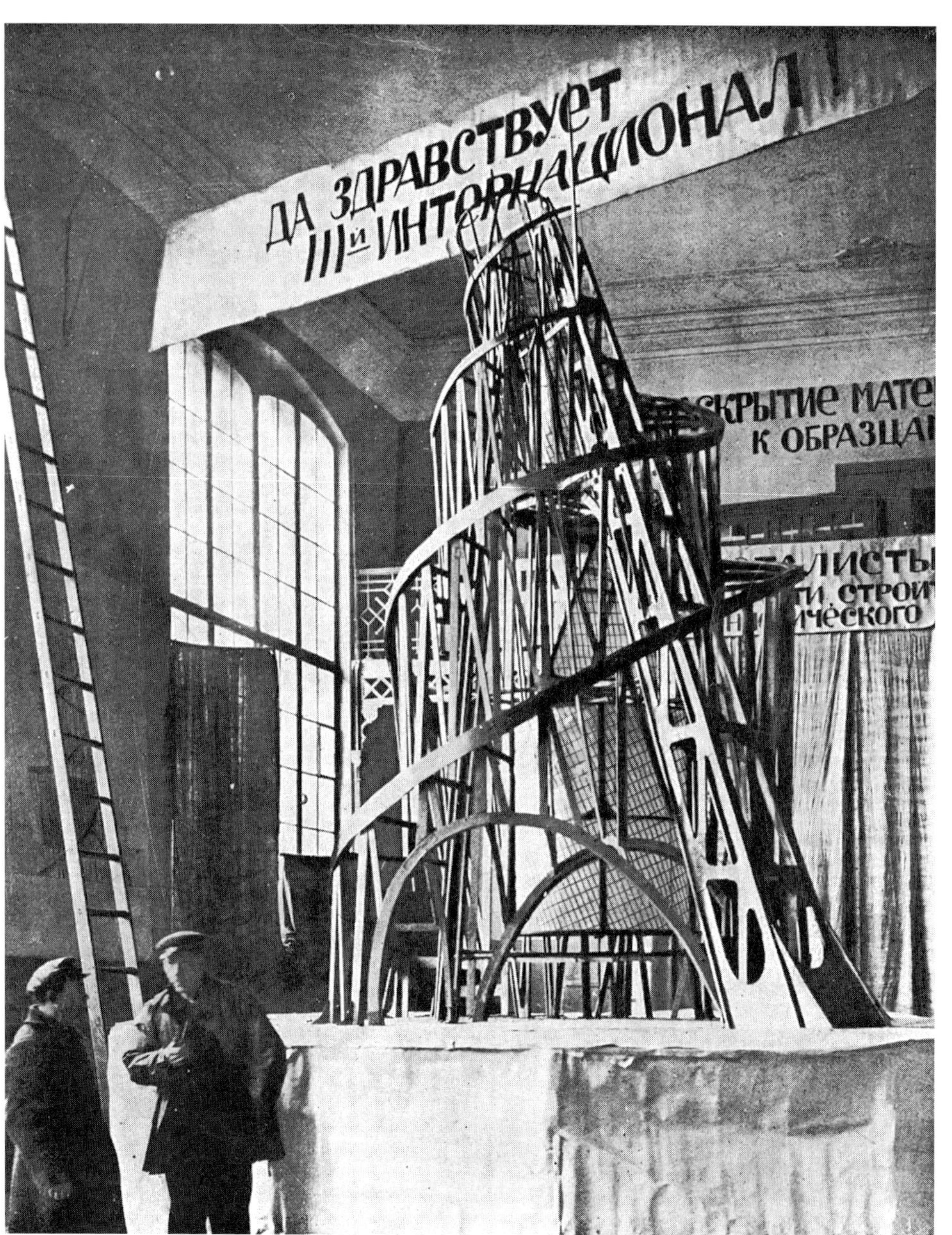

FIGURE 2.2
Vladimir Tatlin with his *Monument to the Third International*, 1920.

Productivism at the Moscow Institute of Artistic Culture (INKhUK) that artists are different from engineers because "*we know how to see*."[3] The single-minded intensity of Tatlin's choice to emphasize touch over vision, material over visual, represents one of the most dramatic shifts in an individual artist's practice in the history of the avant-garde. The critic Abram Efros mustered the requisite pathos in pronouncing the standard negative assessment of this shift in 1924: "I regret that Tatlin descended into Constructivism, his talent is so great and so necessary—I regret that he is inventing and building economical stoves. . . . art is unhappy, it still remembers Tatlin the artist, it could still regard as its own Tatlin the builder, the fantastic architect of the Tower of the Third International."[4] Even within the history of Russian Constructivism, Tatlin's "descent" is one of the most absolute shifts from making visual art to making plain utilitarian objects. His everyday objects are therefore the necessary place to begin the story of the Constructivist socialist object even if they will not be the best place to end it, because they attempt to deny rather than engage with the object desires of modernity.

Although he was recognized as the "father of Constructivism"—born in 1885, he was six years older than Rodchenko and about fifteen years older than the youngest student members of the Constructivist group formed at INKhUK in 1921—Tatlin never called himself a Constructivist, and referred to his own practice as the "culture of materials" to distinguish it from that of the INKhUK Constructivists.[5] During the period of the INKhUK debates in Moscow, Tatlin was teaching in Petrograd, but he was a "corresponding member" of the Institute and occasionally attended meetings. At a meeting in December 1921, even though one of the younger Constructivists attacked him personally, criticizing the "utopianism" of his *Monument*, Tatlin came out in accord with the Productivist program of utilitarian, industrial production. "Life compels us to make new things," he said. "We must unite and work together."[6] He began "working together" with a group of artists to make "new things" in 1922 at his studio, the Section for Material Culture, which was part of the State Institute of Artistic Culture (GINKhUK) in Petrograd. The Tatlin scholar Larissa Zhadova notes that although Tatlin always identified himself as the director of the Section and signed his reports on its work "on behalf of the Group for Material Culture," this seeming individualism was not in conflict with his own conception of the individual in relation to the collective as he had expressed it in a 1919 statement: "The initiative individual is the refraction point of the collective's creativity and brings realization to the idea."[7] The "New Everyday Life" article in *Krasnaia panorama*, though dominated by the two large illustrations of Tatlin himself, speaks anonymously of the work of the Section, mentioning Tatlin's name only in the final paragraph: "The work is carried out collectively by a group of co-workers whose numbers include the artist Tatlin, who is at the same time also the director."[8] In 1924, then, Tatlin presents himself as a collective worker creating the most basic material objects for use in everyday life; as the opening lines of the article put it, the work of the Section experiments with "the reorganization of everyday life" and is based on "calling maximum attention to the simplest things that surround us."

In its emphasis on "the simplest things that surround us," Tatlin's art-into-life project defies the commodity aesthetics and consumer desires that flourished again in revolutionary Russia during the period of the New Economic Policy (NEP). For Tatlin, the everyday life of noncapitalist modernity would be simple and functional. Industrial production would be appropriately altered—by advanced artists like himself—to meet the most pressing daily needs of the masses, rather than to cater to their errant desires. He set up this contrast in the bluntest of terms in a photomontage that he made on the basis of the "New Everyday Life" article shortly after its publication in December 1924, which was likely displayed in the "exhibition room" of the Section for Material Culture (figure 2.3).[9] The lower section of the photomontage incorporates an additional photograph of Tatlin modeling his design for a men's sportswear suit, pasted above and partially obscuring two horizontal images of gentlemen wearing fashionable suits—the upper one distinctly old-fashioned, the lower one more contemporary—cut out of magazines. The earnest contrast between the images of Tatlin and the gentlemen is amplified by the scribbled texts in Tatlin's own hand. On the right, the handwritten lines connected to his picture with an emphatic straight-lined arrow assert the vehement need-based practicality of his sportswear suit: "This clothing is made with the advantage of being warm, not restricting movement, being hygienic and lasting longer." A scrawled curving arrow connects the reproachful text on the left to the fashionable gentlemen: "This clothing restricts movement, is unhygienic, and they wear it only because they consider it—beautiful." The misguided men who covet clothing merely for its beauty represent the old, capitalist way of life, now resurgent in the period of NEP. The cut-and-paste technique of the photomontage asserts that Tatlin's "material culture" will literally eclipse these men and their aesthetic consumer desires, replacing them with consumers who want only simple, unadorned things that fulfill human needs.

Tatlin's particular version of the "socialist object" therefore counters Peter Bürger's worry, in *Theory of the Avant-Garde*, that the art-into-life strategies of the avant-garde courted a collapse of art into the "commodity aesthetics" of mass

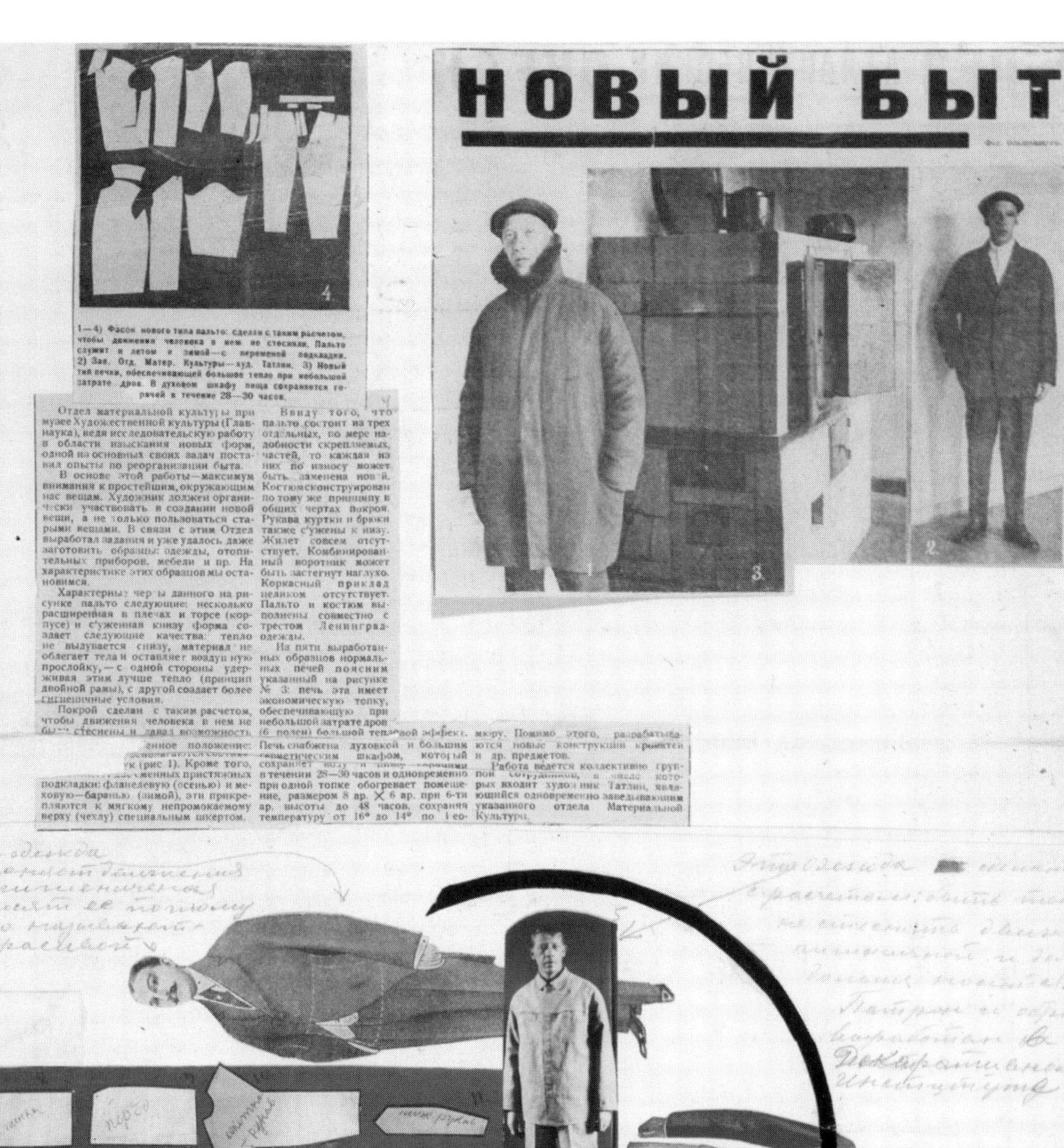

НОВЫЙ БЫТ

1—4) Фасон нового типа пальто: сделан с таким расчетом, чтобы движения человека в нем не стесняли. Пальто служит и летом и зимой—с переменой подкладки. 2) Зав. Отд. Матер. Культуры—худ. Татлин. 3) Новый тип печки, обеспечивающей большое тепло при небольшой затрате дров. В духовом шкафу пища сохраняется горячей в течение 28—30 часов.

Отдел материальной культуры при музее Художественной культуры (Главнаука), ведя исследовательскую работу в области изыскания новых форм, одной из основных своих задач поставил опыты по реорганизации быта.

В основе этой работы—максимум внимания к простейшим, окружающим нас вещам. Художник должен органически участвовать в создании новой вещи, а не только пользоваться старыми вещами. В связи с этим Отдел выработал задания и уже удалось даже заготовить образцы: одежды, отопительных приборов, мебели и пр. На характеристике этих образцов мы остановимся.

Характерные черты данного на рисунке пальто следующие: несколько расширенная в плечах и торсе (корпусе) и суженная книзу форма создает следующие качества: тепло не выдувается снизу, материал не облегает тела и оставляет воздушную прослойку,—с одной стороны удерживая этим лучше тепло (принцип двойной рамы), с другой создает более гигиеничные условия.

Покрой сделан с таким расчетом, чтобы движения человека в нем не были стеснены и давал возможность [illegible] енное положение: [illegible] ук (рис 1). Кроме того, [illegible] менных пристяжных подкладки: фланелевую (осенью) и меховую—баранью (зимой), эти прикрепляются к мягкому непромокаемому верху (чехлу) специальным шкертом.

Ввиду того, что пальто состоит из трех отдельных, по мере надобности скрепляемых, частей, то каждая из них по износу может быть заменена новой. Костюм сконструирован по тому же принципу в общих чертах покроя. Рукава куртки и брюки также сужены к низу. Жилет совсем отсутствует. Комбинированный воротник может быть застегнут наглухо. Корсасный приклад целиком отсутствует. Пальто и костюм выполнены совместно с трестом Ленинградодежды.

Из пяти выработанных образцов нормальных печей поясним указанный на рисунке № 3: печь эта имеет экономическую топку, обеспечивающую при небольшой затрате дров (6 полен) большой тепловой эффект. Печь снабжена духовкой и большим герметическим шкафом, который сохраняет [illegible] в течении 28—30 часов и одновременно при одной топке обогревает помещение, размером 8 ар. X 6 ар. при 6-ти ар. высоты до 48 часов, сохраняя температуру от 16° до 14° по [illegible] мору. Помимо этого, разрабатываются новые конструкции кроватей и др. предметов.

Работа ведется коллективно группой сотрудников, в числе которых входит художник Татлин, являющийся одновременно заведывающим указанного отдела Материальной Культуры.

О.М.К. ДЕЛАЕТ ИЗЫСКАНИЯ НОВОЙ ФОРМЫ ПОВСЕДНЕВНОЙ НОРМАЛЬ-ОДЕЖДЫ

FIGURE 2.3

Vladimir Tatlin, montage incorporating the article "The New Everyday Life," 1924–1925. Cut-and-pasted printed papers, photographs, india ink, and pencil on paper. See plate 1.

culture.[10] Although Tatlin designed his objects to be mass produced, his vision of socialist modernity included industrial production and technology but excluded the commercialized mass culture of capitalism. Yet in their material literalness and emphatic utility his objects threaten to enact a different collapse of the work of art into the mute artifacts of everyday life. They attempt to deny all visual qualities—not only "beauty"—in favor of material qualities of primitive utility such as hygiene and warmth. By purporting to address only consumer need, and not consumer desire, within socialist modernity, they diverge from this book's definition of the socialist object. At the same time, however, they are socialist objects in the sense that Tatlin clearly construed them as active and emotionally affective: his language of affection for his everyday objects, as they heroically beat down capitalist commodities, demonstrates that they function as "comrades" and "coworkers" in his fight against the old everyday life. This chapter will argue that Tatlin's stunning shift from making ambitious art to making stoves and boxy suits should not be understood as a moment of descent or loss for the avant-garde, but as a conscious invention of an active material object through which the modernist principle of "truth to materials"—the will of the medium or the material itself determining artistic form—takes on a social agency.

Tatlin's Primitivisms

Tatlin was well aware of the contradiction between the primitive technology of his wood-burning stove and the advanced technological ambitions of Constructivism: "The time for 'Americanized' stoves in the conditions of our Russian everyday life [*byt*] has not yet arrived," he told the art historian and critic Nikolai Punin. "We need things as simple and primitive as our simple and primitive everyday life."[11] *Amerikanizm* was a buzzword for modernity in early Soviet Russia, with strong positive connotations of advanced industrial technology and inventiveness as well as the obvious negative ones, from a Bolshevik perspective, of capitalist excess. Tatlin is wistful that Russia is not yet ready for the Americanized stoves, just as the Russian economy and engineering resources had been nowhere near adequate for actually building the technological marvel of his proposed *Monument to the Third International*. There were barely enough nails to be found in Petrograd, so the well-known story goes, to build the wooden model of it. But he is also realistic to the point of pessimism: by 1924, more completely than his Constructivist colleagues, he has shed the unrealistic industrial enthusiasm that so gripped the INKhUK Productivists during the years of War Communism. If they understood their dream of the artist-constructor working in socialist industry as being challenged primarily by the demands of the consumerist NEP economy, Tatlin saw the challenge as stemming from the other side: from Russia's historically backward, agrarian economy. He directed his utilitarian objects toward feasibly improving the deeply traditional, outmoded practices of everyday life experienced by the majority of proletarians and peasants, rather than at sustaining the tenuously more modern life experienced by certain classes of urban dwellers, like the Nepmen and members of the intelligentsia, in Leningrad and Moscow.

Tatlin's commitment to "our simple and primitive everyday life" in 1924 significantly recasts the notion of the "primitive" as it functioned in the neoprimitivist movement through which he first entered the prerevolutionary avant-garde around 1911.[12] The neoprimitivist painter Natalia Goncharova promoted Russian peasant subject matter as most appropriate for modern Russian painting, even claiming that native Russian forms such as Scythian statuettes and the wooden dolls of craft fairs had invented cubism long before the Parisians.[13] She and the painter Mikhail Larionov, with both of whom Tatlin was closely allied in the early 1910s, mined native Russian art forms for their flattened formal qualities and their pictorial immediacy: the folk art traditions of the flat, colorful *lubki* (woodcuts), patterned shawls, and wooden dolls; the curvilinear forms and shimmering colors of icons; the bright, flattened figuration of commercial shop signs; and, in the case of Larionov, the crude graffiti of Russian army barracks.[14] One of Tatlin's first major exhibitions of his work, at the avant-garde Donkey's Tail (*Osliny khvost*) exhibition in Moscow in March 1912, included the paintings *Fishmonger* and *Sailor (Self-Portrait)* (figure 2.4), both from 1911, in keeping with the exhibition's theme of "scenes from folk life."

In *Sailor (Self-Portrait)*, Tatlin presents himself in sailor's uniform, recalling his work as a ship's boy in his early teenage years, when he ran away from home and sailed to Bulgaria and Turkey, and his summer work, while attending the art college in Penza in his early twenties, as a professional sailor of ships on the Mediterranean. The painting refers to the pictorial tradition of the *lubok* in its use of opaque areas of a limited palette of blue, gold, and black paint, and in the dramatically contrasting scale of the two tiny, flattened figures framing Tatlin's head, their distance from him signified only by their difference in size, not by the more sophisticated techniques of painterly realism. Even more obviously the painting evokes the icon tradition, in the triangular shape of the face, the stylized curve of brow into nose, the gracefully curving silhouettes of the two small figures, and the gold color and striking white highlights of the face. Tatlin's self-portrait deftly collapses the lower-class masculine image of the sailor, dashing but

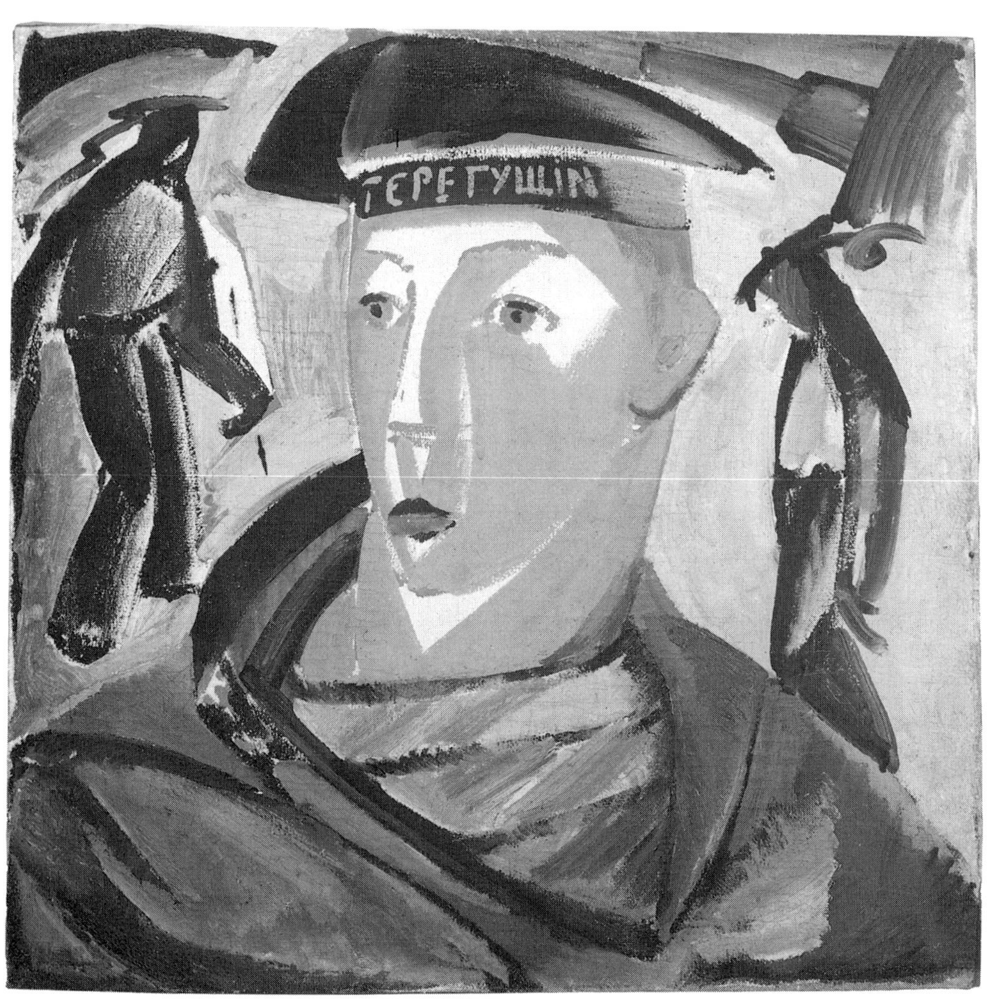

FIGURE 2.4

Vladimir Tatlin, *Sailor (Self-Portrait)*, 1911. Tempera on canvas. Courtesy State Russian Museum, St. Petersburg. See plate 2.

uneducated, with the otherworldly intensity of icon portraits of the saints, to create an arrestingly hybrid image of himself as modern Russian artist. In this model of primitivism, the appropriated native or folk forms themselves signify as inherently modern in the colorful immediacy of their simplified, even crude visual language, promising unmediated access to the authenticity or pleasure or spirituality offered by the subject matter.

Tatlin soon followed a singular path out of this folk primitivism, however, narrowing his focus by 1913 to one strand of the Russian native tradition, namely icons, and by 1915 vociferously disassociating himself from all avant-garde "isms."[15] What so attracted Tatlin's attention in the icon tradition was less its primitiveness than its unique materiality: icon paintings were often highlighted with bright white paint—the technique he used in *Sailor*—as well as gilt, surrounded by elaborate frames made from valuable metals and encrusted with precious stones, metal halos, and even protective metal casings that were opened only on holy occasions.[16] But instead of the precious or ritualized materials of the icon, Tatlin assembled his three-dimensional constructions of the mid-1910s that he called "painterly reliefs" (*Zhivopisnye rel'efy*) and "selections of materials" (*Podbory materialov*) from the detritus of the modern, semi-industrialized city streets. For example, a work like his *Painterly Relief 1915* (figure 2.5), now lost, was made from wood, plaster, tar, glass, and sheet metal. In spite of Goncharova's colorful claim that Russian folk art had invented Cubism long before the French, the relief's jutting forms, framed on the wall in the vertical format of a painting, speak strongly of its debt to the Cubist sculptural collage of Picasso, to whose studio in Paris Tatlin had made a revelatory pilgrimage in the spring of 1914. But if Picasso's Cubist constructions continued to refer to the familiar lexicon of Cubist objects such as guitars and bottles, in order to interrogate the arbitrary nature of the sign in the Western tradition of illusionistic painting, Tatlin's reliefs took as their subject the properties of material itself—the concave curl of glass, the reach of rusted metal.[17]

His reliefs can be characterized as investigations of *faktura*, a fundamental concept of Russian avant-garde art in the early 1910s referring to the way in which a work of art is made, its constitutive materiality. In her detailed account of the term, Maria Gough defines one of the key principles of *faktura* as "materiological determination." Tatlin, she writes, "sought to foster the volition of the material" rather than express his individual artistic will; "reconfiguring himself as the material's assistant, Tatlin thereby partially effaced his own presence within the work."[18] If neoprimitivism had provided a modernist pictorial language for

Tatlin's densely layered self-portrait in *Sailor,* his painterly reliefs participate in a markedly different strand of the modernist project: the attempt to erase artistic will or authorial identity from the work of art in favor of allowing the will of the medium itself to emerge.[19]

Tatlin's effacement of himself from the sculptural work was only a fiction, of course: as Gough also points out, it was Tatlin's subjective act of composition that allowed the assembled materials to find their appropriate form. His artistic choice is evident in the strongly centered, geometric composition of *Painterly Relief* 1915, as well as in the dramatic sweep of the sheets of metal that make up his *Corner Counter-Relief* (*Uglovoi kontr-rel'ef*) of 1915 (figure 2.6). In this lost work, sculpture has vaulted from its usual pedestal on the floor to hang suspended in the air, an angular massing of industrial materials supported by cables that are literally attached to, and dependent on, the corner walls of the room. The "materiological determination" of the work is evident in its investigative, quasi-engineering premise: it tests the weight-bearing capacities of tin and aluminum, as well as the tensile strength of their supporting wires. But at the same time, because the materials do not have to perform any actual function, Tatlin could have assembled them in any number of ways; the work therefore also represents his own compositional choice.

In Gough's analysis, the demand for utilitarian function made by the Constructivist program of 1921 effected the transformation of the meaning of *faktura* from an anti-authorial "materiological determination" to a more conventional functionalism. The political and practical ambitions of the Constructivist program meant that material would no longer determine form, but would become "the instrument" of such external ambitions as the expression of Communist ideology and the fulfillment of a given utilitarian function: "*Faktura* as a principle of materiological determination (form follows material) was replaced by a nascent functionalism (form follows function)."[20] Once form had to follow an external, practical function, it would be determined by the needs of this everyday function, and not by the spirit of the artist as a worker of material. With this functionalism, she continues, the Constructivists retreated from the modernist attack on artistic subjectivity represented by Tatlin's notion of the material itself as generative of artistic form, and opted instead for reinserting the will of the maker in shaping material toward a given external function, in the process leaving art behind entirely in favor of utility.

Gough's text on *Faktura* does not address Tatlin's own later work with utilitarian objects; it contrasts his early reliefs of the 1910s with the later declarations

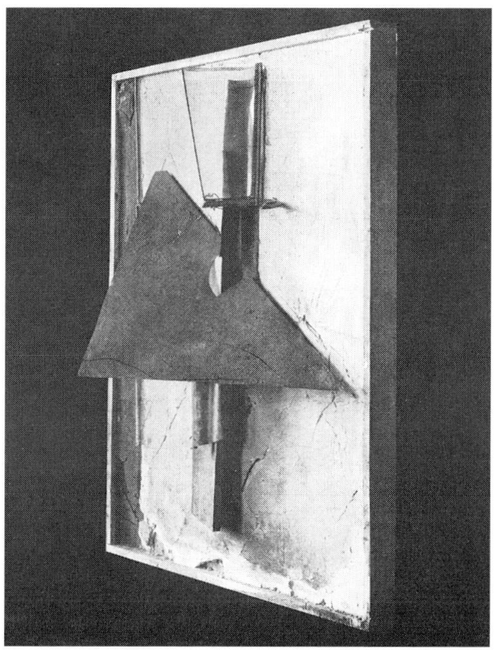

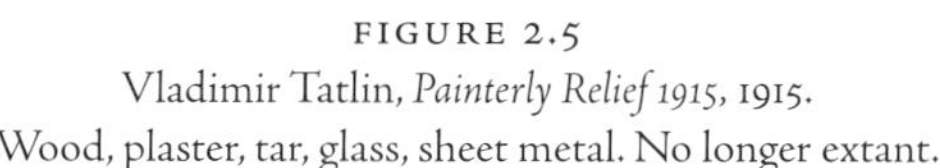

FIGURE 2.5
Vladimir Tatlin, *Painterly Relief 1915*, 1915.
Wood, plaster, tar, glass, sheet metal. No longer extant.

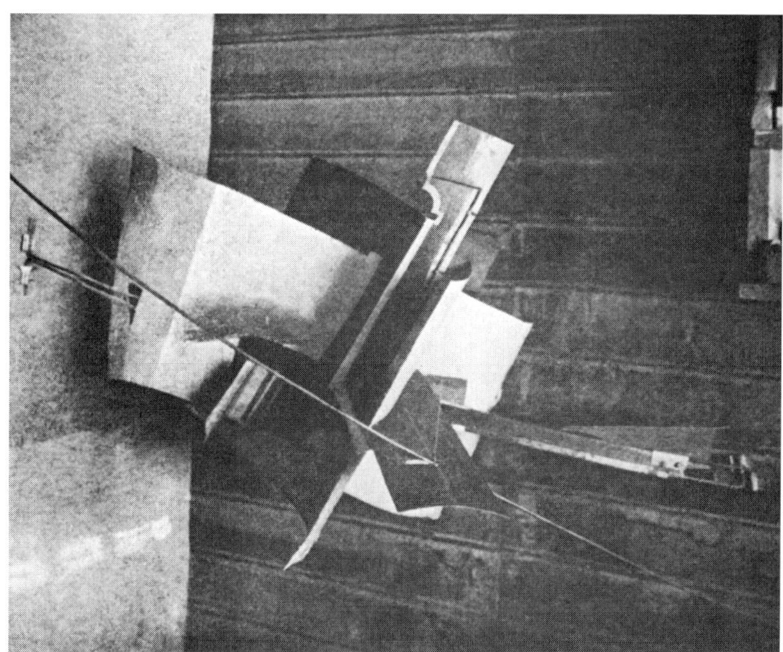

FIGURE 2.6
Vladimir Tatlin, *Corner Counter-Relief no. 133*, 1915. Aluminum and tin sheeting, oil pigment, priming paint, wire, fastening components. No longer extant.

of utilitarianism by Constructivists like Rodchenko and Gan. Analysis of actual utilitarian objects falls outside its scope. It is the argument of this book that detailed critical attention to Constructivist utilitarian objects, including the everyday objects that Tatlin would go on to make in the 1920s, demonstrates that they do not consistently warrant the label of an instrumentalized functionalism. If we examine Tatlin's everyday objects using Gough's helpful notion of "materiological determination," we find that Tatlin did not simply abandon his radical notion of material itself as generative of form. The "volition of the material" and the effacement of the author were maintained, but now in the service not only of artistic experimentation, but of transforming everyday life in socialist Russia.

The everyday objects, in their resolute plainness, seem to insist on the effacement of the author, just as the text of the "New Everyday Life" article downplays Tatlin's leading role in the Section for Material Culture. Tatlin suggests that this effacement is due to the demands of "our simple and primitive everyday life," which do not allow for such individual flourishes as, for example, the technological pyrotechnics of *amerikanizm*. By assigning the explanation for his objects' form to "everyday life" (*byt*), however, Tatlin is offering not a functional explanation but a material one: in Russian language and culture, *byt* has deep ties to materiality. In his everyday objects, then, it will be possible to trace an alternative version of the "volition of the material," in which the materiality of everyday life determines form in a way that is not external to the material, as in functionalism, but intrinsic to it. These objects are Tatlin's contribution to the Constructivist recasting of the key notion of *tselesoobraznost'* (expediency, or, more precisely, "formed in relation to a goal") as a broader psychological and historical principle of the socialist object. The visual anonymity of Tatlin's "primitive" everyday objects therefore connects with, rather than "descends" from, the antisubjective achievement of his avant-garde reliefs.

If neoprimitivism had involved an interest in ethnographic research into folk objects and customs, Tatlin's primitive objects of 1924 were also the result of research into the customs of everyday life, albeit in a less exoticizing form. In one of the reports he submitted in November 1924 on the work conducted by his Section for Material Culture, he listed as one of the Section's three main tasks "Research into everyday life as a certain form of material culture."[21] For Tatlin, then, "everyday life" was not a static category—which, as we shall see, it had been historically in Russia—but one that promised, if properly researched and understood, to inspire new forms in the objects produced by his Section. He conceptualized this research as the logical extension of his earlier investigations of material in his reliefs; as he wrote in another report around the same time, the Section's objective was "to use the accumulated experience on material culture (relief and counter-relief), and apply these experiments to the organization of everyday life, taking mass production into account."[22] Although we do not have a record of the exact nature of the Section's research into everyday life, the objects themselves reveal what Tatlin learned about contemporary Russian *byt* in his research.

"So what kind of life has been predicted by Tatlin and what kind of art does it need?" asked the critic Punin, Tatlin's loyal defender even in the face of his switch from avant-garde experimentation to primitive utilitarian objects. "Tatlin's answer to this fundamental question," Punin admits, "was a stove. Such an answer meant above all that the artist's attention is focused with particular fixity on what is usually called *byt*, not on its higher levels, on that which exceeds it, i.e., on that which somehow originates in *byt* and serves as its elevation and decoration, but on its lower levels of daily human needs."[23] Tatlin would meet these "lower levels" of need with efficient stoves for workers' apartments, patterns for mass-produced hygienic clothing, and formulas for better kinds of utilitarian paints developed in the Section's "Division of Coating Materials," as well as designs for beds, pots, and dishes. Tatlin's "particular fixity" of attention to *byt* challenged the most fundamental categories of Russian culture, in which *byt* was always a category to be transcended—in Punin's terms, to be exceeded and elevated. In his attention to the "low" of everyday life, Tatlin invented a form of artistic primitivism that risked his avant-garde identity far more radically than other modern art movements that have come under the primitivist label.

Bolshevism and *Byt:* Can "Everyday Life" Ever Be "New"?

The question of *byt* in relation to Bolshevism first entered seriously into public discussion in 1923 with the publication of Leon Trotsky's essays on the subject in the party newspaper *Pravda*, collected that same year in his book *Questions of Everyday Life*.[24] It was unprecedented in the Russian intellectual tradition for an author to devote an entire book to theorizing the political significance of everyday life. In premodern Russian, the word *byt* was a neutral term meaning "way of life" or "everyday life," derived from the verb *byvat'*, meaning "to happen, to take place, to be present." The more negative meaning of *byt* as the petty, repetitive daily experience that is the opposite of *bytie*, "spiritually meaningful existence," accrued to the word only in the later nineteenth century.[25] In her history of the meaning of *byt* in Russian culture, Svetlana Boym has argued convincingly that the fundamental distinction in Russian culture is not private versus public, as in the West, but material versus spiritual.[26] In the Russian philosophical opposition between *byt* and *bytie*, the goal was to transcend material *byt* in favor of spiritual *bytie*. In this striving for transcendence, Boym proposes that "*byt* is perceived not simply as unspiritual but also as non-Russian in the higher, poetic sense of what it means to be Russian."[27] This poetic urge toward transcendence also motivated Russian revolutionaries; in their case, however, the transcendence was ideological rather than spiritual, with the goal of collective happiness in a Communist future in this world. The Marxist materialism of the revolutionaries—the philosophical belief that economic existence determines social consciousness—did not exempt them from the traditional Russian contempt for the material side of life, that is to say, for *byt*. In the nineteenth century, Boym writes, "Westernizers and Slavophiles, Romantics and modernists, aesthetic and political utopians, and Bolsheviks and monarchists all engaged in battles with *byt*. For many of them what mattered was not physical survival but sacrifice, not preservation of life but its complete transcendence, not the fragile human existence in this world but collective happiness in the other world."[28]

Trotsky's 1923 articles inaugurated an explosion of public debate about the prospect of a higher form of a "new everyday life" under socialism. The phrase *novyi byt* had cropped up regularly in the utopian atmosphere of the civil war years, loosely signifying a range of ideas from simple strategies for the modernization of backward peasant life to radical collective living arrangements, but these ideas had not occupied official party attention. The party's sudden interest in *byt* in 1923 represented, most broadly, a sense that the New Economic Policy had brought about a breathing spell after the upheaval of the civil war, allowing the new government to turn its attention from seizing power to questions of culture and social life. It also signaled the leaders' worry that the return to a semblance of normality under NEP would result in a bourgeois influence on morality, sexuality, and domestic life. The party responded by engaging more directly in formulating ideas of appropriate habits of daily life under Communism.[29] In the foreword to *Questions of Everyday Life*, Trotsky writes that the idea for his topic came to him from a series of long, impassioned meetings he had with a group of "mass agitators" (*agitatory-massoviki*) from the Moscow Party Committee, during which the participants revealed that their most pressing questions concerned family life and *byt* (VB, pp. 3–4). Throughout his essays, he refers to examples from the lives of these earnest party activists and their uncertainty about the correct form of *byt* for a communist.

In Trotsky's account, *byt* is no longer petty or banal, but a primitive, atavistic force that can undermine the forward movement of the revolution. His essay "In Order to Reconstruct *Byt*, We Must First Come to Know It" characterizes the conservative aspects of *byt* in Marxist terms:

> In questions of *byt* more than anywhere else, the extent to which the individual person is the product rather than the creator of his conditions becomes clear. *Byt*, i.e. the environment and practice of life, even more than economics hides itself "behind people's backs" (to use Marx's expression). Conscious creation in the area of *byt* has had an insignificant place in human history. *Byt* accumulates through people's spontaneous experience, it changes spontaneously . . . and thus it expresses much more the past of human society than its present. (VB, p. 25)

Because it operates behind people's backs "spontaneously"—a term Trotsky uses in the negative Marxist sense of something unrecognized or untheorized—*byt* is a passive force that opposes the conscious creation of new forms of social life, tenaciously preserving a connection to the past of human history. Trotsky continues by reminding his readers that the small proletarian class in Russia has not existed for generations, but has only in the past decades emerged from the poverty and backwardness of the peasantry, specifically tying the everyday life of the contemporary Russian proletariat to a more primitive time. In its material weight, *byt* becomes a literal physical burden that prevents the elevation of proletarian consciousness into socialist modernity.

The crude practices and material objects of traditional village *byt* had been well documented in prerevolutionary ethnography, the only scholarly field that had seriously analyzed *byt*. But ethnographers studied *byt* in the sense of researching the "folk ways" of various groups who were securely "other" to themselves: the peoples of the non-Russian provinces, the peasants of various regions, and the emerging class of industrial workers. By analyzing the significance of the everyday lives of the Soviet proletariat and of party members themselves, Trotsky metaphorically turned this "ethnographic gaze" directly on the "self" of the Bolsheviks, discovering a backwardness that would sabotage revolutionary efforts to construct a new life if it was not investigated and combated.[30] In response to this demand for information on the actual, still largely regressive conditions in which early Soviet industrial workers lived, the newly revamped and Marxist field of the ethnography of the everyday life of workers (*rabochii byt*) intensified its research in the early 1920s.

An indefatigable ethnographer on the staff of the State Russian Museum in Leningrad, for example, E. Medvedev, documented the domestic material lives of Leningrad workers in 1924–1925, leaving files full of meticulously labeled photographs in the photographic collection of the Historical-Everyday Section (*Istoriko-bytovoi otdel*) of the museum.[31] A photograph from Medvedev's research, showing a Leningrad worker's family eating dinner together in 1925, vividly demonstrates the causes for Trotsky's fear of the underhanded effects of traditional peasant *byt* on the Soviet working class (figure 2.7).[32] The worker is Vasilii Trofimovich Smirnov, a riveter at the Nevskii Shipbuilding Factory in Leningrad. This skilled position in heavy industry placed him in the elite of the small Soviet working class. The caption notes that Smirnov's family and visitors from the countryside are eating with him. At first glance this might seem to be an innocuous image of a family dinner, albeit one that openly acknowledges the material poverty of even elite workers in its depiction of the meager meal and the newspapers used as wallpaper. But a viewer like Trotsky would immediately notice that the family members are all eating soup from the same big bowl, just

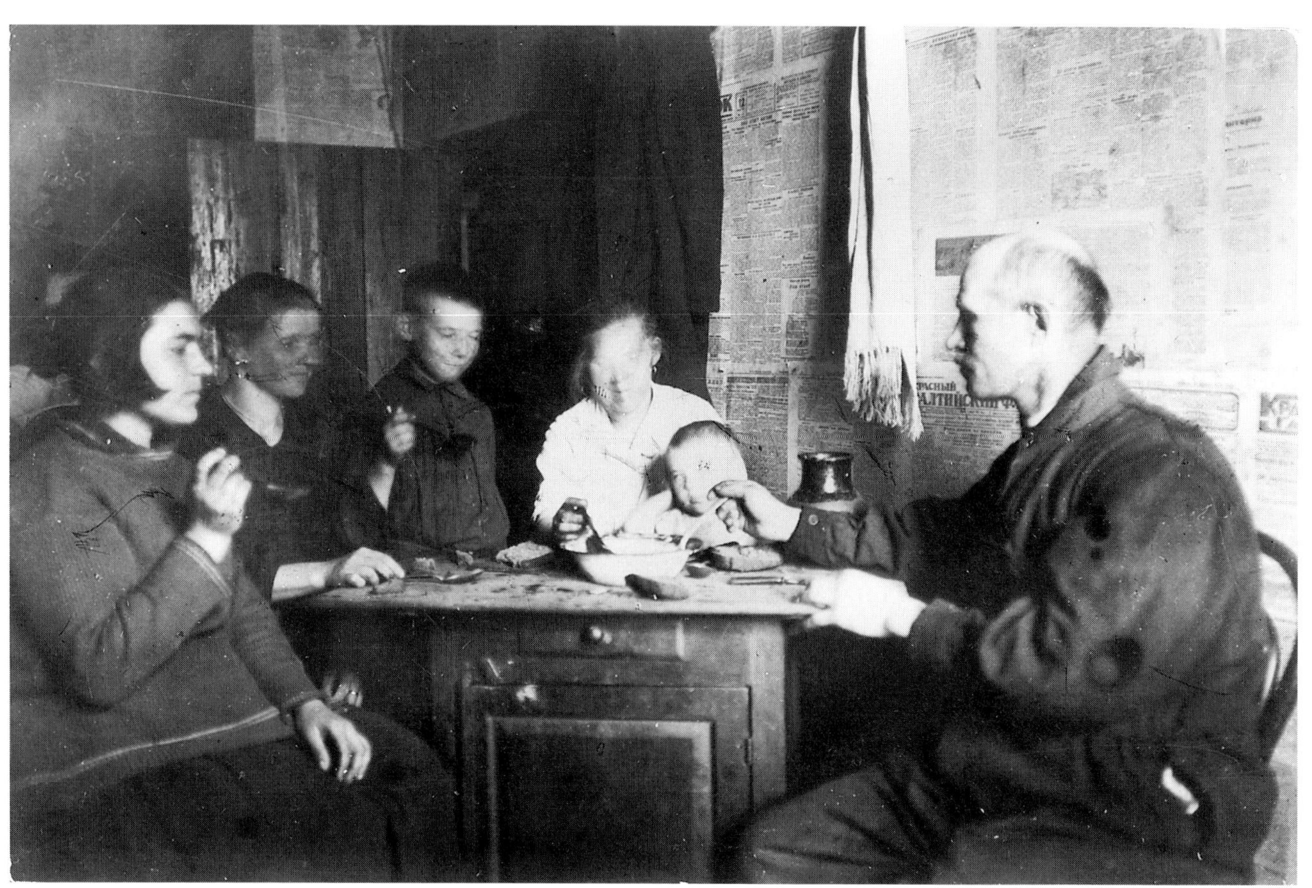

FIGURE 2.7

A worker from the Nevskii Shipbuilding Factory with his family at dinner, Leningrad, 1925. Courtesy Russian Ethnographic Museum, St. Petersburg.

as peasants had always eaten in the countryside—a practice that spread syphilis and other infectious diseases, as Soviet health propaganda continuously warned. The photographer seems to have deliberately posed his subjects to emphasize this dangerous communal supping: with the exception of the infant, all the people in the photograph clutch their offending spoons, two of which are literally poised in midair, and all stare fixedly at the transgressive shared bowl. The photograph therefore corroborates Trotsky's claim, in *Questions of Everyday Life*, that the Russian proletarian is not far removed from his barbarous peasant origins, and the bad habits and even the very material objects of backward peasant *byt* will follow him to his new, urban setting and threaten not only his life, with disease, but his socialist consciousness.

The photograph of Smirnov's family reveals the continuation of the traditional, "irrational" family and domestic relations that, for Trotsky, must be "reconstructed" in order for socialist consciousness to flower. He warns that the most pernicious and long-lasting effects of the proletariat's peasant origins are subjective: the oppressive relations between husbands and wives, parents and children. Trotsky blames these relations on the irrationality of the capitalist and feudal exploitative economic systems, maintaining that "years and decades" of socialist economic growth will be required before the conservatism of "personal and family *byt*" can be reconstructed from top to bottom (VB, p. 26). He identifies three goals for this reconstruction: the liberation of women from domestic slavery, the socialization of child care, and the liberation of marriage from private property relations (VB, p. 30).

As these goals demonstrate, the concept of the "new everyday life" (*novyi byt*) was meant to be liberatory for women. The *novyi byt* campaign, and in particular Trotsky's analyses of gender relations in *Questions of Everyday Life*, can therefore also be understood as a partial response to, or even cooptation of, the feminist voices within Bolshevism. The Bolsheviks, following the standard views of Marxism, held that women's oppression was an effect of capitalist conditions of exploitation, and that proletarian revolution would liberate all workers, male and female.[33] Upon seizing power, the Bolsheviks enacted sweeping new legislation proclaiming women's equality, yet it soon became clear that the revolution had not automatically solved "the woman question." In 1919, the party created the *Zhenotdel* (*Zhenskii otdel* or women's section), which had the contradictory task of propagandizing socialism to women workers and educating them politically, at the same time as it maintained that women had no special needs beyond those of the proletariat as a whole. Beginning in 1920, the *Zhenotdel* was led by the charismatic Bolshevik feminist Aleksandra Kollontai. Yet already by the end of 1921, Kollontai was forced out of the leadership of the *Zhenotdel*, and the section was soon systematically deprived of resources. The section had repeatedly called for greater state attention to problems of *byt*, with little result, and when it called for women's participation in the creation of communal institutions such as daycare centers, public laundries, and dining rooms, the party accused it of "feminist deviationism"—a serious charge that led to it being stripped, by 1923, of any real power.[34] The fact that Trotsky introduced questions of *byt* into public discussion, and called for workers themselves to take the initiative in reconstructing *byt*, therefore suggests that the party deliberately coopted the issue of *byt* from the *Zhenotdel* and its advocacy for women.

The paradoxical decision to debate the problem of *byt* without explicitly framing it as a women's issue resulted from the conflict between the two distinct sides of "the woman question": on the one hand, the Bolsheviks genuinely sought the emancipation of women, but on the other, they feared that backward, nonparty women would impede male party members and workers. While the *novyi byt* campaign in certain ways responded to the demands of the denigrated *Zhenotdel*—for example, it was aimed primarily at liberating women from domestic duties, and specifically critiqued at least some of the patriarchal aspects of marriage—it also turned the issue around to attack women for being themselves the obstacle to creating a new everyday life under socialism, because of their obstinate attachment to home and hearth, tradition and religion, or, more punitively, for their proclivity, either as pampered wives or as prostitutes, for avoiding socially useful, productive labor.[35] The primitiveness and passivity of *byt* that operated "behind the backs" of proletarians, so vividly evoked by Trotsky, became linked in the broader party debates with the fear of the social passivity and political backwardness of peasant and bourgeois women. The *novyi byt* was associated completely with women's issues in practice, if not in its stated theory.

Whether intending to liberate or discipline them, propaganda promoting the *novyi byt* was directed toward women, because everyday life was perceived to be their sphere of influence. Men obviously experienced everyday life as well; but they could not be expected to institute changes at the level of everyday experience, because their roles lay in public or working life. It would be absurd, for example, to imagine a propaganda poster exhorting fathers to place their children in the new cooperative day care centers. In the few examples of *novyi byt* propaganda directly addressed to men—other than public health messages functioning at a lower level of ambition, such as those urging them to wash their hands before eating, or not to spit in the street—they are prodded simply to adhere to the standards of decency of traditional *byt,* in order to make life better for their wives and children. A poster addressing the struggle against profanity, for example, from a series of *novyi byt* propaganda posters from 1923, commands "Don't curse! Foul language disgraces you, worker. Profanity is the legacy of your former enslavement. It sullies the spirit of your children, humiliates your wife and mother."[36]

Another poster from this same series appeals to the male worker to take the role of moral leader in the battle against prostitution, which was considered an aspect of the campaign for the *novyi byt* because of its effects on women, the family, and sexual health. The main text reads: "Having wiped out capitalism, the proletariat will wipe out prostitution" (figure 2.8).[37] The Bolsheviks treated prostitution primarily as a problem of female inequality under capitalism; the woman was a victim of economic circumstances, and it was the responsibility of the new socialist government to combat the problem without further victimizing the woman—even if, in practice, saving women from prostitution sometimes meant incarcerating them in labor camps.[38] The handsome, muscular worker, dressed in strangely timeless white garb and holding a hammer, strides into the picture as a larger-than-life savior, trampling fat capitalists as he takes the hand of the smaller, barefoot woman. The text banners below amplify this obvious visual message of woman as victim in need of salvation: "Prostitution is a great misfortune of humanity. [Male] worker: take care of the woman worker." Unlike most propaganda, however, this poster is unusually vague in its directive: other than not patronizing prostitutes himself, what exactly is the individual male worker whom it addresses being asked to do? A worker pulling a prostitute off the street while she was working would hardly be welcomed by her, unless, theoretically, he were offering to marry and support her—but this would conflict with Bolshevik theory, which condemned traditional marriage, in which the husband supported the wife, as a property relation akin to prostitution. The worker pictured here seems to function more as a highly gendered representation of the proletarian government itself, whose task it is to help women transcend the squalor of the old *byt,* including prostitution. *Byt* was the purview of the male worker only in his role as a protector of the women and children whose presence in effect defined the term.

Trotsky's writings on *byt* do not explicitly attack women, as do those of some of his colleagues, nor does he paint women simplistically as hapless victims; his emphasis is on realistic strategies for the emancipation of women. In his essay "From the Old Family to the New," he admits the difficulty of this proposition: it is one thing for the Bolshevik government simply to legislate the political equality of women and men, another to attempt to establish equality in the workplace, and another, more difficult matter altogether to establish actual equality between the man and woman within the family. At the same time, measures to promote political equality and equality in the workplace—measures the government could realistically enforce—would never have any serious effect without real equality in the home: "Politics are flexible," he writes, "but *byt* is immobile and obstinate" (VB, p. 40). In its passivity, *byt* can never be a site for political action, but rather must be obliterated as a separate sphere of life. Trotsky argues that the only way to promote real equality between women and men is to build up the Soviet economy to the point that it will be rich enough to liberate the family from the material worries that destroy it, and allow women to participate fully in productive labor, through public laundries, dining halls, sewing workshops, and child care.

For this study, the significance of Trotsky's particular articulation of *byt* is the way that he ties socialist subjectivity to the personal relations not just between people, but between people and material objects. His attack on *byt* is an attack on its sheer material weight, pointing to the way that, in the evocative words of Maurice Blanchot, the everyday "tends unendingly to weigh down into things."[39] If we go back to the dictionary and look again under *byt*, we find that in old Russian, one of its original meanings was simply "goods and chattel" or "property."[40] The very term *byt* therefore directs us toward material possessions. Trotsky argues that a *novyi byt* can accomplish equality between women and men only through the virtual elimination of possessions: the complete rationalization of the material order of domestic life from above, by the state. "Only then," Trotsky writes, "will the relation of husband and wife be freed of everything external, foreign, binding, incidental. The one will cease oppressing the other. Genuine equality will be established. The relation will be determined only by mutual attraction" (VB, p. 45).

In this evocation of a love relationship unhampered by possessions or women's traditional dependence on men, and based on true attraction, Trotsky in effect restated Kollontai's famous description of a form of "free love" under socialism. Her concept of a new form of love was not an excuse for promiscuity, as her many critics claimed, but an argument that a woman could become an equal in a romantic relationship only if that relationship were freed of the physical and psychological effects of the property relation, which made women the possessions as well as dependents of men.[41] Kollontai had long been criticized

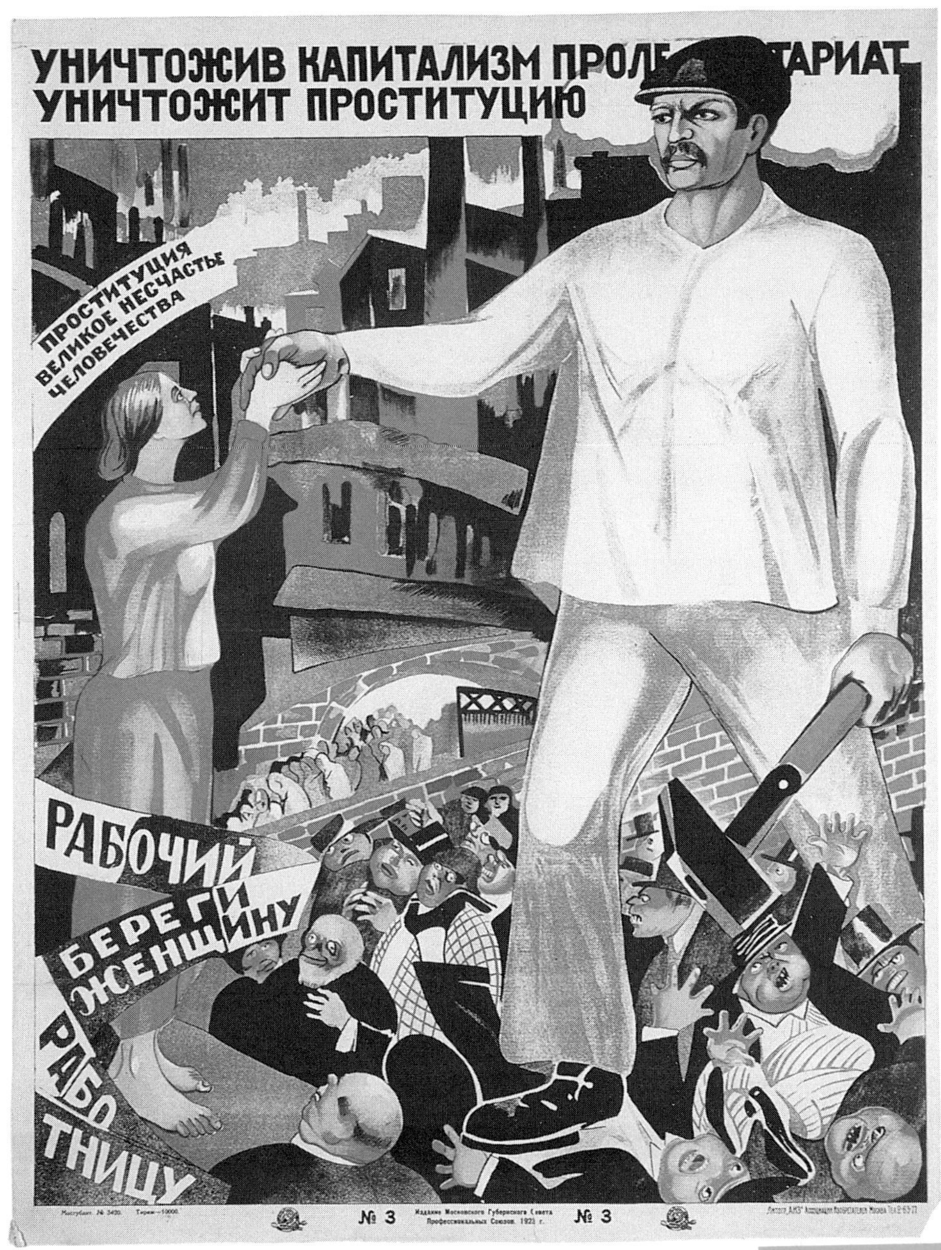

FIGURE 2.8
Poster: "Having wiped out capitalism, the proletariat will wipe out prostitution," 1923. Courtesy Russian State Library Department of Graphics, Moscow. See plate 3.

КООПЕРАЦИЯ
ОСВОБОЖДАЕТ ЖЕНЩИНУ
ОТ ТЯГОТ
ДОМАШНЕГО ХОЗЯЙСТВА.

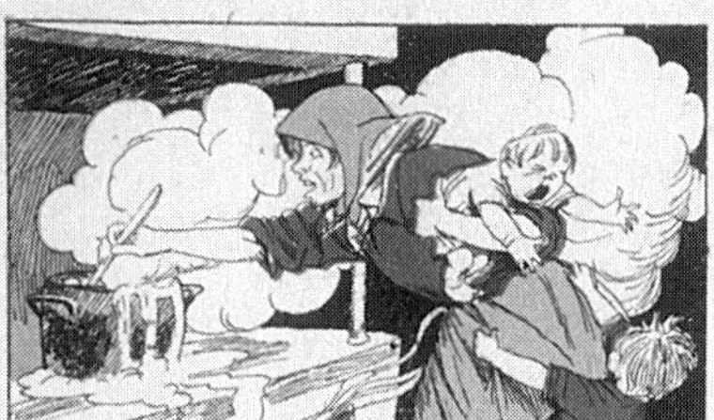

Домашняя кухня.

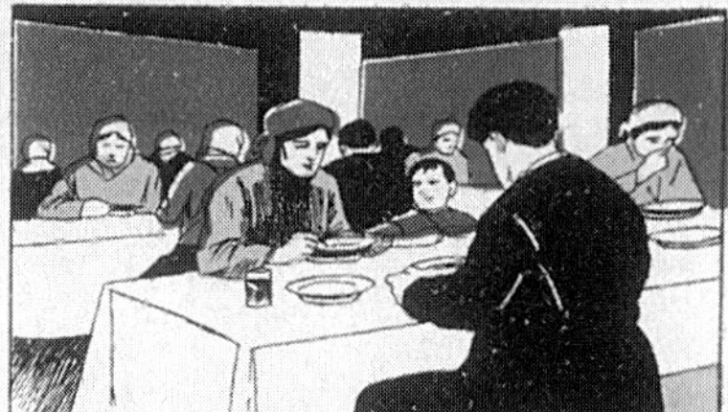

Кооперативная столовая.

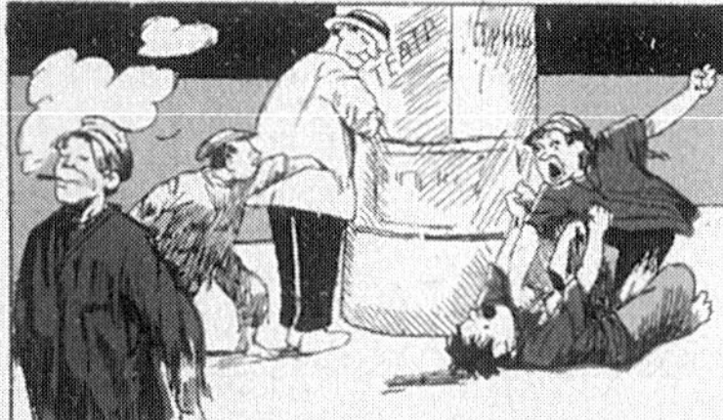

Дети без призора.

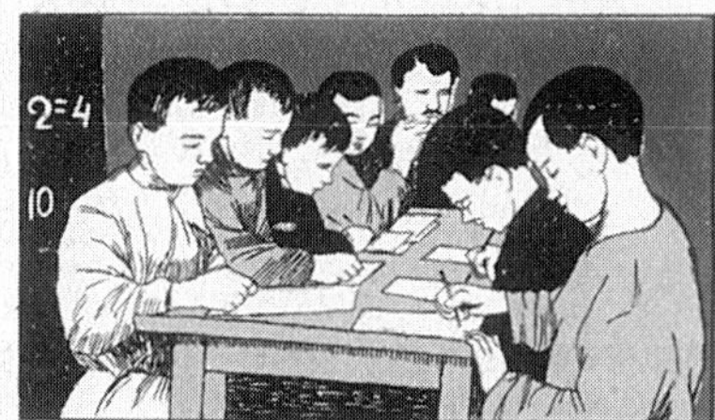

Дети в кооперативной школе.

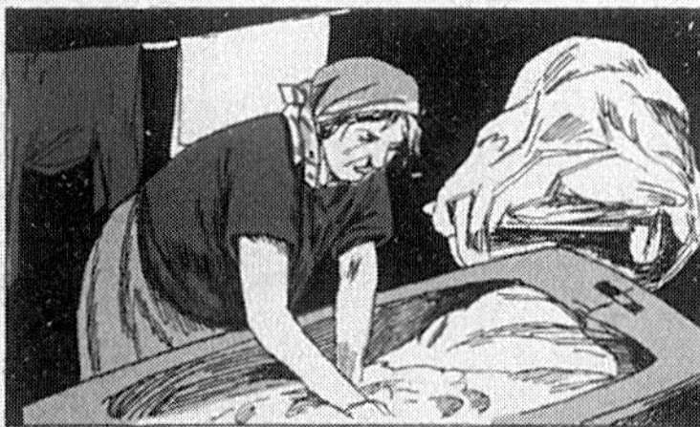

Домашняя стирка.

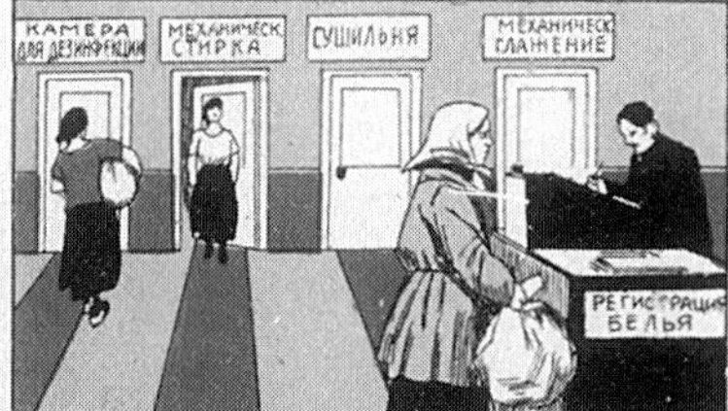

Кооперативная прачечная.

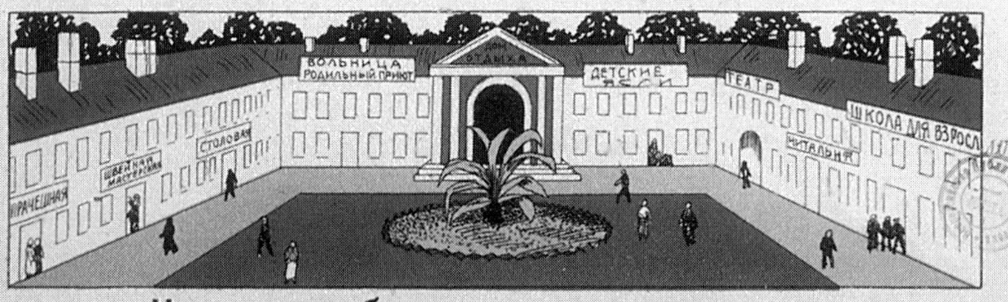

К новому быту через кооперацию.

Донлит № 3589.
Типо-литограф. Госиздата в Новочеркасске.
Отпечатано 2800.

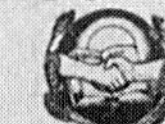

ИЗДАТЕЛЬСТВО
„ЮГО-ВОСТОЧНАЯ КООПЕРАЦИЯ"
Ростов на Дону.

FIGURE 2.9

Poster: "Cooperation liberates woman from the burdens of housekeeping. To the new everyday life through cooperation," 1924. Courtesy Russian State Library Department of Graphics, Moscow.

for her belief in the centrality of a new kind of nonpossessive love for building proletarian culture; Trotsky's similar, if differently framed, point received no such censure.[42] Yet even though Trotsky's vision of a domestic life based on sexual equality bears similarities to Kollontai's explicitly feminist vision, his proposed solution for achieving it ends up reasserting traditionally gendered, hierarchical cultural categories: "human" spiritual relations become possible only with the elimination of matter—which, in his account, is persistently tied to the domestic sphere occupied by women, and therefore understood as feminine.

The association of femininity with matter can be traced back to Aristotle and a set of etymologies that link matter with *mater* and *matrix*, or the womb. "[T]o invoke matter," as Judith Butler has put it, "is to invoke a sedimented history of sexual hierarchy and sexual erasures which should surely be an *object* of feminist inquiry, but which would be quite problematic as a *ground* of feminist theory."[43] From this contemporary feminist perspective, Trotsky and the Bolshevik *byt* reformers, with their undoubted good intentions to emancipate women, can be faulted precisely for taking the association of femininity with matter as the *ground* of their program. Kollontai herself relied on assumptions about women's essential nature in her proposals for improving the lives of women, calling the maternal instinct, and women's instinct to care for children, "natural-biological."[44] In the 1920s, text after text and poster after poster—whether authored by men or women—assumed that women were responsible for the reproduction of material life. The only solution to this burden of responsibility was the total removal of women's domestic duties from the sphere of the home and into the hands of the socialist state. The idea that sexual equality in the home could be brought about simply by sharing tasks between the sexes was essentially inconceivable.[45]

Trotsky's vision of a domestic life literally emptied of "binding" and "incidental" objects instances the Bolshevik urge to clear away the detritus of the private object world, to destroy *byt* in favor of the higher, dematerialized sphere of *bytie*. The antiprostitution poster produces this effect visually, by contrasting the large, simplified white form of the male worker with the cluttered forms of buildings, brick walls, and crowds of people surrounding the woman, who is literally bound by the swirling banners of text. This paradoxical antimaterialism of the *novyi byt* is figured most often in propaganda posters by the ubiquitous before–after pictorial model, such as in a poster from the town of Rostov-on-Don of 1924, whose boldface texts at top and bottom read: "Cooperation liberates woman from the burdens of housekeeping. To the new everyday life through cooperation" (figure 2.9).[46] The term "cooperation" (*kooperatsiia*) referred to stores and services provided by state-affiliated organizations, as distinct from privately held ones. The more freely drawn left side shows three disorderly scenes from the old way of life under capitalism: an overburdened woman cooking in the squalor of a private kitchen; untended children; and a woman doing the backbreaking work of hand-washing linen. People interact with each other and with objects to the point of excess; witness the hot stove and overflowing pot, the fisticuffs and pickpocketing, the soapy water and the body bent forward over the washtub. The highly geometric right side, in contrast, displays parallel scenes ordered and modernized by collective socialist wealth: a state-run cooperative cafeteria, a school, and a laundry complete with a sign reading "disinfecting chamber." The objects have been almost completely removed, and those that remain are uniform and utterly plain: white bowls on white tablecloths on the table, white rectangles of paper on the school desk. If the liberal use of hatch-marks in the drawings on the left side conveys noisy commotion and clutter, the preponderance of simple color fields on the right and bottom invokes a motionless silence.

The poster advertises a *novyi byt* that has liberated woman, but women are still doing the laundry. Their liberation is registered visually only by the spare, geometric spaces on the right side of the poster: the women now glide along the straight, vertical paths in the mechanized laundry on the lower right, seemingly caught in the vacuum left by the elimination of the object world from the touch and control of the individual. In none of the right-hand images do people's gazes meet. Trotsky's dream of revolutionary subjects "freed of everything external, foreign, binding, incidental" becomes, in this admittedly schematic poster, a nightmare vision of subjective alienation. Yet there were many posters like this, as well as schematic "sketches" of domestic scenarios in the many articles on *byt* in the popular press, and they all suggested that in the imaging of the *novyi byt*, the primary aspect of *byt* itself—the everyday object world—would be eliminated. If *byt* will be *novyi*, it will no longer be *byt* at all, but something much closer to *bytie*. The campaign for the *novyi byt* therefore defied the very cultural logic of *byt*. The Bolsheviks could imagine transforming *byt* only by overcoming it, because of their peculiarly Russian brand of Marxism, which was philosophically materialist, at the level of *bytie*, but ascetic and antimaterialist at the level of *byt*.

Lef and *Byt*

When it came to attacking *byt*, there was no great divide between mass propaganda and the avant-garde. A diatribe against *byt* written by Sergei Tret'iakov appeared in a no less pivotal venue than the inaugural issue of the journal *Lef* in March of 1923, in a position piece on Futurism entitled "Where From, Where To?"[47] Tret'iakov's dim view of *byt* has much in common with the antimaterialism of Trotsky and the propaganda posters, though significantly for this study, his focus is not on state interventions into everyday life, but on the role of the Futurist—which is to say, the left artist, such as Tatlin—in creating a new form of socialist life. The article responds to critics, including Lenin, who deemed the Futurist *Lef* group irrelevant to the needs of the new Bolshevik state.[48] Tret'iakov argues that Futurism was never a true school, but rather a "social-aesthetic tendency" (p. 193) uniting artists in their hatred for petty bourgeois art and *byt*. In the ten years since its inauguration in Russia in 1913, he writes, Futurism has grown up, in step with the development of the consciousness of the proletariat and the revolution, into a worldview with the aim of "the production of the new person through the use of art as one of the weapons of this production" (p. 195). The "battle" for the "psychological structure" of this new person will be an "inevitable battle against *byt*" (p. 200).

In his claim that Futurism has battled petty bourgeois *byt* since its earliest incarnation in 1913, Tret'iakov adds to the complex associations of *byt* by pairing it with another key concept in Russian culture, *meshchanstvo*, meaning, approximately, the petty bourgeoisie or the state of being petty bourgeois—often translated into English as "Philistinism." Like *byt*, the word *meshchanstvo* originally had a neutral, institutional meaning: it defined an official stratum of society, namely city dwellers of the lowest rank such as traders, artisans, servants, and soldiers. Only in the mid-nineteenth century did the term take on the negative meanings of bad taste, banality, and materialism that the elite strata of Russian society associated with the *meshchanstvo*.[49] This degraded urban model of *meshchanskii byt* presented the greatest danger to the development of the "new person" after the revolution because it was the model that beguiled the working class: the Russian proletariat was caught between the reality of its primitive *byt* of peasant customs imperfectly transplanted to urban conditions, and its understandable aspirations toward the comforts of *meshchanskii byt*.[50]

Tret'iakov defines *byt*, like Trotsky, in terms that emphasize its atavistic force, but even more explicitly than Trotsky he stresses the reactionary power of the material objects comprised by *byt* (p. 200):

> And by *byt* in the objective sense we mean that stable order and character of objects with which the person surrounds himself and to which, regardless of their usefulness, he transfers the fetishism of his sympathies and memories and in the end literally becomes the slave of these objects. In this sense *byt* is

> a deeply reactionary force, that which in pivotal moments of social change prevents the organization of the will of a class for plotting decisive assaults. Comfort for comfort's sake; coziness as an end in itself; all the chains of tradition and of respect for objects that have lost their practical meaning, beginning with the neck tie and ending with religious fetishes—this is the quagmire of *byt.*

Tret'iakov's metaphors invoke material impediments to physical and spiritual mobility: the person becomes a "slave" to objects; enslavement is enforced by the binding "chains of tradition"; the stultifying "comfort for comfort's sake" of the cozy bourgeois home restrains the person physically like the sticky and enveloping "quagmire of *byt.*" Passive and conservative, *byt* prevents revolutionary action. The person invests his sympathies and memories in objects, rather than in higher goals of social change. By associating *byt* with religious fetishes and the swamp ("quagmire"), Tret'iakov links even modern, urban, *meshchanskii byt* with the primitive peasant *byt* that had been the object of Trotsky's critique.

Tret'iakov's virulent critique of the material objects of *byt* produces the traditional Russian opposition between material and spiritual, *byt* and *bytie.* Futurism, he writes, will involve "not *byt* in its stagnancy and dependence upon the clichéd order of objects, but *bytie*—dialectically experiencing reality, in the process of uninterrupted becoming" (p. 200). Tret'iakov's Futurist, Marxist version of *bytie* will be the realm of the new Futurist personality, who will be energetic, inventive, disciplined. In direct combat with NEP profiteering, which "Americanizes" the personality, the Futurist personality will contribute his entire productive output to the Bolshevik collective: "the Futurist must be least of all the owner of his own production. His battle is with the hypnosis of names and the patents associated with them. . . . It does not matter that people will forget his name—what matters is that his inventions will enter into living circulation, where they will give birth to new improvements and new training" (p. 201). Tret'iakov's critique is directed here more pointedly at exclusive possession, at the social constructions that bind people to material objects, than at objects themselves; he insists, after all, that new objects need to be "invented." But his rhetoric betrays the ascetic Bolshevik impulse to transcend the passive material world of *byt* in order to achieve a more meaningful existence of revolutionary action. Freed from the "clichéd order of objects," Tret'iakov's Futurist will float free with new energy and inventiveness, just like Trotsky's husband and wife "freed of everything external, foreign, binding, incidental."

"Everyday-Life-Creation" and the Active Material Object

Tatlin flew in the face of this avant-garde and Bolshevik antimaterialism. Although the plain functionality of Tatlin's objects worked to deny the structures of acquisitive possessiveness derided by Tret'iakov, he deliberately produced objects that would be immediately useful in "our simple and primitive everyday life" rather than in a Futurist *bytie* or Bolshevik *novyi byt* of gleaming communal cafeterias and public laundries. Tatlin, with his left avant-garde pedigree stretching back to the early 1910s, and his insistence on the collective, anonymous nature of the work of his Section for Material Culture, would seem to be the prototype for Tret'iakov's Futurist inventor, yet he departed from Tret'iakov's vision by deliberately miring himself in the devalued, and, as we have seen, feminized, order of *byt*. The photographs accompanying the article on his work in *Krasnaia panorama* tie him to his everyday objects, as he models the practical clothing and is posed in front of the wood-burning stove. The bold title "*Novyi byt*" at the top of the page is slightly incongruous, compared to most propaganda posters with that title, given the decidedly gritty and nonfuturistic look of the illustrations. His objects seem to be shaped by the needs of *byt*, rather than by his visual invention as an artist. We recall his declaration of 1920: "Distrusting the eye, we place it under the control of touch."

Tatlin's project found its theoretical ally in a different strand of *Lef* thinking, represented by Boris Arvatov. For Arvatov, *byt* was a potentially active force. In his essay "Everyday Life and the Culture of the Thing," he claimed that the creation of proletarian culture "can proceed only from the forms of material *byt*."[51] This culture would emerge not by transcending the material sphere, but by "organically" and "flexibly" working within it in order to transform it in a process of "everyday-life-creation [*bytotvorchestvo*]" (EL, p. 121). Organic and flexible are the right terms to describe Tatlin's willingness to direct his artistic practice toward the kinds of things that were really needed in the contemporary conditions of *byt*, despite the fact that it involved a radically different, and traditionally less valued, kind of "creation" from his previous avant-garde endeavors. Arvatov and Tatlin knew each other through the INKhUK; Arvatov was a strong supporter of Tatlin, and his formulation of a theory of the socialist object clearly shows the marks of his knowledge of Tatlin's work.[52] Conversely, when Tatlin offers a theoretical justification for the "research" work of his Section in his 1924 report, he seems to draw on Arvatov's thinking: "Recognizing . . . that the shaping principle of culture, production and experience is material," he writes, "the Section for Material Culture sets itself the task of: 1) Research into material as the shaping principle of culture. 2) Research into *byt* as a certain form of material culture."[53] This notion of material as an actively "shaping" principle is reminiscent of the "volition of the material" that guided the form of his reliefs, in Gough's propitious phrasing. But if the "volition" of the material in the reliefs was formal, in the sense that the materials themselves determined the form of the final sculptural object, the "shaping" principle of material in *byt* is a social one.

Arvatov had theorized this social version of the "volition of material" in 1922 in his Marxist history of art, "Art and Production."[54] He declared the dualism of *byt* and *bytie* to be a historical artifact of capitalism. In the precapitalist past, he claimed, the artist was simply the most qualified of craftsmen, an inventor and innovator who made things to satisfy the functional demands of *byt*. Both the functional and the visual properties of a thing contributed to its active, almost animate powers of "organizing material *byt*."[55] Under capitalist industrialization, however, the artist feared that mass-machine-production would make him obsolete, and he retreated into specialized craft. This was a mistake, according to Arvatov; the artist should have embraced industrial production, because it represented the most advanced form of human imagination. But instead the artist under capitalism turned to handcrafting luxury objects to satisfy the demands of the eye: "artistic objects were now hidden under glass, that is, they were murdered as objects, and remained only as naked visual forms."[56] The anthropomorphizing verb "murdered" signals the object's extraordinary animation in Arvatov's account. The active totality of the material object within everyday life was violently sundered by bourgeois aesthetics, which rendered the visual into a passive quality, and placed visual objects in glass coffins. His critique of bourgeois aesthetics for isolating the visual from the other senses, and so turning visual objects into spectacles cut off from the social context in which they were made and in which they should have had a social function, is similar to Walter Benjamin's critique of the alienation of the senses under capitalism, and especially fascism, in his essay "The Work of Art in the Age of Mechanical Reproduction."[57] Arvatov's theory of an aesthetics made whole again under socialism imagines that industrial technology will amplify and clarify all the human senses, rather than isolate and alienate them. His theory of material culture is therefore politically ambitious: the material culture of socialism will make the subject critical and conscious, and therefore invulnerable to the lure of capitalism.

This distrust for the eye in Arvatov's history of art, which seemed to entail a total rejection of the visual as an isolated sense, was criticized for denying to proletarian culture the potential political power of the visual arts. In *Literature and Revolution,* Trotsky criticized *Lef* on precisely this point: "to reject art as a means of picturing, of imaging knowledge, is in truth to strike from the hands of the class that is building the new society its most important weapon."[58] Arvatov responded in *Lef* that critics mistakenly took the Constructivists' struggle against easel art—which he calls the most bourgeois form of visual art that oppressively promotes passive contemplation—for a struggle against all visual art. *Lef* does promote visual art, he argues, but only the kind of art that makes sense in the epoch of proletarian dictatorship: "Decisively rejecting living-room and museum oriented easel art, *Lef* is fighting for the poster, the illustration, the advertisement, the photo- and kino-montage, i.e. for those kinds of mass *utilitarian* forms of visual art that are made by means of machine technology and closely connected with the material *byt* of urban industrial workers."[59] Arvatov here endeavors to recapture, under modern conditions of industrial production, the lost relation of the artist to the everyday material life of the community that his history of art ascribes to the precapitalist era.

The theoretical explanation for Arvatov's idealized notion of the active material object that existed before capitalism's isolation of visual art from other forms of making was the concept he called the "monism of things [*veshchnyi monizm*]" (EL, p. 127)—an idiosyncratic development of the nineteenth-century Marxist Georgii Plekhanov's concept of monism, which was itself developed out of Marx's first thesis on Feuerbach.[60] This thesis criticized Feuerbach's dualistic distinction between sensuous objects themselves and those objects as contemplated by human beings. Marx argued for the necessary identity of material with human consciousness: "The chief defect of all hitherto existing materialism (that of Feuerbach included) is that the thing, reality, sensuousness, is conceived only in the form of the *object of contemplation* [*Anschauung*], but not as *sensuous human activity, practice* [*Praxis*], not subjectively."[61] The thing must be understood not only as an object of human thought, as in the idealist view, which distinguishes between thought and matter, but as actually constituted by human praxis, as in the materialist or monist view, which resists that distinction as ideologically motivated. Judith Butler puts this cogently in her philosophical study of matter: "If materialism were to take account of praxis as that which constitutes the very matter of objects, and praxis is understood as socially transformative activity, then such activity is understood as constitutive of materiality itself . . . according to this new kind of materialism that Marx proposes, the object is not only transformed, but in some significant sense, the object *is* transformative activity itself."[62] Arvatov's "monism of things" takes Marx's materialism in a more literal direction, by imagining that not only the "object" in the philosophical sense—in which there is a slippage between material and ideal, matter and spirit—but the "thing" in the material sense will once again have "volition" because of its connection to "sensuous human activity." This socialist "culture of the thing" will return *byt* to being the site of human creativity—of "everyday-life-creation"—that it was before capitalism.

Arvatov's enthusiasm for artistic creativity within *byt* was not shared by many others in the Soviet art world. In an article in the journal *Soviet Art* in 1925, the critic Robert Pel'she ridicules Arvatov and his *Lef* colleague Nikolai Chuzhak for their rejection of painting and sculpture and their obsession with making everyday things as the only appropriate form of artistic activity.[63] Pel'she is responding specifically to articles by Arvatov and Chuzhak in the same issue of *Soviet Art*: Arvatov indicts the return of easel painting during NEP in an essay entitled "Reaction in Painting," while Chuzhak's essay "The Art of Everyday Life" defends "the proletariat's young instinct of healthy dialectical 'thing-ness' [*veshchnost*]."[64] According to Pel'she, the Productivists' insistence on the useful material thing might seem to uphold a Marxist notion of materialism, but it actually reinforces the most banal, bourgeois dualism between matter and spirit, body and soul; it is insufficiently dialectical. He dismisses the "notorious ideology of 'thing-ness'" as *Lef*ist sectarianism and anarchic philosophy that "takes on the character of some kind of fetish, some kind of idolatry."[65] For the Productivists, a picture or a statue are not true "things" because they do not affect the person physically: "the new life will be built and organized only through such a 'thinglike origin' [*veshchnoe nachalo*] of art as a pot, a spoon, a bucket (Comrade Chuzhak really likes dishes)."[66] We have already heard Arvatov's explanation that he was only against pictures and statues in the current historical moment, as they did not correspond to the conditions of contemporary proletarian *byt*. But Pel'she's snide litany of pots and buckets—an obvious invocation of the everyday objects made by Tatlin at that time—and his derisive potshot at Chuzhak for liking dishes reveal the anti-feminine underpinnings of his criticism of the Productivist engagement with *byt*. Pel'she's derision is predictable: in Russian everyday life, men have nothing to do with dishes, and male artists certainly should not descend to that mundane level.

Pel'she's mocking, misleading description of the *Lef*ists' theory of the everyday thing, and his call for a more "dialectical" understanding of Marxist materialism, can be understood as a front for a far simpler response: the traditional Russian rejection of passive and feminine *byt*. Whether or not we are convinced by Arvatov's concepts of a "monism of things" and "everyday-life-creation," it is clear that they contest this particular misogynist tradition.[67] Unlike most of his contemporaries, Arvatov does not feminize *byt* as a category; for him, *byt* is not inherently passive, but a potential site of active creation. Similarly, Tatlin's stated commitment to "research into everyday life" suggests that for him, *byt* is not a passive category, but one that holds the promise of social transformation. He does not distinguish between the significance of his grander artistic projects, like *Monument to the Third International*, and his plain everyday objects, as suggested by an inventory included in one of his production reports on the work of his Section: "material constructions: objects, partly extant, partly made in the studio—the model of the Monument, stove, dishes, dresses."[68] All are presented as the results of his imaginative material experimentation. While neither Arvatov nor Tatlin are explicitly committed to reclaiming *byt* as a feminine area of experience, in the interests of supporting women, they also do not attempt to appropriate and transform *byt* in the interest of making it over into a masculine *bytie*. Arvatov's theory of *byt* and Tatlin's everyday objects cannot be described as intentionally feminist, but they challenge some of the most entrenched gendered categories of Russian culture as part of their goal of creating a better socialist life.

The "Volition of the Material" in Tatlin's Everyday Objects

Tatlin's design for a traditional Russian wood-burning stove was meant to contribute to the heart of the feminine domestic domain: the kitchen. Beyond facilitating women's task of cooking food, the stove also, in typical Constructivist fashion, performed a number of other functions, such as heating the room and providing a source of hot water. The laconic "New Everyday Life" article enumerates the stove's technical specifications, in words likely provided by Tatlin himself:

> this stove has an economical furnace providing a sizable heating effect with a small expenditure of wood (six logs). The stove is supplied with an oven and a large hermetically sealed chamber that keeps water and food hot for 28–30 hours and, at the same time, with only one furnace it can heat a room of 8x6 arshins at a height of 6 arshins for 48 hours, maintaining a temperature of 14–16 degrees Réaumur.[69]

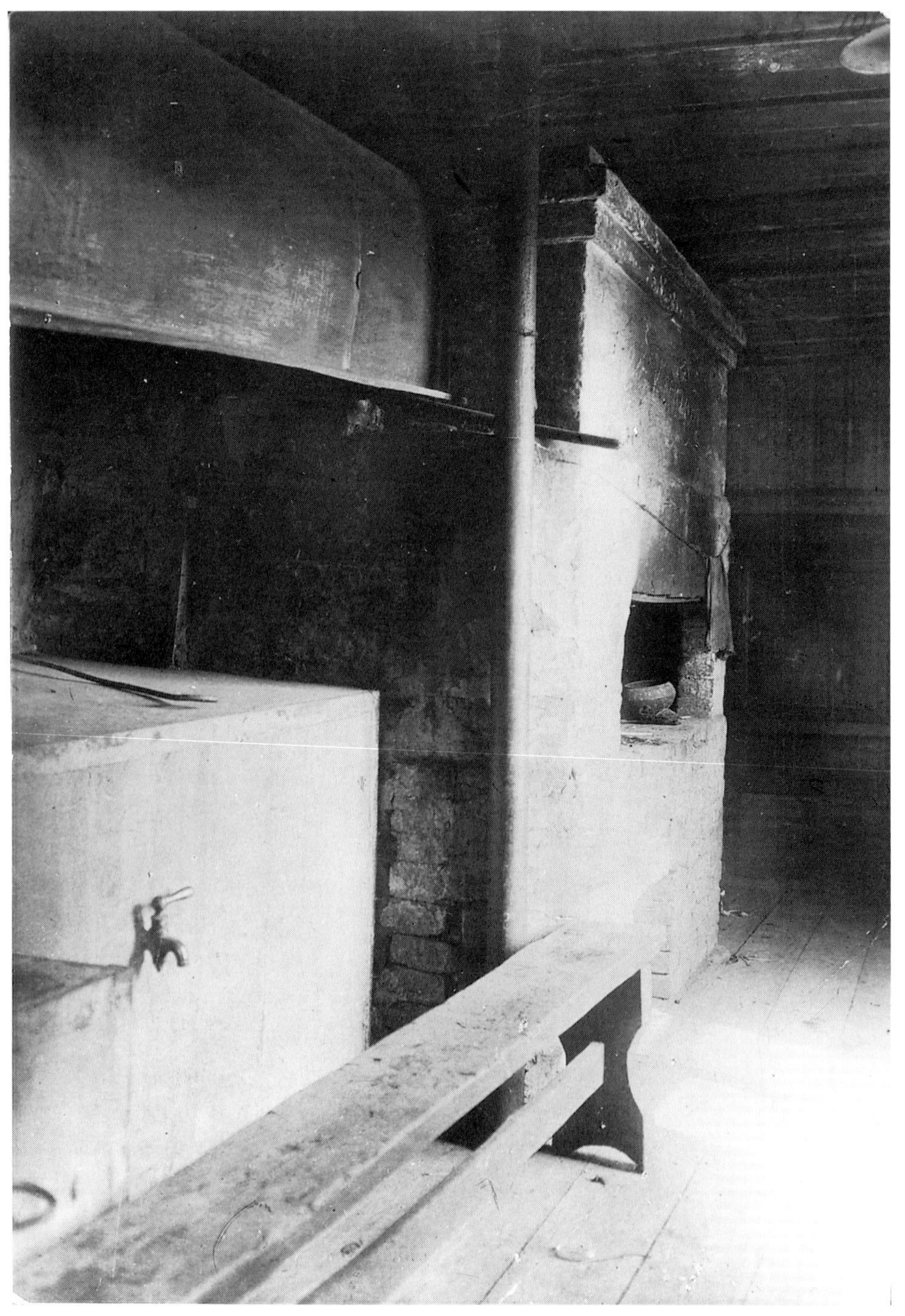

FIGURE 2.10
A stove in the kitchen of textile-factory workers in Smolensk village, 1925.
Courtesy Russian Ethnographic Museum, St. Petersburg.

Tatlin provides no such detailed description of the visual qualities of the stove, keeping the focus firmly on the stove's function. Yet the description, technical as it is, delineates a social function for this object that exceeds a narrow functionalism: as a source of heat, hot water, and nourishment, the stove would anchor the room, and in many cases the entire living space, of the stove's users. It would "organize material *byt*," in the words of Arvatov.

The large wood-burning stove, plain and rectangular in form, had traditionally organized the domestic space of the home in Russian village life. People even slept on it, since it was the warmest place in the house. Such stoves continued to be used in the more modern settings of dormitories and communal houses, as well as in urban apartments, albeit on a necessarily smaller scale. A photograph commissioned by the inquisitive ethnographer E. Medvedev from the Russian Museum shows a typical stove in a communal house occupied by textile-factory workers in Smolensk village, near Leningrad, in 1925 (figure 2.10).[70] The visual form of Tatlin's stove, photographed in the "New Everyday Life" illustration from the same angle as the textile workers' stove, does not differ markedly from the traditional one; the two stoves share such features as the water spigot and the placement and shape of the opening into the range, as well as the general rectangular shape. Tatlin's stove does appear to be functionally advanced: the tiled exterior is more modern and hygienic; his design efficiently condenses the different parts of the larger stove, including the chamber containing heated water, into one structure; it provides glass shutters for the opening into the range, which allows the area above the range to function as the "hermetically sealed chamber" for keeping food heated, and allows the cook to see in without unsealing the chamber; and the stove would smoke less than the iron stoves in wide use at the time, given its sophisticated furnace system.[71] His design in effect maximizes the functional qualities of the traditional stove, making it optimally useful for urban *byt* at that time. A fuel-efficient stove that could keep water and food hot for long periods was especially helpful in cities, where sources of firewood were unreliable and street vendors could charge astronomical prices for it, and where many tall apartment buildings were without hot running water.

The stove design therefore seems to reflect the results of some form of "research into *byt*," and we happen to know the specific nature of the "research" in this case: Tatlin originally designed a version of this stove to meet the needs of his own home. Tatlin did joiner's work all his life, making things like benches and billiard tables, and as early as 1920–1921 he had made two economical stoves for himself, in order to experiment and, more saliently, to heat his apartment.

"Originally," Zhadova writes, "the artist did not attach any professional significance" to the making of these stoves.[72] But when, in the Section for Material Culture, he did begin to attach professional significance to objects that would transform *byt*, he realized that he already had developed an object that responded to the demands of "our simple and primitive everyday life." Developing his earlier, amateur utilitarian stoves into five different prototypes for new kinds of stoves in his professional work in the Section in 1924, he did not embellish them aesthetically. Although Zhadova proposes that the stove resembles a modernist cube, and refers to an article by Kazimir Malevich from 1929 in which he emphasizes the "artistic character" of the stove's form, this seems to be stretching things: the rectangular form derives from the traditions of stove-making more than from geometric modernism.[73] The technical inventiveness of the stove might be related in spirit to the quasi-engineerism of the suspended *Corner Counter-Reliefs* series, but not in form. As Punin declared, if the stove can be called artistic at all, then it will be by virtue of being made by Tatlin the artist, not by virtue of its visual form. This stove, he writes, "could probably be put together by any good stove maker."[74] The volition of material life itself had determined the form of Tatlin's stove.

Tatlin's designs for clothing are similarly plain and functional. Yet his design for a men's sportswear suit made from linen of 1924–1925, which we saw pasted onto the photomontage based on the "New Everyday Life" article (see figure 2.3), has an unusually boxy visual form that differs markedly from contemporary men's clothing.[75] The simple tab collar of the jacket is reminiscent of the traditional Russian peasant shirt, the belted *rubashka*, which had become popular among Communists, but the rest of the jacket does not conform to any traditions of Russian *byt*. As with her analysis of the stove, Zhadova again proposes that his suits were based on "geometric planes" deriving from Cubism.[76] The connection between the squared-off jacket with its cross-shaped seams, on the one hand, and Cubism, on the other, might seem tenuous, but it is supported by a pair of unusual photomontages that he made to document the suit, in which photographs of Tatlin himself modeling the prototype of the suit from front and back are carefully framed by the labeled pattern pieces for the jacket, tacked to the wall (figures 2.11, 2.12). The large, semirectangular shapes of the pattern pieces on the wall recall the irregular shapes of the jutting pieces of sheet metal suspended against the corner walls in *Corner Counter-Relief no. 133* (see figure 2.6), while the framing function of the pattern pieces recalls the triangular piece of sheet metal framed by the conventionally rectangular picture frame in *Painterly Relief 1915* (see figure 2.5). This rectangular painterly relief, with its strong central vertical element

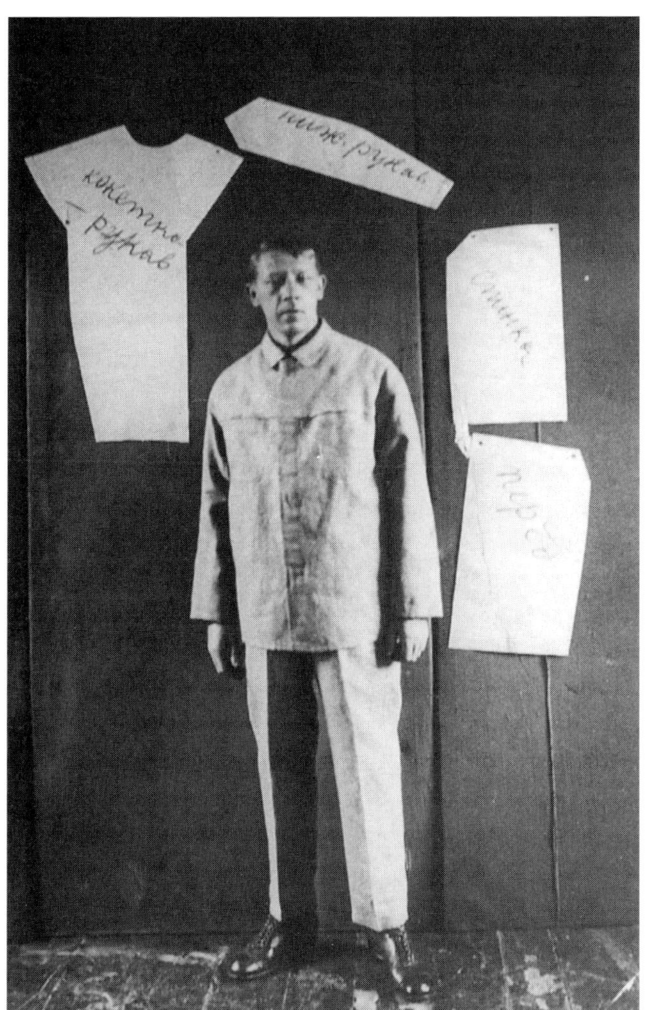

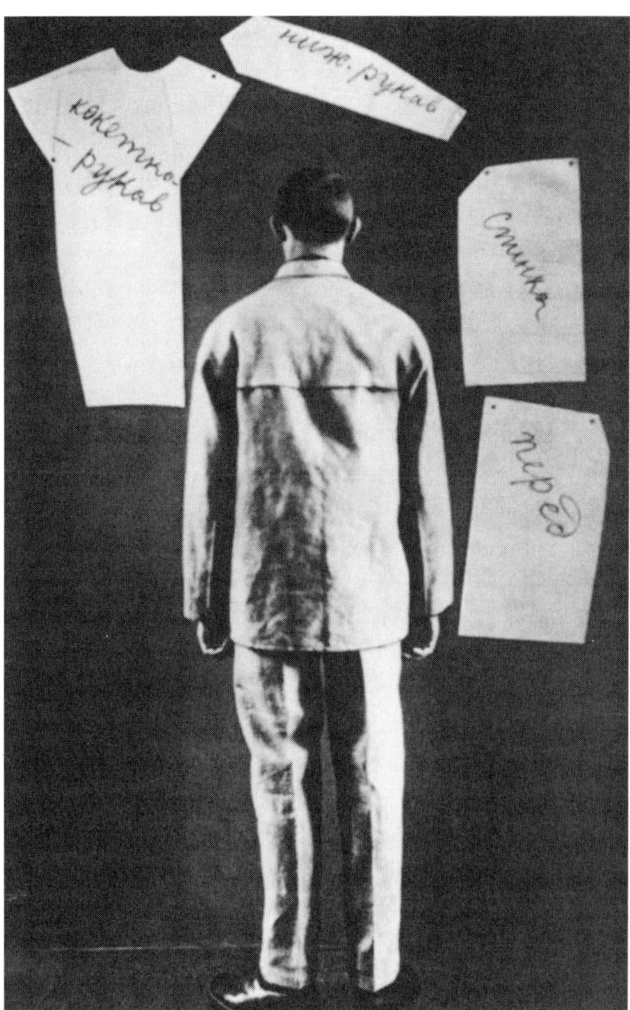

FIGURES 2.11, 2.12
Vladimir Tatlin modeling his men's sportswear suit with pattern pieces, front and back views, 1924–1925.

of a wooden stick, crossed by the sheet metal and glass elements, is echoed by the rectangle of the jacket, as well as the cross formed by the jacket's central vertical and upper horizontal seams. In the case of the suit more than the stove, the form of the object has not been strictly determined by the material demands of *byt*, but also clearly incorporates Tatlin's own visual proclivities, making it less anonymous. In contrast to Punin's claim about the stove, this suit could not have been designed by any good tailor.

Nor would this suit have been designed by a good tailor, because it represented a programmatic rejection of conventional men's dress of the moment in urban Soviet Russia. The actual suit modeled by Tatlin in the photographs was produced as a single prototype example in the factory workshop of the state-owned Leningrad Clothing Manufacturers' Trust (Leningradodezhda), on the basis of a design he had worked out while serving as a member of the Soviet on Standard Clothing at the Institute of Decorative Arts in Leningrad. Tatlin's plan had been for the trust to mass-produce his various standard patterns for clothing, but nothing was ever produced past the prototype stage. The reasons for this become clear if we examine a poster advertisement from Leningradodezhda from around 1924: the slim, natty figure of the man in the drawing, in his elegantly fitted, accessorized suit, underlines the weirdness of Tatlin's stiff, boxy outfit, which is at once rustic and futuristic (figure 2.13).[77] Like other state-owned businesses in 1924, Leningradodezhda was expected to turn a profit and it therefore catered to the tastes of the NEP consumer public, for which, as we have already seen in his angry scribbles denouncing the men in their "beautiful" suits on the "New Everyday Life" photomontage (see figure 2.3), Tatlin had only contempt.

As viewers with an interest in the fate of Tatlin's avant-garde origins in the face of his deliberately anonymous everyday objects, we can identify the vaguely geometric forms of his sportswear suit as a stylistic rebuttal of the cut of fashionable NEP-era suits. But artistic choice tells only part of the story; as with his stove, the motivation for the visual form of the suit also stems from Tatlin's perception of the needs of contemporary *byt*. "This clothing," he had scrawled next to the photograph of his suit, "is made with the advantage of being warm, not restricting movement, being hygienic and lasting longer." The cotton linen fabric of the suit was easier to clean than the traditional wools of men's suits, and therefore more hygienic, while the wide, boxy shape of the jacket was meant not just as a politically motivated visual contrast to elegantly fitted men's suits, but as a more comfortable alternative, allowing freedom of movement to work. Tatlin's unadorned suit functions as a white-collar equivalent to the clothes worn by

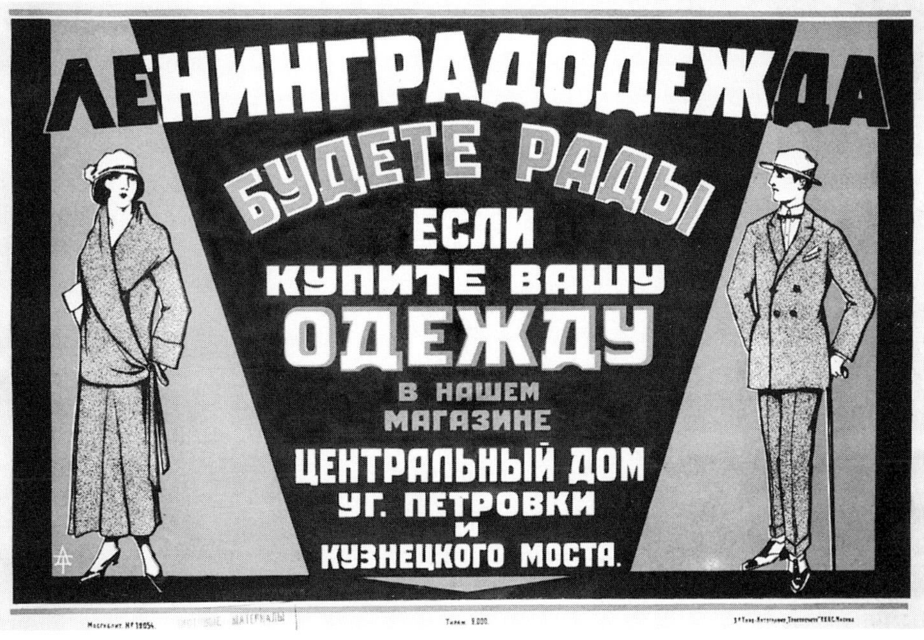

FIGURE 2.13
Advertising poster for Leningradodezhda, c. 1924. Courtesy Russian State Library Department of Graphics, Moscow. Photo by the author.

workers, drawing on the simplicity and practicality of plain work clothes to reinvent the men's suit.

Tatlin's study of workers' clothing joins his own "research into *byt*" with the practices of the professional ethnographers who researched workers' *byt* (*rabochii byt*), such as Medvedev from the Russian Museum. The two photographs of Tatlin in his awkward, rigid stance, posing from the front and the back to ensure that the suit is thoroughly documented, are oddly reminiscent of a pair of actual ethnographic photographs of two workers from the Baltiiskii Shipbuilding Factory in Leningrad in 1924, which lay just across town from Tatlin's studio (figures 2.14, 2.15).[78] They were taken by the photographer K. Kubesh, who worked with Medvedev on several research forays into factories and workers' housing in Leningrad. The two workers posing here in their production clothing (*prozodezhda*) overalls have the somewhat uncomprehending look of the subject who is told to pose as himself—to fully inhabit his assigned role in life and present himself as an object for the documentary photograph. They were even told to turn around to present their backsides to the camera. They stand awkwardly, nervously; the man on the right has his left arm poised, half bent, as if he wasn't able to decide where to put it before the shutter clicked.

The resemblance between the front and back photographs of Tatlin in his suit and the workers in their overalls may be fortuitous, but it forces us to recognize that the anonymous, documentary nature of the photographs of Tatlin is deliberate, because his practice in material culture is allied with the earnest project of research into *byt*.[79] Just as the photographs of the two workers exist to document their clothing, rather than these men as individuals, so the photographs of Tatlin emphasize the qualities of the suit, from front and back, rather than the personality of Tatlin the artist. And just as the workers are photographed at their work site surrounded by industrial equipment, with the man on the right holding a hammer in one hand and another tool in the other, so the photographs of Tatlin's suit emphasize the potentially industrial process for producing it through the display of the simplified pattern pieces surrounding him.[80] The suit's standardization and ease of assembly is guaranteed by the lack of any individualized fitting or tucking or detailing; shaping the suit to the lines of the individual body would respond to the demands of fashion, while Tatlin's goal is to respond to the requirements of efficient mass-production.[81] Practical, hygienic, comfortable, and cheaply mass produced, his suit is expedient (*tselesoobraznyi*) in the broader Constructivist sense of that term, because it responds to his particular vision of the material demands of workers' *byt*—a vision that has more in common with the ethnographic account of a primitive *byt* than with optimistic NEP advertisements touting a modern, urban lifestyle.

Despite Tatlin's earnestness in his photographs, his solidarity with workers and their primitive *byt* only goes so far, of course; unlike the literally anonymous workers depicted in ethnographic photographs, he enters self-consciously into the ethnographic construction of *byt* as an author. His modest, self-effacing modeling of his suit is also belied by the unusual choice of pinning the pattern pieces above and around his head in an elongated halo, creating a theatrical effect; it would have made more sense to pin the pieces next to each other in an arrangement that would mimic the garment itself. He could even be faulted for a certain arrogance in refusing to work within the parameters of the current production of Leningradodezhda, completely ignoring the tastes in clothing of most of the buying public. Although the jacket of Tatlin's suit may look fairly normal to viewers accustomed to clothes from the later twentieth century, when men's casual jackets inspired by various kinds of workers' uniforms—and even, briefly, by Maoist jackets—became popular, in 1924 his suit would have looked peculiar and futuristic to workers from the Baltiiskii Shipbuilding Factory shopping for leisure clothes, or for that matter to anyone but the most dedicated Communist–Futurist.

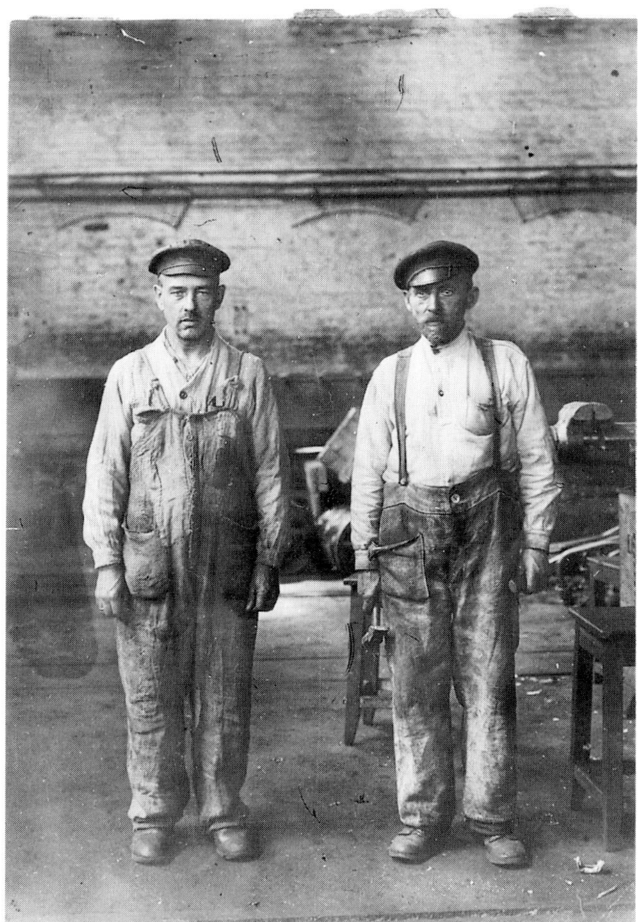

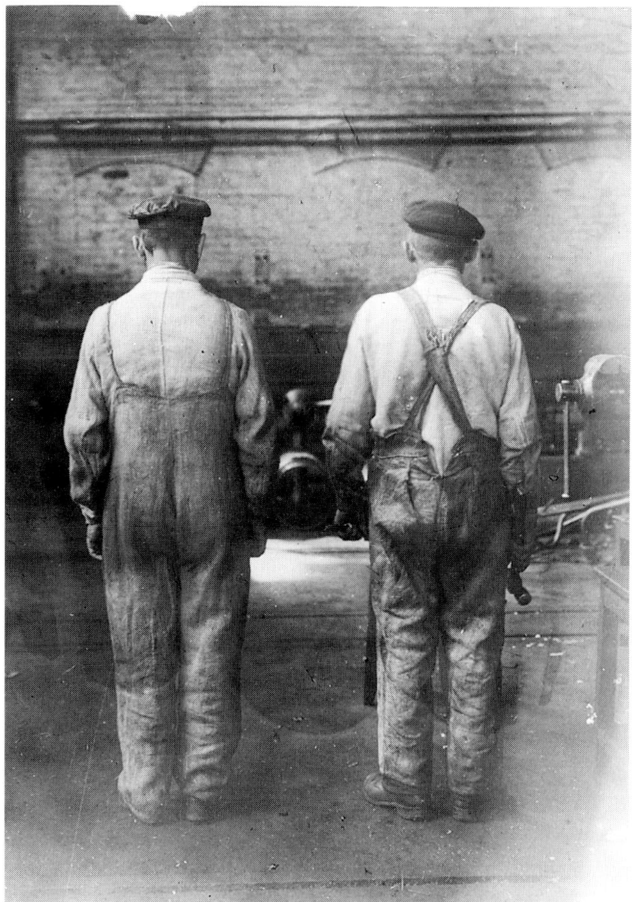

FIGURES 2.14, 2.15
K. Kubesh, documentary photo of workers in production clothing, front and back views, Baltiiskii Shipbuilding Factory, Leningrad, 1924.
Courtesy Russian Ethnographic Museum, St. Petersburg.

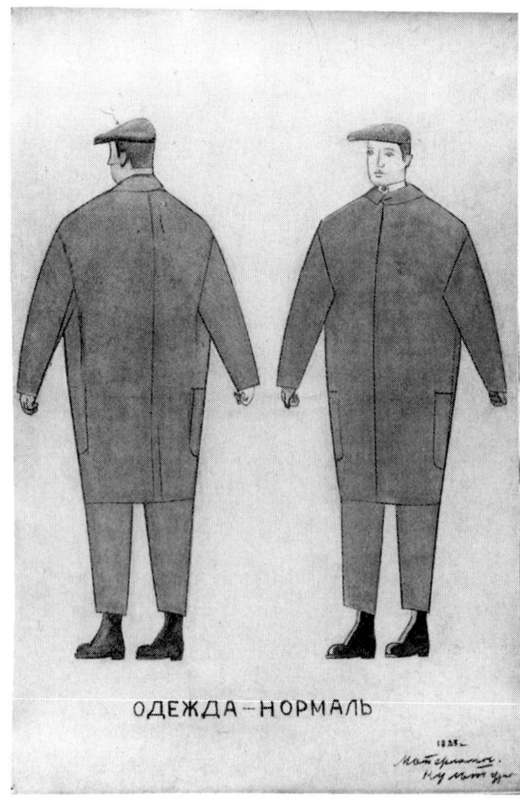

FIGURE 2.16
Vladimir Tatlin, design for a man's coat, 1923. Pencil on paper.

The critic Konstantin Miklashevskii brought up precisely this problem of the paradoxical arrogance of a famous artist suddenly choosing to work within traditionally anonymous craft production. Indignant that Tatlin presumed to have the necessary competence to enter highly skilled craft industries as an engineer or designer, he ridiculed Tatlin's pencil drawing of a design for a man's coat, exhibited at the Petrograd Artists of All Tendencies exhibition in 1923 (figure 2.16):

> Many thousands of craftsmen all over the world have for ages competed to create a coat that would offer maximum expediency. English firms produce coats presenting in this respect the fruits of long practical experience and a high degree of perfection. With one sketch Tatlin, on the other hand, wants to do better and even publicly exhibits drawings that, naturally, are not corroborated by craft skill.[82]

The Productivist counterargument would be that although English manufacturing firms may have years of experience, they do not have the artistic inventiveness of the avant-garde artists, and further, that the designs of such firms are dominated by the profit motive rather than a concern for what kinds of coats will most improve everyday life. Yet Tatlin's primitive sketch showing a hulking man with a tiny head and the rote, vacant face of a fashion sketch has little to offer in the way of avant-garde artistic inventiveness. Nor, seemingly, does the conventionally functional design for the coat, which—as the text of the article on "The New Everyday Life" describes the similar overcoat illustrated there—is wide and full-cut through the shoulders and torso to prevent constriction and facilitate the formation of a layer of warm air; narrow toward the bottom to prevent warmth from escaping; and has extralarge arm-holes to allow unhindered movement of the arms and tapered sleeves, again to retain warmth. The most radical component of the otherwise unremarkable drawing is the carefully lettered caption announcing that this is a "clothing-standard" (*odezhda-normal'*) for mass production rather than a singular creation. This caption would have located it immediately for contemporary viewers within the avant-garde domain of Productivism.

The ornery Miklashevskii may have a point about the "poorness" of this sketch. It represents one of Tatlin's earliest clothing design efforts, before he had begun to work in earnest with the Leningradodezhda trust and the Institute of Decorative Arts. Perhaps Tatlin was jumping the gun by displaying this sketch, in order to announce publicly, in an artistic context, his new commitment to making the most basic objects for everyday life. His later linen sportswear suit was a more complex achievement, uniting technical innovation with his own visual experience from his reliefs; we recall that he had directly articulated this working method in a report on the Section for Material Culture, when he stated that he wanted to "use the accumulated experience on material culture (relief and counter-relief), and apply these experiments to the organization of everyday life." But the criticism that Tatlin's project received, and its failure to enter mass production, stemmed more broadly from the sheer cultural illogicality, in the Russian tradition, of this attempt to "apply" his artistic experiments to *byt*. His art itself was highly valued, but for critics like Efros, Pel'she, and Miklashevskii, the spiritual or intellectual value of his artistic experiments could only be lost when they entered into the material domain of primitive everyday life. Miklashevskii considered Tatlin to be the most talented of the Constructivists, but argued that Tatlin's foray into clothing design "wasted" his great talent. He notes with respect that Tatlin "knows how to install electric lights and doorbells in apartments,

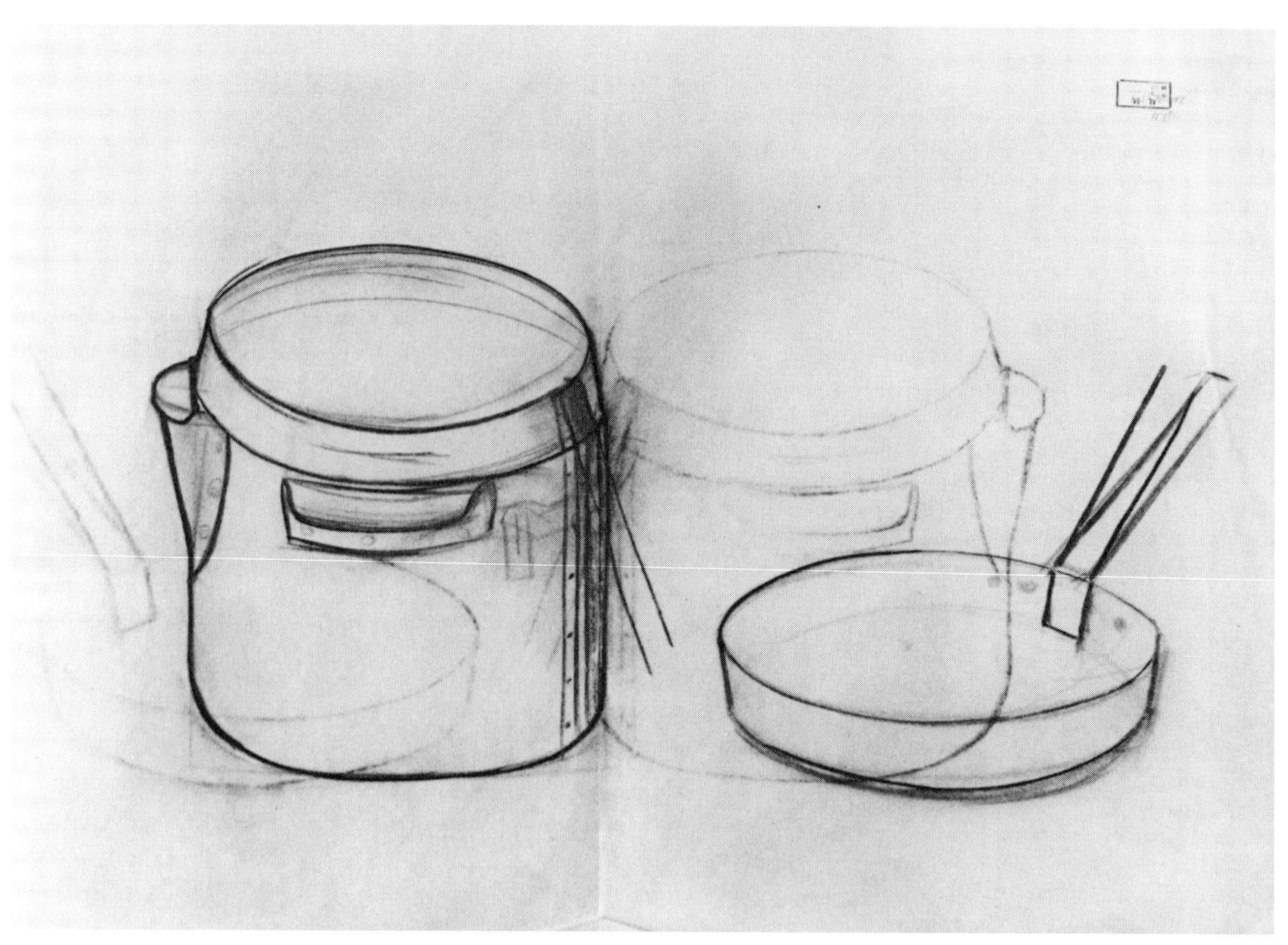

FIGURE 2.17
Vladimir Tatlin, design for a multipurpose metal pot, 1923. Pencil on paper.

how to put together stoves and (as he himself noted . . .) how deftly to tie sailors' knots."[83] An artist who worked as a sailor as a young man, voyaging on sailing ships across the Mediterranean, cuts a romantic figure, especially when his skill at tying sailors' knots shows up again in the taut mounting of his ambitious sculptural *Corner Counter-Reliefs*. Yet when Tatlin recalls the windbreaker and angler's cap that he used to wear as a sailor in his designs for practical winter coats and caps, the romantic narrative falters.[84] His art objects are superior to those of any other artist, according to Miklashevskii, but his misbegotten everyday objects are inferior to those of the average tailor, stove-maker, or tinker.

Perhaps the everyday object with the greatest pathos is Tatlin's failed design for a multipurpose metal pot of 1923 (figure 2.17). Its failure seems more significant because, unlike the ponderous sketch for the conventional overcoat, this sketch of a pot ambitiously attempts to "apply" his experience from the reliefs to an innovative object. The level of ambition seems incommensurate with the extreme modesty of the object itself, which takes its place in Pel'she's dismissive list of the lowly pots, spoons, and buckets favored by the *Lef*ists. The sketch is unfinished, seemingly abandoned when Tatlin couldn't get the parts to assemble right; he was trying for a combination cooking pot and teapot with a lid that would double as a frying pan, but he seems to have run into a problem with the mechanism for getting the long handle of the pan to stay put along the side of the pot. The pot's logic of space-saving and multifunctionality attempts to respond to the material privations of primitive Russian *byt*. But it also calls to mind, however faintly and hauntedly, his *Corner Counter-Relief* of 1915 (see figure 2.6)—in its projected material of metal, its mechanisms of spring tension and balance, the jutting shapes of the lip and handle of the pot, and, especially, the diagonally erect handle of the frying pan, which echoes, these many years later, the bold upward thrust of the relief's central, vertical slice of aluminum sheeting. The abandoned sketch with its shadowy doubled forms—the result of the paper being folded over and the graphite rubbing off on the other side of the paper—is like a ghost of the dramatic visual form of the counter-relief.

Tatlin's attempt to use his experience with visual form to make an everyday object is, in this instance at least, defeated by the volition of primitive material *byt*. The defeat is not just mechanical, in the difficulty of designing an object that through sheer ingenuity could solve the problems of overcrowded kitchens and material poverty, but philosophical, in the cultural impossibility of the jump from advanced sculpture to the pots and pans that represent the lowliest women's work of *byt*. In its failure, the sketch for the multipurpose pot points to the difficulty of the Constructivist reworking of *tselesoobraznost'* from a term meaning pure expediency or functionalism to one encompassing a more social understanding of the goal to be met by a particular form.

The Return of the Eye

The photomontage incorporating the "New Everyday Life" article of 1924-1925 (see figure 2.3) can be read as a rejoinder to the earlier, failed sketch of the multipurpose metal pot. Where the sketch is tentative and ghostly, the photomontage offers a bold, graphic composition in the lower half. The narrow vertical photograph of Tatlin modeling his sportswear suit, cut out from the photomontage in which he is surrounded by the pattern pieces (see figure 2.11), is pasted above the horizontal images of gentlemen in fashionable suits in such a way that Tatlin blocks out only the middle of their legs, leaving the details of their jackets and faces visible. To the left of Tatlin, arranged horizontally in a row, are the four pattern pieces that had surrounded him in the sportswear suit photomontage. They have been recombined to form a rectangular block with a red background that is answered, on the right side of the composition, by a thick black graphic line in the shape of a horizontal combined with a half circle. The horizontal block of pattern pieces on the left and the vertical photograph of Tatlin in his suit in fact combine to form a vivid symbolic image: a hammer. This explains why the photograph of Tatlin has been cut out from the larger original in such a way that the top of it forms a curved arch, to mimic the rounded portion of a hammer. It also explains the presence of the strange, truncated black graphic line on the right: it forms an abstract sickle, with curved blade and straight handle. Tatlin has created a subtle version of the ubiquitous Soviet symbol of the hammer and sickle. In this highly visual object, Tatlin and his everyday material objects become a hammer with which to strike the NEPmen in their fancy suits. Tatlin's visual form elevates itself above, and overcomes by force, the everyday life of NEP.

The metaphor of the hammer as an instrument to smash the old material life, in the Russian tradition of transcending *byt* to achieve a higher *bytie*, had appeared in Nikolai Punin's 1920 essay on Tatlin's *Monument to the Third International.* Punin framed his critical support for the monument around the claim that it should be understood not as an extension of Tatlin's earlier experiments with material in his reliefs, but rather as a triumphant overcoming of material through artistic form. Punin places particular significance on the temporal form of the spiral, in upward movement from the weight of the past toward the unfettered socialist future:

"The form wants to overcome material and the force of gravity; the force of resistance is great and massive; flexing its muscles, the form searches for the way out along the most resilient and dynamic lines that the world knows—spirals. They are full of movement, striving, speed and they are as taut as creative will and an arm-muscle strained with holding a hammer."[85] Punin expresses the visual force of the spiral through the stock Bolshevik image of the muscular proletarian holding a hammer, visualizing the overcoming of material as the literal smashing of matter. The language of art criticism here allies itself with the traditional Russian dualism of *byt* and *bytie*: the artistic form of the spiral, representing the path to a higher *bytie*, provides a "way out" from primitive material *byt*. The antiprostitution propaganda poster showing the hammer-wielding proletarian might almost serve as an illustration for Punin's imagery: massive, larger than life, saviorlike in his white garb, striving and flexed, the worker smashes through the material detritus of *byt* during NEP to elevate the woman worker by saving her from prostitution (see figure 2.8).

Tatlin's photomontage pitting the old against the new also contains the same pictorial elements as the antiprostitution poster. Like the worker in the poster, Tatlin wears a plain, light-colored outfit that is oddly anachronistic, with black boots; he is elevated above the other pictorial elements; he is pictorially associated with a hammer; and he tramples hapless capitalists wearing suits and hats. Tatlin sets himself up as the savior who will rain blows down upon the old *byt* from above, rather than participate in it from within. The composition specifically changes the scene of Tatlin's work in *byt* from the primitive, feminine domain of the kitchen with its pots and dishes, represented above by the photograph of the stove, to the modern and, in this case, masculine domain of *meshchanskii* consumerism. Entering *byt* to "battle" *meshchanstvo* was a far more acceptable avant-garde activity—as we saw, for example, in Tret'iakov's essay on Futurism—than entering the kitchen with a well-designed pot. Setting up this particular image of "battle" in the lower half of the photomontage also subtly shifts the meaning of the illustrations for the "New Everyday Life" article that are pasted onto the upper right half of the image: it pulls the two photographs there of Tatlin into alliance with the active image of the hammer beating the bourgeois gentlemen, and away from the passive connotations of *byt* that would be associated, at first glance, with the stove. The photomontage violently reasserts the authorial presence that had been largely repressed from the visual form of the everyday objects, and marks the vivid return of the "eye" to the "touch" of Tatlin's work in the Section for Material Culture.

Throughout the project, even though the everyday objects did not visually evince a particular Tatlin style, he connected them to his artistic identity through their public presentation. He placed two photographs of himself around the photograph of the stove in the "New Everyday Life" article. The clothing designs were always modeled by Tatlin himself. All of the prototype clothing was cut to his own measurements; only one drawing of a woman's dress survives, and it was never produced as a prototype.[86] This emphasis on the image of his own body, its size and shape as well as its visual presence in almost every public presentation of the objects, connected him to them and compensated for the repression in them of most manifestations of individual artistic form. His need for control over his working process further suggests his intense relation to the objects. According to Zhadova, he exerted complete control over information about the work of the Section: "Tatlin, known for his suspiciousness and his morbid fear of plagiarism, allowed neither employees of other sections nor representatives of the administration onto the premises of the Section for Material Culture—including the director himself, Malevich, a long-standing rival and competitor to Tatlin."[87]

Tatlin revealed a similar desire to impose his individual identity onto the work process, if not the works themselves, in a lecture he gave in 1923 entitled "Down with Tatlinism" (*Doloi Tatlinizm*)—a title that in itself asserts the existence of an entire new "ism" named after himself, even as he purports to criticize it. In the lecture, Tatlin complained that despite his best efforts to enter production, his requests to work in factories were routinely misunderstood or denied by factory authorities. From the audience, Miklashevskii asked him if there was one kind of production that he was particularly interested in working in, and Tatlin responded that "he would need a motorcycle and the right to travel to at least fifteen factories, in order at each one of them to produce the things he needed."[88] On the one hand, Tatlin claims to be a modest worker within collective Soviet production, Miklashevskii points out, but on the other, he acts as if he is a "chosen one" who can contribute to any area of industry, even outside his area of specialty. Miklashevskii continues indignantly: "he's convinced that, dilettante of technology though he is, it will cost him nothing to make new technological things, he has only to get the desire for it and then ride around on a motorcycle from one factory to the next." It is this motorcycle-riding "chosen one" whose technological things will singlehandedly destroy the old *byt* who makes his appearance in the form of Tatlin-as-hammer in the photomontage.

Yet there is another, more modest image of a worker holding a hammer that this Tatlin might also recall: the worker from the Baltiiskii Shipbuilding Factory modeling his overalls in the front and back ethnographic photographs, whose hammer is not a symbolic attribute but an instrument of his labor in the factory (see figures 2.14, 2.15). Tatlin's photomontage may stage an eruption of the authorial agency that had been repressed in his collective work in the Section for Material Culture, but it remains fundamentally faithful to that project's goal of "research into material as a shaping principle of culture." The content of the hammer, after all, is the sportswear suit, one of the Tatlin's material objects that would meet the demands of "our simple and primitive *byt*" and bring about a socialist *novyi byt*. Rather than the hammer smashing matter and transcending material *byt*, in the spirit of Trotsky, Tret'iakov, Punin, and the entire Russian philosophical tradition, Tatlin proposes to use his own, improved form of a material object of the *novyi byt* to work against the *meshchanskii byt* of NEP, in the spirit of Arvatov and the socialist object. His sportswear suit becomes an "instrument" of "everyday-life-creation," not in the sense of an instrumentalized object that is purely functional, but in the sense evoked by Arvatov when he writes that under socialism, the thing will function "as an instrument and as a co-worker" (EL, p. 124). Tatlin demonstrates his emotional investment in his suit as a comrade-object in the tender praise he scrawls next to it, in contrast to the petulant words that he writes about the NEP suits and the men who value them merely for being "beautiful." Tatlin refuses to concede to the commodity desires of modernity. Instead, he imagines that his active socialist objects can organize a modern form of everyday life that will be free of such desires.

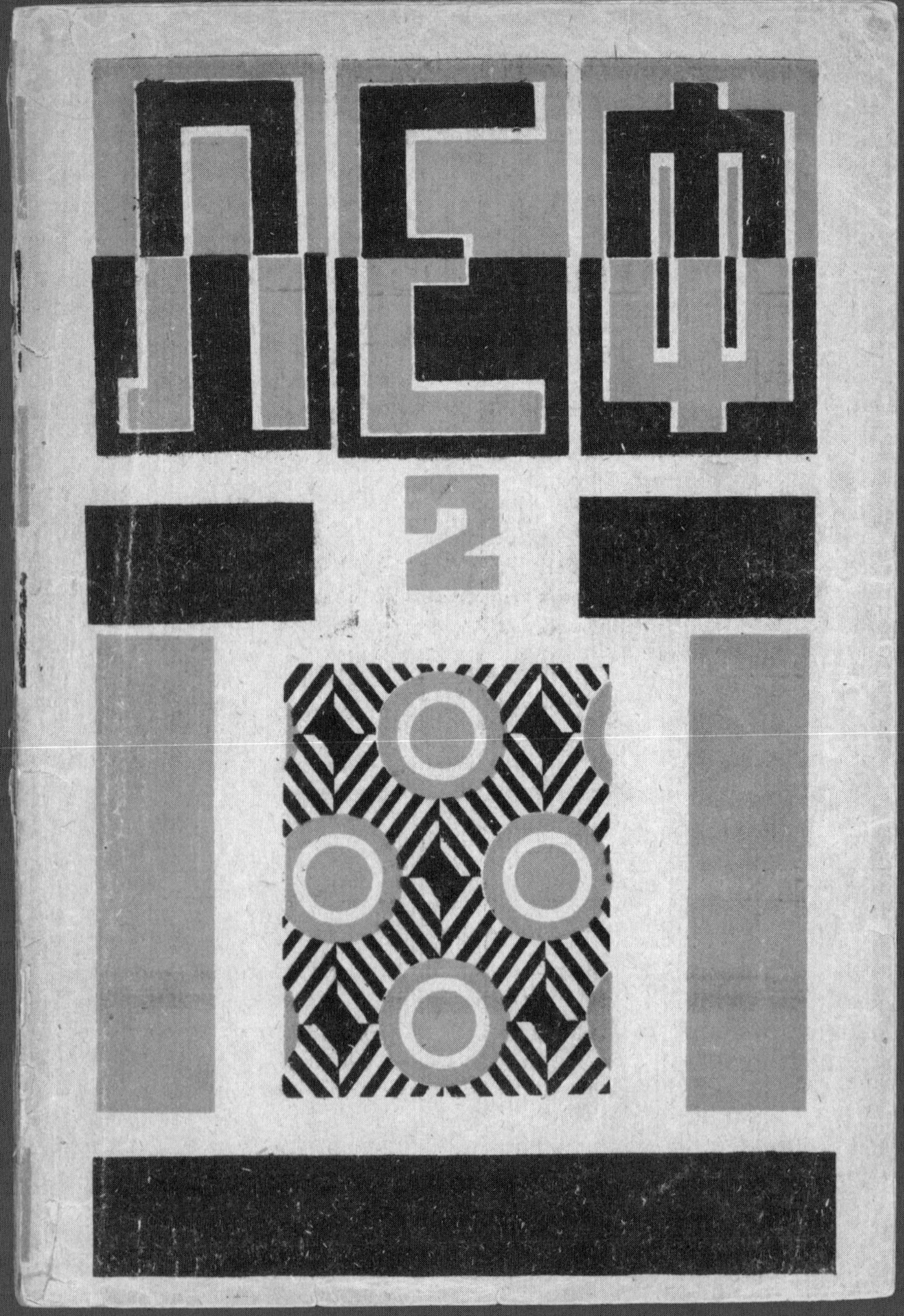

FIGURE 3.1

Aleksandr Rodchenko, cover of *Lef* no. 2 (1924), incorporating Liubov' Popova's fabric design. Gift of the Judith Rothschild Foundation. The Museum of Modern Art, New York. Digital image © The Museum of Modern Art/Licensed by SCALA/Art Resource, N.Y.

CHAPTER 3

THE CONSTRUCTIVIST FLAPPER DRESS

A geometric textile design by Liubov' Popova appeared on the cover of an issue of *Lef* in 1924 (figure 3.1). The issue was dedicated to her because she had died suddenly of scarlet fever at the age of thirty-five in May of that year. In their dedication, the editors wrote, "Popova was a Constructivist-Productivist not only in words, but in deed. When she and Stepanova were invited to work at [the First State Cotton-Printing] Factory, no one was happier than she was. Day and night she sat making her drawings for fabrics, attempting in one creative act to unite the demands of economics, the laws of exterior design and the mysterious taste of the peasant woman from Tula."[1] Working at the First State Cotton-Printing Factory in Moscow in 1923–1924, Popova and her colleague Varvara Stepanova were the only Constructivists to see their designs for everyday, utilitarian things actually mass-produced and distributed in the Soviet economy. Unlike Vladimir Tatlin, who failed, despite his best efforts, to have his designs for everyday objects produced by a factory, they fulfilled the Constructivist brief of entering into collective factory production.

As the celebratory *Lef* dedication makes vivid, Popova and Stepanova were central players in the Constructivist subset of the avant-garde; the Russian avant-garde of the early twentieth century is well known for the unusual prominence of women artists within it.[2] Yet Popova and Stepanova, not their male counterparts, were the ones who worked in textile design, a traditionally feminine area of artistic endeavor associated with the applied and decorative arts rather than advanced industrial production.[3] The story of their textile-design work could therefore be recruited for a history of modernist women artists who have in various ways reclaimed feminized areas of craft for high art—artists such as Anni Albers at the weaving workshop at the Bauhaus; Sonia Delaunay with her Cubist-inspired fabric and fashion; Hannah Höch, whose later Dada collages critically incorporate fabrics and images of domesticity and fashion; Meret Oppenheim with her fur-lined surrealist teacup; as well as a whole generation of second-wave-feminism-inspired artists since the 1970s working in "femmage" styles. But a conscious retrieval of fabric design as a typically feminine practice was emphatically not how Popova and Stepanova themselves articulated their practice. As committed Productivists who had forsworn the individual touch of painting and craft, their stated goals at the textile factory were precisely the scientific and technical ones of Constructivism: the opportunity to develop skills of mechanical drawing, to participate in the factory research laboratory and production decisions, and to see their work enter the process of industrial mass production.

The Constructivist interest in technical and systematic models of making can be described as a move toward transparency. The Productivist Boris Arvatov characterized the development of the ideal form of the modern thing in this way: "the mechanism of a thing, the connection between the elements of a thing and its purpose, were now transparent" (EL, p. 126).[4] The transparent thing demonstrates its expediency or *tselesoobraznost'*—the connection between its material form and its purpose—by showing us how it was made. This rhetoric of transparency dominated Constructivist writings, and it has contributed to our usual definition of Constructivism as an avant-garde that embodies the modernist desire for rationality. But this rhetoric has been too narrowly interpreted in terms of an instrumental utilitarianism. The previous chapter argued that Tatlin's everyday objects respond to the broader social needs of material *byt* (everyday life) and so exceed a narrow functionalism. This chapter pursues a similar argument, demonstrating that Popova and Stepanova's textile and fashion designs deviate from a technological functionalism not because of their connection with craft or decorative art, but because of the way they embody the Constructivist attempt to forge a new form of socialist consumption as the necessary counterpart to socialist production. The transparency and rationality of the Constructivist thing does not preclude it from addressing the famously nontransparent problem of commodity desire. The utilitarian purpose invoked by Constructivist *tselesoobraznost'* is not only the mechanical purpose of the thing but the larger purpose of confronting the phantasmatic power of the commodity object and redeeming it for socialism.

The *Lef* dedication is instructive, because its description of Popova's "creative act" offers a highly economical explanation of this broader interpretation of the key

Constructivist term *tselesoobraznost'*. According to the *Lef* editors, Constructivist *tselesoobraznost'* concerned itself with the material form of things not only in relation to the goal of solving technical problems of utilitarian form ("the laws of exterior design") but also in relation to the task of contributing to the new socialist economy ("the demands of economics") and the need to appeal to consumer desire ("the mysterious taste of the peasant woman from Tula"). Unlike Tatlin, who dismissed the subjective taste of gentlemen who liked to wear "beautiful" suits, Stepanova and Popova committed themselves more deeply and systematically to solving the "mystery" of consumer desire in modernity. The very mundanity of cheap printed cotton fabric, with its absolute usefulness in the "new everyday life" (*novyi byt*) after the revolution, made it an exemplary Constructivist thing. But Popova and Stepanova knew that the real test of their textile-design work at the First State Cotton-Printing Factory would come in clothing design—in the formation, from their fabrics, of three-dimensional things for use in everyday life. Fashion would therefore be the site of their Constructivist intervention into revolutionary material culture, an area of consumer culture that was undeniably associated with femininity.

Byt itself, as the chosen field of action for the Constructivist object, was already, as we have seen, a domain negatively cast as feminine and primitive. In Russian culture, the tenacity of the split between material life (*byt*) and spiritual life (*bytie*) paradoxically supported the rise to prominence of women writers and artists in the early twentieth century; in the context of the hypervaluation placed on literary and, to a lesser extent, artistic achievements, women like the revered poet Anna Akhmatova were able to transcend the usual limitations imposed by their gender. It is therefore all the more perverse and challenging that Popova and Stepanova, as women artists, would take their hard-won Productivist credentials back into *byt*—into its most commercialized and feminized guise of fashion—and aim to make a Constructivist difference there. As Constructivists working within the field of fashion, they acknowledged the individual desires of the female consumer while remaining critical of them and attempting to steer them in more collective directions. This chapter will establish Popova and Stepanova's Productivist commitment to the project of the transparent Constructivist object, as well as their openness to confronting the desires encompassed by fashion commodities—with an emphasis on the former for Stepanova and her designs for sports clothing and on the latter for Popova and her designs for flapper dresses.

Griselda Pollock has suggested that the historical presence of women artists in a "field of representation so powerfully dominated by the beat of men's drums . . .

offers a shift in the pattern of meanings in a given culture."[5] But Popova and Stepanova did not simply shift the meanings within an already-defined field; rather, the shifts they introduced through their textile and fashion work can be understood as foundational to the very formation of the most productive version of the Constructivist object as a socialist object. Tarrying with the feminized domains of the everyday and the commodity were part and parcel of Constructivist art-into-life practice: at this moment, Tatlin was designing stoves and pots and pans for proletarian kitchens, and as we will see in the next chapter, Aleksandr Rodchenko was making cookie advertisements for Mossel'prom, the state-owned agricultural trust.

Constructivist things like pots, cookie ads, and flapper dresses—related as they are to everyday life and commerce—have a distinctly marginal look to them in the context of modern art and in the context of the technological ambitions of the early Constructivist manifestoes. Two important Popova scholars say as much when they write that Popova's fashion experiments, as opposed to her textile designs at the factory, raise the problem of the extent to which her art is Constructivist at all: "If in our analysis of her fabrics we immediately felt the presence of the Constructivist aesthetic (regular geometrism, the use of black and white, the slight graphic tone), then all the phenomena as a whole—clothing and textile design both—clearly exceed the stylistic framework and aesthetic principles of Constructivism."[6]

The argument of this chapter will be the opposite: Popova's flapper dress exceeds our given definitions of Constructivism only because those definitions are too narrow. Seemingly marginal Constructivist things like the flapper dress can instead define Constructivism, if we understand it more expansively. Popova and Stepanova's project, as the most successfully realized example of Constructivist theory, is front and center in the story of the Constructivist object. Their designs both are indebted to and deviate from traditionally feminine forms of artistic practice. They demonstrate that Constructivism itself, as theory and practice, can be understood as an avant-garde that unsettles some of the gendered hierarchies of modernist art.

good model argument

!

Into Production![7]

Popova and Stepanova began to work for the First State Cotton-Printing Factory sometime in the late fall of 1923.[8] It was a massive and well-known factory on the banks of the Moscow River that had been privately owned before the revolution by Emil Tsindel' (figure 3.2); despite its new postrevolutionary name, most people in the early 1920s, including Popova and Stepanova, still referred to it as

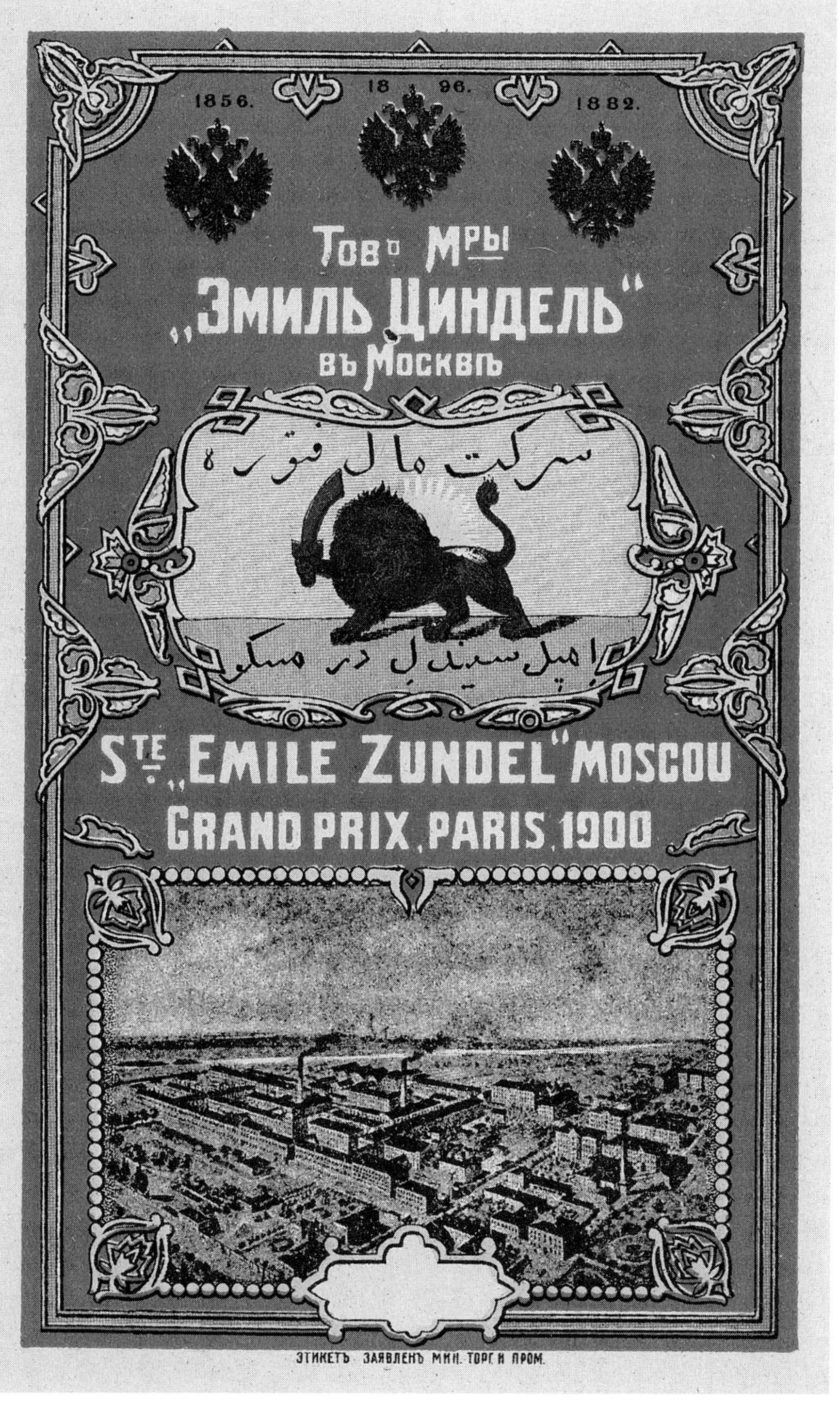

FIGURE 3.2

The Tsindel' Factory, illustrated in the brochure *Societé de la manufacture "Emile Zundel" a Moscou*, 1914. Courtesy Russian State Library, Moscow.

the Tsindel' factory. After years of world and civil war, revolution, and embargo had cut off contact with other industrialized nations, Soviet textile producers, like most other recently nationalized manufacturers struggling to produce efficiently in the shaky postrevolutionary economy, were burdened by outmoded equipment and designs. In an effort to jump start the sorry state of the factory's production, the director, Aleksandr Arkhangelskii, took the creative risk of hiring a pair of avant-garde artists as textile designers. He took the unprecedented step for a Soviet industrial manager of actually heeding the many Constructivist speeches, articles, and manifestoes that declared that the new "artist-constructors" of the left avant-garde held the key to improving the quality and competitiveness of Soviet industry. The Constructivist women were most likely invited to work there, while their male colleagues were not, because of the feminization of the textile industry; in Russia as in other industrialized countries, textile workers were predominantly women. Yet if Popova and Stepanova's gender may have made them natural employee choices for Arkhangelskii, their avant-garde credentials and notoriety landed them the job. They were well known in Moscow for their costume and set designs for the avant-garde theater director Vsevolod Meyerhold, which had been widely discussed in the press, and Stepanova had even made a foray into the discourse of clothing production by publishing an article called "Today's Clothing Is Production Clothing" in *Lef* in early 1923.[9]

When Popova and Stepanova entered the First State Cotton-Printing Factory, they attempted to define their role precisely as that of the Productivist artist-engineer. They wrote a high-handed memo to the factory administration with the following demands:

> 1. Participation in the production sections . . . with the right to vote (on production plans, production models, the acquisition of design drawings and the hiring of workers for artistic work). 2. Participation in the chemistry laboratory to observe the coloring process. 3. The production of designs for block-printed fabrics according to our requirements and proposals.[10]

The third demand was meant to give them the right to determine the types of fabrics printed in relation to their proposed uses—in other words, to connect the "traditional" applied-art aspect of the textile-printing process to the more ambitious one of the shaping or forming of mass-produced objects such as clothing.[11] By voicing their desire to be involved in production decisions and to enter the industrial laboratories of the factory, they attempted to differentiate themselves from traditional applied artists who stayed within the artistic domain of the design departments. They threw themselves into the study of the cotton-printing process, developing an understanding, for example, of the limitations posed by the narrow width of the factory's print rollers and its outmoded conveyor system.

A skeptic might well ask on what grounds Popova and Stepanova expected that they could possibly be qualified to run technical laboratories in factories. Their qualification (*kvalifikatsiia*, a key buzzword of the time), they would answer, was their training as modernist artists. As we have seen, they both had participated in the debates leading to the formation of the Productivist program in 1921 at the Institute of Artistic Culture (INKhUK) in Moscow. According to this program, Productivist artists would combine their skills of advanced artistic analysis of material, form, and process with newly adopted scientific skills of organization and technological proficiency, in order to dynamize the traditional, backward practices of Soviet industry.

Both Popova and Stepanova started out as painters, but they arrived at their joint stint at the First State Cotton-Printing Factory, and the remarkably similar textile designs they produced there, through different paths of artistic development. Popova was born into a rich and cultured family near Moscow in 1889 and received an excellent art education. She had the opportunity to travel in Russia and Europe to look at art and spent a year in Paris studying at La Palette, the studio of the Cubist painters Henri Le Fauconnier and Jean Metzinger. On her return from Paris in 1913, she worked in the studio of Tatlin, who was then developing his reliefs; during this period she successfully exhibited paintings in a Cubist style. In 1916 she switched allegiances and joined the Suprematist group around Kazimir Malevich and developed her own acclaimed Suprematist-inspired language of abstract painting, her *Architectonics* series.

In *Painterly Architectonics with Pink Semicircle* of 1918, vibrantly colored quadrilaterals and a pink circle are layered like so many flat cut-paper collage elements on the surface, invoking Suprematist flatness (figure 3.3). Yet where Malevich's flat quadrilaterals can be read in modernist terms as indices of the picture frame, evacuating any possibility of three-dimensional space, Popova here courts its emergence: the explicitly painterly touch of her brushwork blends colors at certain junctures, producing a chiaroscuro shading that gives occasional solidity, even roundness, to the planes. Some of her quadrilaterals, here and elsewhere in the *Architectonics* series, graze each other at oblique angles, slicing themselves open to grasp other forms within their openings. This drama of interconnected colored forms unfolds here against a backdrop of looming darkness.

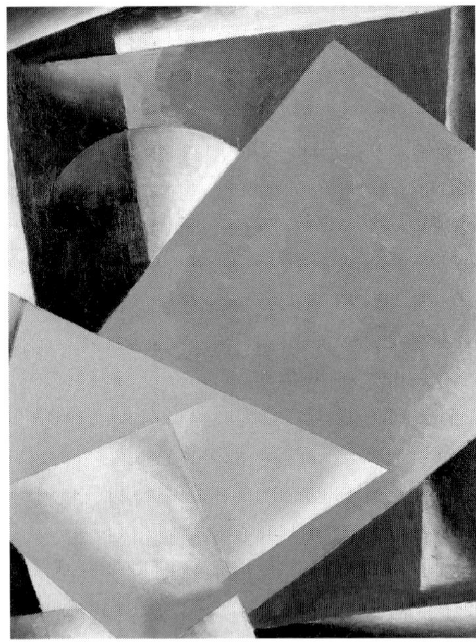

FIGURE 3.3
Liubov' Popova, *Painterly Architectonics with Pink Semicircle*, 1918. Oil on canvas. State Tret'iakov Gallery, Moscow. See plate 4.

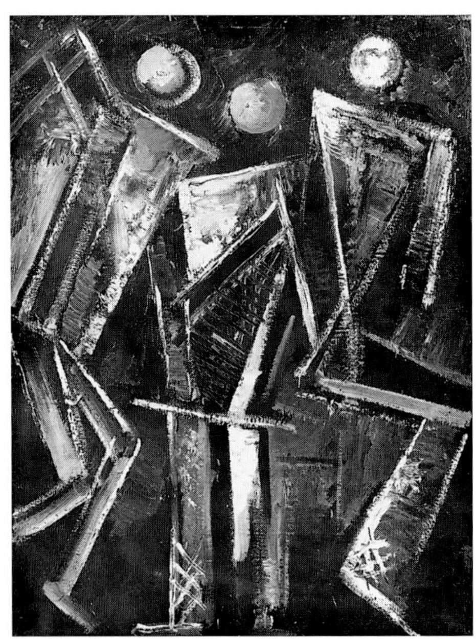

FIGURE 3.4
Varvara Stepanova, *Three Figures*, 1920. Oil on plywood. Private collection.

Emotion and even illusionism lurk, despite Popova's stated intention of achieving a transparency of formal means. In an artist's statement of 1919, she would graphically divide all of painting up into two categories, one positive and one negative. She placed the *Architectonics* works in the positive column under the plus sign, defined in modernist terms by a list of their constituent elements: painterly space, line, color, energetics, *faktura*. In the negative column under the minus sign she placed the term *aconstructiveness*, which she defined as illusionism, literariness, emotion, and recognition.[12] She soon abandoned the *Architectonics* series, however, as if the solidity and interconnectedness of the architectonic planes still suggested too much sensation or narrative, no matter how nonliterary—although the contradiction between her work and her stated intentions gives the *Architectonics* paintings their pictorial force, as it works itself out across their surfaces. She began instead to make even more rigorously flattened and linear compositions, such as her *Spatial-Force Construction* series of 1921.

We should not be surprised to learn that one of her contemporaries, a student at the state art school VKhUTEMAS, where she taught the basic course in painting, spoke of Popova's "domestication of her own, to some extent ladylike (*damskoi*), Suprematism."[13] Although her young admirer—who also praises her beauty and good taste in clothes—hardly uses the adjective "ladylike" here with any specificity, it is not difficult to guess at what he might have meant by this feminine adjective. Today as in 1920, the terms touch, sensation, and interconnectedness are privileged signifiers of the feminine.[14] In the context of avant-garde painting and the debates at INKhUK, "ladylike" was not the adjective an ambitious painter like Popova would want attached to her work. Her *Spatial-Force Construction* paintings of 1921 might be a deliberate rejoinder to this kind of description. Mathematical in their vectored linearity, vehemently material in their use of plywood, impasto oils, and marble dust, and modernist in their irreducible flatness, they meet quite precisely the proto-Constructivist criteria for "plus" painting enumerated by her own statement of 1919.[15]

For most of the period of the debates at INKhUK, Popova resisted the Constructivist group's demand for utilitarianism. Only in November 1921 did she sign a proclamation of artists who renounced easel painting in favor of Productivism. Comparing the richly gradated shading of her *Painterly Architectonics with Pink Semicircle* with the printed fabric of 1923–1924 that had appeared on the cover of *Lef*, the fabric design can be seen as a kind of end point in her consciously Constructivist move away from the individual, sensual touch of painting toward more anonymous, linear forms based on the industrial model of mechanical drawing. The earlier painting's conjuring of spatial illusionism against all odds from the flat Suprematist circles and quadrilaterals is retained but graphically simplified and transformed in the fabric design. The ingenious juxtaposition of alternately directed black and white stripes creates the effect of receding black holes, while bright orange targetlike circles seemingly hover above the background.

Stepanova's fabric designs created similar optical or op-art-like effects, although their origins cannot be traced to her pre-Constructivist painting practices with the same satisfyingly linear logic. Stepanova was younger than Popova by five years, and her background was less privileged. She had gone to art school in Kazan and did not move to Moscow until 1913. There, she became involved with the avant-garde and continued to study painting, but she also worked as a secretary in a factory. Her only major series of paintings to be exhibited, at the Nineteenth State Exhibition in Moscow in 1920, were influenced, like Popova's paintings at that time, by the flat, abstract planes of Suprematism. But she appropriated them for a more traditional style of figuration, turning the quadrilateral planes into torsos and limbs and giving them round heads and little feet; most of her canvases comprise friezelike rows of flattened dancing figures (figure 3.4). These paintings were not as well received as innovations in abstract painting as Popova's efforts of the same period. Stepanova recorded in her diary the responses of contemporary artists and critics to the exhibition. Those who wanted to respond encouragingly used open-ended terms such as "rich," "fresh," "charming," and "intriguing" to describe her work, while others more straightforwardly called it "unformed," "evolving," "lacking definite values," "ungovernable," and "unbalanced" (these last two adjectives were offered by Marc Chagall). All these terms fit within the historical lexicon of male critics confronting women's art. One critic even told her straight out that her paint was overworked and that this was typical of women's art.[16] Later, the Constructivist Konstantin Medunetskii would rudely refer to the figures in these paintings as "tadpoles."[17]

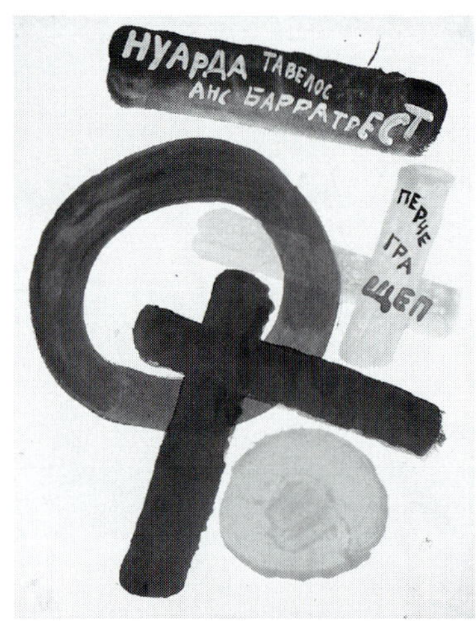

FIGURE 3.5
Varvara Stepanova, illustration for *Rtny Khomle*, 1918. Tempera on paper. Private collection. See plate 5.

Her considerable graphic talent, on the other hand, had emerged in 1918 when she began to produce nonobjective sound poems, such as *Rtny Khomle*, for which she handwrote the evocative sounding nonsense words, surrounding and enveloping them with bright, almost translucent rectangles, circles, thick lines, and grids rendered in brushy, freehand tempera (figure 3.5). These visually forceful and inventive works on paper are more modest in scale and finish than her paintings. Yet clearly she wanted to produce work at a higher level of permanence and finish, which is why she turned to producing the less well-received oil paintings of 1920. In the context of her own artistic history, then, it is not surprising that Stepanova was a founding member of the Working Group of Constructivists at INKhUK, which definitively rejected easel painting in favor of utilitarian work. Stepanova's allegiance to the antisubjective, mechanistic aspects of Constructivism may well have been more vehement and consistent than Popova's because her paintings had not received the same kind of erudite critical acclaim. She became the research secretary of INKhUK in 1920–1921 and would continue to function as an archivist and theorist of Constructivism throughout the 1920s. She was a far more prolific writer than Popova, keeping careful records of avant-garde exhibitions, delivering theoretical papers, and publishing essays.

We can see her at work with a compass in a famous photograph taken by her life partner, Aleksandr Rodchenko, in 1924 (figure 3.6). The photograph has come to function as a sign for Constructivism's rejection of the individual touch of the artist's hand—here reduced to an amorphous blob—in favor of the mechanical precision of the compass. In a notebook entry, Stepanova writes that the factory council at the First State Cotton-Printing Factory criticized her and Popova for drawing with compass and ruler, assuming that they did so because they could not draw.[18] Her implication is that factory councils have no comprehension of the Constructivist view that artistic drawing in the context of industry is obsolete. But perhaps for Stepanova there is also a recognition that her talent does lie with

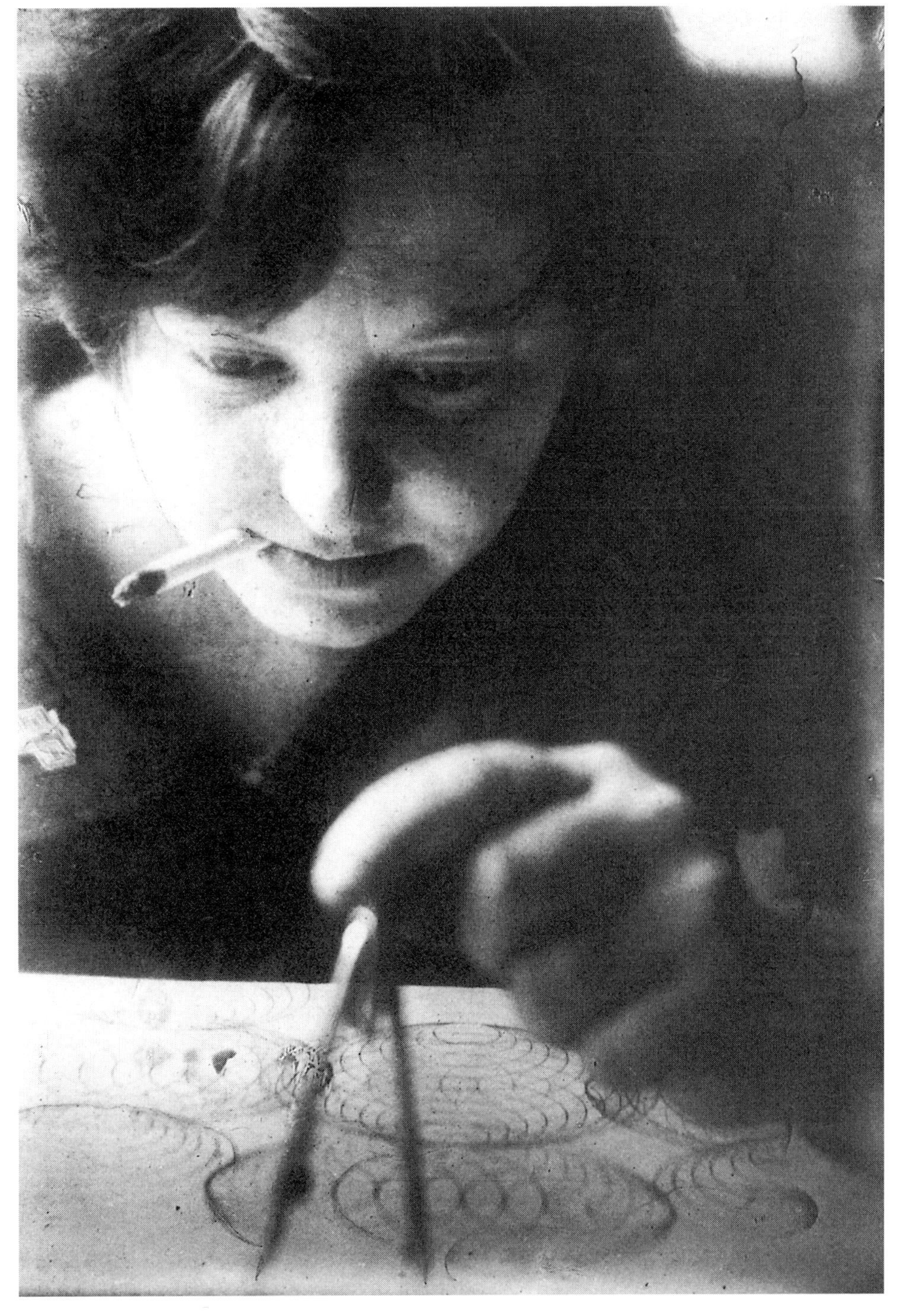

FIGURE 3.6
Aleksandr Rodchenko, photo of Varvara Stepanova drawing with a compass, 1924.

simplified graphic forms, with the ruler and the compass. In a paper on their work at the textile factory delivered at INKhUK in January 1924, she enumerated her and Popova's goals as the eradication of "the high artistic value [placed on] a handdrawn design" and the elimination of "naturalistic design"—she has in mind the traditional Russian floral patterns—in favor of exclusively geometric forms.[19] Yet despite the anti-authorial anonymity associated with mechanical drawing and factory labor, Stepanova's public performance of her Productivist role suggests that it was not, in fact, anti-individual or antisubjective. She developed a strong artistic identity as a Productivist that would prove enabling to her as a woman artist in a way that her identity as a painter had not. Rodchenko's photograph both produces and corroborates this Productivist identity; her hand may be out of focus, but her blurry forefinger is parallelled by her intensely chewed cigarette, and the two parallel lines of finger and cigarette dramatically bisect the central vertical rectangle, the four corners of which are fixed by her intently gazing eyes above and the sharp points of the compass below. The photograph produces her as individual creator as romantically as any painted portrait of the artist at work, but the model of creation is transformed from mystifying inspiration to useful invention.

Popova and Stepanova may have arrived at the textile factory from different artistic origins, but both artists seem to have agreed that their mandate there was to produce geometric designs with consistently vibrating effects, even though such specifically op-art effects, as opposed to merely geometric forms, were nowhere articulated as particularly Constructivist. For Stepanova we have direct evidence that these effects were an explicit goal of her designs; her 1925 course plan for the Textile Faculty at VKhUTEMAS, where she taught, asks students to "plan a bichromatic design in order to create a multi-colored effect" and "compose a design which creates chromatic effects (such as iridescence)."[20] We even have a series of images, from an early sketch to a finished fabric, that demonstrate her disciplined process of working toward the most optical variation of a given design—in this case a design revisiting the motif of the circle and horizontal bars that had appeared in her freehand illustration for *Rtny Khomle* in 1918. The first sketch is clearly made with ruler and compass to ensure the precise dimensions that allow the outer "edges" of the circles to rest exactly on the outer edges of the vertical or horizontal lines that surround them (figure 3.7). Even in nascent, partially sketched form, the design already gives the impression of heavy, striped balls floating against a recessed lattice of lighter stripes, owing to the dark gray stripes that alternate with the red or yellow color inside the balls, as opposed to the simple alternation of white and color stripes in the background. In the intermediate design, she has made two crucial changes that promote a fully optical, vibrating effect (figure 3.8). First, she has placed the balls so that their "edges" abut the red background stripe, rather than the white one, allowing for strong, unbroken stripes of red to bolster the vertical axis of the design, so that the horizontally striped balls no longer seem to float so securely "above" the vertical stripes. Second, she has eliminated the gray color within the circles, so that both circles and background are now structured by white stripes, the dual pictorial function of which contributes to the vibrating effect. In the final variant, which was mass-produced at the First State Cotton-Printing Factory, she has simply turned the circles ninety degrees, so that all the stripes now move in the same direction (figure 3.9). When this logical continuity of vertical stripes is dislocated by the simple shift from white to colored band within the circles, the optical effect is even stronger. With the slight irregularities that result from the weave and stretch of the fabric, on printed cloth the design seems to shift and move.

But if it can be demonstrated that optical patterns were the explicit goal of Stepanova's and Popova's textile designs, it still does not answer the question, What makes these optical patterns Constructivist? Neither artist ever spoke to this directly, but the answer that this chapter proposes is that in its dynamic, optical quality, this piece of cotton fabric, destined for women's dresses, embodies the Constructivist ideal of a mass-produced object of everyday life that has been penetrated and transformed by the processes of production. The fabric is a specifically industrial object because its vibrant colors were perfected in the factory's chemistry laboratory, and its small, repeating pattern of balls on stripes responds to the limitations imposed by the narrow printing presses at the factory. According to Arvatov, the dynamism of the socialist thing results from its condition of industrial production—for Marx, the most powerful unleashing of human energy and imagination in history—and its purpose is to import this dynamism into the passive, consumerist lethargy of everyday life (*byt*) under capitalism (EL, p. 121). Tatlin had also designed his stove, suit, and multipurpose pot to bring technical ingenuity into backward *byt*, but the plain, even muted visual forms of his objects reflected his perception of Russian *byt* as primitive and therefore not yet in need of "Americanized" flourishes. In contrast, the vibrating opticality of the Constructivist fabric patterns, while not integral to the structure or production of the cotton cloth itself, was meant to convey the invention and creativity of the industrial production process through its very visual form. The skilled human labor that produced the fabric is rendered transparent in its material form, lending the fabric itself the animation of its makers.

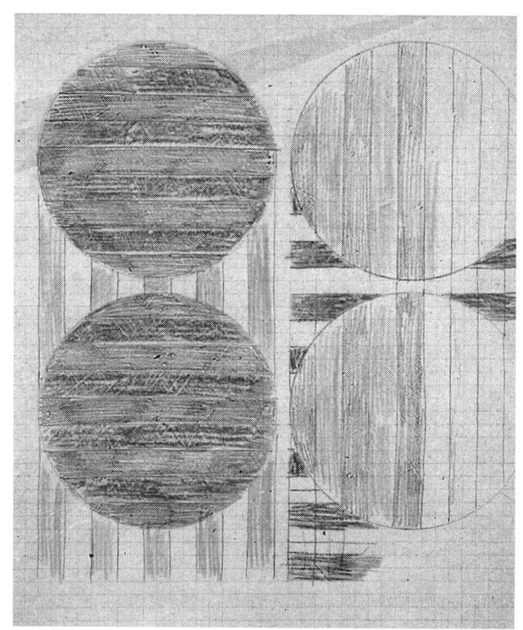

FIGURE 3.7
Varvara Stepanova, preliminary sketch for fabric design, 1923–1924. Color crayon on paper.

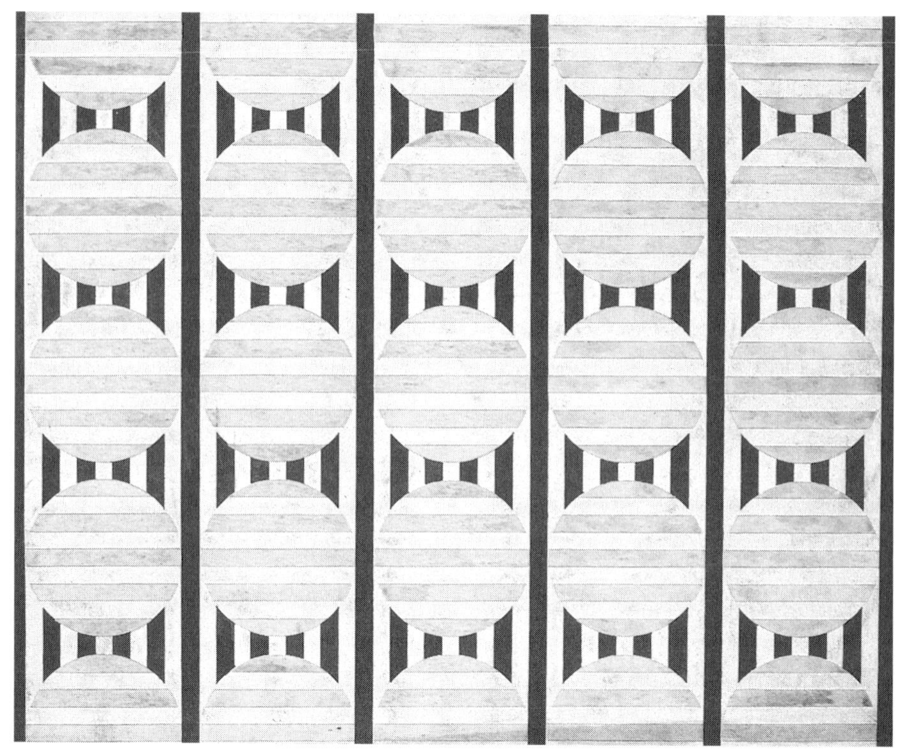

FIGURE 3.8
Varvara Stepanova, intermediate sketch for fabric design, 1923–1924. Gouache on paper.

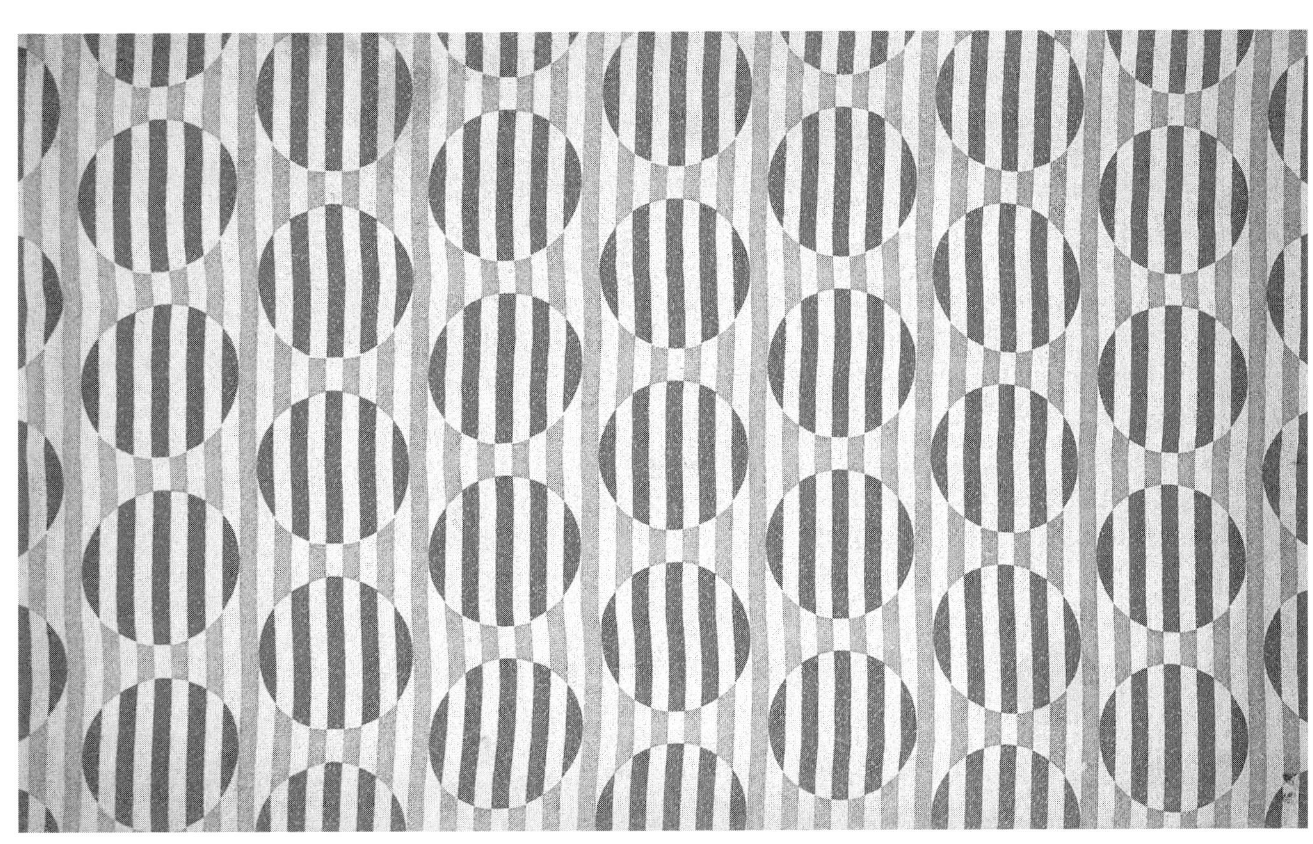

FIGURE 3.9
Varvara Stepanova, weaving sample of final version of fabric, 1923–1924. Private collection. See plate 6.

The work of Popova and Stepanova at the First State Cotton-Printing Factory fulfilled, as far as was possible in the Soviet context, Arvatov's vision of the culture of the thing as presented in his 1925 essay "Everyday Life and the Culture of the Thing." In this essay, we recall, he attempted to imagine how socialism will transform passive capitalist commodities into active socialist things. The essay took as its subject matter the industrial things in Western modernity and the technical intelligentsia that invented them. According to Arvatov, the technical intelligentsia organized the advanced technological things of industry through its work, but as "a group of hired organizers" (EL, pp. 125-126) it did not possess the things it organized; its everyday life was therefore structurally less affected by the commodity form. Popova and Stepanova, as designers at the factory fulfilling the role of the technical intelligentsia, were uniquely well placed to realize Arvatov's vision.[21] As self-consciously revolutionary artists, they had already begun to renounce bourgeois forms of *byt* in their own lives—helped along by the appalling living conditions in Russia during the civil war—and as women, they had of necessity a more practical and experiential investment in *byt*. Now, as technical design workers in the factory, they were in a position consciously to imbue their everyday objects with the dynamic qualities derived from technological modes of construction. Their vibrating fabric designs can be seen to embody precisely those "physiological-laboring capacities of the organism" that made the thing into an "instrument" and a "co-worker" (EL, p. 124). The set of demands they had addressed to the factory managers in their memo, demanding participation in the chemistry laboratories and production decisions, was their passport to becoming full-fledged members of a new, socialist technical intelligentsia. They would unite the advanced experience already available to this class in the West with the socialist economy of the USSR—the step that was missing in the West. "I suppose we have a proletariat in the West and an ideology of proletarian culture in Russia," Arvatov had said after hearing Stepanova's paper on Constructivism at INKhUK. "We have Constructivist ideologists in Russia, and technological industry in the West. This is the real tragedy."[22]

Corroborating Arvatov's pessimism, and perhaps predictably, Popova and Stepanova's Constructivist requests to be more than traditional designers were largely denied by factory management. They were not invited to work in the factory's research laboratory; in fact, they did not even work in the factory's design atelier, but rather at home in their studios. They went to the factory only to drop off their designs, as depicted in a caricature that appeared in Rodchenko and Stepanova's homemade newspaper of 1924, *Nash gaz*: it shows Popova on her way

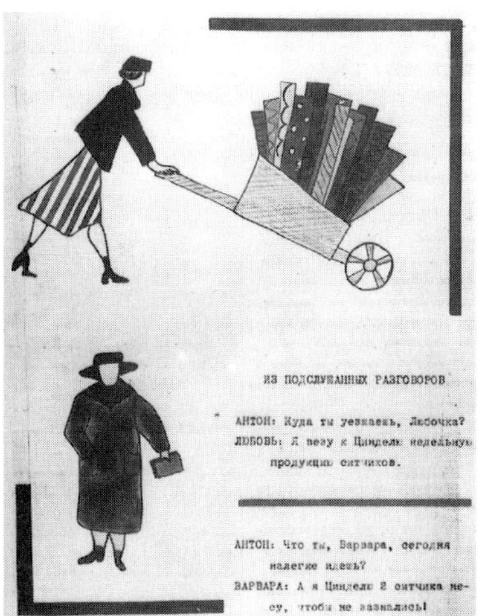

FIGURE 3.10
Aleksandr Rodchenko, caricature of Popova and Stepanova in *Nash gaz*, 1924.

to the factory pushing a wheelbarrow filled with designs ("I'm taking my weekly production of designs to Tsindel'!" she says), while Stepanova herself is hand carrying two new designs to the same destination (figure 3.10).[23] They were prevented from fulfilling the role of the technical intelligentsia by conservative industrial management, which was too pressured by the financial problems of running a newly nationalized factory to have the luxury of experimenting with left avant-garde schemes for industrial improvement. Arvatov's dream of a technical intelligentsia transformed by the collectivizing forces originating in production was paradoxically further from being realized in socialist Moscow than, say, in capitalist Chicago.

The Socialist Thing in the NEP Marketplace

Soviet industry was caught between socialism and capitalism in 1923 because it was operating under the semicapitalist and market-based New Economic Policy (NEP). Soviet state-owned enterprises competed on the NEP market with private ones, and many of them advertised to solicit consumers. A 1923 advertisement for fabrics from the Mossukno state textile trust in Moscow conveys the inherent contradictions of Bolshevik capitalism (figure 3.11). It shows turbaned black boys unfurling bolts of cloth from above, while a female figure modeling fabrics on a stage is ogled from below. These familiar orientalizing and sexualizing strategies from bourgeois visual culture are here deployed, however, to address putatively proletarian consumers: the onlookers include a Red Army soldier with a red star on his cap on the lower left and a red-kerchiefed working woman on the right. Women wearing kerchiefs were familiar fixtures from propaganda posters, whether wearing them tied in front, to signify a peasant woman, or in back, to signify the woman worker. The text of a huge poster from 1923, for example, proclaims that "the new everyday life [*novyi byt*] is the child of October," while the graphics show a kerchiefed woman worker who emancipates herself by kicking out her domestic stove and washboard—signs of primitive Russian *byt*—and striding into factory production with the help of new collective services such as public dining rooms and nurseries, pictured on the upper right (figure 3.12). The transposition of this giant red woman from the *novyi byt* poster into a docile member of a fashion show audience in the Mossukno advertising poster is exactly the kind of contradiction that defined NEP. Tatlin refused to address the everyday life of commodified display and fashion represented by the Mossukno ad, and designed his everyday objects to respond to the primitive living conditions depicted on the lower left of the *novyi byt* poster. Popova and Stepanova designed textiles and clothing that attempted to confront the models of *byt* represented by both the advertising and the propaganda poster, because the lives of Soviet women were circumscribed by both of them.

In militaristic language paralleling the visual language of the striding, kicking woman of the propaganda poster, the Bolshevik art critic Iakov Tugendkhol'd wrote that with her textile design work Popova had made "a breach in the Bastille of our factory conservatism."[24] Most critical rhetoric cast Popova and Stepanova as pioneers; the Bolshevik rhetoric of the liberation of woman under socialism permeated public language, even if no one actually analyzed the role of women artists in the avant-garde with any seriousness.[25] But the heroic aspect of their entry into the factory was tempered by the prosaic economic fact that they had been hired to help boost sales. The Russian Republic may have been socialist, but during NEP the First State Cotton-Printing Factory had to balance its budget and turn a profit. Hiring the Constructivists proved moderately successful in this regard. Although all told they worked at the factory for barely a year, several dozen of their fabrics were printed and distributed throughout the Soviet Union and were seen widely on the streets of Moscow. Tugendkhol'd, who was by no means a constant supporter of Constructivism, also wrote, "Last spring, without even knowing it, all of Moscow was wearing fabrics which Popova had designed."[26]

Popova and Stepanova were fully aware that their work at the First State Cotton-Printing Factory had to respond to the market; in the same memo to factory management in which they demanded participation in production, they also enumerated two final demands: "4. Contact with tailors, fashion ateliers and magazines. 5. Work on promoting the products of the factory in the press, advertising and magazines. Our participation could also take the form of work on designs for window displays."[27] This marks their difference from Tatlin, whose work in clothing design ignored the practices of the NEP clothing market. Popova and Stepanova understood their Productivist work in fabric design to be inseparable from broader questions of the market—and in the case of fabric designs, these questions specifically meant fashion.

Soviet women were routinely assailed with enormous images of emancipated women on propaganda posters, at the same time that Soviet publishing houses printed advertisements like the one for Mossukno fabrics and resumed the publication of prerevolutionary women's fashion magazines. *Housewives' Magazine* (*Zhurnal dlia khoziaek*), for example, had been started in 1913 and combined practical and fashion advice for women with more weighty literary and political issues, including women's rights and the legalization of abortion; the magazine

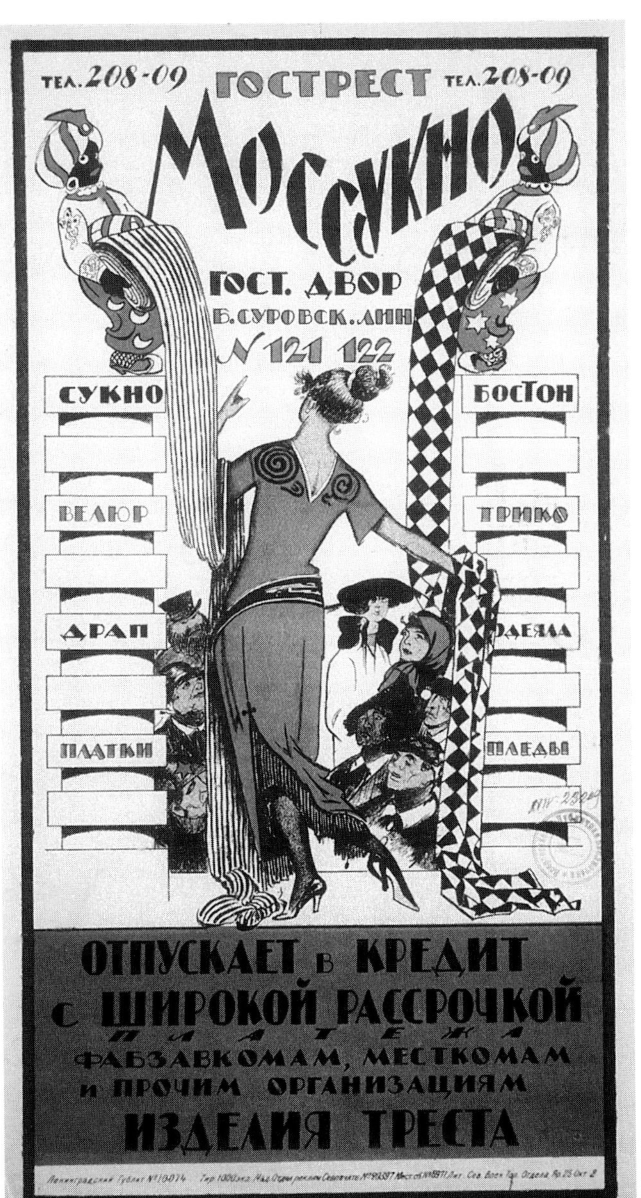

FIGURE 3.11
Advertising poster for the Mossukno state textile trust, 1923.
Courtesy Russian State Library Department of Graphics, Moscow.

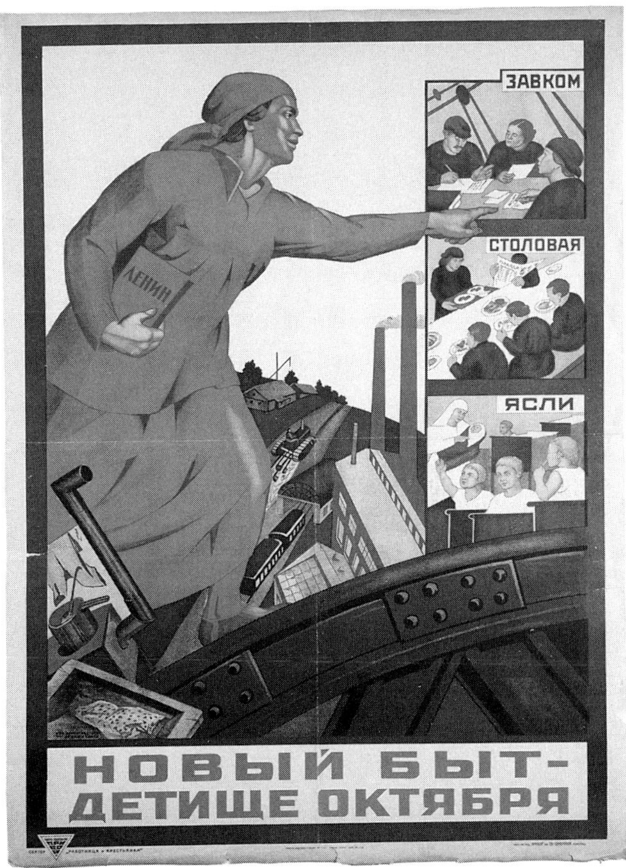

FIGURE 3.12
Poster: "The new everyday life is the child of October," 1923.
Courtesy Russian State Library Department of Graphics, Moscow.
See plate 7.

exemplified the tradition of bourgeois liberalism, clearly oriented toward the relatively small demographic group of literate, middle-class urban women. It ceased publication in 1917 owing to the upheaval of the revolution but returned in 1922 as a publication of the State Publishing House. How did the Bolshevik press reconcile egalitarian socialist ideals with Parisian fashion trends? After all, Walter Benjamin, preeminent theorist of mass culture and socialism, would ask optimistically in his *Arcades Project*: "Does fashion die (as in Russia, for example) because it can no longer keep up the tempo?"[28] His question implies that only the tempo of actual social change brought about by revolution can obliterate finally the lure of fashion's endless cycle of novelty. Yet an editorial in the first postrevolutionary issue of *Housewives' Magazine* in 1922 put the lie to his optimism, answering his question in a resounding negative: "our readers may think that fashion has died out . . . but our old friend fashion, powerfully ruling the female half of the human species, has no intention of dying!"[29] The editorial goes on to describe the length and pleating of the season's skirts, while other articles in the same issue offer serious discussion of the new Soviet laws on women's rights and the development of communal kitchens. This and all issues of the magazine carried several double-spread pages of Parisian fashion patterns, which were clearly its main selling point. The content of the magazine encompasses both socialist enlightenment and fashion, without attempting to theorize how socialism might transform fashion. This was the question that preoccupied Popova and Stepanova.

The question of how socialism might transform consumer culture specifically in the context of NEP Russia also preoccupied Arvatov. His essay "Everyday Life and the Culture of the Thing" had imagined industrial things in faraway America, but in 1925 he wrote another essay, "Art and the Quality of Industrial Production," which confronted the present conditions of the Soviet economy and was therefore more open to questions of actual consumer desire.[30] Soviet industry, he warns in this essay, is currently in a dismal state, lagging far behind the advances of Western industry. Factory design departments, when they exist, are staffed with old-fashioned, academic graphic artists who tend simply to replicate existing patterns, some ten or twenty years old. Before World War I, textile factories had relied primarily on patterns imported from Paris. With most trade agreements with the West nullified by the Bolshevik victory in the civil war, no new patterns were arriving from Paris in the early 1920s. For these reasons, Soviet mass-produced things lack the "'elegance,' 'fashion,' 'originality,' 'stylishness,' 'contemporaneity' (for example, in the English spirit, Americanized, etc.), 'chicness,' 'pleasantness,' and even 'opulence'" that consumers seek (p. 40). Arvatov admits that satisfying consumers with the qualities they desire "is undoubtedly a question of the quality of production" (p. 40). Therefore, even though it goes against his own theoretical convictions, Arvatov reluctantly endorses enlisting the help of applied artists to add the missing sense of "style" to Soviet commodities, raising their market value. Here he seems to have in mind leftist artist-Productivists like Popova and Stepanova at the First State Factory, even if they are not yet functioning fully as Constructivist artist-engineers.[31]

Arvatov suggests, in this essay, that a *tselesoobraznyi* thing is one that succeeds in its purpose of satisfying consumer desires for fashion and stylishness as well as in the more standard Constructivist purpose of transparently performing its technical function. Some of the terms on his list of current Soviet consumer desires are clearly negative; "elegant" and "chic" and "opulent" are unequivocally the adjectives of wealth. But the other terms are not so distant from the supposedly more "rationalized" consumer desires that he associates with contemporary industrial development in America and Britain. Industrial production there, he claims, is represented by "the most convenient, comfortable, dynamic, everyday-economic, machinized thing" (p. 41). Even if the Soviet desired qualities are not yet quite as fully rational as these, they are clearly legitimate enough for Arvatov to harangue his imagined readers—managers of Soviet trusts or other government planners who were, unfortunately, unlikely readers of the magazine *Soviet Art* in which the essay appeared—to hire applied artist-constructors in order to begin to satisfy them.

But this solution can only be temporary, he cautions, because using applied artists to beautify products is a "market-oriented" approach that "indulg[es] the subjectively taste-determined, individualistic demands of the consumer" (p. 41). He pulls back from fully endorsing the more open-ended understanding of the "purpose" served by *tselesoobraznost'*, calling for the eventual entry of true Productivists into industry in order to combat this "subjectively taste-determined" approach, which is causing Soviet industry to lag behind the more fully rationalized industry of the West. The artist must use her creativity not for "fantasizing," not for "decoration from without," but for "real technical construction" (p. 41). These are the same terms that he uses in "Everyday Life and the Culture of the Thing"; the thing must be fully transparent in its construction rather than covered over by fantasy. He may point, in this essay, to the special circumstances of the present NEP economy, but he holds fast to his assertion that in the West, as in the Soviet Union, the future will lead "to the mass, collectivized calculation of the needs of society and their rational satisfaction, and thus to planned productive invention" (p. 41). The socialist object falls somewhere between these two poles: acknowledging and aiming to satisfy the commodity desires of modernity, but committed to the belief that eventually, in some fully achieved socialist, industrial utopia, these desires can be fully rationalized to the benefit of all.

eventual goal

Stepanova and the Limits of Production Clothing

Stepanova's brief article "Today's Clothing Is Production Clothing," published in *Lef* in 1923, takes a typically hard Constructivist line against fashion; written by a woman artist, it serves as a powerful rebuttal to the newly reappeared NEP fashion magazines and their claims about the fashion desires of "the female half of the species." Store-window displays with their wax mannequins, Stepanova writes, will become a thing of the past because they reflect the old bourgeois *byt*, while contemporary clothing can only be understood in action: "Fashion, which psychologically reflects our everyday life [*byt*], habits and aesthetic taste, is giving way to clothing organized for working in various branches of labor."[32] This kind of utilitarian work clothing was called *prozodezhda* (production clothing), and it could be broken down into even more specialized categories, called *spetsodezhda* (special clothing). The form of this clothing should be determined exclusively by the "more precise and specific demands" posed by its function, with no decoration or ornamentation; to use Arvatov's term, the function and mode of making of this clothing will be transparent in its form. Stepanova names as examples "the clothing worn by surgeons, pilots, workers in acid factories, firemen and members of arctic expeditions."[33] With the exception of surgeons, all of these professions were exclusively male at that time. These examples buttress the strong antifeminine rhetoric of the entire article, as Stepanova dissociates herself from anything culturally related to femininity—*byt*, the decorative, the store window, the wax mannequin.

In the avant-garde context of *Lef*, Stepanova's rhetoric mimes the language of Bolshevik economic planners and clothing industry specialists. Her terms appeared in the proclamation "On the Provision with *Prozodezhda* and *Spetsodezhda* of Workers in Coal Mines" of October 1920, signed by no less of a Bolshevik official than Lenin himself.[34] Her essay has much in common with the technical publications of the textile and clothing industries of the time, which similarly promoted the eradication of handicraft production in favor of industrial mass production and the rationalization of clothing designs.[35] By allying her text rhetorically with the technical language of the garment industry, Stepanova asserts the distance of her own artistic project from fashion. Here as elsewhere in her practice, her vehement commitment to the engineering and production model of art, which was generally associated with masculine areas of experience, signals her desire to distance herself from the usual expectations of her gender—expectations that we have already seen revealed in the way that male critics discussed her paintings in 1920.[36]

Stepanova's article on production clothing was published before she began to work at the First State Cotton-Printing Factory. She had not, at that point, had any practical experience with mass-producing things to be sold in the NEP marketplace or with the possibility that her Constructivist designs would be used by consumers in their everyday lives in non-Constructivist ways. A few years later, however, Stepanova wrote an important text that takes up the question that the fashion magazines, and she herself initially, had refused: How might socialism transform fashion? The magazines had blithely assumed that the two could coexist; she herself, in 1923, had claimed that socialism would obviously destroy fashion. This 1928 essay, "The Tasks of the Artist in the Textile Industry," conveys both her continued commitment to the model of the artist-Productivist and, more surprisingly, a new understanding of fashion as an emblem of modernity and an object of socially meaningful consumer desire.[37] Stepanova's clothing designs maintain allegiance to the standard Constructivist model of transparency; in this respect, she functions in this chapter as something of a foil to Popova, whose direct forays into fashion design strain more fully against the limits of that model. But in her writings and her teaching Stepanova indicated her broader understanding of the socialist thing as an object of individual, opaque desires as well as collective, transparent ones—the kind of understanding that would come to the forefront, in Popova's work, in her actual dress designs.

Aside from a few garments that she made for her own use, Stepanova did not design clothes incorporating her mass-produced fabrics. This points to the contradictory nature of the fabric-design work for her. At the factory she was designing thin, printed cotton calicoes destined primarily for traditional women's garments such as dresses, skirts, and scarves, or for domestic objects like curtains and tablecloths, but these were exactly the kinds of traditional objects of *byt* that she had criticized in 1923 because they "psychologically reflect" our "habits and aesthetic taste." In her 1928 article, she notes that printed cotton fabrics are already becoming obsolete, and that the artist in the textile industry must concentrate on developing new kinds of fabrics, such as the knitted fabrics (*trikotazh*) that have already begun to proliferate in the West. She acknowledges, in effect, that even her own greatest Constructivist triumph, her work at the First State Cotton-

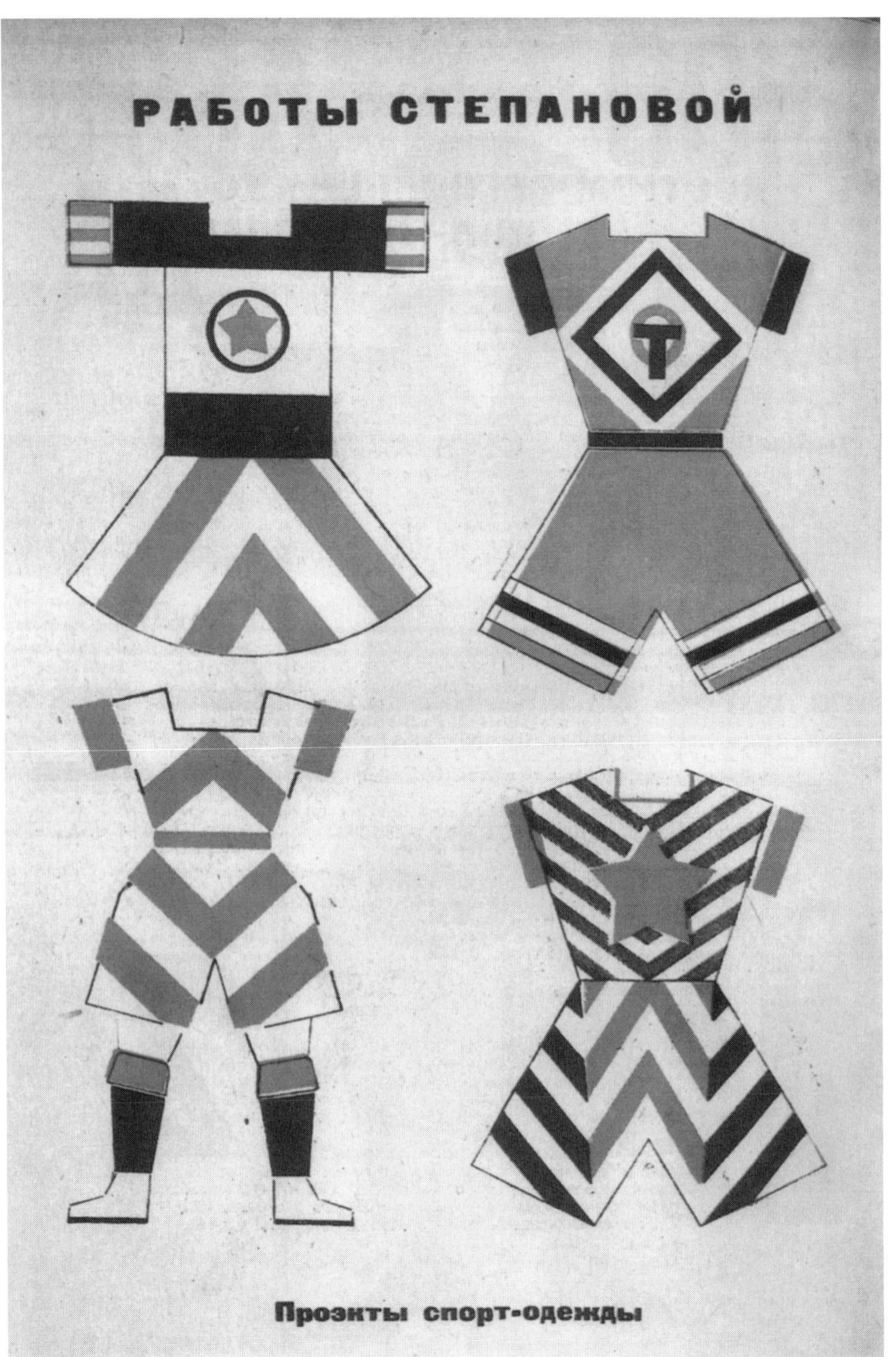

FIGURE 3.13
Varvara Stepanova, designs for sports clothes, 1923. See plate 8.

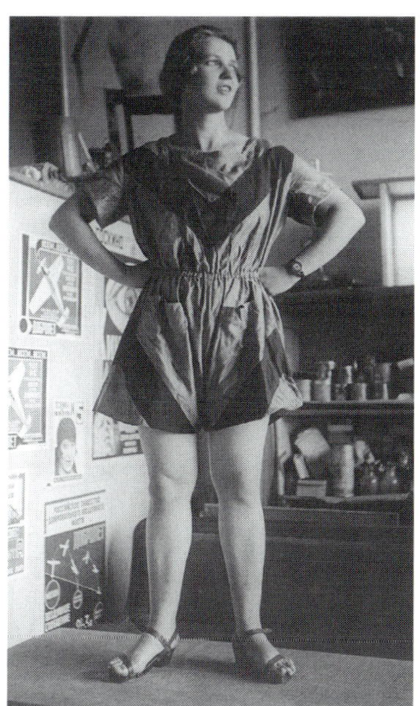

FIGURE 3.14
Aleksandr Rodchenko, photo of Evgeniia Zhemchuzhnaia in sports clothing designed by Stepanova, 1924.

Printing Factory, had been doomed from the perspective of her own larger goals of replacing traditional fashion with rationalized clothing. Her attempt to use optical designs to infuse calico cloth with the dynamism of production was therefore in retrospect merely a partial, applied-art contribution to improving the quality of Soviet fabric production rather than a total transformation of the object.

Stepanova's many clothing designs of the early 1920s did not, therefore, incorporate the draping effect of soft calico fabrics. They rather inclined toward stiff, even boxy, forms in simple geometric designs that stemmed from appliquéd fabrics rather than printed ones. They were for the most part not everyday clothes but rather clothes designed for specific utilitarian functions: so-called sports costumes that she designed through her involvement in staging agitational performances at the pedagogical faculty of the Academy of Communist Education in Moscow; *prozodezhda* for actors in theatrical productions; and a few designs for women's "professional suits." Unlike her fabric designs, which were mass-produced in the here-and-now of Moscow in 1924, her clothing designs seemed to be destined for a different, Constructivist world—not Tatlin's primitive *byt*, but a vibrant, austere, and vigorous future. Her clothes do not address specific, historically experienced bodies, structured within deeply ingrained gender hierarchies. They rather bypass contemporary *byt* completely in favor of imagined public spaces for the staging of an egalitarian, androgynous order.

Her designs for sports clothes that illustrated her 1923 article in *Lef* exemplify this new order (figure 3.13). Their form was determined by function. Their bold graphic patterning was not decorative, she claimed, but was justified by the need to differentiate teams on the playing field; she classified them as a form of *spetsodezhda*. The four outfits—one with a skirt, three with shorts—are drawn using the flat planes of circles, triangles, and rectangles from the pictorial lexicon of Suprematism. As in Suprematism, these designs reduce the visual image to the most basic geometric shapes inherent in representation. The drawings do not portray the body in action, which, according to her text, was the only way that production clothing could be seen. They rather evoke human bodies conforming to a geometric order—an appropriate visual metaphor for athletic bodies disciplined by the emerging ideology of proletarian *fizkul'tura* (physical culture). A photograph of Stepanova's friend Evgeniia Zhemchuzhnaia modeling a version of one of the shorts outfits in Stepanova's studio attests to the ruin of these androgynous, geometric lines when they enter into contact with a real body that gives off heat and has rounded limbs (figure 3.14). Yet in photographs from the performance of *An Evening of the Book*, an agitational student theater piece promoting literacy designed by

Stepanova in 1924 at the Academy of Communist Education, the multiplication of this same shorts costume on a whole row of young female bodies of uniform height and size suddenly enables it to live up to the dynamism of the drawings (figure 3.15). The costumes create a continuous geometric pattern from body to body, like a fabric design, suggesting a direct connection between Stepanova's optical designs and the futuristic, mechanistic vision of the human body as a disciplined collective machine that is so often attributed to Constructivism. The girls function literally as human signboards; large letters spelling out the word *antrakt* (intermission or *entr'acte*) are attached to their backs, one per body, with the first and last girls bearing exclamation points rather than letters (figure 3.16). Their bodies become the linguistic sign—the exclamation point—that most closely corresponds to pure agitational address.

This collective of young girls in Stepanova's sports costumes demonstrates a version of the body possible in performance, but not experienced in the everyday life of Moscow in 1924, in which females always wore skirts. Though there is no record of Stepanova's view of how gender difference would be affected by socialism, she does seem to suggest that the socialist future would be more androgynous, and more egalitarian, in a poster she made to advertise yet another agitational play, performed at the Academy in 1923 (when it was still called the Academy of Social Education): *Through Red and White Glasses* (figure 3.17). On the lower left of the poster, under the phrase "through red glasses," Stepanova has drawn three fairly schematic red figures, two males and a female, dressed in three varieties of boxy *prozodezhda*. The female figure is just as straight-edged and rectangular as her male counterparts; her gender is discernible only by the rounded line of her jaw and the slight fullness of the style of her short hair. The counterparts to these figures on the right side of the poster appear under the phrase "through white glasses." Here there are four white figures dressed in conventional upper-class clothes, and again there is one female, but she is strongly differentiated from the male figures, drawn with a caricatured feminine body: she has enormous round breasts, a tiny waist, wide hips, and full thighs.

Stepanova's specifically androgynous vision also took form in a unisex clothing design for a performance at the Academy of Communist Education, documented by an evocative photograph of male and female students of the Academy all dressed in the exact same costume (figure 3.18). The dark striped pattern of the pants, in particular, seems designed to override the conventional signs of gender difference. The illusion of a diamond-within-a-diamond design when the legs of the pants are pressed together makes the lower half of the

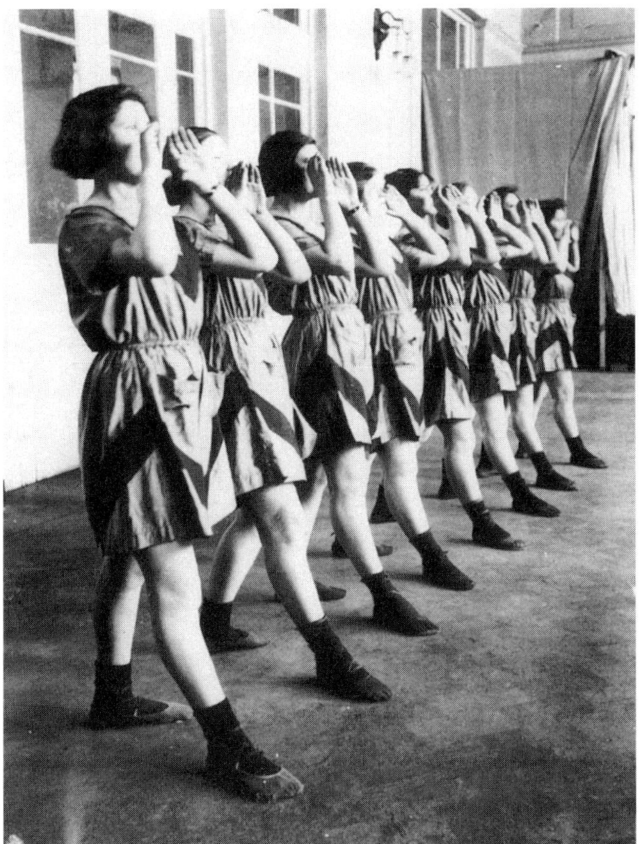

FIGURE 3.15
Students in sports clothing designed by Stepanova, in performance of *An Evening of the Book*, 1924.

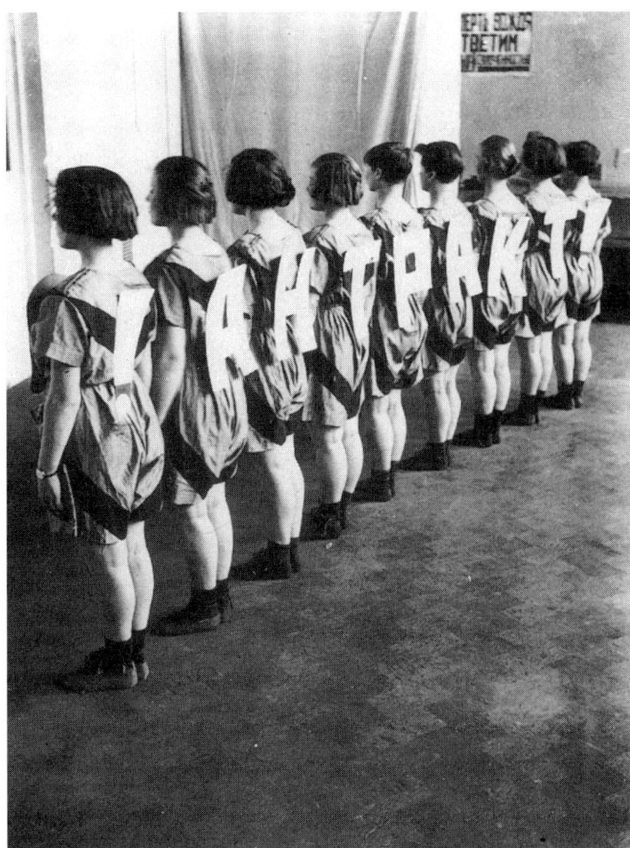

FIGURE 3.16
Students in sports clothing designed by Stepanova, spelling out *!antrakt!* (intermission), in performance of *An Evening of the Book*, 1924.

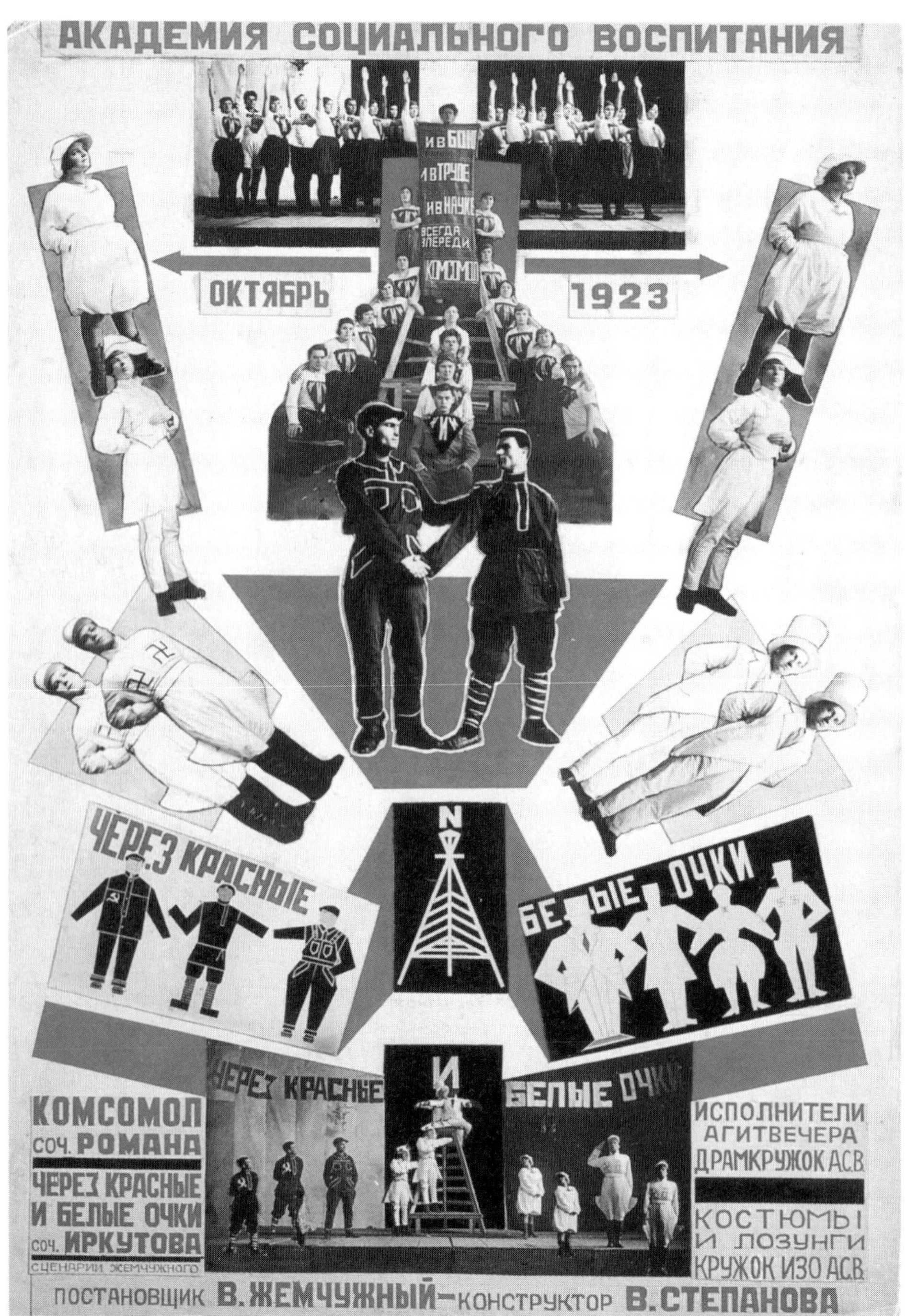

FIGURE 3.17

Varvara Stepanova, poster for the agitational play *Through Red and White Glasses*, 1923.

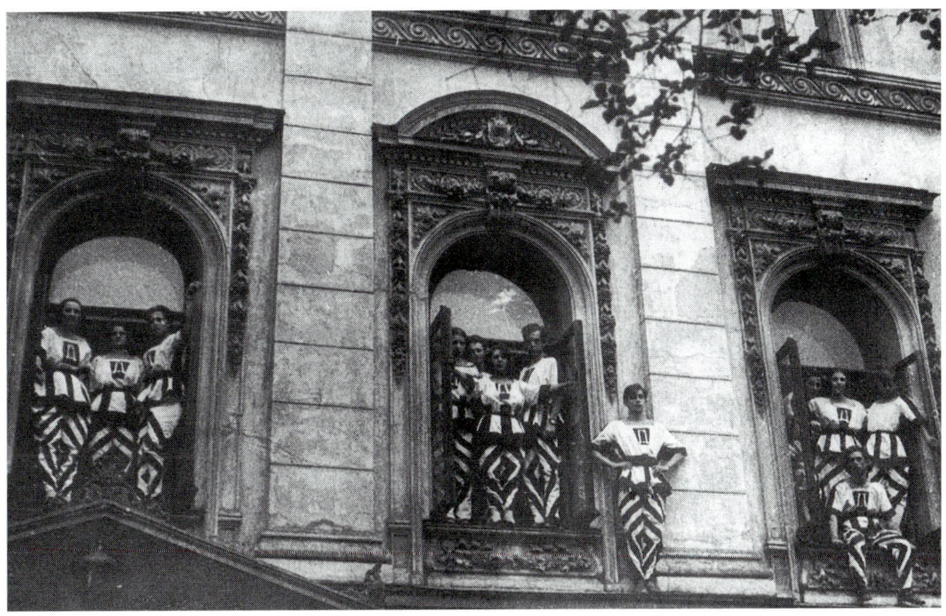

FIGURE 3.18
Students at the Academy of Communist Education dressed in costumes designed by Stepanova, 1924.

students' bodies look like some completely third, hermaphroditic appendage—phallic in its form but distinctly vaginal in its patterning, with the lines emanating out from the "central core" of the diamond shape.[38] Throwing open the windows and filling them, their androgynous costumes minimizing natural differences between bodies, the young students proclaim a hybrid new constructed order against the naturalism of the ornate ironwork vegetation of the window frames on the prerevolutionary building. It may be a coincidence that the students were photographed posing in the upper-storey windows of the school, of all places—it is an odd site for a group snapshot—but this photograph might also stage Stepanova's explicit rebuttal of the class and gender hierarchies of the fashion displays of the contemporary store window.

Critical as Stepanova may have been of the store window, her mass-produced fabrics, like the others produced by the factory, necessarily entered the commercial spaces of NEP Moscow. A photograph by Rodchenko shows bolts of her optical fabric of striped balls floating on a recessed lattice of stripes, which we saw develop from the earliest sketch stage, on display in a fabric store window in 1924 (figure 3. 19). Framed sketches of women's fashions are placed on top of the fabric, suggesting its availability for being sewn up into fashionable dresses rather than rational *prozodezhda*. Bunched together and softly draped in the typical style of

Russian commercial displays of the time, the thin calico fabric loses some of its modernist optical effect. Compared, however, to another fabric store window display in the newly renovated Passazh Arcade in Leningrad in 1924—the kind of arcade that was the subject of Benjamin's *Arcades Project*—the geometries of Stepanova's pattern look markedly different from the formal and highly ornamental lace patterns and the array of old-fashioned floral prints on offer there, destined for the overcrowded bourgeois interiors that survived during the period of NEP (figure 3.20).

A Soviet film from late 1924 provides some backhanded evidence that this contrast between Stepanova's fabric and its visual surroundings was recognized, that its offer of a visual sign of rationality, and even of modernity itself, was taken up by cultural producers beyond the confines of the *Lef* group. In the comedy *The Cigarette Girl from Mossel'prom*, a big hit for the Soviet film industry, a young and pretty cigarette girl from the state-owned Mossel'prom company temporarily becomes the mistress of a visiting evil American capitalist, but is thankfully brought back into the Bolshevik fold by the end through the intervention of the bumbling comic hero who adores her. Another, older female character who is attempting to snag the hero for herself wears a dress made from the same optical fabric pattern designed by Stepanova, but here with the light and dark colors reversed. A still from the film shows these three characters in an uncomfortable moment: the woman in the Stepanova fabric on the left, the hero in the middle, and the cigarette girl—complete with her special Mossel'prom portable cigarette case hanging from her neck—on the right (figure 3.21). Another still shows a scene of the hero kneeling before the woman in the Stepanova dress, and it gets exactly right the way that the fabric's bright optics rebel against the faded florals of the outdated wallpaper, against the impossibly primitive primus stove (the ubiquitous single propane burner) and bucket that announce the pathos of Russian *byt*, and against the actress's own full body, which is not conventionally flattered by the busy pattern (figure 3.22). The film designers recognize that Stepanova's fabric is meant to signify dynamism, rationality, and mechanization, even as these meanings are used to poke mean-spirited fun at this ungainly woman clutching her pot lid, the futuristic fabric rendering her almost clownish. By placing the fabric in a context that points up its clownishness, and by domesticating it into a fashionable flapper-style dress with a decorative white collar, the film designers most likely also got a chance to mock the Productivist pretensions of the zany Constructivists. But they nonetheless utilized the dynamic meaning that the optical design was meant to offer, even if only in lampooning it.

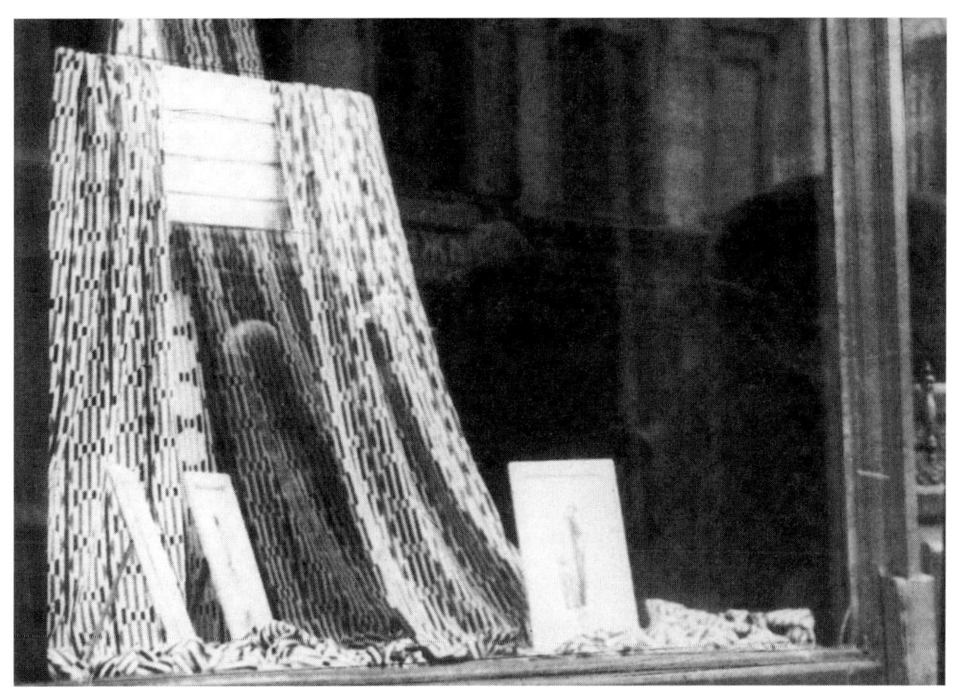

FIGURE 3.19
Aleksandr Rodchenko, photo of Stepanova's fabric in a store window, 1924.

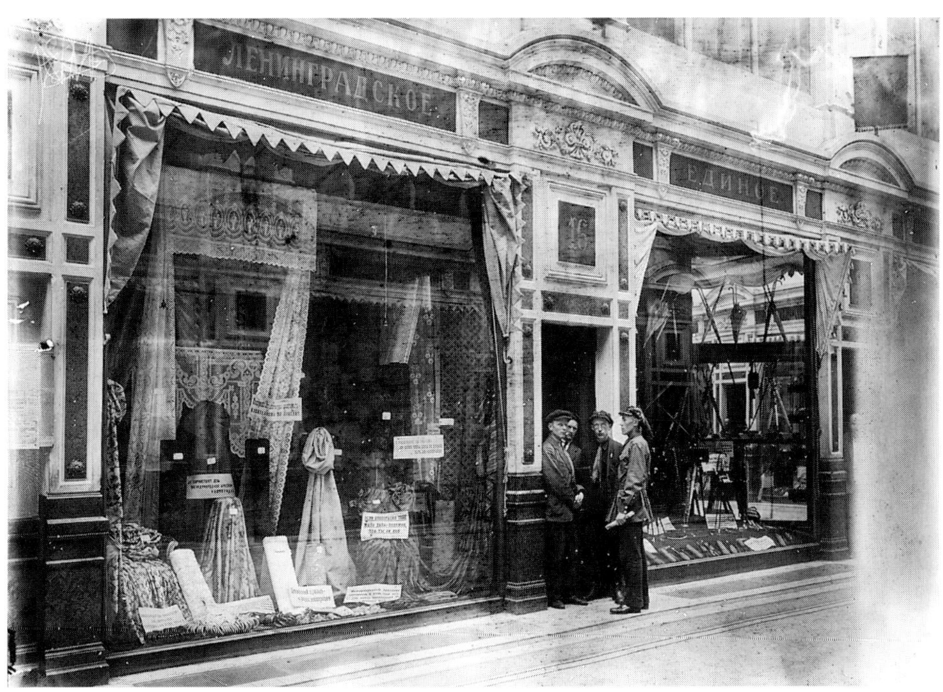

FIGURE 3.20
Fabric store window display, Passazh Arcade, Leningrad, on "International Cooperatives' Day," July 5, 1924. Courtesy Central State Archive of Film and Photographic Documents, St. Petersburg.

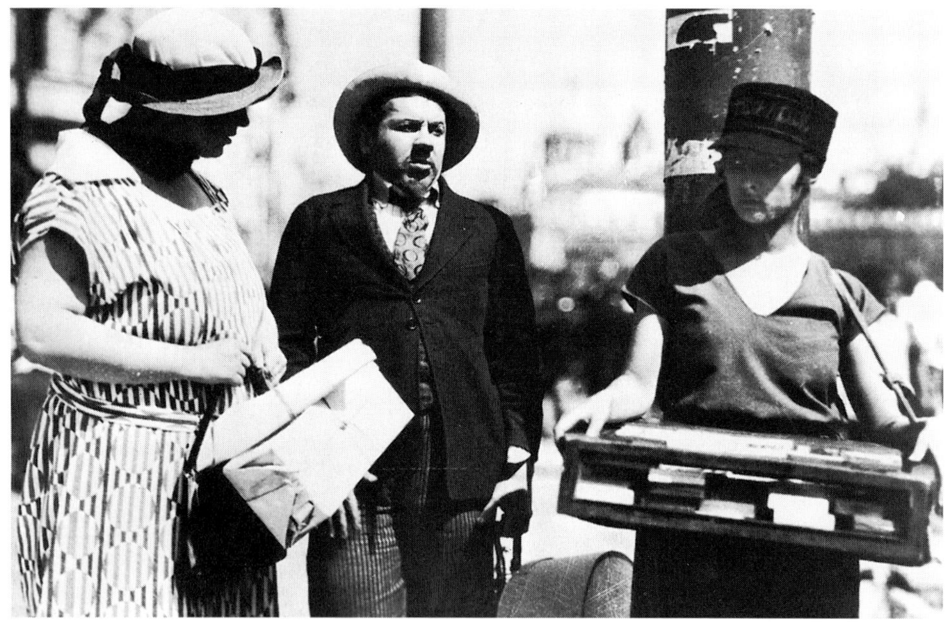

FIGURE 3.21
Film still from *The Cigarette Girl from Mossel'prom*, 1924. Iulia Solntseva as the cigarette girl is on the right. Courtesy Pacific Film Archive.

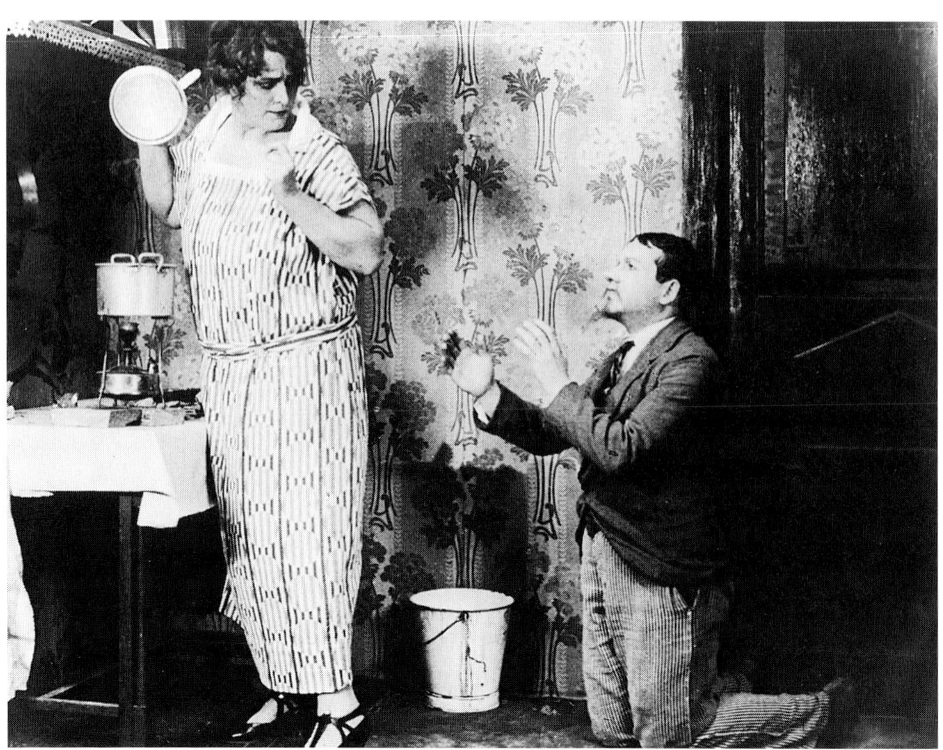

FIGURE 3.22
Film still from *The Cigarette Girl from Mossel'prom*, 1924. Courtesy British Film Institute.

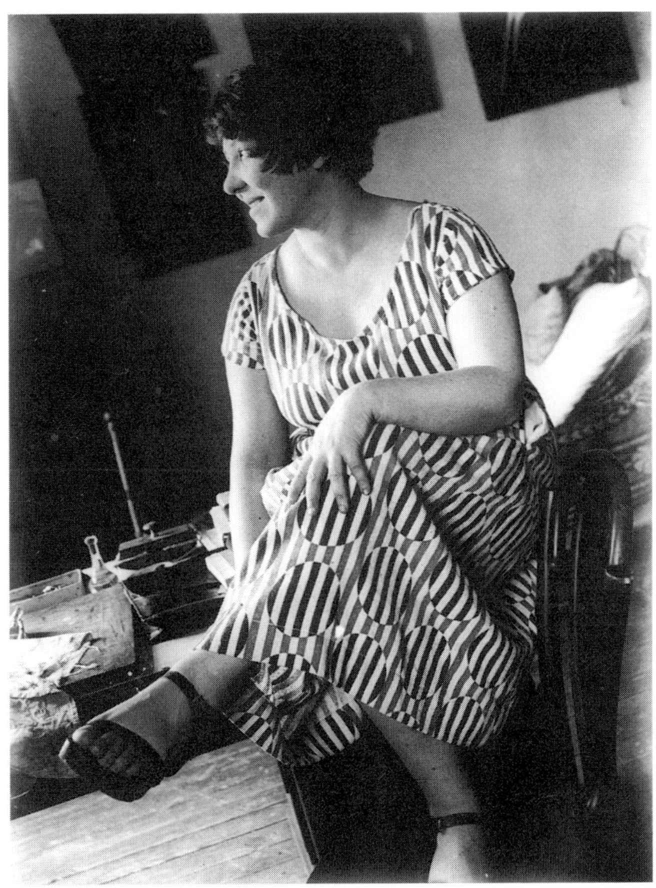

FIGURE 3.23
Aleksandr Rodchenko, photo of Stepanova wearing a dress of her own fabric, 1924.

While Stepanova's own utilitarian clothing designs signaled her desire to move toward a strictly rational form of clothing, there are other signs of her willingness to work within the market structures of fashion during NEP. Her work designing calico prints, despite her misgivings, emblematizes that willingness, and there are indications that she welcomed or even anticipated the uses to which her fabrics were put once they entered the NEP market. Her obvious pleasure in wearing a traditionally feminine dress made from her optical fabric as she poses dreamily for a photograph by Rodchenko in 1924 offers one indication (figure 3.23); so does her interest in having Rodchenko document the presence of her fabric in a store window, as we saw above. In her 1928 article, she concludes that the fundamental task of the artist–textile worker is to stop making textile drawings as an abstraction and to take an active part in forming them into clothing—"to force his way into the *byt* and life of the consumer and find out what gets done with the fabric after it leaves the factory."[39] This conclusion was based on a more elaborate plan from her teaching methods at VKhUTEMAS in 1925. She had students keep a notebook on them at all times for recording the fabrics and clothes they observed on the streets. These were her requirements:

> (a) direct observation of the current designs for fabrics produced by the Soviet textile industry, with sketches
> (b) study of the evolution of changes in so-called "fashion" and analysis of it
> (c) observation of the current situation, with the goal of devising methods for a conscious awareness of the demands imposed on us by new social conditions.[40]

She acknowledges that the "current situation" of fashion must be studied, understood, and, to an extent, designed for, even as she urges her students ultimately to move toward projects that will depart from the conventions of fashion and respond to the "new social condition" of an egalitarian socialist economy. In opposition to Boris Groys's well-known accusation that Constructivism aimed for a "total work of art," Stepanova's conscious, if guarded, openness to exploring consumer desire in everyday life offers evidence that Constructivism was rather a practice that was open to being adapted to the needs of everyday life, such as they were in the hybrid context of NEP Russia in the early 1920s.[41] This was a source of its strength as an avant-garde art-into-life practice rather than a sign of its failure.

Stepanova's guarded openness to fashion was acceptable to her, however, only as a part of the Constructivist insistence on the exalted role of the artist in improving Soviet industrial production. In her 1928 essay, she complains that the artist in the textile industry has been forced to remain a mere applied artist, a handicraft decorator, rather than the kind of independent participant in production who invents new dyes, for example, or new structures and materials for cloth. This complaint was fully justified, we know, by her own disappointing experience at the First State Cotton-Printing Factory. A reference to the automobile industry in her opening paragraph suggests just how industrial, and non-craft-oriented, her ambitions for artists in the textile industry were: "How many textile drawings of the last decade do we know," she asks, "that could be favorably compared to the exterior design of even only the latest model of the Ford automobile?" (p. 190).

This comparative lack of achievement on the part of the textile artist resulted not only from the applied-art tradition of the textile industry but also from the very character of textile production as an industrial form. The textile is a flat plane that resembles the surface of a drawing or a painting, trapping the textile artist within traditional artistic practices rather than encouraging her to develop the principle of *tselesoobraznost'* (p. 191)—to invent new ways of projecting the textiles into three-dimensional forms, as artists can in other industries. The Soviet artist–textile worker must take an active part in this purposive forming of textiles into clothing, which will result in a new form of socialist fashion: "Fashion in a planned socialist economy will take a completely different form and will depend, not on competition in the market, but on the improvement and rationalization of the textile and garment industry" (pp. 191–192). Clothing under socialism would be responsive to history, not the market. Clothes would still fall out of use, not because they start to look funny when the market generates novel fashions, but rather because the conditions of *byt* will have changed, necessitating new forms of clothing (p. 192). Yet the socialist rationalization of fashion would not mean the end of fashion (p. 191):

> It would be a mistake to think that fashion can be eliminated, or that it is only an unnecessary appendage of a speculative character. Fashion accessibly offers a set of the predominant lines and forms of a given slice of time—the outer signs of an epoch. It never repeats the forms it has already found, but steadily and consistently takes the path of rationalization, just as, step by step, our *byt* is becoming increasingly rationalized.

She has not completely changed her hard-line view of 1923; the market structures that organize fashion must eventually cede to a more rational organization of clothing. But she acknowledges fashion as a valuable expression of the experience of modernity, and, in an even more surprising departure from the rigorously antifeminine as well as antifashion rhetoric of her 1923 essay in *Lef*, she goes on to suggest that fashion is valuable because it both expresses and produces liberation from gender hierarchies.

Stepanova compares the development of men's and women's clothing over the past decade in the West as well as in Russia. The influence of the uniform from World War I had temporarily rationalized men's clothing, she claims, but this tendency did not last, and it reverted to more traditional forms. In contrast, women's clothing had changed dramatically; she does not have to remind her readers that in the same ten years, short skirts and loose, long-waisted dresses replaced the long skirts, fitted waists, and even corsets that persisted through the 1910s. These empirical observations then lead her to make a statement that is extraordinary for a woman artist who never otherwise publicly expressed any views on gender: "The appearance of woman over the last decade exhibits an exceptional picture of her emancipation. In these ten years women's dress has been rationalized to such an extent that it has come to represent in and of itself almost the greatest achievement of contemporary urban *byt*" (p. 191). The unexpected passion with which she announces the importance of the changes in women's fashion that she has experienced in her own adult life (from age twenty-four to thirty-four) demonstrates her understanding of the significance of clothing for the individual female wearer as well as for the collective.

Popova's "Flapper Dress"

If Stepanova acknowledged the importance of fashion in her writings, if not directly in her practice, Popova's interest in fashion was more straightforward. She designed many fashionable dresses and even two window displays for a fashion store in Moscow. Unlike Stepanova, whose interest in designing stiff, androgynous clothing, primarily in the vein of sports and production clothing, precluded making designs that utilized the softer, more traditional cotton calico fabric that she designed at the First State Cotton-Printing Factory, Popova took up the role of the artist-Productivist that Stepanova would recommend in her 1928 article. She took her two-dimensional fabric-design work to the next level of *tselesoobraznost'* by shaping it into three-dimensional objects to be used in everyday life. She attempted to intervene directly in the Soviet fashion industry in order to improve it, even if, unlike her fabrics, her dress designs were not mass-produced.

Popova's clothing designs based on her own fabrics aimed for the "chicness" that Soviet consumers wanted and which Soviet products lacked, according to the list of desirable consumer qualities that Arvatov had enumerated in his essay on "Art and the Quality of Industrial Production." In Arvatov's terms, Popova would fall squarely into the category of the temporary fix offered by the left applied artist: improving the quality of backward Soviet production, first, by making dynamic designs for the already outmoded cotton calico fabrics and, second, by making these mass-produced Soviet fabrics appeal to consumers by projecting them into designs for "elegant" coats and "stylish" flapper dresses. (The term "flapper dress" is not Popova's; I use it to evoke the familiar vision of the loose-fitting, drop-waisted style of dresses from the 1920s rather than the figure of the flapper herself.)[42] The "current" and ostensibly temporary interest in consumer desires that Arvatov allows for in his essay is not, however, only a temporal condition of Popova's objects but a structural one. Popova's work shows Constructivism to be a practice that is as much about meeting the needs of consumption as about a fantasy of production.

Popova did not write about her fashion designs, so we can analyze her theory of the Constructivist thing only from the things themselves. Unlike Tatlin's clothing designs, oriented toward hygiene and warmth, or Stepanova's, oriented toward a rationalized future, Popova's clothes set up a deliberate confrontation between the rational product of socialist industry and the commodity fetish. They point to the fundamental problem in Marxist thought raised in the opening pages of this study: What happens to the individual fantasies and desires organized under capitalism by the commodity fetish and the market after the revolution? How will the desire for the mass-produced objects of industry be organized under socialism? How will consumers suddenly forget all their fetishistic desires, inculcated by the capitalist market, and relate to objects in a purely rational way (Arvatov's "rational satisfaction")? The very idea of a Constructivist flapper dress addresses this question by proposing an object that would attempt to harness the power of the commodity fetish—its ability to solicit individual desires—for socialism. The final portion of this chapter will argue that Popova's flapper dresses are not merely routine commercial designs that are marginal to her "real" practice as a Constructivist but are important contributions to an expanded understanding of the Constructivist theory of the socialist object.

The Soviet garment industry was one of the most backward of Russian industries. In 1917, only 3 percent of all clothing was produced industrially, with the rest made in small artisanal workshops or at home.[43] The many foreign dress patterns published in magazines like *Housewives' Magazine* were directed at women sewing at home or ordering dresses from workshops; the idea of fashionable clothing available to everyone at mass-market prices was still largely utopian. Left artists like Popova were not alone in confronting the problem. The state-owned Moscow Garment-Producing Trust, for example, established an Atelier of Fashions to improve Soviet clothing production. In 1923 it briefly published a journal, *Atelier,* which illustrated sketches of Western European as well as Russian fashions (figure 3.24). The magazine was discontinued after one issue for its elitist bias; the recommended textiles for the kinds of dresses it published—crepe de chine,

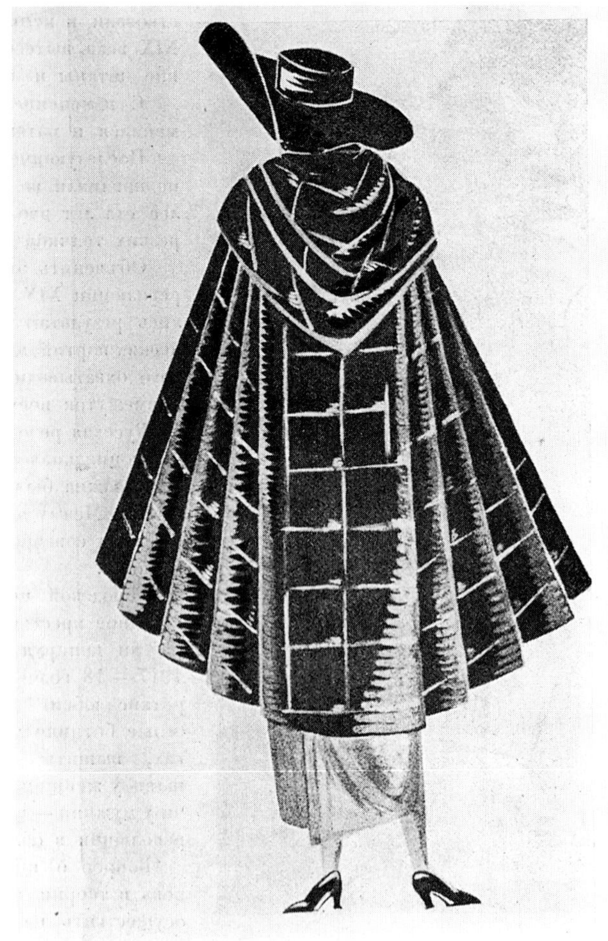

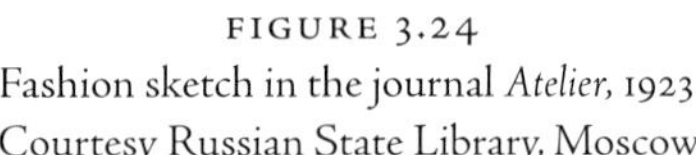

FIGURE 3.24
Fashion sketch in the journal *Atelier*, 1923.
Courtesy Russian State Library, Moscow.

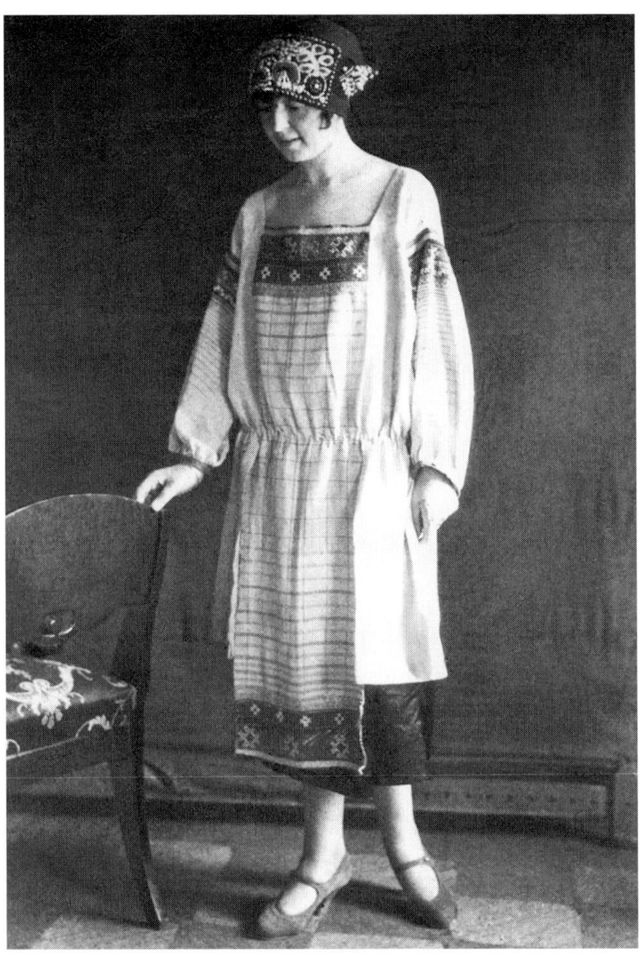

FIGURE 3.25
Nadezhda Lamanova, dress incorporating a Russian embroidered towel, 1923.

cheviot, and cashmere—were available in Russia only to the well-connected few, and the complicated fluting and accordion-pleating of the designs were beyond the skills of women at home or the capabilities of Soviet mass production.

This kind of elitist fashion was also contested, surprisingly enough, by the most celebrated professional fashion designer in prerevolutionary Russia, Nadezhda Lamanova, who turned her talents after the revolution toward inventing a feasible fashion. In an attempt to circumvent the serious shortages of materials that often arose in the chaotic NEP economy, as well as the high prices charged by private traders, some of Lamanova's dress designs incorporate curtains or bed linens that would already exist in the household, or traditional Russian folk handicraft cloths that, owing to state subsidizing of the lucrative handicraft industry, were still cheap and widely available on the Soviet market in 1923. One of her dresses is styled from an ornamental embroidered dishtowel that forms a kind of smock over a simple dress of coarse homespun linen (figure 3.25). Lamanova's response to the backwardness of the clothing industry was to meet it head on, by designing for thrifty handicraft production at home. But practical as it was, her solution did not address the central problem: the need to develop the mass production of clothing. It was not *tselesoobraznyi* in Constructivist terms, or in the terms of Tatlin's "material culture": the material form was not the most appropriate one for the larger purpose of the thing. The goal of Constructivism was to enter mechanized mass production because it represented the most advanced form of human creation; Constructivism therefore always distanced itself strenuously from the craft traditions of applied art, which it considered to be backward.[44]

In contrast to *Atelier*, Popova the artist-engineer designed *tselesoobraznyi* Constructivist dresses, the forms of which fully and appropriately responded to the limits imposed by the Soviet conditions of mass production. For example, she designed a dress out of the optical fabric that had appeared on the cover of *Lef*, but here in blue on black, rather than orange on black (figure 3.26). Its main visual interest stems not from the expensive fabrics and complex cuts of the fancy *Atelier* designs but from the bold geometric graphics of Popova's own fabric design based on her formal experience as a modernist painter. The dress has an elongated silhouette and a decorative collar, much like the dress made from Stepanova's fabric in the movie *The Cigarette Girl from Mossel'prom*, but Popova has re-created the stylish effects of Western fashion through highly simplified means. The dress is plainly and fully cut and is given its shape by being tied with a large simple sash rather than by tailoring; it is ornamented by an oversized collar that is attached to the top of the dress in a rudimentary way; and it is made from available, affordable, mass-produced printed cotton from the First State Cotton-Printing Factory. It is ready for mass production.

Popova's flapper dress could also be described in less flattering terms as *clumsily* simple. The collar resembles a large bunched napkin, and the voluminous cheap printed cotton fabric does not drape as gracefully as the flapper style demands. Compare it, for example, with a very similar dress toward the right of a spread of foreign fashions illustrated in *Housewives' Magazine* in 1925, which has a more carefully measured and sewn collar, a more tailored cut, and a more discreet geometric print (figure 3.27). The clumsiness of Popova's dress is even more apparent in an extraordinary reconstruction of the design made in 1985 by Elena Khudiakova, an architecture student in Moscow who faithfully re-created a number of Popova and Stepanova designs (figure 3.28).

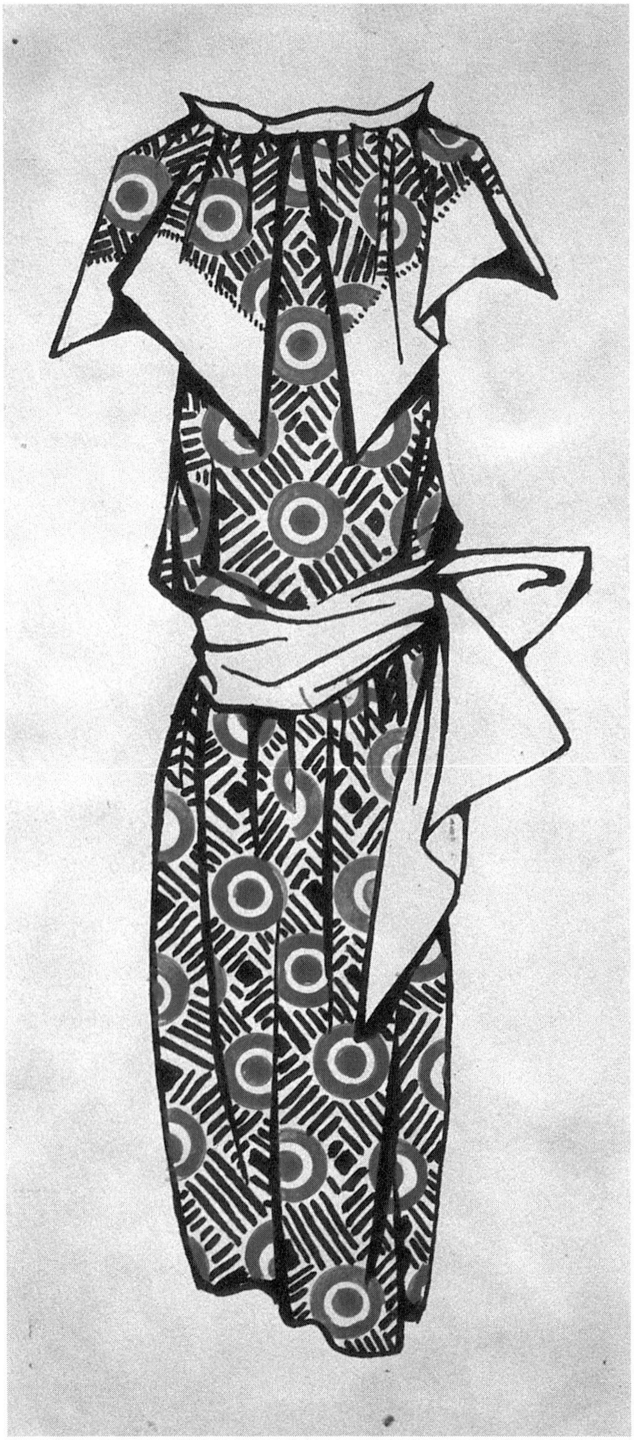

FIGURE 3.26
Liubov' Popova, design for a dress, 1923–1924.
Courtesy Dmitrii Sarabianov. See plate 9.

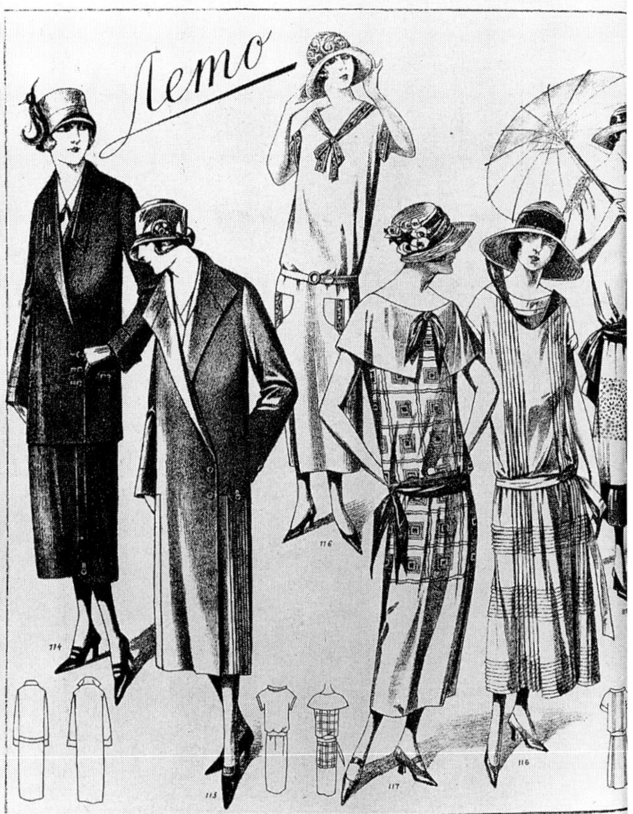

FIGURE 3.27
Foreign fashion patterns illustrated in *Housewives' Magazine*, 1925.
Courtesy Russian State Library, Moscow.

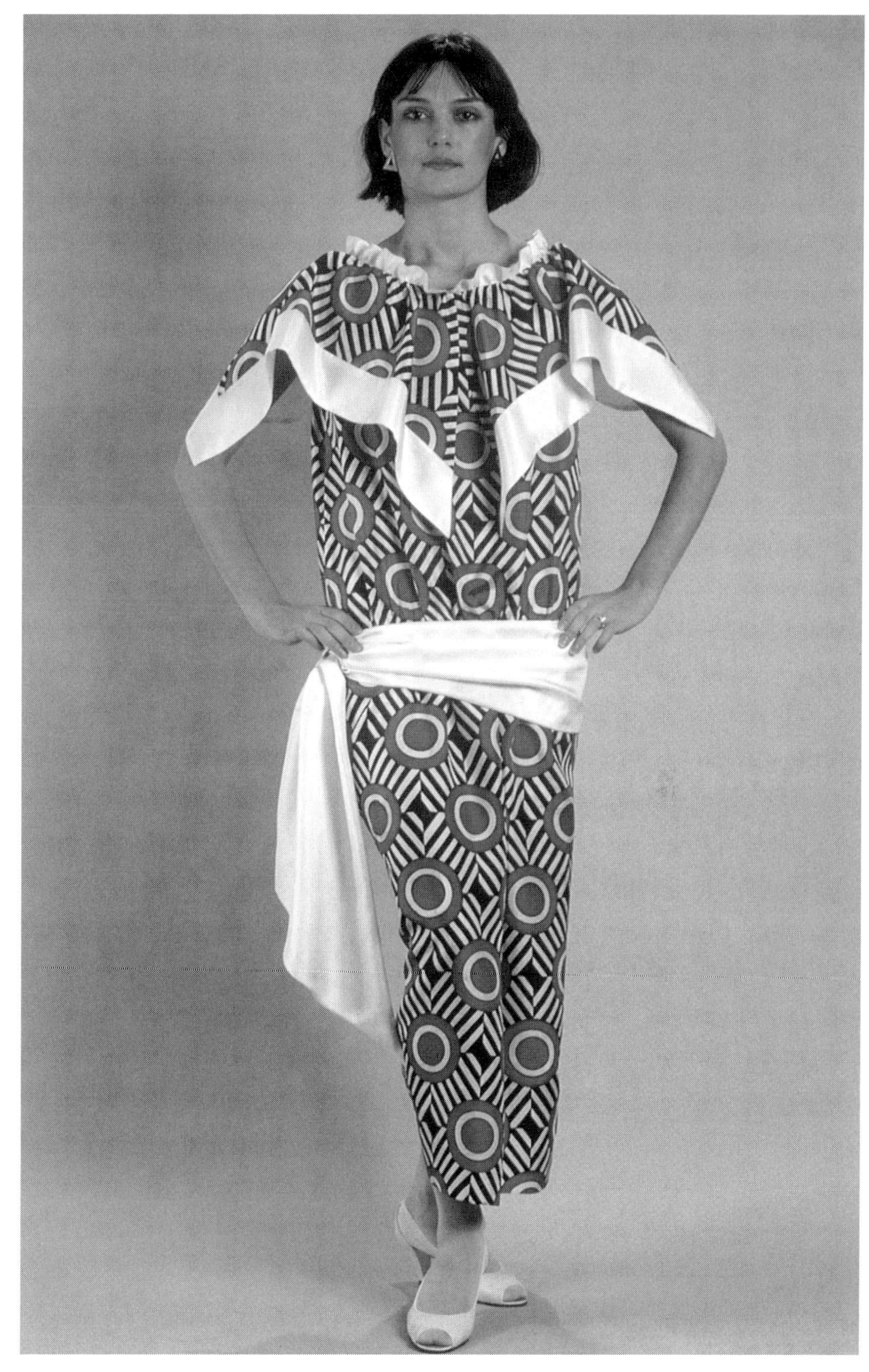

FIGURE 3.28
Elena Khudiakova, reconstruction of Popova dress design, 1985. Modeled by Khudiakova.

The argument proposed here is not, however, that Popova's design is a failure, a sign that she had ventured, in her Constructivist fervor, into an area of practice for which she was not trained—a criticism leveled frequently at the Constructivists.[45] Rather, this dress is an object that shows us how it is made; it hides nothing, but rather renders its mode of production transparent. It wants to wear its Constructivist heart on its fashionable sleeve, as it were; it wants to incorporate the consumer fantasy of fashion into the Constructivist rhetoric of transparency. The purpose of this flapper dress is not only to clothe a female body efficiently but to elicit the belief that, in wearing this dress instead of a Western or NEP-produced one, the woman who wears it is more rational and more emancipated (to use Stepanova's term) than nonsocialist wearers of flapper dresses. This belief is elicited through—and will eventually take the place of—the fantasies of femininity that normally function to give such a dress its exchange-value on the market. It becomes an "instrument" of social change, as in Arvatov's description of the socialist object as "an instrument and as a co-worker" (EL, p. 124). This understanding of Popova's dress design adds a layer of meaning to Arvatov's description of the ideal transparency of the industrial thing: "the mechanism of a thing, the connection between the elements of a thing and its purpose, were now transparent, compelling people practically, and thus also psychologically, to reckon with them" (EL, p. 126). Popova's flapper dress project acknowledges addressing consumer fantasy as a necessary purpose of the socialist object, even if the goal is to direct the fantasy of the consumer (to "compel her psychologically") away from purposeless decoration and ornament and toward more *tselesoobraznyi* and transparent objects that embody the creativity of industrial production.

Despite its obviously feminine and fashionable aspects, in its transparency this flapper dress bears a surprising resemblance to Popova's most famous clothing designs, which are usually considered to be more properly Constructivist than her dresses: her *prozodezhda* costumes designed in 1921 and used for Meyerhold's production of *The Magnanimous Cuckold* in 1922 (figure 3.29). The flattened, highly simplified, and perfectly symmetrical drawing of an outfit of shirt, skirt, and apron for a female character called Actor no. 5, for example, is largely composed of the floating quadrilaterals that had made up Popova's Suprematist paintings, rendering the construction of the clothing as transparent as the truth-to-materials ethos rendered her paintings understandable as modernist works that were about the process of painting. The flat black rectangles of the apron have been replaced, in the flapper dress, by the softer forms of the enormous sash and handkerchief

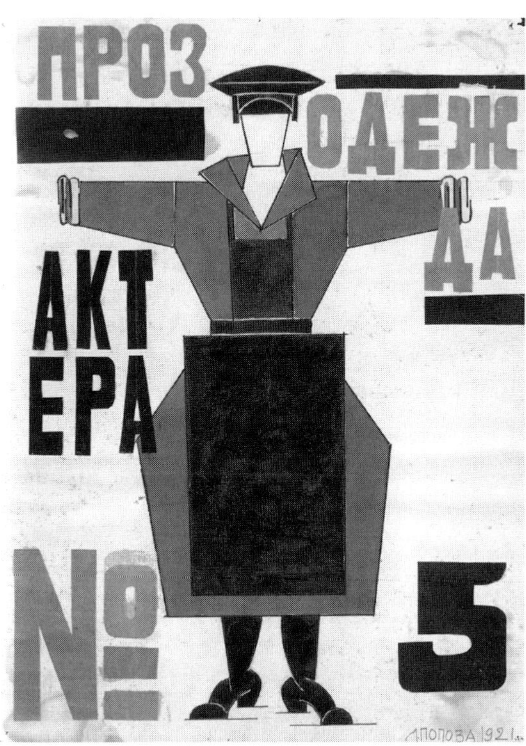

FIGURE 3.29
Liubov' Popova, design for production clothing for actor no. 5, 1921. Gouache, india ink, cut-and-pasted paper. Courtesy Dmitrii Sarabianov.

collar, but the design is still a transparent one in which materials and parts speak for themselves and nothing is hidden.

For Marx, the industrially produced object becomes a commodity fetish when the real value of the object—its labor value—is replaced by its exchange-value on the market. Laura Mulvey clarifies this in semiotic terms when she writes that Marx's fetish derives from a failure of inscription; the sign of (labor) value should leave an indexical trace on the object, but the commodity's success depends on the erasure of the marks of production. The object must enter the market with a seductive sheen.[46] If the desirability of the capitalist commodity on the market is based on the invisibility of the industrial labor process, then by refusing to pull off the slickly accomplished sheen of fashion, Popova's dress "breaks the spell of the commodity," to use a Benjaminian phrase. Through its very material forms, the dress reveals its own recent birth as a hybrid socialist object in the conditions of the semisocialist, semimarket economy of the New Economic Policy.

Popova's dress challenges the usual function of the fashion commodity not only by succeeding in preserving the traces of labor but also by refusing to produce the seamless sheen of femininity—the glossy surface that, in the psychoanalytic scenario, covers over and disavows the fantasy of the female body's lack.[47] Not just labor value, but the labored production of femininity, is made visible in the bunched-napkin collar of her dress. Unlike the similar collar on the dress in the fashion drawing in *Housewives' Magazine*, which drapes delicately over the model's shoulders calling attention to her throat and breastplate, Popova's massive collar broadens the model's shoulders and obliterates her chest. It becomes a sign for the failed attempt to produce an appropriately feminine surface armor. In this willful androgyny, the dress unexpectedly resembles the *prozodezhda* costumes for the *Magnanimous Cuckold* because we know that Popova considered her designs for these costumes to be androgynous. The men's and women's costumes were identical, except that women were given skirts instead of pants, and a text by Popova reveals that for her this distinction was so natural that she did not even notice it: "there was a fundamental disinclination to making any distinction between the men's and women's costumes; it just came down to changing the pants to a skirt."[48] Combined with Popova's embrace of mechanical drawing, mathematics, and industrialism, this interest in androgyny suggests a conscious will on her part to resist the conventional signs of sexual difference in her Constructivist things. Her flapper dress is best understood as a design that continues this utopian resistance to conventional gender hierarchies rather than temporarily deviating from it into conventional, commercialized femininity.

On the level of the unconscious, it is possible to read the optical pattern of the fabric itself as a refusal to make the female body cover over the fantasy of its lack. In its visual form, the fabric pattern resists the veil of femininity as Freudian fetish, as well as the commodity fetish. Sewn up into this bizarre dress, the op-art design of receding black holes and protruding blue targets, which seems so abstract and anonymous when viewed as a flat image, begins to resemble an apotropaic proliferation of vaginal "central core" forms across the model's body. One line of targets lines up along the central axis of the body, and in Popova's sketch (see figure 3.26) the circle over the area of the crotch is broken up by the fold of fabric into two half circles, forming a vulvar shape. It is as if the dress deliberately fails to perform its role as the feminine fetish that allays male fears of castration. If we recall Stepanova's harlequin-like sports costumes for the students at the Academy of Communist Education, with the suggestively vaginal form created by the pattern on the pants, we find ourselves with examples in the work of both artists of the repressed sign of femininity bubbling up in the context of purportedly androgynous, Constructivist clothing designs. In the case of Stepanova's design, this eruption, along with the suggestively phallic shape of the pants when the legs are pressed together, might be read as a sign of the sexuality repressed from her clothing designs more generally. But in the case of Popova, the errant sign of the repressed female body that surfaces here stands for the contradictions entailed in trying to combine a feminine fashion form with Constructivist transparency. The pressure of the attempt to hold both aspects in solution is made visible in the clumsy forms of the dress itself, which would most likely have been too antifetishistic to function as a commercially successful feminine commodity had it reached the NEP market in 1924. The dress addresses and resists that market, pushing at the limits of Constructivist transparency or truth-to-materials, but also, like Stepanova's designs, upholding them.

What happens when the Constructivist flapper dress pushes so hard at the limits of transparency that it almost achieves the sheen of the commodity? Popova's most overtly commercial fashion image, a window display design of 1924, offers an example of this kind of flapper dress (figure 3.30). It presents summer clothing in the window of a Moscow fashion studio in 1924; as in the fashion sketch from *Housewives' Magazine*, the printed cyrillic word is *leto*, or summer. The earnest transparency of the previous dress, and the demands of the strapped Soviet economy, seem long forgotten, replaced, by a stroke of montage, with a sinuous model, an elegant, flowing frock, and an ostentatious motorcar that appears to be speeding toward us. The patterned fabric of the dress is not one of Popova's more complex optical designs, but a slightly more conventional horizontal stripe pattern contrasted with a decorative piping of vertical stripes. We seem to be far from the young students dressed in Stepanova's androgynous sports costumes filling the windows of the Academy of Communist Education, far from Stepanova's cautious relation to fashion as something to be studied and negotiated, but ultimately transcended. We seem to be, in fact, squarely inside the "commodity phantasmagoria." How might this image be redeemed for socialism? Can there be such a thing as a Constructivist flapper dress?

For Benjamin, fashion was one of the dominant wish-images of modernity, occupying the entire Konvolut B of his *Arcades Project*.[49] This project attempted to imagine not just a Marxist revolution but the transition to socialism that would follow it, to imagine a form of socialist culture that would reactivate the original promise of the creativity of industrialism while delivering it from the commodity phantasmagoria of capitalism that prevented its realization.[50] The Constructivists

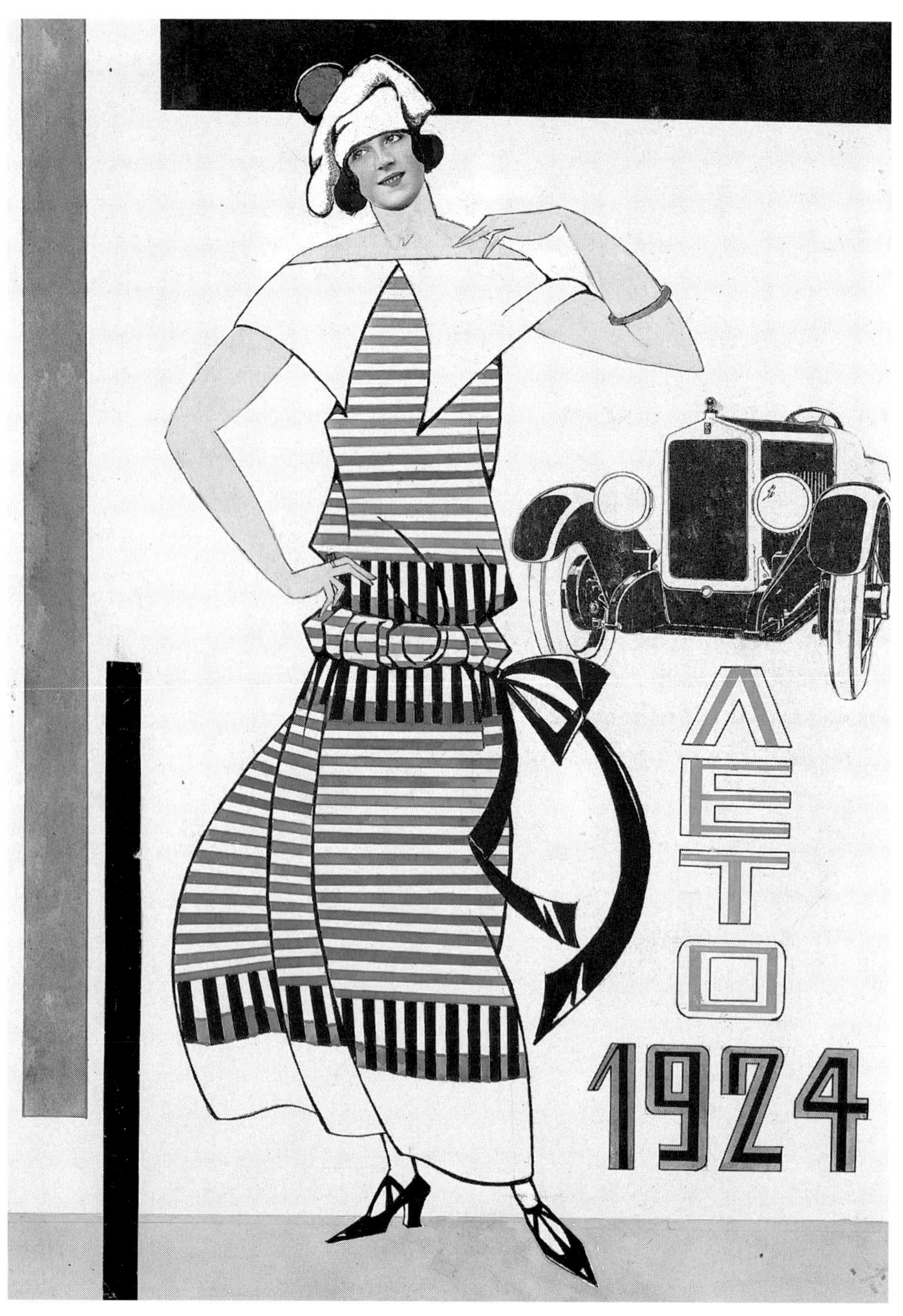

FIGURE 3.30
Liubov' Popova, design for a window display, 1924. India ink, gouache, cut-and-pasted printed papers, varnish on paper. Photo courtesy State Tret'iakov Gallery, Moscow. See plate 10.

and Benjamin share not only the core Marxist belief that a socialist future—once freed from the commodity phantasmagoria—would embrace the creative material abundance made possible by industrial modernity, but also the more specific, and stranger, belief that the success of this socialist culture would depend on the very material forms of modern things. Benjamin theorized the dialectical moment that would break the spell of the commodity; this break with the past will come when the presence of mythic wish-images of the ur-past—the myth of "a humane society of material abundance"—are made visible to the dreaming collective in the newest technological forms.[51]

Benjamin critiques the endless novelty of fashion as an instrument of capital that makes the subject—particularly the female subject—forgetful of history and so prevents historical change.[52] This forgetful subject, lulled by the phantasmagoria of capitalism, is the very subject of "the dreaming collective." Fashion reifies the human capacity for change into the inorganic commodity, the "realm of dead things," replacing the natural engendering of human life (the natural condition of birth) with novelty's inescapable cycle of eternal recurrence.[53] But in other entries in Konvolut B, Benjamin calls attention to the utopian promise of fashion. The mass production of clothing beginning in the nineteenth century led to a democratization of style; the new industrial abundance of fashion challenged the "natural" social hierarchies of class based on the accidents of birth, making visible the mythic wish-image of, precisely, "a humane society of material abundance."[54] This is why Benjamin's question about fashion in Soviet Russia, which we have already considered, is phrased so uncertainly: "*Does* fashion die (as in Russia, for example)?" Perhaps it should not die, after all, because it is the locus of the wish-image that must be redeemed in the new material forms of modernity in order to engender a utopian future. The conditions of actual social change brought about in Russia by the defeat of capital and the "birth" of the revolution might stop fashion's eternal cycle of repetition and reawaken its utopian promise as a force of social change.

The Constructivist object is born from the rhetoric of transparency, but it points, not just to its mode of making, but also to its historical situatedness, to its place within the wish-images of modernity. Popova's photomontage window display design could, for example, be analyzed within the standard rhetoric of transparency as a typically leftist avant-garde image that aims for a disruption or laying bare of the device of consumer fantasy. The argument that the pictorial technique of montage disrupts the sheen of the bourgeois spectacle, calling attention to the construction of ideology within it, is a familiar one from modernist art history. The obvious fragmentation of the woman's body in the window display—the way it is cobbled together pictorially, its parts out of proportion—could serve to illustrate Benjamin's critique of fashion as an inorganic commodity, the falsely animated dead forms of which turn the real, living woman into a "gaily decked-out corpse."[55]

But the interpretation offered here is rather that the montage engages with the wish-image of fashion as something that must be redeemed by the form of the Constructivist dress. The dislocations of this montage work to make the body of the female figure more, rather than less, vital. Her elongated silhouette mimics those of the figures in the insipid fashion drawings of the time, such as the ones in *Housewives' Magazine*, but she goes them one better. She has the same ridiculously tiny, pointed feet below and small head above, but, in between, a massive, sensual body explodes out of the picture, with immense rosy arms, one of them lifted in an autoerotic gesture to touch the bare flesh of the exposed pink shoulders. The dress swirls around her body, clinging to reveal its contours, and Popova has brushed in a ruddy, reddish glow to liven up the black-and-white cheeks of her cut-out photographic face. Through her sheer size and pictorial force, this figure broadcasts not only the dynamic qualities of the contrasting stripes of the Constructivist dress but the powerful wish-image of the bodily freedom and confidence of an urban woman in 1924, only recently freed from the tightly fitted waists and full-length skirts that Popova herself wore as a young woman.

Popova's window display can serve as an illustration of Stepanova's exhilarated statement that contemporary fashion represents the emancipation of woman, that it "represent[s] in and of itself almost the greatest achievement of contemporary urban *byt*." Although the elegantly subdued figures in the fashion spread in *Housewives' Magazine* are technically wearing similarly comfortable clothing, Popova's giant, unfettered, collaged woman, disproportionate and bursting out of the frame, insists pictorially on her emancipation. As Benjamin wrote in "One-Way Street," the modern advertisement "all but hits us between the eyes with things as a car, growing to gigantic proportions, careens at us out of a film screen."[56] The juxtaposition of the female figure with the speeding car is almost ham-handedly insistent on the dynamism, activity, and contemporaneity of the woman and the dress. Like Stepanova, who invoked the artist-constructors at the Ford motor company as models for Constructivist textile worker-constructors, Popova in this design syntagmatically borrows the veneer of industrial achievement of the motorcar to promote the modernity of her dress. The car is after all a more standard symbol of the "greatest achievement of contemporary urban *byt*" than

Stepanova's—and Popova's—proposed symbol of women's fashion. Although it might surprise us to see an expensive status commodity like a fancy car in a Constructivist image, even more than seeing a flapper dress, the motorcar at that time in the Soviet Union symbolized modernity and progress as much as wealth; Moscow in 1924 was, we should recall, still primarily a city of horse-drawn carriages.

For the Constructivists, who unbeknownst to Benjamin went further than any of his contemporaries toward realizing his theory, the mass production of cheap, high-quality Constructivist textiles was meant to democratize fashion and disseminate the creative technological forms of modernist art throughout everyday life.[57] There is no shortage of proof to back up this claim about the Constructivist dedication to egalitarianism. The critic Ivan Aksenov, for example, reported that two days before her own death from scarlet fever, and deep in grief over the death of her child who had just succumbed to the same illness, Popova still "experienced great happiness upon ascertaining . . . that fabrics covered with her designs were selling widely in the countryside and in working-class neighborhoods."[58] According to Tugendkhol'd, Popova had said that "not one of her artistic successes ever gave her such deep satisfaction as the sight of a peasant woman or a worker buying lengths of her material."[59] In the obituary he wrote for her, he noted that her fabrics were transforming the tastes of working-class women: "This spring, the women of Moscow—not the Nepmankas, but the workers, the cooks, the service workers—began dressing themselves up. Instead of the former petty bourgeois little flowers, there appeared on the fabrics new and unexpectedly strong and clear patterns."[60]

In this window display, then, Popova deliberately inhabits the capitalist language of fashion advertising in order to take up its wish-imagery of abundance. The display's redemptive quality stems from Popova's deeply personal investment in it. Montage, which Popova otherwise rarely used, is not deployed critically but, rather, parodically to emphasize the sheer overload of images available for her investment of desire. Note the long cut-out rectangle of shiny green paper along the left border that picks up the green of the pom-pom on the hat and the numbers on the lower right; the curl of the sash that fits just so within the space framed by the car wheel and the vertical text; or the way the tiny photograph of the model's face—the only element literally cut out from commercial advertising—is dwarfed by the freakish enormity of the shoulders and arms. Popova's choice to experiment with the montage technique can help us to understand the meaning of her Constructivist flapper dress. She has borrowed the montage technique here as a visual strategy precisely for its personally parodic effect.

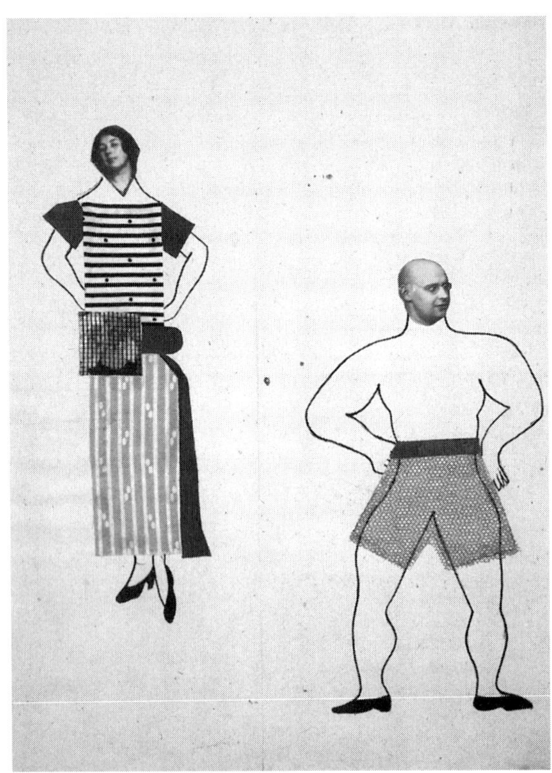

FIGURE 3.31
Aleksandr Rodchenko, caricature of Popova and Rodchenko in *Nash gaz*, 1924. Photomontage.

Popova seems to be looking specifically at the photomontage caricature of herself and Rodchenko that appeared in Stepanova and Rodchenko's "newspaper" *Nash gaz* of 1924, which parodies the kind of gender and class divisions that Constructivism tried to break down (figure 3.31). On the right side of the image, Rodchenko's bespectacled photographic head sprouts a massive drawn-in boxer's body in boxing shorts, spoofing the Constructivist as working-class strongman—a spoof sharpened by the conspicuous absence of male equipment revealed by the absurdly lacy boxer shorts and the oddly geometric, upward-pointing phallic shape formed by the space between his legs. On the left side of the image, and on the other side of a parodic gender divide, Popova's face is pasted onto a body striking a haughty pose in an elaborate flapper dress, complete with jumbo belt buckle and preposterously long sash—the female artist-Constructivist tricked out as bourgeois fashion plate. That the caricature took this particular form suggests that Popova was used to being teased by her colleagues for her style of dress and upper-class ways.[61]

Listen to Rodchenko, reminiscing about first meeting Popova in 1915 when they participated in an exhibition together: "Popova, who was one of the rich, related to us with condescension and scorn, because she considered us to be unsuitable company, a class that she wanted nothing to do with. . . . She almost never talked with me, and came by only rarely, leaving behind her in the gallery the scent of expensive perfume and the memory of beautiful clothing."[62] This is the Popova who emerges from the caricature, certainly, appropriately juxtaposed with a proletarian-boxer Rodchenko. But the crucial point is that Popova had a change of heart and committed herself to socialist goals and therefore began to disassociate herself from her previous self-presentation. As Rodchenko himself added at the conclusion of the above passage in his memoirs: "later, after the revolution, she changed a lot and became a real comrade."[63] The figure in Popova's window display design mimics almost exactly the *Nash gaz* caricature of her—right down to the position of the feet, the right arm on the hip, and the angle of the tilted head—suggesting that Popova's window display is shot through with a self-aware and self-mocking humor at her own investment in fashion, the unpreventable bubbling up of her haute-bourgeois feminine upbringing that marks her difference from colleagues like Stepanova and Rodchenko.

Popova's ironic identification with the figure in the window design expands the Constructivist rhetoric of transparency, as it is usually understood. Popova's investment of personal desire in the thing does not immediately return it, however, to the structure of the fetish, which names the "incomprehensible mystery of the power of material things," according to William Pietz.[64] Constructivism proposes, rather, that the power of material things *can* be rendered comprehensible, to the benefit of makers and users alike, without diminishing it. We recall Arvatov's claim that things that are *tselesoobraznyi* can still also have "humanity" and "emotionality," and can still be "the embodiment of human thought."[65]

It is of course always risky to exploit the recourse we have to biography, and so to imply that Popova's upper-class feminine identity can somehow explain the particular "emotionality" of her rational Constructivist things.[66] But it gave her particular knowledge and experience that allowed her to produce the window display as such an extreme, but therefore also effective, example of the Constructivist thing as a transparent socialist counterpart to the commodity fetish. The *tselesoobraznost'* of Popova's window design is that it is formed in relation to the goal of confronting consumer desire. It gives form to that desire through forms gleaned from her own desires—which, as Rodchenko's memoirs show, are perhaps imperfectly socialist but are changing in a socialist direction—

in order to encourage a similar socialist change in the desires of the mass of female consumers. In this sense, it functions as a "co-worker" or "comrade" in the struggle to invent a *novyi byt*. The window design offers the mythic wish-images represented by the motorcar and the model, but it redeems them through the dress made from Constructivist fabric, which is not mythic, but actually obtainable, because it is mass-produced by Soviet industry for the purpose of being affordable and easily available to working women. Possession is no longer exclusive.

As women Constructivists, Popova and Stepanova took different paths with their Constructivist things. Stepanova's artistic successes derived from her embrace of the antisubjective language of technology, an embrace that was conditioned by her less positive experiences as a woman painter. She upheld the standard Constructivist rhetoric of transparency, pushing at its limits only in her writings; her clothing designs stick tenaciously, even exhilaratingly, to a model of transparency and egalitarian androgyny that has no truck with commercial feminine fashions. Popova's willingness to risk experimenting in the feminized area of the fashion commodity led, by contrast, to the more surprising and densely layered meanings of the Constructivist flapper dresses. This willingness most likely resulted from her more secure artistic identity; she was less in need of the authority conferred by the technological model of artistic making. Her flapper dresses refute the parodic gender polarization of the *Nash gaz* caricatures, suggesting that androgynous sports costumes are not the only alternative to the clothing of bourgeois femininity or proletarian masculinity.

A photograph of Popova with her students at VKhUTEMAS in 1922 captures the precariousness of her fashion project (figure 3.32). She sits in the middle of the group, wearing a white pom-pom on her hat. This pom-pom, standing out defiantly from the drabness of a sea of Muscovites bundled against the indoor winter cold, reaches across a gulf to join with the green pom-pom perched on the hat of the female figure in her window display. We need both these images to make sense of the Constructivist project: the grim determination, out of the severe material privations of the postrevolutionary years, to mass-produce transparent utilitarian objects for use in everyday life—and the dream of creating a socialist form of modernity in which the phantasmatic power of objects would be redeemed for the benefit of everyone.

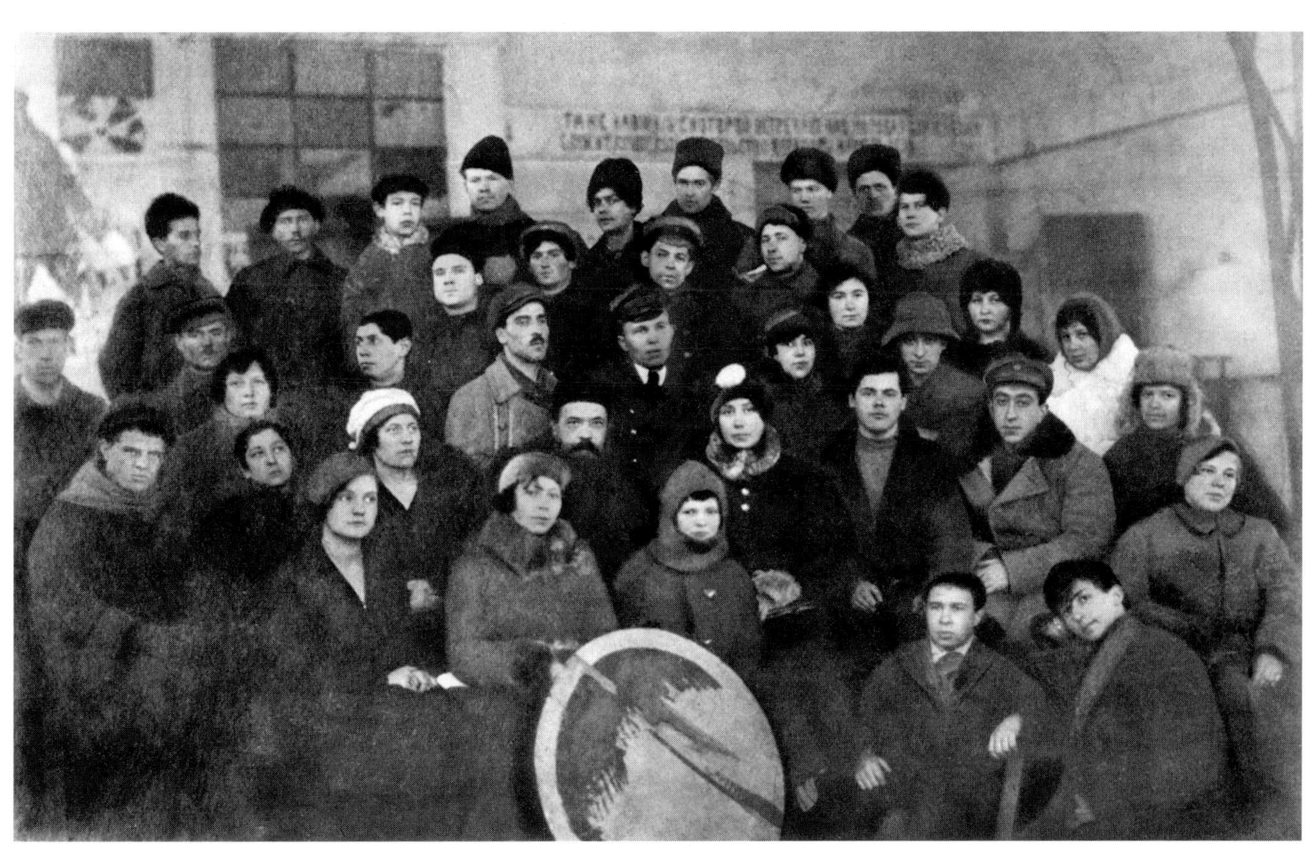

FIGURE 3.32
Group photograph of Popova with her students at VKhUTEMAS, 1922.

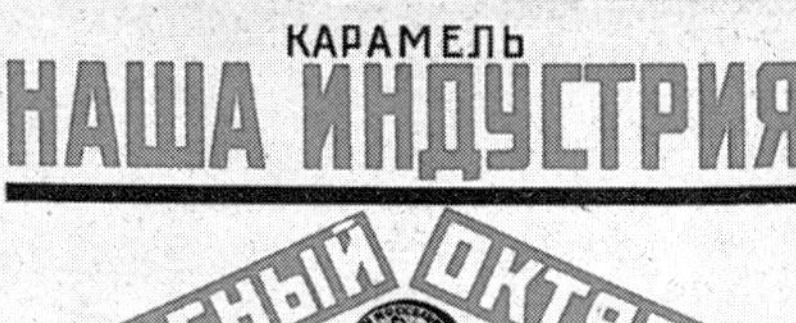

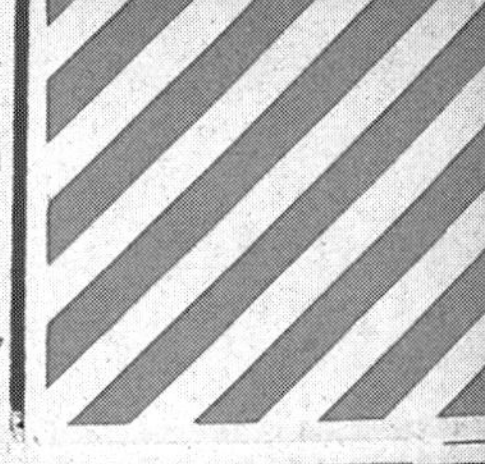

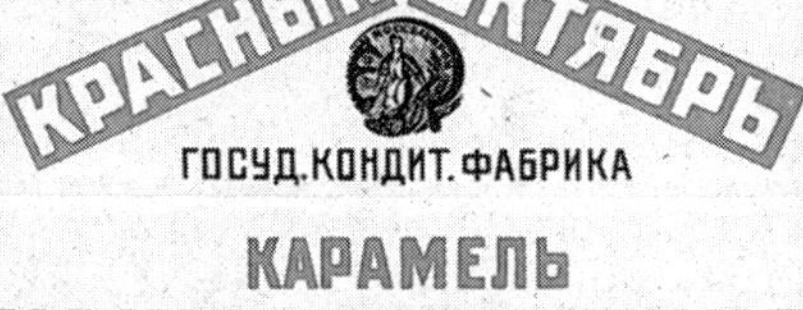

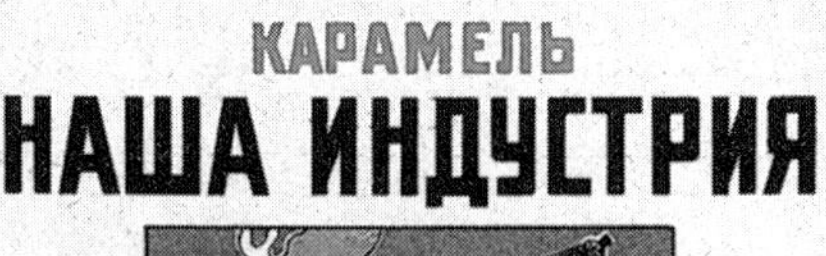

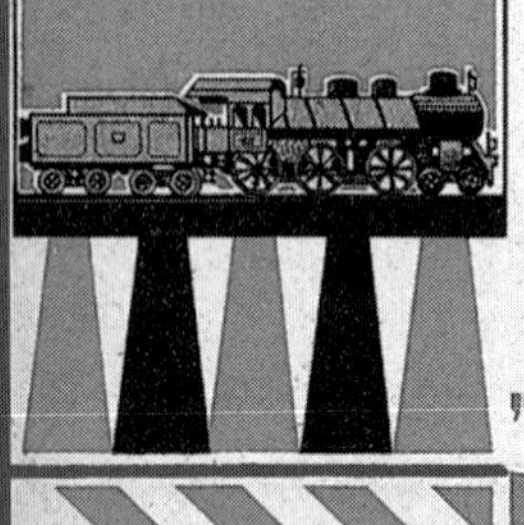

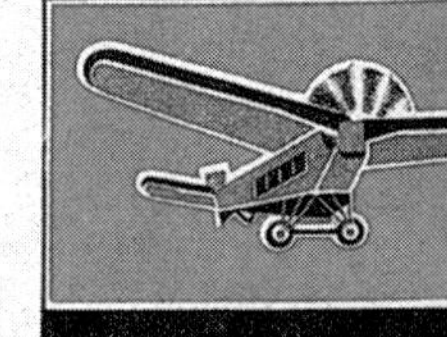

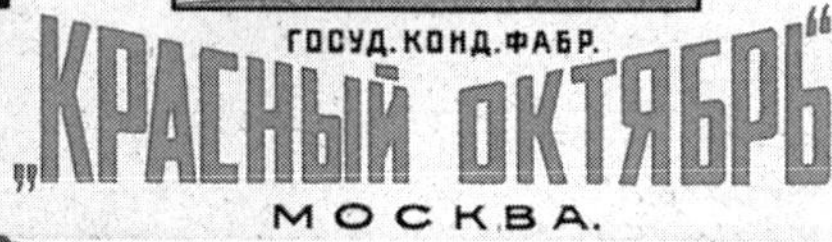

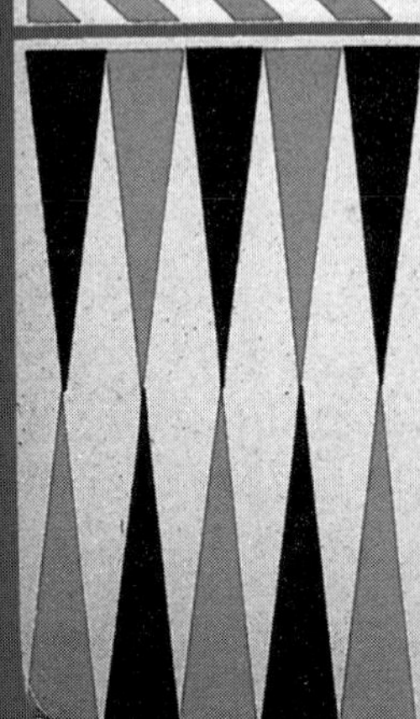

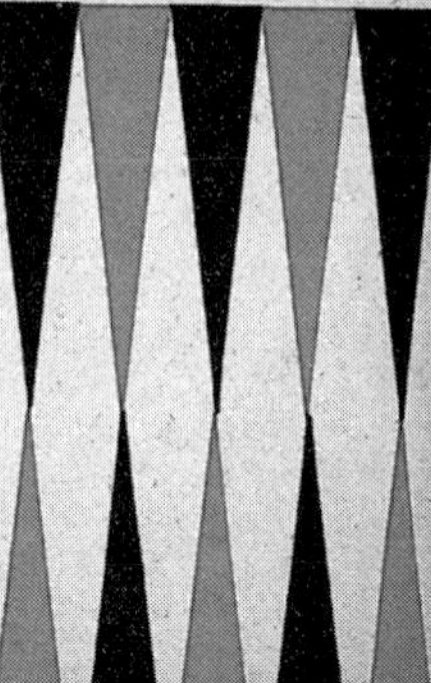

FIGURE 4.1
Aleksandr Rodchenko, box for Our Industry caramels, 1923. See plate 11.

CHAPTER 4

CONSTRUCTIVIST ADVERTISING AND BOLSHEVIK BUSINESS

In the summer of 1923, the Constructivist Aleksandr Rodchenko and the poet Vladimir Mayakovsky formed a two-man commercial design business called *Reklam-Konstruktor* (Advertising-Constructor), producing advertising and packaging for Soviet state-owned enterprises. One of their main clients was Mossel'prom, a Moscow organization uniting state industrial enterprises that processed agricultural products. In late 1923 Rodchenko designed a small cardboard box for *Nasha industriia* (Our Industry) brand caramels, produced by Mossel'prom's Red October factory (figure 4.1). Rodchenko's vibrating orange- and black-striped graphics are reminiscent of Liubov' Popova's and Varvara Stepanova's optical fabrics, which rolled off the presses of the First State Cotton-Printing Factory in 1923–1924 to be used in potentially transformative ways by Soviet consumers in their everyday lives.

But if Popova and Stepanova could claim to have entered directly into the Soviet factory to produce their fabrics, "our industry" and "the factory" figure on the caramel box only as signs. Further, if the fabrics were socialist objects in themselves, where is the socialist object in the commercial graphic design? Most of the designs were standard two-dimensional advertising images, and not objects at all. The little cardboard box was made to contain caramels that are socialist in the sense that they were produced by a Soviet state-owned factory, but they are clearly not socialist objects made by Constructivists. The proposal of this chapter will be that the socialist object in this instance is the combination of the Constructivist graphic design with the Soviet commercial product. The designs transform modest products like caramels, cigarettes, cookies, and pacifiers into active objects, offering diagrams or maps of how the prerevolutionary desires for commodities that still dominate in the period of the New Economic Policy must be redeemed into more conscious and collective desires for objects in the socialist future. The Rodchenko–Mayakovsky business venture tackles even more explicitly the highly temporal Constructivist question raised in the previous chapter by Popova's flapper dresses: How will our desire for the mass-produced objects of industry be organized and harnessed for socialism after the revolution?

There is a powerful pathos in the way that the optically vibrating modern graphics dress up the small, flimsy cardboard box and the old-fashioned engravings of machinery—a pathos that matches that of a state confectionery factory naming caramels after a Soviet industry that as yet barely exists. The staccato, accelerated language of abstract pattern is in palpable visual tension with the almost nineteenth-century feel of the pictures of industry, which resemble illustrations in a contractor's catalog or a primary school textbook. The tension is also temporal, between the immediacy of the graphics and the narrative time of the pictures, in which the crane emits puffs of smoke and the airplane propeller whirs around. In contrast to Rodchenko's bold, framing graphics, the outmoded engravings summon childhood memories of "modernity" in the adult consumer of 1923, evoking the idea of "industry" as it might have seemed to a child at the end of the previous century. Together they form what Walter Benjamin calls in the *Arcades Project* a dialectical image—"that wherein what has been comes together in a flash with the now to form a constellation."[1] In the terms of Benjamin's analysis of the revolutionary potential of mass culture, the little caramel box turns out to be deliberately theoretical in its pathos, rather than simply pathetic, as it attempts to harness childhood fantasies of abundance experienced in individual histories for the collective Bolshevik fantasy of an industrialized future just around the corner.

This interpretation of the commercial design work accords it greater significance within the Constructivist project than did most of Rodchenko's contemporaries.[2] The Productivist theorist Osip Brik, for example, in his article "Into Production!" in the first issue of *Lef*, applauds Rodchenko for his Productivist desire to enter production not as an applied artist, but as a Constructivist who will produce new, high-quality things. But in the current economic situation of NEP, Brik complains, "when everything is concentrated on 'quantity,' what talk can there be of qualification!" Artists, economic planners and "philistines" are not yet ready to accept "the iron constructiveness of Rodchenko's constructions." In response to this inhospitable climate, Brik writes, "Rodchenko is patient. He will wait. Meanwhile he is doing what he can—he is revolutionizing taste, clearing the ground for the future material culture that will be not aesthetic, but expedient [*tselesoobraznyi*]."[3] Brik's language of "iron" constructiveness emphasizes the masculine creativity of production, while the more passive terminology of "waiting," "doing what he can," and "clearing the ground" characterizes the mundane, repetitive nature of the tasks of everyday life. Brik is right to point to the transitional nature of the advertising project in "revolutionizing taste," but he is less convincing in his characterization of it as passive, or as peripheral to real Constructivism, because the commercial graphics offer an interpretation of the transition to the socialist object that is crucial to the development of that object. They offer an interpretation of the socialist object before it exists. Just as the cheap Mossel'prom caramels are the transitional objects of young Soviet industry, placeholders for the more ambitious products of heavy industry to be produced in the future, so the Constructivist advertisements interpret this transitional moment in consumer desire in the hope of clarifying the relation to the object that will be required when the socialist object of Constructivism fully arrives.[4]

With few exceptions, the commercial graphics have not been analyzed as a central practice of the Constructivist project.[5] This is no doubt at least in part a result of their quirky visual forms that depart so radically from the "iron" imagery of Constructivist engineerism. (The art historian Paul Wood once defended them as being more significant than the "endearingly dotty" designs that they appear to be.)[6] More centrally, though, these ads and packages, made with the specific aim of selling the products of a certain firm more effectively—even if it is a Soviet state firm—seem to have departed from the avant-garde "art-into-life" ambitions of Constructivism to collapse too directly into the "life" of commercial mass culture, becoming, as Peter Bürger puts it, a "false sublation" of art into life in the form of "commodity aesthetics."[7]

This chapter will propose, however, that the Rodchenko–Mayakovsky commercial graphics blur Bürger's distinctions between avant-garde and mass culture. The advertisements confront the problem of postrevolutionary desire with the same theoretical rigor as Mayakovsky's celebrated poem "About This" of 1923, and develop in a novel way the visual strategies of the more widely acknowledged avant-garde projects of Constructivism, such as photomontage and sculpture, in order to imagine a new order of active, comradely objects and a differently organized consumer desire under socialism.

A Modernist Collaboration: "About This"

Much more than is usually suspected, the Constructivist advertisements bear a strong resemblance, both in their visual structure and in their ideological relation to commodity desire, to the more characteristically modernist collaboration that preceded them: Rodchenko's famous series of photomontages, made in the spring of 1923, illustrating Mayakovsky's long poem "About This" (*Pro Eto*).[8] The photomontages are universally regarded as prime examples of the new modernist medium of photomontage in the 1920s. The text of "About This" is both a love poem written to Mayakovsky's lover Lili Brik, wife of his friend and *Lef* theorist Osip Brik, and a poetic indictment of the continuation of the old forms of everyday life (*byt*) after the revolution.[9] Like the caramel box, the poem takes up the temporal problem of the transition to socialism—from the old bourgeois *byt* of possessions, including the lover as a possession, to an as yet unknown form of a new everyday life (*novyi byt*) of new relations to material objects and to people. The complex temporal structure of the poem—with juxtaposed scenes and images spanning from the dinosauric past to the thirtieth century—refuses any idea of a linear transitional path from the old *byt* to the new. Its temporal jumps and contradictions are instead suggestive of the more dialectical temporal structure of revolution proposed by Benjamin, in which the past and present collide to illuminate the future.

The poem chronicles Mayakovsky's response to a two-month separation imposed by Lili Brik in late December of 1922. In his despair at their separation and his fear of losing her, he became a recluse, living alone in his tiny room, while she carried on her everyday life, entertaining at home and socializing at the houses of friends. The poem intertwines two main narratives: Mayakovsky's present-day attempts to contact Lili, on the one hand, and his dialogue with the narrator of a poem he wrote some seven years before called "Man" (*Chelovek*, 1915). The persona of the older poem, a Christlike figure who threatens to commit suicide by jumping from a bridge into the Neva river in Petrograd, represents a purer version of Mayakovsky himself, when he was a younger Bolshevik Futurist preparing for revolution, rather than a financially successful poet in danger of settling down into the complacent postrevolutionary *meshchanskii* (petty bourgeois) *byt* of NEP. His love for Lili becomes tangled up in his worries about his own identity as a revolutionary because in his imagination she is tied to all the domestic things and practices that threaten to divert him from the purer path of his former self.[10] This personal conflict enacts the larger Bolshevik conflict between revolutionary ideals and the stasis of *byt*—a dualism within which, as we have seen, woman was equated with *byt*, just as Lili Brik stands for *byt* in "About This."[11]

Mayakovsky published "About This" as the controversial centerpiece of the first issue of the avant-garde journal *Lef*, of which he was editor-in-chief, provoking dissent within *Lef* ranks about the relation of the personal to the political from the very start. Manuscript versions of the poem reveal that Mayakovsky methodically edited out many of the personal references, consciously attempting to transform the poem into a more general indictment of *byt*. At an April 1923 reading of the work, for example, he emphasized that in "About This," much more than the love story, "the crucial thing is: our way of life [*byt*] . . . a way of life which hasn't changed at all and which is now our vilest enemy, and turns us into philistines [*meshchane*]."[12] "About This" skewers the new Communist bureaucrats of NEP who, in the view of committed revolutionaries like Mayakovsky, were especially guilty of promoting the traditional *meshchanskii byt* of urban Russia, threatening to nullify the political changes that had been so hard won through revolution and civil war. Despite Mayakovsky's efforts to emphasize the poem's larger political critique, however, the Productivist critic Nikolai Chuzhak criticized it harshly in the next issue of *Lef* for its unproductive obsession with *byt*, material possessions, and the personal love story: "Everything is moved by *byt*. 'My' house. 'She,' surrounded by friends and servants. . . . 'he' listens at doors, genius that he is, rushing back and forth from *meshchanins* to *meshchanins*. . . ."[13]

Just as Chuzhak contends, the poem has Mayakovsky scurrying back and forth between his own family's Moscow apartment and apartments where Lili might be, pleading with the people there to fly with him to Petrograd to save the man on the bridge contemplating suicide from his poem of 1915—pleading, essentially, that they give up the security and warm, cozy surroundings of their NEP-era Christmas parties to travel back in time, as well as through the cold and snow, to a moment of revolutionary purity. No one heeds his pleas. This betrayal of both himself and the revolution leads to a dramatic staging of Mayakovsky's crucifixion by the forces of *byt*. He can only be saved by what the linguist Roman Jakobson, in his elegiac essay on the poet, calls his "constant infatuation with a wonderful future."[14] In the final section of the poem Mayakovsky projects himself into the thirtieth century where he pleads with a chemist to resurrect him (p. 103):

Resurrect me
I want to live my full share!
Where love won't be the servant
of marriages
lust
bread.
Damning the bed,
getting up from the warm spot on the stove
love will stride throughout the universe.

The dream of a higher, more spiritual and collective form of love appropriate to the dematerialized *novyi byt*, liberated from ties of materiality like private beds, has strong affinities to the Bolshevik campaign for a *novyi byt* that was emerging at this moment. This campaign, as we have seen, was burdened by an impossible temporal structure in which *byt* could become *novyi* only by being destroyed, or transformed completely into its conceptual opposite of *bytie*, or higher spiritual existence. Mayakovsky's vision of the thirtieth century resembles nothing so much as the many propaganda posters for the *novyi byt* showing the socialist future as a space evacuated of domestic objects.

Mayakovsky's vision also expresses in poetic language the same idea articulated in more sober prose by Sergei Tret'iakov in the same inaugural issue of *Lef* as the poem, in his essay "Where From, Where To?"[15] In that essay Tret'iakov had written, we recall, that people are slaves to the objects that envelop them in the "quagmire of *byt*." The hero of the essay, the nameless Futurist inventor, sets an example by freely giving away his entire production to the collective. Unlike Chuzhak, Arvatov, and the other *Lef* theorists and artists who were attempting to theorize a transformation of everyday life in all its materiality into a positive revolutionary force, Tret'iakov and Mayakovsky seem to espouse the more standard Bolshevik vision of a dematerialized *novyi byt*, such as Trotsky's dream of a new "relation of husband and wife [. . .] freed of everything external, foreign, binding, incidental" in a world of state-run public nurseries, laundries, and cafeterias (VB, p. 45). In his negative review of the poem in *Lef*, Chuzhak asserts that the utopian ending of "About This" does not tackle any realistic solutions to the persistence of the old *byt* in the new society. Mayakovsky avoids the crucial problem of the transition to socialism, including the necessary transformation of the material life of the everyday.[16]

The dramatic temporal gap between the cluttered present and a fantasy future magically freed of possessions is only one image of the poem, however. A contrasting and equally powerful image—and one more closely connected to the "transitional" narratives of the Rodchenko–Mayakovsky commercial graphics—is that of the conflicted identity of Mayakovsky the lover who is deeply implicated in the present day *byt* that he inhabits. Looking for Lili at the apartment of Fekla Davidovna, a female acquaintance, Mayakovsky the narrator encounters banal introductions over drinks and tea, and a dance of mice, bedbugs, cockroaches, and the objects of *meshchanskii* Soviet decor: samovars, geraniums, canaries, family pictures. The objects threaten to close in on him, like Tret'iakov's quagmire of *byt*: the glinting samovar "wants to envelop you in its samovar arms" (p. 84). Old and new symbols intermingle in the motley mix of early Soviet *byt*; among the wall decorations, "Jesus tips his thorny crown and bows politely, and Marx, bitted and haltered in a pink frame, pulls his full weight in the middle-class ménage."[17] With professed horror, Mayakovsky the narrator recognizes—by his height, his skin, his clothes—none other than himself among the bourgeois objects and social rituals in this ménage: "One of them / I recognized / As like a twin / Myself / My very own self" (p. 84). Roman Jakobson refers to this "terrible double" of the poet as the "owner-purchaser" who must be contrasted with the "inventor," and he famously characterizes Mayakovsky's relation to *byt* as an element of his constitution of himself as a subject: "If we should attempt to translate Mayakovsky's mythology into the language of speculative philosophy, the exact equivalent of this enmity [for *byt*] would be the opposition of 'ego' and 'not ego.' It would be impossible to find a more adequate name for the enemy."[18]

Yet Mayakovsky's recognition of himself enjoying the Christmas festivities in Fekla Davidovna's apartment can also be understood, conversely, to soften the structuralist opposition of Jakobson's statement. The stark philosophical binary of heroic self perpetually pitted against the dissolving power of the old *byt* certainly figures in Mayakovsky's character and his work, but the temporal confusion and ironic doubleness of "About This" suggest that his identities as ascetic Bolshevik and as owner–purchaser lover must be reconciled, since both involve love in different ways. The interrelatedness of the two aspects of his identity is manifested in his riven voice, as he projects himself into the innocent but also brutal figure of the bear: "I paw at my ears—/ in vain! / I hear / my / my own voice / the knife of my voice cuts me through my paws" (p. 75). The voice of the man on the bridge from seven years before chastises the present narrator (p. 76):

So, it seems, you're worming your way into their caste?
You're kissing?
    eating?
        getting a paunch?
You yourself
    intend to clamber mincingly
        into their *byt*
into their family happiness?!

The previous Mayakovsky persona accuses his present self of being weakened by the emotional comfort of his personal love relationship with Lili and the material comforts of the *meshchanskii byt* in which it unfolds. The present Mayakovsky hyperbolizes the opposition between revolutionary ideals and the "family happiness" of *byt*, indicting his own mother (p. 82):

October thundered through
                punishing
                    judging.
You
    under its fire-feathered wing
set a place
    and laid out the chinaware.

This hyperbole is so extreme that it seems almost to mock the standard Bolshevik ideology of a feminized, antiheroic *byt* that stands in the way of revolution. Why should the innocuous, practical objects that support the simple practices of everyday life, such as sitting down at table to eat from chinaware, be opposed to the masculine metaphor of revolution in thundering narrative movement across the map of history? Why, the poem seems to ask, are we so attached to these conceptual oppositions? Why are they the only ones that can motivate us—motivate me, Vladimir Vladimirovich Mayakovsky—toward revolutionary work?[19] His table-setting mother is after all only another personification of himself. He has set the table, grown a paunch, fallen in love.

Love is the poem's unnamed trickster, the desire that the new socialist life must dialectically incorporate. In the poem's title, the "this" of "About This" refers to love, although it is never spelled out. The first section begins with the question: "About what—about this?" (p. 65) and expands on "this theme" all the way through to the last two rhyming lines of the section. The first of these invokes the image of learned heads that have beaten themselves against this unnamed theme, and ends on the word "foreheads" (*lbov*); the second consists of the enigmatic sentence: "The name of this theme is: . . . !" (p. 66). The missing word signaled by Mayakovsky's ellipsis is "love" (*liubov'*). The imaginative restoration of the letter "iu" and concluding soft sign to *lbov* is an emblem for Benjamin's dialectical image: "what has been comes together in a flash with the now to form a constellation." What better constellation to represent the now of a dialectical socialist culture than the scientific foreheads (*lbov*) of the *novyi byt* to which have been restored the elided letters of a love (*liubov'*) that had been thought too domestic, too philistine, too feminine?

Rodchenko's illustrations take their cue from the incorporation, expressed by this verbal image, of a personal and literal love into the organized spaces of the revolution. The sober foreheads of scientific socialism and the *novyi byt* are represented by the stringently Constructivist compositional forms, which organize the chaos of photographic images evoking themes of love and the old bourgeois *byt*. Rodchenko's repeated use of photographs of Mayakovsky and Lili Brik made the photomontage illustrations into a kind of document of the actual affair, putting right back in all the direct personal references that Mayakovsky had deliberately and somewhat coyly left out of the text.[20] The text of the poem, for example, opens with an anonymous dedication "to her and to me" (p. 65), while Rodchenko's famous cover image for the book version shows an intense close-up photograph of Lili's face, leaving no doubt as to the object of "this" love. The proliferation of photographs of Mayakovsky himself across and within the photomontages emphasizes the rivenness of Mayakovsky's identity as revolutionary and as lover. The photomontages confirm the doubleness of the poetic text: the highly organized compositional forms create juxtapositions of images from Mayakovsky's personal narrative and the old bourgeois *byt* that are highly critical, and yet this imagery is retained and rendered dynamic and vivid.

Of the eight published montage illustrations by Rodchenko, the fourth one most directly confronts Mayakovsky's relation to the clutter of *byt* (figure 4.2). It was published in the book version of the poem with an old-fashioned caption drawn from lines from the poem: "And the century stands / as it was / Unwhipped / the mare of *byt* won't budge" (p. 84). One reading of the montage could affirm it as a successful evocation of this gendered verbal image of the obstinate mare of the old *byt*, depicted in the profusion of specific objects of feminine domesticity mentioned in the poem, like samovars and place-settings.[21] The innocuous silver butter knife partially obscures the photograph of Mayakovsky on the upper left, taking on a sinister quality like the upright bar of a prison cell. The stem of the crystal candy dish next to it on the right repeats the vertical, emphasizing Mayakovsky's entrapment. The old-fashioned cut black paper silhouette of a wife pouring tea from a samovar for her husband, balanced on top of the candy dish, is a heavy weight pressed against the heart of the poet—or a cruel crystal ball showing that the *byt* of the Soviet future will be no different from the bourgeois *byt* of the nineteenth century. On the center right, a stereotypical capitalist or NEP profiteer, replete with bow tie and monocle, similarly entraps another photograph of Mayakovsky within his ample belly. The objects that immure Mayakovsky also feminize other male figures. Two Red Army soldiers on the lower left slouch and grin foolishly as they take their tea and cake in the shadow of the samovar. At the top center, another soldier is trapped within an oval silver serving tray, his legs cut off by its edge and transformed into ineffectual little handles. Instead of a gun, he holds two giant silver teaspoons. The placement of the large photograph of Mayakovsky on the left in his workers' cap can then be read as an attempt to project a masculine sense of discipline, embodied in his direct, almost accusatory gaze, against the tide of all of the objects of bourgeois feminization. The image might even be understood to set up a visual struggle between a *byt* abandoned to the feminine, on the one hand, and a more organized *novyi byt* transformed by the multiplication of rigidly phallic images: the upright knife and the two-spoon double phallus. In this way it distinctly resembles, in spirit rather than form, the antiprostitution propaganda poster of 1923 that we examined in chapter 2 (see figure 2.8), which also includes a heroic, saviorlike male figure, gazing intently and wearing a workers' cap, who fights against a sea of fat, bald capitalists in suits representing the old *byt*.

A different reading of Rodchenko's montage, however, can emerge from the doubleness of meaning made possible by the profusion of imagery inherent to the photomontage form. Rodchenko sets up a contrast between the two photographs of Mayakovsky: the first, on the left, has him glaring purposefully out at the viewer in his workers' cap, "punishing / judging," like October itself in the poem, while in the second, on the right, the symbolic cap is now on his knee, and his raised eyebrows and gesticulating hands imply a comical, self-ironizing monologue: "kissing? / eating? / getting a paunch?" Is he trapped inside the gilt frame of the mirror on the ladies toiletries table, or is he comfortably ensconced? Rodchenko emphasizes the ease of Mayakovsky's fit within the mirror's frame by precisely fitting the measure of his photographic figure to the mirror's ornate pedestals and

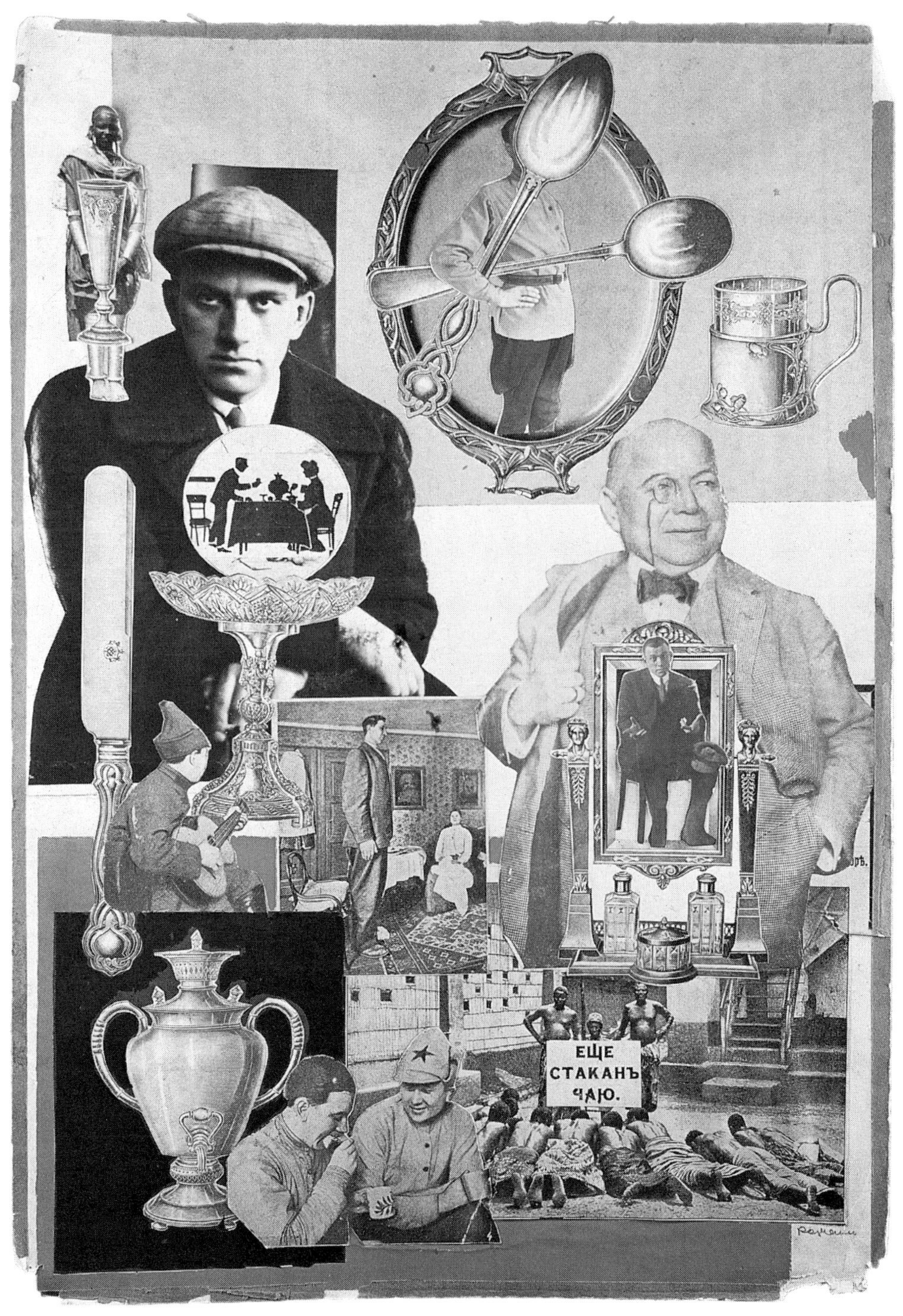

FIGURE 4.2

Aleksandr Rodchenko, illustration for Vladimir Mayakovsky's "About This," accompanied by the lines "And the century stands / as it was / Unwhipped / the mare of *byt* won't budge." Maquette for book illustration, 1923. Cut-and-pasted printed papers and gelatin-silver photographs with india ink on cardboard. Scala/Art Resource, N.Y. See plate 12.

the cut-glass crystal bottles that form part of the mirror set. He also heightens this sense of Mayakovsky's ease by juxtaposing this photograph with a strange kind of mirror image directly to its left: a medical documentary photograph of the real-life giant Fedor Makhnov, a victim of glandular disease.[22] Not only does Makhnov's enormity make him look pitifully trapped within his family's bourgeois living room, but the photograph fortuitously poses him in front of a framed portrait of Marx hanging on the wall, tying the image firmly back to Mayakovsky's poetic narrative of the appearance of Marx himself enframed on the wall within "the middle-class ménage" of Fekla Davidovna's apartment. Unlike Makhnov, whose very glands naturally entrap him within the spaces of bourgeois *byt*, the famously tall Mayakovsky can and does fold his great height into these spaces. Rodchenko's photomontage confirms Mayakovsky's self-recognition within the ménage, emphasizing the poem's concession that Mayakovsky's protest against the old *byt* is a fiction—"I recognized / As like a twin / Myself."

Benjamin Buchloh has interpreted Rodchenko's exuberant return to figurative imagery in these photomontages, after years of almost exclusively abstract visual practice, as a sign of his "relief at having finally broken the modernist ban on iconic representation."[23] In the sheer profusion of photographic quotation from mass-produced sources, the montages do appear to revel in the storytelling power that was banned, or at least severely reduced, in the linear, geometric designs of Rodchenko's other work of the time. But Rodchenko's use of figurative imagery has a purpose beyond antimodernist rebellion: he has harnessed figurative photographic images to his larger, Constructivist project of organization or systematization. The photomontages, despite their superficial similarity to the more heterogeneous Dadaist photomontages with their effects of disruption and "shock," are in fact highly organized according to the principles of linearity and geometry of other Constructivist works. The formal composition of the montages becomes a narrative device in itself: it is the mechanism that organizes the objects and emotions from the old, private *byt* into a legible story. This legibility is a necessary step in the transition to a socialist future of collective objects and emotions.

Rodchenko turns the Constructivist concern with construction and engineering into a metaphoric device by literally buttressing the "Mare of *byt*" montage at the four corners with images referring to the theme of tea drinking, to which Mayakovsky returns repeatedly in the poem as a sign of the most conventional *meshchanskii byt*. A samovar gets pride of place on the lower left, and on the upper right, a prominent photograph of a traditional Russian tea

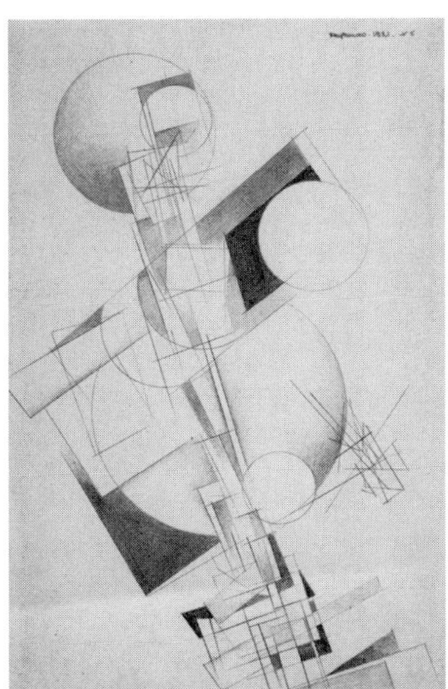

FIGURE 4.3
Aleksandr Rodchenko, *Constructive Composition no. 5*, 1921. Pencil on paper.

glass set in an ornate metal holder floats solo against the pinkish rectangle that forms the background. The seemingly incongruous images of Africans in the remaining two corners illustrate Mayakovsky's lament in the poem that even curly-headed negroes in Africa now lap up their tea (p. 82). He invokes Africa in typically colonialist terms as an uncivilized Eden that is powerless to resist the encroaching bourgeois civilization. But the implicit suggestion that his beloved revolution is as subject to corruption as unspoiled African culture indicates that for him, "primitive" Africa is a positive term. Rodchenko seizes on this vivid image, punctuating the photomontage at the top left with a photograph of a richly dressed African woman standing erect, her body obscured by an overlaid image of a giant silver goblet. On the bottom right, a group of Africans lie prone on the ground before a ruler or religious figure. His body is obscured by a superimposed advertising-type signboard on which is written, in prerevolutionary Russian lettering, "Another cup of tea."

This narrative "construction" of the montage is emphasized by other compositional elements drawn from the Constructivist repertoire: the repetition of geometric forms like the rectangle, circle, and oval; the linear patterning of the cutlery; and the organization of the photographic elements against a background of monochromatic rectangles. These forms can all be found in the graphic constructions by Rodchenko and others that were made for the composition–construction debates at the Institute of Artistic Culture (INKhUK) in 1921, such as Rodchenko's *Constructive Composition no. 5* (figure 4.3). In the context of those debates, Rodchenko had said that composition, which he associated with aesthetics and taste, had to be replaced by construction: "All new approaches to art arise from technology and engineering and move towards organization and construction."[24] Two of Rodchenko's other photomontages for "About This" evoke not only the forms of Constructivist drawings, but the actual engineering-oriented sculptural constructions of early Constructivism. One montage illustrates Mayakovsky's narrative of his unsuccessful attempts to call Lili on the telephone and the "troglodyte" beast of jealousy that motivates him (pp. 71–72) (figure 4.4); the other illustrates the lines devoted to Mayakovsky's "bearification" (pp. 72–73), when he becomes a bumbling beast that is both a figure of jealousy in Russia, and more generally a figure for someone too brutish to conform to the bureaucratic niceties of his complacent NEP-era colleagues in the Soviet cultural sphere (figure 4.5). As a bear he floats away on a river of his own tears, which turns into the Neva River in Petrograd. There he meets the younger revolutionary version of himself, standing on the Nevsky bridge above him, contemplating suicide.

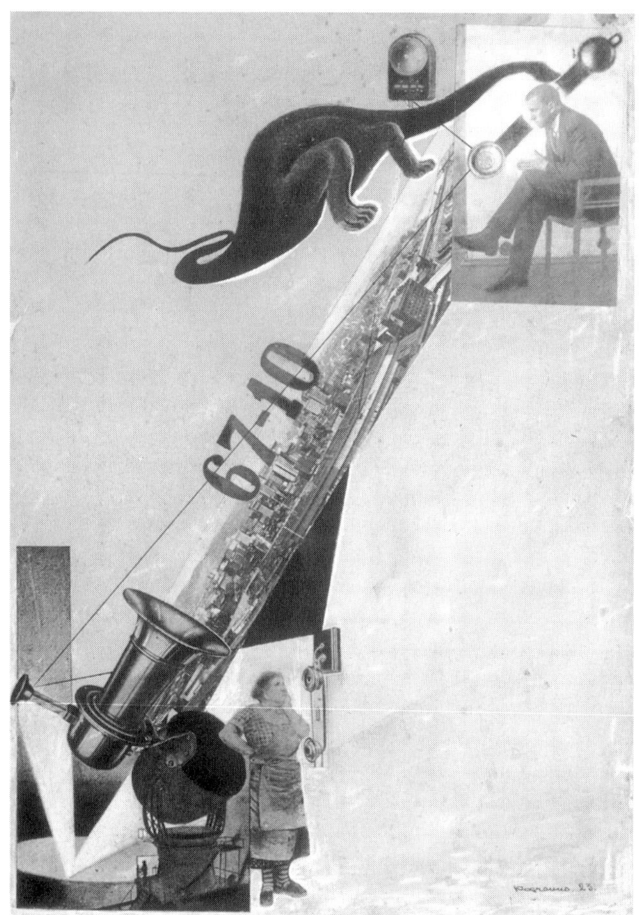

FIGURE 4.4
Aleksandr Rodchenko, illustration for Vladimir Mayakovsky's "About This," accompanied by the lines "Out of the cord / jealousy came crawling / a cave-dwelling troglodyte monster." Maquette for book illustration, 1923. Cut-and-pasted printed papers and gelatin-silver photographs with india ink on cardboard.

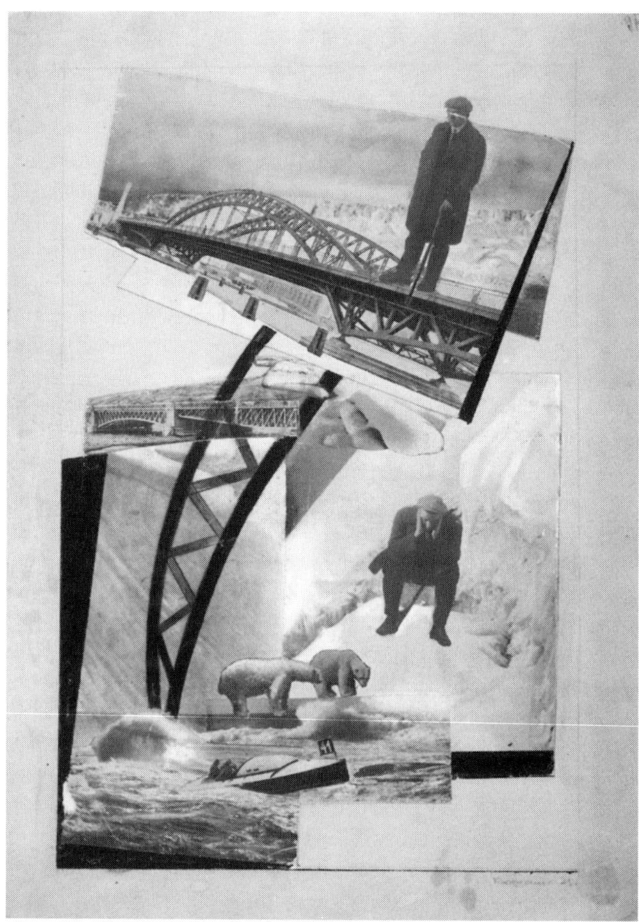

FIGURE 4.5
Aleksandr Rodchenko, illustration for Vladimir Mayakovsky's "About This," accompanied by the lines "I paw at my ears — / in vain! / I hear / my / my own voice / the knife of my voice cuts me through my paws." Maquette for book illustration, 1923. Cut-and-pasted printed papers and gelatin-silver photographs with india ink on cardboard.

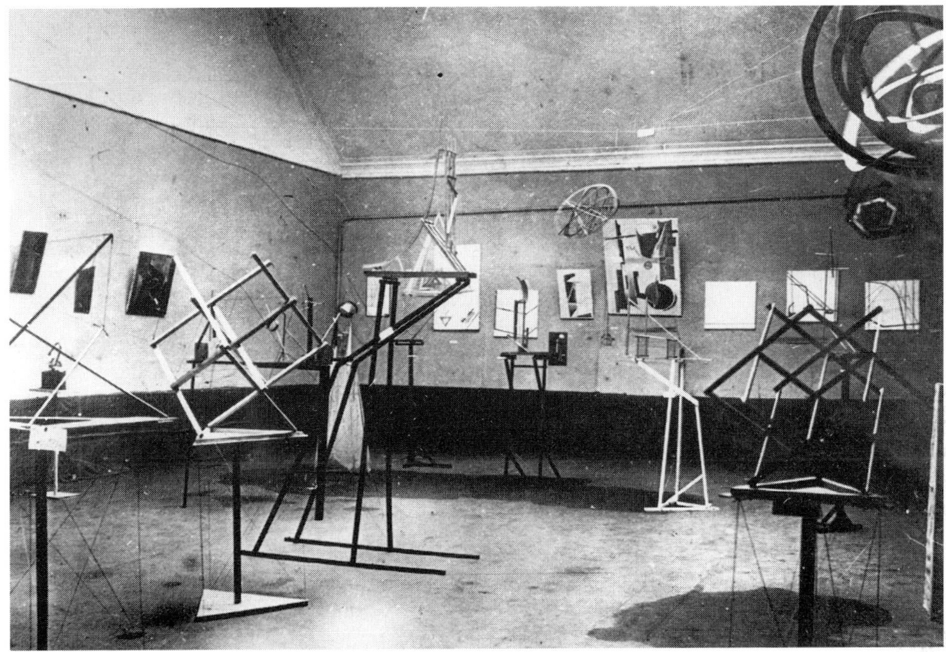

FIGURE 4.6
Installation view, Second Spring Exhibition of the OBMOKhU, Moscow, 1921.

Stepping back from the intricate montage of dinosaurs, cityscapes, projectors, icebergs, and bears that makes up these compositions, and taking in their overall structure, we see that they resemble the architectural or engineering constructions of the Constructivists Karl Ioganson and the Stenberg brothers. Three of Ioganson's structures are visible in the foreground of an installation photograph of the Second Spring Exhibition of the OBMOKhU (Society of Young Artists) in Moscow in May–June 1921 (figure 4.6). The three structures on the floor in the center of the photograph, resembling bridges or cranes, are by the Stenbergs; four works from Rodchenko's *Spatial Constructions* series hang from the ceiling. The "About This" troglodyte montage, with its central, diagonal, elongated, and rectangular image of a city braced by taut telephone wires, is constructed like one of Ioganson's "cold structures," in which tensile wires hold together pieces of wood into a rigid structure based on the engineering principle of "tensegrity."[25] The bear montage combines photographic images of the kinds of actual bridges that provided models for the Stenberg brothers' sculptures with a soaring, inked-in bridgelike form that connects the two scenes in which photographs of Mayakovsky are placed: one representing the man on the bridge from 1915, the other showing the current, conflicted Mayakovsky of NEP, sitting helplessly with his hands covering his ears. The two polar bears represent the unreconstructed doubles of the latter Mayakovsky, while in the troglodyte montage, the modern, suit-wearing poet, seated elegantly with his legs crossed, squares off against his troglodytic self, the dinosaur emerging from the ancient past.[26]

The photomontages enact Mayakovsky's acknowledgment of the "troglodytic" and "bearified" aspects of himself that rear up from the past and cannot be shed on the command of the revolution; the organizational element that secures the pictorial meaning of these juxtapositions of Mayakovsky's selves is Constructivist engineerism. The "About This" photomontages therefore function as an unexpected counterpart to the abstract, engineering-oriented works of early Constructivism, suggesting that "organization," like other key Constructivist terms such as transparency and expediency, was not necessarily predicated on a rejection of figurative images or of the personal desires represented by them. In these photomontages, and in the commercial graphics to follow, images of these desires were retained but reorganized in order to imagine the socialist future. They would be the means for the dialectical transformation of the present transitional moment of NEP.

The Transition to Advertising: Rodchenko and Mayakovsky's Business Partnership

Rodchenko and Mayakovsky's earliest advertisements, made in the summer of 1923 only a few months after the "About This" illustrations, employ a similarly cluttered visual style of figurative profusion, as well as a similarly ironic tone about the bourgeois objects of everyday life. Unlike the more unified, stringent style of their fully developed commercial graphics, these early ads are more spontaneous and untutored in form, allowing us to see more clearly the close theoretical connection between them and "About This." They reveal the same ironic doubleness of protest against and desire for the objects of the old *byt*, and they similarly attempt to organize that desire in the service of a transformed *novyi byt*.

The advertising business began as something of a fluke at the end of June 1923, when Mayakovsky solicited an advertising commission from the state department store GUM (the State Universal Store, *Gosudarstvennyi Universal'nyi Magazin*). GUM occupied the grand prerevolutionary arcade of Moscow, located directly on Red Square, selling privately manufactured and imported goods as well as the products of state factories. Mayakovsky enlisted Rodchenko's collaboration on the advertising project, and they produced five advertisements over the course of three days.

One of the first commissions of what would become their *Reklam-Konstruktor* business was an object-cluttered advertisement for the women's department of GUM, published in the magazine *Krasnaia Niva* (Red Field) on June 30, 1923 (figure 4.7). Mayakovsky's jingle wryly addresses the pervasive nature of consumption in capitalist—or in this case, NEP semicapitalist—society: "There is no room for doubting or thinking—everything for the woman is only at GUM." Or, as she might be instructed today: "Don't think, shop." Like something out of Jean-Gerard Grandville, the nineteenth-century French caricaturist who so entranced Walter Benjamin, the scattered objects of Rodchenko's visual design float in a fantastic commodity phantasmagoria above the figure of the woman at the lower right, as if they were all caught on the same breeze that has filled and lifted the umbrella on the upper right. The boots, stockings, gloves, blouse, coat, scarf, and hairpieces are uncannily animate, as if they are so many metonyms for the woman, who is herself a cut-out figure from a magazine or catalog.

A day later, a similarly ironic advertisement for the men's department at GUM took up an entire page in the Sunday edition of the widely read, large-format newspaper *Izvestiia* of July 1, 1923 (figure 4.8). Mayakovsky's text knowingly plays on the truism that the spiritual identity of the bourgeois is only ever the sum total of his possessions: "Everything that the heart, body, or mind requires—everything for the person is available at GUM." The objects depicted by Rodchenko are the commodities that constitute masculine bourgeois identity: bow tie, collar, bowler hat, pipe, watch, fountain pen, boots, shirts, briefcase, a book of Pushkin, and, explicitly from the West, a Big Ben brand folding set of nail clippers and a box of Pony Post brand cigars. In both these ads, Rodchenko mimics exactly the visual style of the old-fashioned print advertisements that still predominated in the Soviet print media, such as one for another state department store, Mostorg, printed in *Izvestiia* on November 18, 1923 (figure 4.9). The central text of this ad announces a pre-Christmas sale of holiday gifts, and the depicted array of objects floats in an enticing jumble within two vertical borders.

In their jokes at the expense of bourgeois acquisitiveness and their use of traditional visual forms, these early GUM advertisements seem to take a lighthearted approach to the business of advertising. Although Mayakovsky published some critical articles at this time about Soviet advertising, in which he advocated the study of contemporary German advertising and the development

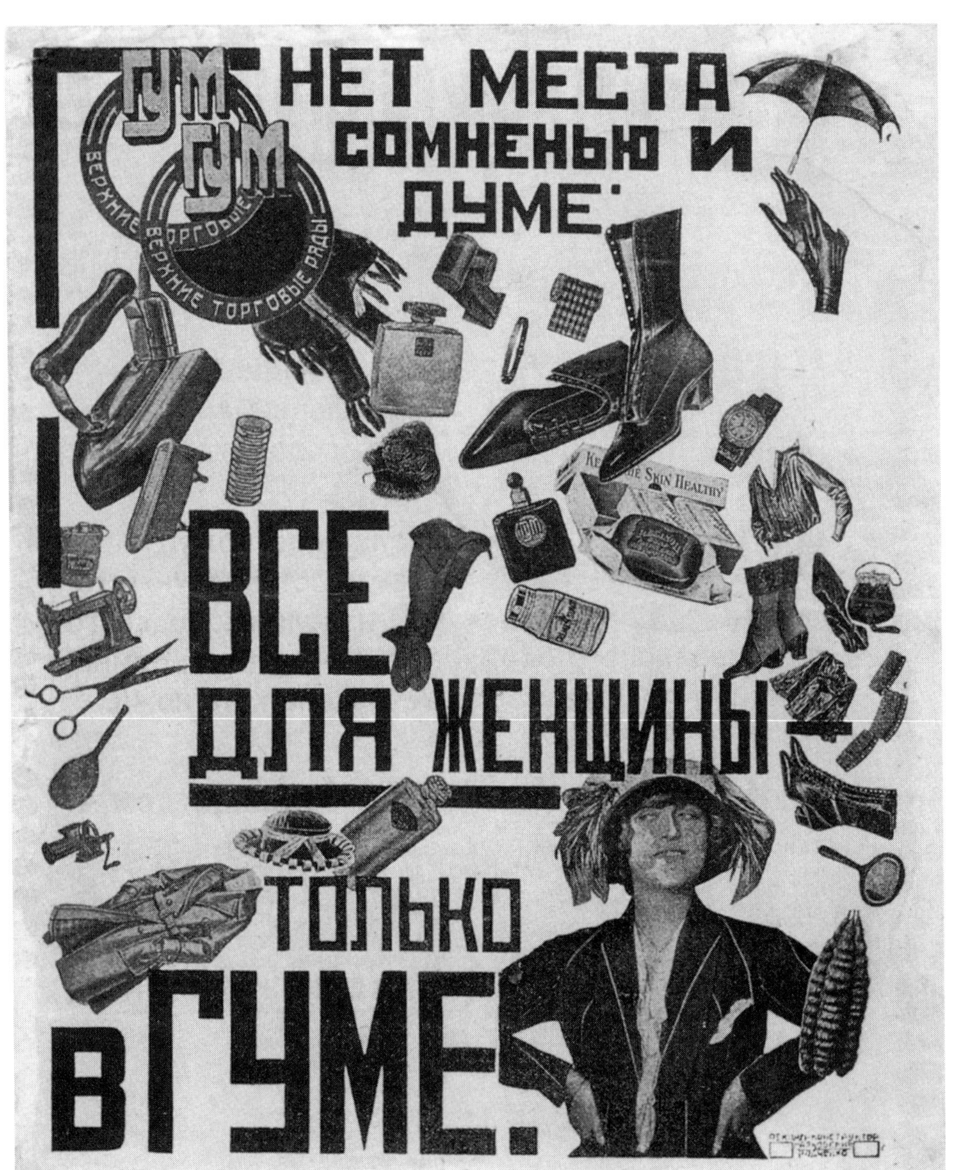

FIGURE 4.7
Aleksandr Rodchenko and Vladimir Mayakovsky, advertisement for the women's department at GUM, 1923.

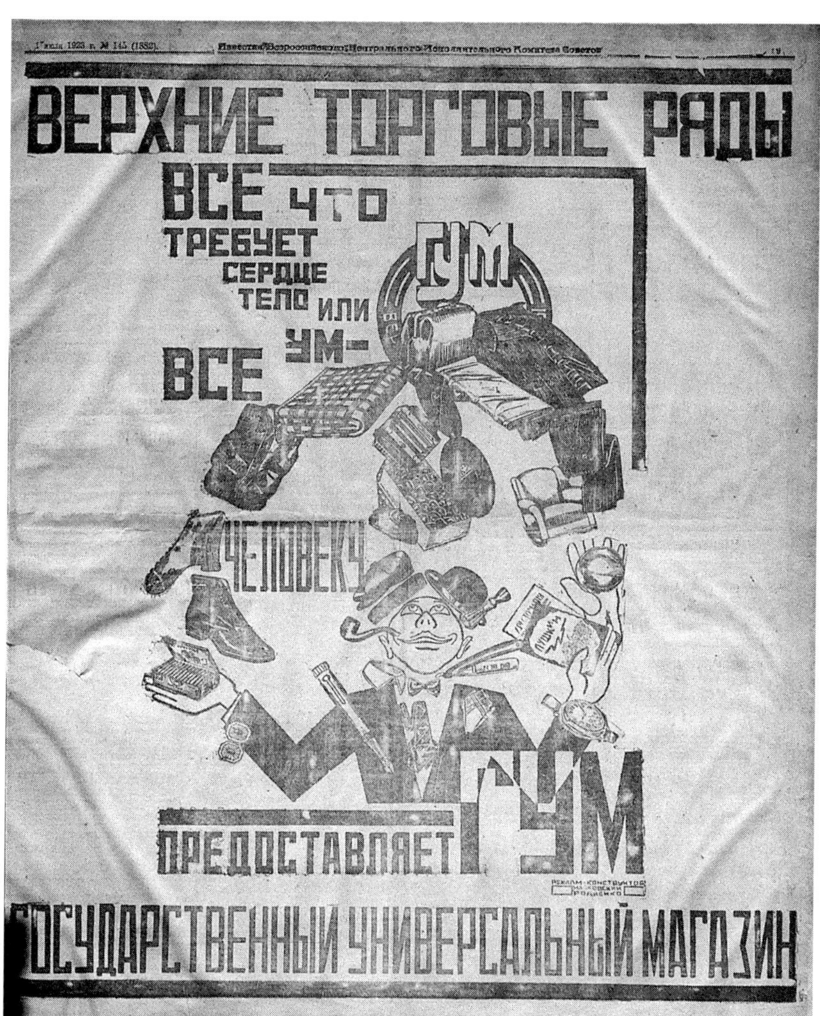

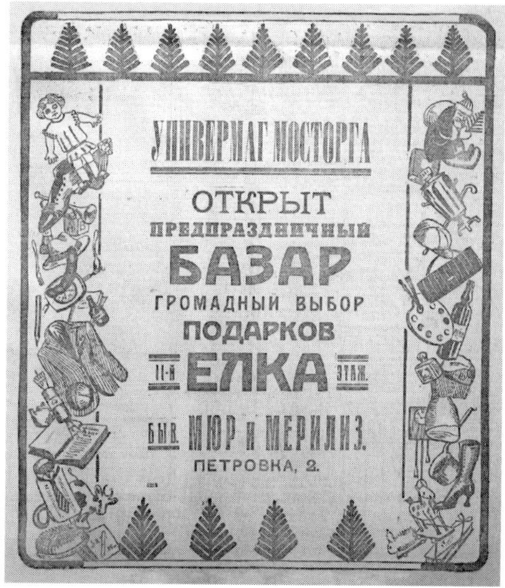

FIGURE 4.9
Advertisement for a pre-Christmas sale at the Mostorg department store in *Izvestiia*, November 18, 1923. Courtesy State Historical Library, Moscow.

FIGURE 4.8
Aleksandr Rodchenko and Vladimir Mayakovsky, advertisement for the men's department at GUM in *Izvestiia*, July 1, 1923. Photo by the author.

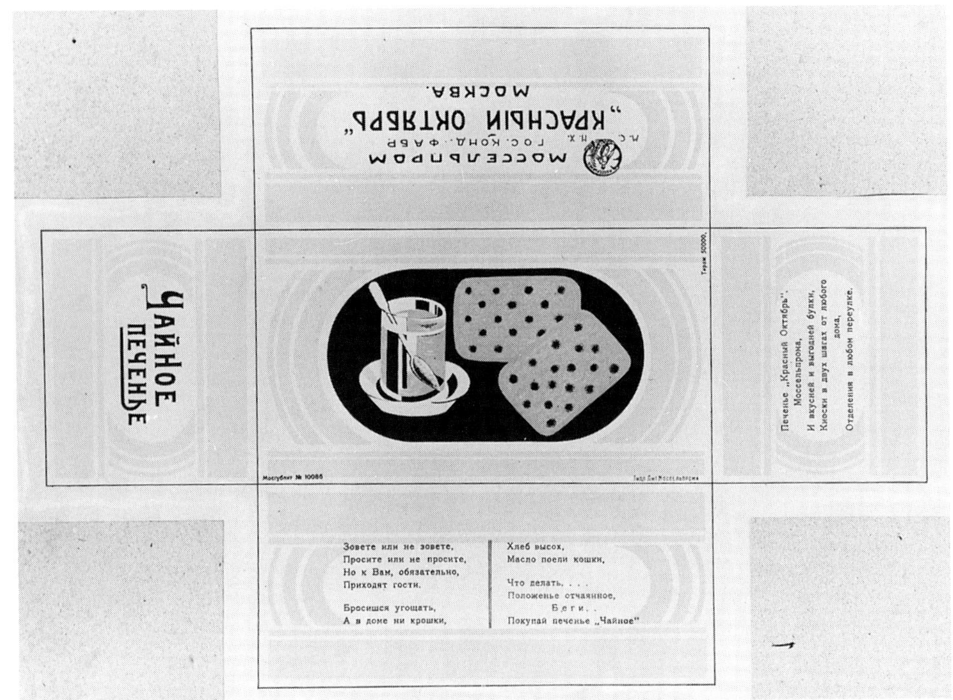

FIGURE 4.10
Aleksandr Rodchenko and Vladimir Mayakovsky, box for Mossel'prom tea cookies, 1923. Private collection.

of more sophisticated publicity campaigns for Soviet products, there is no evidence that either Mayakovsky or Rodchenko ever concerned themselves with studying advertising as a specific set of professional skills.[27] They seem instead to have assumed that they could take care of the simple business of advertising wares as well as any jingle-writer or applied artist trained in an advertising agency. The humor of their GUM ads is based on a rueful acknowledgment of the excessiveness of consumption, which was ideologically justified if it could bring Nepmen into GUM to spend money in a state-owned store. The little man in the GUM ad is a figure for the bourgeois acquisitiveness and possessiveness that Mayakovsky and Rodchenko had so artfully skewered in "About This." One of their slightly later package designs, a cardboard box for Red October Tea brand cookies from Mossel'prom from the fall of 1923, even goes so far as to celebrate, perversely, the very tea drinking that Mayakovsky had so viciously derided in "About This" (figure 4.10). In place of the cut-out photographic reproduction of the tea glass that had been placed in critical juxtaposition with other mass-cultural images in the "Mare of *byt*" photomontage, Rodchenko here simply draws a prosaic picture of the typical Russian tea glass with two cookies. Mayakovsky's little poem printed on the side of the box, far from railing against the *meshchanskii byt* represented by tea drinking, teasingly conjures an impromptu tea party:

Call them or don't call them
Invite them or don't invite them
No matter what you do,
Guests will drop by your house.

You decide to offer them something to eat
but there isn't a crumb in the house
The bread has gone stale
The cats ate the butter.

What is to be done . . .
The situation is desperate . . .
R u n
buy some Tea brand cookies.

Nikolai Chernyshevsky and Vladimir Il'ich Lenin's portentous question "What is to be done?" (*Chto delat'?*) no longer refers to radical politics, but to the "desperate situation" of the host with no treats to offer the guests.[28]

This modernist irony was the simplest way for the revolutionary artist and poet to approach the distasteful commercial task of advertising. But the proposal of this chapter is that casual irony would not define the advertising project for them. Their commercial design work, like their collaboration on "About This," confronts the contradiction between revolution and the object desires of everyday life, and like Rodchenko's photomontages, attempts to master those desires for a potentially more organized future. Even the early men's department ad for GUM, while seemingly composed of a jumble of objects akin to the Mostorg Christmas ad, is also an image of organization: the cartoonish man attempts to juggle all the commodities, to control them by keeping them circulating in some kind of orderly circular trajectory rather than succumb to the total structuring of his identity by the commodity. He is a figure for Mayakovsky, who battles against the engulfing tide of objects in Fekla Davidovna's apartment even as he enjoys the party, and for Rodchenko the Constructivist, who will confront rather than sidestep the phantasmatic power of the commodity object in order to harness it for socialism.

The difference between the two GUM ads for the men's and women's departments, in which the man juggles his objects while the woman is simply one of them, might illustrate quite neatly the gendered difference between the protesting revolutionary Mayakovsky and the self-indulgent bourgeoise Lili

Brik produced by the text of "About This," at least at one level of meaning. But Mayakovsky's GUM slogans are equally damning for both sexes. Further, the significance of the visual difference between the images can be read not as a sign of Rodchenko's participation in the standard association of woman with commodity, but as a knowing illustration of that assumption, because the illustrations are as double-edged as Mayakovsky's text in "About This." The pig-faced man is more petit-bourgeois buffoon than effective juggler, while the woman's expression and pose might best be described as jaunty or quizzical, as if she is keeping her head while brushing off the cascade of commodities. The depiction of male control in the face of the commodity is mobilized pictorially only in order to expose it as a fiction, just as Mayakovsky's own immunity to the objects and comforts of *byt* are exposed as a fiction in "About This." Even Rodchenko and Mayakovsky's earliest, most off-the-cuff ads, then, have much in common with their more celebrated modernist collaboration on the poem.

Although the first Rodchenko–Mayakovsky collaborative advertisements appeared in late June 1923, both artists had separately become interested in the field some time before. Rodchenko had begun independently to make advertisements and logos for Dobrolet, the voluntary share society for the development of Soviet aviation, in the spring of 1923. (One of his Dobrolet pins, depicting a schematic airplane, is visible on Stepanova's lapel in his famous photograph of her drawing with a compass in 1924 [see figure 3.6].) In his memoirs, he recounted how one evening around this time, he was sitting in a cafe with Mayakovsky and the poet Nikolai Aseev when the two poets began to joke about the lame slogans on the Dobrolet posters, commenting that it must have been a second-rate poet who had written them even though they knew full well that it had been Rodchenko himself:

> I got offended and started to scold them for the fact that they weren't writing texts for advertisements, and that I had come up with my verses by chance. . . . I don't know whether this gave the needed spur to Mayakovsky, or whether he had already made up his mind and therefore made a point of noticing my poster, but shortly thereafter he suggested that we should do the GUM advertisements.[29]

As Rodchenko suspected, advertising had been on Mayakovsky's mind that spring. He had published his article "Agitation and Advertising," arguing for the political importance of advertising, on June 10 in a small Ekaterinburg magazine. In this article he wrote:

> We understand perfectly well the power of agitation. . . . The bourgeoisie understands the power of advertising. Advertising is industrial, commercial agitation. No business, even the most reliable, keeps going without advertising. It is a weapon born of competition. . . . We cannot leave this weapon, this agitation on behalf of trade, in the hands of the NEP-men, in the hands of the bourgeois foreigners trading here.[30]

This kind of defense was necessary not only because the avant-garde community and the art press paid little attention to advertising, but because it was generally considered by committed Bolsheviks to be a politically suspect activity.[31]

Bolsheviks who had spent their formative years as underground agitators, in and out of tsarist prisons and exile—Mayakovsky himself had joined the Bolsheviks at age fourteen, and had been imprisoned for six months at age sixteen, five of them in solitary confinement—were shocked at the idea of running a government that required them to engage directly in business as trade and tax officials or as commercial and industrial managers.[32] As Lenin put it with some exasperation at the Eleventh Party Congress in March 1922:

> The point is that the responsible communist—even the best, who is certainly honest and devoted, who in the past endured imprisonment and did not fear death—does not know how to carry on trade, because he is not a businessman. He did not learn to trade, does not want to learn, and does not understand that he must start learning from the beginning.[33]

In early Soviet Russia, the compromise with the NEP business world was demanded by the vanguard Bolshevik party itself, complicating further the avant-garde's traditional opposition to mass commercial culture. By overcoming their antibourgeois scruples and following Lenin's command to "learn to trade," Rodchenko and Mayakovsky challenged the central modernist myth, as outlined by Bürger, of the necessary autonomy of the avant-garde from mass culture; their work was critical, avant-garde, and commercial at the same time.

The advertising business became firmly established in fall 1923. The first collaborative Rodchenko–Mayakovsky ads had appeared in quick succession from June 30 to July 3, including those for GUM, and Mayakovsky on his own had written the text and drawn the picture for an advertisement for Mospoligraf that appeared on July 1 in the journal *Krasnaia niva*. But Mayakovsky then left for a long trip abroad, interrupting the new venture. As soon as he returned in late

September, however, work for GUM recommenced, augmented from October 2 on with the work for Mossel'prom and eventually also for Rezinotrest, the State Rubber Trust, Chaieupravlenie, the State Tea Directorate, Gosizdat, the State Publishing House, and further work for Mospoligaf. Their work was concentrated most heavily in the last three months of 1923 and the first months of 1924, though it continued at less breakneck pace throughout 1924 and into early 1925. Even within the brief eight-year tenure of NEP (1921–c. 1928), there were significant fluctuations in official policy on the permissibility of private manufacture and trade in response to both party and popular outrage at the unexpected prosperity of the Nepmen. For example, the government launched a major crackdown on private trade in the late fall of 1923, and the situation stabilized and again became congenial to private business only in early 1925. This meant that Rodchenko and Mayakovsky entered into their business venture at the height of the power of private trade, and stayed on for the duration of the battle against the private sector that continued for more than a year, right in the middle of NEP.

We have an account of how they worked from Rodchenko's memoirs, written in 1939. Mayakovsky ran the business side of things; with his fame and compelling personal presence, he acted as the customer representative. In the mornings, he would visit the various customers, delivering completed orders and receiving payment. He would also take new orders and occasionally solicit new customers, carrying with him a portfolio of their work that Rodchenko had put together. He sometimes received statistical material and other product information that he would have to read through. In the evenings, Rodchenko would stop by his house to pick up the new texts he had written during the day and receive payment for the previous day's work. Rodchenko would then return home to his studio, where his students from the art school VKhUTEMAS would help him realize his designs, often through the night. The Rodchenko–Mayakovsky business successfully colonized one whole sector of public visual culture in Moscow with Constructivist values. Rodchenko's hyperbolic claim for the scope of their work has often been cited: "All of Moscow was covered with our work. . . . We made about fifty posters, about one hundred signboards, wrappers, containers, illuminated advertisements, advertising columns, illustrations in magazines and newspapers."[34]

They developed a graphic visual language and critical approach in their advertising that can be characterized as specifically Constructivist in the most meaningful sense of that term: they used the same visual and poetic forms derived from the modernist experimentation that led to other Constructivist works, in order to promote a more conscious and organized relation to socialist commodity objects. At their best, their ads present a crisp diagramming of the excess of desire that defines capitalist consumption. The solutions that the ads offer to this excess continue to explore the doubleness of revolutionary desire that formed the heart of "About This." Some of their ads develop a language of protest against excess that emphasizes utility and collectivity, as in Mayakovsky's utopian thirtieth century, while others depart from a model of use-value to interpret sympathetically the pervasiveness of commodity desire that continued to dominate in the transitional era of NEP, as in Mayakovsky's self-recognition as the contented lover within *meshchanskii byt*.

Mossel'prom: A Case Study of Bolshevik Business

Two of Rodchenko and Mayakovsky's earliest efforts for Mossel'prom, from the first days of October 1923, embody the utilitarian, firmly anti-NEP strand of their project. In these posters advertising cooking oil and bread (figures 4.11, 4.12), Mayakovsky's jingles address working-class Soviet consumers directly and without irony.[35] In the cooking oil ad, the slogan reads: "Cooking oil. Attention working masses. Three times cheaper than butter! More nutritious than other oils! Nowhere else but Mossel'prom." The bread advertisement announces: "Workers: High prices and NEP shouldn't scare you. Buy cheap bread! Discounts starting at 15%. In all the stores and kiosks of Mossel'prom, two steps from any home."

In early October 1923, consumer prices rose to their highest level since the inception of NEP. The situation was so acute that the government closed many private businesses, slashed state credit to private traders by more than half, arrested or restricted the trading privileges of private NEP business people, and began to consider regulating prices for consumer staples—all measures that contradicted the market principles of NEP.[36] Appearing at a moment of crisis-level high prices, these oil and bread ads speak in commonsense terms to an audience presumed to have limited resources. Mayakovsky's slogans do not appeal to an order of fantasy beyond the products' use value as nutritious, everyday foods. That is left to Rodchenko's performative Constructivist graphics, which establish the mundane oil bottles and loaves of bread within the field of desire for all things modern. Rodchenko deploys an array of effective graphic devices: the geometric blocking of the visual space; the wide, evenly spaced, almost vibrating stripes; and, most strikingly, the use of a central geometric shape—the circle surrounding the oil bottles, the diamond enclosing the bread—ringed by an outline of white against the stripes, causing the shapes to stand out like targets. The modernist glamour of the graphics rubs off onto the dull but useful products. Most strikingly, in the

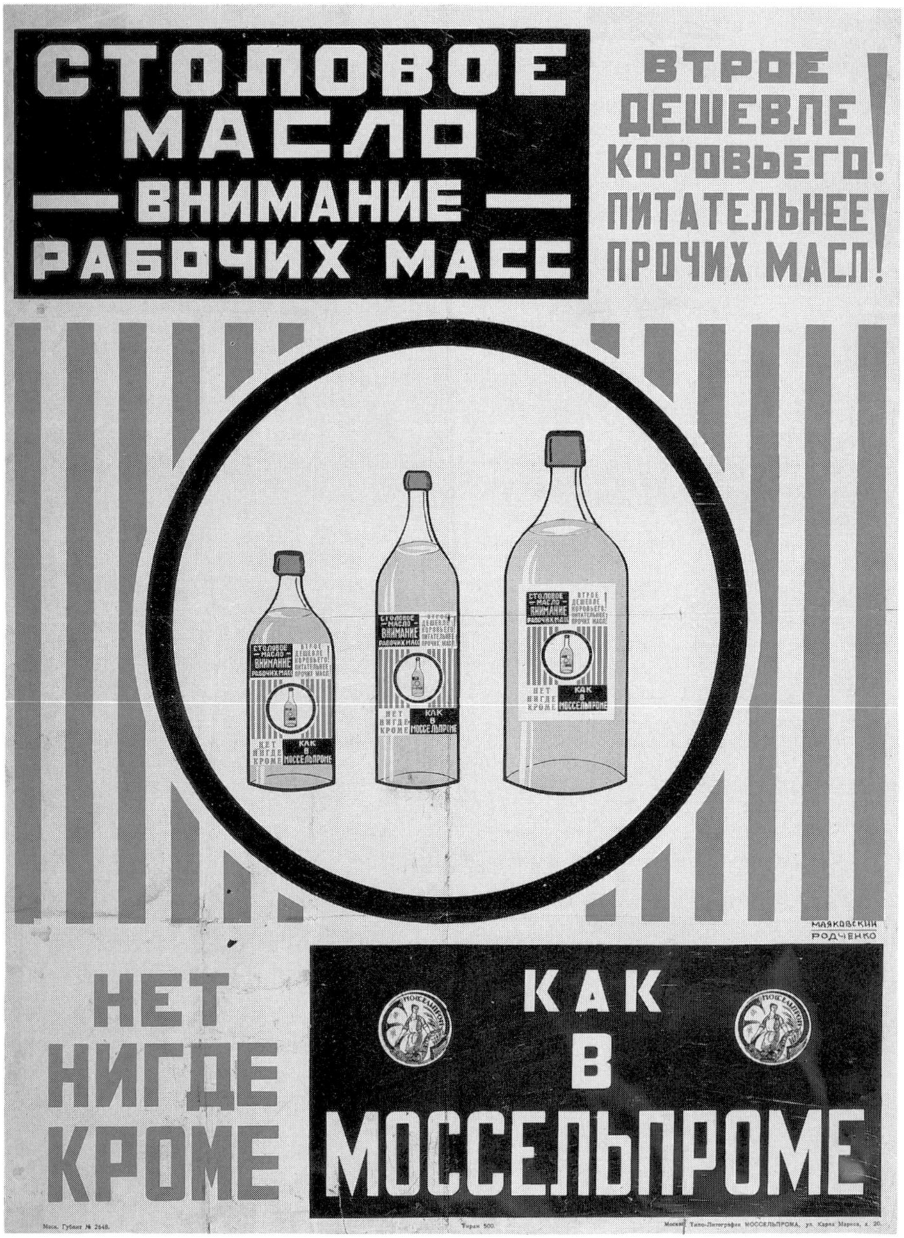

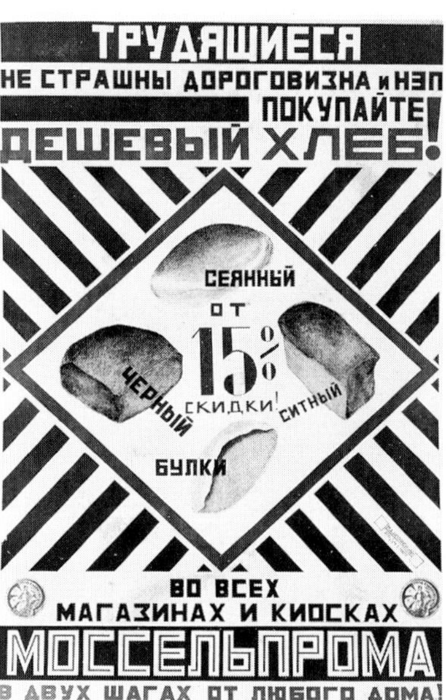

FIGURE 4.12
Aleksandr Rodchenko and Vladimir Mayakovsky, advertisement for Mossel'prom bread, 1923. Private collection.

FIGURE 4.11
Aleksandr Rodchenko and Vladimir Mayakovsky, advertising poster for Mossel'prom cooking oil, 1923. Merrill C. Berman Collection. See plate 13.

oil ad, the labels on the bottles repeat the poster itself in an effect of *mise-en-abîme*, suggesting an infinite progression and regression of socialist objects not only into the future but also into the past.

These ads assure workers that they are not at the mercy of price-gauging private NEP businessmen for their daily staples. They also demonstrate the particular verbal and visual style of the Rodchenko–Mayakovsky venture that would become a valuable commercial trademark for Mossel'prom. They function almost as a pointed critique of Rodchenko's earlier, more ironic design efforts in the GUM ads, which bore a greater resemblance to the standard advertising imagery of the day than to his own modernist practice. He draws the oil bottles in the same deliberately simplified style as he drew the tea glass on the Tea Cookies box, but this time he frames them with red, vertical stripes that align perfectly with the bottles, animating their red caps and red-striped labels to make them part of a dynamic surface pattern. The bread advertisement uses photographic images of loaves of bread cut out from other mass-reproduced images, just as in the GUM ads, but instead of forming a juggled or floating jumble of objects, these four loaves are geometrically organized to fill each corner of the diamond. The optical effect of inward movement created by the angled graphic lines rushing in from each corner of the composition further highlights the individual loaves. Both texts also contain what would become Rodchenko's typographic signature in the Mossel'prom series: large, stylized exclamation points as tall as two or three lines of text. The catchy jingle from the cooking oil ad, "Nowhere else but Mossel'prom" (nee-gdye-krom-ye-kak-v-mos-sel'-prom-ye), would become an element of almost all their future Mossel'prom ads, and became a popular catchphrase in 1920s Moscow. In his autobiography, Mayakovsky wrote that "in spite of the derisive whooping of the poets, I still consider 'Nowhere else but Mossel'prom' to be poetry of the highest qualification."[37]

When the oil and bread ads appeared in print form in the newspaper *Izvestiia*, they stood out from the surrounding ads not only by their politicized language of class identity and bodily need, but by their size and striking visuals. As a state-owned enterprise, Mossel'prom received favorable rates on advertising space in the state-monopolized press.[38] It could afford more space, and more expensively illustrated ads, than smaller enterprises, as the page on which the cooking oil ad appeared on October 5, 1923, demonstrates (figure 4.13). The most extreme NEP-era contrast is with the small ads to the upper left of the oil ad; one announces in Latin letters the "Dinai Fox-Trot, Koncert-Cabaret," and to its left appears a notice in cyrillic of another cabaret named the "Ampir," open from three o'clock in the afternoon until four o'clock in the morning. These cabarets halls were the expensive haunts of the NEP profiteers.

It is not surprising that Constructivist advertisements would speak in a pro-Bolshevik, anti-NEP-business language, yet the picture of the *Reklam-Konstruktor* advertising business is more complicated. Rodchenko and Mayakovsky entered into the venture as businessmen, and became involved in the contradictions of the NEP-era business world. Mayakovsky, for example, proved himself to be an astute businessman by putting together an official price list for the various artistic labor costs involved in their commercial design work. This list was submitted to, and approved by, the Tariff-Regulating Department of the Section for Fine Arts of the Moscow Region Union of Art Workers. The list is detailed, and the prices are high: from 100 to 150 rubles for large, complex posters; from 30 to 60 rubles for more modest ones; 15 rubles for a candy wrapper; 30 rubles for a larger chocolate bar wrapper; 40 rubles for one side of a box, but 30 rubles per side for a box decorated on all sides; and so on.[39] (Although the value of the ruble fluctuated in the unstable NEP economy, we can get a sense of the meaning of these prices by considering that in the Mossel'prom annual report covering October 1923 to April 1924, workers at the Moscow factories are reported to earn between 18 and 21 rubles per month.)[40]

The letter with which this price list was submitted on May 15, 1924, signed by Mayakovsky, Rodchenko, and the Constructivist Anton Lavinskii, attempted to put an antibusiness, proto–planned economy spin on their understandable desire to be guaranteed uniformly high prices on their labor:

> We are the *Lef* group, executing all manner of industrial-artistic work for many different government and public institutions. Despite the uniformity of the work and the possibility of setting a single, firm price on it, on each new occasion we are forced to argue about the price with people who often have no understanding of the character and appropriate remuneration of artistic labor.
>
> In view of this, we request that you discuss and confirm . . . a firm price for certain basic aspects of our art. These prices will first of all defend the artist from the random tastes of the employer and save the artist from superfluous and humiliating trade negotiations, and secondly, they will guarantee for the institution the correctness of the sum requested by the artist.[41]

Their desire to avoid humiliating negotiations with uninformed employers was certainly genuine, and partly motivated by a distaste for the business world, but

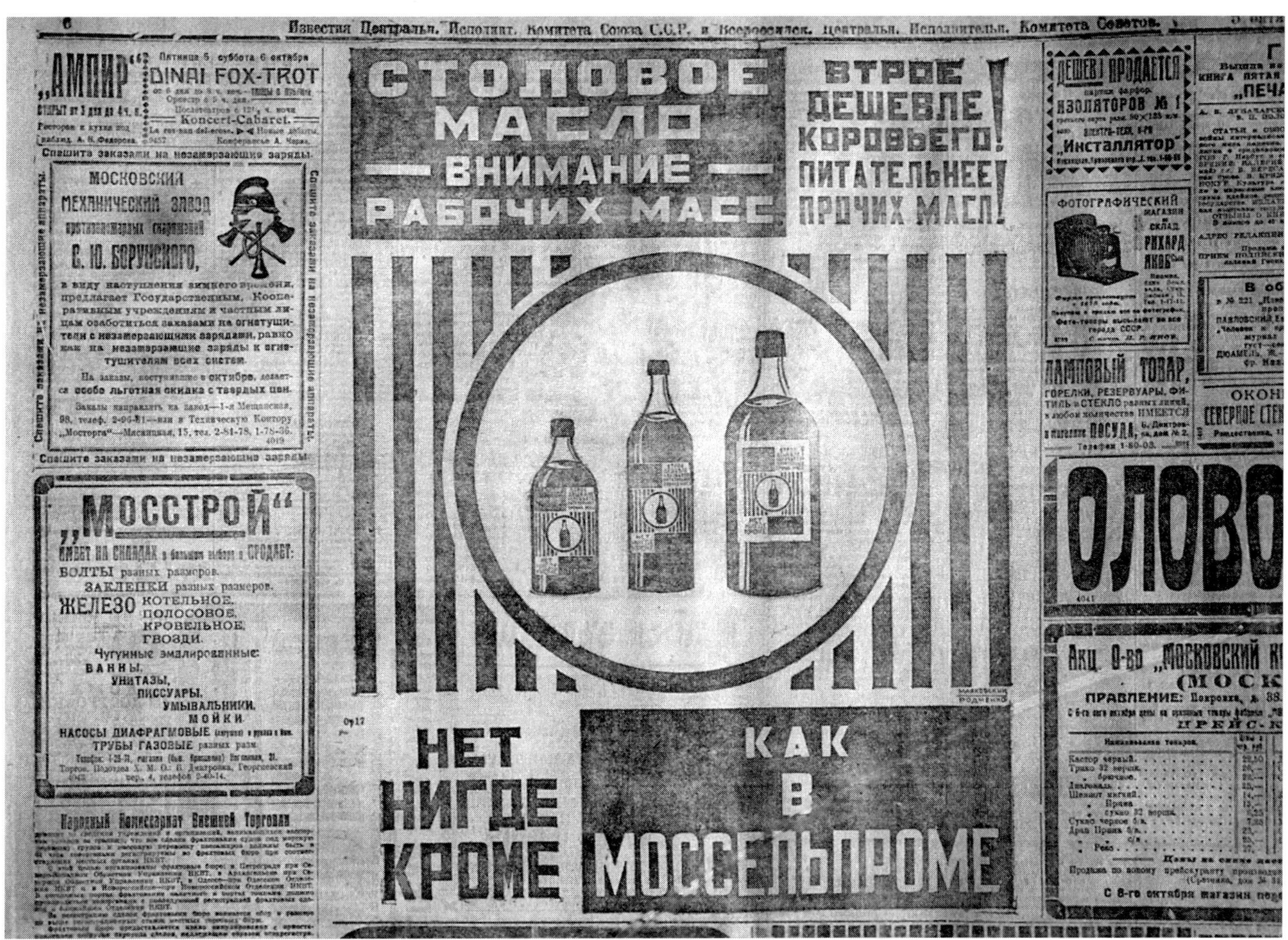

Известия Центральн. Исполнит. Комитета Союза С.С.Р. и Всероссийск. центральн. Исполнительн. Комитета Советов.

„АМПИР"

DINAI FOX-TROT

Konzert-Cabaret.

Спешите заказами на незамерзающие заряды.

МОСКОВСКИЙ МЕХАНИЧЕСКИЙ ЗАВОД

С. Ю. БОРУЦКОГО,

в виду наступления зимнего времени, предлагает Государственным, Кооперативным учреждениям и частным лицам озаботиться заказами на огнетушители с незамерзающими зарядами, равно как на незамерзающие заряды к огнетушителям всех систем.

„МОССТРОЙ"

ИМЕЕТ НА СКЛАДАХ в большом выборе и ПРОДАЕТ:

БОЛТЫ разных размеров.

ЗАКЛЕПКИ разных размеров.

ЖЕЛЕЗО КОТЕЛЬНОЕ. ПОЛОСОВОЕ. КРОВЕЛЬНОЕ. ГВОЗДИ.

Чугунные эмалированные:

ВАННЫ,

УНИТАЗЫ,

ПИССУАРЫ,

УМЫВАЛЬНИКИ,

МОЙКИ

НАСОСЫ ДИАФРАГМОВЫЕ

ТРУБЫ ГАЗОВЫЕ разных разм.

Народный Комиссариат Внешней Торговли

СТОЛОВОЕ МАСЛО

— ВНИМАНИЕ —

РАБОЧИХ МАСС

ВТРОЕ ДЕШЕВЛЕ КОРОВЬЕГО!

ПИТАТЕЛЬНЕЕ ПРОЧИХ МАСЛ!

НЕТ НИГДЕ КРОМЕ

КАК В МОССЕЛЬПРОМЕ

ДЕШЕВО ПРОДАЕТСЯ

ИЗОЛЯТОРОВ № 1

„Инсталлятор"

ФОТОГРАФИЧЕСКИЙ МАГАЗИН и СКЛАД РИХАРД ЯКОБСОН

ЛАМПОВЫЙ ТОВАР,

ГОРЕЛКИ, РЕЗЕРВУАРЫ, ФИТИЛЬ и СТЕКЛО

ПОСУДА

ОКОН

СЕВЕРНОЕ СТЕ

ОЛОВО

Акц. О-во „МОСКОВСКИЙ К

ПРАВЛЕНИЕ:

ПРЕЙС-К

С 8-го октября магазин

FIGURE 4.13

Aleksandr Rodchenko and Vladimir Mayakovsky, advertisement for Mossel'prom cooking oil in *Izvestiia*, October 5, 1923. Photo by the author.

it was also motivated by their need to earn money in that world. Their position exemplifies the inherent contradiction of the idealistic notion of the artist-constructor or left cultural worker entering production in step with the proletariat. Like Popova and Stepanova at the First State Cotton-Printing Factory, although they wanted to participate in socialist production, Rodchenko and Mayakovsky interacted not with workers on the factory floor, but with the managers and specialists of NEP enterprises known as "red managers" or "red industrialists." Often of bourgeois origins, these managers had been businessmen before the revolution and were hired by Soviet businesses to improve profits. They were responsible for marketing and were therefore the very employers with "random tastes" with whom Mayakovsky had to negotiate. The letter and price list present the artists as hired laborers protecting themselves from management as a way to deflect any perception that their work as highly paid, skilled specialists placed them in a managerial position equivalent to that of the red managers.[42]

As one of the more financially successful state industrial concerns, Mossel'prom epitomized the contradictions of socialist production during NEP, when state companies had to employ the marketing and labor practices of capitalism to compete with private businesses. It included confectionery and cigarette factories, bakeries, a sausage and canned goods factory, two breweries, and a number of restaurants, cafeterias, and pubs. In addition to everyday necessities, the various Mossel'prom factories thus also produced inexpensive luxuries, which were precisely the kinds of commodities that were widely sold by private traders: their low overhead and transportability made them easy to sell from mobile sites such as kiosks and sidewalk stands. Most private traders were forced to operate on a small, flexible scale because state imposition of restrictions and taxes was both severe and unpredictable. Mossel'prom products that profited the state therefore competed directly with imported and privately made goods, placing the Rodchenko–Mayakovsky advertising venture at the heart of the NEP struggle to produce a socialist form of consumption that would equal and surpass the capitalist one.

Mossel'prom was one of the Soviet enterprises that made progress in this endeavor. After recovering from early financial difficulties, especially those caused by the shortages of raw materials suffered by most early Soviet factories, in mid-1923 Mossel'prom started turning a healthy profit. By October of 1924, the director, V. Krasnov, could deliver a relaxed and glowing annual report to a management meeting, stressing the new acquisitions of the organization in the previous year, such as the venerable Einem confectionery factory, its strong credit standing, its profitability, and its excellent record of steadily decreasing the credit given to private traders and the amount of raw materials purchased from them.[43] Yet the financial success of Mossel'prom as a Soviet state enterprise did not guarantee that it could operate according to egalitarian socialist labor principles. We learn from Krasnov, for example, that workers in a Mossel'prom brewery lived in beer barrels owing to lack of housing.[44] He also reported on the wages of Mossel'prom factory workers (between 18 and 21 rubles per month, as mentioned above) without referring to the massive income disparity between workers and management. The payrolls of the Mossel'prom white-collar workers held in the Mossel'prom archives reveal that in 1924 they earned from 120 to 225 rubles per month, with a very few managers earning 250 rubles and the two vice-directors earning 360 rubles per month.[45] These illegally high salaries were made possible through the addition of special, personal salaries, called *spetsstavki*, above and beyond the more modest baseline salaries, which hovered around 100 to 120 rubles per month.

An unexpected name appears on the Mossel'prom managerial payroll starting in October 1924: *Lef* theorist Osip Brik, author of "Into Production!," earning a full 250 rubles per month.[46] Brik is listed as the Manager of the Cultural Bureau, under the Pubs Section of the Department of Retail Trade. Turning up in the archive in the minutes of business meetings and in internal memos, Brik appears to have held a prosaic, full-time managerial job at Mossel'prom for at least a year—a fact never mentioned in the extensive biographical literature on this pivotal figure in the Soviet left avant-garde, or in the exhaustive documentation of the triangular relationship of Osip Brik, his wife Lili Brik, and Mayakovsky.[47] Brik was using his skills to promote progressive culture in a popular venue—agitational theatrical entertainments in the Mossel'prom pubs, including the well-known "Blue Blouse" players—and earning a good paycheck in hard times. The fact is significant because it fills out the picture of the complex allegiances engendered by NEP. Osip Brik was the colleague of the very philistine managers with "random tastes" whom Rodchenko and Mayakovsky derided. Brik probably derided them for their philistinism too, but he was charged with increasing the profitability of the Mossel'prom pubs, just as his manager colleagues were charged with increasing the sale of caramels, cookies, and cigarettes, and he took the charge seriously.

Brik also turned his business acumen to the debates on advertising, publishing two articles on the subject in the magazine *Zhurnalist* (Journalist). In the first, written in June 1923 in support of Mayakovsky's imminent plans to enter advertising, Brik asserts that "advertising not only promotes commerce, it also promotes culture; it has an enormous agitational and cultural significance, especially in our peasant Russia."[48] He chooses the fire extinguisher as his example of a modern commodity that legitimately requires advertising to peasants, because it would provide valuable protection for wooden peasant huts. On the other hand, he cautions, ads for liquor, expensive perfumes, and cosmetic powders have little cultural significance. Writing a year later in the same magazine, however, after viewing Mayakovsky and Rodchenko's many advertisements—including some for Mossel'prom beer and the GUM ladies' department with its perfumes and cosmetics—and about to begin a managerial job in a NEP enterprise himself, he is more open to the cultural significance of commodity desire in the broader sense. He recognizes that the goal of advertising is not simply to inform consumers of the existence of a useful thing, but to create the need for that thing in the consumer: "there are cases when it is necessary *to create a contingent of buyers,* i.e. to convince people to buy who had not considered buying this thing, to whom it seemed that the suggestion of buying this commodity could never be directed at them."[49]

Brik's language is almost identical to that of Marx in his most complex articulation of the dialectic of production and consumption, in the introduction to the *Grundrisse*. Criticizing the simplistic notion that use value is only about satisfying bedrock bodily need, Marx writes:

> Hunger is hunger, but the hunger gratified by cooked meat eaten with a knife and fork is a different hunger from that which bolts down raw meat with the aid of hand, nail and tooth. Production thus produces not only the object but also the manner of consumption, not only objectively but subjectively. Production thus creates the consumer. [It] not only supplies a material for the need, but it also supplies a need for the material.[50]

Although Marx himself would not elaborate a socialist theory of consumption, his brief remarks here demonstrate that provoking or soliciting consumer desire cannot be understood as the exclusive domain of profiteering capitalist business practices, but is the very basis of the development of mass production. Brik concludes his article by pointing to "the enormous significance in business of mastering the wishes of the customer."[51] In his view, then, socialist advertising must confront the desire of the consumer more generally, and not only in bona fide instances of the desire's impeccable "cultural significance."

Constructivist Advertisements as Transitional Objects: Between Capitalist Past and Socialist Future

Rodchenko and Mayakovsky's earnest advertisements for nutritious cooking oil and cheap bread from Mossel'prom, and Brik's proposed advertisement for the culturally significant fire extinguisher, promoted the fulfillment of genuine human needs, as opposed to the endless commodity desire promoted by capitalism. The stern contrast between fire extinguisher and cosmetic powders in the Brik essay, and between the illicit late-night cabarets and upright oil bottles on the *Izvestiia* newspaper page, is what we would expect from left cultural workers in NEP Russia. Yet some of the Rodchenko–Mayakovsky advertisements enact the contrast between capitalist past and socialist future within the space of the images themselves, offering, like Brik's essay, a critical analysis of the mechanisms of object desire in the transitional moment of NEP. In a double critique, both socialist austerity and capitalist excess are subjected to interpretation.

Rather than attempting to eradicate or denigrate any memory of the capitalist past—the usual strategy of the before–after style of Bolshevik propaganda posters—some of Rodchenko and Mayakovsky's commercial graphics deliberately recall the wish-images of the past by invoking outmoded verbal and visual images. Their advertisement for Shutka brand Mossel'prom cigarettes of October 4, 1923 (figure 4.14) incorporates images of the actual Shutka cigarette box, with its old-fashioned and markedly prerevolutionary design featuring a gypsy-type woman with a red flower in her hair (figure 4.15). In a different strategy from the *mise-en-abîme* effect of the labels on the bottles in the cooking oil poster, which produced a totalizing system of austere socialist objects stretching from the past into the future, the double presence of the gypsy woman in this advertisement allows a familiar material object from the capitalist past to remain visible in the present of Mossel'prom. The graphics follow the format of all Rodchenko's cigarette ads for Mossel'prom: two large, attention-grabbing exclamation points border the image at left and right, against a background of two vertical blocks of color that also extend across the bottom of the image in a third horizontal block, on which the "Nowhere else but Mossel'prom" slogan appears. The center of the image always includes the brand name and one or more pictures of the cigarette box itself, as well as a rhyme by Mayakovsky.

Like Rodchenko's inclusion of the prerevolutionary image from the cigarette box, Mayakovsky's rhyme evokes a temporal doubleness. At the most obvious level of meaning, it picks up on the brand name Shutka, which means "joke": "Not as a joke, but seriously: tastier than oranges, more perfumed than roses."

The sensuous pleasures of oranges and fresh roses were expensive luxuries on the NEP market, while low-quality, state-produced tobacco (Shutka was the lowest-category tobacco, Sort IIB, that Mossel'prom sold) was affordable to everyone.[52] The rhyme consciously invokes working-class camaraderie: "we don't need the Nepman's oranges." But it also evokes a specific, nineteenth-century romance that hinges on cigarettes, namely, Georges Bizet's popular opera *Carmen*. The title character Carmen is a gypsy girl who works in a tobacco factory. She wears strongly scented flowers in her hair and eats oranges; the city square in Seville, which forms the setting for several key scenes in the opera, is populated with cigarette girls and orange sellers.[53] Rodchenko and Mayakovsky promote a collective nostalgia for smoking by invoking the sexualized image of the cigarette girl—both the fictional gypsy Carmen and the inevitable contemporary association with Mossel'prom cigarette girls—and the vaguely revolutionary associations of Bizet's operatic narrative, in which the character of Carmen was granted a strong proletarian earthiness. Mayakovsky's literary allusion to Carmen might seem to be at odds with the more ham-handed proletarian appeal of his rhyme, but it has the fortunate

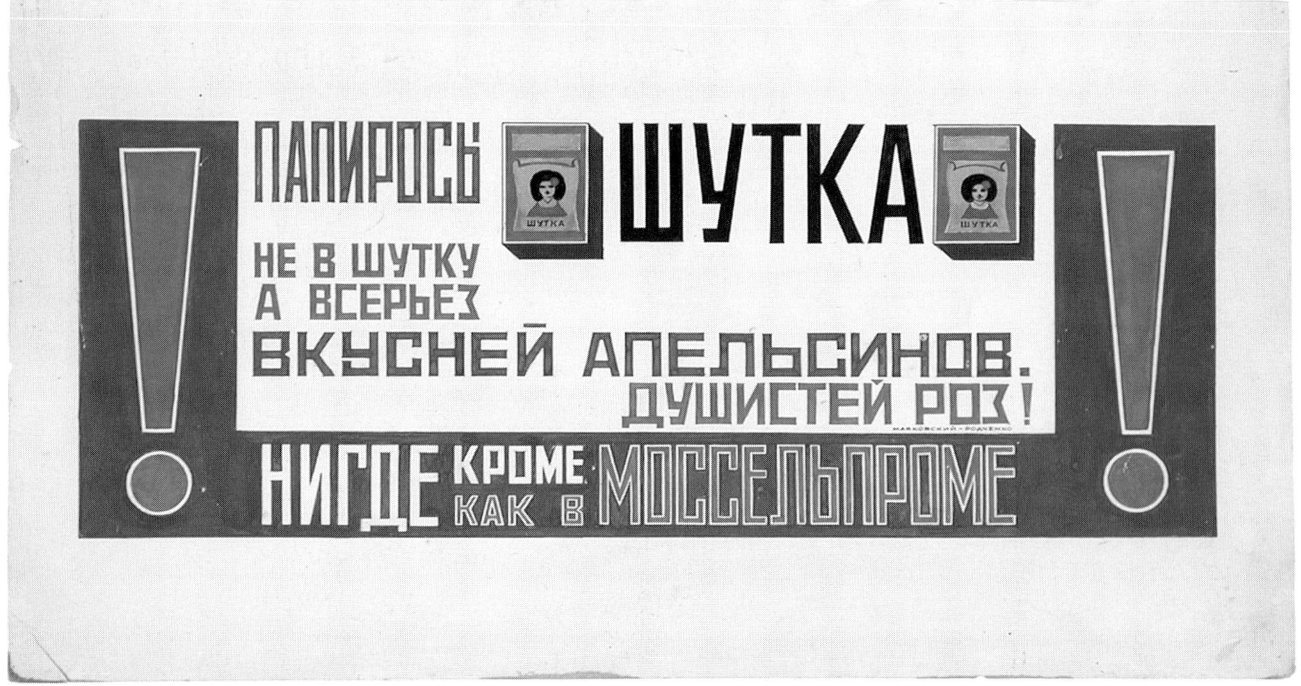

FIGURE 4.14
Aleksandr Rodchenko and Vladimir Mayakovsky, advertisement for Mossel'prom Shutka cigarettes, 1923. Gouache maquette. Howard Schickler Fine Art. See plate 14.

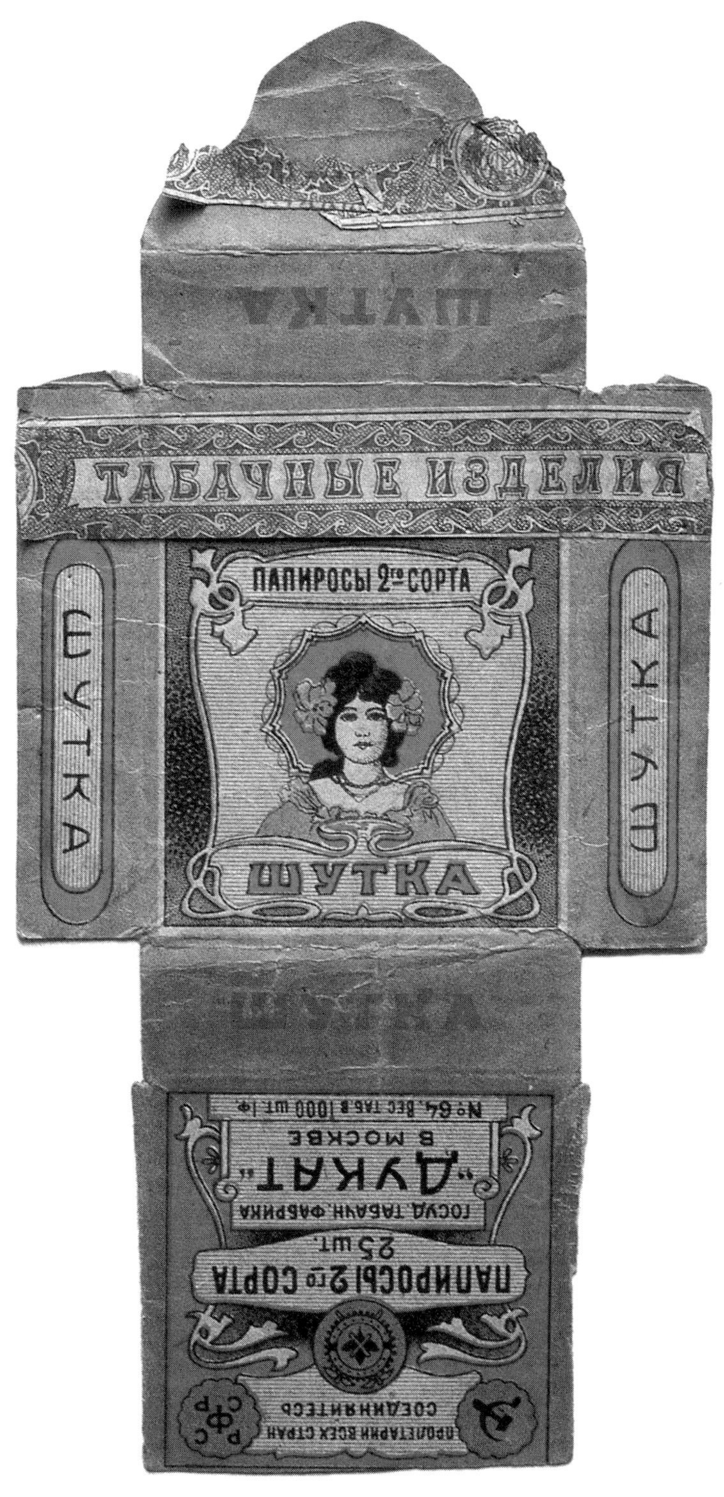

FIGURE 4.15
Box for Shutka cigarettes, early 1920s. Courtesy State Mayakovsky Museum, Moscow. Photo by the author. See plate 15.

effect of transforming the cheaply exploitative, exoticized female image on the original cigarette box into a more specific image of proletarian female power.

This complex verbal and visual image of nostalgia is graphically framed by Rodchenko's tall exclamation points. They function almost as indexical signs in the sense that they urge a directional emphasis, a "look here!," like Louis Althusser's famous example of the policeman shouting "Hey, you there!," or the pointing finger of propaganda posters.[54] An anonymous poster of 1924, for example, which was part of the government campaign exhorting workers to shop in state cooperative stores rather than the disorganized world of the private NEP traders, shows a humorless kerchiefed woman pointing directly out at the viewer (figure 4.16). The campaign fostered an image of woman as politically conscious and socially responsible; the poster's slogan announces: "Woman worker/homemaker! YOU are the principal consumer. Go to the cooperative store." Paradoxically, the gypsy woman on the Mossel'prom Shutka box and the stern, red-kerchiefed woman pointing out from the poster were both images of femininity disseminated by Soviet state-owned printing presses in 1923–1924. The Shutka ad proposes that the model of conscious, self-aware consumption represented by the woman in the poster is attainable without sacrificing all desires from the past; Rodchenko's organizing graphics and Mayakovsky's allusive rhyme attempt to redeem the romantic, sexualized image of the gypsy woman for a newly conscious proletarian consumer.

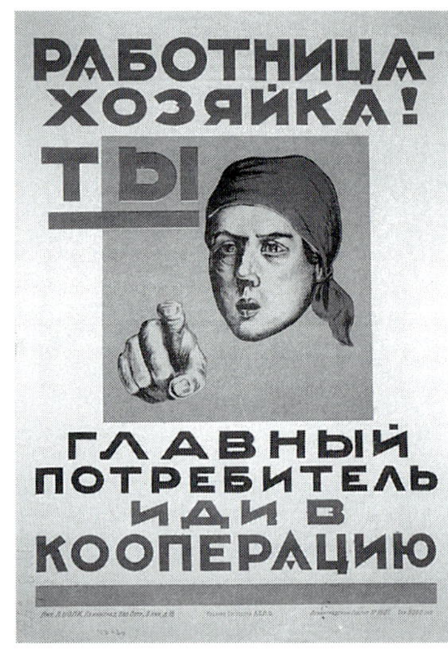

FIGURE 4.16
Poster: "Woman worker/homemaker! You are the principal consumer. Go to the cooperative store," 1924. Courtesy Russian State Library Department of Graphics, Moscow. Photo by the author.

The incorporation of a desire stemming from the prerevolutionary past is more explicit in Mayakovsky's slogan for Mossel'prom Red October brand cookies. In their advertising poster of October 6, 1923, the little girl proudly declares: "I EAT cookies from the Red October factory, the former Einem" (figure 4.17). Einem was a major confectionery factory and well-known brand name before the revolution, so the slogan reminds viewers of the former life of this commodity. Rodchenko's image echoes this nonrevolutionary effect by incorporating a photographic image of a girl's head that is strangely reconfigured by the addition of eye shadow, thinly penciled brows, and bright red lipstick, giving her the vaguely lascivious look of an adult flapper that is not at all like the wholesome little Communist girl one would expect to eat the Red October brand. Yet his use of photomontage and the modernist framing graphics characteristic of all his Mossel'prom designs—the wide stripes of blue color and the geometric shape of the hexagon framing the central image—are the visual counterparts of the new brand name Red October, pointing toward the organized, collective future. The cavalcade of ten large Red October cookies jostling their way into the girl's mouth, the first in line already forcing itself in beneath the strip of her little white teeth,

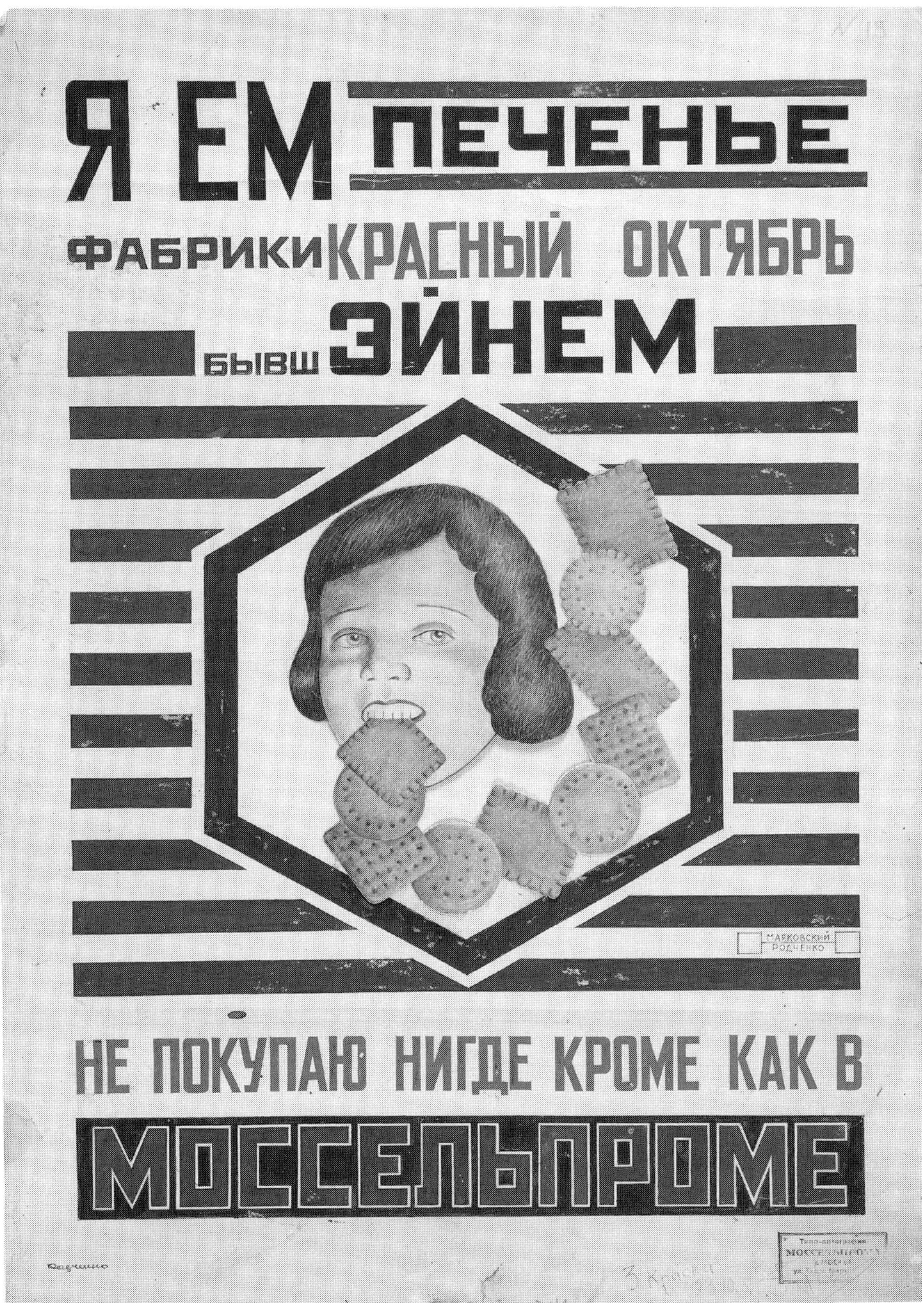

FIGURE 4.17
Aleksandr Rodchenko and Vladimir Mayakovsky, advertising poster for Red October cookies, 1923. Howard Schickler Fine Art. See plate 16.

makes this an iconic image of socialist consumption as literal ingestion. The hooklike shape and yellowish-brown color of the train of cookies even mimic the depiction of the human digestive system in anatomical drawings, while the layered shapes of the cookies also resemble children's building blocks, suggesting the gradual, additive nature of this transitional process of transforming consumption. The NEP girl's ingestion of the socialist Red October cookies can be read as a metaphor for the transformation of the Soviet subject by the socialist object.

She announces that she eats socialist Red October cookies instead of Einem cookies, pointing toward the socialist future but reminding early Soviet viewers of Einem's capitalist past. A prerevolutionary Einem poster from the early 1900s, designed by the Menert brothers, also used an image of a little girl, in this case a giant, skipping lightly across a yellow Moscow River from the Kremlin toward the Einem factory, which lies on an island in the Moscow River to this day (figure 4.18). This poster's advertising slogan, "My first step is for Einem cookies," is also in the little girl's own voice, suggesting that in his Red October rhyme, Mayakovsky took his cue from this prerevolutionary ad or others like it. His jingle in fact insistently returns us to the nostalgic desire for this past, turning as it does on the rhyme between the girl's declarative "I eat!" (*Ia em!*, pronounced ya-yem) and the name "Einem" (eye-nyem) with the name Red October (*krasnyi oktiabr*) momentarily de-emphasized in the middle: "Ia em pechenie fabriki Krasnyi Oktiabr, byvshii Einem." "Byvshii" is the past participle of the verb "byt'," meaning to be, so the "having been" of Einem echoes after the comma, as it were, preserving the past desires lodged in its name. Rodchenko's typography emphasizes the word "Einem," centered just above the hexagon, by its size and thickness, at the visual expense of "Krasnyi oktiabr'," in thinner red lettering above it, to play up the temporal effect of Mayakovsky's rhyme.

Rodchenko's design itself produces this temporal effect: the spiral of photographic cookies snaking their way into the girl's mouth have their point of origin "outside" the image, just below the word "Einem," so that even though they are now Red October cookies, they can still be read as objects originating in the past and entering into the present of Red October, because the spiral is an inherently mobile, temporal form. The spiral of cookies breaches the border of the hexagon. Like the circle at the center of the cooking oil ad, the hexagon seems to cite deliberately the forms of Rodchenko's hanging *Spatial Constructions* series of 1920–1921, all of which had originated as flat geometric forms (figure 4.19). *Spatial Construction no. 10* begins its life as a flat, two-dimensional hexagon of plywood painted the color of metal, with a series of concentric hexagons carved straight

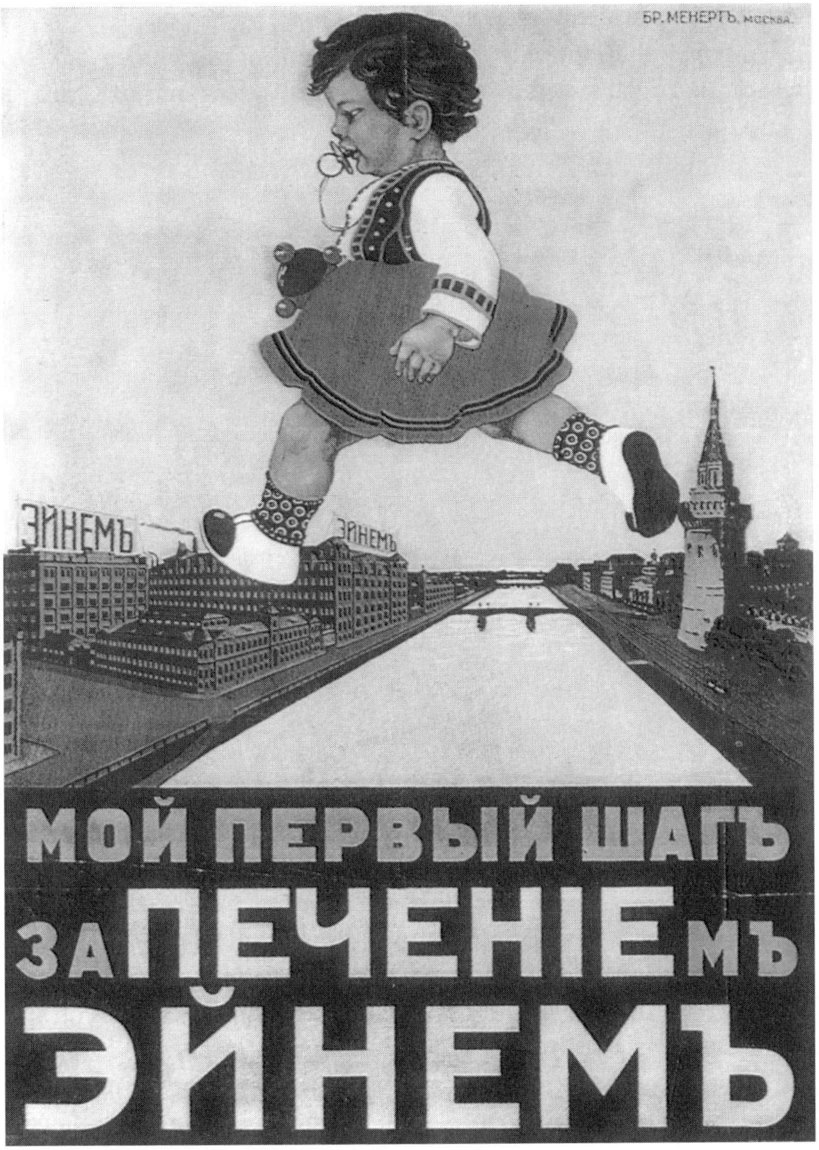

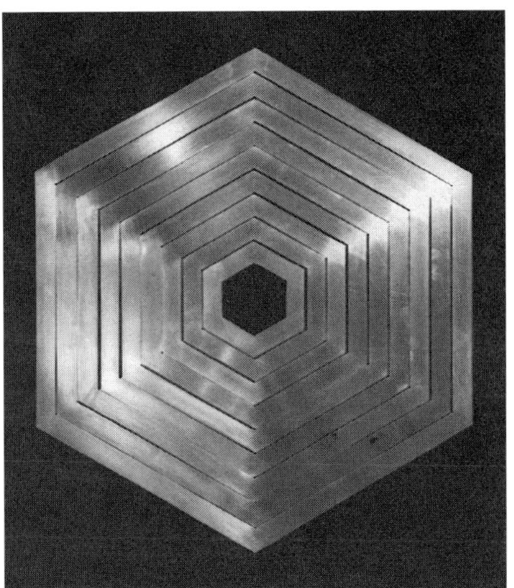

FIGURE 4.19
Aleksandr Rodchenko, *Spatial Construction no. 10* (closed view), 1921 (reconstruction by Aleksandr Lavrent'ev).

FIGURE 4.18
Menert Brothers, advertising poster for Einem cookies, early twentieth century. Courtesy Russian State Library Department of Graphics, Moscow. See plate 17.

through its surface. When each concentric section is opened out to a different point in space and the structure is suspended from above—as in the triangular, oval, hexagonal, and circular structures suspended from the ceiling in the installation photograph from the Obmokhu exhibition (see figure 4.6)—these lightweight constructions are infinitely transformable within the transparent logic of their own system. Their parts respond to air currents or human touch; but as set systems, rather than socialist objects, they do not respond to the social world, to culture, or to history. The Our Industry caramel box also begins life as a flat form, but will take on multiple aspects when its flaps are creased or folded or fitted into slots to form a resealable container, extending the systemic logic of transformation into the social world of NEP consumption. Later, in Rodchenko's design for a workers' club of 1925, this functional logic will reappear in the fold-out furniture designs. In the Red October poster, Rodchenko breaks the self-enclosed, logical system of his hexagonal spatial construction with the spiraling line of photographic reproductions of mass-produced cookies, which bring the sweet taste and sentimental associations of Einem into the Constructivist world of Red October. This curving spiral of cookies is the conceptual counterpart of the spiral effect of the labels on the oil bottles, where the *mise-en-abîme* produced the temporal sensation of infinite progression and regression into future and past. Yet it is also the conceptual opposite, because the cookie spiral carries the past of Einem into the present of Red October, while the oil bottle labels attempt, in more straightforwardly Bolshevik fashion, to obliterate the capitalist past.

Walter Benjamin imagined that the dreaming collective of bourgeois culture would awaken from the "dream sleep" of the commodity phantasmagoria into a socialist culture when the wish-images of what he called the "ur-past"—the mythic, egalitarian society of material abundance—would be made visible in the newest technological forms. Wish-images of the harmonious ur-past had left their traces embedded in the mass material culture of the recent, outmoded past—for him, in the material culture of the arcades, in the past of his grandparents—and would have to be redeemed in the new material forms of modernity in order to engender a socialist future.[55] Rodchenko's designs carry out Benjamin's prescription to the letter: they refer to the traces of the recently outmoded past—the old-fashioned engravings of industrial machinery on the Our Industry caramel box, or the little girl from the prerevolutionary Einem poster—and attempt to awaken them, through the citation of Constructivist objects like the *Spatial Constructions* series and modernist graphics, into the "now" of Mossel'prom.

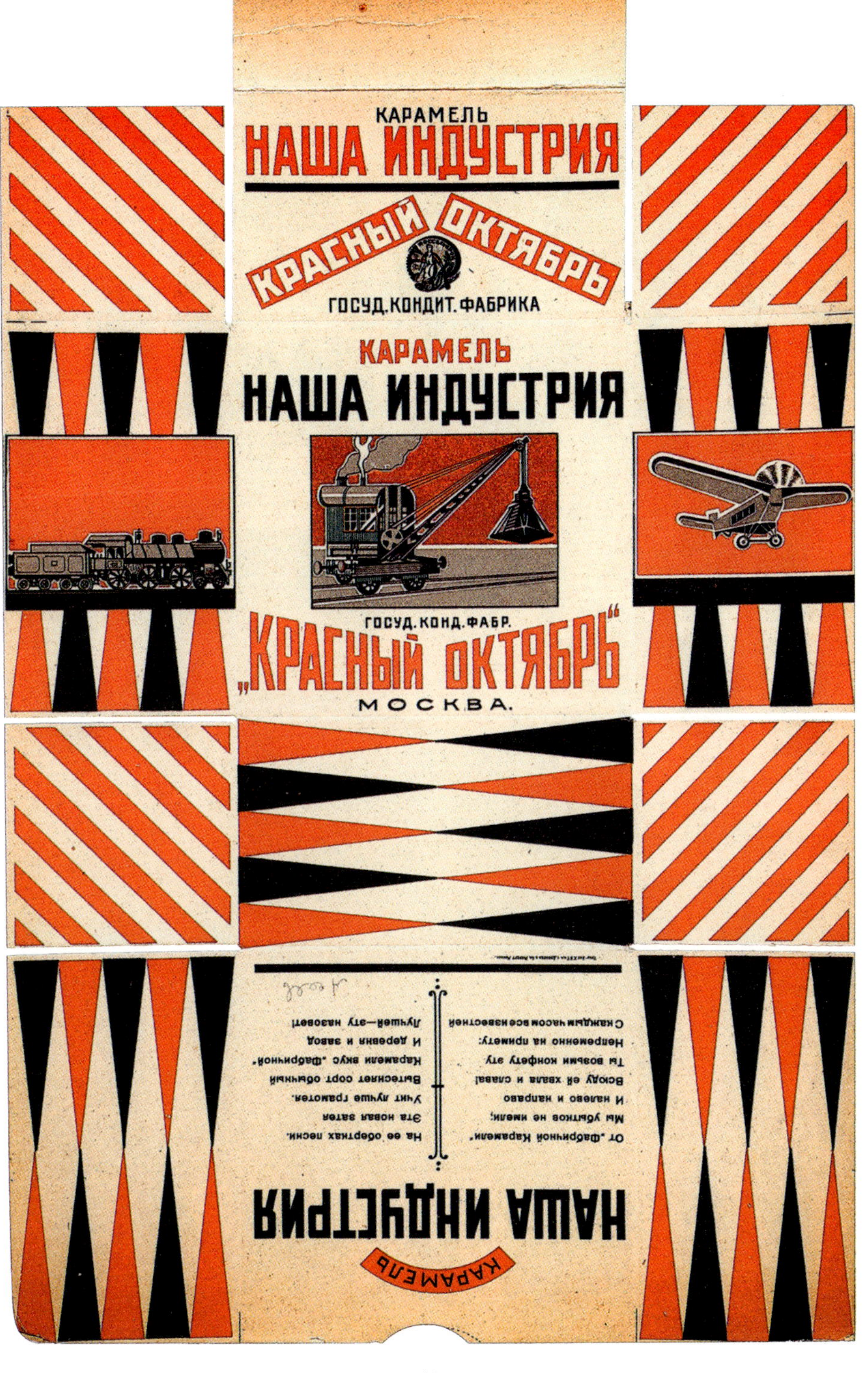

PLATE II

Aleksandr Rodchenko, box for Our Industry caramels, 1923.

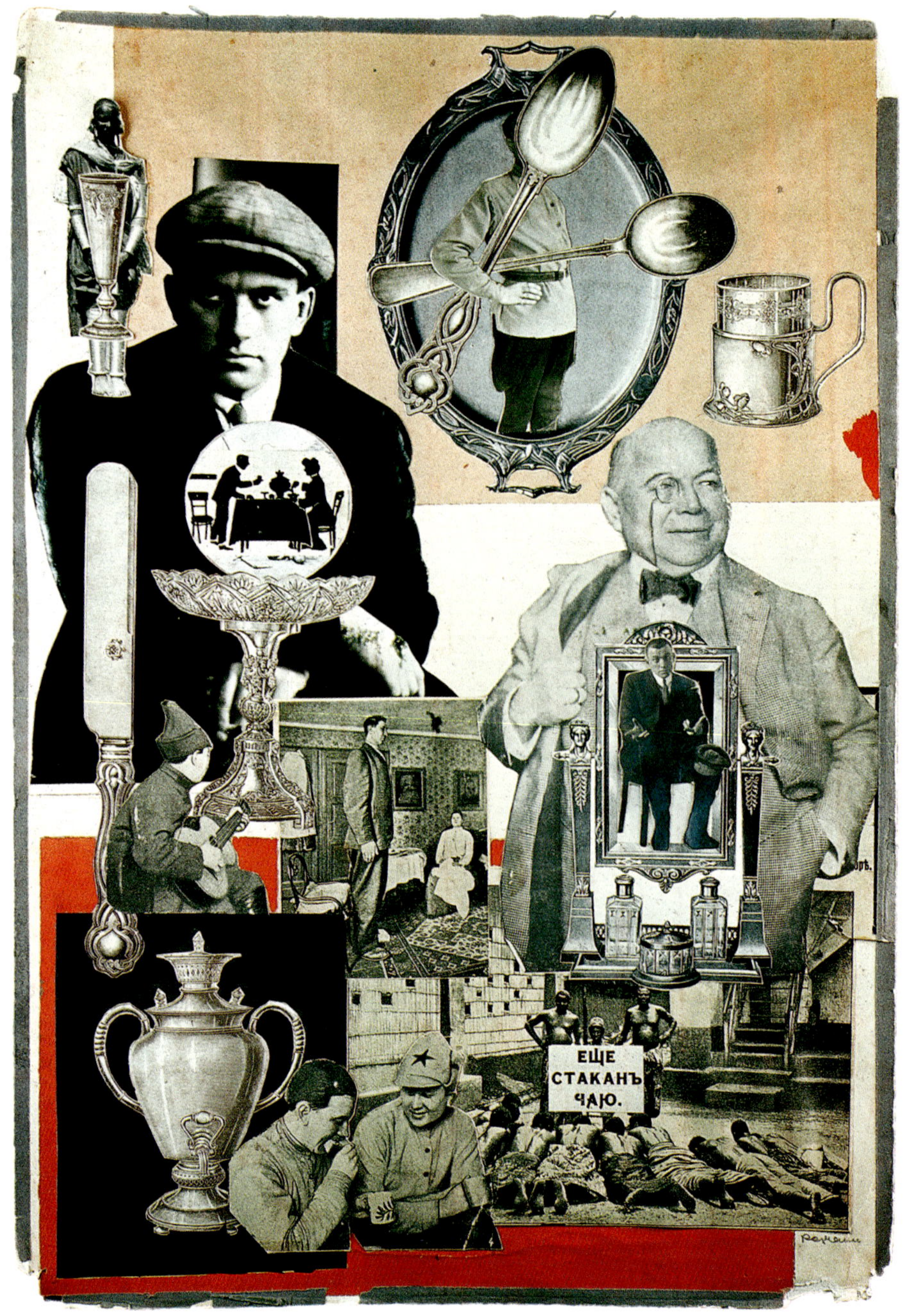

PLATE 12

Aleksandr Rodchenko, illustration for Vladimir Mayakovsky's "About This," accompanied by the lines "And the century stands / as it was / Unwhipped / the mare of *byt* won't budge." Maquette for book illustration, 1923. Cut-and-pasted printed papers and gelatin-silver photographs with india ink on cardboard, 1923. SCALA / Art Resource, N.Y.

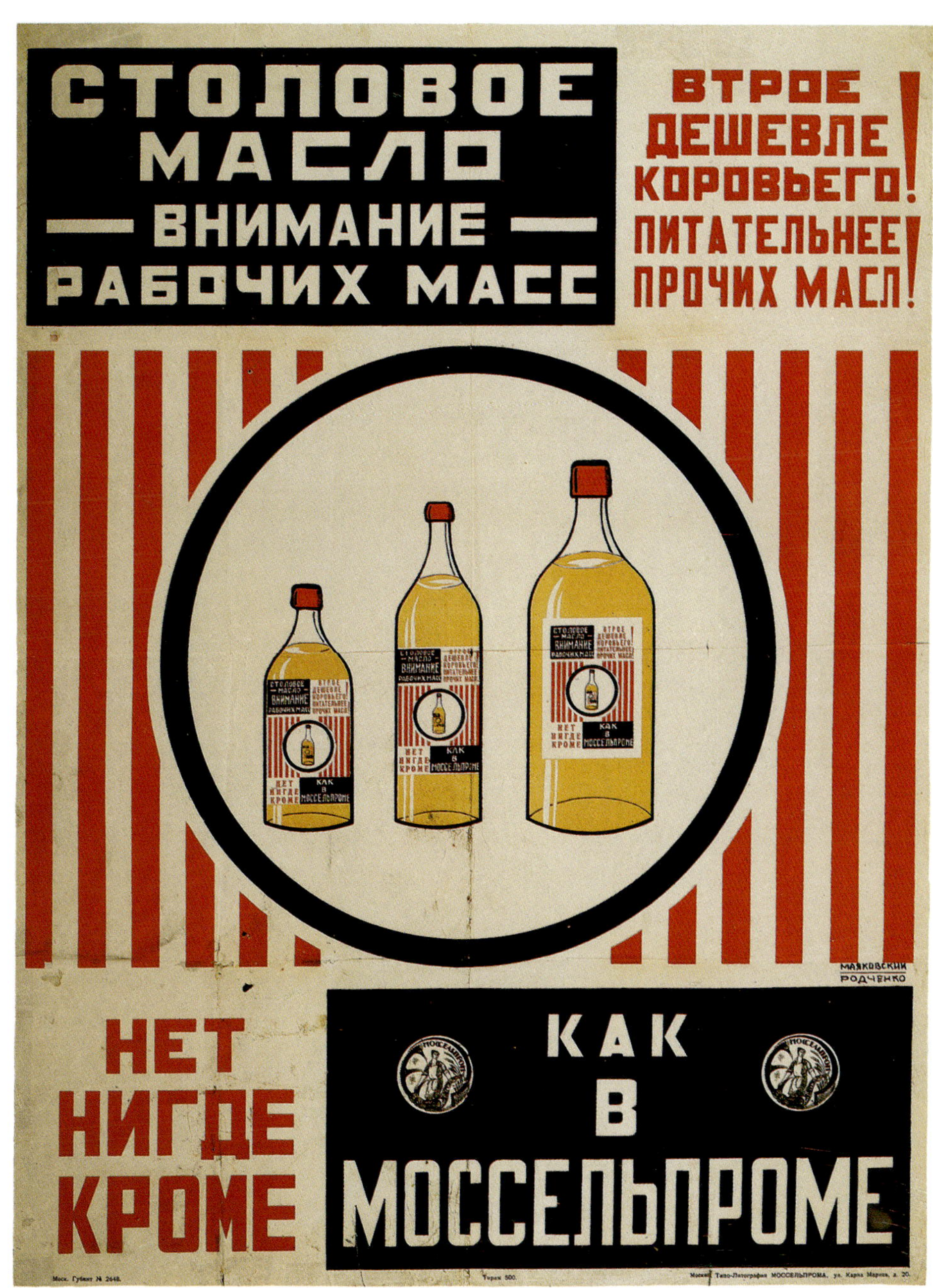

PLATE 13
Aleksandr Rodchenko and Vladimir Mayakovsky, advertising poster for Mossel'prom cooking oil, 1923.
Merrill C. Berman Collection.

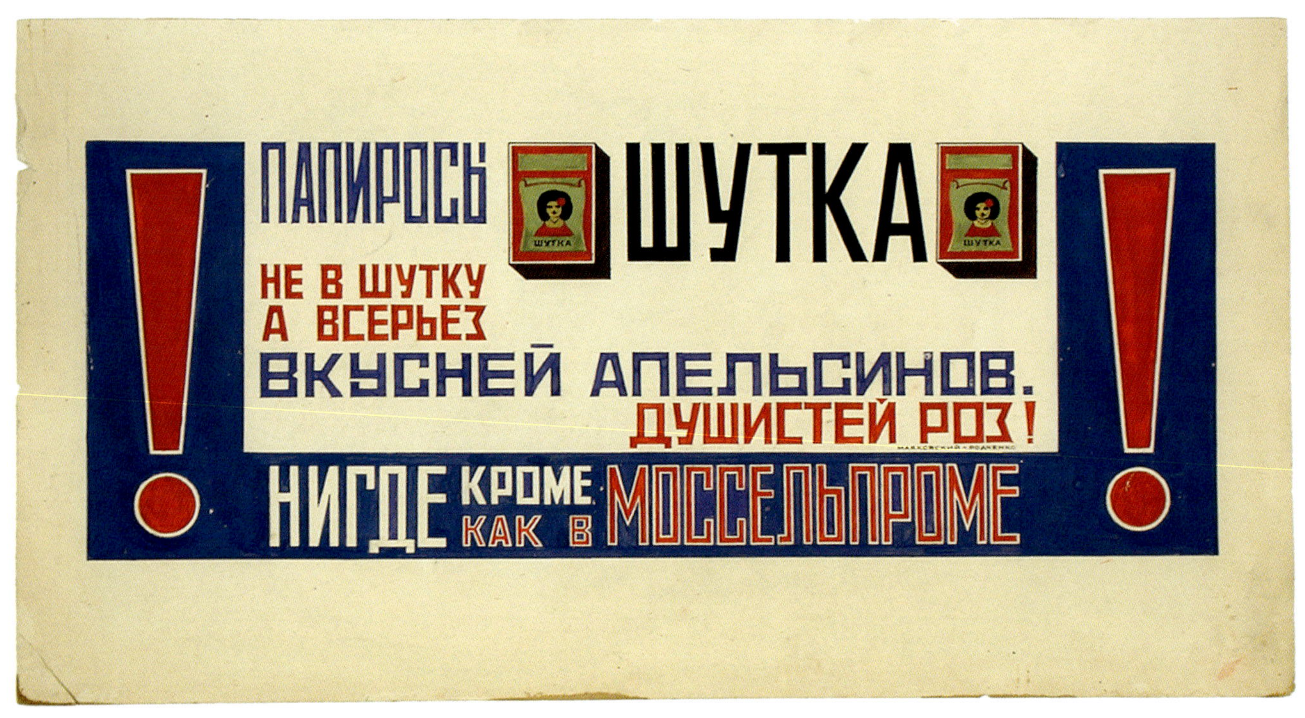

PLATE 14
Aleksandr Rodchenko and Vladimir Mayakovsky, advertisement for Mossel'prom Shutka cigarettes, 1923. Gouache maquette. Howard Schickler Fine Art.

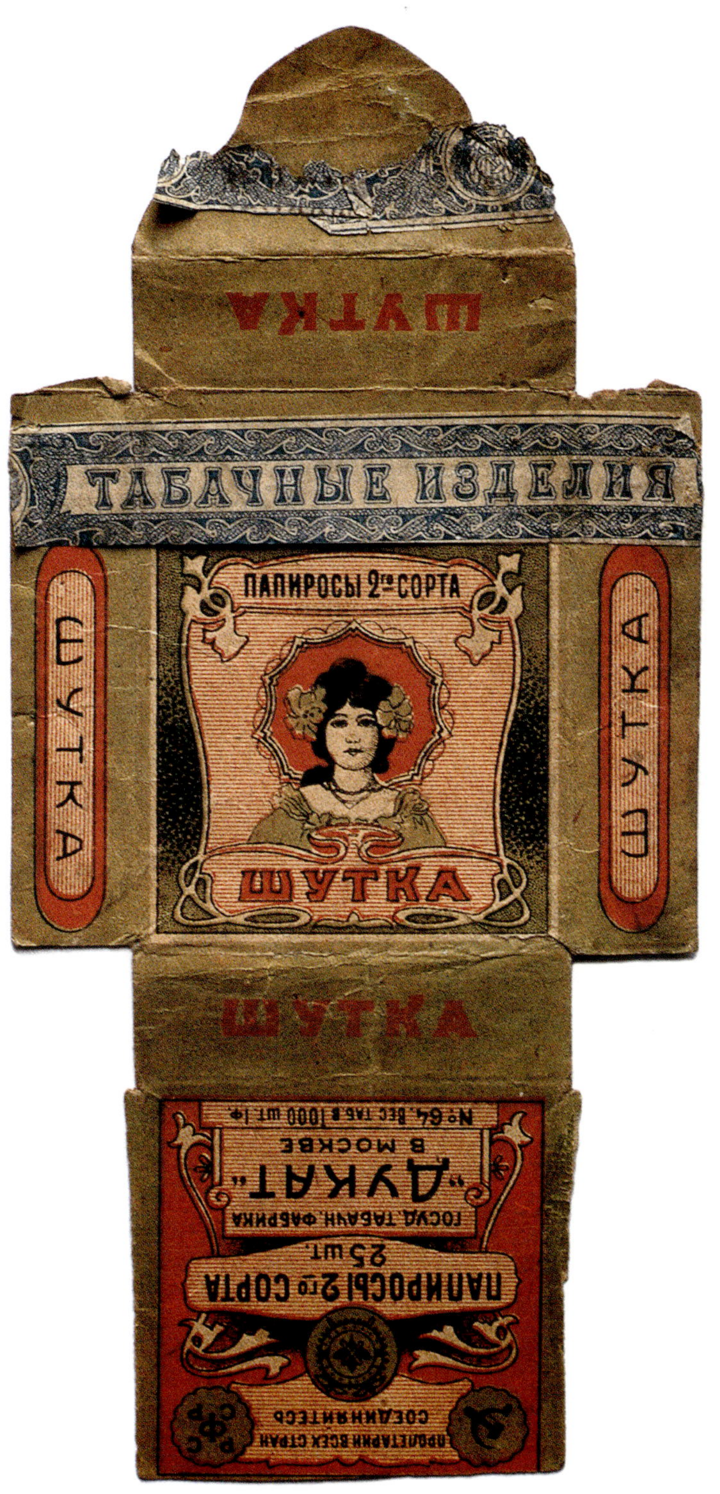

PLATE 15
Box for Shutka cigarettes, early 1920s. Courtesy State Mayakovsky Museum, Moscow. Photo by the author.

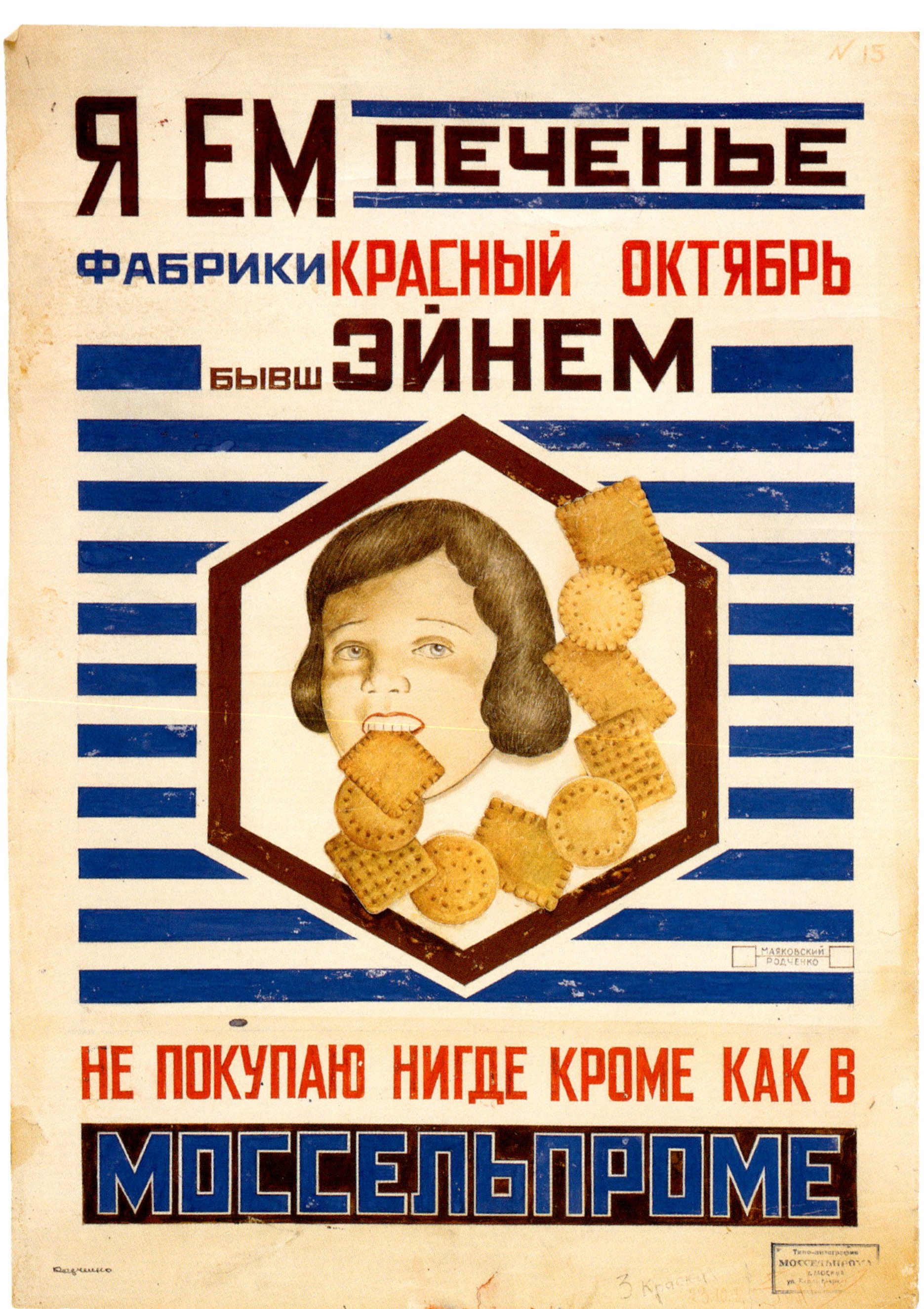

PLATE 16
Aleksandr Rodchenko and Vladimir Mayakovsky, advertising poster for Red October cookies, 1923.
Howard Schickler Fine Art.

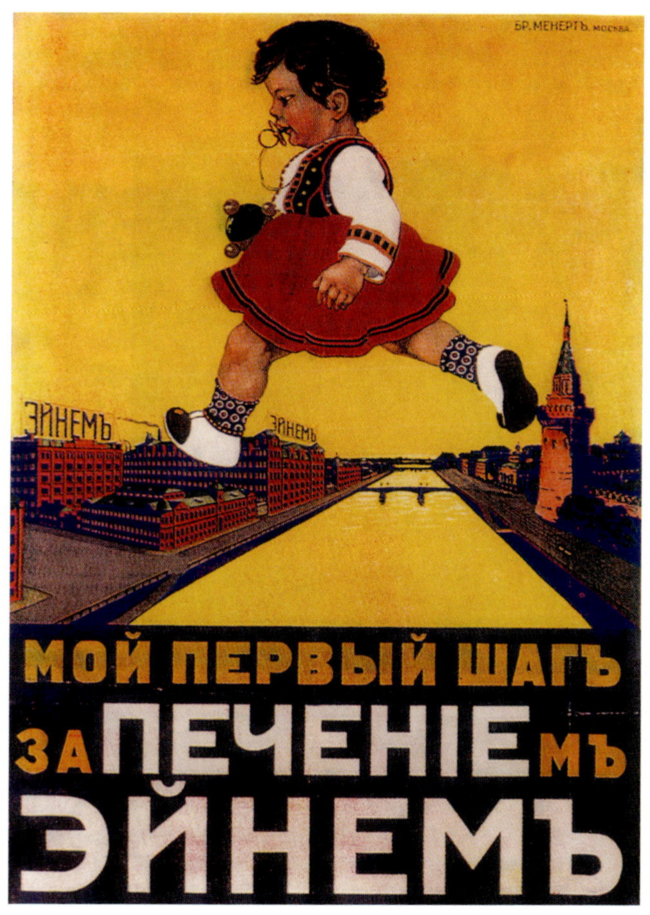

PLATE 17
Menert Brothers, advertising poster for Einem cookies, early twentieth century. Courtesy Russian State Library Department of Graphics, Moscow.

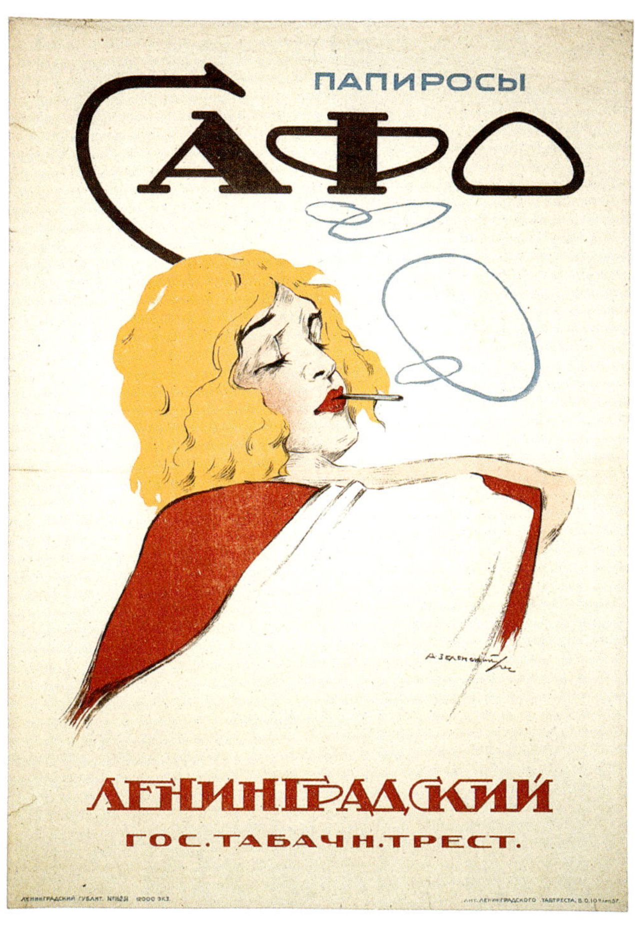

PLATE 18
Aleksandr Zelenskii, advertising poster for Sappho cigarettes, ca. 1925. Courtesy Russian State Library Department of Graphics, Moscow.

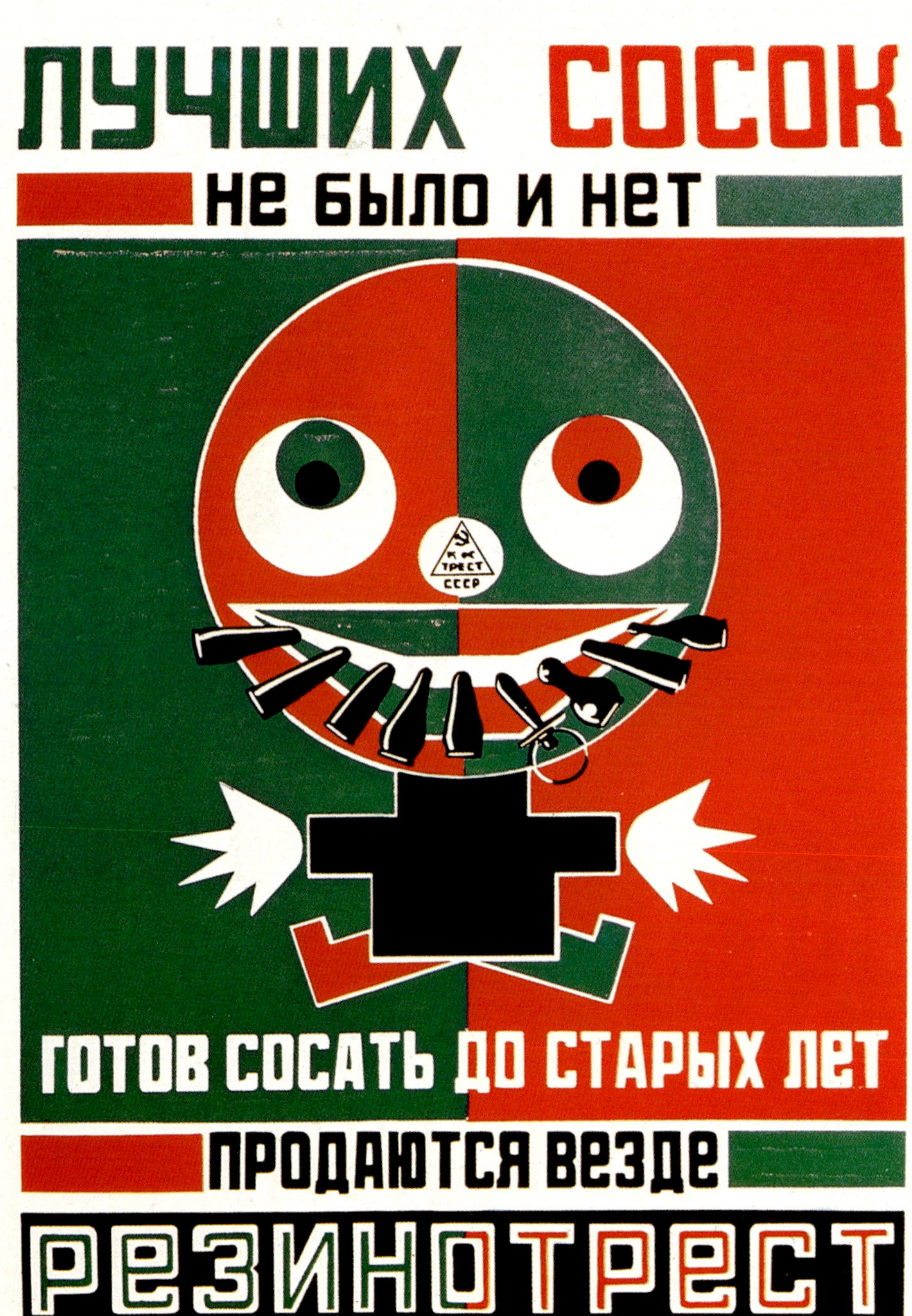

PLATE 19

Aleksandr Rodchenko and Vladimir Mayakovsky, advertising poster for Rezinotrest pacifiers, 1923 (reconstruction by V. A. Rodchenko). SCALA / Art Resource, N.Y.

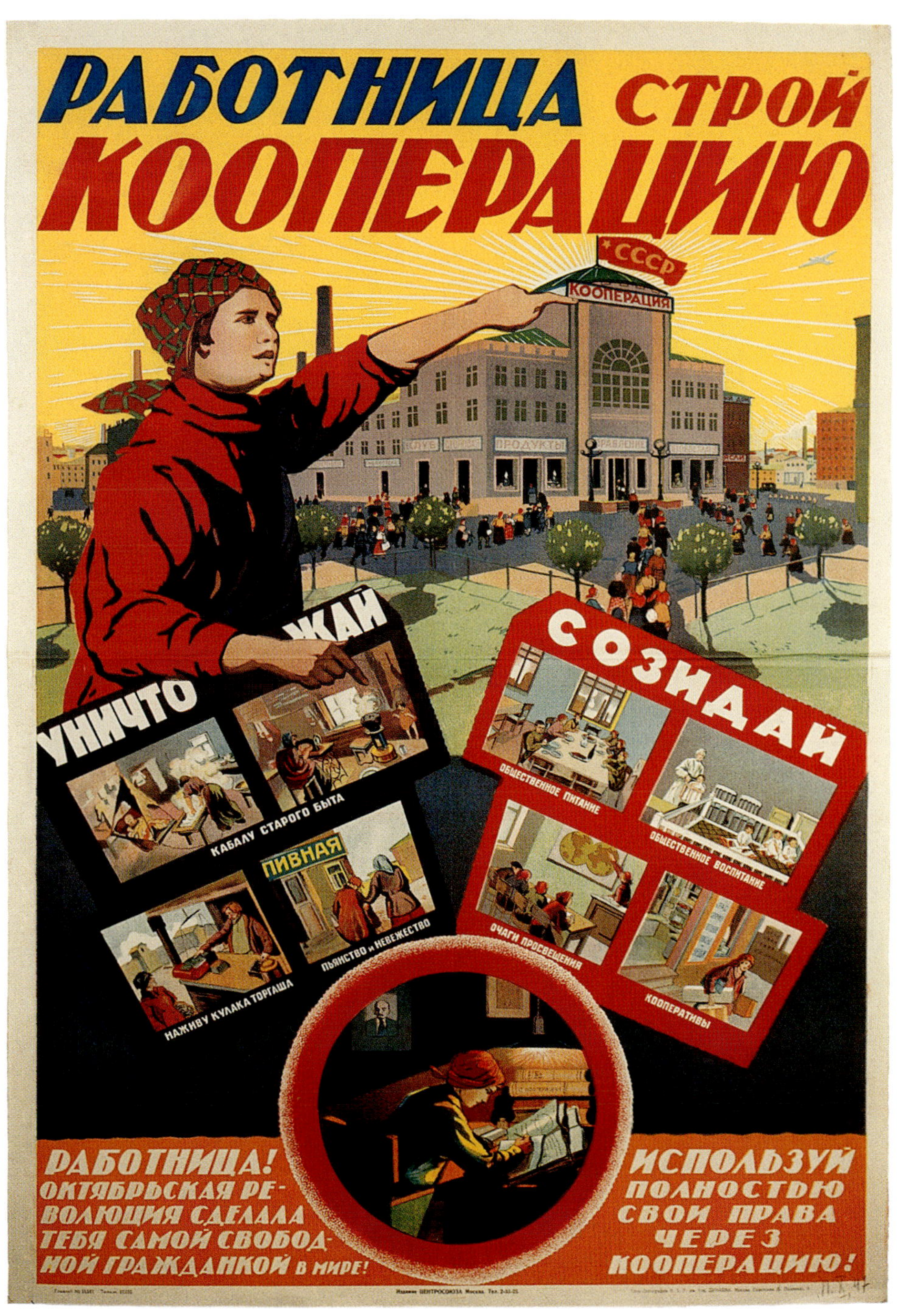

PLATE 20

Poster: "Woman worker, build cooperation!", Moscow, 1925.
Courtesy Russian State Library Department of Graphics, Moscow.

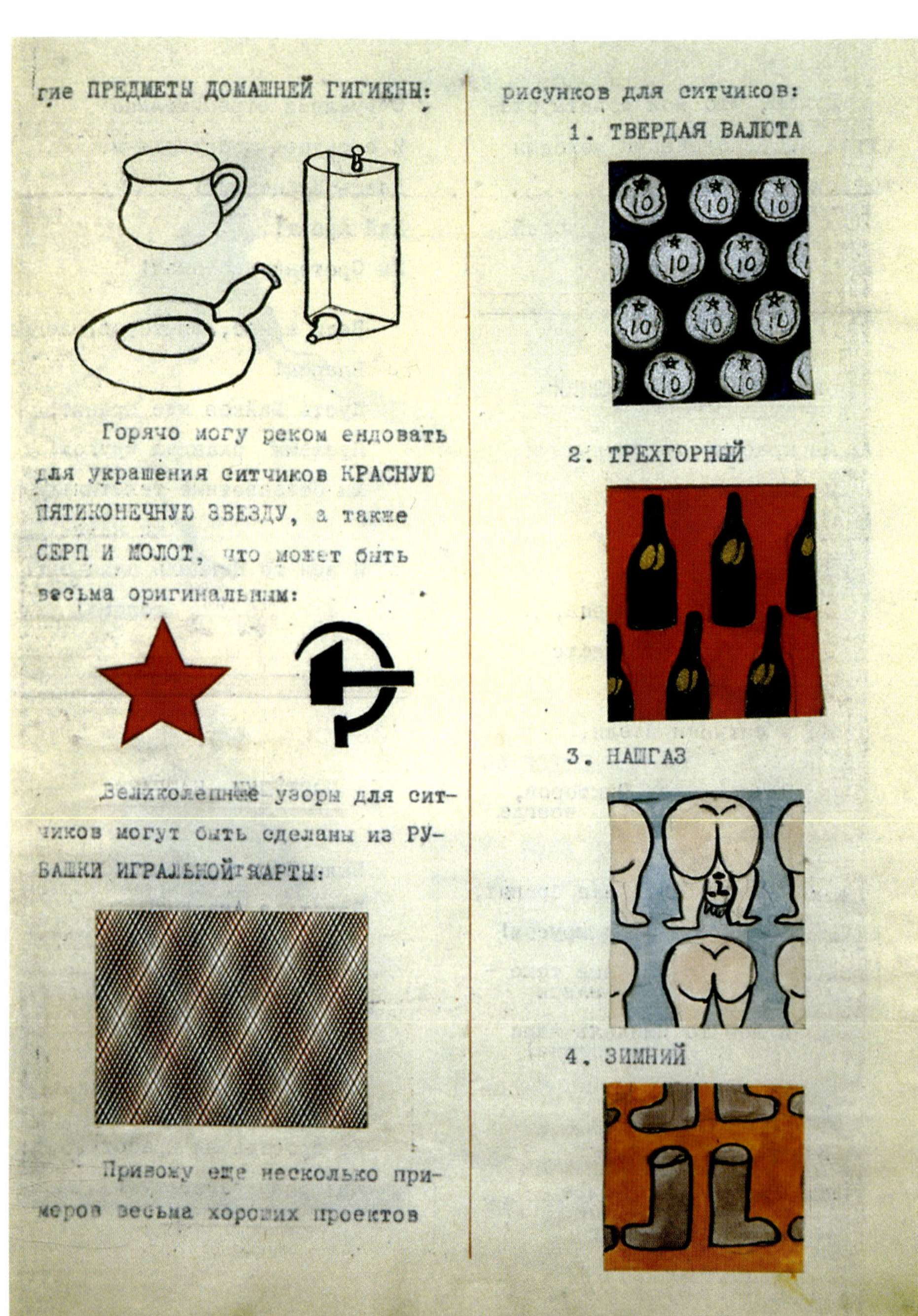

гие ПРЕДМЕТЫ ДОМАШНЕЙ ГИГИЕНЫ:

Горячо могу реком ендовать для украшения ситчиков КРАСНУЮ ПЯТИКОНЕЧНУЮ ЗВЕЗДУ, а также СЕРП И МОЛОТ, что может быть весьма оригинальным:

Великолепные узоры для ситчиков могут быть сделаны из РУБАШКИ ИГРАЛЬНОЙ КАРТЫ:

Привожу еще несколько примеров весьма хороших проектов рисунков для ситчиков:

1. ТВЕРДАЯ ВАЛЮТА
2. ТРЕХГОРНЫЙ
3. НАШГАЗ
4. ЗИМНИЙ

PLATE 21

Aleksandr Rodchenko, page with ideas for fabric patterns in *Nash gaz*, 1924.

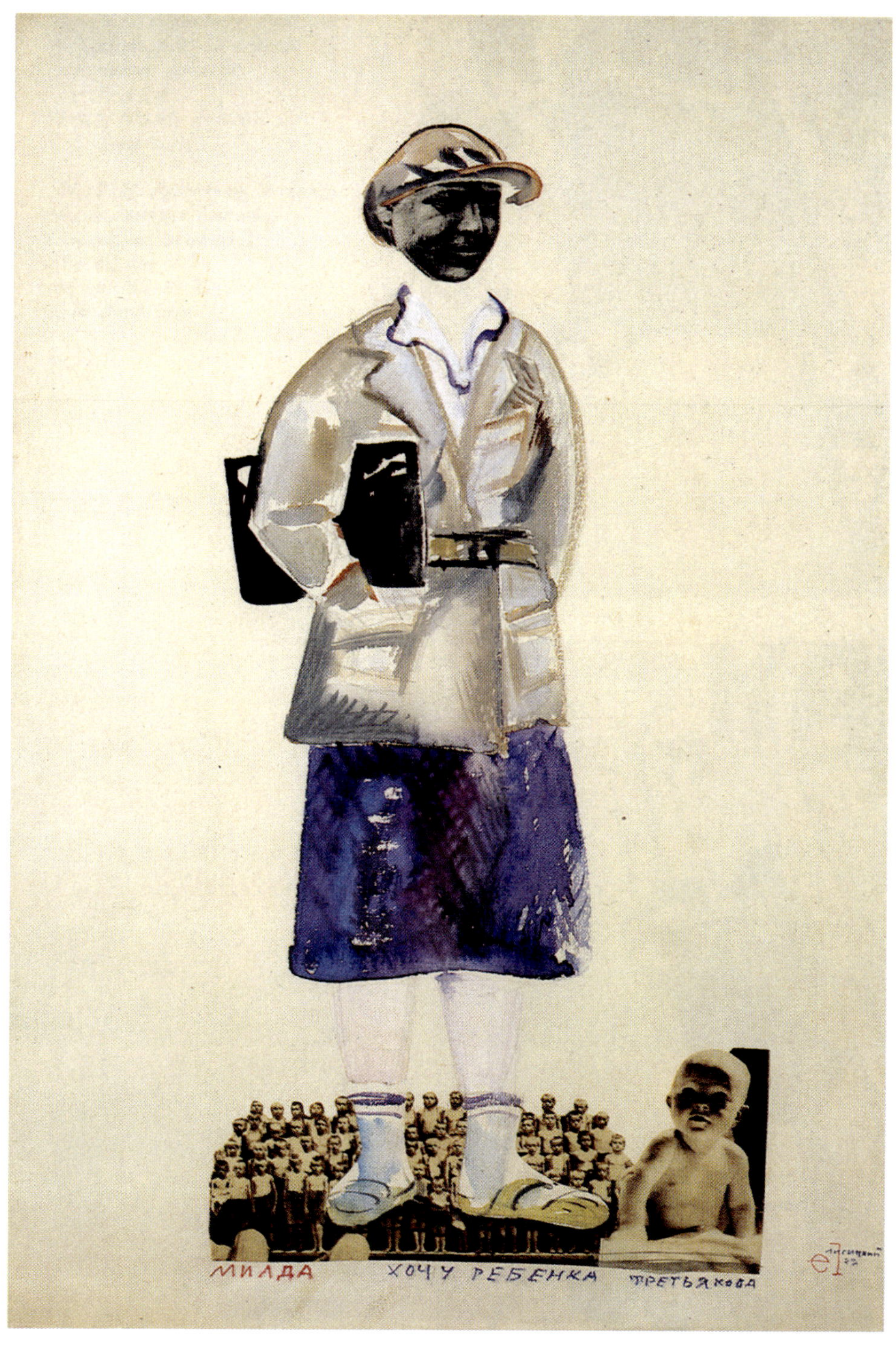

PLATE 22

El Lissitzky, costume design for Milda in *I Want a Child!*, 1929. Watercolor, pencil, and collage on pasteboard.

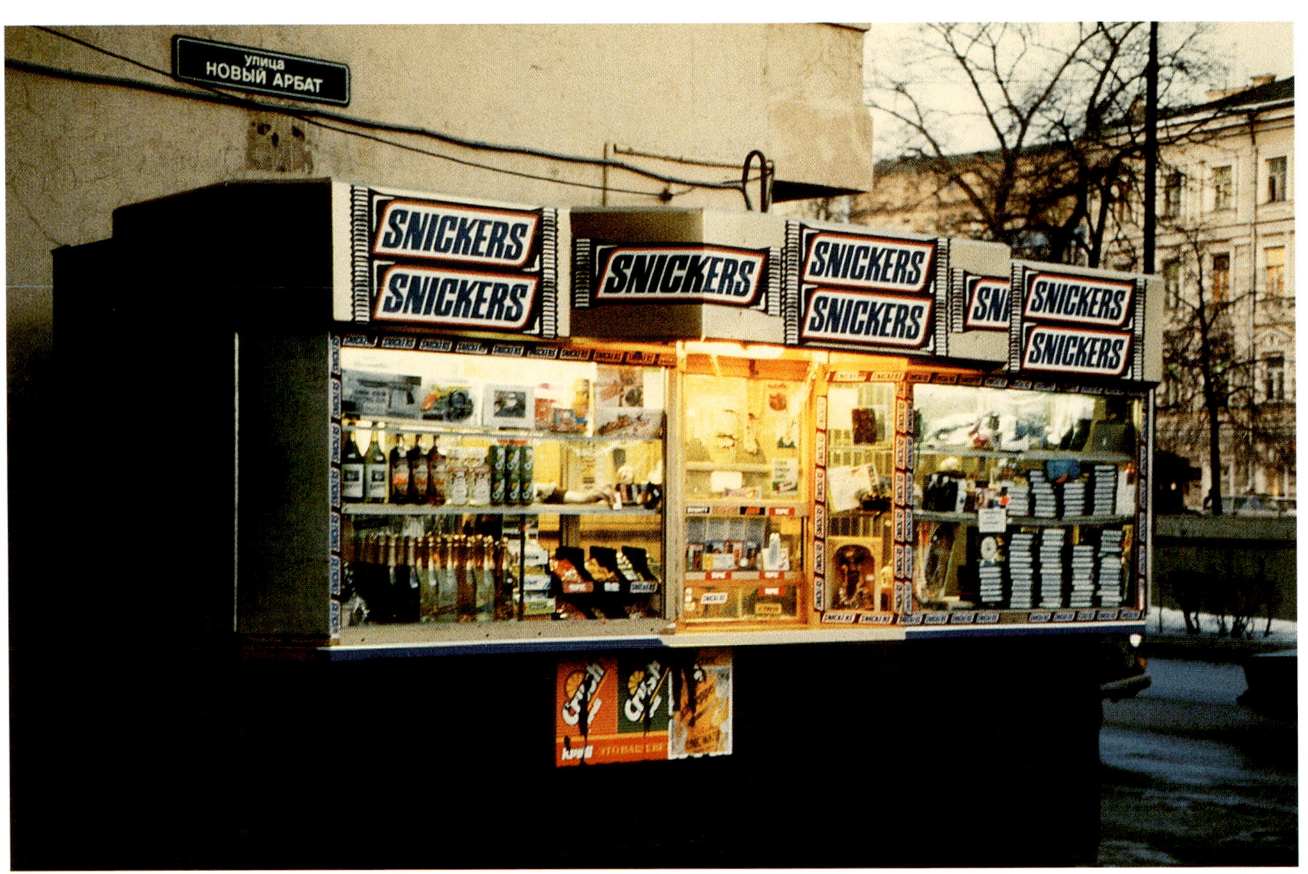

PLATE 23

George W. Kresak, photograph of Moscow kiosk, 1994. Courtesy George W. Kresak.

The figure of a child is an ideal, even hackneyed icon for the promise of the future. But Roman Jakobson asserts that, paradoxically, "the constant infatuation with a wonderful future is linked in Mayakovsky with a pronounced dislike of children," because they represent "the evil continuum of specific tomorrows that only prolong today."[56] He cites Mayakovsky's play *The Bedbug*, in which a bureaucratic doctor contends that a woman who has committed suicide could not have done it "from love," because love is an emotion of continuity, not rupture: "love makes you want to build bridges and have children," the doctor insists.[57] For Mayakovsky, children represent the continuation of today, the bridge between today and the tomorrows that will be unchanged, and therefore they cannot be revolutionary figures. The images of children that crop up in the Rodchenko–Mayakovsky graphics might therefore be understood to have a less literal and more psychoanalytic function: they invoke the oral drive of infancy as described in detail by the psychoanalyst Melanie Klein, with its greed and aggression toward the "part object" of the mother's breast, as a model for comprehending adult desires for the transitionally socialist consumer objects of NEP.[58]

The methods of psychoanalysis, and the broader psychoanalytic idea that the sexual drives support or underpin the desire for things, were well known in intellectual circles in Russia at this time, including the *Lef* circle.[59] This knowledge helps to explain Mayakovsky's anguished conflation of his love for Lili Brik with his pleasure in things, and it surfaced as well, as we have seen, in Sergei Tret'iakov's criticism of the person who "transfers the fetishism of his sympathies and memories" to objects and so "becomes the slave" of objects.[60] Rodchenko and Mayakovsky's working process provides evidence for their deliberate mobilizing of the oral drive as a literalization of desire for the object at its most originary level. The ads were always initiated by Mayakovsky's rhymes, which he scrawled on bits of paper, accompanied by doodled pictures, and passed on to Rodchenko. Rodchenko stated forcefully in his memoirs that he did not make use of these sketches, owing to Mayakovsky's satiric, folk-engraving (*lubok*) style of drawing; he wrote, "The text was always accompanied by a drawing, which he wasn't able not to make, even though he said every time: 'here, I drew this, but of course you don't need it, I just did it to work things out.'"[61] But if we examine the previously unpublished Mayakovsky sketches that are housed in the Manuscript Department of the State Mayakovsky Museum in Moscow, it becomes clear that Rodchenko often took Mayakovsky's sketches as a starting point, and that these sketches often suggested an oral theme. In Mayakovsky's original sketch for a 1923 ad for *Posol'skie*

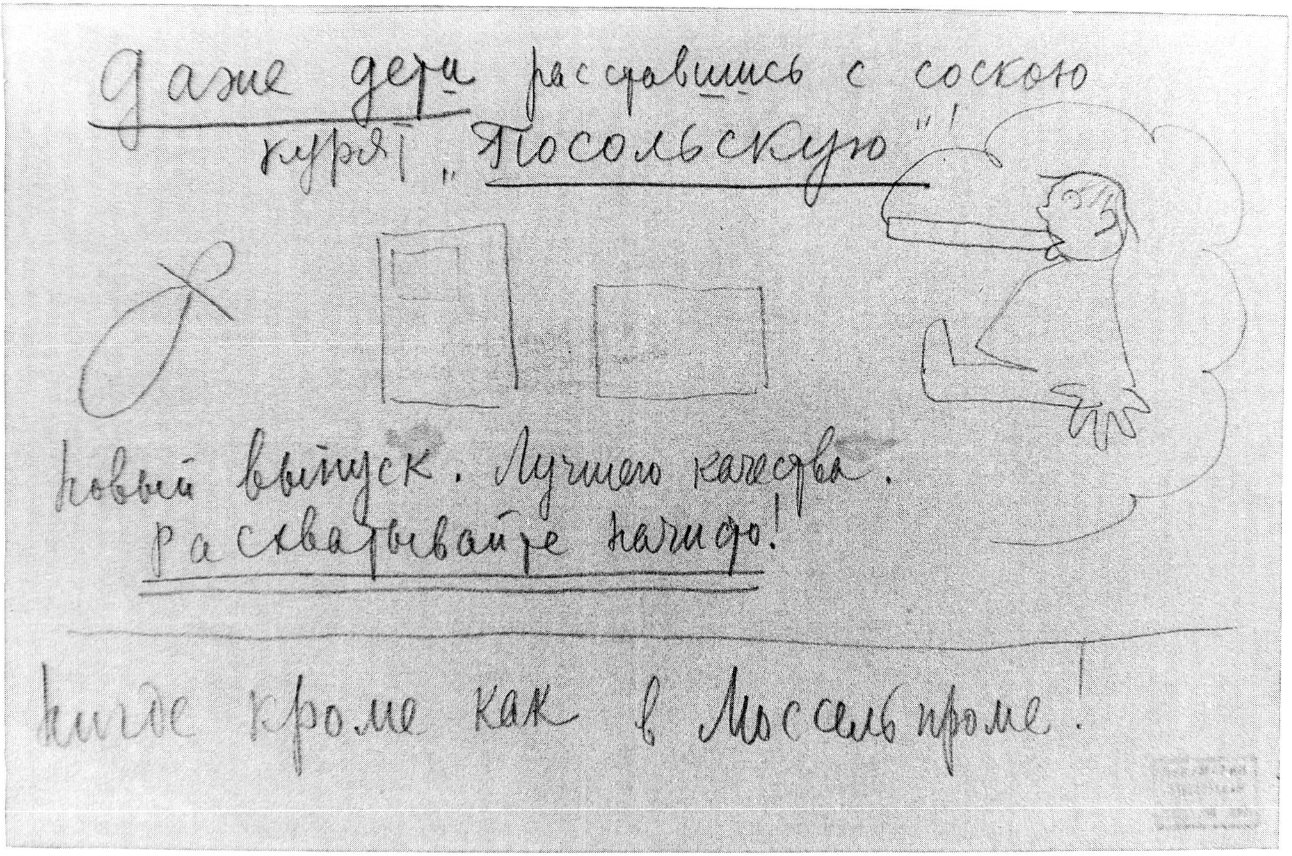

FIGURE 4.20
Vladimir Mayakovsky, sketch for Embassy cigarettes advertisement, 1923. Pencil on paper. Manuscript Department, State Mayakovsky Museum, Moscow.

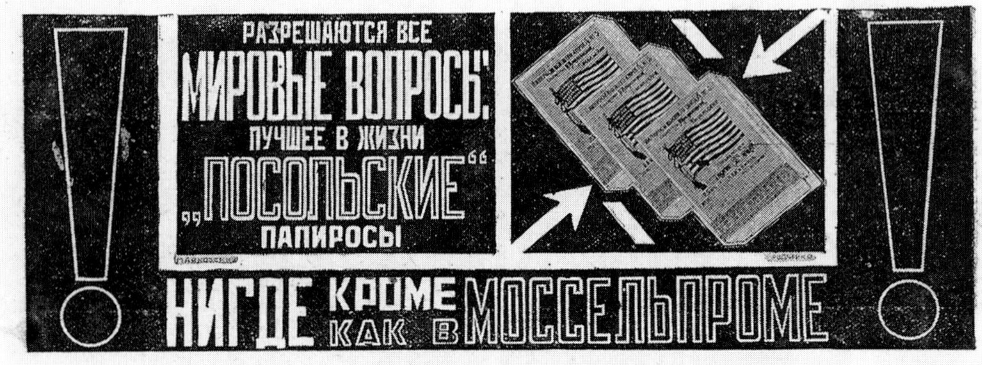

FIGURE 4.21
Aleksandr Rodchenko and Vladimir Mayakovsky, advertisement for Embassy cigarettes, 1923. Private collection.

(Embassy) cigarettes, for example, he accompanies his dubious slogan "Even children, giving up their pacifiers, smoke Embassy" with an even more questionable drawing of a child sitting in wide-eyed shock, a giant smoking cigarette stuffed in his mouth (figure 4.20). Although it is unclear from the archival records, it seems likely that it was Rodchenko who nixed this entire concept, which went perhaps too far in the other direction from innocent bourgeois images of childhood like the prerevolutionary Einem ad. The final version of the Embassy ad as it was printed, with its plainly organized composition incorporating three layered images of the actual cigarette box, and no gagging children, was far more conservative and appropriate to the brand name. Mayakovsky's new rhyming slogan read "All questions of world peace have been decided. Embassy cigarettes are the best" (figure 4.21).[62]

In another Mayakovsky sketch, unaccompanied by a slogan but with the phrase "at Mossel'prom" written sideways through the drawing, a man with a large bald head has what appears to be a cookie clamped in the opening of his enormous mouth (figure 4.22). These drawings point to what we might call Mayakovsky's oral fixation, because as preliminary sketches they are almost a kind of automatic writing that unconsciously accompanied his "real" creative work of composing the rhymes. If we think of the many photographs of Mayakovsky taken by Rodchenko at this time, with his prominently shaved head and ever-present cigarette in his mouth, the sketch might even be read as a schematic self-portrait, suggesting that Mayakovsky quite literally imagined consumer desire in terms of his own (figure 4.23). His poetry is full of references to the mouth and lips, which eat, kiss, chew, spit, suck, and swallow, and to his own shouting voice emanating from his mouth. The mouth is the key interface between the outer world and Mayakovsky's own self.[63] The psychoanalytic model of the greedy infant suspended in the oral phase, who must learn to control his aggression and accept that the gratification provided by the breast is not his to command, is therefore not an altogether unlikely figure for the revolutionary poet who wants a new way of life to come to pass immediately but must control his impatience and find partial substitute activities—such as making innovative advertising for cheap Soviet cookies—on the way toward a fully realized socialist culture.

The Red October cookies are the NEP-era substitutes or placeholders for the grander socialist objects that will eventually be produced by socialist industry, and can be understood as analogous to what the psychoanalyst D. W. Winnicott called the "transitional objects" of the oral phase of early infancy: the pacifier or chewed-on corner of the blanket.[64] The transitional object, which Winnicott also

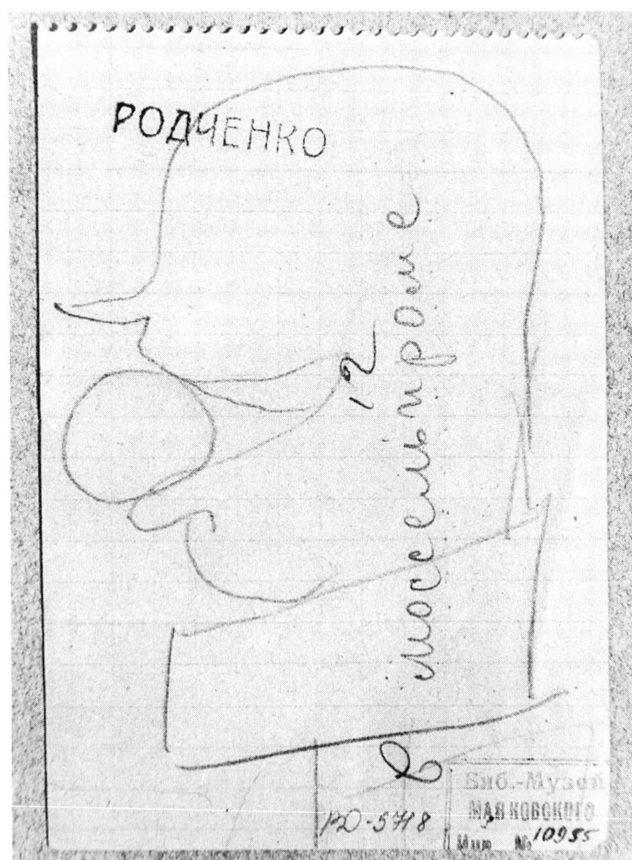

FIGURE 4.22
Vladimir Mayakovsky, sketch for unidentified Mossel'prom advertisement, c. 1923. Pencil on paper. Manuscript Department, State Mayakovsky Museum, Moscow.

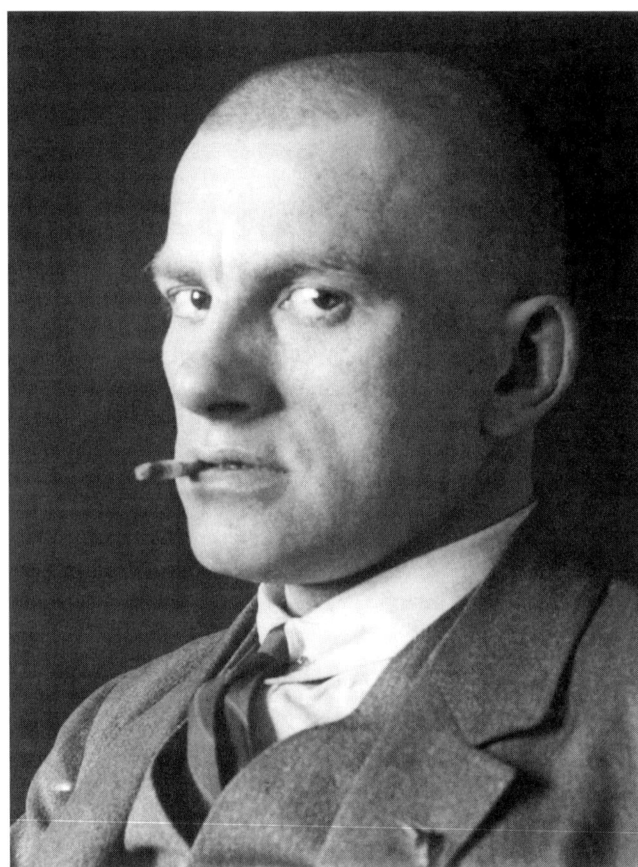

FIGURE 4.23
Aleksandr Rodchenko, photo of Vladimir Mayakovsky, 1924.

calls "the first not-me possession," allows the infant to adjust to the "reality principle" of the absence of the gratification of the mother's breast—the true desired object. The true desired object of the Constructivists is the socialist object, which will use the most advanced technological forms of industry to amplify the sensory experience of its human user, and awaken him or her from the dream sleep of the commodity phantasmagoria. But in the moment of NEP, the Constructivists adjust to the reality principle that the large-scale production of such objects is not yet possible, and concentrate their graphic efforts on laying bare the processes of the most originary, bodily level of object desire. Their advertisements are "transitional objects" that explore the transition from the fetishistic capitalist desires fomented by the commodity to the equally strong, but now explicit and comprehensible desires for the semisocialist objects of NEP—an exploration that will eventually result in fully organized desires for socialist objects themselves.[65]

In the case of the Red October cookies ad, the visual image of aggressive orality stems, unusually, from Rodchenko. The little sketch that accompanied Mayakovsky's scrawled rhyme provides only the basic setup for Rodchenko's image, with no oral emphasis: a floating female head framed within an oval in the center of the composition, with text above and below (figure 4.24). Rodchenko transforms the generalized, oval shape of Mayakovsky's frame into the specific shape of the hexagon—the shape of one of his own *Spatial Constructions*—and he opens up Mayakovsky's harmless, closed oval of cookies into a larger spiral of active cookies on the move.[66] The only unusual aspect of Mayakovsky's sketch that Rodchenko partially retains is the adult character of the female head; Mayakovsky's schematic depiction of an apparently adult woman is an odd image to accompany the childish slogan of "I eat cookies!" The adult aspect of the girl refuses the innocent and banal image of temporal continuity associated with children, and instead emphasizes the sexualized nature of the figure's oral desire. The bodily literalness of Rodchenko's Mossel'prom advertisements works to make the sexual nature of object desire legible and even comical, as an antidote to the standard mystification and eroticizing of the commodity.

Compare the female figure in Rodchenko's ad with that from a contemporary advertisement for the Leningrad State Tobacco Trust, by the poster artist Aleksandr Zelinskii (figure 4.25). The product is Sappho brand cigarettes, and the image of the yellow-haired, heavily rouged woman, eyes closed in a seemingly narcotic trance induced by the cigarette nestled between her bright red lips, could be a figure of Benjamin's "slumbering" collective. The Constructivist advertisements refuse such veiled, fetishistic imagery that intimates an oral sexuality in favor of

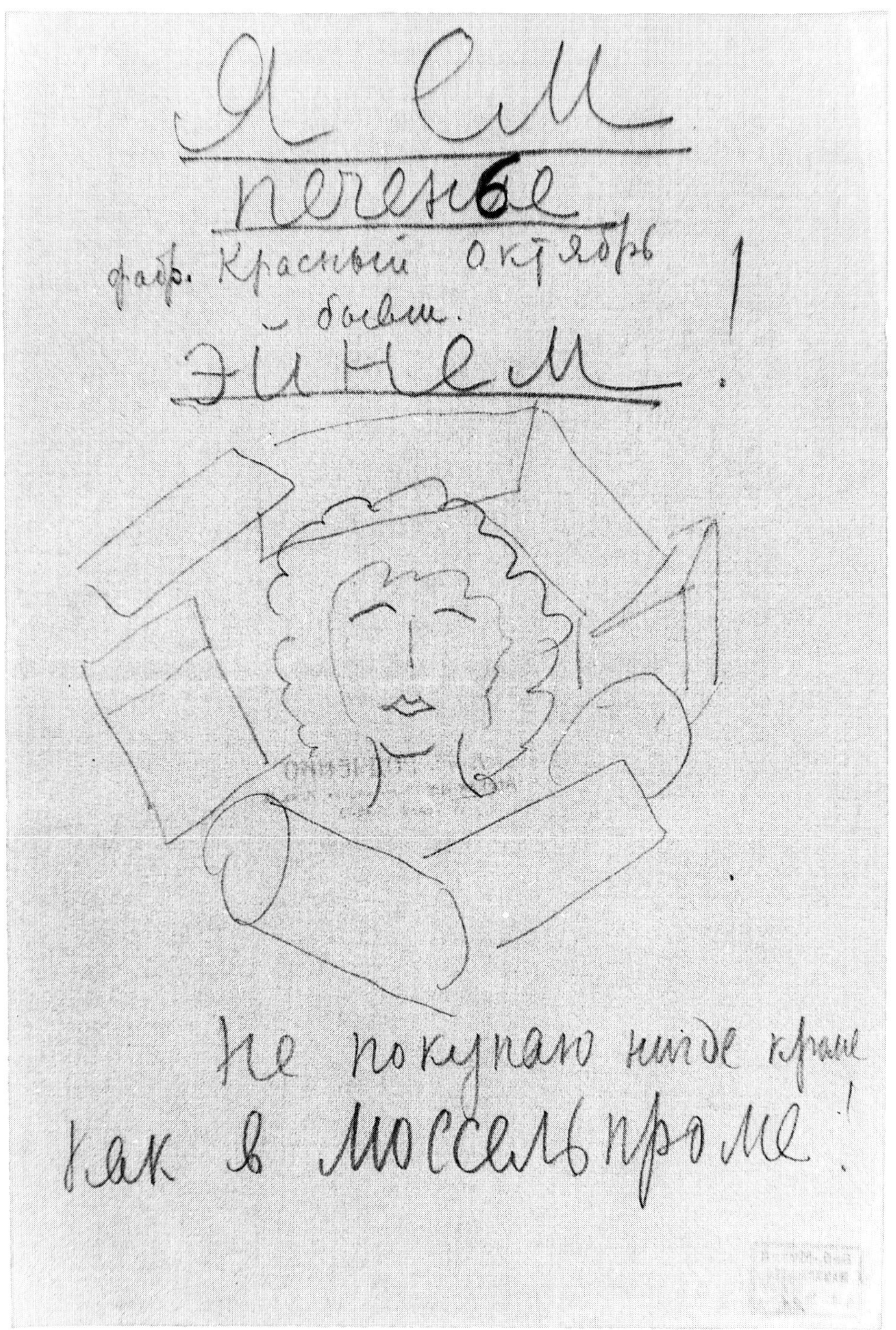

FIGURE 4.24
Vladimir Mayakovsky, sketch for Red October cookie advertisement, 1923.
Pencil on paper. Manuscript Department, State Mayakovsky Museum, Moscow.

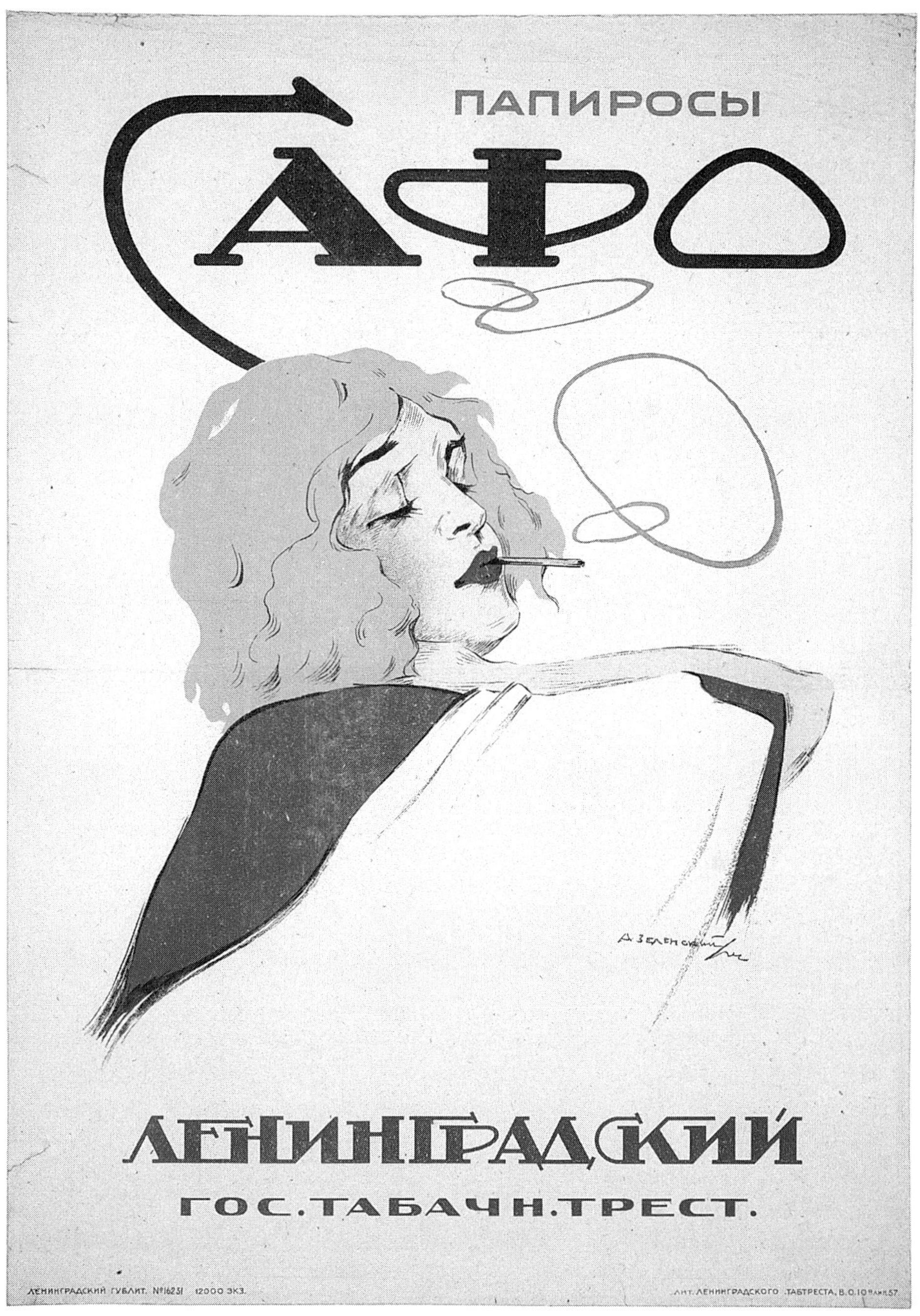

FIGURE 4.25
Aleksandr Zelenskii, advertising poster for Sappho cigarettes, c. 1925.
Courtesy Russian State Library Department of Graphics, Moscow. See plate 18.

a more explicit depiction of the oral drive. The objects of industrial mass culture have a powerful hold on the human subject, the Constructivist ads seem to say; the difference between capitalism and socialism is that under socialism the nature of that hold will be articulable to the subject, even if it cannot be immediately altered or overcome. The Constructivist drive toward transparency was not just material, as in the systematic *Spatial Constructions* series or Popova's clumsy flapper dress or the spare forms of the Workers' Club, but psychological, offering the critical understanding of the excessive nature of consumer desire—the "flash of recognition"—that would be necessary for waking up from the commodity phantasmagoria of capitalism. It is this transparency of object desire that the ads map out, contravening Peter Bürger's claim that when avant-garde art enters into life as a form of mass culture, "it is an art that enthralls."[67]

The Red October girl grasps the first cookie firmly between her white teeth (rather than pressing it seductively between red lips, as "Sappho" does with her cigarette) and she directs a sly, knowing look out at us as she does so (again in contrast to Sappho's closed eyes). She will crunch her way through the spiral of cookies until her present meets and confronts the desires lodged in the cookies' past, like the game in which two people start eating a rope of licorice from either end until their mouths meet in a sticky kiss. This kiss would be a dialectical image in Benjamin's sense, the then and the now meeting in its constellation.

The Rodchenko–Mayakovsky poster that presents the most densely dialectical image of their collaboration, economically literalizing the concept of the protosocialist object as a "transitional object," is their well-known advertising poster of 1923 for rubber pacifiers made by Rezinotrest, the State Rubber Trust (figure 4.26). Mayakovsky's sketch for the ad shows a childishly rendered round head with dots for eyes and nose, and a banana-shaped mouth from which five pacifiers protrude upward, as if the little figure is sucking on all five pacifiers at once (figure 4.27). Mayakovsky's terse, clever slogan makes use of the Russian word for pacifier, *soska* (or, in the genitive plural, *sosok*), which literally means "sucker": *"Luchshikh sosok ne bylo i net, gotov sosat' do starykh let"* (There have never been, nor are there now, better suckers. They are ready for sucking until you reach old age). Scrawled above his avidly sucking figure, the deliberate perversity of the rhyme emerges. Why would you want a pacifier that you could suck on until old age, unless you had a bit of an oral fixation? But then, why would you want a pacifier at all? No baby actually wants a pacifier; the baby wants the breast, but is given the pacifier as a substitute for the real nourishment, a placeholder that makes waiting possible—precisely the "transitional object." We recall that

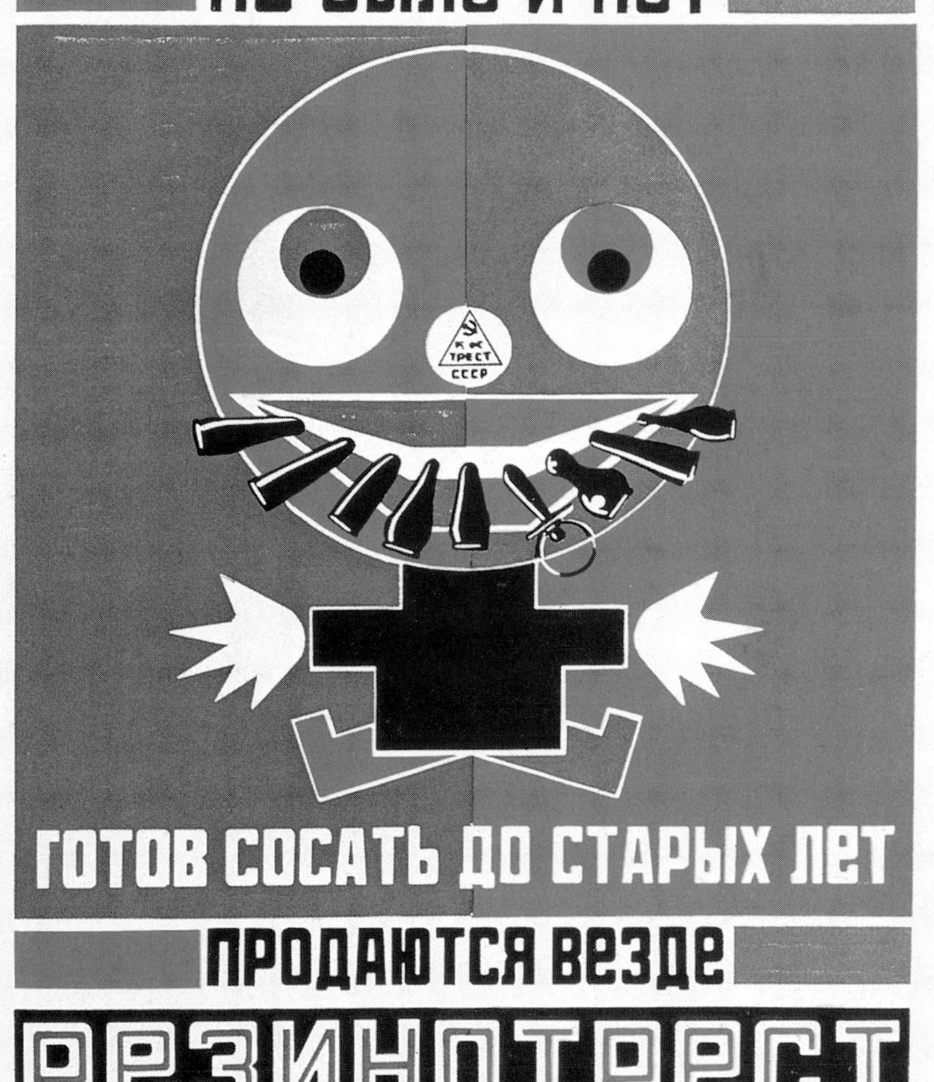

FIGURE 4.26
Aleksandr Rodchenko and Vladimir Mayakovsky, advertising poster for Rezinotrest pacifiers, 1923 (reconstruction by V. A. Rodchenko). Scala/Art Resource, N.Y. See plate 19.

Mayakovsky's sketch for the Embassy cigarettes advertisement directly analogized the childish pacifier with that adult object of oral pleasure, the cigarette—another object of temporary oral placation that does not satisfy a genuine need.

The advertisement proposes the Rezinotrest pacifier as the ultimate socialist object for the transitional period of NEP. It is a commodity on its way to becoming the comradely object of the future, what the Productivist theorist Boris Arvatov called "the thing as the fulfillment of the physiological-laboring capacities of the organism" (EL, p. 124). This "physiological" capacity of the thing is as yet imaginable only on the most primitive, direct level of the gratification of the mouth. The oral desire of infancy is excessive and irrational by definition, as Mayakovsky's sketches of the gleefully sucking little figure in the pacifier ad, as well as of the gagging child in the Embassy cigarettes ad, demonstrate.

Rodchenko's final version of the pacifier poster, however, performs a Constructivist organization of this image of oral desire that intervenes in its excessiveness, attempting to direct and clarify it. The little figure is no longer actively sucking; rather, the pacifiers themselves become active objects, determining the pace and direction of the oral pleasure as they point like bullets into the mouth. Only one of the nine pacifier-type objects even looks like an actual pacifier, with the conventional ring hanging from its end; the rest of the variously shaped objects might more accurately be characterized as rubber nipples for glass baby bottles, which would also be called by the generic name "soska" in Russian. As substitutes for the breast, they enact the incarnation of the breast described by Melanie Klein, in whose psychoanalytic scenario the part-object of the breast can be an object of aggression by the devouring infant, but also an object of threat toward the infant.[68] The violence of this threat is heightened by the affinity of some of the pacifier shapes for bullets and even of the single, abstractly rendered pacifier with a ring on it for a hand grenade, and by the way that the outstretched white hands of the little figure resemble stylized explosions. This sadistic aspect of the oral drive is also emphasized by the highly controlled composition. It is rigidly blocked out in geometrically divided sections of color: note the strict symmetry of all elements (except the pacifiers) and the careful alternation of red and green in the lettering at top and bottom, the background, the two sides of the head, the eyes, the mouth, and the legs. The visual organization of the modernist graphics has seemingly spilled over into organizing the bodily content of the image.

Rodchenko and Mayakovsky's uncompromising, if playful, demonstration of the vicissitudes of object relations offers a politicized contrast not only to eroticized

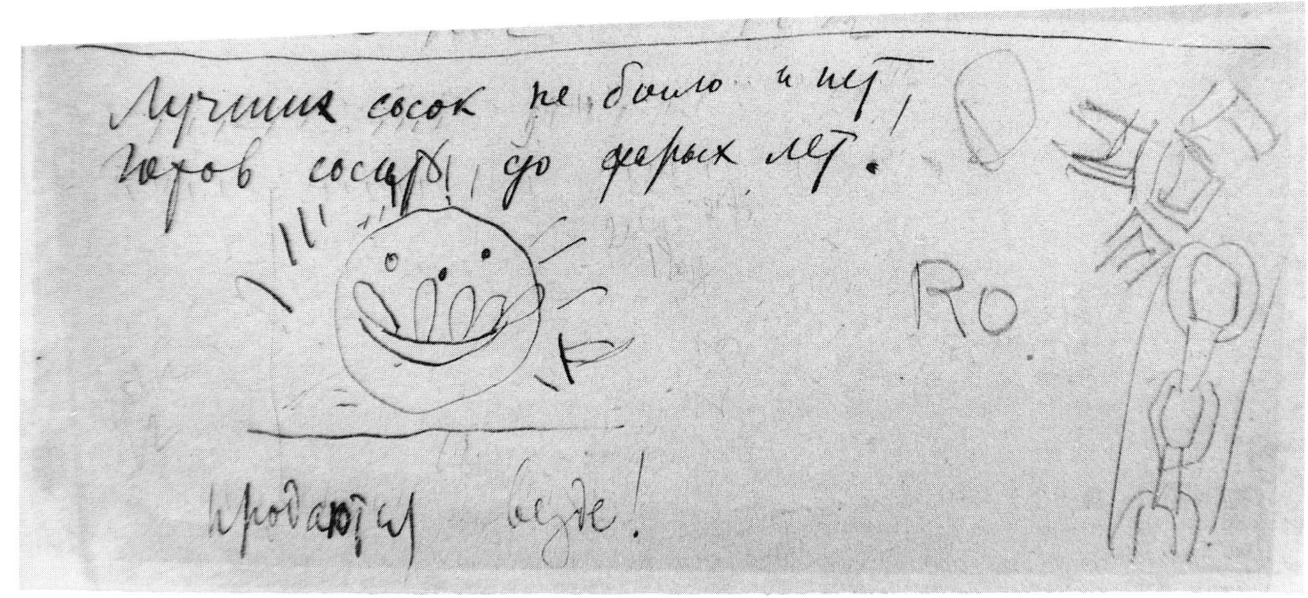

FIGURE 4.27
Vladimir Mayakovsky, sketch for Rezinotrest pacifier advertisement, 1923. Ink on paper. Manuscript Department, State Mayakovsky Museum, Moscow.

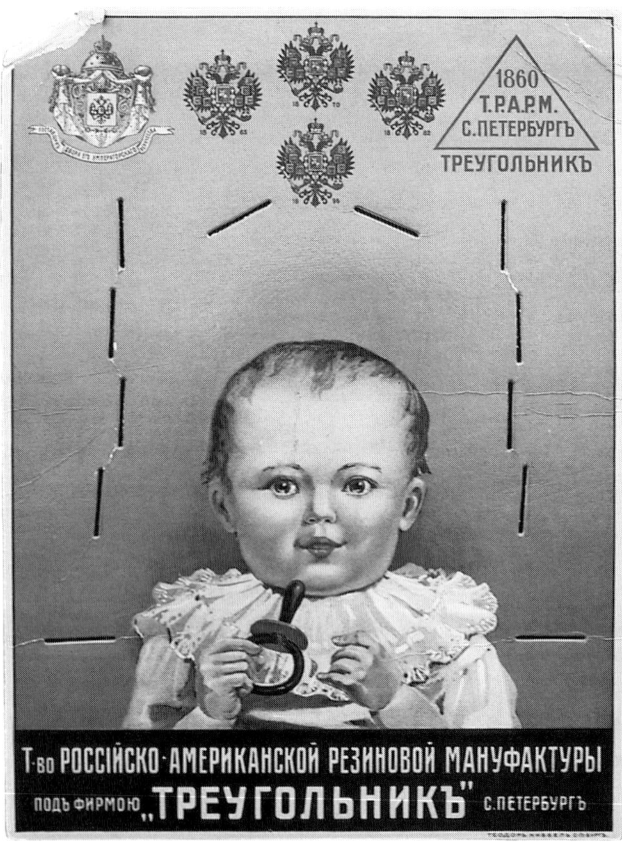

FIGURE 4.28
Promotional packaging for Treugol'nik pacifiers, early twentieth century.
Courtesy Russian State Library Department of Graphics, Moscow.

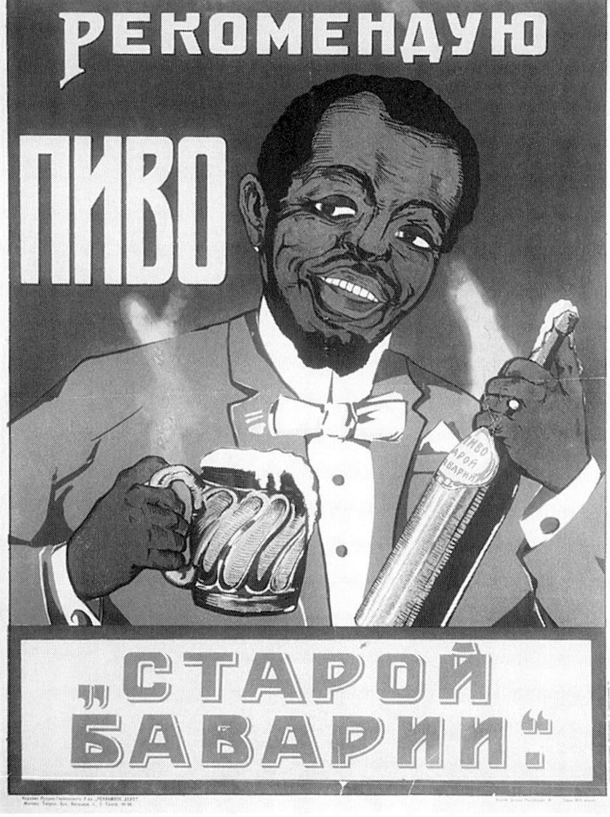

FIGURE 4.29
Advertising poster for Old Bavaria beer, c. 1925.
Courtesy Russian State Library Department of Graphics, Moscow.

images such as the Sappho cigarette advertisement but also to the sentimental images of childhood that uphold the bourgeois continuity of the family, such as the prerevolutionary Einem advertisement. Specifically, Rodchenko's little cartoon figure in the Rezinotrest poster proposes a Constructivist antithesis to the advertising images of the prerevolutionary incarnation of Rezinotrest, the Russian-American rubber company Treugol'nik (Triangle). An early twentieth-century piece of Treugol'nik display packaging for pacifiers, for example, depicts a cherubic round-faced baby, framed by a fancy white lace collar and imperial eagles (figure 4.28). Once again Rodchenko cites the prerevolutionary brand name of the product by placing the triangular Treugol'nik symbol, seen on the upper right of the display board, inside the circular nose of his figure, although now the Soviet term *trest* and a hammer and sickle symbol have replaced the previous wording inside it. But his little figure refuses the myth of a timeless realm of happy childhood conjured by the baby in the prerevolutionary image. Its huge, lolling white eyes, thick-lipped grin, and white-gloved hands invoke the blackface comedy of the 1920s. Blackface, jazz, and the figure of the negro more generally were symbols of modernity in NEP-era Soviet culture.[69] In a more conventionally racist example, an anonymous Soviet poster advertisement from the mid-1920s depicts a black waiter in a bow tie serving a beer, with the text "I recommend Old Bavaria beer" (figure 4.29). The modernity of this image of the dressed-up negro serving man lies in its inevitable associations with exoticism and colonialism, while Rodchenko's blackface figure, through its rigorous, rhythmic blocking of alternating colors and geometric forms, is more closely tied to the staccato rhythms of jazz as an alternate manifestation of modernity.

The Rezinotrest pacifier poster is dense with the past it is attempting to shed. Mayakovsky's rhyme invokes the very span between childhood and old age that his revolutionary Futurism rejected, while behind the frantically modern figure of the blackface comedian lurks the happy baby of the Triangle Rubber Company display board. The pacifiers and rubber nipples themselves represent the new everyday life not only in being made by the state-owned Rezinotrest company, but in their invocation of the mass bottle-feeding of infants in state-run nurseries replacing the breastfeeding mother at home. Yet this new everyday life is invaded throughout by the persistence of the old everyday life under capitalism that was dominated by the greedy desire for endless commodities, represented by the excess of nine pacifiers, none of which is an object of genuine need.

This persistence is made most explicit in the *mise-en-abîme* represented by the third pacifier from the right: the tiny details of two white shapes on this black pacifier repeat the form of the head and outstretched arms of the little figure itself. The baby sucks on pacifiers in an infinite loop, and no amount of geometric compositional organization, or socialist economic organization, will change the fact that the desire of this gaping mouth is infinite. What is possible, however, is that this desire be comprehended—rather than repressed—and eventually harnessed for socialism through the socialist object. In this diagrammatic poster, to quote Benjamin on the dialectical image once again, "what has been comes together in a flash with the now to form a constellation." The spiral of cookies in the Red October advertisement also formed a *mise-en-abîme* of sorts, because of the temporal nature of the spiral form. Yet the cookie spiral itself is imperfect: the cookies seem to progress in an orderly alternation between quadrilateral and circular cookies, but this alternation is broken at the point to the right of the girl's mouth where two rectangular cookies are juxtaposed; further, the two circular cookies on the right break the pattern of cookies evenly layered one on top of another in a row, by being superimposed over both of their neighbors. The fractured nature of this spiral might suggest a break in the *mise-en-abîme*, a point of insertion for the "flash" of the socialist object that will intervene into the endlessness of commodity desire and redirect it toward socialist ends.

The Red October ad was deemed successful enough to be chosen for placement, in horizontal format, on large signboards on top of the Mossel'prom kiosks that dotted Moscow. Rodchenko captured the fragility of any notion of organized, collective consumption in NEP Russia when he photographed one of these signboards *in situ* in 1924 (figure 4.30). At that time Mossel'prom did not even have an organized system of permanent stores, but sold most of its wares through makeshift kiosks such as the rickety one seen here, or through itinerant street vendors such as the cigarette girls. Chomping on her cookies, surrounded by Mayakovsky's rhymes and Rodchenko's graphics, the Red October girl grinning down from her perch on the kiosk embodies the Constructivist entry into Soviet everyday life. Just as the privileged poetic interface between Mayakovsky and the surrounding world was the mouth, so this makeshift image of aggressive oral abundance in the midst of the barren Moscow street must be seen to constitute one of the central rather than marginal Constructivist interfaces with *byt*—with the gentleman in a suit and hat glimpsed from the back rushing off; with the peasant or costumed Bolshevik in his belted blouse striding off toward the right; and with the peasant women in kerchiefs sitting on the dusty ground at the left, likely selling some itinerant wares of their own laid out before them. In his book *Art and Production*, Boris Arvatov wrote that "the activity of the artist-engineer will become a bridge from production to consumption."[70] But Rodchenko and Mayakovsky did not make ads that functioned as simple bridges, because they recognized that the transition from the capitalist commodity to the socialist object would be not a linear passage but a dialectical one. The individual fantasies and desires organized under capitalism by the commodity fetish needed to be comprehended and rescued for the future socialist world of plenty.

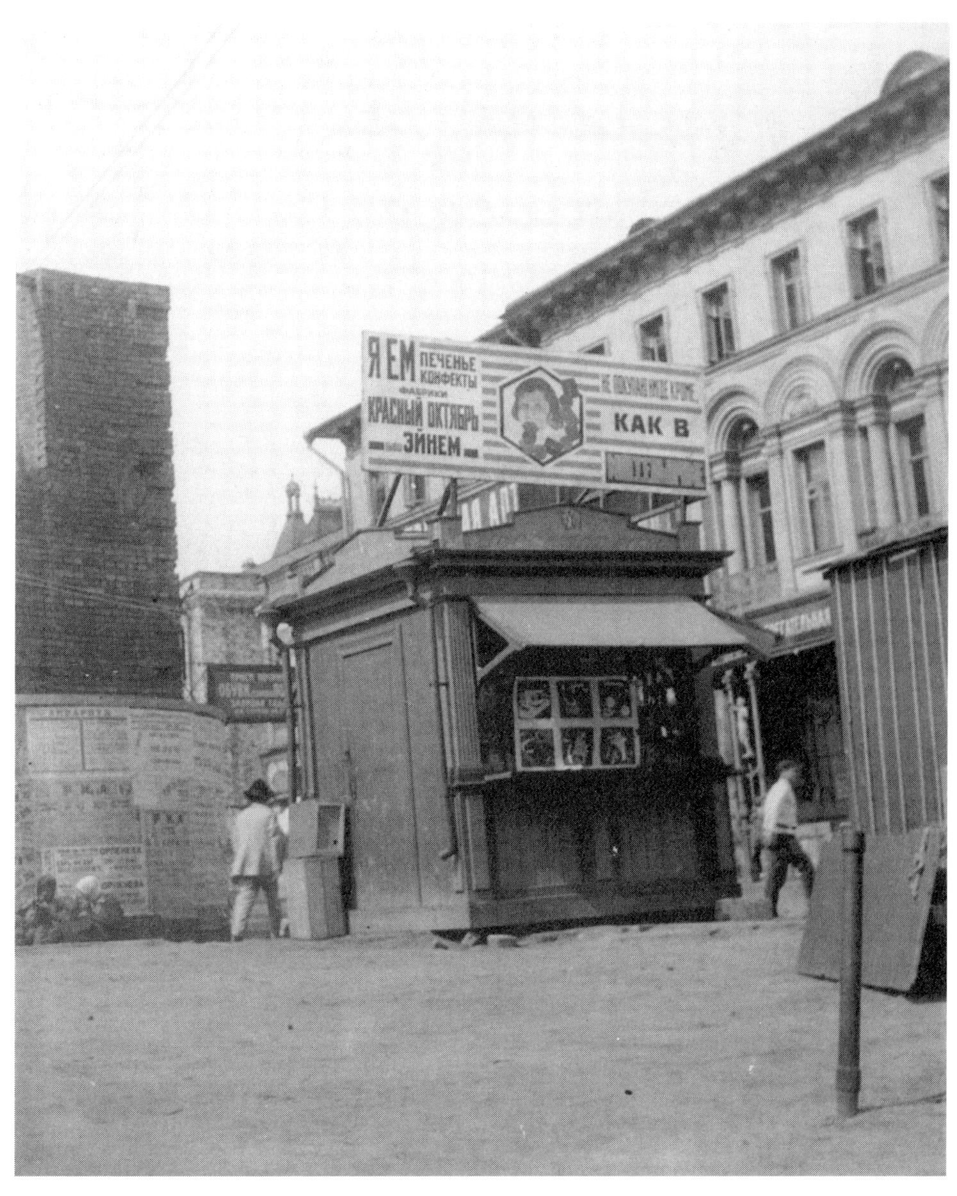

FIGURE 4.30
Aleksandr Rodchenko, photo of his Red October cookie advertisement on a Mossel′prom kiosk, Moscow, 1924.

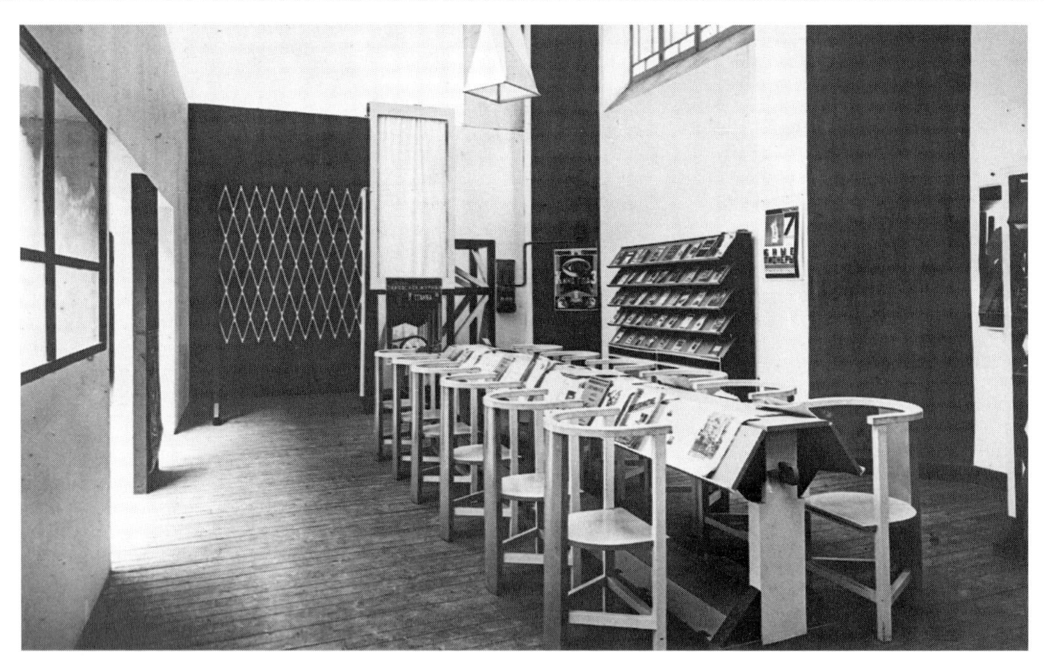

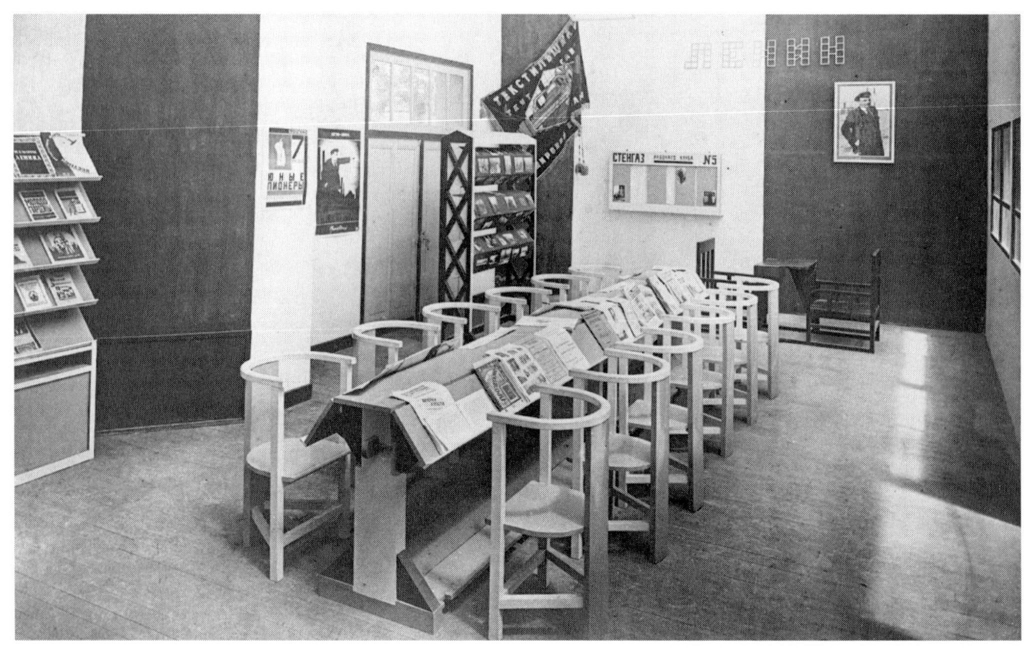

FIGURES 5.1, 5.2

Aleksandr Rodchenko, workers' club interior (view with speaker's platform [top] and with case for wall newspaper [bottom]), Paris, 1925. Alfred H. Barr, Jr. Papers. The Museum of Modern Art Archives, New York. Digital image © The Museum of Modern Art/Licensed by SCALA/Art Resource, N.Y.

CHAPTER 5

RODCHENKO IN PARIS

This chapter returns to the words of Aleksandr Rodchenko, written in a letter from Paris in 1925, that opened this book: "The light from the East is not only the liberation of workers, the light from the East is in the new relation to the person, to woman, to things. Our things in our hands must be equals, comrades, and not these black and mournful slaves, as they are here."[1] Rodchenko was in Paris on his first and only trip abroad to arrange the Soviet section of the Exposition Internationale des Arts Décoratifs et Industriels, for which he built his most famous Constructivist "thing," the interior of a workers' club (figures 5.1, 5.2). Rodchenko's lucidly spare, geometric club embodies the rationalized utilitarian object of everyday life proposed by Boris Arvatov, and Rodchenko's invocation of the socialist object from the East as a "comrade" corresponds to Arvatov's theory of the new industrial object as an active "co-worker" in the construction of socialism (EL, p. 124). Yet there is something uncanny about the stark, constrained order of the workers' club that exceeds Arvatov's theory, a visual uncanny that corresponds to the curious intensity and emotion of Rodchenko's verbal plea for "our things in our hands." This chapter will propose that the object desires that were mapped by the eccentric Constructivist advertisements also find expression in a central Constructivist object like the workers' club. Even in its seemingly most orthodox modernist form, the Constructivist object confronted the field of desire that is organized, under capitalism, by the commodity.

Rodchenko's letters are a response to the psychic and sensory overload of the Parisian commodity world; the visual forms of his object from the East must somehow cogently respond to his new, intimate knowledge of the Western commodity and its extraordinary power to organize desire. On the other hand, despite the rhetoric of his letters, Rodchenko knew very well that "East" and "West" were not quite so cleanly opposed in 1925. The West had industrial technology, while Russia was only beginning to industrialize, but Moscow was no haven from the commodity, because the New Economic Policy had unleashed a vital if idiosyncratic commercial culture. The Paris Exposition itself was as much a trade fair as an exhibition, and the Soviets were there because they hoped to participate lucratively. The evidence we have from Rodchenko's encounter with Parisian consumer culture in 1925 offers an especially vivid articulation of the Constructivist theory of a socialist object that encompasses, rather than represses, the desires organized by the Western commodity fetish, even as its goal is to construct new, transparent relations between subject and object that will lead to the collective ideal of social utopia illuminated by "the light from the East."

Soviets in Paris: The Official Idea of a "Socialist Thing"

Rodchenko's socialist thing from the East differed fundamentally from the idea of a socialist thing promoted by the official program of the Soviet delegation to the Paris exposition. The exposition was one of the first large-scale opportunities for the Soviet Union to present itself as a powerful trading nation on the international scene. The French government had not even officially recognized the Soviet Union until late October 1924, and did not issue the invitation to participate in the exposition until November 1, 1924, a scant five months before its scheduled opening. An exhibition organizing committee was hastily assembled, and by January 1, 1925, the committee had hired Rodchenko to travel to Paris as artistic executor of the exhibits, as well as to build his proposed workers' club on-site.[2] The committee chose to support the Constructivist workers' club as a highly visible symbol of the new political structure and everyday life of the Soviet Union, and to hire a radical avant-garde artist to give the boldest, most innovative form to the display of Soviet objects, in order to ensure that the Soviet exhibition would live up to the openly modernist goals of the international organizing committee of the exposition.[3] The rules of the exposition stated that it was "open to all manufacturers whose produce is artistic in character and shows clearly modern tendencies. . . . the real way to be modern is to find the form which best fits the function, taking into account the material."[4] Exhibition organizers hoped to foster the development of an international decorative style using modern materials such as reinforced concrete and steel, in forms appropriate for the modern world of the automobile, airplane, and hydroelectric dam.

Yet the majority of the exposition's pavilions and exhibits—especially some of the more lavish French contributions—made use of rich materials that had little to do with the relation between form and function. The grand salon within the French model *Residence of a Collector,* designed by E.-J. Ruhlman, for example, contained expensively upholstered furniture crafted from rare woods, *objets d'art* and a grand chandelier.[5] A writer in the journal *L'amour de l'art* dismissed the entire exposition as immoral, because exhibitors spent millions of francs to build temporary pavilions that they filled with sumptuous decorative art aimed only at the privileged classes.[6] Another critic reported that "les ouvriers causent: 'on ne peut se loger à Paris, et *ils* font des palais pour exposer les chaussures de leur poules'" (the workers are muttering: "we can't afford to live in Paris, and *they* build palaces to show off the shoes of their whores").[7] Rumors of the luxurious nature of the pavilions being set up at the exposition had already reached Moscow by the time the Soviet Union received its invitation to participate, affording the exhibition organizers an excellent opportunity to distinguish the Soviet section from other contributions both in terms of modernist originality and a refusal of material ostentation—the latter virtually assured by the small budget allotted to the project.

The organizers elected to give pride of place to the avant-garde theater designs, architectural projects, and graphics produced after the revolution. In a photograph of the grand entrance to the halls assigned to the Soviet Union in the Grand Palais, Rodchenko–Mayakovsky advertisements for Mossel'prom cigarettes and Rezinotrest are visible on the left wall, Constructivist textiles frame the door at left and right, and the doorway itself frames a new, smaller model of Tatlin's *Monument to the Third International* that he produced for the occasion (figure 5.3). (A decidedly non-Constructivist sculptural bust of Lenin takes center stage at the top of the stairs.) But the Soviet exhibits also promoted the Soviet Union's Eastern exoticism and folk traditions, albeit appropriately framed ideologically in order to differentiate these from the same picturesque exoticism that had been promoted under the tsars. (At the Eleventh World Exposition in Paris in 1900, for example, the Russian Imperial government erected an enormous Muscovite fortress.) These traditional decorative art objects were socialist not in form, but only as a result of their production under putatively socialist conditions. With Soviet industry in 1924 still recovering from war and revolutionary upheaval, the products of the traditional craft industries of Russia and the republics were some of the few things that the Soviet Union had to sell on the international market, making the decorative arts exhibition an opportunity for Soviet self-promotion. The brand of nationalism promoted by the official Soviet program was urbane and

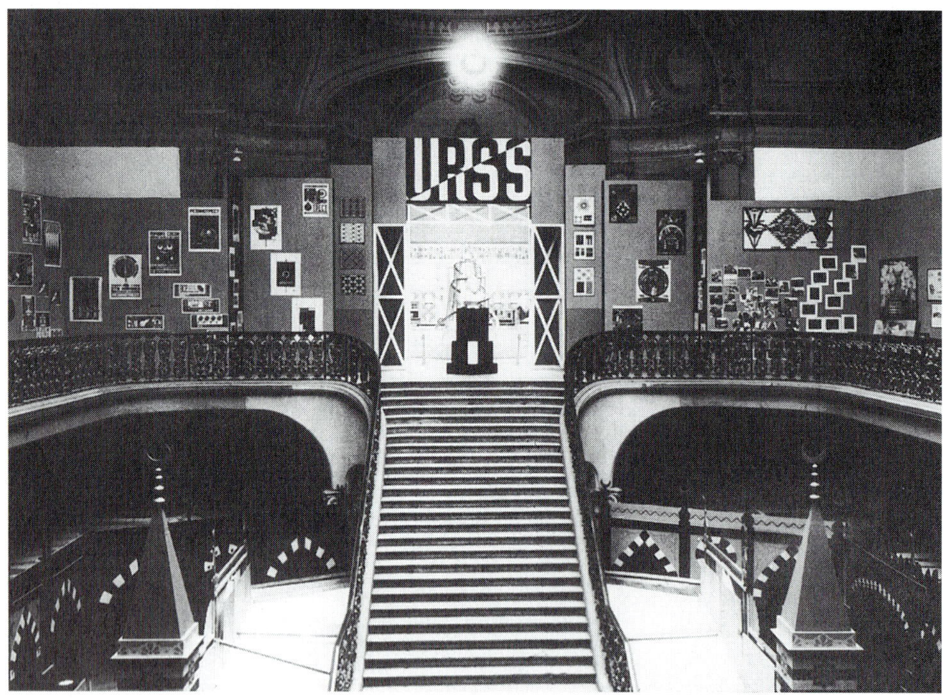

FIGURE 5.3
View of entrance to the Soviet exhibits at the Grand Palais, Paris, 1925.

utilitarian: it stressed the national specificities of Russia and the Soviet Republics insofar as this would ensure interest in their exotic products, but at the same time it attempted to represent the USSR as a modern, well-organized trading nation on a par with Western powers.

The committee's announcement of the architectural competition for the Soviet pavilion therefore asked architects to express the idea of the USSR as both a workers' and peasants' government, and as a brotherly union of separate nationalities; to emphasize both socialism and national specificity.[8] In contrast to the expensive marble of other pavilions, the winning design by the architect Konstantin Mel'nikov was constructed entirely of inexpensive wood and glass, appropriate materials for a temporary structure that required maximum visual access (figure 5.4).[9] The two-storey walls of glass flooded the interior with light, and the structure had been so ingeniously designed for a temporary exhibition that it had literally been unpacked from a suitcase: the wooden components had been measured out and cut to order in Russia, then shipped to Paris for quick assembly (and eventual disassembly) on site. The orientation of the pavilion and a tall open-framework stand, which rose high above the front entrance with the letters "URSS" at its top, took full visual advantage of the pavilion's small allotted plot of ground among the trees, and of its close proximity to the bombastic Italian

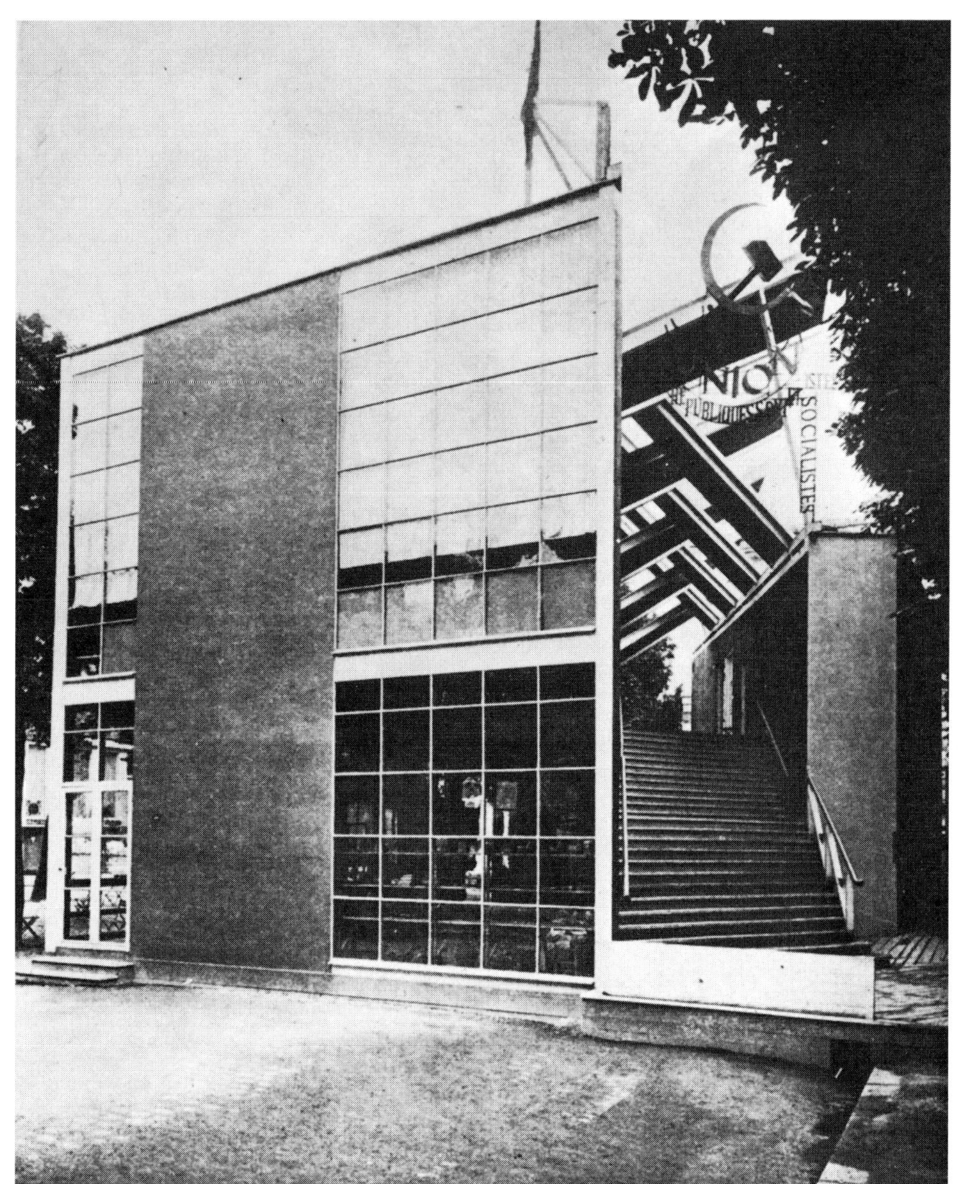

FIGURE 5.4
Konstantin Mel'nikov, Soviet pavilion, Paris, 1925.

pavilion for contrast. The tone was broadly nationalist, evoking both Soviet optimism and the Russian tradition of building out of wood. The pavilion took its place among the international modernist elite; only Le Corbusier's building matched its status as an example of a truly modern building at the exposition.

In their ideas of Soviet self-presentation in Paris, Mel'nikov recalls, he and Rodchenko understood each other perfectly: "In architecture I fought against 'the palace,' while in the design of the exhibits, he fought against 'the store,' because in the past an exhibition essentially did not differ from a big arcade [*passazh*]."[10] The organizing committee certainly wanted to avoid the display and ostentation of the other pavilions, in order to capitalize on the Soviet Union's image as newly rationalized and creatively efficient after the revitalization brought about by the revolution. But although the committee agreed wholeheartedly with Mel'nikov's "antipalace" rhetoric, the very arcade-like nature of the exhibition was what made it valuable to the young Soviet Union, trying to promote itself as a trading partner with developed countries in order to secure valuable hard currency. The overriding purpose of the exhibit was to present the most salable items of Soviet light industry and craft to the international buyers who attended the exhibition: porcelain, glass, flatware, and textiles from the state manufacturing trusts; carved wooden figures, painted wooden trays, appliquéd peasant blouses, and gorgeously printed flowered wool shawls of traditional Russian craft production; carpets and embroidered cloths from the Caucasus; furs from Archangel; and the ubiquitous black lacquered objects from Palek, mentioned in many reviews as the most memorable Soviet exhibits aside from the pavilion itself.[11] The influential Soviet critic Iakov Tugendkhol'd defended this commercial focus on national crafts by stating that it would be a caricature of the ideals of international Communism to imagine that it would eliminate national differences, because these differences provided "popular freshness" to art; each nation within the Soviet Union had to be encouraged to develop the possibilities of its own *genius loci*, rather than submit to a cosmopolitan, international style.[12]

The official invitation to submit exhibits to the exposition, distributed in November 1924, stressed its economic benefits, stating that participants would have the opportunity for "the conquest of new sales markets."[13] This openly commercial rhetoric was distasteful to the members of the exhibition organizing committee, all of whom, as academics, artists, or museum functionaries, were members of the cultural intelligentsia. Soon a heavy-handed representative from *Narkomvneshtorg* (the National Commissariat of Foreign Trade) was brought onto the committee to ensure that trade goals were accorded equal status with artistic ones.[14] The dual status of the exposition as part art exhibition and part trade fair, and the Soviet Union's ambiguous status as both a revolutionary state and a nation eager for trade, raised difficult questions: Should retail sale by participating Soviet businesses be allowed? Would it be permissible to bring duplicates of official exhibits that would be for sale? How should items be sold—through shops, kiosks, or a grand auction at the end of the exhibition?[15] The committee came to the reluctant decision that copies of exhibited items could be made available for retail sale.[16] *Narkomvneshtorg* took responsibility for drawing up a price list, and eventually Mel'nikov was commissioned to design wooden *Torgsektor* (trade section) kiosks to be erected next to the Soviet Pavilion for the purpose of selling native handicrafts and state-produced artistic goods (figure 5.5).

Mel'nikov's Torgsektor kiosks ironically functioned as the "arcade" or "store" that he had praised Rodchenko for resisting in his exhibition design. The kiosks themselves were rigorously modern and expedient in their design, like his pavilion; they were constructed out of lightweight wood, painted a crisp combination of red, white, and gray, and their diagonally sloping roofs directly echoed the interlaced beams above the diagonal stairway of the pavilion. But they contrasted incongruously with the often ornate objects on display within them, such as, for example, the porcelain figurines by the popular artist Natalia Dan'ko, who

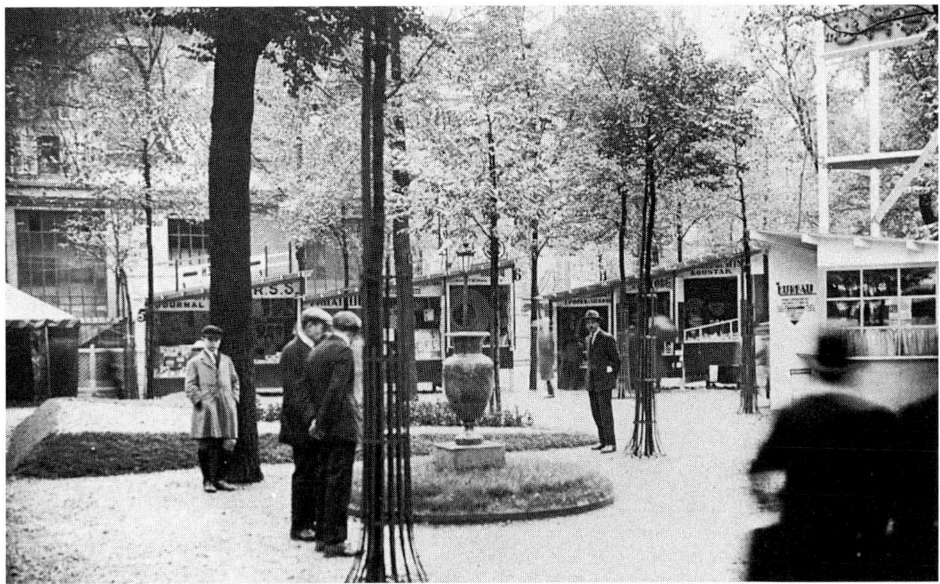

FIGURE 5.5
Konstantin Mel'nikov, Torgsektor kiosks, Paris, 1925. Courtesy Avery Architectural and Fine Arts Library, Columbia University in the City of New York.

specialized in continuing the Russian tradition of porcelain figurines but with newly Soviet themes; in her chess set, for example, the king is a worker in delicate porcelain overalls, the queen a peasant girl carrying a sheaf of wheat intermixed with corn flowers. Such traditional decorative knickknacks represent "socialist objects" on the official terms of the Soviet delegation to Paris. These were precisely the kinds of objects to which the Constructivists most strenuously objected: old decorative forms churned out by Soviet factories, either completely unchanged from prerevolutionary molds and patterns, or merely decorated on the surface with new "revolutionary" subject matter.

The Transparency of the Constructivist Object

In pointed contrast to the traditional crafts on display, and for sale, in the Soviet section, Rodchenko's workers' club was derived entirely from new forms based on the postrevolutionary program of Constructivism. Constructing the modular, movable furnishings of the club interior out of cheap, lightweight wood, and using open-frame construction, Rodchenko was intent on conserving materials and eliminating excess weight and bulk. The objects in the club have the social function of materially organizing the leisure time in the everyday lives of workers, but like his Mossel'prom advertisements, they are formally related to his earlier *Spatial Construction* series, such as his *Spatial Construction no. 9* of 1921 (figure 5.6). Like the hexagonal *Spatial Construction no. 10* that we examined in the previous chapter, this spatial construction is made of plywood painted the color of metal, and originates as a thin, flat circle of wood with a series of concentric circles carved through its surface. When each concentric section is opened out it forms a three-dimensional structure that is infinitely transformable, but only within the constraints of its own system. This formal logic reappears in the speaker's platform of the club, where these expanding and collapsing forms take on a utilitarian purpose in the foldout screen for projecting slides and the contractible bench and speaker's stand (figure 5.7, and visible at the back of figure 5.1). Other objects in the workers' club also operate like the speaker's platform: the side flaps of the long central table can be lowered for a more comfortable reading position; the chess ensemble in the back of the room, under the poster of Lenin, consists of two chairs separated by a nifty revolving chessboard on hinges; above it, the case for the "wall newspaper" allows for daily changes (see figure 5.2).

Critics have doubted the theoretical feasibility, or even the political integrity, of the Constructivist attempt to take the self-referential, systemic structures that were so revelatory as modern art and harness them for utilitarian tasks in

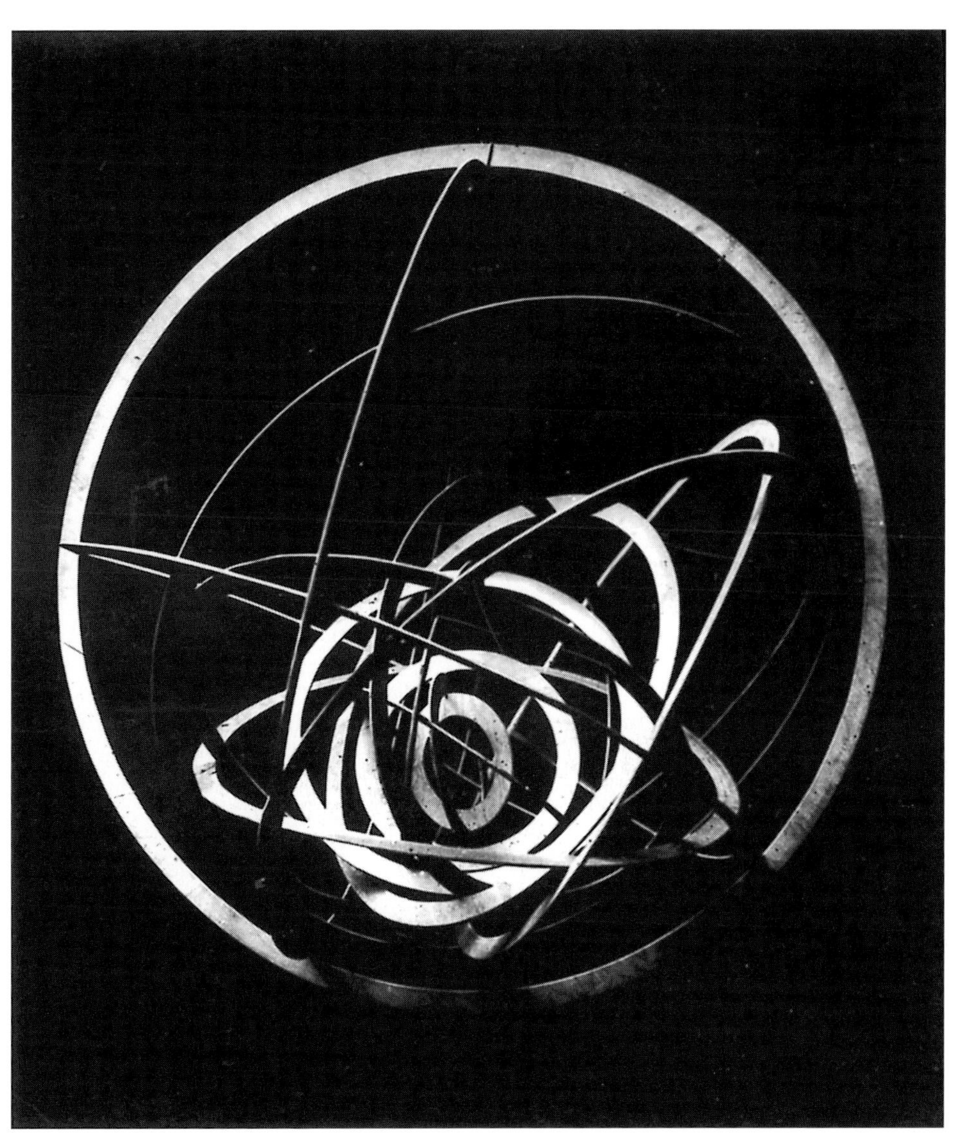

FIGURE 5.6
Aleksandr Rodchenko, *Spatial Construction no. 9*, 1921. Painted plywood. Photo Howard Schickler Fine Art.

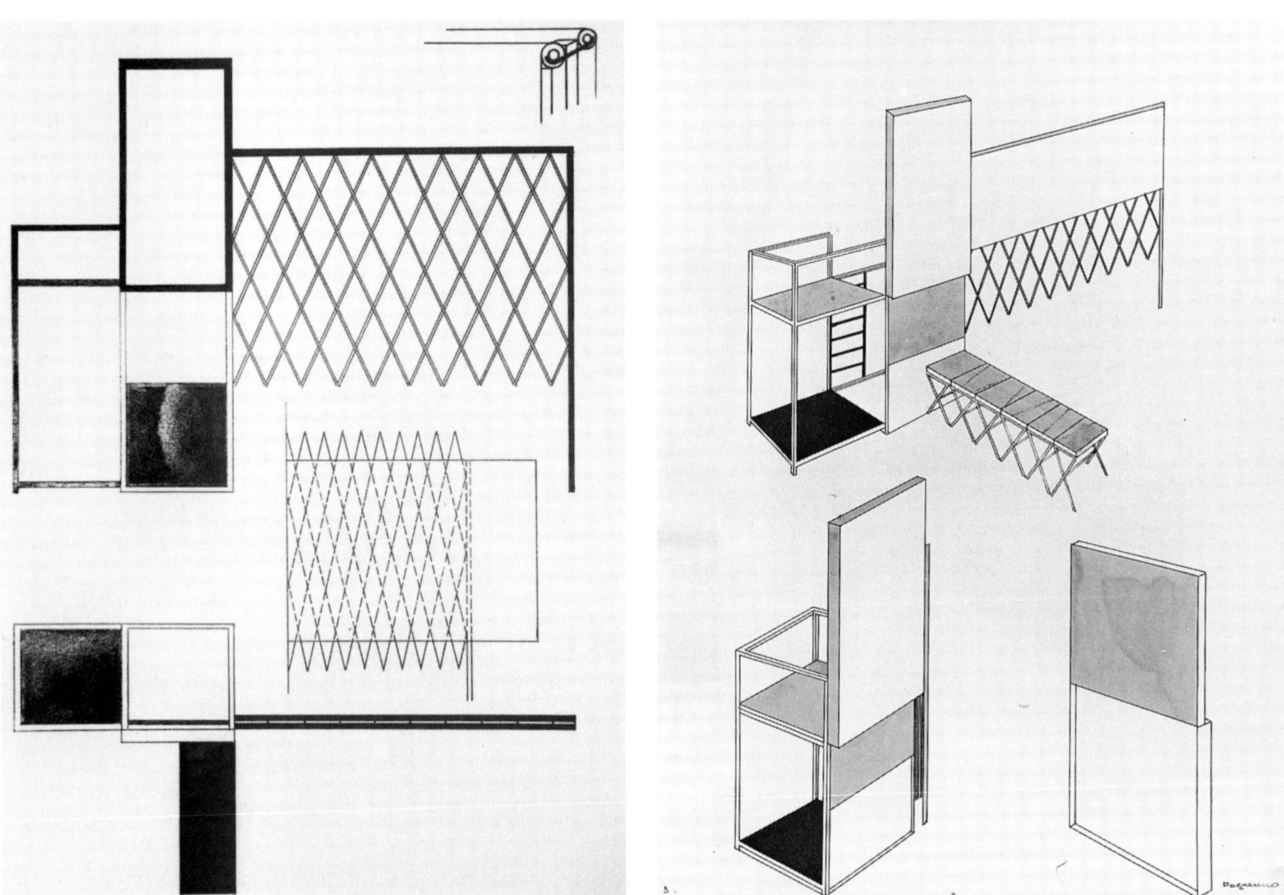

FIGURE 5.7
Aleksandr Rodchenko, drawings for workers' club speaker's platform. India ink on paper. Private collection.

transforming everyday life. The contemporary Soviet version of this critique of Constructivism was made forcefully by Tugendkhol'd in his review of the Paris Exposition, in which he lumped the "spiritless geometry" of the Russian Constructivist exhibits together with the rationalized geometry of those of the Esprit Nouveau group of France, exemplified by Le Corbusier's exhibit of a starkly furnished house as a "machine for living" complete with a maid's room. Tugendkhol'd had little patience for utopian technicism, from the left or the right: "The fetishism of the machine, the worship of industry—here is the pathos of this group of artists, serving in essence as the ideologues of the large-scale capitalism flourishing in France. [. . .] the whole 'new spirit' or 'new style,' of which these 'utopians' are capable, leads to . . . sun baths for workers on flat, East-facing roofs."[17] He warned the Constructivists against their participation in this "new style," because metaphors of a "light from the East" can be so easily converted to mere compensatory sun baths rather than revolution; helping to align people with the products of modern industry most often simply facilitates their subjection to its capitalist logic. This concern reappears in Manfredo Tafuri's dark vision of modernist utopianism, for example, as well as in Jean Baudrillard's postmodern critique of modern design.[18]

Hubertus Gassner has offered a provocative analysis of Rodchenko's *Spatial Constructions* series of 1921, describing these works as "transparent" systems that metaphorize and organize both the body and the unconscious—only to claim that the utilitarian turn in Constructivism destroyed the purity of these systemic forms by harnessing them in the service of Soviet modernization and industrialization.[19] According to Gassner, because the hanging construction allows for nothing that exceeds determination by the system, the Constructivist artist-engineer achieves organized self-consciousness through the very process of making it:

> If the structure is completely systematic in its inner logic and entirely transparent in its making or functional modes, i.e., if the object is "constructed throughout," it appears as a homologous model of the producer's unconscious of which he has become fully aware. The artistic subject becomes as transparent as his creation. The previously impenetrable dark of his subconscious and body is illuminated and rendered transparent through the exposure of the logic of their functional modes.[20]

Gassner's confidence that the conscious subject can become "fully aware" of her unconscious desires in this way may be overly optimistic about the possibility of achieving psychoanalytic self-knowledge, but precisely this fantasy of a transparent relay between the consciousness of the maker and the consciousness of the object fuels the most utopian ideal of the Constructivist object. Gassner further identifies a compelling homology between the Constructivist object and the human body:

> In the Constructivist universe, objects exist solely as organs of human activity. They adjust to people's actions, expand and die with them, while constantly renewing their own shape and function. The Constructivist objects are congruent counterparts of the subject. Therein lies their utopian potential. Ideally, they would have transformed material reality into an unrestricted space in which free people could act.[21]

The Constructivist object as a "congruent counterpart" of the human subject, an object that "expands and dies" with the human body, brings us close to what Rodchenko might mean when he calls the object a "comrade." Yet Gassner claims that the displacement of this homology between the body and the object onto utilitarian tasks—the transition, that is, from the *Spatial Constructions* series to the workers' club—would lead only to the subjection of human bodies to the forces of industrialism. Gassner returns us to the dystopian conclusions of Tugendkhol'd and Tafuri. The Constructivists failed to transform reality into a space of freedom, he concludes, because the moment of perfect transparency, which is also a fleeting moment of pure autonomy for the art object because it is responsible only to its own coherent system, is destroyed when the self-referential structures have utilitarian imperatives imposed on them from outside the system—or, in other words, when they are brought into contact with history.[22]

Yet Gassner's insights into the bodily and unconscious functioning of the nonutilitarian Constructivist object can also be used to support, instead, a claim for its utopian potential precisely in its utilitarian form. For Gassner offers an analysis of the uncanny content of the Constructivist object: its doubling of the human body. In Marx's definition of commodity fetishism, the system of exchange inverts social relations, resulting in "material [*dinglich*] relations between persons and social relations between things."[23] Hal Foster has suggested that in this trading of semblances between producers and products, "the commodity becomes our uncanny double, evermore vital as we are evermore inert."[24] In contrast to Marx, Arvatov's theory of the Constructivist object attempts to recuperate for proletarian culture this notion of thinglike relations between producers, and of social relations between newly active and materially appropriate things. Constructivism aims, in effect, to remake or harness the uncanny of the commodity—its ability to act as the doppelgänger for the human producer—for socialist ends. The uncanny effect of an object stems from its evocation of a repressed desire; the uncanny (*das Unheimliche*), Freud says, "can be shown to come from something repressed which *recurs*."[25] In the uncanny this recurrence provokes anxiety, but the socialist object would make a space within the uncanny (a home within the *Unheimliche*) that could also be the site of release from or acknowledgment of the repressed desire. For the "secret nature" of the uncanny is that this recurrence is "in reality nothing new or foreign" (nothing *unheimlich*), "but something familiar and old-established in the mind" (something *heimlich*), which is why Freud insists that *das Heimliche* cannot be differentiated from *das Unheimliche*.[26] In its uncanny animation, the Constructivist object will be the figure of the automaton, working to align human subjects with the modernizing "light from the East," but in its very embodiedness it will also mark out a homely space for the potential humanizing of the unhomely products of industrial culture, bringing those products into the human field of desire.

For Gassner, the meeting of the perfect, transparent, systemic Constructivist structure with the material history of the industrial commodity compromises the object and obviates its interest, whereas the argument of this book is that precisely this compromise defines the Constructivist "socialist object." For as this study has detailed, the material circumstances of Russian Constructivism in 1925 were not the univalent "drive toward industrialization and modernization" described by Gassner, but rather the hybrid situation of NEP. As an autonomous art object, the transparent Constructivist structure functions as a metaphor of perfection, not as an actor in history; conversely, as an actor in the actual material, historical, and bodily circumstances of NEP Russia, the utilitarian Constructivist object loses its perfection, and a good bit of its transparency, but it gains in its potential ability to organize the object-desires of modernity as an alternative to the commodity form.

Letters from Paris

Rodchenko's letters home to Stepanova document the profound shock of the self-proclaimed modernist artist and engineering enthusiast upon encountering the sheer technological and material magnitude of fully developed modernity. He notes with surprise that there are no horses on the streets at all (Letters, March 24, p. 10). The letters express his experience of Western modernity through his relation to the objects of the Parisian commodity world; in Paris without any knowledge of the French language, the objects spoke to him with that much more resonance. "The first thing that met my eyes in Paris—we arrived at night—was the bidet in the hotel room and in the morning today, a man selling indecent postcards" (Letters, March 23, p. 10). These first objects he describes are specifically bodily and sexual; in the letters that follow, he will return repeatedly to the power of commodities to structure bodies and identities. He quickly finds himself transformed by this commodity world.

Immediately upon arrival he took advantage of the highly favorable ruble exchange rate and bought himself a new suit, shoes, suspenders, collars, socks, and more. Later he notes: "I have to buy myself a damned hat, I can't walk around in my cap because not a single Frenchman wears one, and everyone looks at me disapprovingly, thinking that I'm a German" (Letters, April 1, p. 13). He confides to Stepanova his every purchase, such as the pair of night slippers he had to buy to keep his feet warm at night, having forgotten his *valenki*, the traditional Russian felt boots. He shares his culinary experiences, describing with care what he eats for each meal and how much it costs; he likes the coffee and the Chablis, but dislikes Brie and Roquefort, and oysters make him want to throw up. The very rhythms and bodily sensations of his everyday life are transformed: he now goes to bed early and gets up early, like the French and unlike Russian bohemians. He mentions the hot running water in the hotel room repeatedly: "I've become a complete Westerner. I walk around clean, shave every day, wash myself all the time" (Letters, March 24, p. 10), and later chides her for expressing curiosity about his new appearance, assuring her that there is nothing interesting about his idiotic new outfits—he feels repulsive in them (Letters, April 5, p. 15). His debonair demeanor in a photograph in which he slouches elegantly against the railing of the outside landing of the Soviet Pavilion suggests, however, that this bodily transformation was not entirely without its pleasures (figure 5.8). With his relaxed pose and half smile into the distance, he looks just as at ease lounging here in his buttoned vest and natty little shoes as he does standing erect with hand on hip in his heavy work-boots and homemade *prozodezhda* (production clothing) in the 1922 photograph by Mikhail Kaufmann that shows him in his Moscow studio surrounded by his series of *Spatial Constructions* in their collapsed, archivable form (see figure 1.1).

A watercolor self-caricature (figure 5.9) captures his dilemma of identity in Paris, where he is by turns an ascetic Bolshevik, a technology-oriented Constructivist, a provincial, Slavophilic Russian, and a desiring subject of everyday life whose desires are organized by the commodity.[27] Dressed in new clothes, taking pictures with his brand new Parisian-purchased camera, he is interpellated by the Parisian object world. Yet his new hat is perched precariously on his trademark shaved head, and he pictures himself observing the city through the distancing

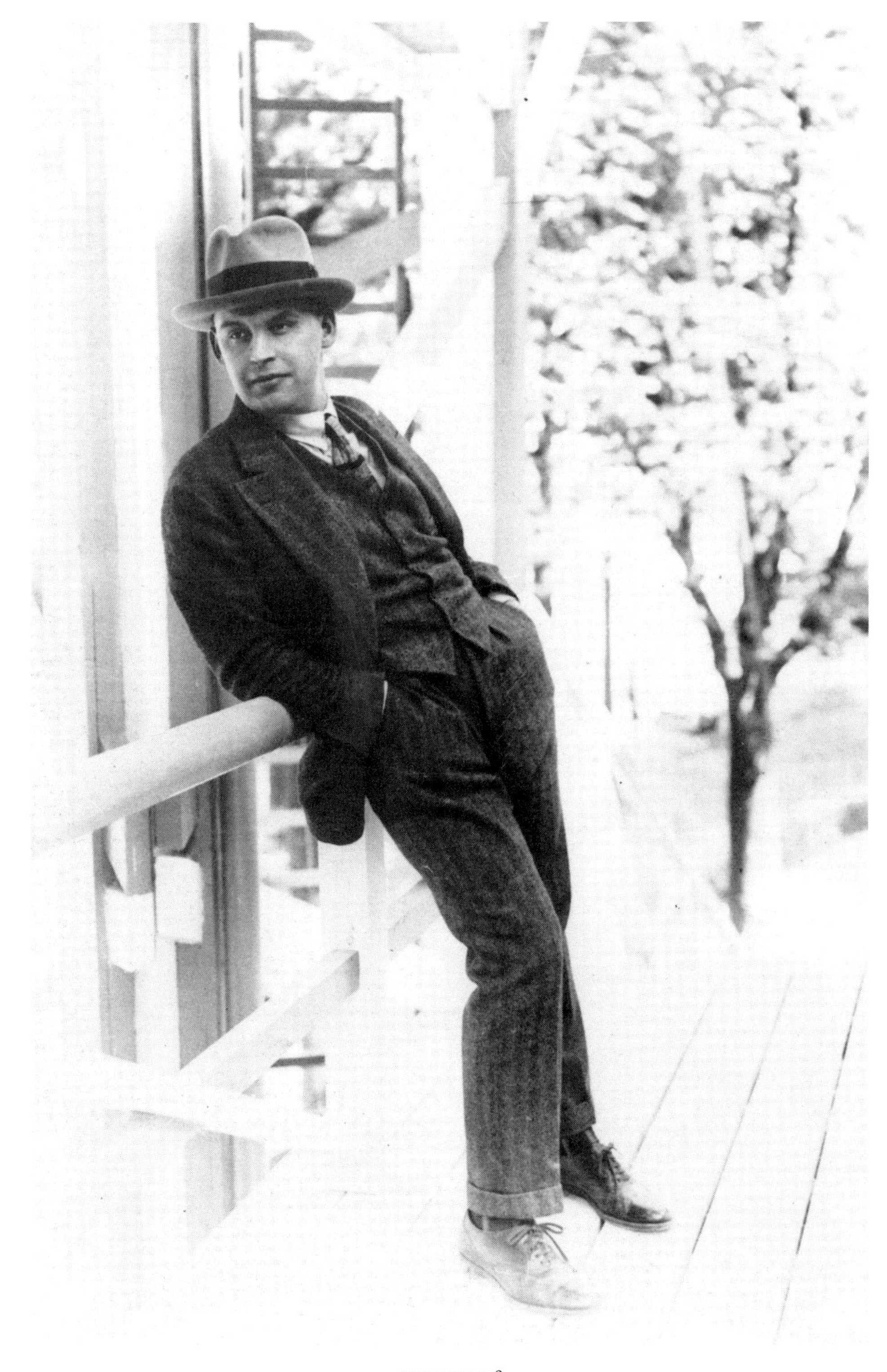

FIGURE 5.8
Aleksandr Rodchenko at the Soviet pavilion, Paris, 1925. Private collection.

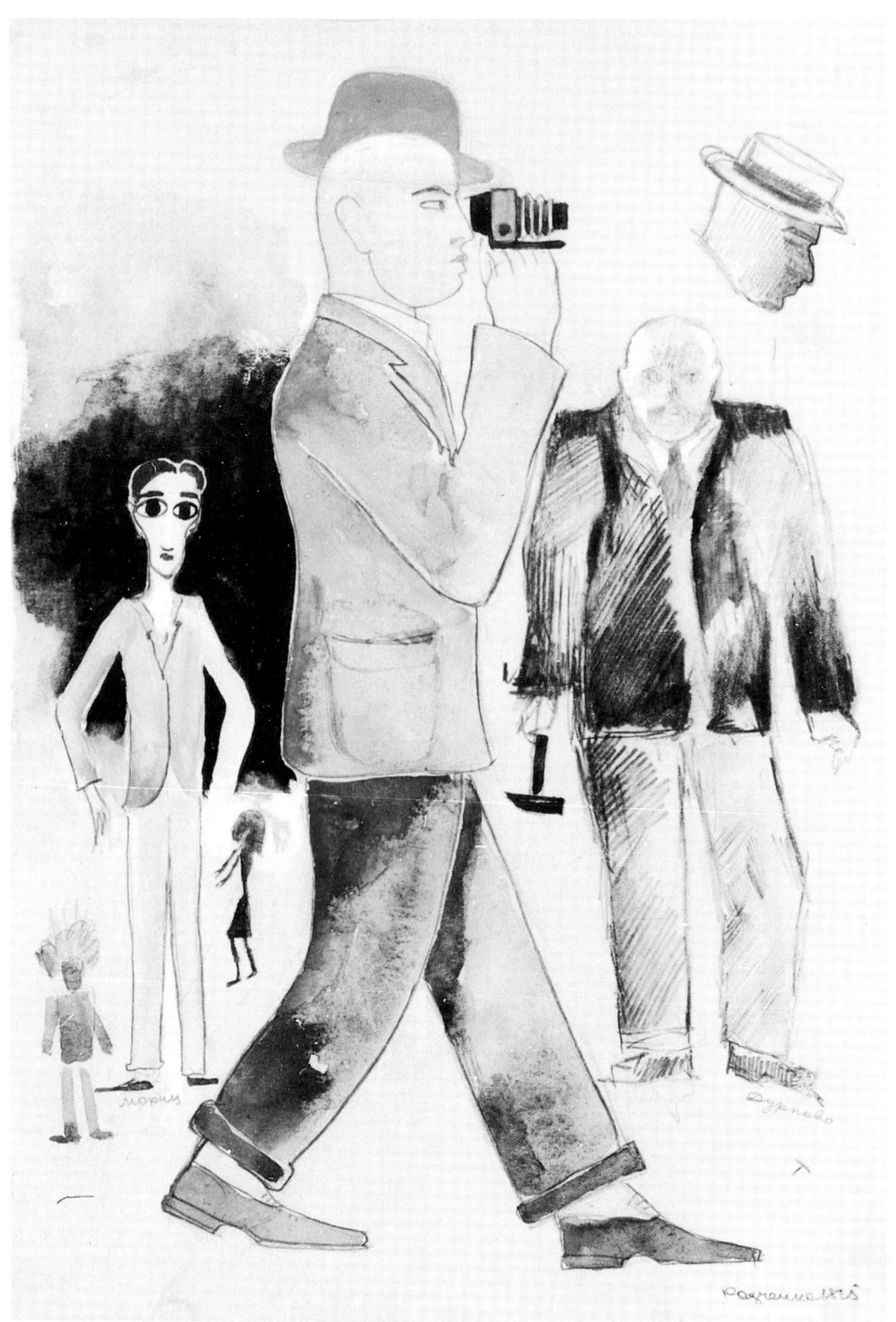

FIGURE 5.9
Aleksandr Rodchenko, self-caricature, Paris, 1925. Watercolor. Private collection.

eye of the camera, as the critical Constructivist from the USSR. Rodchenko's upright posture, purposeful stride, strong jawline and mechanically amplified eye wage a winning battle against the trouser cuffs and hat brims and pointy shoes for visual dominance; the overall effect is of the straight-backed Constructivist transcending both costume and surroundings. The caricature playfully acknowledges his own vulnerability to the pleasures of Western commodities but also maintains the need for a Constructivist remaking of the commodity into a thing that can be an active, useful comrade to the human subject.

The object as comrade, by responding to and working with the human body, affects not only the physical qualities of that body, but psychic ones as well—extending into the nontransparent reaches of the commodity. When he buys his new "ICA" brand camera, for example, he writes to Stepanova its exact measurements, lens size, and speed, and calls it "splendid." His purchase of a "Sept" brand movie camera merits an even lengthier, technically detailed description concluding with the phrase "I am terribly happy"; as he describes its technical features he inserts the phrase "I am sitting and turning it around in my hands," revealing that of course his delight in the camera exceeds its technological appropriateness and becomes tied up with the sheer sensual pleasure of possession and the fantasies triggered by that possession.[28] Rodchenko senses that this interweaving of conscious, functional Constructivist object pleasure with the phantasmatic pleasures of commodity possession might compromise his confidence in the object "from our point of view." For as his text reveals, the orchestration of his body by bourgeois clothing and modern hygiene is only the outwardly visible sign of the inevitable orchestration of his desire by the commodities around him. The letters are filled with references to things in the abstract, to the ways that these things incite his own desire behind the back of his proclaimed disgust for them. "I see masses of things and don't have the possibility of buying them" (Letters, March 27, p. 13). Or again: "Here there are millions of things, they make the head spin, I want to buy everything by the wagonload and bring it home" (Letters, May 4, p. 20).[29]

There is a progressing metaphoric collapse between material objects and the unsettling sexuality that they organize. He mentions repeatedly not only the bidets, but also the perverse insinuation of the ubiquitous double beds. Moving into a new hotel room, he reports "again a bidet, and a 3- or 8-person bed" (Letters, April 8, p. 16).[30] Noting that all the women wear short, tight skirts, they later become in shorthand "tight women" and finally simply "tight buttocks," linked in metaphoric chains of bad objects: "these tight women and hats and endless bidets" (Letters,

April 2, p. 14). These bad objects cannot be pried apart from the good ones: "[Westerners] create industry of high quality, and again it is offensive, that on the best ocean liners, airplanes and so on, there are and will always be again these fox-trots, and powders, and endless bidets" (Letters, March 25, p. 12). The word "endless," the phrase "there are and will always be," and the repetition of the word "again" signal Rodchenko's emerging understanding of the inescapable locking together of the desires lodged in commodity fetishes—the fox-trots, powders, and bidets—with the technological promise of industrial production—the ocean liners and airplanes. Rodchenko resists the idea that the desires orchestrated by the powders and bidets should have a place in the Constructivist universe of transparent relations between people and things.

He explicitly links the powder-using Parisian women with the passivity of the commodity: they are immobile, merely decorating the world rather than acting in it, lined up as in a store window, quantified as at a cash register. He sums this up in a terse sentence: "The cult of woman as thing" (Letters, March 25, p. 12). Later he elaborates that the women are even worse than the things, because they are produced as if from a pattern, all exactly alike, according to fashion (Letters, May 2, p. 19). The most extreme example of the objectification of women is the cabaret show, which Rodchenko describes for Stepanova with theatricalized horror:

> Here there are masses of theaters where the entire evening, naked women in expensive and enormous feathers walk on and off the scene in silence against expensive backdrops and that's all, they walk through and that's it. [. . .] And they are silent and don't dance and don't move. But simply walk through . . . one . . . another . . . a third . . . five at once, twenty at once . . . and that's it . . . I can't even begin to describe exactly what this "nothingness" is for, what this "thing" is for, what it means when it seems that only a man is a person, and women are not people, and you can do anything with them—that is a thing. . . (Letters, May 2, p. 19; ellipses original except for bracketed instance)

This passage expands on what Rodchenko means when he calls for a "new relation to the person, to woman, to things." Rodchenko's reaction to the cabaret suggests a typically ascetic, moralizing reaction against sexual display and fashion that might best be rectified, in Bolshevik style, by imposing standards of purely functional, less sexualized clothing like Stepanova's sports clothes as well as public decency laws.

But the repeated sexual references in his letters suggest that he is alert to the erotic power of the Parisian commodity world, and criticizes its form—the passivity and patterning of commodities and of women—rather than its content. He wants the things, after all, "by the wagonload." He is able to imagine a different, socialist form of fashion that would redeem the short tight skirts: his letters to Moscow are full of observations for Stepanova, who was just concluding her work designing textiles for the First State Cotton-Printing Factory, on the appealing and useful aspects of Paris fashion. He details for her the colors and styles of women's coats, skirts, stockings, and shoes, and notes that "the fashions here are truly interesting" (Letters, March 24, pp. 10–11).[31] A few days later, he writes to her that he has heard about a technology that allows one to print fabric and make fashionable clothing at home; "I'm now thinking that on my return, I will build you a studio for production and printing" (Letters, March 28, p. 13).[32] This suggests the possibility of an active, Constructivist form of fashion that would retain the phantasmatic power of the Parisian fashions, but would no longer render women as passive objects. The "light from the East" would then entail a more conscious and egalitarian model of modern, urban self-display, and not just the imposition of moralizing constraints.

In spite of Rodchenko's repeated references to women as things in Paris, and his assertion in the above passage on the cabaret that "only a man is a person," in other passages he is on the cusp of acknowledging the fact that men are just as vulnerable to the commodity as women. After his declaration of the "cult of woman as thing," he turns his attention to man: "and again man, creating and building, is all in a flutter with this '*great fever,*' this *world-wide syphilis of art*" (Letters, March 25, p. 12). That is to say, man should be productive, but the fever of commodity consumption has ruined him as well. He does not openly include himself in this indictment of Parisian men, but as we have seen, he acknowledges his own implication in the desires of consumption at other moments in the letters.

The power of his letters stems from their earnest grappling with a desire to participate in the commodity world of the West, as well as with the converse desire to escape to the imagined East. His observations of the fox-trotting public make him long for the East: "how simple, how healthy is this East, this you can see clearly only from here" (Letters, March 25, p. 12). He specifies at least one version of the transparent "new relation to woman" that he associates with the nonthreatening, noneroticized East: describing the anti-Bolshevik Russian émigrés who sit in cafes and literally cry when they hear Russian songs, he reflects, "I am sure that if I was told today that I would never return to the U.S.S.R., I too would sit in the middle of the road and cry—'I want my mommy.' Of course, these are two different mommies: their mommy is Russia, mine is the U.S.S.R." (Letters,

March 27, p. 12). The Soviet Union becomes equated with healthy reproductive sexuality, with maternal safety and authority, suggesting that the relation of stern mother to good son is one model for the organized relations of desire that Constructivism seeks. Rodchenko addressed his letters to Stepanova, who lived in their Moscow apartment with their newborn baby daughter, Varvara, and his mother, Ol'ga Evdokimovna. The exclusively female and familial nature of his audience made it all the more natural for Rodchenko to act the part of the good Communist son in Paris, dismissive of his newfound elegance in bourgeois clothing, horrified by what he saw in his forays to dance halls and cabarets, seized by a desire to tidy things up: "it is simply necessary to wash everything, clean it all up, and set a goal for it" (Letters, April 2, p. 15). On a visit to the Olympia dance hall, he sees heavily made-up women in skimpy dresses dancing the fox trot, and calls them "ugly and endlessly terrifying" (Letters, March 25, p. 11). Two sentences later he notes again that "I wash myself endlessly with hot water," suggesting that his new pastime of bathing is a response not only to the availability of modern plumbing, but also an obsessive reaction to the muck of the commodity that surrounds him.

The sexuality projected onto this muck is the opposite of that of the "healthy" East. In his description, the commodified Parisian women are distinctly nonmaternal. Writing about women subjected to the whims of fashion to the point that ugly women are now in vogue, he invokes specifically nonreproductive imagery of women's bodies: he sees women "with thin and long hips, without breasts and without teeth and with disgracefully long hands topped with red stains, women in the style of Picasso, women in the style of 'negroes,' women in the style of 'hospital inmates,' women in the style of 'the dregs of the city'" (Letters, March 25, p. 12).[33] In this metaphoric orgy, Rodchenko's observations about the commodity's assault on the productive subject extend to its effect on the reproductive subject.

The importance of his letters, for this study, is not what they reveal about the form of his particular, individual desires—these are not our concern—but rather what they can reveal about the phantasmatic content that he projects onto his Constructivist objects. This distinction becomes crucial as we examine the specifically anal-erotic aspect of this nonreproductive sexuality he associates with the Parisian object world, to which we were first alerted by the "tight buttocks" and "endless bidets." He closes this letter about women as "the dregs of the city" with a particularly lurid outburst: "we will eat feces in a silver wrapper, hang dirty panties in a golden frame and copulate with a dead bitch" (Letters, March 25, p. 12).

The short skirts on the "tight buttocks," it turns out, conceal soiled underwear, and the bidets are meant for washing bottoms as well as genitals. We can turn to Freud here for the most precise interpretation of the theoretical significance of this aspect of Rodchenko's letters. His metaphors of excess and filth, and his corresponding desire for authoritarian control and rationalization, not to mention his repeated references to washing and cleaning, all point to the relevance of the classic psychoanalytic model of anal erotism for analyzing his picture of the relation between Western commodities and Soviet socialist objects.[34] The previous chapter argued that Rodchenko's Mossel'prom advertisements attempted to diagram consumer desire through the model of the oral drive, because as the earliest infantile stage of desire it corresponded to the primitive NEP economy, which was itself "transitional." The object world that he encountered in Paris was far more excessive and sophisticated, occupying a more advanced stage of capitalism and therefore more likely to evoke the formation that Freud characterized as anal erotism—for Freud, a character formation deeply tied to the hoarding of wealth within capitalist modernity. Rodchenko's goal is to clean up the Parisian objects and bring them home to the simple, healthy East, where he hopes that the excesses of this more mature model of modernity can be avoided.

It is in this broader cultural sense that an anal-erotic reading of his letters can be significant. Witness his description of the Paris commodities that are "decorated on the outside and coldly decorate Paris, but on the inside, like black slaves, concealing catastrophe, they carry their black labor" (Letters, May 4, p. 20).[35] His desire to pry apart the tightly shut buttocks, to open up the cold Paris objects and shed the light from the East onto the black catastrophe concealed in their interior, takes the form of a sexual fantasy of nonreproductive anal penetration projected onto the objects. But it is also a Constructivist fantasy of freeing the "black and mournful slaves" from their commodity labor in order to transform their work into the productive labor of the comrade.

Ideally, the system of modern production and consumption in the West should function as transparently and effectively as its vast systemic technology of sewage and plumbing (the bidets and hot water), resulting in regulated consumption and clean bodies and streets. But Rodchenko phantasmatically identifies the excessive, irrational desire for the commodity that he witnesses in Paris with excess shit that cannot be contained by the best plumbing in the world. In another caricature from Paris, Rodchenko sketches the entrance to the Soviet pavilion with a small figure of a bourgeois gentleman wearing a top hat that may be a spoof on the pavilion's designer, the architect Mel'nikov (figure 5.10).

Rodchenko has exaggerated the size of the exit sign in the stairwell, but the pointing hand of the gentleman and the receding letters of the word seem to indicate that the sign points into the building rather than out of it. He has changed one letter in the French word for "exit," so that the sign reads *"sortir"* instead of *"sortie."* In Russian, *"sortir"* means lavatory. We find ourselves back in the bathroom with Rodchenko, this time inside the light and transparent Soviet pavilion. The joke lies in evoking the opposite of what is true: the pavilion as socialist object conceals no black catastrophe of excess commodity desire within it. Or perhaps the caricature refers to the fantasy of the bodily processes as a regulated system in the East; the flushing public toilet is an apt metaphor for the logical architectural system of Mel'nikov's pavilion—a wishful metaphor, because the Russian East was notorious for its primitive plumbing.

Constructivism imagined a form of modernity that embraced the technology and efficiency of the regulated systems of modern urban life—mass production, motorized transport, plumbing, sewage—but without the commodity form, which sullied its transparency with fetishistic desires. The plumbing without the bidets. "Why did I have to see it, this West," laments Rodchenko, "I loved it better without having seen it. Take its technology from it, and it remains a rotten pile of manure, helpless and decrepit" (Letters, April 2, pp. 14–15). The pile of stinking manure represents not shit as the regulated product of the body's system, but as the eroticized excess of the capitalist system, cropping up in soiled panties and silver bonbon wrappers. While Rodchenko's letters produce a fantasy of the East as the site of regulated systems and transparent desires for both bodies and objects, the kinds of desires crucial to the phantasmatic power of the commodity find their way into the very form of the rational Constructivist objects he made in Paris, turning them into objects that can fully meet the commodity on its own terms.

Walter Benjamin in Moscow

Walter Benjamin's pilgrimage to the Soviet East in the winter of 1926–1927 is the converse of Rodchenko's trip to the Parisian West a scant two years earlier, and like Rodchenko in Paris, Benjamin frames his writings about his experiences around the object-world he encounters there. His essay "Moscow" offers a vivid description of the space of the Moscow street with its overflow of goods:

> In Moscow goods burst everywhere from the houses, they hang on fences, lean against railings, lie on pavements. Every fifty steps stand women with cigarettes, women with fruit, women with sweets. They have their wares in

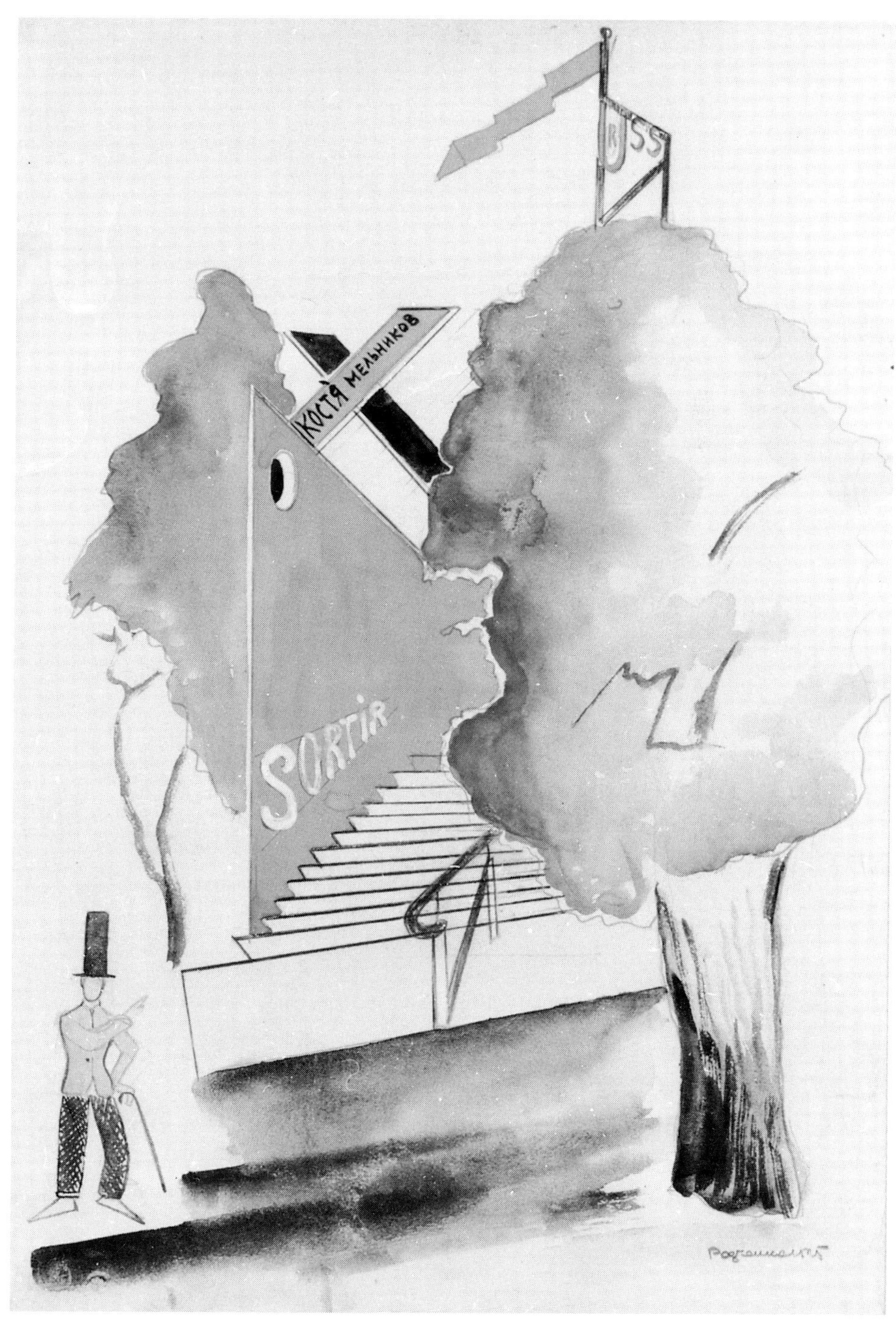

FIGURE 5.10
Aleksandr Rodchenko, "Sortir" caricature, Paris, 1925. Watercolor. Private collection.

> a laundry basket next to them, sometimes a little sleigh as well. A brightly colored woolen cloth protects apples or oranges from the cold, with two prize examples lying on top. Next to them are sugar figures, nuts, candy. One thinks: before leaving her house a grandmother must have looked around to see what she could take to surprise her grandchildren.[36]

This passage appears already on the second page of his essay, signaling Benjamin's conviction that the petty consumer-object-world of Moscow would have as much to tell about revolutionary life as literary debates or organized political meetings held in workers' clubs. The exquisite, unruly dream-objects that the individual encounters—shiny apples and spun-sugar figures—must add up to the collective utopia adumbrated by more public monuments such as the workers' clubs. Benjamin juxtaposes lyrical depictions of Moscow's primitive street trade with his descriptions of the radically changed lives of the members of the intelligentsia, which are ascetic and politicized to a degree unknown in Berlin or Paris. "[W]hat distinguishes the Bolshevik, the Russian Communist, from his Western comrade," Benjamin writes, "is [h]is unconditional readiness for mobilization. The material basis of his existence is so slender that he is prepared, year in, year out, to decamp" (M, p. 107).

In his analysis of industrial modernity, Benjamin discovers a potential political force in the way the fragile and fleeting formations of individual fantasy congeal into, or are centered on, objects that individuals share—objects that are all alike, and whose very sameness and reproducibility inspire the dream of a collective wish-image. But Benjamin compares the "wild variety" of the Moscow street trade not to other cities of modernity but to "the South," referring to Capri and Naples—the sites, in his personal spatial history, of the "mythological," premodern childhood of industrial culture.[37] Benjamin in this way recognizes the political implications of the transitional nature of the hybrid object-world of NEP-era Moscow. "Shoe polish and writing materials, handkerchiefs, dolls' sleighs, swings for children, ladies' underwear, stuffed birds, clothes hangers," he enumerates, "—all this sprawls on the open street, as if it were not twenty-five degrees below zero but high Neapolitan summer" (M, p. 101). In this list, most of the objects are probably handmade, though some of them—the clothes hangers, the shoe polish, the ladies' underwear—have likely bolted from factory assembly lines directly into the snow. Bypassing the store windows and fixed price labels that constitute such a crucial site in modern consumption, they signal the disorganization and incompleteness of the Soviet system of production and distribution. The primitive and temporary structure of exchange in Moscow is represented by the rickety kiosks of the Sukharevskii market, in which "cloth and fabric form buttresses and columns; shoes, *valenki*, hanging threaded on strings across the counters, become the roof of the booth" (M, p. 102). The "Moscow" essay goes far beyond the conventional wisdom of historians that the Russian revolution was doomed because it took place in an underindustrialized nation. Benjamin identifies the problem in the disjunction between the utopian potential of the collective fantasies located in the profusion of objects and the different utopia enacted in the asceticism and monumental aspirations of the official forms of Bolshevik collectivity. These two utopias must be brought into congruence. The second utopia can succeed only if it is made to confront and harness the first.

For Benjamin, the fairy tale represents the collective tradition of a liberating narrative of nature's alignment with human beings that counteracts, rather than reinforces, capitalism's myths of progress and monumentality—myths to which socialism also falls prey.[38] A small object that caught Benjamin's imagination figures the possibility of infusing modern socialist industry with the promise of the prerevolutionary fairy tale. In his diary entry of January 12, 1927, Benjamin notes: "Today in the Kustarny [Handicraft] Museum I bought a lacquer box on whose cover a female cigarette vendor is painted against the ground of black. . . . the word *Mosselprom* is visible on the vendor's apron."[39] In the "Moscow" essay, however, having thought through the profound strangeness of this object, he calls her more evocatively "the Soviet 'Madonna with the Cigarettes'" (M, p. 114). Although we have no image of this object, it isn't hard to imagine the deep, shiny black ground of the traditional lacquer box from Palek with a young maiden painted in bright shades of red, orange, gold, and green. But instead of a Marian icon or a fairy tale princess or peasant lass, we see a modern woman who wears the Mossel'prom apron, pert cap, and portable display case of cigarettes hanging from her neck and open at her belly.

The Mossel'prom cigarette girl had already been cemented as a new, socialist sex symbol in the Soviet imagination by the film *The Cigarette Girl from Mossel'prom* of 1924, in which Stepanova's fabric, as we have seen, was used for a dress for one of the female characters. The dark-eyed actress Iulia Solntseva starred as the ambitious cigarette girl, and she can be seen in a still from the film wearing the portable cigarette display case (see figure 3.21). She dispenses the cheapest form of commodity pleasure available, and one of the few commodities that the Soviet state excelled at producing (Mossel'prom alone produced over twenty-two brands of cigarettes). Benjamin's Palek box offers a quintessentially modern figure of femininity—independent, sexual, dispensing sensuously pleasurable commodities, herself possibly a commodity—superimposed onto a cultural object-form that usually offered more traditional, "Eastern" figures of femininity from ancient folk tales or the narratives of the Orthodox church. The modern fairy tale of the commodity, so closely allied with femininity in its passivity, desirability, and possessibility, replaces earlier fairy tales in which women play similarly prescribed roles. One imagines Benjamin's wonder at this object stemming from his interest in the fairy tale, in the possibility that the modern, Soviet tale of Mossel'prom could harness the collective desire of past fairy tales in order to create a utopian version of socialist consumption. One wonders how Benjamin would have responded to Rodchenko's Mossel'prom caramel box.

Rodchenko the Constructivist might seem to be allied exclusively with Benjamin's ascetic Communist, insisting on camping within a "slender" material existence like the spare, modular, movable furniture of his workers' club. But Rodchenko's intense reaction to the object-world of the West, which caused him to refer repeatedly, in his letters, to his fantasy of objects in the East, participates in Benjamin's certainty about the utopian political promise of the mass commodity. The comparison with Benjamin's essay forces the question of the status of Rodchenko's letters as a contribution to the theory of the Constructivist object. Benjamin had written to Martin Buber, the publisher who commissioned the Moscow essay: "my presentation will be devoid of all theory. . . . I want to write a description of Moscow at the present moment in which 'all factuality is already theory.'"[40] What if we were to agree, with Martin Buber, to read Rodchenko's anecdotal and everyday description of the Paris object-world as struggling to express the profound structural differences between capitalism and socialism, at the level of the commodity and bodily experience? Rodchenko's less consciously articulated insights into the workings of desire in the Western system of consumption, and his use of these insights to fuel his fantasy construction of a model of socialist consumption (the light from the East) provide another piece of evidence that the theory of the Constructivist object did not imagine a world without commodity desire but rather imagined objects that could deliver that desire from capitalism for the benefit of the new socialist culture.

The Constructivist theory of the object shares Benjamin's doubt in the implicit Marxist faith that once socialist relations of production have been achieved, industry and technology will automatically generate a socialist imagination capable of producing a new culture. Rather, as Susan Buck-Morss writes in her study of Benjamin's Arcades project, "progressive cultural practice [for Benjamin] entails bringing both technology and imagination out of their mythic dream states, through making conscious the collective's desire for social utopia, and the potential of the new nature to achieve it by translating that desire into the 'new language' of its material forms."[41] What Buck-Morss calls the "new nature"—that is, the man-made object-world of modernity—has the potential to foster the flowering of collective desire through a "new language" of objects. Benjamin focuses his text on the object-world of Moscow because the past and present desires lodged in the chaotic realm of NEP objects will have to become the source of the collective fantasy that will sustain the future of the Soviet experiment. Benjamin's conception of the commodity's dream-power—of the individual consumer's shifting, mobile, unruly fantasy relations to modern commodities—departs from the model of the commodity fetish, both in Marx's sense (because Benjamin devotes much more attention to the political significance of the desires subsumed for Marx under the category exchange-value) and in the popular-Freudian sense (because the Benjaminian consumer doesn't fixate on the object).

In Constructivism, the "new language" of the forms of the "new nature" will organize the individual desires of the new Soviet consumer in a particular collective direction. For Benjamin, this directing of the object's dream-power would compromise its utopian potential, even though, in the Soviet case, he would be in conflicted agreement with the political goals of such a fixation. By suggesting that the Constructivist object also makes a place for the less fixed workings of desire, this book proposes that Constructivism included aspects of Benjamin's hope that a progressive political relation between private fantasies and collective goals could be articulated through the object.[42]

Benjamin strikes a note of optimism in his assessment of Bolshevik commodity politics. Noting that "people here have not yet developed European consumer concepts and consumer needs" (M, p. 117), he suggests that there may be a strategic reason for this lack: "it is possible that . . . an astute Party stratagem is involved: to equal the level of consumption in Western Europe, the trial by fire of the Bolshevik democracy, at a freely chosen moment, steeled and with the absolute certainty of victory" (M, p. 117). This is, then, the ultimate test of Bolshevism: to provide the level of consumer abundance known in the West, but democratically and humanely, in a way that will foster the individual desires lodged in material objects for the benefit of the collective. The moment can be freely chosen, but victory must be certain, because its failure would signal the failure of the revolution. Benjamin hopes that the delay is indeed a party stratagem, and not merely the result of temporary economic scarcity, because he sees clearly that the party could outgrow its asceticism and begin to pursue privatized consumption for its members without ensuring a democratic consumption for the collective: "should the European correlation of power and money penetrate Russia, too, then perhaps not the country, perhaps not even the Party, but Communism in Russia would be lost" (M, p. 117).

This prescient statement signals exactly the course of events in the Soviet Union: the country survived, the party survived, but the dream of Communism was lost. The Constructivists, alone among left cultural radicals in Russia in the mid-1920s, shared Benjamin's certainty about the link between daily practices of consumption and power, between material objects and the survival of the revolution.

"Thing and Idea" in NEP Moscow

In contrast to Benjamin's success at writing an account of Moscow in which "all factuality is already theory," the influential literary critic Viacheslav Polonskii, writing in the party newspaper *Izvestiia* in early 1927, blasted *Novyi Lef* for publishing Rodchenko's letters because they contained no ideas, but only the banal facts of Rodchenko's daily experience in Paris: "They have no content. There are no ideas in them. There are not even any curious observations. . . . The author simply did not see anything significant, and what he did see—bidets, buttocks, collars and authentic Chablis—is all embarrassment and shame."[43] The opposition between Benjamin's philosophical confidence in the truth lodged in objects, on the one hand, and Polonskii's derision of Rodchenko's assessment of Parisian commodity culture, on the other, signals a worry about a form of materialism that seemed to threaten a higher realm of ideas that pervaded Soviet culture during NEP.

For Polonskii, Rodchenko's descriptions of his improved dress and personal hygiene embodied the caricatural travails of a Bolshevik from the wild East when he meets the civilized West. Polonskii's authorial strategy is particularly mean-spirited and effective: he simply lists quotations from Rodchenko's letters, taken out of context and removed from the diaristic rhythm that lends them the power of their mounting hysteria. His purpose is to take a swipe at *Novyi Lef*'s new literary program promoting the genre of "factography," or the "literature of fact." If Rodchenko's letters are representative of this new genre, then it is clearly a petit-bourgeois-decadent (*meshchanskii-upadochnicheskii*) one. The very notion of a literary genre based exclusively on factual reportage deliberately challenged the Russian literary tradition of the novel that is a meditation on the moral fate of humanity or the travel essay that turns out to be a comment on the fate of Russia.

For Polonskii, Rodchenko's letters are a particularly ignominious example of an unfortunate genre that replaces literary ideas with mere factual description—"collars, hats, buttocks—who needs this?" He takes the moral and literary high road, suggesting what Rodchenko should have been observing in Paris: the Louvre, for example, and the Musée Carnavalet, in which monuments to the struggle of the French proletariat are collected.

Polonskii deliberately quotes Rodchenko's mantra of the "tight buttocks and endless bidets" with almost greater frequency than the letters themselves, in order to insinuate Rodchenko's perverse anal investment. He implies that Rodchenko attempts to cover over this private perversion through recourse to provincial Eastern moralizing against the West. Rodchenko's interest in buttocks and bidets is merely "decadent"; his interest in collars and Chablis is *meshchanskii*; and his stories of French cigarettes sampled, meals and baths taken, traffic avoided on the street, are simply *bytovye*, that is to say, everyday and banal. The argument of this chapter, in contrast, has been that Rodchenko's fixation on sexualized objects stems not only from his individual desire, but from his insight into the systemic nature of capitalist consumption, the ways in which it mimics and exceeds the body's functions in a grotesque but effective mapping of the human body onto the body politic.

Polonskii's critique typifies the opposition in Russian culture between *byt* and *bytie*, between the banal materiality of everyday life on the one hand, and the higher, spiritual, literary, and ideological realms of existence, on the other. Constructivism's interest in *byt* and materiality, and *Lef*'s opposition to literary tradition, had drawn the ire of the literary and cultural establishment since the early 1920s, so it should come as no surprise that *Novyi Lef*'s new "literature of fact" should merit such strong criticism in the Bolshevik Party newspaper. Polonskii's critique also reflects its moment of writing in early 1927, the period of the economic austerity regime and rationing of consumer goods that signaled the approaching demise of NEP and the initiation of the Five-year Plans. The space for Constructivist fantasizing about changing objects and practices of commodity consumption, which was paradoxically facilitated by NEP and its encouragement of consumerism, was beginning to be eliminated by the lead-up to the plans' drive toward heavy industrialization. Rodchenko's letters, with their attention to the workings of Parisian commodity culture and their fantasizing about the possibility of constructing a utopian material culture in the USSR, belong to the earlier, different era of high NEP. They ring slightly out of tune with the new austerity regime of early 1927. This is perhaps one important reason why

Novyi Lef chose to publish them in 1927: to return the attention of the left artistic intelligentsia to the Constructivist debate on the transformation of *byt* through the transformation of material culture.

An article in the mass magazine *Zhurnal dlia zhenshchin* (Magazine for Women) in 1925 entitled "Thing and Idea," by A. Zavedeev, shows that the Constructivist concern with things was not the exclusive province of the left intelligentsia.[44] Amid the illustrations of the latest fashions from Paris and advice columns to housewives, Zavedeev offers a startlingly Constructivist acknowledgment that the desire for material things is proper in a socialist society, because things are no less important than ideas, while calling, at the same time, for a more rational and organized relation to things. Before the October Revolution, he writes, Muscovites had no idea where things came from; they simply paid for them and took them for granted. But the commodity shortage and constant devaluation of money during the civil war suddenly made people acutely aware of things; all people's thoughts became material. In a similar vein to Arvatov, Zavedeev writes that this was to a certain extent a healthy, needed change from the prerevolutionary bourgeoisie's helpless separation from the world of use-values. But this constant awareness of objects puts people in danger of becoming fanatics of objects. Zavedeev captures the contradiction of commodity culture in Russia during NEP. In the West, the constant and total availability of commodities, limited only by access to wealth, incites fetishism. In Russia, commodity fetishism is always inflected by the experience and fear of complete lack due to the spotty distribution system in state stores and cooperatives, the elements of chance and luck involved in street trade, and the possibility of encountering fantastically inflated prices at any moment, owing to currency instability and the sellers' market produced by incomplete distribution systems under NEP. "We must eliminate such an abnormal, even idolatrous relation to things," he exhorts his female readers. The socialist economy will soon bring about the end of the commodity deficit, and further, "our consciousness is sufficiently materialized by new, real values, by the spilled blood and sweat of our generation, so that we will never return again to the old illusions of ideas. We know the authentic value of things. They are the firm ground of our ideas and the heaven of our prosperity." He hopes that the future will bring about a reasonable human relation to objects that will fall somewhere between capitalist commodity fetishism, Bolshevik asceticism, and the overvaluation of commodities produced by the particular economic structures of NEP. This "reasonable" relation will come about in a utopian future when Communism has produced an object-world as rich as capitalism's, but without commodity fetishism.

A large, colorful propaganda poster from 1925 seems to illustrate the rational future of shopping imagined by Zavedeev, right down to the depiction of bright rays of sun suffusing a socialist "heaven of prosperity" (figure 5.11).[45] The text at the top commands "Woman worker, build cooperation," and a giant figure of a woman worker wearing the requisite kerchief organizes the image with her insistent pointing. The orderly socialist consuming collective is depicted through the unfortunate visual device of images of people standing in long lines around a massive building with entrances labeled "Grocery Store," "Public Cafeteria," "Club," "Nursery," and so on; lines were a reality of Soviet consumption in 1925 and continued to be so for the life of the Soviet Union and beyond.[46] The smaller pictorial inserts in the lower half of the poster show the before–after scenes customary in *novyi byt* propaganda posters. The "before" pictures are dark and painterly in style, jumbled in content, and shown in vertiginous perspective (see figure 5.12), while the "after" pictures are geometrically ordered, precisely drawn representations of silent, emptied spaces (see figure 5.13). On the left, bordered in black, the text commands "DESTROY the cabal of the old *byt,* the profit of the kulak trader, drunkenness and ignorance," while on the right, bordered in bright red, the text exhorts "CREATE public dining halls, public education, centers of enlightenment, cooperative stores." The young woman emerging from the cooperative store in one of the inset pictures on the lower right appears to be the same woman who is bent over a mathematics textbook under the watchful eye of Lenin in the circular inset at bottom center. Because the acquisition of objects is now well organized by the cooperative, she can concentrate her full energy on the acquisition of ideas—unlike the illiterate peasant women shown in the left-hand pictures. Yet, except for her proletarian red kerchief, the pretty young woman resembles a bourgeois lady exiting a boutique after a successful shopping trip, weighed down with interesting packages tied up with string. This image of individual pleasure in excessive shopping symptomatizes the object desires to which Zavedeev, and the Constructivists, directed their attention, but which were repressed in the standard Bolshevik conception of rationalized collective consumption.

We have an image that Rodchenko made in 1924 that attempts to navigate the terrain of the commodity desires of NEP with more complexity than the before–after format of the propaganda poster, in which the wages of capitalist excess are securely placed on the left side, and the utopian ideals of harmonious socialism are meant to be legible on the right, with no representations of the excessive desires that will have to be organized under socialist consumption.

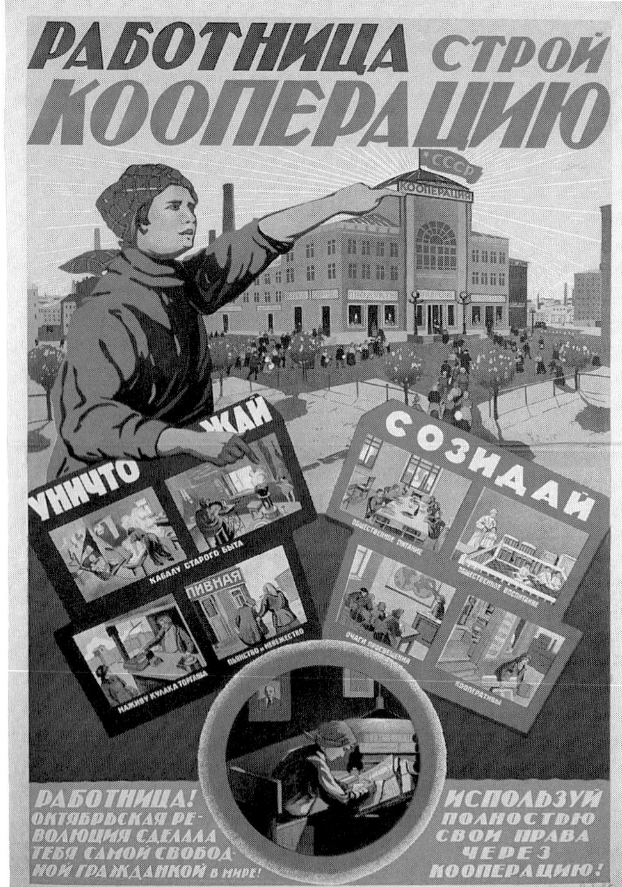

FIGURE 5.11

Poster: "Woman worker, build cooperation!," Moscow, 1925. Courtesy Russian State Library Department of Graphics, Moscow. See plate 20.

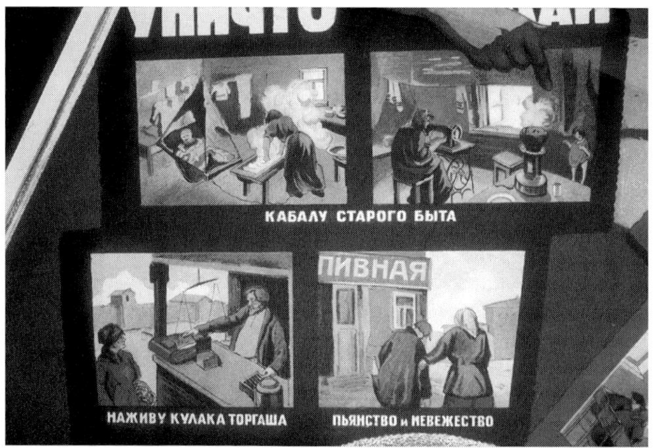

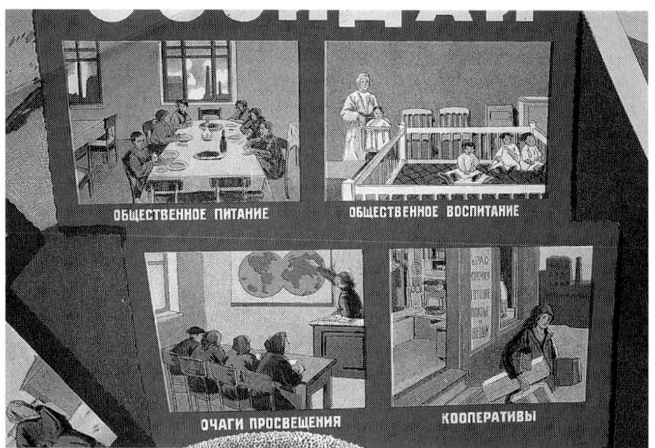

FIGURES 5.12, 5.13

Poster: "Woman worker, build cooperation!," Moscow, 1925, details of left and right insets. Courtesy Russian State Library Department of Graphics, Moscow.

гие ПРЕДМЕТЫ ДОМАШНЕЙ ГИГИЕНЫ:

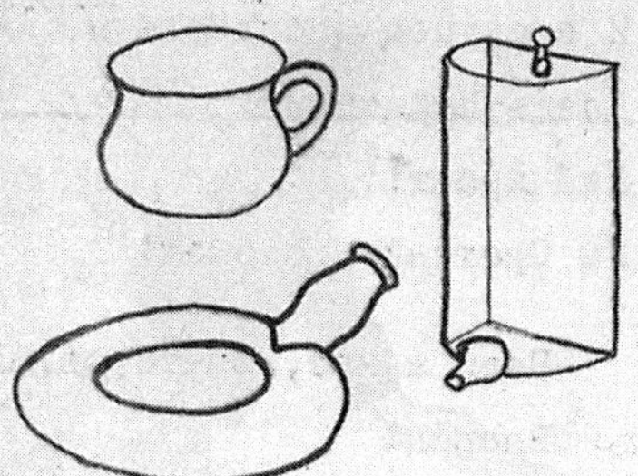

Горячо могу реком ендовать для украшения ситчиков КРАСНУЮ ПЯТИКОНЕЧНУЮ ЗВЕЗДУ, а также СЕРП И МОЛОТ, что может быть весьма оригинальным:

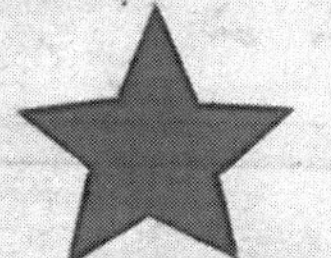

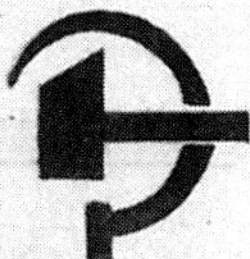

Великолепные узоры для ситчиков могут быть сделаны из РУБАШКИ ИГРАЛЬНОЙ КАРТЫ:

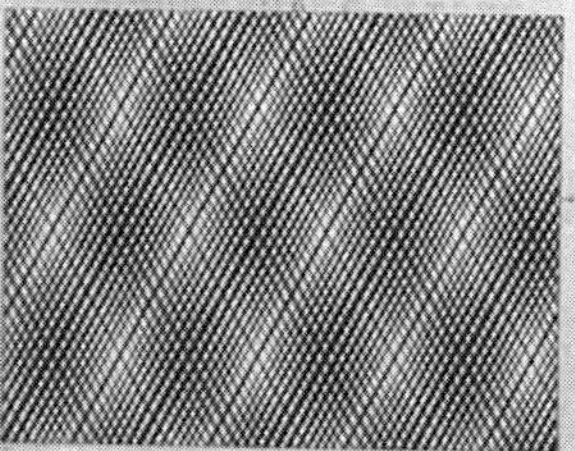

Привожу еще несколько примеров весьма хороших проектов рисунков для ситчиков:

1. ТВЕРДАЯ ВАЛЮТА

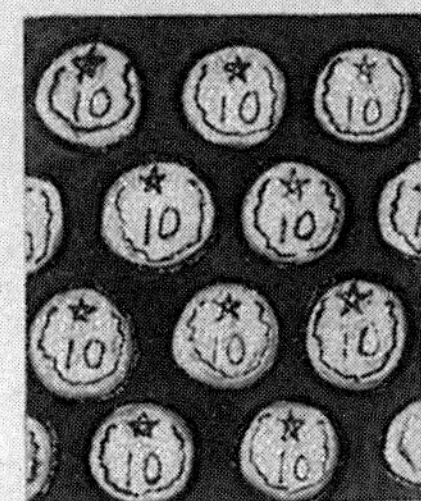

2. ТРЕХГОРНЫЙ

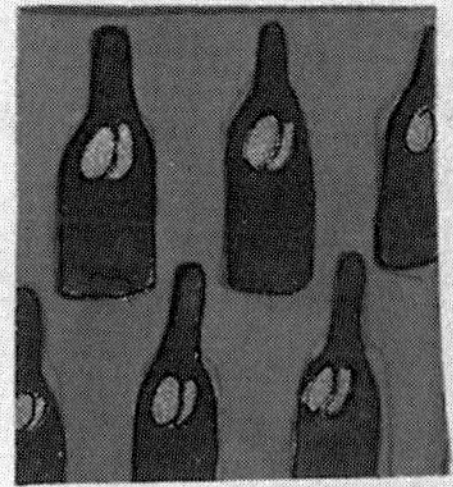

3. НАШГАЗ

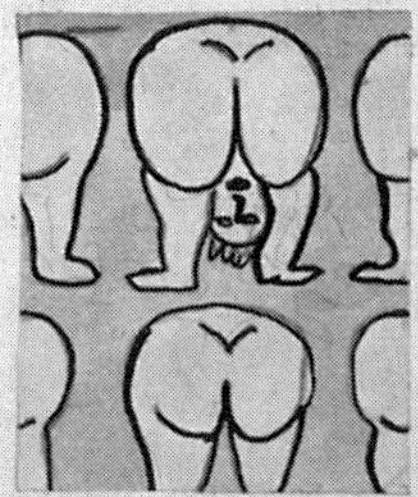

4. ЗИМНИЙ

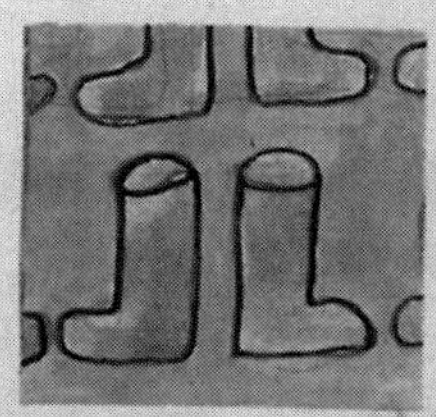

FIGURE 5.14
Aleksandr Rodchenko, page with ideas for fabric patterns in *Nash gaz*, 1924. See plate 21.

A page of drawings and text from the homemade newspaper *Nash gaz*, the image maps the regulated system of the human body onto the object system (figure 5.14). In the typed text, Rodchenko jokingly offers unsolicited advice to young Constructivist textile designers about appropriate motifs. On the upper left, above the drawings of toilet parts, the visible line of text completes the sentence: "It is indecent to draw . . . objects of domestic hygiene."[47] He facetiously suggests that the red star or hammer and sickle, by then already banal elements of Soviet iconography, would provide highly original fabric motifs, as would the backs of playing cards—as indicated by the illustration of a card on the lower left, which does resemble his own fabric designs (he made only a few) as well as some of Stepanova's. He then presents four more ideas for fabric patterns: number one, on the top right, "hard currency"; number two, "Triple Peaks," the name of a brand of state-produced Mossel'prom beer; number three, "Nash gaz," which can also be read as "our gas" and has the same connotations as in English; and number four, "winter," with a picture of *valenki*, the traditional felt boots.

For all its playfulness, the image organizes the pathological excess of the commodity system by mapping it onto a grid. The overarching structure of the grid is provided by the concerns of production: the need to develop patterns for mass-produced Constructivist textile designs. The four sets of pattern possibilities on the right all represent objects that can be exchanged on the market, broadly speaking. Presented as relatively the same size, in identical boxes, in the same repeating format, they appear as objects of consumption organized on an assembly line. All four pictures suggest by their uneven edges that they have been cut out from a larger sheet of the same design, setting up the sensation that if not for Rodchenko's cutting and ordering, the coins and beer bottles and bare bottoms and *valenki* would continue on in endless horizontal and vertical rows, just as the system of commodity exchange is seemingly limitless.

But the ordered grid is also a figure for the human body as a microcosm of the NEP economy. Read vertically, the four pictures evoke the human subject in shorthand terms: money as the structuring abstraction; beer as a mass commodity to be ingested; the anus as site of excretion and sexual part-object; and the boot as base. The *valenki* refer to the lowest level of the Soviet economy: most often handmade, for sale on the street, as Benjamin noted, as well as in stores, they are preindustrial objects of the peasant economy. Fuzzy *valenki* are also associated with Russian traditions of home, hearth, and family; we need only recall Rodchenko lamenting to Stepanova from his lonely hotel room in Paris that he remembered his *valenki* with fondness. The currency and mass-produced beer bottles, on the other hand, represent the financial and productive institutions of the Soviet state. Finally, the bare bottoms figure the body as a system of ingestion and excretion. In the deficit-ridden and inflationary economy of NEP, oral ingestion becomes a kind of lowest-denominator metaphor for the complex processes of consumption, as in Rodchenko's advertisement for Red October cookies from Mossel'prom. The picture of the bare buttocks on the *Nash gaz* page invokes the other half, as it were, of this bodily process of consumption-as-ingestion, linking up with the drawings of the toilet seat and tank on the upper left to form the other term of the overtly excretory axis on the page. This image prepares us for one of the forms that Rodchenko's anal-erotic analysis will take in his letters from Paris, namely, a fantasy of control and regulation. For Rodchenko, the fantasy of the regulated system of bodily processes—what goes in gets processed, with the waste efficiently eliminated—contrasts comfortingly with the pathology of the system of capitalist exchange, in which surplus value feeds endlessly into a monstrously expanding system. The bodily map provided by the *Nash gaz* page is the equivalent of the pointing figure in his caricature of Mel'nikov from Paris, which identifies the Soviet pavilion as the site of the regulated body and the efficiently flushing toilet.

This reading of the image is nothing, however, if not a standard Constructivist reading, which attempts to fix and regulate the meanings of the body, the better to align it with the requirements of socialist production—of textiles, in this case. But the image also speaks to the uncontrollability of the body, which will always be the wild card in any attempt to regulate human actions and desires. For the bare buttocks labeled "our gas" also invoke the involuntary fart as the opposite of bodily control and obedience. The rows of little figures bent over and baring their vulnerable bottoms, when analyzed in combination with the references in Rodchenko's letters to "tight buttocks" and to objects concealing black catastrophe in their interior, also refer us to another erotic formation that Rodchenko projects onto his Constructivist objects. The buttocks in the picture are open and pink, rather than "tight" and "black"; one could say that the drawing attempts to penetrate the inside of the body and render it transparent.

The proximity of the phallic shapes of the beer bottles, in picture 2, and of the columnar shapes of the *valenki*, in picture 4, emphasize the vulnerability of the buttocks in picture 3. In a visual intermingling of the two registers of the body and the commodity, the labels on the beer bottles mimic the shapes of the buttocks below. Rodchenko and Mayakovsky's 1925 advertisement for Triple Peaks beer shows the double label that was a feature of the bottle design (figure 5.15).

As Rodchenko developed his *Nash gaz* image, these innocent double labels became linked with the image of the buttocks, as they would be even within the context of his own advertisement's visual and verbal language of conscious, rationally motivated consumption (Mayakovsky's slogan proclaims: "Triple Peaks Beer drives out hypocrisy and moonshine"). The active bottle of Triple Peaks beer sends out graphic red lightning bolts that look to painfully burst the sides of the smaller bottles of moonshine, causing the coils from the still that emerge from them to resemble, instead, streams of gaily curliqued white liquid spewing from the bottle tops.[48] Even the yellow quadrilateral that forms the background to the drama of the bottles has a distinctly phallic connotation in the Constructivist repertoire of forms: in Stepanova's 1922 costume designs for *The Death of Tarelkin*, a male costume is drawn with this quadrilateral form between his legs, at crotch level, pointing upward, while an adjacent female costume has the same form between her legs, but upside down and pointing downward (figure 5.16). This reading of Rodchenko's state beer advertisement as, at its deepest level of meaning, a visual metaphor of anal rape, might confirm the most dystopian account of Constructivism as a rationalizing movement that supports the Soviet state in its authoritarian assault on the individual consumer.

And yet, the playful representation of the exhibitionist bare bottoms in the *Nash gaz* image, seemingly inviting inspection or erotic caress, indicates that the visual metaphor of anal erotism as deployed by Rodchenko is not purely sadistic but reversible into its opposite, lending a doubleness to the beer ad's intervention into the erotics of Soviet consumption during NEP.[49] Rodchenko's images show us a body that is potentially explosive and obscene (farting) and pervaded with non(re)productive desires, broadening the standard Constructivist metaphor of the body as a regulated system that can be aligned with the industrial system of objects. The page from *Nash gaz* begins as a search for appropriate patterns for Constructivist textiles and ends up functioning as a map of the widest possible scope of the Constructivist object.

Constructivist Objects in Paris

The straight-backed chairs of Rodchenko's club, with their rigid encircling arms that contain the sitter, seem to insist on the modernizing version of Constructivism that aims to rationalize the lives of subjects in alignment with the modern productive system—the ultimately dystopian version elaborated by Tafuri, Tugendkhol'd, Baudrillard, and Gassner.[50] But as much as the page from *Nash gaz*, the club can also be understood as an object that confronts the commodity's hold

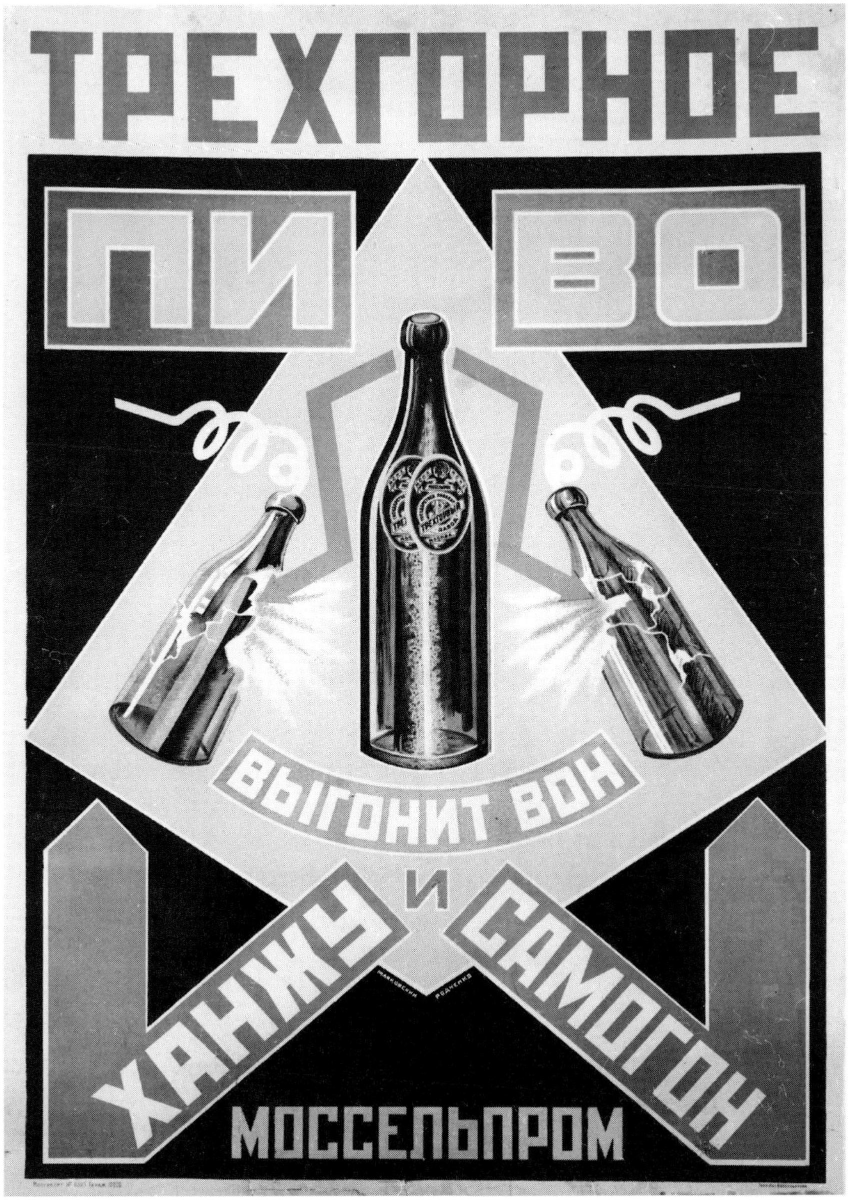

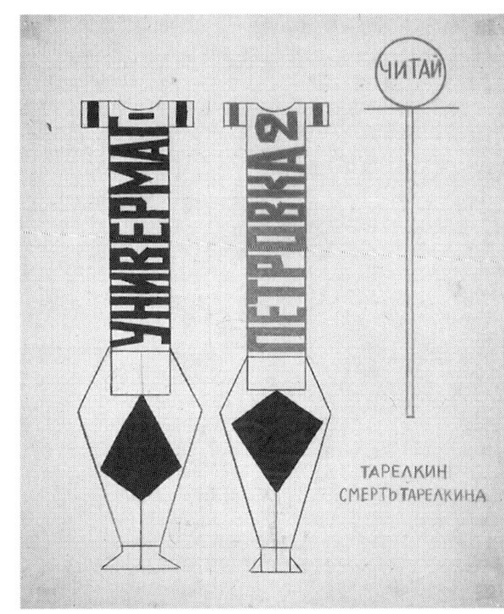

FIGURE 5.16
Varvara Stepanova, costume designs for *The Death of Tarelkin*, 1922. Gouache and pencil on paper.

FIGURE 5.15
Aleksandr Rodchenko and Vladimir Mayakovsky, advertising poster for Triple Peaks beer, 1925. Howard Schickler Fine Art.

on the body and on fantasy. The club was not simply a show design, dreamed up by Rodchenko to impress Parisian viewers with Communist asceticism. At home he would go on to work for the Moscow Proletkul't, where he taught a furniture production workshop that carried out modest commissions for outfitting Moscow workers' clubs, always on tight budgets.[51] He also could not have avoided participating in the earnest debates about the efficacy of the workers' clubs, which included theoretical questions of the role of clubs in the formation of the *novyi byt*, the role of women in clubs, the use of art and drama circles and of cultural films, and the appropriateness of dancing, as well as material questions of hygiene and decor.[52] As his letters show, the Parisian public he was most interested in addressing was the proletariat—the only people in Paris who were producers like him and, therefore, in his imagination, less vulnerable to the diverting pleasures of consumerism. He notes with delight that workers in Asnières have access to all kinds of inexpensive amusements, such as restaurants and cafes, that Russian workers do not have. He sentimentalizes the innocent, authentic pleasures of workers' culture; after a pleasant stroll in the suburbs of Paris he reports that "the workers play football, walk around with their arms around each other, dig in their kitchen-gardens and dance in cafes" (Letters, March 28, p. 13).[53] The fact that he sees no contradiction between his pristine workers' club and the French workers digging in the soil in their small gardens, between his club's promotion of sober leisure activities and the workers dancing in cafes, indicates the warmth of his own conception of his club as a Constructivist object. In his vision, the thing as "comrade" will participate in this kind of spontaneous everyday life, helping to organize it, certainly, but not to dehumanize it.

In the face of the real-life camaraderie of workers strolling with their arms around each other in the suburbs of Paris, just how did Rodchenko imagine the inanimate objects in his club to be "comrades"? Rodchenko begins to offer an answer when he expands on his notion of the thing as comrade: "Things take on meaning, become friends and comrades of the person, and the person learns how to laugh and be happy and converse with things" (Letters, May 4, p. 20). Presumably things can "converse with" people only through bodily sensations or through fantasy. The club as a Constructivist object cooperates with the body's movements, certainly, but its system might seem to be too fully regulated and transparent to allow a space for individual fantasy. It therefore works to make its human counterparts more uniform and regulated, like itself. Although the social content of this uniformity is the progressive Marxist ideal of a collectivity of workers enjoying nonalienated leisure, this definition of the Constructivist object is that of the cold, rationalizing modernist nightmare feared by Tafuri and other critics. But the Constructivist object in Rodchenko's hands will not, or will not only, be cold or removed in its transparency, it will not be against the body. Expanding and collapsing, encircling and extensive, folded in and disappearing, it is like the human body in its vulnerability. It offers its modern technological forms up to us, inviting us to project our human wishes and fantasies onto it. It suggests an alternative definition of the Constructivist object as the modernist dream of the new forms of industrial modernity brought down to human scale.[54]

The speaker's platform offers an especially poignant example of Gassner's "expanding and dying" capacity of the object (see figure 5.7). The orthogonal view, on the left, illustrates the way the speaker's platform opens horizontally, with special attention to the flexible wooden lattices that can be expanded to form the backbone of the screen, and to the little set of pulleys, illustrated at the top right, that guarantees the smooth functioning of the system. The axionometric view, on the right, shows how the stand can extend out into space—from the short, flat rectangle on the lower right, it expands upward and outward on all sides, asserting itself several meters into the surrounding room. There is an uncanny pathos in this object, as if it knows its own potential for grandeur but is always ready to fold itself down and in and away when it is not wanted, aware also of its own mortality. In its closed form, it is a mere blank surface, with no signifying markers—like a person with eyes and mouth closed. But when it opens itself up, it fully reveals the inner logic of its system—we see and understand every joint, every crossed wooden lattice, every step and board that flips up and around and over to form the speaker's platform, the bench, the screen. The uncanny of this object is the return of the same projection of anal-erotic desire that manifested itself in Rodchenko's letters and the *Nash gaz* page. The speaker's platform, like the Parisian objects and the drawing of the rows of pink buttocks, provoke the urge to pry open the "tight buttocks," to flip the body forward and over and shed light on the opening that conceals the tightness and interior blackness of those buttocks. In this way, the very material form of his club responds to the desires called up by his encounter with the Parisian commodity world, even as it also responds as a socialist ordering of those desires into a legible system.

Rodchenko writes tenderly of the cleanliness and illumination of his club, of the way its material forms repulse the Paris manure, symbol of the eroticized excess of the commodity system: "It's true that it's so simple and clean and light that you would never willingly track dirt into it" (Letters, June 1, pp. 20–21).[55] Rodchenko projects his desire onto his technological forms, warming and humanizing them for their collective social function. Even if the content of this desiring projection may not be rendered fully conscious, as Gassner would have it, in the final material incarnation of the object, neither is it repressed. It can begin to be recognized and directed toward collective ends.

In the sense that his club responds to both socioeconomic demands and the demands of the human body, including unconscious ones, it offers one possible answer to Benjamin's question:

> When and how will the worlds of form that have arisen in mechanics, in film, machine construction and the new physics, and that have overpowered us without our being aware of it, make what is natural in them clear to us? When will the condition of society be reached in which these forms or those that have arisen from them open themselves up to us as natural forms?[56]

The Constructivist object ideally would utilize only the most modern technology and work to "make it clear" and "open it up" to the human subject as a comrade would in conversation: "the person learns how to laugh and be happy and converse with things." Yet Rodchenko's club interior, while ingeniously designed in the geometric, functionalist forms of the international modern movement, is in fact handcrafted out of wood; like the traditional printed cotton calico fabric, and the printed cardboard of the Mossel'prom caramel box, it is not a bona fide example of the newest mass-produced technological inventions. His economical use of the wood was necessitated by the budgetary restraints on the exhibition, but it also represented Constructivism's overall commitment to coping with the material scarcity of the NEP economy by eliminating waste and excess. The use of painted wood for building his club, as for Mel'nikov's pavilion—both were painted red, gray, and white to Rodchenko's specification—called to mind traditional Russian craft. In Benjamin's brief article entitled "Russian Toys," published soon after his return from Moscow, he praises the primitive, artisanal forms of these wooden toys: "The spirit from which these products emanate—the entire process of their production and not merely its result—is alive for the child in the toy, and he naturally understands a primitively produced object much better than one deriving from a complicated industrial process."[57] This description is close to Arvatov's words about the ideal modern thing: "the mechanism of a thing, the connection between the elements of a thing and its purpose, were now transparent" (EL, p. 126). With his speaker's platform, Rodchenko asserts that the object can best be a comrade to human beings when it shows us how it was made, just as, for example, Popova's flapper dress had done.

As opposed to the hyperstimulation of the endless commodities produced by industrial culture, the single speaker's platform attempts to provide, within its flexible and transparent forms, an alternative kind of variety. This Constructivist object, as much as Rodchenko's Mossel'prom ads, negotiates the different economies of the object—the traditional, often wooden, peasant object of the past, the meager NEP commodity of the present, and the technologically advanced, mass-produced industrial object of the socialist future. The very fragility of the wooden forms of the club—the delicate vertical beams of the chairs, the openwork sides to the bookcases, the latticework of the folding screen—contributes to an appealing, antimonumental element in its vision of the future. The club objects are not only eternal, frozen monuments to industrial progress, but also flexible, movable, and temporary, like human beings.

This is the uncanny doubleness of Rodchenko's club: under its carapace of simplicity and lucidity lies an intense conflictedness about the object. The object will be flexible and open like the speaker's platform, the site of erotic fancy and mobile embodiment, but it will also be austere and hyperrationalized, like the constraining, straight-backed chairs. The tension between these two versions of utopia gives the Constructivist object its pathos, and its historicity. Buck-Morss writes about Benjamin's *Arcades Project*: "A materialist history that disenchants the new nature in order to free it from the spell of capitalism, and yet rescues all the power of enchantment for the purpose of social transformation: this was to have been the goal of Benjamin's fairy tale."[58] If we substitute "materialist practice" for "materialist history," we get an excellent definition of utopian Constructivism: a materialist practice that frees the new technical and industrial forms from the spell of the commodity in Marx's sense of reification and exploitation, but which does so without depriving those mass-produced forms of their ability to become the shared, collective sites of individual formations of fantasy.

On one level, Constructivism diverged from Benjamin's fairy tale by attempting to bring the body and its desires fully into alignment with the new material forms of the socialist object, to fix the mobile and unruly formations of individual fantasy with the organizing power of the new, socialist object that would replace the commodity fetish. But on another level, the Constructivist object made a home for the "enchanted" workings of an unfixed fantasy and a desiring embodiedness. In the end, the proposal of this book is a difficult and fragile one, as fragile as the latticework screen of Rodchenko's speaker's platform: even if this enchantment of the object was not stated explicitly and can be uncovered only through a critical reading of images, texts, and objects, its status is not simply that of the repressed underside of the conscious theory of Constructivism—the repressed bodiliness that would haunt all of the rationalist utopian projects of the 1920s—but rather a component of the theory of the socialist object itself. Rodchenko's workers' club is a space in which the subject will, certainly, be lined up with the light, but he will also, crucially, be encouraged to acknowledge and experience, like Rodchenko himself, his unfixed desires.

A review article of the Paris Exposition in the Soviet journal *Rabochii klub* (Workers' Club) offers partial evidence for this fragile claim. The author reports that large groups of admiring French workers visited Rodchenko's club. "Now this—this is our club," exclaimed one French worker, as he "lovingly stroked the case for the wall newspaper with his hand." (The case is visible on the back wall of the club in figure 5.2.) The author continues, "almost every worker . . . was drawn precisely to stroke one or another of the things in the club, and to stroke it lovingly."[59] The club, then, provoked a sensuous response that was an extension of the transparent relay of appropriate movements and activities that it consciously solicited as a Constructivist object. This sensuous response can be read precisely as an expression of an unfixed phantasmatic response. The report of the ideologically motivated Bolshevik author may be exaggerated, and the response of the Parisian workers themselves may be untrustworthy evidence, and yet this anecdote provides a nostalgic image for the Constructivist dream. The austere, *unheimliche* forms of the club invite the workers oppressed by capitalist industry to enter into the unsparing ideological light of the visiting Bolsheviks, and once there they find not only order and bracing constraint but a home for the play of fantasy.

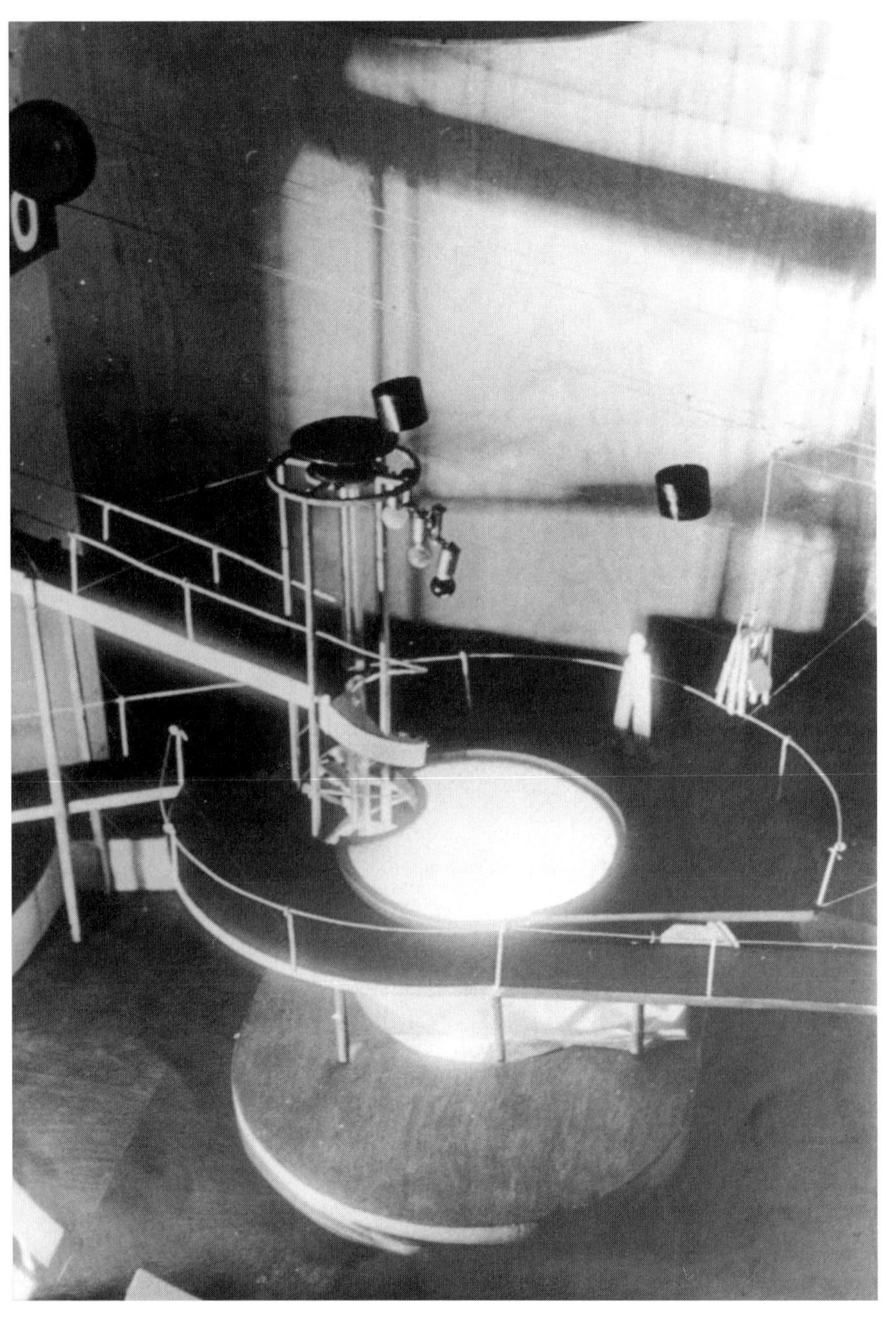

FIGURE 6.1
El Lissitzky, model of the stage design for *I Want a Child!*, 1929. Courtesy Russian State Archive of Literature and Art. © 2004 Artists Rights Society (ARS), New York / VG Bild-Kunst, Bonn.

CHAPTER 6

EPILOGUE: THE LAST POSSESSION

The previous chapter ended on a note of nostalgia for the Constructivist dream of the socialist object. This nostalgia set in already in the Constructivists' own practice not long after Rodchenko returned from Paris in the summer of 1925, because the period in which the Constructivist object found a place in Soviet production and consumption turned out to be brief.

In his memoirs "Working with Mayakovsky," Rodchenko famously boasted about their advertising work: "We completely conquered Moscow and completely set in motion, or rather, changed out, the old tsarist-bourgeois-Western style of advertisements with new, Soviet ones."[1] The success of their advertisements was followed by the triumph of his workers' club in Paris, which was so successful with the Parisian public, particularly Communists and workers, that the Soviet government presented it as a gift to the French Communist Party after the Exposition Internationale closed. Rodchenko was anxious to return home to the Soviet Union to continue his "conquest" of Moscow with Constructivist objects. But he was not to be offered such an opportunity for wide-scale intervention into public space again. Rodchenko returned from France to find that his services in commercial design were no longer required. In a more subdued passage from his memoirs that is less well known, he describes the moment: "Then this work stopped. Mossel'prom hired the artist Iuon, and Iuon, of course, no longer gave us any work. The company of RAPP and MAPP, of course, drove us out of everything and attempted in everything to criticize and liquidate our work."[2] RAPP and MAPP were the acronyms, respectively, for the Russian and Moscow Associations of Proletarian Writers, and Konstantin Fedorovich Iuon was an illusionistic easel painter with a preference for landscapes and genre scenes.

The citation of this detail from Rodchenko's memoirs is not meant to rehash the argument that ultimately, traditional painterly illusionism would triumph over modernist experimentation in Russia because it appealed more to the tastes of the masses. The success of so much of the Constructivist work discussed in this book has provided contrary evidence to that argument. Rather, the point is that Rodchenko and Mayakovsky, as well as other Constructivists, were deprived of key sites of intervention into Soviet production and consumption starting around 1926, precisely at the moment that Soviet state enterprises were moving toward becoming the exclusive suppliers of everyday goods, once competition from NEP manufacturers, traders, and importers was slowly being eliminated with the gradual dismantling of NEP. Constructivist objects continued to exist in the later 1920s: Stepanova and Rodchenko designed books and journals, Rodchenko designed objects for film and theater projects, and Tatlin and Rodchenko continued to teach at VKhUTEMAS until 1929, where their students produced highly regarded works of industrial design. In addition, the artist El Lissitzky, who had returned to the Soviet Union from Europe only in 1925 after an absence of several years, become associated then with Constructivism. He undertook a number of practical designs for furniture, typography, photomontage, and exhibitions, and taught at the wood and metalwork faculty at VKhUTEMAS.[3] But the rhetoric around these Constructivist objects of the later 1920s was no longer on the fervent level of Rodchenko's "our things in our hands" or Arvatov's "culture of the thing." The emotional rhetoric of the active object, participating as a "comrade" or "coworker" in the creation of socialist modernity, became less sustainable as the transitional period of NEP came to a close and it became clear that Soviet industry would not make a place for Productivism in its most ambitious and expansive definition.

The Constructivist dream of the comradely object had a final, valedictory resurgence in Sergei Tret'iakov's eugenic play *I Want a Child!* of 1926, a cautionary parable about the difficulty of this dream and its potential redirection into other cultural forms. The resurgence was a short-lived one because the play, completed in September 1926 and destined for the theater of Vsevolod Meyerhold, was censored in early 1927. Meyerhold was eventually given permission by the censors, in December 1928, to mount it in his theater exclusively as a "discussion piece" only if certain of the most problematic parts were rewritten, and El Lissitzky was commissioned in early 1929 to design the production, but the set was never built and the play was never performed.[4] Despite its unfortunate fate, the play is instructive because it brings together all the key beliefs about the socialist object after its demise, offering a dissection of its promises and pitfalls. The Constructivist objects we have examined in this book were all directed toward the body of the new Soviet consumer: Tatlin's stove, supplying warmth and the means of cooking food; Tatlin's, Stepanova's and Popova's clothing designs, providing warmth and hygiene or, alternatively, sartorial tools of self-fashioning; the Rodchenko–Mayakovsky ads, directing oral desires; and Rodchenko's *Nash gaz* page, mapping bodily functions, and his workers' club, contributing a space for the working body at rest. This Constructivist address to the body of the new consumer through the material object takes the form, in *I Want a Child!*, of the literal production of new bodies. Instead of Soviet industry producing comradely objects, the scientific control of reproduction will lead to the production of new comrades themselves. The play imagines the eugenic child itself as a collective socialist object.

In *I Want a Child!*, an unmarried party member named Milda, whose extensive public organizing work to benefit the collective leaves no time for marriage or children, suddenly realizes that she wants to have a child. As an agronomist well-versed in eugenics as well as Leninism, Milda decides that the prospective father must be of 100 percent healthy proletarian stock. Rationalist and antiromantic, she searches out an appropriate specimen. Fixing her sights on the brawny young worker Iakov from the local construction site, she propositions him to father her child. She offers him a contract stating that after conception she will make no claims for his support of her or the child, nor will she ask him to play the roles of husband or father in any way. After considerable discussion he agrees to her terms, and they begin to have sex. As soon as she conceives, she severs all ties with him. Their son is raised communally in collective Soviet children's institutions. She allows Iakov no fatherly access, despite his pleas. In the play's conclusion, set four years later in 1930, Iakov catches a glimpse of his son when the child wins first prize in a "Healthy Baby" contest—displayed as an object of collective consumption, rather than of traditional, individual parental pride.

Developed in the West, eugenics was a science that imposed the industrial disciplines of scientific quality control and rational planning onto the sexed body of the individual citizen. In the context of this play by a left avant-garde writer, eugenics becomes a means to produce a specifically socialist Soviet subject who will be, from his or her very conception, collectively owned and communally oriented. If, in a socialist society, all objects belong to the collective, then the only remaining possession is the body—and, in the case of parents, their children. Tret'iakov imagines a future in which the male body offers up its sperm, the female body offers itself up to the invasive eye of science, and both parents willingly give up their child—their last possession—to the institutions of the collective.

"In *I Want a Child!*," Tret'iakov said, "love is placed on an operating table."[5] The play rejects traditional dramatic formulas for building emotion around its potboiler plot, and instead presents the actions of all the characters as questions for discussion. The inner reaches of private dramas will be laid out for vivisection on the operating table, or better yet, placed under a microscope. This is Tret'iakov's description of the opening shot of the film script that he wrote in 1928 on the basis of the play (and which was also censored, in 1929):

> In the shot a million fibers are moving and this movement looks like a ripened field, swayed by the wind in one direction. On this swaying there appears a huge, semi-transparent sphere, glimmering with radiating filaments from the luminous nucleus at its center. This sphere rolls on the swaying field. The delicate flagella with their fat little heads, wriggling swiftly, move toward the sphere. They surround the sphere with twitching rays on all sides. One of them pierces the membrane of the sphere. This membrane becomes glassy as soon as it is pierced, grows turbid, and through the murk one can see how the head of the flagellum moves toward the nucleus and joins with it. With a sharp movement this entire picture is jerked out of the shot. This is Milda the agronomist-cattle-breeder working with the microscope.[6]

The round glass eye of the inquisitive microscope, rendering visible this heroic narrative of fertilization, offers a dramatic visual metaphor for the script's narrative of the penetration of Bolshevik ideology into every aspect of Soviet *byt*. El Lissitzky's stage set, designed as a small-scale model in 1929 but never built, would have made the stage into a transparent glass circle, lit from below and open to the audience on all sides, similarly invoking an all-seeing Bolshevik state (figure 6.1). Devoid of traditional props—or, to use the unabridged theatrical term, "properties"—Lissitzky's bare stage emphasized the rationalizing and antimaterialist aspects of Tret'iakov's play, clearing a space for social practice unencumbered by possessions.

Their use of these metaphors of visibility leave Tret'iakov and Lissitzky open to the charge that their work imagined Soviet subjects as fully rationalized objects of surveillance by the disciplining Soviet state. This would confirm the horror story told by Boris Groys: the totalizing impetus in the Russian avant-garde paved the way for the repression and totalitarianism of Soviet society under Stalin.[7] Tret'iakov's interest in eugenics in *I Want a Child!* only exacerbates this critique, because eugenics attempts to master the very raw materials of the subject, neutralizing all negative physical and psychological aspects inherited from the capitalist past at the level of the germ plasm. This goal provides fuel for Groys's sweeping argument that the avant-garde, like the Bolsheviks themselves, wanted to obliterate all remainders of past culture in order to remake society in its own totalizing image.

But in *I Want a Child!*, the lived experience of *byt* continually interrupts grand Bolshevik plans for a *novyi byt*. Tret'iakov investigates the human effects of the transition to the new world of socialism, rather than offering a blithe narration of its achievement. Despite its seemingly uncompromising, futuristic vision, Tret'iakov's play, like Constructivism more broadly, shares Walter Benjamin's insight that a future socialist culture will succeed only if it can reactivate the original promise of the creativity of industrialism—the human desires lodged in the material objects of the recent past—while delivering it from the commodity phantasmagoria of capitalism that prevented its realization. Tret'iakov's play provocatively extends this Constructivist reactivation of the creativity of industrialism through its objects onto the territory of the human body itself, using the device of eugenics to imagine a parallel reinvention of procreativity through industrial technology. Like Constructivist socialist objects freed from the pernicious effects of the commodity form, Tret'iakov's socialist form of reproduction would be delivered from the consequences of capitalism: possessiveness, the alienation of labor, and patriarchal social forms of male dominance and female passivity. The transitional nature of Tret'iakov's play, set within the socially chaotic context of NEP but looking toward the socialist future, was meant to awaken the contemporary Soviet audience from the "dream sleep" of capitalism into a socialist culture. Holding the past, present, and future in a fragile solution, this "constellation"—to use Benjamin's evocative term once again—offers counterevidence to Groys's indictment of the avant-garde for its attempt to obliterate the past and present to create a totalized future.

A Feminist Eugenics?

Tret'iakov's choice to take up the theme of eugenics is an instance of his engaged response to highly topical debates on the topic of sexual *byt*. There was widespread popular interest in the theory of eugenics in the Soviet Union in the 1920s, but eugenics fit into the officially sanctioned versions of the *novyi byt* primarily only in its "positive" guise, in which people with desirable traits would be encouraged to reproduce with each other, as a component of organized sexuality on the traditional familial model.[8] According to the mass-oriented magazine *Hygiene and Health of the Worker and Peasant Family*, in an article by Dr. Bernatskii written in 1928, one of the key conditions that must be met in choosing an appropriate marriage partner for healthy offspring is "the necessity of definite and sharply expressed sexual characteristics, physical as well as spiritual (the male principle and the female principle)."[9] A woman is "more caressing than a man, her movements are light, her voice is softer, she is tidier and neater, she is more observant of details, she loves coziness and cleanliness. In a word, she is 'feminine.'"[10]

The model of eugenics that Tret'iakov deploys in *I Want a Child!* challenges such traditional assumptions about gender. The central character of Milda is defined by her conscious refusal of traditional femininity; she is the opposite of the objectified women that so horrified Rodchenko in Paris. She embodies instead the figure of the androgynous and asexual Bolshevik woman who emerged in the popular imagination in the civil war years.[11] In her first appearance in the play, she is dressed in a man's suit, standing with her back to the audience in the worker's club attached to the construction site (*stroika*) that is the play's setting. She has dedicated herself to public organizing work at the site, giving lectures at public meetings and fighting to establish a children's day care center at the workers' club. When the workers Iakov and Grin'ko enter the club, Grin'ko mistakes Milda for a male friend, grabbing her from behind. Upon seeing his mistake, he pushes Milda away, exclaiming "That's not a person, that's a woman [*ta tse zh ne chelovek, ta tse zh baba*]" (KhR, p. 210)—a slang reworking of the traditional Russian proverb "A chicken is not a bird, a woman is not a person" (*Kuritsa ne ptitsa, zhenshchina ne chelovek*). Grin'ko's scornful misogyny is applied with special venom to the androgynous and authoritative Bolshevik woman.

The rest of the play contests the traditional construction of femininity that supposedly justified this misogyny. A key scene in this contestation unfolds when Milda has invited Grin'ko's comrade Iakov to her room for an "interview" and propositions him to sire a child with her. She seduces him into sleeping with her through the ruse of physical transformation, aided by the commodity objects associated with bourgeois femininity. Iakov responds negatively to her proposition at first, but Milda disappears behind a screen, emerging a few minutes later transformed: hair waved, face made up and powdered, dressed in a tight, low-cut dress. The "soldier-woman" (*soldat baba*), as Grin'ko calls her (KhR, p. 224), achieves her goal of conceiving a child without a husband or a traditional family—a goal directly contradicting conventions of femininity—by taking on the masquerade of store-bought femininity. When Iakov asks her wonderingly how she managed to transform herself, she answers with customary frankness, "The way all such things are done. From the parfumerie. From the hair dresser" (KhR, p. 227). Yet after this initial scene of seduction, Milda returns to her normal, unfeminine self;

there are no more mentions of makeup or dresses. Tret'iakov invokes the familiar dramatic ploy of the transformation of the ugly duckling into the swan, only to defuse its power by refusing to maintain the transformation. The feminine beauty revealed by the transformation is no more natural than the masculine plainness that preceded it. Both are constructed, with the help of everyday objects like powder, perfume, curling irons, and dresses—or soldier's trousers and sturdy boots.

In solving the narrative problem of how to get this unfeminine rationalist interested in having a child at all, Tret'iakov does not resort to traditional gendered assumptions about women's natural longing for motherhood, but rather invokes the powerful rhetoric of production. When a father of an infant asks Milda whether she has a child, and she says no, he responds: "But a good product would come from you. Your pelvis is one hundred twenty centimeters and you would produce a lot of milk" (*A produkt by u vas khoroshii vyshel. Taz santimetrov sto dvadtsat i moloka by mnogo dali*, KhR, p. 214). The proposal that reproduction could be understood within the structures of organized production—her body a well-equipped factory, her breasts providing adequate raw materials, her good health ensuring flawless products—provides the impetus for her sudden desire to have a child. The Constructivists took rational industrial production as their model for artmaking after the revolution; in *I Want a Child!*, it also becomes the model for human decisions about sex and reproduction.

Yet more traditional models of sexual desire also crop up in the play, both by design—in order to signal to the audience the tenacity of the old *byt*—and in certain cases seemingly unconsciously, suggesting the limits of Tret'iakov's own ability to think beyond the contemporary ideology of sex and gender. Milda's selection of Iakov as the father of her child, for example, is explained not only by his proletarian pedigree, but by his possession of the masculine gender characteristics deemed desirable by Soviet proponents of "positive" eugenics. Once Milda realizes that she wants a child, her friend, a doctor, offers to introduce her to a eugenically appropriate candidate for fatherhood: a handsome doctor who stems from an old family of the intelligentsia. She meets her friend at his office at the *stroika* to be introduced to this other doctor, but from his window she catches sight of the rugged figure of Iakov, at work on the actual construction project itself. The police have come to arrest the leader of some hooligans who had recently committed a gang rape of a young woman, and Iakov is vocally defending them: women themselves provoke rape, he says, by wearing perfumes and powder and wiggling their buttocks (KhR, p. 223).[12] Hearing this speech, Milda exclaims "Hooligans!," but her doctor friend replies that Iakov and his comrades are not hooligans at all, but merely strong, healthy young men: "No consumption, no neurasthenia, no venereal disease—exhibition pieces" (KhR, p. 223). Seemingly in response to this affirmation of Iakov's health, Milda starts a conversation with him. Yet the scene suggests that not only his health attracted Milda, but also his display of rough masculine sentiment in his defense of the vicious rape.

Milda's choice of the manly Iakov is made more immediate and visual in the film script. Milda is in her friend the doctor's office when the second doctor enters briefly. In this man, her friend assures her, flows the blue blood of the intelligentsia; he will produce excellent offspring. Tret'iakov then describes a montage of changing, successive portraits of pedigreed people over the course of three hundred years, ending with the portrait of the handsome doctor (KhR-S, p. 40). This montage provides a literal image of eugenics: the positive traits of past generations are passed down through time, creating a link between the past and the future. Yet the almost *mise-en-abîme* effect of the infinite progression of similar portraits through time is stopped at the present moment. There is no montage of the doctor's future offspring coming forward, as it were. The reason for this becomes apparent later, when Milda sees this same blue-blooded doctor bandaging the hand of an injured worker: "During the bandaging the contrast was striking between the pale, refined face of the doctor and his narrow, aristocratic hands and the bronze, cast-iron, snub-nosed workers" (KhR-S, p. 40). Through eugenics, class politics will be imposed onto the very germ plasm, protecting the future from the unwanted class characteristics of the presocialist past. Hard-muscled, bronzed masculinity wins out over the pampered, feminized upper-class male body. The favorite Bolshevik symbol of the rough, handsome worker is here presented alongside the teachings of contemporary medical discourse, such as those of Dr. Bernatskii, that the combination of masculine men and feminine women created the healthiest families and offspring.

This scene on the *stroika* celebrating stereotypical proletarian masculinity is in line with the relatively benign understanding of popular eugenics that existed then in the Soviet Union, but it is at odds with the critique of gender stereotypes that dominates the rest of the play. This discordance is an instance of Tret'iakov's "discussion piece" style, in which visions of the rational, gender-egalitarian reproduction of the future are continuously intertwined with the eruption of desires from the past that complicate their realization. Or it may signal that his radical vision of a future socialist sexuality—in which a woman could be as swayed by the ideology of production as by traditionally gendered desire—could not be imagined unconditionally from the perspective of the present.

Industrial Production: An Imperfect Model for the Future of Sex

Tret'iakov stages his most powerful criticism of eugenics by framing it as a problem of productive labor: by projecting industrial models of rational production onto the body, the play proposes, eugenics also risks carrying the exploitative labor practices of the capitalist past into the future. Milda's search for a proletarian specimen to father her child is portrayed as double edged. In their first interview, Iakov answers Milda's questions about his background because he assumes that she is yet another of the many writers gathering information on the everyday life of workers at that time. His friend Grin'ko boasts to Milda that Iakov's father and grandfather were both metal workers from the Putilov metalworking factory, making him nothing less than a "count" of the working class. Iakov is unaware that he is being looked over like a potential stud on a stud farm, though this becomes clear later in the pivotal scene in which Milda finally propositions him. She says to him pedantically "You know that there is production. This is when products are made in factories or from the earth, and there is reproduction—this is when human stock itself is renewed, or more simply—people are born" (KhR, p. 226). Iakov answers patiently that he understands. She continues on in a eugenic vein, explaining that bad conditions of production lead to a low-quality product, just as incorrect conditions of reproduction—disease, alcoholism, idiotism—lead to bad people. When she finally manages to tell Iakov that she wants to conceive a child with a healthy worker, and that she has chosen him, he immediately objects that he already has a fiancée. Milda offers him the crucial explanation: "I don't want a husband. I want a child. You yourself aren't necessary to me. I need your spermatozoa."

This scene challenges conventional wisdom about the passivity of feminine sexuality, for Milda knows what she wants, explains it frankly, and is not embarrassed to ask for sex. But it also presents eugenics in a critical light, because it enacts the central problem of Marxism itself: the alienated relation of the producer to the product of his labor. Milda has selected Iakov because of his Putilovskii proletarian pedigree, and yet she demands of him what has always been demanded of the proletarian: that he produce a product and then give it up, to be alienated from it forever. The body's natural production of sperm and the production of metal machine parts through factory labor are not comparable forms of production, yet the metaphor of alienated labor is made fully intentional: Iakov responds angrily to Milda's proposition by asking "What am I, a stallion?" (*Zherebets ia zavodskoi, chto li?*) (KhR, p. 227). Tret'iakov puns here on the standard term for "stallion," *zavodskoi zherebets*, which literally means "factory stallion."

In the Constructivist vision of a socialist future, as this book has argued, the alienation of the worker from the object of his labor will be eliminated not only through the Communist transformation of the means of production, but through the very form of the objects produced: socialist objects will be comrades of the worker, rather than alienating commodities to be possessed by someone richer than himself. This Constructivist dream of a *novyi byt* without possessions provides the context for the powerful justification that Milda offers Iakov for her exploitative demand on his reproductive labor: the product in question, the healthy part-proletarian child, will belong to the collective rather than to Milda herself. Later she will state explicitly that the child will be raised primarily in the children's house (*detdom*) and the kindergarten (*detskii sad*, KhR, p. 233). She wants Iakov to give up his sperm to her, not just to fulfill her personal wishes for a child, but to benefit the Soviet collective. This is a private, bodily counterpart to the public, economic demand made by the Bolshevik Party of the Soviet proletariat: accept a continuing alienated relation to your labor, just as under capitalism, because the product of that labor is now expropriated by the State, which "represents" you.

Already in 1923, writing in *Lef*, Tret'iakov had imagined that in the socialist future, the human subject—personified in the character he called the "Futurist inventor"—would no longer latch onto fetishized objects, but would willingly part with the products of his creative labor, offering them to the collective.[13] Three years later, in *I Want a Child!*, Tret'iakov has Milda's friend Distsipliner speak lines that carry this battle against possession from production into reproduction:

> To hell with husbands. . . . What do you say to a syringe? The government will give the best spermatozoa to the best women producers. . . . It will take these children at its own expense and develop a breed of new people. . . . there will be scientific control over the person not only during upbringing, not only during birth, but even at the moment of conception. (KhR, p. 221)

The tone of the scene suggests that this outburst is to be viewed as eccentric and dystopian, but the simple fact that Distsipliner is identified as an inventor suggests that he is a figure for Tret'iakov's heroic "Futurist inventor," who speaks Tret'iakov's own disciplining desire for a socialist future in which both the products of creative invention—socialist objects—and the products of Soviet reproductive bodies under "scientific control"—eugenic children—will belong to the collective. No human characters in Tret'iakov's story experience artificial insemination with a syringe or a "scientifically controlled" conception. But by making Milda's character an agricultural expert involved in animal breeding, Tret'iakov alludes to this more futuristic, and potentially coercive or "negative," model of eugenics. The possibility that the character of Distsipliner expresses aspects of Tret'iakov's own extreme views, camouflaged by the "discussion play" format, is suggested by the similarities between Distsipliner's scripted outbursts and a brief, two-page introduction to the film script of *I Want a Child!* that Tret'iakov wrote in late 1928 or early 1929. In this text, he expresses his exasperation with people who irresponsibly pass on their venereal diseases, tuberculosis, malaria, and neuroses to their children, rivaling his crotchety tone in *Lef* in 1923, where he denounced the material clutter and inefficiency of contemporary Russian *byt*, and even the backward Russian people themselves, citing their "inability to walk intelligently down the street, to get on to a streetcar, to exit a lecture hall without shoving each other."[14] He calls for sexual practices to become organized in the same way that other everyday practices have become organized under the *novyi byt*. In terms reminiscent of Rodchenko's indictment of Parisian sexuality, he blames the disorganized state of sexuality on the institution of bourgeois marriage, whose basis in economics and the ideology of possession leads to dissipation and sexual fever.

Unlike the more conventional advocates of a new socialist sexuality, Tret'iakov imagines a future social order in which reproduction is no longer organized according to patriarchal marriage structures, and children become collective social objects rather than private fetishes. The whole enterprise of reproduction must shed its structures of possession and become more collective:

> Only where the former form of marriage is smashed and great responsibility is assumed by the individual, the former "small proprietor," the present "co-worker," before his or her comrades in life and before future generations, will it be possible to return to conception the purity, all the clarity and social responsibility, that it lost choking in orgasms and gonococci. (KhR-S, pp. 33–34)

In his emphasis on the sexual partner as a "comrade in life" and his critique of the former status of the lover as a "proprietor" of another person, Tret'iakov echoes Aleksandra Kollontai, who, as we have seen, argued that women in traditional romantic relationships were the possessions as well as dependents of men,[15] and Rodchenko, who wrote from Paris that women should be equals and comrades, and not objects to be possessed. Yet Tret'iakov's quest for an act of conception characterized by "purity" and "clarity," and his demand that vision and transparency replace the desiring body "choking in orgasms and gonococci," leave no room for a differently desiring body. He cannot imagine an alternative sexual desire.

The Socialist Object as a Model for the New Soviet Subject

The Constructivists and *Lef* writers may not have advanced a new model of socialist sexual desire, but they did imagine new forms of object desire under socialism, through their theorization of the socialist object as a rejoinder to the commodity fetish. In Tret'iakov's play it is not surprising, then, that the problem of how to reconcile old attachments to material objects with a *novyi byt* that will be without possessions continually stands in for the larger dilemma of reconciling old forms of sexual desire with new ones. He elaborately stages an entire domestic and private object world to reveal the desires of his characters and to delineate their identities.

In one scene, a group of women in the communal kitchen of Milda's building sit enveloped in steam that comes damping out from an enormous array of bubbling pots on the *primusy*, or primus stoves (single propane burners) surrounding them. Within the setting of this literal material density—the exclusive province of women in the new as in the old *byt*—they gossip about how Milda has been bringing a young worker to her room at night, and worry that she will steal their husbands and spread syphilis to their families. This communal but otherwise old-fashioned kitchen—inefficient, low-tech, and overcrowded, the antithesis of the gleaming collective dining rooms of propaganda posters—is the object-equivalent of the women's old-fashioned, if legitimate, female response to newfangled, Bolshevik notions of "free love" in the context of their low-income lives. These neighbors' voices are also heard through the thin walls from the next room during the seduction scene; an older female voice laments that "the Bolsheviks are copulating" (KhR, p. 228), an unflattering if not inaccurate verb to describe the Bolshevik seduction devised by Tret'iakov. A material object has given Milda away: her squeaky bed. Tret'iakov forces Milda's future visions of the *novyi byt* into constant mediation with the imperfect present.

A key scene demonstrates that firmly rooted beliefs about possessions and their significance will always interrupt the futuristic visions of characters like Milda. The day following Milda's successful seduction of Iakov, he expresses his newfound feelings for her through an object: he comes uninvited to her room to hang a pair of curtains that he has just found at a good price at the Smolenskii market. Her room was "like a garage," he says, and addressing her with an affectionate diminutive, he asks "It's nice that I brought you some comfort, isn't it, comrade Milka?" (KhR, p. 228). He went to the market, the heart of the free NEP marketplace, to bring home a decorative domestic object that demonstrates his pleasure in the fact that they are building a family together. His gesture is misbegotten, yet it illustrates the difficulty of any scheme that will attempt to do away with the objects of individual *byt* and the proprietary emotions they embody. Arvatov had argued, we recall, that the expedient socialist object would not deprive things of their "humanity" or "emotionality."[16] The Constructivist difference would be that the "humanity" of things would now be one that had shed the negative qualities of human beings under capitalism, but maintained the positive human qualities of reason and emotion in socialist form.

The ultimate socialist object in Tret'iakov's play, characterized by both rationality and "emotionality," is the eugenic baby. Genetically purged of the capitalist traits of the past, a literal embodiment of the creativity of production, the eugenic child will be an object of properly socialist desire and emotional affect, existing in public nurseries and kindergartens rather than in the materially and emotionally cluttered lap of the family. The final scene of the play, which takes place at a Healthy Baby contest set four years later in 1930, displays the eugenic baby as a perfected product of socialist reproduction. In this imagined future, the *stroika* has been completed. Banners proclaim "Healthy parents mean a healthy new generation"; "A public children's day care center means the liberation of the woman worker"; and "Healthy conception—healthy pregnancy" (KhR, p. 235). The first prize for one-year-old babies is awarded jointly to a boy—the second son of Iakov and Milda—and a girl—the daughter of Iakov and his wife. This is the moment when Iakov gets his alienated product returned to him, for he is announced as the father of Milda's son, and therefore gets to beam with double pride at having sired not one but two first-prize children. Public display for the approval of the collective replaces the private, exclusive relation of possession fostered by traditional family structures.

In his journalistic style, Tret'iakov seems to have gotten the idea for the ending of his play from the immediately contemporary announcement of the first Soviet Healthy Baby contest (Konkurs zdorovykh detei), sponsored by the magazine *Hygiene and Health of the Worker and Peasant Family* and announced in September of 1926, as Tret'iakov was finishing his play.[17] The judging of the contest would supposedly be based entirely on scientifically objective and measurable characteristics, such as weight and "skin tone." The magazine devoted two successive cover images in early 1927 to the young winners of the contest, producing a pair of somewhat inexpert photomontages of babies (figures 6.2, 6.3); most of them are

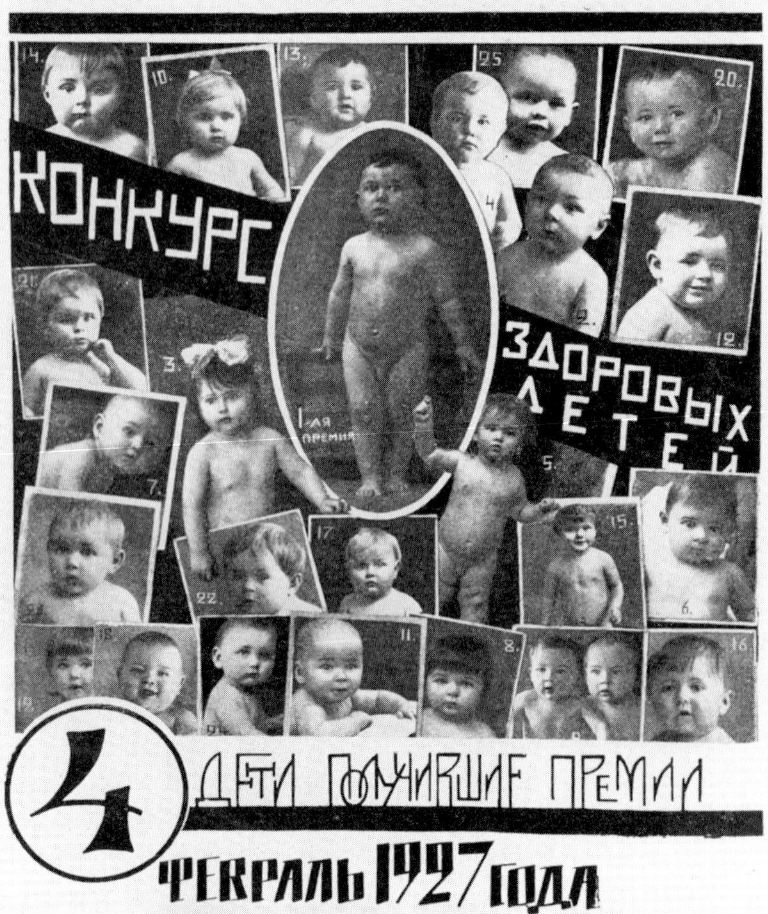

FIGURE 6.2
Cover of *Hygiene and Health of the Worker and Peasant Family* no. 4 (1927), announcing the prize winners in the first Soviet Healthy Baby Contest. Courtesy Russian State Library, Moscow.

ГИГИЕНА и ЗДОРОВЬЕ
РАБОЧЕЙ и КРЕСТЬЯНСКОЙ СЕМЬИ

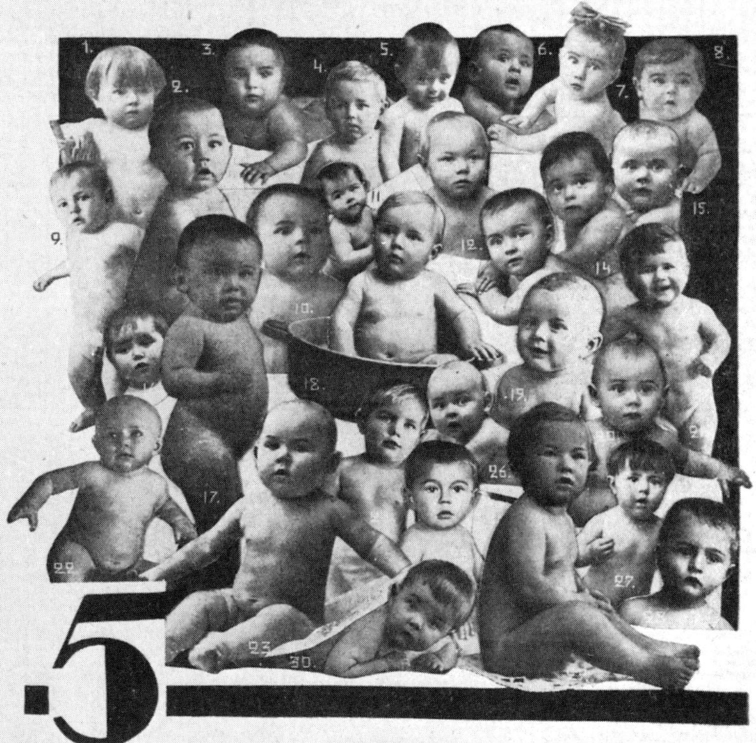

5

МАРТ 1927 ГОДА

Дети признанные лучшими на конкурсе „Здоровых Детей“
(Фамилии на 2 стр. обложки).

FIGURE 6.3
Cover of *Hygiene and Health of the Worker and Peasant Family* no. 5 (1927), announcing the results of the first Soviet Healthy Baby Contest. Courtesy Russian State Library, Moscow.

plump, as desired, while the quality of their skin tone must be left to the imagination, as it is not revealed by the grainy newsprint of the cheap paper. The public and festive nature of the contest was meant to strengthen the magazine's propaganda for the hygiene and health components of the *novyi byt*.

Yet even in this triumphal ending for his eugenic theme, Tret'iakov inserts "discussion questions": is eugenics really necessary, when the regular love union of two healthy working people, Iakov and his wife, can result in as healthy a baby as the more rationally organized union of Iakov and Milda? Are the emotional losses entailed by the rationalization of reproduction justifiable? This question is posed by an exchange between Milda and Iakov in which she tells him that she breast-fed the baby until it was time to send it away to the *detdom*. He asks if she did not find it difficult to tear herself away from the baby, and she responds "It's always hard to tear yourself away. Do you think it was easy for me back then to let you go?" (KhR, p. 236). Even the rationalist Milda expresses regret at giving up her lover and her child, signaling the difficulty of relinquishing all the possessive desires of the past. Tret'iakov may have hoped at one level for the implementation of Milda's rationalist, collective utopia—perhaps even replete with syringes and sperm banks—but his play leaves the impression that if the new Soviet subject is predicated on the destruction of the past, rather than on a redemption of its desires, it will not be a subjectivity that anyone will want to live.

A Theater without Properties: Lissitzky's Transparent Stage Design

If *I Want a Child!* offers a complex depiction of the lived contradictions of the *novyi byt*, its planned staging in the Meyerhold Theater seemed to downplay its material contradictions and to present, instead, a proto-totalitarian microcosm of Soviet citizens being relentlessly surveyed by an all-seeing state. Lissitzky's model set departs radically from the settings described in Tret'iakov's stage directions. Instead of depicting the *stroika*, the workers' club, or the crowded communal building, Lissitzky's plan completely reconfigured the traditional theatrical space of audience and stage to emphasize total visual access and surveillance; only the red banners promoting healthy childbirth, taken from the stage directions for the final scene of the Healthy Baby contest, follow Tret'iakov's intent. Lissitzky's own words provide the most cogent description of his work:

> The stage is fully merged with the auditorium by the construction of an amphitheatre. For the play itself a new area in the theatre is created, a "ring" that rises from the orchestra pit. The actors emerge from below, from the

> depth of the orchestra pit, from above, out of the balconies, and from the sides across bridges: they no longer have anything to do with the stage. Props roll down ropes from above and disappear into depth after every scene. Light sources move together with the actors, who perform on a transparent floor.[18]

The central ring of the stage was accessible by two ramps that extended to the sides of the theater, as well as by a bridge that connected one of the balconies with a spiral staircase leading down to, and piercing, the ring platform, which was raised above the ground on pillars. Far above the stage, Lissitzky constructed a set of pulleys and ropes with which to transport furniture and props from the upper balconies to the stage. In his model of the stage set, collapsible chairs are suspended above the stage, ready to be deposited on it by the pulley system. The production of the play would be as fully rationalized as industrial production, with the pulley system providing an assembly-line structure to minimize the labor of actors and stage hands.

Lissitzky's transparent and open space responds ironically to the cluttered and claustrophobic spaces of the communal building in Tret'iakov's script. Rather than materially enacting these crowded spaces, the spare transparency of the set figures the total visibility and surveillance made possible by the material closeness and nosy neighbors of Soviet *byt*, as well as by the mechanisms of party control over peoples' personal lives, such as informants and the secret police. The tissue of domestic objects that serves to complicate the rationalizing rhetoric of Tret'iakov's play are removed from the scene, to be replaced, conceptually at least, by the spectators on all sides who will participate in the discussion of the piece. There is good reason to believe that Lissitzky's design was produced in accordance with the wishes of Meyerhold, who had hired him to design the set specifically for the limited, experimental "discussion" format of the play that the censors had authorized.

The stage design of a luminous glass circle, lit from below, may have been suggested to Lissitzky by Tret'iakov's film script, which opens with the image of the sperm and ovum observed through the round, illuminated lens of Milda's microscope. Lissitzky's design responds to this microscope image not only structurally, at the level of the glass eye of the microscope as an instrument of penetrating vision, but at the level of content. The wriggling sperm penetrating the glassy sphere of the ovum under the microscope take the visually appropriate form, in Lissitzky's model stage set, of the spiral staircase that penetrates the transparent glass circle of the stage in order to open it up and make it more efficient as a productive unit within the assembly-line of the set.

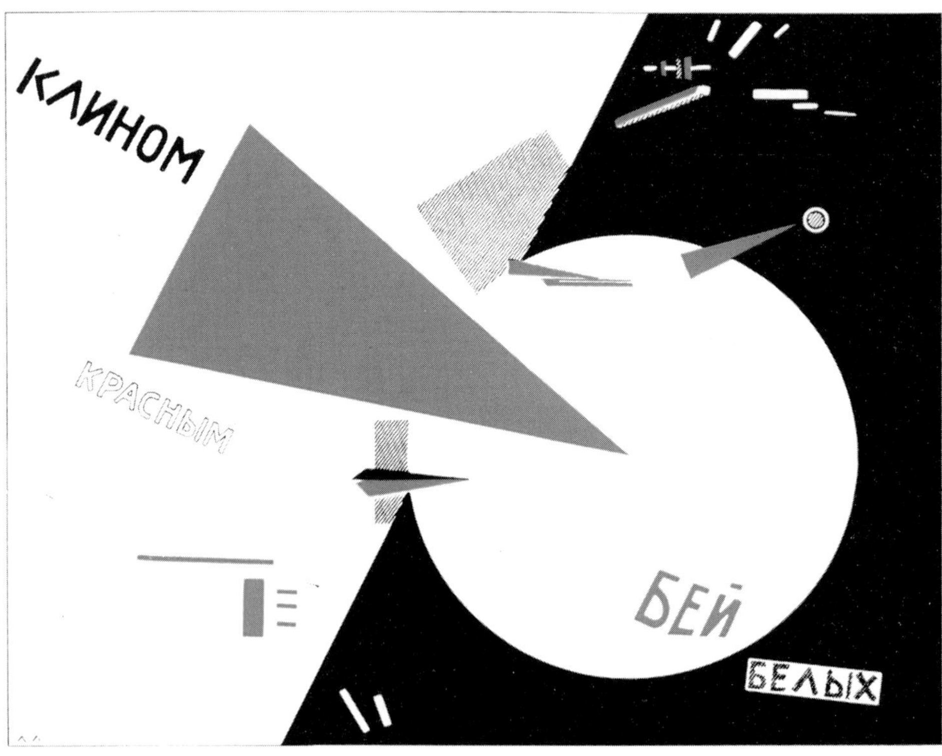

FIGURE 6.4
El Lissitzky, *Beat the Whites with the Red Wedge*, 1919. Poster.

The penetrated circle had appeared before in Lissitzky's work, most famously in his 1919 civil war propaganda poster *Beat the Whites with the Red Wedge* (figure 6.4). The sexual violence of this image is expressed, if not explicitly acknowledged, in Jean-François Lyotard's celebration of the poster as an icon of modernist abstraction: "To beat the whites with the red wedge is not only to win the Civil War, improve the economy, and build collectivism; it is also to force the wedge into all the white zones of experience. . . . the closed, all-enveloping roundness of white investment must everywhere be opened and pierced by red sharpness."[19] The floating geometric forms of Lissitzky's Suprematist composition represent not only the penetration of the White Guard front by the Red Army, but the fantasy of the complete penetration of traditional Russian social life by the invigorating sharpness of Bolshevik ideology. This reading of the significance of the motif of the penetrated circle, which emphasizes the totalitarian potential of Lissitzky's set, Tret'iakov's play, and Meyerhold's proposed staging of it, supports Eric Naiman's conclusion that "if Boris Groys is correct and there is a direct line connecting the Russian avant-garde with Stalin's governance, that line surely runs through Meyerhold and *I Want a Child!*"[20] Naiman demonstrates that Meyerhold's plan for mounting the play as a "discussion piece" involved an Orwellian notion of "discussion": it would be carefully controlled and scripted in order to ensure that "all questions will be treated correctly."[21]

But the Russian avant-garde was not monolithic, and Lissitzky and Tret'iakov are not identical with Meyerhold. The form of Lissitzky's stage design stems from his own aesthetic repertoire, and is not necessarily deployed only to fulfill Meyerhold's plan; recall that, writing in the opening issue of his journal *Veshch'/Gegenstand/Objet*, he stated that "we do not wish to limit the production of artists" to pure utility.[22] Lissitzky's open glass stage and spiral staircase might be read very differently, for example, as his formal response to a description of the play given by Tret'iakov in a 1927 interview: "Not a play that closes in an aesthetic circle, but one that begins on the aesthetic trampoline of the stage and unfolds in a spiral, winding its way through the audience's arguments and through their extratheatrical experience."[23] Lissitzky's spiral staircase literally winds its way up from the stage, connecting with a bridge to the balcony with audience seating. The spiral is a uniquely temporal graphic form, figuring always the movement from a point in the past toward an infinitely expanding future—in the case of Constructivist works like Tatlin's *Monument* or Rodchenko's Red October cookie advertisement, specifically the movement from the capitalist past toward the socialist future. Lissitzky's spiral staircase rising dramatically out of the flat stage stands as a graphic figure for a more voluntary and contested dissemination of Bolshevik visions of the future than the model of the penetrating eye of the microscope.

There is no evidence that Tret'iakov himself wanted to stage the play as a scripted discussion; his intention was for the audience member to experience a genuine challenge to his or her own subject position through the aesthetic form of a theater that rejected cathartic narrative and identification with heroes in the bourgeois tradition. Lissitzky's bare stage could be read, then, as his interpretation of Tret'iakov's call for a stage as an "aesthetic trampoline"—a space cleared of the trappings of bourgeois culture, the better to facilitate the posing of new questions. It is a visual interpretation that partially contradicts Tret'iakov's textual emphasis on the emotional significance of the material objects remaining from the old *byt*, but it does not therefore necessarily dovetail with Meyerhold's desire to control audience participation.

These are the two sides of the *Lef* avant-garde coin: the dream of the transparent relay between human subject and socialist object that eliminates alienation but redeems the desires lodged in the past for the socialist future; and the nightmare transparency of the rationalized public sphere of total control and

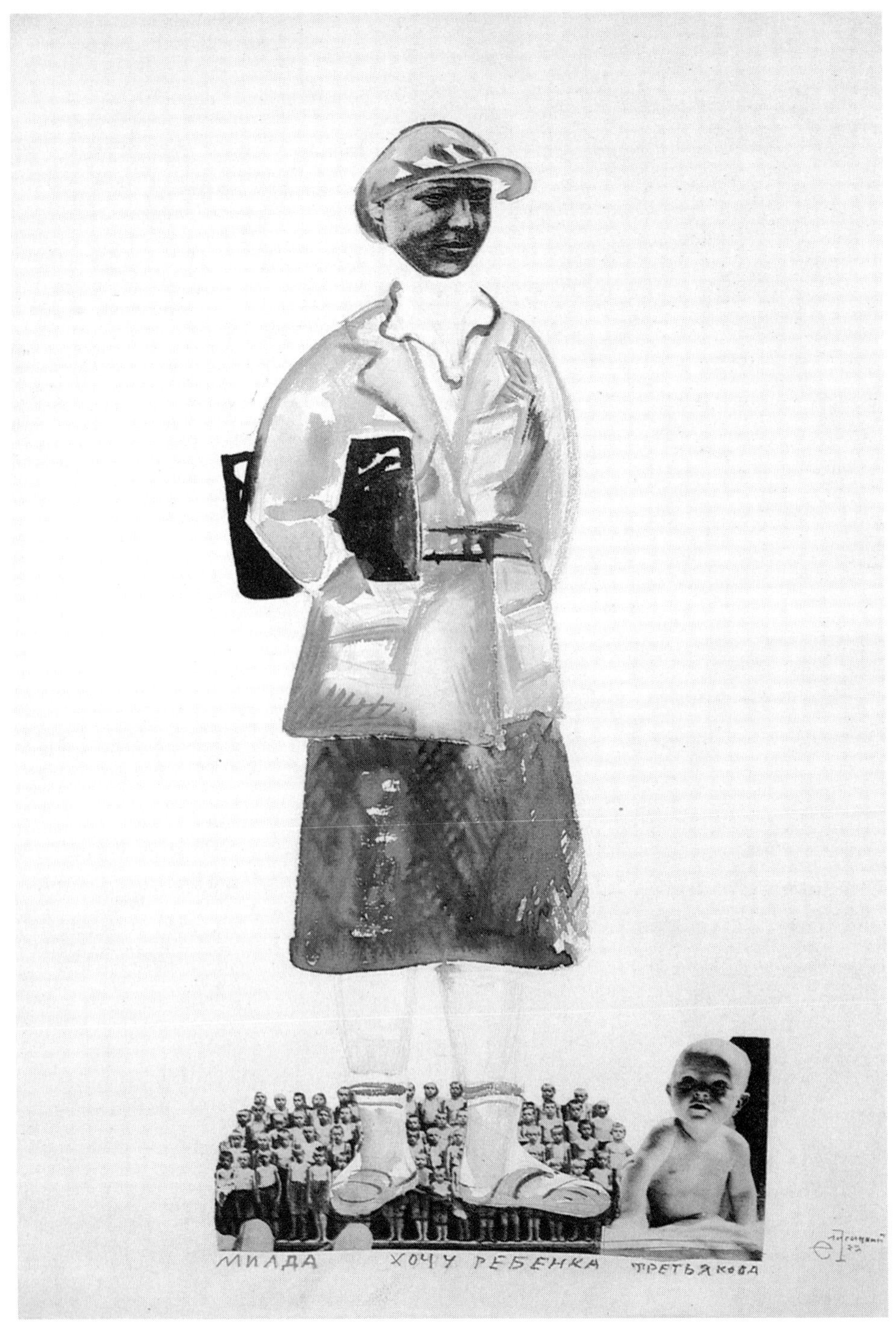

FIGURE 6.5

El Lissitzky, costume design for Milda in *I Want a Child!*, 1929. Watercolor, pencil, and collage on pasteboard. © 2004 Artists Rights Society (ARS), New York / VG Bild-Kunst, Bonn. See plate 22.

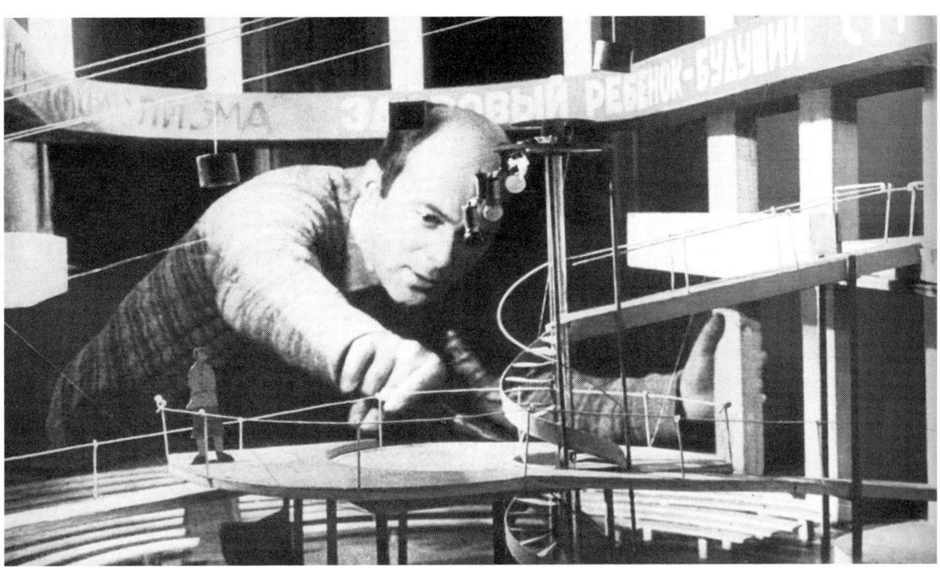

FIGURE 6.6
El Lissitzky at work on the model of his stage design for *I Want a Child!*, 1929.
© 2004 Artists Rights Society (ARS), New York / VG Bild-Kunst, Bonn.

visibility. In conclusion, two images from *I Want a Child!* can stand for these two possibilities. The first is a photomontage by Lissitzky depicting his costume design for the character of Milda, made in 1929 (figure 6.5). It maintains all the tensions and contradictions of Tret'iakov's text, at the level of form as well as content. It combines a delicate watercolor drawing of Milda's clothing, juxtaposed jarringly with a black-and-white photographic image to represent her face. This face is far too small for the body, and it is decidedly masculine, as well as surprisingly Asian in its features when the play clearly specifies Milda's ethnicity as Latvian. Milda's watercolor feet float incongruously above photographs of skinny schoolchildren and a single naked baby, who resembles any one of the plump contestants from the first Soviet Healthy Baby contest. Lissitzky's visual image parallels the montage-like form of Tret'iakov's text, while its content similarly suggests that the futuristic, imagined character of Milda will have to be brought together in a "dialectical image" with the conditions of present Soviet *byt*—signaled here through the documentary photographs of Soviet children—in order for the "flash of recognition" for contemporary viewers to take place.

The second image, also from 1929, is a photograph of Lissitzky leaning into the model of his stage set to adjust the fragile railing around the glass circle (figure 6.6). This photograph might be read as the literalization of the nightmare, in which the Constructivist has become pure Stalinist puppeteer, rearranging social space as if it were composed of cardboard human figures and toy objects. This image supports the notion of a direct line between the avant-garde and Stalin; but, as this book has proposed, the Russian avant-garde contained many lines, the most promising of which could have led toward a very different kind of socialist object and socialist subject.

Afterword

My conception of the "socialist object" of Constructivism emerged from my experience of living in Moscow from 1992 to 1994, soon after the fall of the Soviet Union. There was a palpable disjunction in researching the revolutionary avant-garde while everyone around me was busy dismantling the effects of the revolution. Paul Wood had just written about this paradox in his 1992 essay "The Politics of the Avant-Garde," which spoke of the "floods" and "avalanches" of new research on the avant-garde that disregarded its Marxist politics, invoking the specter of "the academic researcher padding noiselessly through carpeted libraries or, indeed, faxing documents from one international center of learning to another."[24] My plan as a researcher, in deliberate contrast to this menacing image, was to write a history of Constructivism in relation to the Bolshevik campaign for a "new everyday life" that would foreground an as yet unexplored aspect of its revolutionary practice. Yet as I researched this topic, I kept encountering signs that this practice was not as straightforward as the Constructivists would have wished. The ideas for the "new everyday life" kept getting recast or sidetracked by the circumstances of NEP, and I found more and more references, in all kinds of sources, to the problem of the thing (*veshch'*).

At the same time, in my everyday life I encountered my own problems with things. From the living-room windows of my eighth-floor apartment in downtown Moscow, I looked down on a sea of makeshift kiosks surrounding the Kievskaia Metro station, signs of the wrenching transition that Russia was making to a market economy. Vendors there sold everything from apples to cotton panties to kitchen faucets. The wild disjunction between the urban, industrial setting and the anarchic modes of consumption permeated my everyday life, as I negotiated the kiosks and street vendors, the inefficient state stores with their long lines, and the shiny and exclusive hard-currency supermarkets, to acquire daily necessities. Suddenly I had my own "flash of recognition" that this daily negotiation could be a source for understanding the Constructivist object. I realized that Constructivism attempted, in the 1920s, to enter into a similarly chaotic and transitional consumer culture of street vendors, fledgling Soviet cooperatives, and private luxury establishments for rich Nepmen, in order to promote the revolutionary transformation of everyday life.

It became clear to me that although Constructivism had in fact, as I had hypothesized, developed an alternative revolutionary practice, it was one that had to develop its original Marxist goals in innovative directions in order to respond adequately to the transitional moment of NEP. I had to rethink my preconceptions about the politics of Constructivism, which led me to the idea of the "socialist object" as an object moving toward the socialist future, but still confronting the power of the capitalist commodity. I thought a lot about the connections between the politics of consumption and political power that year in Moscow, because from my kitchen window, on the other side of the apartment, I had a view of the White House, home of the new Russian parliament. On October 4, 1993, it was shelled by Russian troops and tanks on the order of President Yeltsin, and I watched it burn (figure 6.7). Living literally between the kiosks and the bombed-out White House that year, I resolved to write an historical account of Constructivism as a flexible Marxist theory of culture that might offer some insight into our post-Soviet, globalized world.

Any account of Constructivist utopianism offered today will be valedictory, as we inevitably look back at it from this post-Soviet perspective. The Constructivist theory of the socialist object was an attempt to imagine a utopian model of socialist consumption to accompany the process of industrialization that was only then beginning in Russia—to preempt the development of the alienated, consumerist form of modernity that already existed in the industrialized West, as well as the differently alienating, production-oriented form that had the potential to arise in the Soviet Union. But as it turned out, technological modernization would come to Russia only at the expense of an advanced consumer culture; these two halves of modernity would not meet in the lifetime of the USSR. After the final failure of the long Soviet experiment in controlled consumption, the impoverished post-Soviet population of Moscow was inundated with the cheapest commodities of international corporate capitalism. As my friend Yura put it back then, all we Russians got out of this harsh economic "shock therapy" was *vsiacheskikh snikersov*—"all kinds of Snickers" (figure 6.8). The cruel joke of Snickers bars as a kind of consolation prize from the global economy, rendered even more absurd by the "-ov" ending of the genitive plural form demanded by Yura's locution in Russian, can stand for the historical failure of the notion of egalitarian consumption. The Constructivist attempt to rescue the enchantment of the commodity for socialist ends still stands in stark and instructive contrast.

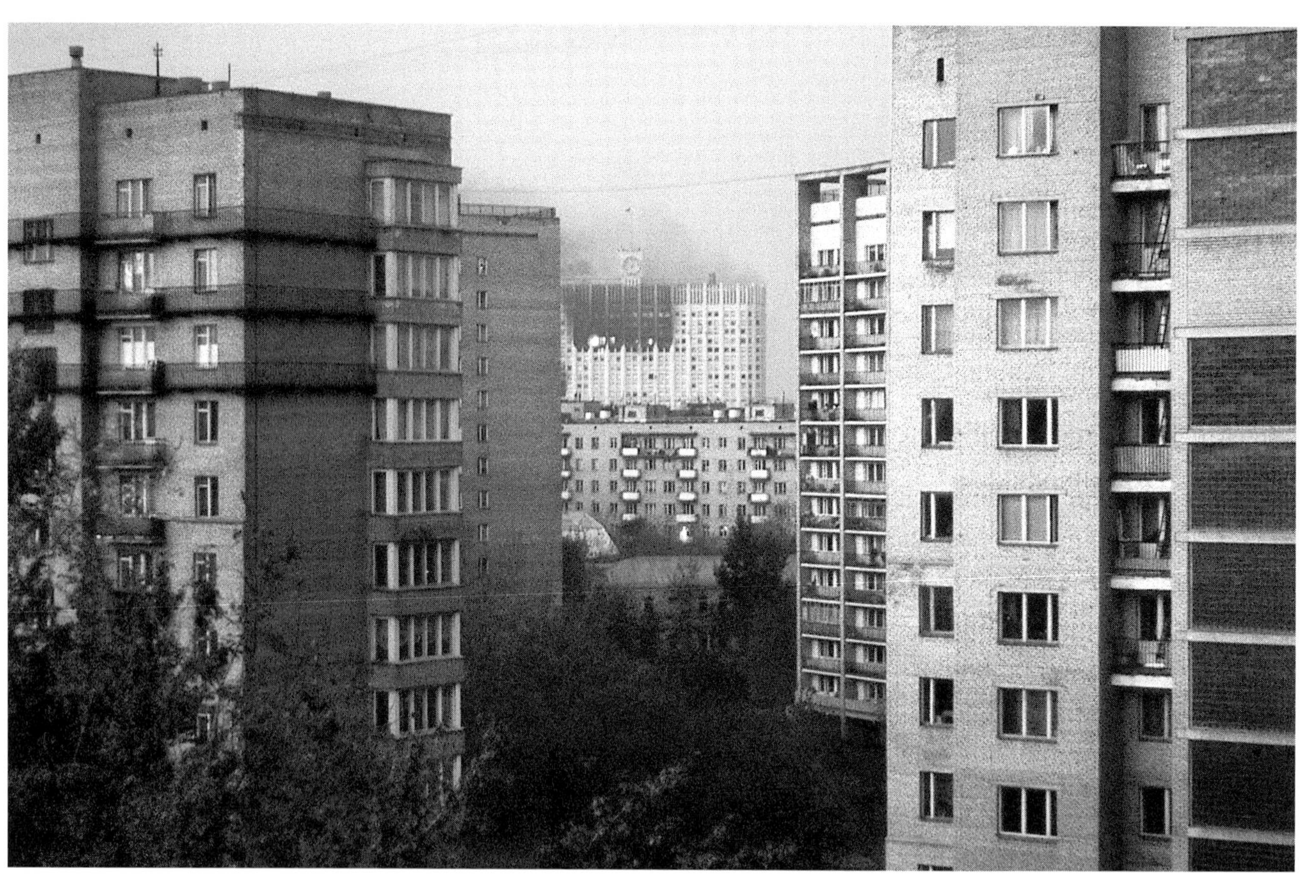

FIGURE 6.7
View of the Russian parliament building from the author's kitchen window, Moscow, October 4, 1993. Photo by the author.

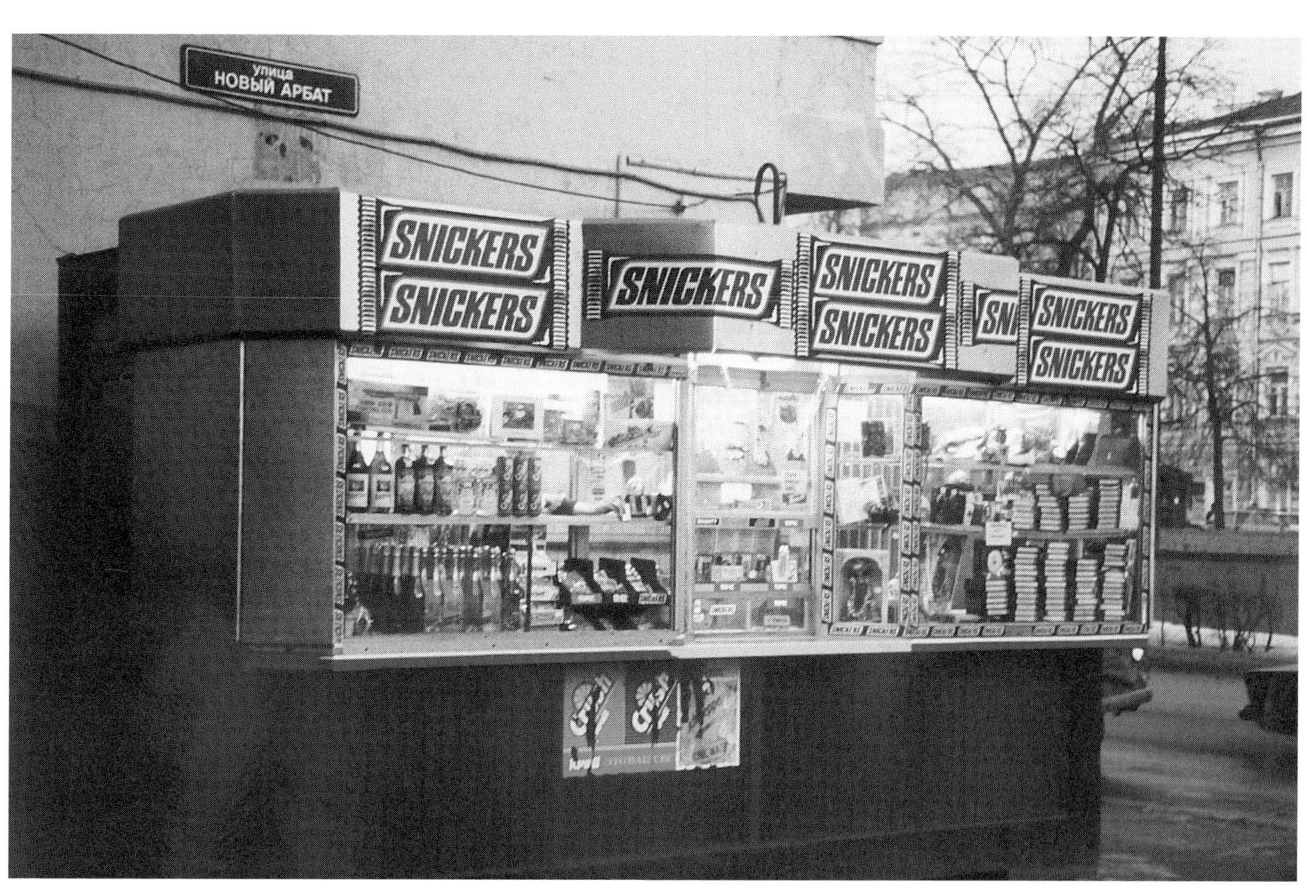

FIGURE 6.8
George W. Kresak, photograph of Moscow kiosk, 1994. Courtesy George W. Kresak. See plate 23.

NOTES

CHAPTER ONE

1. Aleksandr Rodchenko, "Rodchenko v Parizhe. Iz pisem domoi," *Novyi Lef* no. 2 (1927): 20 (letter of May 4, 1925). All translations from the Russian in this book are my own, unless otherwise noted. The most complete version of Rodchenko's letters from Paris in English is Aleksandr Rodchenko and Varvara Stepanova, "Letters to and from Paris (1925)," trans. Galina Varese with Mike Weaver and Galin Tihanov, *History of Photography* 24 , no. 4 (winter 2000): 317–332.

2. Catherine Cooke cautions that the common practice of rendering the term *bezpredmetnyi* as "nonobjective" in English is confusing, because in its original use by the painter Kazimir Malevich, it meant more specifically "having no subject"—in opposition to traditional painting with recognizable subject matter. I am continuing the practice of translating *predmet* as "object" in the term *bezpredmetnyi* because of the emphasis in this study on the problem of the material artifact (*predmet*) or thing or object (*veshch'*) within the Russian avant-garde. See Catherine Cooke, *Russian Avant-Garde Theories of Art, Architecture, and the City* (London: Academy Editions, 1995), p. 15; in this book, Cooke offers critical discussion of the usual translations of several key terms from the Russian avant-garde lexicon.

3. NEP was pronounced as a word, rather than spelled out as an acronym, and was frequently neologized, as in "Nepman" and "Nepmanka." The policy was not officially discontinued until the 1930s, but it was effectively terminated by the onset of the first Five-Year Plan in 1929, and had already been gradually dismantled by a series of laws severely limiting private enterprise enacted in 1927–1928.

4. Peter Bürger, *Theory of the Avant-Garde,* trans. Michael Shaw (Minneapolis: University of Minnesota Press, 1984). The term "avant-garde" (in Russian *avangard*) was not the one that Russian modernist artists of the 1910s and 1920s used to describe themselves, although it is the standard term applied to them by later Russian and Western art historians. These artists described themselves, and were referred to by critics, first by the generically applied term "Futurists" and then simply as "left" (*levyi*) artists. From the early 1910s, Futurism was a blanket term for the most formally advanced artists who exceeded the by-then acceptable mainstream modernism of Impressionism and Cézannism; after the revolution, the term "left" artists came to encompass former Futurists who were committed to pursuing art-into-life strategies, and therefore the term functions similarly to Bürger's use of the term "avant-garde."

5. Ibid., p. 50.

6. Hal Foster has disputed Bürger's claim that Russian Constructivism's critique of the autonomy of art is institutional as well as conventional, noting that "if the historical avant-garde focuses on the conventional, the neo-avant-garde concentrates on the institutional." He arrives at this conclusion by rehearsing Rodchenko's well-known claim that his triptych painting of the primary colors, made in 1921, had achieved "the end of painting." As Foster notes, this gesture demonstrated nothing about the institution of art, but only the conventionality of painting. See Hal Foster, "Who's Afraid of the Neo-Avant-Garde?," chapter 1 in *The Return of the Real: The Avant-Garde at the End of the Century* (Cambridge, Mass.: MIT Press, 1996), p. 17. But Rodchenko's gesture with the red, yellow, and blue canvases was made in 1921, at the time Constructivism was still being formulated; this study examines the substantial later evidence, in the work of Tatlin, Popova, and Stepanova as well as

Rodchenko in nontraditional, extra-artistic settings, of a turn from the conventional critique to the institutional.

7. Bürger, *Theory of the Avant-Garde*, p. 54.

8. Ibid.

9. Ibid., p. 114, n. 21.

10. For a detailed and sympathetic account of Lennon's relation to the New Left and political radicalism in general, see Jon Wiener, *Come Together: John Lennon in His Time* (Urbana and Chicago: University of Illinois Press, 1984).

11. Andrei Belyi, cited in Boris Groys, *The Total Art of Stalinism: Avant-Garde, Aesthetic Dictatorship, and Beyond*, translated by Charles Rougle (Princeton: Princeton University Press, 1992), p. 20.

12. This basic definition of art historical modernism, which has been the starting point for significant revisions and criticisms over the last thirty years or so, was articulated most famously by Clement Greenberg in the context of mid-century American painting: the self-critical attention given by advanced artists, beginning in the second half of the nineteenth century, to the materials, processes of making, and structures of reception that are inherent and exclusive to particular art forms. Greenberg lays out this definition of modernism most starkly in "Modernist Painting," *Art and Literature* (spring 1965), reprinted in Clement Greenberg, *The Collected Essays and Criticism*, vol. 4, ed. John O'Brian (Chicago: University of Chicago Press, 1986–1993), pp. 85–93.

13. "Polozhenie Otdela izobrazitel'nykh iskusstv i khudozhestvennoi promyshlennosti NKP po voprosu 'o khudozhestvennoi kul'ture,'" *Iskusstvo kommuny* no. 11 (1919): 4, quoted in Christina Lodder, *Russian Constructivism* (New Haven: Yale University Press, 1983), p. 79. Lodder's comprehensive study was the first to synthesize archival documentation of the INKhUK debates into a detailed account of the practices and personalities of the movement. On the INKhUK, see pp. 78–98. The term *tekhnika* was used broadly at this time, with a meaning extending beyond technique to "technology." The meaning of the term *faktura* extends far beyond the English "facture" and was much disputed; for a comprehensive history and analysis of the term, see Maria Gough, "*Faktura*: The Making of the Russian Avant-Garde," *Res* 36 (1999): 32–59.

14. V. V. Kandinskii, "Skhematicheskaia programma rabot Instituta khudozhestvennoi kul'tury po planu V. V. Kandinskogo" (1920), in Ivan Matsa, *Sovetskoe iskusstvo za 15 let: materialy i dokumentatsiia* (Moscow and Leningrad: Ogiz-Izogiz, 1933), p. 126; on the psychological research, see p. 127; on the spiritual, see p. 134.

15. Selim O. Khan-Magomedov, *INKhUK i ranii konstruktivizm* (Moscow: Architectura, 1994), pp. 36–37. Future references to this book will be cited parenthetically in the body of the text as "*INKhUK*." Khan-Magomedov narrates the INKhUK discussions that led to the development of Constructivism, including many direct citations from unpublished archival sources in private collections. As Khan-Magomedov notes in an early chapter of the book, Vladimir Tatlin was generally recognized at the time as the "forefather" of Constructivism (p. 20), but as a resident of Petrograd and therefore only a corresponding member of INKhUK, he did not participate in the early INKhUK discussions. For one example of Tatlin's statements against the "merely personal" in art, see "The Work Ahead of Us" (1920), translated in Larissa Alekseevna Zhadova, ed., *Tatlin*, (New York: Rizzoli, 1988), p. 239.

16. *Tselesoobraznost'* is usually translated into English as "expediency," but I offer my clunkier and more literal translation because current English usage favors the opportunistic or self-interested meaning of "expedient," rather than the primary and neutral meaning of "suitable for achieving a particular end."

17. Two other working groups were also formed at this time, based on professional rather than ideological groupings: the group of architects and the group of sculptors.
18. "Programma rabochei gruppy konstruktivistov INKhUKA," private archive, Moscow; cited in Khan-Magomedov, *INKhUK*, p. 95. The program is published in its entirety in *INKhUK*, pp. 95–96. An edited version of the program was published in the journal *Ermitazh* no. 13 (1922): 3–4. Lodder provides a comprehensive account of the content of the program in *Russian Constructivism*, pp. 94–98.
19. Aleksandr Lavrent'ev states that the use of Communist terminology resulted from the influence of Gan, who deliberately "politicized" the creative activities of Constructivism. Rodchenko and Stepanova split with Gan in 1923; the latter went on to form his own splinter group of Constructivists. Gan's writings did contain far more references to Communism than those of any other Constructivists, as exemplified by his 1922 book *Konstruktivizm*. Yet the writings of Rodchenko and Stepanova after the split with Gan continued to express strong support for socialism, but simply contained less Marxist jargon, suggesting that the fundamentally socialist "political" orientation of Constructivism cannot be ascribed only to Gan, nor can he be accused of taking Constructivist creative work in a direction contrary to the artists' own aims. See Lavrent'ev's commentary in Peter Noever, ed., *Rodchenko—Stepanova: Budushchee—edinstvennaia nasha tsel'*, 171–172 (Munich: Prestel Verlag, 1991).
20. This is Khan-Magomedov's interpretation of the minutes of the meetings (*INKhUK*, p. 97).
21. "Programma rabochei gruppy 'obzhektivistov' INKhUKa," April 14, 1921, manuscript, private archive; reproduced in its entirety in Khan-Magomedov, *INKhUK*, pp. 75–76; citation from p. 75.
22. Draft statement of the Working Group of Objectivists, spring 1921, private archive, cited in Khan-Magomedov, *INKhUK*, p. 74; the ellipsis is Khan-Magomedov's.
23. The definition of "production art" worked out by INKhUK theorists was highly specific. The still amorphous term "production art" had first been debated in the revolutionary publication *Iskusstvo kommuny* (Art of the Commune) in 1918; a collection of essays published by the state publishing house in 1921 entitled *Art in Production*, although it contains an essay by Brik, does not yet represent the position that would be worked out later in the INKhUK. Several of the essays, while using the new term "production art," actually espouse the more traditional idea of applied art, in which the artist is valued for beautifying the products of industry. See *Iskusstvo v proizvodstve* (Moscow: IZO Narkompros, 1921).
24. Catherine Cooke called *formoobrazovanie* an "often wild process" and defined it as "giving some 'shape' to that *bezobrazie* or 'imagelessness' which is chaos." She warned that it is sometimes translated a bit too tamely as "design." See Cooke, *Russian Avant-Garde Theories of Art*, p. 15.
25. See Khan-Magomedov, *INKhUK*, p. 231. The aim of his book more generally is to set the record straight in the interest of "historical fairness," by assembling the archival facts to prove, first, that the form-creating research of the INKhUK artists was in fact fundamental to the development of Constructivism and Productivism (p. 18), and second, that the Productivists cut off the promising artistic experimentation of the Objectivists and Constructivists before it had been organically completed. Khan-Magomedov also sketches out the "atmosphere of tension" between artists and theorists in INKhUK in his *Rodchenko: The Complete Work* (Cambridge, Mass.: MIT Press, 1987), p. 114. In his most recent book, which he states is "the completion of [his] research over many years on the creative tendency of

Constructivism," Khan-Magomedov continues to elaborate on his thesis that Constructivism was primarily a creative, artistic movement of form-creation that must be understood as separate from—and in a complicated relation to—the theory of Productivism. See his *Konstruktivizm: kontseptsiia formoobrazovaniia* (Moscow: Stroiizdat, 2003); citation from p. 15. Drawing on archival sources, heavily illustrated, and wide-ranging in scope—from the nineteenth-century origins of Constructivism in Russian technology through Constructivist architecture and "post Constructivism"—the book offers a comprehensive account of the practitioners, theorists and works of the Constructivist movement.

26. "Transcript of the Discussion of Comrade Stepanova's Paper 'On Constructivism,'" December 22, 1921, private archive, trans. James West in *Art into Life: Russian Constructivism, 1914–1932* (New York: Rizzoli, 1990), pp. 74–79. Arvatov urges artists to enter the polytechnical institute on pp. 74, 75, and 78. Fragmentary citations from the discussion in the original Russian are given in Khan-Magomedov, *Konstruktivizm*, pp. 200–202. An outline of the paper given by Stepanova, which summarized the theory of Constructivism with an emphasis on its rejection of art, has been assembled from her draft notes; see "Konstruktivizm," pp. 163–169, in Varvara Stepanova, *Chelovek ne mozhet zhit' bez chuda: pis'ma, poeticheskie opyty, zapiski khudozhnitsy*, ed. V. A. Rodchenko and A. N. Lavrent'ev with N. C. Lavrent'ev (Moscow: Sfera, 1994).

27. Bubnova's comments are translated in *Art into Life*, p. 78; translation modified. Fragments of her commentary are given in Khan-Magomedov, *INKhUK*, p. 202.

28. Stepanova's comments are translated, in significantly different form, in *Art into Life*, p. 78; my translation is based on fragments of her comments in Khan-Magomedov, *INKhUK*, p. 202.

29. Excerpts from Rodchenko's contributions to the INKhUK debate, April 22, 1922, private archive, translated in Khan-Magomedov, *Rodchenko*, p. 115; the ellipsis is Khan-Magomedov's.

30. Excerpts from Brik's contribution to the INKhUK discussion held on December 26, 1921, cited in Khan-Magomedov, *INKhUK*, pp. 205–206; Boris Kushner, lecture delivered at INKhUK on April 6, 1922, cited in Lodder, *Russian Constructivism*, p. 101. Only one of the four lectures given by Kushner at INKhUK in the spring of 1922 was published; see Boris Kushner, "Organizatory proizvodstva," *Lef* no. 3 (1923): 97–103. The other three are summarized in Lodder, *Russian Constructivism*, pp. 100–101, and in greater detail, with substantial fragments cited from the archival texts in Khan-Magomedov, *Konstruktivizm*, pp. 206–210.

31. El Lissitzky and Ilya Ehrenburg, "Blokada Rossii konchaetsia," *Veshch'* no. 1–2 (March–April 1922): 1–4, reprinted in *El' Lisitskii, 1890–1941* (Moscow: Gosudarstvennaia Tret'iakovskaia galeria), pp. 74–75; the words in all caps are original.

32. Osip Brik, "Chto delat' khudozhniku poka?," (What Can the Artist Do for Now?), April 13, 1922, shorthand report of the meeting, manuscript, private archive, cited and translated in Lodder, *Russian Constructivism*, p. 100; large portions of the shorthand report are cited in Khan-Magomedov, *Konstruktivizm*, pp. 202–206, though only a fragment of this particular passage is cited, on p. 204. In the opening lines of this lecture, Brik succinctly captures the "transitional" nature of Constructivist practice: "What can the artist do for now, in this transitional time, when the conditions have not yet been born in which our program, proposed by Marx—production art—can be realized" (p. 202). In Rodchenko's response to this lecture, he pleaded for INKhUK to take a more practical approach to imagining the artist's entry into production:

Let us assume that they show us factories; or that an outside person comes from a factory, from a plant, and broadens our horizons. For now we cannot go there. They won't let us in.... Of course we look at ships and planes with great interest, but we need details. Perhaps INKhUK could organize visits, for if we go there on our own it is one thing, but if we go as a scientific delegation it is another (Khan-Magomedov, *Rodchenko*, p. 115, translation modified; different fragments of this quote are cited in the original Russian in Khan-Magomedov, *Konstruktivizm*, p. 205).

33. *Art into Life*, p. 76.

34. The left artists had learned to expect that they could participate in shaping the material world of socialism through their experiences in official posts of authority in Bolshevik institutions during the civil war. Since most well-established artists were wary of supporting the seemingly unstable Bolshevik government, the marginal Futurist avant-garde seized the chance to enter into the center of decision making about arts administration under the new government, declaring their support for the Bolsheviks soon after the October Revolution. Future Constructivists organized mass agitational celebrations of the one-year anniversary of the October Revolution in 1918, participated in the reorganization of art schools under the aegis of the Bolshevik state, and held high-level administrative positions in the Department of Fine Arts (IZO Narkompros) in 1919–1920. Rodchenko, for example, as head of the Museum Bureau, was in charge of acquiring artworks for provincial and other museums, and Tatlin headed the plan for monumental propaganda for the Moscow IZO until he moved to Petrograd in mid-1919. (In this study, I refer to the city of St. Petersburg by the name by which it was known on the date being discussed: St. Petersburg until 1914; Petrograd 1914–1924; Leningrad 1924–1992; and St. Petersburg since 1992.)

35. V. I. Lenin, speech to the Tenth Party Congress, March 1921; cited in Alan M. Ball, *Russia's Last Capitalists: The Nepmen, 1921–29* (Berkeley: University of California Press, 1987), p. 17. The preceding paragraph on War Communism, and the general account of the policies of NEP given here, are based on Ball's "Introduction: The War Communism Prelude," pp. 1–12, and his chapters 1 and 2, "Building Communism with Bourgeois Hands," pp. 15–37, and "NEP's Second Wind," pp. 38–55.

36. Ball, *Russia's Last Capitalists*, p. 16.

37. V. I. Lenin, cited in Ball, *Russia's Last Capitalists*, p. 18.

38. The return of the term *barin* is noted in the memoirs of the Menshevik leader F. I. Dan, *Dva goda skitanii* (Berlin, 1922), p. 253, cited in Ball, *Russia's Last Capitalists*, p. 16.

39. Sergei Tret'iakov, "LEF i NEP," *Lef* no. 2 (1923): 70. Lace curtains, potted fichus trees, and especially porcelain elephants—traditionally arranged across a mantel or other surface in a group of seven elephants of descending size—were the ubiquitous and much-derided symbols of the return of petty bourgeois (*meshchanskii*) taste under NEP.

40. Ibid., p. 71.

41. Ibid., p. 78.

42. Osip Brik, "V proizvodstvo!," *Lef* no. 1 (1923): 108.

43. Boris Arvatov argued that it was not by chance that groups of easel painters were reemerging now that the market had once again become the basis of economic relations under NEP. See Arvatov, "Reaktsiia v zhivopisi" (Reaction in painting), *Sovetskoe iskusstvo* no. 4–5 (1925): 71.

44. The publication of the journal *Lef* was subsidized from 1923–1925, and again, briefly, in its reincarnation as *Novyi lef* (New *Lef*) in 1927–1928; Constructivists held teaching positions at the state art school VKhUTEMAS; and Constructivists won a number of commissions from various state enterprises, especially in the mid-1920s, several of which form the topics of the chapters of this book.

45. Lodder, *Russian Constructivism*, p. 145. She emphasizes that her assessment of the Constructivist lack of success "does not diminish the value of [their] investigations themselves."

46. Ibid., p. 181. She notes that the one exception to the Constructivist lack of success in industry was the mass production of Constructivist textiles (the topic of chapter 3 of this study), but that in this case the role of the artists did not differ much from that of traditional applied artists, and therefore did not represent a true example of the work of the artist-constructor in industry (p. 145).

47. Ibid., p. 178. In addition to "decline," she uses the terms "confinement" and "limited" in chapter 6 of her study, entitled "Confinement: Photomontage and the Limited Design Task." Benjamin Buchloh has contested this view of Constructivism's compromise with realism, stating that when Constructivism is judged by critics like Lodder to have failed in its modernist project, "criteria of judgment that were originally developed within the framework of modernism are now applied to a practice of representation that had deliberately and systematically disassociated itself from that framework in order to lay the foundations of an art production that would correspond to the needs of a newly industrialized collective society." See Benjamin Buchloh, "From *Faktura* to Factography," *October* 30 (fall 1984): 108. Although the present study questions Buchloh's overly optimistic description of Soviet society as already industrialized and collective, it does attempt to answer his call for new, historically appropriate "criteria of judgement" for understanding Constructivism's choices in the 1920s. Buchloh confronts Lodder's account of Constructivism's "decline" by focusing on what might be characterized as the most burning issues in Constructivist history for modernism—that is, on explaining the break between the abstract modernist interest in the materials of art (*faktura*) of the years 1920–1921, when Constructivism was being formulated, and the return to illusionism in the program of documentary and propaganda photography known as factography adopted by Constructivist artists in the late 1920s. Much of the later photography—especially Rodchenko's—while illusionistically reflecting reality, is also universally acknowledged as a high point in the history of modernist photography; so Buchloh in effect singles out for analysis the moments of Constructivism variously legitimized by the modernist canon, even as he critically questions that canon's assumptions. This book, in contrast, focuses on the problematic middle period of Constructivism from 1923 to 1925, which Buchloh's essay does not engage—the period that includes objects such as the stove, the overcoat, the cookie advertisements, and the flapper dress. These objects are analyzed here as closely related to the earlier modernist ambitions of their makers, and are accorded as much significance as factography in Constructivism's attempt to "correspond to the needs of" postrevolutionary Soviet society.

48. Paul Wood," The Politics of the Avant-Garde," in *The Great Utopia: The Russian and Soviet Avant-Garde, 1915–1932* (New York: Guggenheim Museum, 1992), pp. 1–24.

49. Ibid., p. 10.

50. Ibid., p. 5. Wood proposes an interpretation of the "politics of the avant-garde" that is novel in its specificity: he argues that the Constructivists were likely associated with the Left Opposition within the party during the 1920s (see pp. 13–17). The Left Opposition first formed loosely in 1921, calling for an economic plan that emphasized heavy industry and the collectivization of labor within it, as opposed to the semicapitalist, consumer-oriented policies of NEP. These demands, Wood points out, reflected those of the Constructivists, whose program of "art into production" was based on the idea of a strong industrial base that would be open to rational organization imposed by Constructivist artists, rather than subject to the whims of the market and the consumer. Under the leadership of Leon Trotsky, the Opposition gathered force briefly in 1924, and then again to a much greater extent in 1927. Wood offers compelling circumstantial evidence for linking the beliefs and practices of left cultural figures with the political platform of the Left Opposition, yet there is no direct evidence that the center of "political" activity among artists like Tatlin, Stepanova, Popova, or Rodchenko—or even among the more actively political Productivist theorists—lay in the rallies or political meetings of the Left Opposition or, for that matter, of the party center. Wood's interpretation follows a party-history model of political art that cannot do full justice to the political ambitions of Constructivist practice. The argument of this book is that the Constructivists invented—however fleetingly—a new model of political art that reconceptualized the material practices of everyday life according to their diverse concepts of what socialism meant, rather than through centralized party politics.

51. Ibid., p. 10.

52. Leah Dickerman has similarly challenged Lodder's evaluation of Constructivism's "compromise," although she takes graphic design and photography, rather than utilitarian objects, as her examples of Constructivism's flexible development from the original Productivist goal of entering industry. In her argument, "among the most significant of Rodchenko's reconceptualizations of his artistic role is that of the creative producer engaged in a fundamental way with the mass media." See Leah Dickerman, "The Propagandizing of Things," in *Aleksandr Rodchenko*, ed. Magdalena Dabrowski, Leah Dickerman, and Peter Galassi (New York: The Museum of Modern Art, 1998), p. 97, n. 7.

53. Boris Groys, *The Total Art of Stalinism*, p. 9.

54. Margarita Tupitsyn, for example, implicitly contests Groys when she writes of El Lissitzky's design work of the later 1920s:

> No matter how much the design principles of the 1920s were degraded in the late examples of Soviet propaganda material, they should not be viewed as precursors of socialist realist methodology. Instead, they are concluding examples of agitational objects, as they had been envisioned since the Constructivists refuted painting in the early 1920s. . . . avant-garde practitioners were perpetually changing course, not only because of shifting political events but also because of the resistance of artists to accept a single mode of artistic production and distribution. With that aim, the Soviet avant-garde disjointed itself . . . from socialist realism, which defended static artistic strategies and depended on the status quo.

See Margarita Tupitsyn, with contributions by Matthew Drutt and Ulrich Pohlmann, *El Lissitzky: Beyond the "Abstract Cabinet": Photography, Design, Collaboration* (New Haven and London: Yale University Press, 1999), pp. 201–202. Paul Wood offers a sustained critique of Groys, focusing on the way his argument collapses the early Bolshevik model of socialism with the Stalinist one, in "The Politics of the Avant-Garde," pp. 6–8.

55. Groys, *The Total Art of Stalinism*, p. 25 and p. 26, respectively. For Arvatov, he writes, "the goal of art [is] the creation of a closed, autonomous, internally organized, self-contained whole that does not refer to anything outside

itself, except, perhaps, in the functional sense . . . all that remains for the artist is to fulfill limited functions within the framework established by the unitary '[Communist] party command'" (pp. 25–26). His charge that Arvatov and *Lef* subordinated art to Communist Party directives forms part of his larger argument about the avant-garde's will-to-power and its attempt to make opportunistic use of the party's political power to achieve its own totalizing artistic project. He provides no concrete evidence for this claim, however, other than stating that "*Lef*'s language gradually became more 'Communistic'" (p. 25). None of the Arvatov texts examined in this study corroborate Groys's account of Arvatov's view of art, nor do they articulate any sense of a "unitary party command" to be followed.

56. The text in which Arvatov most directly confronts the demands of NEP is "Iskusstvo i kachestvo promyshlennoi produktsii" (Art and the Quality of Industrial Production), *Sovetskoe Iskusstvo* no. 7 (1925): 39–43. This text is discussed in chapter 3.

57. No known photograph of Arvatov exists, so I reproduce here the only extant likeness of him: a drawing by Petr Galadzhev published in the theater magazine *Zrelishcha* in 1922.

58. This is the assessment of Arvatov offered by Christina Lodder, who provides an account of his ideas, as well as a brief biographical sketch, in *Russian Constructivism* (see pp. 105–108; 239); and by Maria Zalambani, "L'art dans la production. Le débat sur le productivisme en Russie soviétique pendant les années vingt," *Annales: Histoire, Sciences Sociales* 52, no. 1 (1997): 41–61. Zalambani attributes what she sees as a theoretical demand for the denial of artistic creativity to Arvatov, who "en prenant part au débat, délimitera le domaine de l'imaginaire des artistes, 'mettra de l'ordre' dans leurs idées et les soumettra à une stricte analyse matérialiste" (p. 45). See also Zalambani, "Boris Arvatov, théoricien du productivisme," *Cahiers du monde russe* 40, no. 3 (1999): 415–446. Khan-Magomedov characterizes Arvatov as "the most devout and uncompromising adherent of the idea of production art," and notes that it was "not by chance" that he was called "the Sainte Juste of Lef" (*Konstruktivizm*, p. 210).

59. Russian State Archive of Literature and Art (RGALI), f. 941, op. 10, ed. kh. 23.

60. The information that his psychiatric illness stemmed from shell shock is taken from Lodder's biographical sketch. Arvatov's initial hospitalization for "severe nervous illness" in 1923 was reported in *Lef* no. 3 (June–July 1923): 40–40a. The journal published two letters written to newspaper editors to protest the mean-spirited portrayal of Arvatov by the poet Dem'ian Bednyi, who published a ditty critical of Lef in *Rabochaia Gazeta* (Workers' Newspaper) in which he referred to "Arvatov, carted off to the crazy house." A letter written to the National Commissariat of Health on Arvatov's behalf in 1935, from his friends Sergei Eisenstein, Sergei Tret'iakov, Viktor Shklovsky, Osip and Lili Brik, and Nikolai Aseev, mentions the specific diagnosis of schizophrenia. Such a severe diagnosis seems incompatible with Arvatov's lucid intellectual output; in the tense atmosphere of the mid-1930s leading up to the Terror, "schizophrenia" may have functioned as a sort of cover term for mental illness. They were petitioning that Arvatov not be transferred from his sanatorium near Moscow to another one in the more distant provincial town of Riazan'. See RGALI, f. 1923, op. 1, ed. kh. 1579.

61. Boris Arvatov, *Iskusstvo i proizvodstvo. Sbornik statei* (Moscow: Proletkul't, 1926). This is his only major text to be translated into other languages; see *Kunst und Produktion* (Munich: C. Hanser, 1972) and *Arte, produzione e rivoluzione proletaria*, ed. Hans Gunther and Karla Hielscher (Rimini and Florence: Guaraldi, 1973).

62. Boris Arvatov, "Byt i kul'tura veshchi

(k postanovke voprosa)," in *Al'manakh proletkul'ta* (Moscow: Proletkul't, 1925), pp. 75–82; for an English translation, see "Everyday Life and the Culture of the Thing (Toward the Formulation of the Question)," trans. Christina Kiaer, *October* 81 (summer 1997): 119–128. Future references to this translation will be cited parenthetically in the body of the text as "EL." See also my introduction to this text, "Boris Arvatov's Socialist Objects," *October* 81 (summer 1997): 105–118, from which the present discussion is partly drawn.

63. Arvatov gives the word *veshch'* a deliberately broad range of meanings throughout the essay ("the system of things" stands for "material culture"; "the world of things" includes "the world of material processes"), meanings that would be narrowed by the use of the more historically and theoretically specific term "object." The Soviet Academy of Science dictionary defines the word *veshch'* as "1. Any inanimate object (*predmet*), usually man-made." See Akademiia Nauk SSSR, Institut Russkogo Iazyka, *Slovar' sovremennogo russkogo literaturnogo iazyka*, vol. 2 (Moscow-Leningrad: Izdatel'stvo Akademii nauk SSSR, 1951), p. 263. The same dictionary defines the more specific term *predmet* as "1. Any concrete material phenomenon, perceived by the organs of touch" (ibid., vol. 11 [1961], p. 130). Art historian Elena Sidorina, in her comprehensive analysis of Arvatov, argues that he actually meant the *veshch'* as a semiotic sign, to be perceived visually and aesthetically, rather than as a literal material thing. Her analysis attempts to recuperate the Constructivist object for modernist art, but lessens its impact as an object meant to participate in the practice of everyday life. See her *Skvoz' ves' dvadtsatyi vek: khudozhestvenno-proektnye kontseptsii russkogo avangarda* (Moscow: Russkii mir, 1994).

64. In chapter 1 of *Capital*, Marx famously makes the analogy to fetishism "in the misty realm of religion," where "the products of the human brain" are projected onto wooden idols. See Karl Marx, *Capital*, vol. I, trans. Ben Fowkes (New York: Vintage, 1977), p. 165. On the origins of Marx's use of the concept of the fetish, see W. J. T. Mitchell, *Iconology: Image, Text, Ideology* (Chicago and London: University of Chicago Press, 1986), chapter 6, "The Rhetoric of Iconoclasm: Marxism, Ideology, and Fetishism."

65. Marx, *Capital*, vol. I, p. 165. Arvatov cites this passage in his discussion of the aesthetics of easel art in *Iskusstvo i klassy* (Moscow-Petrograd: Gosudarstvennoe izdatel'stvo, 1923), p. 52.

66. Marx, *Capital*, vol. I, p. 166.

67. Ibid.

68. "Technical intelligentsia" translates *tekhnicheskaia intelligentsia*, a specific and highly motivated class term. Historically, the intelligentsia was the intellectual or educated sector of the bourgeoisie in Russia, a social group that emerged in the second half of the nineteenth century. Bolshevism aimed to eradicate the bourgeoisie as a class, but it recognized the need for preserving the technical skills of the bourgeois engineers, scientists, and administrators who were needed for the practical tasks of building socialism. By referring to this same group of people in America as the "technical intelligentsia," Arvatov offers them social legitimation in Soviet terms: they are partially exonerated for their bourgeois class status. The members of the artistic intelligentsia in Arvatov's *Lef* circle, by stressing their role as technicians—of texts or of art objects—attempted to identify themselves with the technical intelligentsia—the one group of the bourgeoisie recognized as useful to the Bolshevik state. On the complex history of the Russian intelligentsia's relation to the Western technical intelligentsia and to Bolshevism in the context of the avant-garde, see Hubertus Gassner, "The Constructivists: Modernism on

the Way to Modernization," in *The Great Utopia: The Russian and Soviet Avant-Garde, 1915–1932*, pp. 298–319 (New York: Guggenheim Museum, 1992), here p. 306.

69. For a lucid analysis of the key Constructivist term *ustanovka* (positioning), see Maria Gough, "Switched On: Notes on Radio, Automata, and the Bright Red Star," in *Building the Collective: Soviet Graphic Design, 1917–1937*, ed. Leah Dickerman (New York: Princeton Architectural Press, 1996).

70. Boris Arvatov, "Segodniashnie zadachi iskusstva v promyshlennosti" (The tasks today of art in industry), *Sovetskoe iskusstvo* no. 1 (1926): 86.

71. Victor Margolin, *The Struggle for Utopia: Rodchenko, Lissitzky, Moholy-Nagy: 1917–1946* (Chicago: University of Chicago Press, 1997), p. 83. Margolin does go on to analyze Rodchenko's objects as a form of design, writing that we can "interpret Rodchenko's work as a designer during the NEP years most effectively as an attempt to create a new narrative of design for a revolutionary society" (p. 84). Khan-Magomedov has consistently advanced the interpretation that the Constructivists can be understood as progenitors of professional Soviet design; a number of the first generation of students of Constructivist teachers at VKhUTEMAS would go on to professional work that more closely resembled the concept of professional design than the piecemeal and idiosyncratic efforts of the Constructivist artists themselves in the 1920s. On the connections between Constructivism and later design, see Selim O. Khan-Magomedov, *Pionery sovetskogo dizaina* (Moscow: Galart, 1995) and Alexander N. Lavrentiev and Yuri V. Nasarov, *Russian Design: Tradition and Experiment, 1920–1990*, trans. Flora Fischer, from the German (London: Academy Editions, 1995).

72. See Christina Lodder, "The VKhUTEMAS and the Bauhaus," in *The Avant-Garde Frontier: Russia Meets the West, 1910–1930*, ed. Gail Harrison Roman and Virginia Hagelstein Marquardt (Gainesville: University Press of Florida, 1992), pp. 196–237, especially the protests of VKhUTEMAS students in 1922 when asked about their similarities to the Bauhaus (pp. 199–200).

73. Terry Eagleton, *The Ideology of the Aesthetic* (Cambridge: Basil Blackwell, 1990), p. 13.

74. These definitions are offered by Susan Buck-Morss in *Dreamworld and Catastrophe: The Passing of Mass Utopia in East and West* (Cambridge, Mass.: MIT Press, 2000): 101.

75. Susan Buck-Morss, "Aesthetics and Anaesthetics," *October* 62 (fall 1992): 22. Buck-Morss here explains the origins of the word "phantasmagoria": "The term originated in England in 1802, as the name of an exhibition of optical illusions produced by magic lanterns. It describes an appearance of reality that tricks the senses through technical manipulation."

76. Walter Benjamin, *The Arcades Project*, trans. Howard Eiland and Kevin McLaughlin (Cambridge, Mass.: Belknap Press of Harvard University Press, 1999), section N, "On the Theory of Knowledge," p. 462 (N2a,3).

CHAPTER TWO

1. "Novyi byt," *Krasnaia panorama* no. 23 (December 4, 1924): 17, translated as "The New Way of Life" in Larissa Alekseevna Zhadova, ed., *Tatlin* (New York: Rizzoli, 1988), p. 407. The article was published anonymously, but Zhadova states that "Tatlin himself probably participated in preparing the texts and the photographs for it" (p. 407). Anatolii Strigalev and Jürgen Harten go even further than Zhadova, arguing that "an analysis of the text (and illustrations) leads to the conclusion that the most likely author was the artist himself." See Anatolii Strigalev and Jürgen Harten, *Vladimir Tatlin Retrospektive* (Cologne: DuMont Buchverlag, 1992), p. 274. As the term *byt* will come up throughout this chapter, it may be helpful to non-Russian speakers to know that it is pronounced, approximately, "beet."

2. V. E. Tatlin, T. Shapiro, I. Meerzon, and P. Vinogradov, "Nasha predstoiashchaia rabota," *VIII s"ezd sovetov. Ezhednevnyi biulleten' s"ezda* no. 13 (January 1, 1921): 11, translated as "The Work Ahead of Us" in Zhadova, *Tatlin*, p. 239; Zhadova notes that the statement was written on December 31, 1920.

3. Excerpts from Rodchenko's contributions to the INKhUK debate on April 22, 1922, private archive, translated in Khan-Magomedov, *Rodchenko*, p. 115.

4. A. Efros, "Vosstanie zritelia," *Russkii sovremennik* no. 1 (1924): 276, cited and translated in Zhadova, *Tatlin*, p. 406.

5. The critic Alfred Kemeny called Tatlin "the father of Constructivism" at an INKhUK meeting on December 8, 1921. See "Protokol zasedaniia INKhUKa," December 8, 1921, private archive, Moscow, cited in Lodder, *Russian Constructivism*, p. 96. In Tatlin's brief "Autobiography," a manuscript written in 1929, he acknowledges his relation to Constructivism: "The influence of my art is expressed in the path taken by the Constructivists, of whom I am the founder." See Zhadova, *Tatlin*, p. 265.

6. The young Constructivist Konstantin Medunetskii's attack on Tatlin's Tower at this INKhUK meeting on December 26, 1921 and Tatlin's own contribution to the discussion at this meeting are cited in Khan-Magomedov, *INKhUK*, pp. 209–211.

7. Vladimir Tatlin, "The Initiative Individual in the Creativity of the Collective," translated in Zhadova, *Tatlin*, pp. 237–238. Zhadova lists the names of the seven other artists who at various times worked in the Section's "Group for Material Culture" (p. 250).

8. "Novyi byt," *Krasnaia panorama*. The original Russian text is legible in figure 2.1; translated in Zhadova, *Tatlin*, p. 407, translation modified.

9. On its display, see Zhadova, "Tatlin, the Organizer of Material into Objects," in Zhadova, *Tatlin*, p. 143.

10. Bürger, *Theory of the Avant-Garde*, p. 54.

11. Nikolai Punin, "Rutina i Tatlin," in N. Punin, *O Tatline*, ed. I. N. Punina and V. I. Rakitin (Moscow: Literaturnoe-khudozhestvennoe agenstvo "RA," 1994): p. 71; translated in Zhadova, *Tatlin*, as "Routine and Tatlin," p. 405, translation modified. The first part of the quotation is cited by Punin as a direct quote from Tatlin, the second part as a paraphrase. This essay by Punin was written in 1924 but remained unpublished during his lifetime.

12. The movement was self-described as "neo-primitivist"; see the booklet by Aleksandr Shevchenko, *Neo-primitivizm. Ego teoriia. Ego vozmozhnosti. Ego dostizheniia* (Moscow, 1913), translated as "Neoprimitivism: Its Theory, Its Potentials, Its Achievements," in John Bowlt, ed., *Russian Art of the Avant-Garde: Theory and Criticism, 1902–1934*, pp. 41–54 (New York: Viking Press, 1976).

13. Natalia Goncharova, "Pis'mo k redaktsii Russkoe slovo" (1912), Russian State Library, Moscow, Manuscript Division (259.3.14), translated as Appendix no. 2 in Jane Sharp, *Russian Modernism between East and West: Natal'ia Goncharova and the Moscow Avant-Garde, 1905–1914* (Cambridge: Cambridge University Press, 2005). Despite Goncharova's enthusiasm for native Russian forms, she and the rest of the Russian avant-garde were well informed about, and openly indebted to, recent French painting such as fauvism, primitivism, and Cubism.

14. For a discussion of how Russian neoprimitivism combined "authentic" folk culture with more "debased" forms of commercial or urban folk imagery, see John E. Bowlt, "A Brazen Can-Can in the Temple of Art: The Russian Avant-Garde and Popular Culture," in *Modern Art and Popular Culture:*

Readings in High and Low, ed. Kirk Varnedoe and Adam Gopnik (New York: Abrams, 1990), pp. 134–58.

15. The booklet *Vladimir Evgrafovich Tatlin 17/XII–1915*, which Tatlin wrote with the artist N. Udaltsova, states: "I have not belonged and do not belong to Tatlinism, Rayism, Futurism, The Wanderers, or any other groups." Cited in Larissa Zhadova, "Tatlin—proektirovshchik material'noi kul'tury," *Sovetskoe dekorativnoe iskusstvo* 77/78 (1980): 205, n. 6.

16. Interest in the icon tradition had recently been revived in avant-garde circles by a major exhibition of icon painting held in Moscow in 1913, to celebrate 300 years of the Romanov dynasty. On the evidence linking Tatlin's work of the 1910s to icons as well as Cubism, see Maria Gough, "*Faktura*," p. 52, and Lodder, *Russian Constructivism*, pp. 8–13.

17. The semiotic approach to Cubism was first proposed by Rosalind Krauss, in her analysis of Cubist collage: "The extraordinary contribution of collage is that it is the first instance within the pictorial arts of anything like a systematic exploration of the conditions of representability entailed by the sign." See Rosalind Krauss, "In the Name of Picasso" (1980) in her *The Originality of the Avant-Garde and Other Modernist Myths* (Cambridge, Mass.: MIT Press, 1985).

18. Gough, "*Faktura*," p. 52.

19. Gough's argument about the radicality of Tatlin's "attack on the concept of artistic subjectivity" draws on the classical distinction between art and non-art in Aristotle: "For a thing to be art, the driving force in the becoming of that thing had to be located in the producer; if located within the thing itself, as in a work of nature, or in a thing that is produced out of necessity as in a work of utility, that thing was not art" ("*Faktura*," p. 59).

20. Gough, "*Faktura*," p. 58.

21. Vladimir Tatlin, "Report of the Section for Material Culture's Research Work for 1924" (November 10, 1924), reprinted and translated in Zhadova, *Tatlin*, p. 256. This report was presented on the request of his superiors at the State Institute of Artistic Culture (GINKhUK), of which the Section formed a part, because they were dissatisfied with the version of the report he had presented to them ten days earlier. His scholarly claims of "research" may reflect an attempt to fill out the work plan of his Section in order to placate his skeptical superiors.

22. Vladimir Tatlin, "Report of the Section for Material Culture's Work for 1923-1924" (November 1, 1924), reprinted and translated in Zhadova, *Tatlin*, p. 255.

23. Punin, "Rutina i Tatlin," p. 71; translated in Zhadova, *Tatlin*, p. 405, translation modified.

24. L. Trotskii, *Voprosy byta* (Moscow: Krasnaia nov', 1923). Future references to this book will be cited parenthetically in the body of the text as "VB." It has been translated as Leon Trotsky, *Problems of Everyday Life and Other Writings on Culture and Science* (New York: Monad Press, 1973).

25. Again, it may be helpful to non-Russian speakers to know that *bytie* is pronounced, approximately, "beet-ee-yeh."

26. Svetlana Boym, *Common Places: Mythologies of Everyday Life in Russia* (Cambridge, Mass.: Harvard University Press, 1994), p. 83. She supports her claim with an account of Muscovite legal history as well as readings in Russian literature, including Dostoyevsky. See the section entitled "Private Life and Russian Soul," in *Common Places*, pp. 73–102.

27. Boym, *Common Places*, p. 31.

28. Ibid. Technically there were no Bolsheviks until 1903, when the Russian Social Democratic Party split into the Bolshevik and Menshevik factions, but there was a strong Marxist intellectual tradition in late nineteenth-century Russia. Trotsky contested this sacrificial understanding of Bolshevism, stating that "The Workers' Government is neither a spiritual order, nor a monastery" (VB, p. 33). Yet throughout the 1920s, the ideal persisted of the party or Komsomol (Young Communist League) member as ascetic and self-sacrificing, sober, simply dressed, devoting his free time to organizational work, and forsaking family and personal concerns. See Eric Naiman's many references to articles in the Soviet press on this topic in the mid-1920s, and his discussion of the Russian intelligentsia's tradition of asceticism, in *Sex in Public: The Incarnation of Soviet Ideology* (Princeton: Princeton University Press, 1997).

29. These reasons for the upsurge in Party interest in *byt* in 1923 are offered by Elizabeth A. Wood, in *The Baba and the Comrade: Gender and Politics in Revolutionary Russia* (Bloomington: Indiana University Press, 1997), pp. 194–197. Wood proposes that the shift from the violence of the civil war to the attempt to introduce new ways of living can be understood as an instance of Michel Foucault's description, in *Discipline and Punish*, of a shift in strategies of power from a regime of punishment to one of discipline (p. 279, n. 16). See Foucault, *Discipline and Punish: The Birth of the Prison*, trans. Alan Sheridan (New York: Vintage, 1979). On the extensive publications on the *novyi byt*, see also Eric Naiman, *Sex in Public*, and Victor Buchli, *An Archaeology of Socialism* (Oxford: Berg, 1999). Buchli argues that the actual implementation of ambitious *novyi byt* programs for public child care and so on—as opposed to discussions and propaganda—did not begin until around 1930.

30. On the ethnographic gaze, see, e.g., Trinh T. Minh-ha, *Woman, Native, Other: Writing, Postcoloniality, and Feminism* (Bloomington: Indiana University Press, 1989).

31. The photographic collection of the *Istoriko-bytovoi otdel* of the State Russian Museum was transferred to the Hermitage, which donated it to the photographic archive of the Russian Ethnographic Museum in St. Petersburg in 1954. It is cataloged as *fond* 133 on the everyday life of workers (*rabochii byt*).

32. Photographic archive of the Russian Ethnographic Museum, St. Petersburg, f. 133, no. 276.

33. In this view, the so-called bourgeois feminists of the prerevolutionary years who had urged women to fight for equal rights, including the right to vote, within the existing tsarist system, represented a selfish, separatist deviation from the main workers' struggle. On the history of Russian feminism, see Richard Stites, *The Women's Liberation Movement in Russia: Feminism, Nihilism, and Bolshevism, 1860–1930* (Princeton: Princeton University Press, 1978); on this history with particular attention to the role of Aleksandra Kollontai, see Beryl Williams, "Kollontai and After: Women in the Russian Revolution," in *Women, State, and Revolution: Essays on Power and Gender in Europe since 1789*, ed. Siân Reynolds (Brighton, Sussex: Wheatsheaf, 1986), pp. 60–80; Barbara Evans Clements, *Bolshevik Feminist: The Life of Aleksandra Kollontai* (Bloomington: Indiana University Press, 1979); and Beatrice Farnsworth, *Aleksandra Kollontai: Socialism, Feminism, and the Bolshevik Revolution* (Stanford: Stanford University Press, 1980).

34. The history of the *Zhenotdel* presented here is based largely on Elizabeth Wood, *The Baba and the Comrade*; for the accusation against the *Zhenotdel* of "feminist deviationism," see p. 197; on *Zhenotdel* consternation at the success of Trotsky's discussion of *byt*, after its own efforts had failed, see p. 195.

35. On party anxieties during NEP about women as an antirevolutionary influence, see Wood, *The Baba and the Comrade*, pp. 200–208.

36. This poster is cataloged under the heading P2.X in the Department of Graphics, Russian State Library, Moscow. P2 signifies a poster (*plakat*) from the period 2 (designating 1921–1925); X signifies the category "*Byt* of

workers of the city and country." It forms no. 2 of a series of four posters produced for the Moscow Region Soviet of Trade Unions by the Literary Organization AIZ (Assotsiatsiia Izobretatelei Moskvy). The text of the poster uses almost verbatim quotations from Trotsky's article entitled "The Struggle for Cultured Speech" in *Questions of Everyday Life*, and another poster in the series, depicting the struggle against bootlegging (no. 4), appears to be a direct response to Trotsky's condemnation of workers' alcoholism.

37. This poster forms no. 3 of the series of posters mentioned in the previous note.

38. See Wood, *The Baba and the Comrade*, pp. 111–116. On prostitution under early Soviet rule, see also Wendy Z. Goldman, *Women, the State, and Revolution: Soviet Family Policy and Social Life, 1917–36* (Cambridge: Cambridge University Press, 1993), and Natalia B. Lebina and Mikhail V. Shkarovskii, *Prostitutsiia v Peterburge* (Moscow: Progress-Akademiia, 1994).

39. Maurice Blanchot, "Everyday Speech," *Yale French Studies* 73 (1987): 19.

40. Vladimir Dal', *Tolkovyi slovar' zhivogo velikorusskogo iazyka*, vol. 1 (1863–66; Moscow: Russkii iazyk, 1978).

41. Kollontai presented her vision of the new love most famously in her essay "Make Way for Winged Eros! A Letter to Working Youth," published in 1923 in the journal of the Komsomol; see Aleksandra Kollontai, "Dorogu krylatomu Erosu! (Pis'mo k trudiashcheisia molodezhi)," *Molodaia gvardiia* no. 3 (1923): 111–124. She imagines that under Communism, erotic love will be "winged" as opposed to "wingless," characterized by (1) emotional equality between men and women, (2) the end of the feeling of property between lovers, and (3) comradely sensitivity on the part of both men and women (p. 123). In her interpretation of Kollontai's "winged eros," Barbara Evans Clements describes it as "eroticism with the possessiveness removed"; see Clements, *Bolshevik Feminist*, p. 227.

42. On the specific attacks on Kollontai's article on "Winged Eros," see Clements, *Bolshevik Feminist*, pp. 232–235, and Farnsworth, *Aleksandra Kollontai*, pp. 324–325. One of the most scathing attacks was written by the *Lef*ist Boris Arvatov, in "Grazhd. Akhmatova i Tov. Kollontai," *Molodaia gvardiia* no. 4–5 (1923): 147–151. He criticizes her for the "feminist subjectivism" of her insistence on a specific "female point of view" (p. 148); concentrating on the female personality only detracts from the larger class struggle, which, when won, would naturally eliminate gender inequality. He advocates that the "emotional-psychological differences that exist between man and woman must be studied and practically coordinated not from the female and not from the male point of view, and not mutually, but scientifically, i.e., outside the individual" (p. 148). Significantly, he frames his disagreement with Kollontai around method rather than substance: he does not deny that historical differences between the sexes exist, or that they have prevented women from achieving independence. The passion with which he argues the importance of this difference in method, and the length and detail of his review, suggests that he took "the woman question" more seriously than his *Lef* colleagues, who rarely addressed it. He also signals his respect for Kollontai, despite his critique, when he writes parenthetically "I personally beg the author's pardon" (p. 148) after accusing her of "subjectivism."

43. Judith Butler, *Bodies That Matter: On the Discursive Limits of "Sex"* (New York: Routledge, 1993), p. 49; on *mater* and *matrix*, see p. 31.

44. Kollontai, "Dorogu Krylatomu Erosu," p. 119, n. 1. Elizabeth Wood argues that Kollontai and others in the women's section "perpetuated stereotypes of women" (*The Baba and the Comrade*, pp. 199–200) and concludes that "basic gender divisions remained unquestioned" (p. 207).

45. I have come across no suggestions in the *byt* literature or visual propaganda that men should participate in household tasks as a way of alleviating women's burdens. Elizabeth Wood states that "although occasional articles discussed the possibility of a new division of domestic labor within the household, they were rare" (*The Baba and the Comrade*, p. 207). The only evidence she offers for the existence of these "occasional articles" is the example of one containing an anecdote about a husband who considered himself a martyr because he agreed to watch the baby occasionally while his wife attended political meetings, since he was home writing his party reports anyway—an example that more properly contradicts the idea that domestic labor could be shared harmoniously (p. 282, n. 71). The Bolshevik claim that women's oppression is the fault of capitalist oppression of all workers, rather than the result of men dominating women, denies that men have anything to gain from the oppressive construction of gender roles. Yet this example of the disgruntled husband who has to watch the baby demonstrates what contemporary feminists, such as Christine Delphy, have long argued, namely that the double oppression of women benefits oppressed men as well as Capital. See Christine Delphy, *Close to Home: A Materialist Analysis of Women's Oppression*, trans. Diana Leonard (Amherst: University of Massachusetts Press, 1984), chapter 9, "A Materialist Feminism *Is* Possible."

46. This poster is cataloged under the heading P2.XI.3 in the Department of Graphics, Russian State Library, Moscow. P2 signifies 1921–1925; X signifies "*Byt* of workers of the city and country"; and the number I signifies a subgroup of the category X for *Byt*, namely, "Woman in the USSR."

47. Sergei Tret'iakov, "Otkuda i kuda?" *Lef* no. 1 (1923): 192–203. Future references to this article will be cited parenthetically in the body of the text.

48. On the fraught relationship between *Lef* and the party, and the intellectual schisms within *Lef*, see Halina Stephan, *"Lef" and the Left Front of the Arts*, Slavistische Beitrage vol. 142 (Munich: Sagner, 1981), and Edward J. Brown, *Mayakovsky: A Poet in the Revolution* (New York: Paragon House, 1988).

49. For a discussion of the meanings of *meshchanstvo* in Russian cultural history, see Boym, *Common Places*, pp. 66–73. See also Vera Dunham's foundational study of the rise of a particular Soviet version of *meshchanstvo* under Stalin, *In Stalin's Time: Middle Class Values in Soviet Fiction* (Durham: Duke University Press, 1990).

50. Trotsky had also acknowledged that some members of the Russian proletariat had their origins in the *meshchanstvo*, which hampered the formation of a socialist proletarian consciousness as much as peasant origins. See Trotsky, *Voprosy byta*, p. 25.

51. Boris Arvatov, EL, p. 121. Although Arvatov published frequently on literature and art in the journal *Lef*, his writings specifically concerning *byt* appeared in other journals, or in his books.

52. Arvatov and Tatlin had collaborated on a failed venture to set up a production laboratory at the Novyi Lessner factory in Petrograd in 1921. On the relations between them see Larisa Zhadova, "Tatlin, the Organizer of Material into Objects," p. 152, n. 34, and Lodder, *Russian Constructivism*, p. 93.

53. Tatlin, "Report of the Section for Material Culture's Research Work for 1924," cited in Zhadova, *Tatlin*, p. 256.

54. Boris Arvatov, "Iskusstvo i proizvodstvo," *Gorn* no. 2 (7) (1922): 103–108. This article was reprinted in his *Iskusstvo i klassy*, pp. 1–13.

55. Arvatov, *Iskusstvo i klassy*, p. 11.

56. Ibid., p. 12.
57. See Walter Benjamin, "The Work of Art in the Age of Mechanical Reproduction," in *Illuminations*, ed. Hannah Arendt, trans. Harry Zohn (New York: Schocken Books, 1978), pp. 217–251. In Susan Buck-Morss's interpretation of this essay, the spectacular and "anaesthetizing" nature of the "commodity phantasmagoria" of capitalism prepared the masses not only to be passively manipulated by the fascist leaders, but to become the passive observers of this manipulation, to take pleasure in viewing their own destruction. See Buck-Morss, "Aesthetics and Anaesthetics," p. 38.
58. L. Trotskii, *Literatura i revoliutsiia* (Moscow: Izdatel'stvo politicheskoi literatury, 1923 [1991]), p. 111.
59. Boris Arvatov, "Utopia ili nauka?" (Utopia or science?), *Lef* no. 4 (1924): 18.
60. See Georgii Plekhanov, *The Development of the Monist View of History, Selected Philosophical Works*, vol. 1, trans. Andrew Rothstein (Moscow: Progress, 1974).
61. Karl Marx, "Concerning Feuerbach," in *Early Writings*, trans. Rodney Livingstone and Gregor Benton (London: Penguin, 1974), p. 421.
62. Butler, *Bodies That Matter*, p. 250, n. 5.
63. Robert Pel'she, "O nekotorykh oshibkakh 'Lefovtsev'" (On some mistakes of the *Lefists*), *Sovetskoe iskusstvo* no. 4–5 (1925): 13–22.
64. Boris Arvatov, "Reaktsiia v zhivopisi," and Nikolai Chuzhak, "Iskusstvo byta," *Sovetskoe iskusstvo* no. 4–5 (1925): 3. The word *veshchnost'* used by Chuzhak is a neologism derived from the word *veshch'* (thing), and means, roughly, "the state of being a thing." Although it appeared with some frequency in this kind of writing at the time, it was not a real word to be found in the dictionary; it differed significantly in tone, if only slightly in syllables, from the dictionary word *veshchestvennost'*, meaning "materiality."
65. Pel'she, "O nekotorykh," p. 17; he uses the terms "*Lefist* sectarianism" and "anarchic philosophy" on p. 16.
66. Ibid., p. 16.
67. We have seen evidence above, in note 42 of this chapter, of Arvatov's strong interest in the correct approach to "the woman question" in his review of Kollontai's essay on "Winged Eros"; see Arvatov, "Grazhd. Akhmatova i Tov. Kollontai."
68. Records of the meeting of the Standing Commission of the Museum of Artistic Culture, September 3, 1923, cited in Zhadova, "Tatlin, the Organizer of Material into Objects," p. 135.
69. "Novyi byt," *Krasnaia Panorama*; the original Russian text is legible in figure 2.1; translated in Zhadova, *Tatlin*, p. 407, translation modified. An arshin is a Russian measure equivalent to 28 inches.
70. Photographic archive of the Russian Ethnographic Museum, St. Petersburg, f. 133, no. 325.
71. Descriptions of the stove can be found in Punin, "Rutina i Tatlin," p. 68, translated in Zhadova, *Tatlin*, p. 403; and in Zhadova, "Tatlin, the Organizer of Material into Objects," in Zhadova, *Tatlin*, p. 140.
72. Zhadova, "Tatlin, the Organizer of Material into Objects," p. 152, n. 42. The information about the first stoves that Tatlin made for his home in 1920–1921 comes from the recollections of his nephew, S. S. Tatlin.
73. Zhadova, "Tatlin, the Organizer of Material into Objects," p. 140. She refers to Kazimir Malevich, "Konstruktivnaia zhivopis' russkikh khudozhnikov i konstruktivizm," *Nova generatsiia* (Kharkhov) no. 8, 1929, reprinted in A. C. Shatskikh and G. L. Demosfenova, eds., *Kazimir Malevich: Sobranie sochinenii v piati tomakh*, vol. 2 (Moscow: Gileia, 1998), pp. 198–206. In this article, Malevich argues that Tatlin's utilitarian objects were made "under the control of those painterly-spatial senses that come under the formulation of the fourth stage

of cubism" (p. 203), but he also states that with the stove, it is especially difficult to resolve the question of its artistic-painterly side.

74. Punin, "Rutina i Tatlin," p. 68, translated in Zhadova, *Tatlin*, p. 403, translation modified.

75. The date given in illustration captions for the linen sportswear suit in Zhadova, *Tatlin*, and other publications is 1923–1924, but another Zhadova text offers evidence that it must have been made in early 1925. Tatlin's final scribbled line pointing to the suit, on the photomontage of the "New Everyday Life" article, states that "the pattern and sample were produced at the Institute of Decorative Arts," and according to Zhadova, Tatlin became a member of the Soviet on Standard Clothing at the Institute only in 1925. She therefore states that the sportswear suit "represents the very last work by Tatlin in the area of clothing (1925)." See Zhadova, "Tatlin—proektirovshchik material'noi kul'tury," p. 218, n. 40; p. 219, n. 44. Similarly, the photomontage incorporating the "New Everyday Life" article (figure 2.3) is usually dated 1924, but as it includes the photograph of Tatlin in his sportswear suit, it more likely dates from early 1925.

76. Zhadova, "Tatlin, the Organizer of Material into Objects," p. 144.

77. This poster is in the Department of Graphics, Russian State Library, Moscow, cataloged under R2, which signifies an advertisement (*reklam*) from period 2 (designating 1921–1925). Zhadova claims that "Tatlin's point of departure in dress design was the plasticity of the human body," but this does not seem to be borne out by the evidence of his sportswear suit, nor by that of his designs for bulky overcoats. See Zhadova, "Tatlin, the Organizer of Material into Objects," p. 143.

78. Photographic archive of the Russian Ethnographic Museum, St. Petersburg, f. 133, nos. 257–258. These two photographs could more properly be said to document working life, rather than everyday life, but the focus of the photographs is the clothing worn by the men, rather than their labor.

79. The argument presented here that Tatlin's project of "material culture" was suffused by an ethnographic understanding of *byt* differs from Zhadova's claim that Tatlin's project should be seen in relation to the modern concept of "design," and that it had "very little in common with the idea of material culture as used in archaeology, anthropology and ethnography." See Zhadova, "Tatlin, the Organizer of Material into Objects," p. 134.

80. The illustrations for "The New Everyday Life" article also included explicit documentation of the pattern pieces for the warm overcoat modeled by Tatlin. The text states that the coat consists of removable linings of flannel or lamb's fur, depending on the season, emphasizing its readiness for industrial assembly.

81. Zhadova claims that Tatlin had "worked out a constructive, economical, logically simplified cutting method" that would have been useful in the serial production of clothing in factory workshops. See Zhadova, "Tatlin, the Organizer of Material into Objects," p. 144.

82. Konstantin Miklashevskii, *Gipertrofiia iskusstva* (Petrograd: 1924), p. 61.

83. Ibid., p. 66. He is referring to Tatlin's statements at a 1923 lecture at the Section for Material Culture, entitled "Down with Tatlinism" (*Doloi Tatlinizm*). Miklashevskii's brief report on this lecture is the only documentation of its contents that remains.

84. Zhadova makes this connection between his designs for coats and sailors' work clothes, particularly his interest in making waterproof coats out of "vulcanized material," with button-in lining. She notes that Tatlin was descended from Dutch shipbuilders, the Van Tatlings, who had been brought to Russia by Tsar Peter I. See Zhadova, "Tatlin, the Organizer of Material into Objects," p. 143.

85. Nikolai Punin, "Pamiatnik III Internatsionala," in N. Punin, *O Tatline*, p. 20; translated as "The Monument to the Third International" in Zhadova, *Tatlin*, p. 345, translation modified. In her study of Tatlin's monument, Gail Harrison Roman notes that, because of Trotsky's condemnation of "Cosmism" and mysticism, "Trotsky's reluctance to support the Tower is more understandable given Punin's assertion that the spiral element of the Tower would facilitate escape from earthly bounds." See Gail Harrison Roman, "Tatlin's Tower: Revolutionary Symbol and Aesthetic," in *The Avant-garde Frontier*, p. 55. But as we have seen, Trotsky had himself expressed his longing for a life freed from material bonds, and in my reading of Punin's essay, his similar desire is no more mystical or spiritual than Trotsky's.
86. Zhadova also calls attention to the ways in which Tatlin's clothes were all designed for his measurements, and modeled only by him, but without explaining her reasons, she concludes not that this was an assertion of his individuality, but rather that this demonstrated that "Tatlin's values were truly and fundamentally democratic." See Zhadova, "Tatlin, the Organizer of Material into Objects," p. 144.
87. Zhadova, *Tatlin*, pp. 252-253. In a further anecdote, she reports that "on the night before [an exhibition at GINKhUK] opened, evidently in order to preserve secrecy, Tatlin took the critic Isakov and another acquaintance into the Section's exhibition by breaking the door leading from his apartment to the display room."
88. Miklashevskii, *Gipertrofiia iskusstva*, p. 60.

CHAPTER THREE

1. "Pamiati L. S. Popovoi," *Lef* no. 2 (1924): 4. The text refers to the factory as the "former Tsindel," which was its prerevolutionary name.
2. This aspect of the Russian avant-garde is often mentioned, although surprisingly little scholarship exists on it; until recently, the Galerie Gmurzynska catalog *Russian Women Artists of the Avantgarde, 1910-1930: Exhibition, December 1979–March 1980* (Cologne: Die Galerie, 1979) and M. N. Yablonskaya, *Women Artists of Russia's New Age, 1900-1935* (London: Thames and Hudson, 1990) were the only major publications to address women artists as an entity within the avant-garde. This changed with the publication of the catalog to the exhibition *Amazons of the Russian Avant-Garde*, ed. John E. Bowlt and Matthew Drutt (New York: The Solomon R. Guggenheim Foundation, 2000). (The title of the exhibition stems from a phrase applied to the artists by their contemporary, the poet Benedikt Livshits.) The catalog essays attempt to answer the question why such an unusual number of women reached prominence within the Russian avant-garde (six women artists were represented in the exhibition). Ekaterina Dyogot's catalog essay, "Creative Women, Creative Men, and Paradigms of Creativity: Why Have There Been Great Women Artists?," pp. 109-127, in particular, offers a theoretical, feminist account of the gendered cultural categories that supported the prominence of women artists.
3. On the ties between the decorative arts and femininity in the Russian context, see Briony Fer, "The Language of Construction," in *Realism, Rationalism, Surrealism: Art between the Wars*, ed. Briony Fer, David Batchelor, and Paul Wood (New Haven and London: Yale University Press, 1993).
4. The meaning of the Productivist term "transparency" (*prozrachnost'*) as I use it in this study parallels that of the semiotic term "indexicality" as used by Maria Gough in her discussion of Rodchenko's *Hanging Spatial Constructions* series of c. 1920: "Rodchenko elaborates a nascent principle of deductive or indexical structure: the very structure of the work reveals the process of its production." See Gough, "In the Laboratory of Constructivism:

Karl Ioganson's Cold Structures," *October* 84 (spring 1998): 113. As Gough points out, Rosalind Krauss first demonstrated the importance of the index for analyzing modernist art; see "Notes on the Index: Part 1" and "Part 2" in Krauss, *The Originality of the Avant-Garde and Other Modernist Myths* (Cambridge, Mass.: MIT Press, 1985). The index, as defined by Charles Sanders Peirce, is a sign that has an existential bond with its object; for example, a footprint in the snow. (See C. S. Peirce, *Collected Papers of Charles Sanders Peirce*, 8 vols., ed. Charles Hartshorne and Paul Weiss [Cambridge: Harvard University Press, 1931–1958], vol. 2.) While the notion of indexical structure may offer a productive heuristic device for analyzing Rodchenko's systemic *Spatial Constructions* series, it cannot be transferred unchanged to an analysis of utilitarian Constructivist things; the indexical model of transparency cannot encompass the opacities introduced by the historical situatedness of the thing.

5. Griselda Pollock, *Differencing the Canon: Feminist Desire and the Writing of Art's Histories* (London and New York: Routledge, 1999), p. 124.

6. Dmitri V. Sarabianov and Natalia L. Adaskina, *Popova*, trans. Marian Schwartz (New York: Harry N. Abrams, 1990), p. 304. Christina Lodder, in *Russian Constructivism*, makes a similar argument: she calls Popova's elegant dress designs a "deviation" from the defined objectives of Constructivism (p. 152). Lodder also emphasizes the traditional nature of textile design itself, arguing that it should actually be seen as a "pragmatic retreat" from the Constructivist ideal, and that it is only through the connection with clothing design projects that it can be understood as part of the larger project, which she defines as "the restructuring of the entire environment in accord with Constructivist principles" (p. 151).

7. The title of this section is borrowed from Osip Brik's article "V proizvodstvo!"

8. No definitive archival evidence of the terms of their employment at the factory, including the exact starting date, has yet been uncovered. But contemporary accounts suggest that they were invited to work there by the director in the fall of 1923, and that they were certainly working there by January of 1924. Popova was still working for the factory at the time of her death in May 1924. According to the art historian Alexander Lavrentiev, who is also Stepanova's grandson, Stepanova continued working there until 1925; Khan-Magomedov specifies that she worked there until only the beginning of 1925 (Khan-Magomedov, *Konstruktivizm*, p. 382). For synthetic accounts of the available sources for this history, see Lavrentiev, *Varvara Stepanova: The Complete Work*, trans. Wendy Salmond (Cambridge, Mass.: MIT Press, 1988), pp. 79–84; Sarabianov and Adaskina, *Popova*, pp. 299–303; Lodder, *Russian Constructivism*, pp. 146–152; Tatiana Strizhenova, *Soviet Costume and Textiles, 1917–1945*, trans. Era Mozolkova (Moscow, Paris, Verona: Flammarion, 1991), pp. 135–147; and Khan-Magomedov, *Konstruktivizm*, pp. 382–389.

9. See Varvara Stepanova, "Kostium segodniashnego dnia—prozodezhda," *Lef* no. 2 (1923): 65–68. Popova designed the set and costumes for Meyerhold's 1922 production of *The Magnanimous Cuckold*, while Stepanova similarly designed his production of *The Death of Tarelkin* in the same year.

10. V. F. Stepanova and L. S. Popova, "Memo to the Directorate for the First State Cotton-Printing Factory," unpublished manuscript, 1924, The Rodchenko–Stepanova Archive, Moscow. Cited in A. N. Lavrent'ev, "Poeziia graficheskogo dizaina v tvorchestve Varvary Stepanovoi," *Tekhnicheskaia estetika* (1980): 25. Translated in Strizhenova, *Soviet Costume*, p. 136, translation modified.

11. This interpretation of the memo is offered by Lavrentiev, *Stepanova*, p. 81.

12. Liubov' Popova, "Statement from the

Catalog for the 'Tenth State Exhibition: Non Objective Art and Suprematism,'" 1919. Reproduced in the original and in translation in Sarabianov and Adaskina, *Popova*, pp. 346–347.

13. Boris Rybchenkov, "Rasskazy B. F. Rybchenkova," in Natalia Tamruchi, ed., *Prostranstvo kartiny: Sbornik statei* (Moscow: Sovetskii khudozhnik, 1989), p. 294. Rybchenkov wrote these memoirs in 1979; his romanticizing memories of Popova's attractively feminine personal qualities, with the hindsight of almost sixty years, do seem to color his recollection of the qualities of her paintings, which he goes on to describe as naive and more suited for printing on children's fabrics than for the development of abstract art. But his memoirs, unreliable as they may be, do signal the possibility of such a gendered reading at the time.

14. For an evocative theoretical account of touch and femininity within a history of painting, see Ewa Lajer-Burcharth, "Pompadour's Touch: Difference in Representation," *Representations* 73 (winter 2001): 54–88.

15. Briony Fer has discussed Popova's *Spatial Force* paintings in parallel terms, emphasizing that Popova was deliberately renouncing the traditional sense of an artist's self, with its connotations of individual nuances, including masculine and feminine, in favor of a more rational and scientific conception of making. In particular, Fer calls attention to Popova's interest in mechanical drawing. See Fer, *Realism, Rationalism, Surrealism*, p. 129, and also "What's in a Line? Gender and Modernity," *Oxford Art Journal* 13, no. 1 (1990): 77–88.

16. See the account of her diary entries describing these responses to her paintings in Lavrentiev, *Stepanova*, pp. 43–44. The critics contrasted her work to the analytic abstraction of Aleksandr Rodchenko, whose work was exhibited next to her paintings at the same exhibition.

17. See Medunetskii's remark in "Transcript of the Discussion of Comrade Stepanova's Paper 'On Constructivism,'" p. 74.

18. Varvara Stepanova, "Registration of Textile Samples," c. 1924, notebook in the collection of the Rodchenko-Stepanova Archive, Moscow, translated and cited in Strizhenova, *Soviet Costume*, p. 147.

19. Varvara Stepanova, "O polozhenii i zadachakh khudozhnika-konstruktivista v sittsenabivnoi promyshlennosti v sviazi s rabotami na sittsenabivnoi fabrike," paper delivered at INKhUK, January 5, 1924, translated and cited in Lodder, *Russian Constructivism*, p. 151.

20. Varvara Stepanova, "Organizational Plan of the Programme for a Course in Artistic Composition at the Faculty of Textile of the VKhUTEMAS, 1925," in *Costume Revolution: Textiles, Clothing, and Costume of the Soviet Union in the Twenties*, trans. Elizabeth Dafinone, from the Italian (London: Trefoil, 1989): 178. These two points of the teaching program (the final two points of section 1, parts L and M), cited here from the English translation, are curiously omitted from this document in a later publication of Stepanova's writings in Russian. See Varvara Stepanova, *Chelovek ne mozhet zhit'*, p. 184.

21. See the public discussion between Stepanova and Arvatov on the subject of the artist's role in industry in "Transcript of the Discussion of Comrade Stepanova's Paper," especially p. 78.

22. "Transcript of the Discussion of Comrade Stepanova's Paper," p. 76.

23. The newspaper was produced by Rodchenko and Stepanova for their friends; its title *Nash gaz* was short for *"nasha gazeta"* (our newspaper). Like the English word "gas," *gaz* here can also be read in the senses of joking and of farting. The newspaper is in the collection of the Rodchenko–Stepanova Archive, Moscow. The full text and images of the newspaper have not been published; the most complete publication of it to date appears in English only, translated by Alexander Lavrentiev, in a small, limited-edition catalog: *Ornament and Textile Design*, ed. Katerina Drevina, Varvara Rodchenko, and Alexander Lavrentiev (Moscow: Manege Gallery, 1990). According to Lavrentiev, the illustrations in *Nash gaz* were done by Rodchenko, while Stepanova finalized the texts and carried out the overall graphic design (conversation with the author, April 2002). The tone of this particular caricature is jocular, but it seems that once again, Popova is depicted as more successful than Stepanova, with her massive output of fabrics.

24. Tugendkhol'd, cited in Natalia L. Adaskina, "Constructivist Fabrics and Dress Design," *Journal of Decorative and Propaganda Arts* 5 (summer 1987): 157.

25. There is a commonplace assumption among non-Soviet specialists that the early years of the Soviet Union were an unprecedented period of women's liberation and sexual emancipation. Sweeping legal reforms instituted by the Soviets immediately after the Revolution did in fact accord women a level of equality before the law unrivaled in any country, and there was lively public debate in the 1920s about the possible forms of a new, Communist sexuality. But more recent scholarship in Soviet history has burst this utopian bubble, demonstrating that actual sexual or women's liberation was very limited in the 1920s and was in many ways eliminated by the 1930s. See, e.g., Elizabeth Wood, *The Baba and the Comrade*; Eric Naiman, *Sex in Public*; Wendy Z. Goldman, *Women, the State, and Revolution*; and Frances Lee Bernstein, "'What Everyone Should Know about Sex': Gender, Sexual Enlightenment, and the Politics of Health in Revolutionary Russia, 1918–1931," Ph. D. dissertation (Columbia University, 1997).

26. Tugendkhol'd, cited in Adaskina, "Constructivist Fabrics and Dress Design," p. 157.

27. Quoted in Lavrent'ev, "Poeziia," p. 25; translated in Strizhenova, *Soviet Costume*, p. 136, translation modified and expanded.

28. Benjamin, *The Arcades Project*, p. 71 (B4,4).

29. "Modnaia khronika," *Zhurnal dlia Khoziaek* no. 1 (1922): 3.

30. Boris Arvatov, "Iskusstvo i kachestvo promyshlennoi produktsii," *Sovetskoe iskusstvo* no. 7 (1925): 39–43. Future references to this article will be cited parenthetically in the text.

31. In the issue of *Lef* dedicated to Popova, Osip Brik praised the "enormous cultural value" of Popova and Stepanova's experiment in working at the First State Cotton-Printing Factory. See Brik, "Ot kartiny k sitsu" (From Painting to the Textile Print), *Lef* no. 2 (1924): 34. Yet some *Lef*ists remained skeptical of the Constructivist credentials of the project; Nikolai Chuzhak, for example, derided their work in the factory for being "little applied art cotton prints" (*prikladnicheskie "sitchiki"*) rather than contributions to the machine production of textiles. See Chuzhak, "Iskusstvo byta," p. 10.

32. Varvara Stepanova, "Kostium segodniashnego dnia—prozodezhda" (1923), in Stepanova, *Chelovek ne mozhet zhit'*, p. 181.

33. Ibid., p. 182. In another section of the article she also lists the following kinds of specialized, primarily masculine clothing: "pilot's uniform, chauffeur's uniform, protective aprons for workers, football shoes, waterproof coat, military service jacket" (p. 181).

34. Cited in Strizhenova, *Soviet Costume*, p. 53.

35. On the imperative within the garment industry to convince workers to give up their handicraft mentality, see, e.g., *Tekhnika i iskusstvo shveinoi promyshlennosti* (Technology and Art of the Garment Industry), no. 2, 1925.

36. In a diary entry from 1927, Stepanova reports on a meeting of the editorial board of the journal *Novyi lef*, in which the board attacks Dziga Vertov and she comes to his defense. The other board members accuse her of defending him for personal reasons, and laugh at her even as she protests loudly. She writes that "they say I am 'that kind of woman'—I drink vodka, I play ma-jong." This anecdote goes some way toward explaining why a woman artist would try to avoid calling attention to her gender, because it could so easily be used against her. See *Chelovek ne mozhet zhit'*, p. 206.

37. Varvara Stepanova, "Zadachi khudozhnika v tekstil'nom proizvodstve," in Peter Noever, ed. *Rodchenko–Stepanova: Budushchee—edinstvennaia nasha tsel'* (Munich: Prestel Verlag, 1991), pp. 190–193. The manuscript is in the Rodchenko–Stepanova Archive in Moscow. A significantly shortened version of the essay, with a different title, was published in the newspaper *Vecherniaia Moskva* on February 28, 1928; an English translation of this shortened version was published in Lavrentiev, *Stepanova*, p. 180.

38. "Central core" imagery was the term invented by Judy Chicago to describe what she called the essentially female image of the vaginal form, and which she claimed to see in the work of most women artists. See Chicago, *Through the Flower: My Struggle as a Woman Artist* (Garden City, N.Y.: Anchor Books, 1977). As further evidence that Stepanova was aware of the genital signification of the abstract patterning of her costume designs, see her double design for male and female costumes for *The Death of Tarelkin*, which are identical except for a geometric form at crotch level on the male costume that points upward, suggesting a phallic shape, while the same similarly placed form on the female costume points downward, suggesting a vaginal one (see figure 5.16).

39. Stepanova, "Zadachi khudozhnika v tekstil'nom proizvodstve," p. 192. Future references to this article will be cited parenthetically in the body of the text.

40. Stepanova, "Organizational Plan," in *Chelovek ne mozhet zhit'*, p. 185.

41. See Boris Groys, *The Total Art of Stalinism*, discussed in chapter 1.

42. Sarabianov and Adaskina argue that Popova's dress designs were oriented not toward working women such as office workers, teachers, or sales clerks, and certainly not toward the proletarian woman worker, but rather toward "a more artistic type" from the "gay twenties . . . the artist, the film star" (*Popova*, p. 303)—in other words, the flapper. But there is much evidence to suggest that this style of dress was worn by a range of urban, working women in Russia, including proletarian women on special occasions. My argument is that Popova was working against just such class hierarchies within fashion.

43. Strizhenova, *Soviet Costume*, p. 9.

44. See, e.g., Boris Arvatov, "Iskusstvo i proizvodstvo."

45. See, e.g., the discussion in chapter 2 of Konstantin Miklashevskii's criticism of Tatlin's attempt to design a winter coat, despite the fact that he possesses none of the qualifications of a professional coat-maker, in his *Gipertrofiia iskusstva*, p. 61.

46. Laura Mulvey, "Some Thoughts on Theories of Fetishism in the Context of Contemporary Culture," *October* 65 (1993), especially pp. 9–11.

47. Mulvey makes this connection between the sheen of the commodity fetish and the glossy surface of the filmic or photographic image of the female movie icon, which covers over the threat of castration posed by the female body that "lacks" the phallus (ibid.).

48. Popova, "Introduction to the INKhUK Discussion of the *Magnanimous Cuckold*," manuscript, translated in Sarabianov and Adaskina, *Popova*, pp. 378–379.

49. On the wish-image, see Benjamin, *The Arcades Project*, p. 4 (from the "Exposé of 1935"); on Marx and the "phantasmagorical" commodity, see pp. 181–182 (G5,1) (quote from Otto Rühle).

50. Susan Buck-Morss writes that the *Arcades Project* "put forth the notion that socialist culture would need to be constructed out of the embryonic, still-inadequate forms that preexisted in capitalism." See Buck-Morss, *The Dialectics of Seeing: Walter Benjamin and the Arcades Project* (Cambridge, Mass.: MIT Press, 1989), p. 123. Buck-Morss's interpretation of the *Arcades Project* has been an invaluable guide for me to Benjamin's text and stands in my view as a major contribution to the theory of modernity in its own right.

51. This interpretation is elaborated in Buck-Morss, *The Dialectics of Seeing*; on the "humane society," see p. 274; on new foms, see p. 146; on the ur-past and the dream, see pp. 116–117.

52. "Fashions are a collective medicament for the ravages of oblivion. The more shortlived a period, the more susceptible it is to fashion." See Benjamin, *The Arcades Project*, p. 80 (B9a,1).

53. On "the realm of dead things," see Benjamin, *The Arcades Project*, p. 70 (B3,8) (I have used Buck-Morss's translation here [p. 101] in place of Eiland and McLaughlin's "world of the inorganic"); on the "overcoming" of birth and death, see p. 79 (B9,2); on "the ridiculous superstition of novelty" see p. 74 (B5a,2), quote by Paul Valéry.

54. On the "revolution" in cotton prints and the changing dress of the lower classes: "Every woman used to wear a blue or black dress that she kept for ten years without washing, for fear it might tear to pieces. But now her husband, a poor worker, covers her with a robe of flowers for the price of a day's labor." J. Michelet writing in 1846, quoted in Benjamin, *The Arcades Project*, p. 78 (B8,3); see also (B6a,3). Susan Buck-Morss cautions that the entries describing fashion as an indicator of social change are more predominant earlier on, and that in the 1930s the entries on fashion become increasingly critical. See Buck-Morss, *The Dialectics of Seeing*, p. 98 and p. 403, n. 97.

55. Benjamin, *The Arcades Project*, p. 63 (B1,4). I have used Buck-Morss's translation of this phrase (*The Dialectics of Seeing*, p. 101).

56. Walter Benjamin, "One-Way Street," in *Reflections*, trans. Edmund Jephcott, ed. Peter Demetz (New York: Schocken Books, 1978), p. 85.

57. I say "unbeknownst" to him because Benjamin, in his relationship with the Soviet producer of children's theater, Asja Lacis, and on his two-month visit to Moscow in 1926–1927, clearly became acquainted with the more straightforwardly agitational and ascetic practices of the literary and artistic avant-garde. He does not seem to have been aware of the more commercial or everyday practices of the Constructivists, such as dress designs or advertisements, that are emphasized in this study. See *Walter Benjamin: Moscow Diary*, trans. Richard Sieburth (Cambridge, Mass.: Harvard University Press, 1986).

58. I. A. Aksenov, "Posmertnaia vystavka L. S. Popovoi," *Zhizn' iskusstva* no. 5 (February 3, 1925): 5.

59. Cited in Adaskina, "Constructivist Fabrics and Dress Design," p. 157.

60. Iakov Tugendkhol'd, "Pamiati L. Popovoi," *Khudozhnik i zritel'* vol. 6, no. 7 (1924): 77.

61. In another caricature from this series—the one discussed above showing Popova and Stepanova taking their fabric designs to the factory (see figure 3.10) —Popova is again depicted as fashionably dressed in a short, swingy skirt, angular jacket, tiny high-heeled black boots, and an elegant hat. This is an amusing getup for someone pushing a wheelbarrow down the street, but again, it suggests that fashionable feminine attire was a reliable source of Popova jokes.

62. Aleksandr Rodchenko, *Opyty dlia budushchego: dnevniki, stat'i, pis'ma, zapiski* (Moscow: Grant', 1996), p. 60.

63. Ibid.

64. In William Pietz's important material and historical account of the fetish, it is a material object that is both deeply personal and

collective. But I have attempted here to support the Constructivists' own assertions that their things, in their transparency, should no longer be understood in terms of the structure of the fetish. See Pietz, "The Problem of the Fetish, pt. 1," *Res* 9 (spring 1985): 14.

65. Boris Arvatov, "Segodniashnie zadachi iskusstva v promyshlennosti," p. 86.

66. On the uses and abuses of biography for reading the work of women artists, see Anne Wagner, *Three Artists (Three Women): Modernism and the Art of Hesse, Krasner, and O'Keeffe* (Berkeley: University of California Press, 1996). As she puts it, an artist's "position as a woman does not have fixed, predictable consequences" (p. 6).

CHAPTER FOUR

1. Benjamin, *The Arcades Project*, p. 462 (N2a,3). The poem printed on the back of the Our Industry caramel box is, unusually, not by Mayakovsky, but by his *Lef* colleague, the poet Nikolai Aseev.

2. *Lef* published Rodchenko's logo designs for Dobrolet, the voluntary share society for the development of Soviet aviation, in its second issue in 1923, and in its first issue of 1924 (issue no. 5), it published two of his advertising posters for Rezinotrest, the State Rubber Trust. The art historian Osip Beskin, defending Constructivism in a debate in the pages of the journal *Soviet Art* in 1925, mentions the militancy and energy of Rodchenko's and the Constructivist Anton Lavinskii's advertisements for state organizations and illustrates Rodchenko advertisements for a Dziga Vertov film and for Mospoligraf, the polygraphic and office supply trust. But aside from the two Rezinotrest posters illustrated in *Lef* (for pacifiers and balls), the many ads for everyday household items, foods, and cigarettes are never singled out for comment or illustration. See O. Beskin, "Otvet napravo—zapros nalevo," *Sovetskoe iskusstvo* no. 6 (1925): 6–16.

3. Osip Brik, "V proizvodstvo!," p. 108.

4. In proposing that Rodchenko's commercial graphics are interpretive or analytical, my argument coincides with Victor Margolin's claim that Rodchenko's objects are "rhetorical." Yet I depart from Margolin's view when he suggests that they are rhetorical or experimental as opposed to being actually involved in the revolutionary transformation of material reality. Because the commercial graphics were widely distributed as packaging and posters, reproduced in newspapers and magazines, and placed on top of Mossel'prom kiosks throughout Moscow, their rhetoric can instead be understood to have contributed significantly to the mass material and visual culture of Moscow in 1923–1925. See Victor Margolin, *The Struggle for Utopia*, ch. 3.

5. The main exceptions are Margolin, *The Struggle for Utopia*, and Leah Dickerman, "The Propagandizing of Things," in *Aleksandr Rodchenko*, ed. Magdalena Dabrowski, Leah Dickerman, and Peter Galassi (New York: The Museum of Modern Art, 1998), pp. 62–99.

6. Paul Wood, "Art and Politics in a Workers' State," *Art History* 8, no. 1 (1985): 118.

7. Bürger, *Theory of the Avant-Garde*, p. 54.

8. The poem was first published, unillustrated, in the inaugural issue of *Lef*: V. V. Maiakovskii, "Pro Eto," *Lef* no. 1 (1923): 65–103. Future citations from the poem will be from this edition, and will be noted parenthetically in the body of the text. Translations from the poem are my own unless otherwise noted; I have tried to convey the sense of the words, at the expense of preserving rhythm and rhyme. A book version of the poem illustrated in black and white with Rodchenko's photomontages was published by the state publishing house, Gosizdat, in 1923. The large and colorful original maquettes for these illustrations are in the collection of the State Mayakovsky Museum, Moscow.

9. The affair began in 1915, when as a young Futurist poet, Mayakovsky had, unbidden, recited his poem "A Cloud in Pants" in the bourgeois home of Lili and Osip Brik. This initiated an arrangement that would last until Mayakovsky's suicide in 1930: Lili, Osip, and Mayakovsky became a kind of family, living together for long periods and sustaining their friendships through the vagaries of Lili and Mayakovsky's romantic relationship. Theirs is one of the more famous of twentieth-century literary affairs and has been documented in works such as Bengt Jangfeldt, ed., *Love Is the Heart of Everything: Correspondence between Vladimir Mayakovsky and Lili Brik, 1915–1930* (Edinburgh: Polygon, 1986).

10. Contemporary accounts of Brik make it clear that she did not deny her upper-middle-class origins or espouse asceticism. Witness Viktor Shklovsky's rather nasty description of her: "Brik loved things—earrings in the shape of golden flies and antique Russian earrings. She had a rope of pearls and was full of lovely nonsense, very old and very familiar to mankind. She knew how to be sad, feminine, capricious, proud, shallow, fickle, in love, clever and any way you like. Thus Shakespeare described woman in his comedy." See Shklovsky, *Mayakovsky and His Circle*, trans. and ed. Lily Feiler (New York: Dodd, Mead, 1972), p. 79.

11. At issue here is the gendering of the cultural category of *byt* in Mayakovsky's work, rather than the gendered nature of the actual love affair between Mayakovsky and Lili Brik. Their letters suggest that their relationship, while highly unconventional in the openness with which they conducted their affair, upheld many of the conventions of masculinity and femininity. He, physically huge and rugged, focused his poetry on himself and his conflicted subjectivity, and signed his letters *"schen"* (puppy); she, physically smaller, signed her letters "kitty" and produced no epic poetry. But like other literary and artistic women of her extraordinary generation in Russia, Lili Brik also defied the conventional associations of woman with domesticity and *byt*. Intelligent, well-educated, and a perceptive reader of poetry and prose, she promoted Futurist and later Constructivist projects through her contacts in Russia and abroad, and became a classic literary salon hostess to the Futurists, Formalists, and the *Lef* group.

12. The quotation from this public reading is taken from Brown, *Mayakovsky*, p. 232. Brown also discusses the manuscript versions and Mayakovsky's process of self-censorship, pp. 232–233. (The parenthetical translation is Brown's, the bracketed one is my addition.)

13. N. Chuzhak, "K zadacham dnia," *Lef* no. 2 (1923): 150.

14. Roman Iakobson, "O pokolenii, rastrativshem svoikh poetov" (1930), in *Smert' Vladimira Maiakovskogo* (The Hague: Mouton, 1975), p. 22. Translated in Roman Jakobson, "On a Generation That Squandered Its Poets," in *Roman Jakobson: My Futurist Years*, trans. Stephen Rudy and ed. Bengt Jangfeldt and Stephen Rudy (New York: Marsilio, 1992), p. 228.

15. Sergei Tret'iakov, "Otkuda i kuda?"

16. Chuzhak writes: "At the end of the poem, we see 'there is a way out.' This way out is **the faith that 'in the future everything will be different,' there will be some kind of 'amazing life'**... I think that this is the faith **of despair.... This is not an exit, but a no-exit situation"** ("K zadacham dnia," p. 151). The use of boldface type is in the original text.

17. This translation is taken from Brown, *Mayakovsky*, p. 243; the lines in the original Russian text appear on p. 84.

18. Iakobson, "O pokolenii," pp. 13–14; translated in Jakobson, "On a Generation That Squandered Its Poets," pp. 216–217, translation modified. Brown writes that in Fekla Davidovna's apartment, Mayakovsky

recognizes his own "well-organized alter ego," the commercial propaganda poet—for Brown, the side of Mayakovsky that prevented him from fulfilling his promise as a true poet (*Mayakovsky*, p. 259).

19. The self-serving nature of the feminization of everyday life within Russian literary and philosophical culture is suggested by a passage of a letter that Mayakovsky wrote but never sent to Lili, during the period he was writing "About This": "There are two main features to my character: 1) Honesty . . . 2) Hatred of all forms of constraint. This is the cause of all the 'squabbles,' hatred of domestic constraints . . . even the forced bringing home of some purchase from the shops, the very tiniest chain, brings on feelings of nausea, pessimism and so forth. . . ." On the basis of this passage, his aversion to *byt* would seem to stem as much from a desire to avoid domestic duties as from a deep conviction that daily activities of consumption interfere with higher revolutionary commitments. See his diary letter no. 113, in Bengt Jangfeldt, ed., *Love Is the Heart of Everything*, p. 130.

20. Rodchenko himself had not yet begun taking photographs in 1923, so the photographs of Mayakovsky and Lili Brik that he used for the "About This" photomontages were commissioned for the occasion from the studio photographer Abram Shterenberg, and supplemented by photographs by two other photographers (only their surnames, Vasserman and Kapustianskii, are given on the inside front cover of the original publication), as well as by snapshots from Mayakovsky's collection. See the Ars Nicolai facsimile edition of the original publication of the poem, including German and English translations, an essay by Aleksandr Lavrent'ev, and supplementary illustrations: Vladimir Maiakovskii, *Pro Eto* (Berlin: Ars Nicolai, 1994). In his essay, Lavrent'ev states that Rodchenko found the other images for these photomontages in German youth magazines that he bought in Moscow, such as *Junge Welt*, *Die Woche*, and *Moderne Illustrierte Zeitschrift* (p. 76).

21. My reading of Mayakovsky's text and Rodchenko's photomontages concentrates on their representation of everyday objects in order to connect this project to their subsequent commercial design work. For a suggestive approach to their collaboration that stresses how the photomontages mediate the split between Mayakovsky as original poetic subject and Mayakovsky as mass-produced media image, and which offers alternative analyses of many of the same elements of the images that I analyze here, see Stephen C. Hutchings, "Photographic Eye as Poetic I: Maiakovskii's and Rodchenko's *Pro Eto* Project (1923)," *History of Photography* 24, no. 4 (winter 2000): 300–308.

22. Makhnov's image appeared in the popular press as a medical curiosity; five years after Rodchenko used it in his montage, the same photograph was used to illustrate an article on the hormonal causes of gigantism and dwarfism in a popular health magazine. The subject is identified there as "the giant Fedor Makhnov." See V. Oppel', "Chto takoe vnutrenniaia sekretsiia?," *Gigiena i zdorov'e rabochei i krest'ianskoi sem'i* no. 6 (1928): 8–9.

23. Benjamin Buchloh, "From *Faktura* to Factography," p. 98.

24. "Protokol zasedaniia INKhUKA," January 1, 1921, manuscript, private archive, Moscow, cited in Lodder, *Russian Constructivism*, p. 88.

25. Christine Schick first drew my attention to the affinities between the troglodyte photomontage and Ioganson's structures ("LEF and the West: Constructivism and Dada in Rodchenko's *Pro Eto*," unpublished paper, Department of the History of Art, University of California, Berkeley, 2000). On the tensegrity principle, the OBMOKhU exibition and the important distinctions in the mode of reference to engineering between the works of Ioganson, the Stenbergs, and Rodchenko, see Maria Gough, "In the Laboratory of Constructivism: Karl Ioganson's Cold Structures," *October* 84 (spring 1998): 90–117.

26. He complains that a troglodyte beast from the ancient past has crawled into the telephone cord, only to go on to admit "No one crawled or is crawling into the telephone, / there is no troglodyte mug / I myself am at the telephone" (p. 72).

27. On Mayakovsky's writings on advertising, see Leah Dickerman, "The Propagandizing of Things," p. 67.

28. Lenin wrote his famous book *What Is To Be Done?* on party strategy in 1902, giving it the title of the scandalous novel about the "new people" of the left Russian intelligentsia written by the radical Nikolai Chernyshevsky in 1863.

29. Rodchenko, "Rabota s Maiakovskim," in Varvara A. Rodchenko, ed., *A. M. Rodchenko: Stat'i, vospominaniia, autobiograficheskie zapiski, pis'ma* (Moscow: Sovetskii khudozhnik, 1982), p. 65. The 1939 manuscript "Rabota s Maiakovskim" (Working with Mayakovsky), held in the Manuscript Department of the State Mayakovsky Museum, Moscow, is Rodchenko's account of the history of their collaboration. Much of it is published, in significantly different versions, in V. A. Rodchenko, ed., *A. M. Rodchenko*, pp. 53–82 and Aleksandr Rodchenko, *Opyty dlia budushchego*, pp. 203–259. The latter version is translated in Aleksandr Rodchenko, *Experiments for the Future: Diaries, Essays, Letters, and Other Writings*, ed. and with a preface by Alexander N. Lavrentiev, trans. and annotated by Jamey Gambrell, with an introduction by John E. Bowlt (New York: The Museum of Modern Art, 2005).

30. Vladimir Maiakovskii, "Agitatsiia i reklama," *Tovarishch Terentii* 14 (June 10, 1923); reprinted in his *Polnoe sobranie sochinenii*, vol. 12 (Moscow: Gosudarstvennoe izdatel'stvo Khudozhestvennoi literatury, 1959), pp. 57–58. Translated in Elena Chernevich, "Introduction," in Mikhail Anikst, ed., *Soviet Commercial Design of the Twenties*, trans. Catherine Cooke (New York: Abbeville Press, 1987), p. 23, translation modified.

31. For a detailed account of the history and politics of Soviet advertising during NEP, see Randi Cox, "'NEP without Nepmen!': Soviet Advertising and the Transition to Socialism," in Christina Kiaer and Eric Naiman, eds., *Everyday Life in Early Soviet Russia: Taking the Revolution Inside* (Bloomington: Indiana University Press, 2005), pp. 119–152.

32. On Mayakovsky's political activities in his youth, see Brown, *Mayakovsky*, chapter 2.

33. V. I. Lenin, *Polnoe sobranie sochinenii*, fifth ed., vol. 45, p. 98, cited and translated in Ball, *Russia's Last Capitalists*, p. 19.

34. Rodchenko, "Rabota s Maiakovskim," in V. A. Rodchenko, ed., *A. M. Rodchenko*, p. 67.

35. Rodchenko made the cooking oil poster on October 2, 1923, and the bread poster on October 4, 1923, according to the receipts for payment for the posters that Mayakovsky submitted to Mossel'prom. These receipts are held in the Manuscript Department of the State Mayakovsky Museum, Moscow, in the file (*papka*) on "Agitreklama: Dokumenty," item numbers 7921–7976.

36. Price regulation was in fact adopted in late December. The economic crisis that came to a head in October 1923 is known as the "scissors" crisis, referring to the visual image of the graph depicting the relation between the price paid to the peasant for agricultural produce, which was low, and the price of manufactured consumer goods, which was prohibitively high. This meant that the peasantry had little incentive to market surplus grain and was unable to purchase manufactured goods. The reasons for the crisis and the possible solutions to it were complex; blaming the NEP middlemen for the high consumer prices was one convenient strategy. For a detailed discussion of the economic situation at this time, see Edward Hallett Carr, *A History of Soviet Russia: The Interregnum 1923–1924* (London: Macmillan, 1954) and Ball, *Russia's Last Capitalists*, chapter 2, especially pp. 39–44.

37. Cited in Vasilii Katanian, *Maiakovskii: Khronika zhizni i deiatel'nosti*, fifth ed. (Moscow: Sovetskii pisatel', 1985), p. 259.

38. On the details of pricing policies for advertisements in the Soviet press in the 1920s, see Randi Cox, "'NEP without Nepmen!'"

39. The price list is held in the Manuscript Department of the State Mayakovsky Museum, Moscow, item number 7965.

40. V. Krasnov, *Kratkie svedeniia o rabote Mossel'proma s oktiabria 1923 g. po aprel' 1924 g.* (Moscow, 1925).

41. "V tarifno-normirovochnyi otdel sektsii izobrazitel'nogo iskusstva moskovskogo gubernskogo soiuza rabotnikov iskusstva [1924]," published in Maiakovskii, *Polnoe sobranie sochinenii*, vol. 13 (Moscow: Gosudarstvennoe izdatel'stvo Khudozhestvennoi literatury, 1961), p. 209.

42. Paul Wood discusses the Constructivists' self-consciousness about their complicated positions as skilled specialists aligned with management in his "Art and Politics in a Workers' State," pp. 112–114.

43. See Krasnov, *Kratkie svedeniia o rabote Mossel'proma*.

44. Ibid., p. 12. He was forced to admit this fact because it had been exposed by the writer Dem'ian Bednyi in a recent newspaper article. He states that building workers' dormitories is a top priority for Mossel'prom management, but he cautions that they are not a group of private capitalists, but rather servants of the workers' government, and therefore do not have control over their own profits to help their workers.

45. Central State Archive of Moscow Oblast' (TSGAMO), f. 1033. (Mossel'prom), op. 2, d. 191.

46. TSGAMO, f. 1033 (Mossel'prom), op. 2, d. 191, p. 34. The last record of payment to him is dated April 9, 1926. He may have stopped working there earlier but continued to receive back pay; on this possibility, see f. 1033, op. 3, d. 134, p. 131.

47. See the minutes of a meeting on January 8, 1925, at which Brik gave a report to which the highest management responded with demands for greater financial efficiency in his department, in TSGAMO, f. 1033, op. 9, d. 3, p. 77, and also the memo in f. 1033, op. 2, d. 212, p. 217. Brik's job was to manage the cabaret and theatrical entertainments that were performed at many of the seventy-six Moscow pubs. He describes how he reorganized the pub entertainments in a short book entitled *Estrada pered stolikami (v poiskakh novoi estradi)* (The stage in front of the little tables: in search of the new stage) (Moscow-Leningrad: Teakinopechat', 1927), but from his description it sounds like the kind of single-task consulting job typical for a cultural worker like himself, rather than the full-time position that it appears to have been. His job as a Mossel'prom manager was not something he actively tried to hide, so much as something he did not consider central to his public image. (This raises the question of another biographical fact about his working life that was not part of his public persona, namely, his work for the Cheka.) Brik's position at Mossel'prom is mentioned briefly, with no details or discussion, by a researcher who uncovered the information for an article on Mossel'prom; see V. R. Aronov, "Firmennyi stil' Mossel'proma v sovetskoi Rossii 20-30-kh godov," in *Stranitsy istorii otechestvennogo dizaina*, Tekhnicheskaia estetika, vol. 59 (Moscow: VNIITE, 1989), pp. 91–108. The only mention of Brik having anything beyond a consulting job at Mossel'prom in the biographical literature is in the brief memoirs of L. Varshavskaia; she remembers walking as a little girl in 1925 with Lili Brik past the famous, modernist Mossel'prom office building in Moscow (which had one wall decorated by Rodchenko), when Lili pointed to Osip's office and said that he worked there. See L. Varshavskaia, "Chto Ia pomniu," in Anatolii Valiuzhenich, ed., *Osip Maksimovich Brik: Materialy k biografii* (Akmola, Kazakhstan: Niva, 1993), p. 166.

48. Osip Brik, "Iskusstvo ob"iavliat'," *Zhurnalist* no. 6 (1923): 26.

49. Osip Brik, "Kakaia nam nuzhna reklama," *Zhurnalist* no. 10 (1924): 62.

50. Karl Marx, *Grundrisse: Foundations of the Critique of Political Economy (Rough Draft)*, trans. Martin Nicolaus (Middlesex: Penguin, 1973), p. 92. The notebooks that make up the *Grundrisse* were not published until 1939, so Brik could not have been referring directly to Marx's words, though he was well informed in Marxism. For the publication history of the *Grundrisse*, see the foreword by Nicolaus, p. 7.

51. Brik, "Kakaia nam nuzhna reklama," p. 61. "Mastering the wishes of the customer" translates his phrase *ovladevanie pokupatel'skoi volei.*

52. The collective pleasure of cigarette smoking was one of the democratic pleasures of modernity, cutting across social classes, and the cigarette became, especially after World War I, one of modernity's ubiquitous symbols. The erotics of the cigarette dominate the photographs that we have of Russian avant-garde figures from the 1920s, including many of Rodchenko's photographs of Stepanova (see figures 1.4 and 3.6). Harnessing the pleasures of smoking for the cause of the revolution would transform one of the prime commodities of modernity into a socialist object. On the cultural and literary history of the cigarette, see Richard Klein, *Cigarettes Are Sublime* (Durham: Duke University Press, 1993).

53. In act 1, scene 6, Carmen throws a flower to Don Jose, who comments on its strong scent; in act 2, scene 5, a festive scene at an inn, Carmen buys treats for the guests: a dish of oranges, sweets, crystallized fruits, and Manzanilla. See Georges Bizet, *Carmen*, trans. Nell and John Moody (London: John Calder, 1982). I am indebted to Jonathan Neil for suggesting the connection between Mayakovsky's Shutka rhyme and Bizet's *Carmen* ("Advertising Diction: Russian Constructivist Cigarette Advertising during the New Economic Policy [NEP]," unpublished paper, Department of Art History and Archaeology, Columbia University, 1997).

54. See Louis Althusser, *Lenin and Philosophy*, trans. Ben Brewster (New York: Monthly Review Press, 1971), p. 174.

55. On "awakening," see especially section K (Dream City and Dream House, Dreams of the Future, Anthropological Nihilism, Jung) in Benjamin, *The Arcades Project*, and Susan Buck-Morss's evocative gloss of this idea, in *The Dialectics of Seeing*, chap. 8, esp. pp. 265–275.

56. Iakobson, "O pokolenii," pp. 22–23, translated in Jakobson, "On a Generation That Squandered Its Poets," p. 228.

57. Iakobson, "O pokolenii," p. 30, translated in Jakobson, "On a Generation That Squandered Its Poets," p. 239.

58. Melanie Klein's theory of object-relations, and in particular of the mother's breast as a part-object, is elaborated in her essay "Some Theoretical Conclusions Regarding the Emotional Life of the Infant," in *Developments in Psychoanalysis*, ed. Joan Riviere (New York: Da Capo Press, 1983), pp. 198–236.

59. On the history of psychoanalysis in Russia, see Aleksandr Etkind, *Eros nevozmozhnogo: istoriia psikhoanaliza v Rossii* (St. Petersburg: Meduza, 1994), in English as *Eros of the Impossible: The History of Psychoanalysis in Russia*, translated by Noah and Maria Rubins (Boulder: Westview Press, 1997). Arvatov demonstrates his familiarity with psychoanalysis in an essay

of 1923, where he writes that it is time we recognized that in the experimental research of figures such as Freud, Jung, and Adler "are collected the richest living, everyday materials; that the scientific organization of psychic life is turning, before our very eyes, from utopia to existing reality." See "Grazhd. Akhmatova i Tov. Kollontai," p. 150. This essay, discussed above in chapter 2, note 42, was his critical response to the Bolshevik feminist Aleksandra Kollontai's famous essay, "Make Way for Winged Eros!" ("Dorogu Krylatomu Erosu!"). The psychoanalytic definitions of the oral drive, of sadism and masochism and their reversibility, were most likely not directly available to Rodchenko, but it is highly possible that he read Arvatov's essay with its praise of psychoanalysis, because he designed the cover of the issue of the journal *Molodaia gvardiia* in which it was published.

60. Tret'iakov, "Otkuda i kuda?," p. 200.

61. Rodchenko, "Rabota s Maiakovskim" in V. A. Rodchenko, ed., *A. M. Rodchenko*, p. 67.

62. While more conservative, Rodchenko's final version of the Embassy cigarette ad still deploys the technique of incorporating a non-Soviet, nonsocialist image into the composition: the cover design of the Embassy cigarette box is dominated by the American flag.

63. Shauna Toh proposed the concept of the interface, especially the oral interface, in her analysis of Mayakovsky's relation to *byt* ("Mayakovsky's Interface with *Byt*," unpublished paper, Department of Art History and Archaeology, Columbia University, 1997).

64. D. W. Winnicott, "Transitional Objects and Transitional Phenomena: A Study of the First Not-Me Possession," *Yearbook of Psychoanalysis* 10 (1954): 64–80.

65. The transitional aspect of Constructivist advertisements can be compared to the contemporary notion of "transitional" houses in Soviet architecture. One of the most famous of these experiments is the Constructivist architect Moisei Ginzburg's design for the Narkomfin Communal House, built in Moscow by the Russian Ministry of Finance in 1928–1930. With its designated communal spaces for child care, dining, laundry, and leisure activities, and with its array of apartment units ranging from traditional self-sufficient family dwellings to smaller units without kitchens to the extreme of dormitory rooms, it was designed to serve as a "social condenser," easing its inhabitants from their individualistic, bourgeois, and patriarchal living habits into communal, socialist, and gender-egalitarian ones. See Victor Buchli, *An Archaeology of Socialism*.

66. Victor Margolin has called attention to Rodchenko's advertising technique of showing "the product itself as an active object." See Margolin, *The Struggle for Utopia*, p. 117.

67. Bürger, *Theory of the Avant-Garde*, p. 54.

68. "The frustrating (bad) object is felt to be a terrifying persecutor, the good breast tends to turn into the 'ideal' breast which should fulfill the greedy desire for unlimited, immediate and everlasting gratification . . . the idealized breast forms the corollary of the persecuting breast." See Melanie Klein, "Some Theoretical Conclusions," pp. 201–202. The concept of the inherent reversibility of the aims of the drives originated with Freud; see, e.g., Sigmund Freud, "Instincts and Their Vicissitudes" (1915), in *General Psychological Theory: Papers on Metapsychology*, ed. Philip Rieff (New York: Collier Books, 1963).

69. See S. Frederick Starr, *Red and Hot: The Fate of Jazz in the Soviet Union, 1917–1980* (New York: Oxford University Press, 1983).

70. Arvatov, *Iskusstvo i proizvodstvo*, p. 119.

CHAPTER FIVE

1. Aleksandr Rodchenko, "Rodchenko v Parizhe. Iz pisem domoi," *Novyi Lef* 2 (1927): 20 (letter of May 4, 1925). Further references will be cited parenthetically in the body of the text as "Letters"; the date of the letter and page number from this publication will be given. A different, expanded version of the letters, but with some of his personal or subjective commentary omitted, was published in Aleksandr Rodchenko, *Opyty dlia budushchego*, pp. 135–169, translated in *Experiments for the Future*, pp. 148–186.

2. The meetings of the exhibition organizing committee are documented in the *Protokoly zasedanii vystavochnogo komiteta otdela SSSR Parizhskoi Mezhdunarodnoi Vystavki Dekorativnogo Iskusstva*, Russian State Archive of Literature and Art (RGALI), f. 941, op. 15, d. 13. The committee was led by Petr Semenovich Kogan, a literary critic and historian and president of the Academy of Artistic Sciences. Walter Benjamin, as a visiting literary figure in Moscow, had some dealings with Kogan, who did not impress him: "went to see Kogan, the president of the Academy. I was not surprised by his inconsequentiality; everybody had prepared me for it." See Benjamin, *Walter Benjamin: Moscow Diary*, trans. Richard Sieburth (Cambridge, Mass.: Harvard University Press, 1986), p. 70. The committee also included, among others, Nikolai Bartram of the Toy Museum (whom Benjamin also met in Moscow), art historian David Arkin, painter David Shterenberg, critic Iakov Tugendkhol'd, and theater administrator V. E. Morits.

3. The committee had selected Rodchenko's proposed design for the club after viewing sketches by a number of artists. It had also considered including many different model rooms representing diverse, if not contradictory, aspects of Soviet life. In addition to the workers' club, the only room finally completed, and the rural reading room (*izba-chital'naia*), which was included as a miniature model, there had been plans for a "world of the child" house to be completed by Nikolai Bartram of the Toy Museum, a workers' dormitory room, a "house of the peasant woman," a peasant theater, and a businessman's room (*komnata delovogo cheloveka*). See *Protokoly* no. 6, p. 23; no. 17, p. 64; no. 18, p. 74.

4. *Reglement* (Imprimerie National: Paris, 1922), cited in *Design 1920s: German Design and the Bauhaus, 1925–32; Modernism in the Decorative Arts, Paris, 1910–30*, prepared for the course team by Tim Benton, Charlotte Benton, and Aaron Scharf (Milton Keynes, England: Open University Press, 1975), p. 63.

5. The grand salon is reproduced as illustration 113 in *Design 1920s*; the comparison between this *Pavillon d'un Collectionneur* and Rodchenko's workers' club is made in Margolin, *The Struggle for Utopia*, pp. 94–95.

6. Gabriel Mourey, "L'Exposition des Arts Décoratifs et Industriels de 1925: Les tendances generales," *L'amour de l'art* no. 8 (1925): 285.

7. Jacques-Emile Blanche, "L'Exposition internationale de l'Art decoratif moderne," *Les Nouvelles Litteraires* no. 140 (June 20, 1925): 1.

8. *Protokoly* no. 6, December 5, 1924, p. 24.

9. On Mel'nikov's pavilion, see S. Frederick Starr, *Melnikov: Solo Architect in a Mass Society* (Princeton: Princeton University Press, 1978); S. Frederick Starr, *K. Mel'nikov: Le Pavillon Sovietique* (Paris: L'Equerre, 1981); and Selim. O. Khan-Magomedov, *Konstantin Mel'nikov* (Moscow: Stroiizdat, 1990).

10. Interview with Konstantin Mel'nikov, in B. Brodskii, *Khudozhnik, gorod, chelovek* (Moscow, 1966), pp. 15–16, cited in Khan-Magomedov, *Konstantin Mel'nikov*, p. 90.

11. One critic ended his long review of the Soviet section with the exhortation: "Allez voir les boites de Palek." See Leandre Vaillat, "A l'Exposition de 1925: U.R.S.S.," *Le Temps* (June 5, 1925): 3. The catalog to the Soviet section of the exhibition provides a full explanation of the exhibits, with illustrations. See *L'Art Décoratif et Industriel de l'U.R.S.S.* (Moscow: 1925). The exhibition comprised the following sections:

in the pavilion itself, the ground floor was filled with crafts and local manufacture from the various republics; the second floor contained the exhibition of Gosizdat, the State Publishing House; a gallery on the Esplanade des Invalides contained the workers' club as well as the model of the rural reading room (*izba-chital'naia*) executed by the Woodwork Faculty (*Derfak*) of VKhUTEMAS; and the six halls assigned to the Soviet Union in the Grand Palais contained (1) handicrafts from Russia and the republics; (2) works from VKhUTEMAS; (3) graphics, advertisements and architectural designs; (4) porcelain and glass; (5) textiles; and (6) theater design.

12. Iakov Tugendkhol'd, "L'Element national dans l'art de l'URSS," in *L'Art Décoratif et Industriel de l'U.R.S.S.*, pp. 27–28.

13. The printed notice is included in *Protokoly* no. 4, November 29, 1924, pp. 17–18.

14. The *Narkomvneshtorg* representative who was brought in was G. B. Iurgenson; see *Protokoly* no. 6, December 5, 1924, p. 21. He played his policing role well; soon committee members were devoting as much energy to business concerns as to artistic ones. See, e.g., *Protokoly* no. 11, December 22, 1924, p. 46.

15. *Protokoly* no. 7, December 8, 1924, p. 25.

16. Each participating business would be charged for the exhibition space allotted to it, with the price determined by the amount of space needed and the number of exhibited items, just as at a regular trade fair. See *Protokoly* no. 17, January 2, 1925, p. 67.

17. Iakov Tugendkhol'd, "Stil' 1925 goda. (Mezhdunarodnaia vystavka v Parizhe)," *Pechat' i revoliutsiia* no. 7 (1925): 42. My ellipsis is noted by the brackets; unbracketed ellipsis in the original.

18. See Manfredo Tafuri, "U.S.S.R.–Berlin, 1922: From Populism to 'Constructivist International,'" in Joan Ockman, ed., *Architecture, Criticism, Ideology* (Princeton: Princeton Architectural Press, 1985), pp. 121–181. Tafuri concludes that the utopian vision of Russian Constructivism led, in both the USSR and in Europe, to an apolitical ideology of technicism and total organization that was completely available to capitalism. For Jean Baudrillard's critique of the elitism and repressiveness of so-called utilitarian modern design, see *For a Critique of the Political Economy of the Sign*, trans. Charles Levin (St. Louis: Telos Press, 1981), especially his critique of the Bauhaus in chap. 10, "Design and Environment."

19. Hubertus Gassner, "The Constructivists: Modernism on the Way to Modernization," in *The Great Utopia*, pp. 298–319.

20. Ibid., p. 317.

21. Ibid., p. 318.

22. Ibid., p. 314. In linking the downfall of the Constructivist avant-garde to their loss of autonomy, and so to their loss of a critical position in relation to the Soviet state, Gassner seems to agree with Peter Bürger's view of the necessary autonomy of the avant-garde. Gassner suggests that the Constructivists' decision to throw in their lot with the Soviet campaign for industrialization stemmed not from a commitment to socialism, but from their self-interested struggle to maintain a power base within the Soviet system, after their initial success at taking over organizational posts in museums and art education was curtailed around 1920 (pp. 315–316). He offers no concrete evidence to support this suggestion, however.

23. Karl Marx, *Capital*, vol. I, p. 166.

24. Hal Foster, *Compulsive Beauty* (Cambridge, Mass.: MIT Press, 1993), p. 129.

25. Sigmund Freud, "The 'Uncanny'" (1919) in *Studies in Parapsychology*, ed. Philip Rieff (New York: Collier Books, 1963), p. 47. While Foster emphasizes the ways that the uncanny recalls infantile anxieties of blindness, castration, and death, Freud specifies that any kind of emotional affect, once repressed, can be the source of the "uncanny."

26. Freud, "The 'Uncanny,'" p. 47.

27. Rodchenko's letters fit the cultural trope of the Russian intellectual's epistle from Paris. As Svetlana Boym has noted, such travelers' accounts "combine personal and national self-fashioning"; since Peter the Great, "every journey of a Russian nobleman to Europe provokes a reflection on the fate of Russia." Her paradigmatic example is Dostoyevsky's "Winter Notes on Summer Impressions," in which France epitomizes self-interested individualism while Russia represents a higher level of community and spirituality. Rodchenko takes up the Dostoyevskian metaphors, but he transfers them from problems of human personality, freedom, and liberty to the liberation of things—and the source of object liberty in the East is not Russian spirituality, but the Bolshevik Revolution. See Boym, *Common Places*, pp. 74–75.

28. The details of his camera purchases were not included in the *Novyi Lef* version of the letters, perhaps because they were deemed too banal in their technicism. They did appear in the version published in Aleksandr Rodchenko, *Opyty dlia budushchego*, letters of May 2 (p. 151) on the Sept camera, and of May 23 (p. 160) on the ICA.

29. The phrase about the "millions of things" appears in *Novyi Lef* under the heading of the letter of May 4 but in fact stems from an undated letter from around May 10; see Aleksandr Rodchenko, *Opyty dlia budushchego*, p. 156.

30. Double beds were often negatively deployed in early Soviet literature as symbols of bourgeois sexuality. See Olga Matich, "Remaking the Bed: Utopia in Daily Life," in *Laboratory of Dreams: The Russian Avant-Garde and Cultural Experiment*, ed. John Bowlt and Olga Matich (Stanford: Stanford University Press, 1996): 59–78, and Birgitta Ingemanson, "The Political Function of Domestic Objects in the Fiction of Aleksandra Kollontai," *Slavic Review* 48, no. 1 (1989): 71–82.

31. The sentence on the interesting fashions was not published in the *Novyi Lef* version of the letter but appears in Aleksandr Rodchenko, *Opyty dlia budushchego*, p. 137.

32. This section on the home studio appears under the heading of March 28 in *Novyi Lef* but is actually from a letter of March 30, which is published in its entirety in Rodchenko, *Opyty dlia budushchego*, p. 140. The opportunity for Stepanova to print fabrics at home had become more relevant with the termination of her work at the First State Cotton-Printing Factory.

33. Rodchenko's description of women "in the style of negroes" is most likely a jab at the elongated and angular bodies of primitivist art, particularly Picasso's. His criticism of "women in the style of Picasso" seems quite clearly not to refer to Picasso's solid, bucolic, and maternal *rappel à l'ordre* women of the early 1920s, but rather to the famous pre-Cubist canvases that had been widely studied in Moscow avant-garde circles during the 1910s. Rodchenko later declares that he has discovered that the most beautiful women in Paris are the "negresses" who work as domestic help; he sees them in the cinema, where he likes the way they laugh infectiously at Chaplin films (Letters, April 19, p. 18). This comment carries its own racist baggage in the form of stereotyping, but it also shows that he equates ugliness not with the actual black women he encounters, but with the popular and artistic representational "style of 'negroes.'"

34. See Sigmund Freud, "Character and Anal Erotism" (1908) and "On the Transformation of Instincts with Special Reference to Anal Erotism" (1917), both in Philip Rieff, ed., *Character and Culture* (New York: Collier Books, 1963), pp. 27–33 and pp. 202–209, respectively.

35. In a rhetorical move of displacement, Rodchenko makes the slave—whom he, as a Marxist, knows to be a blameless victim of imperialism—into the active agent of catastrophe. The black body of the slave is

here a metaphor for the bodily density of the commodity, but for Rodchenko it appears that the metaphor of the slave's "black labor" is more related to dirt and excrement than to actual slave labor.

36. Walter Benjamin, "Moscow," in *Reflections*, ed. Peter Demetz, trans. Edmund Jephcott (New York: Schocken Books, 1978), p. 98. Future references will be cited parenthetically in the body of the text as "M."

37. See Susan Buck-Morss, "Spatial Origins," chap. 2 in *The Dialectics of Seeing*, pp. 25–43.

38. Buck-Morss argues for the importance of the complex metaphors of childhood and the fairy tale in Benjamin's philosophical thought. See "Dream World of Mass Culture," chap. 8 in *The Dialectics of Seeing*, pp. 253–286.

39. Benjamin, *Walter Benjamin: Moscow Diary*, p. 75.

40. The letter, dated February 23, 1927, is published in *Walter Benjamin: Moscow Diary*, p. 132. The phrase "everything factual is already theory" was taken from Goethe's writing on the "ur-phenomenon." See Susan Buck-Morss's discussion of Georg Simmel's study of Goethe and its influence on Benjamin in Buck-Morss, *The Dialectics of Seeing*, pp. 71–77.

41. Buck-Morss, *The Dialectics of Seeing*, p. 125.

42. My reading of Constructivism in relation to Benjamin suggests that there are certain similarities between the surrealist and Constructivist approaches to objects, contradicting the usual assumption that whereas surrealism explored the dream-relation to modern objects as a way to critique capitalist reification, Constructivism simply repressed desire and the dream in favor of constructing a new, reified socialist-industrial object.

43. Viacheslav Polonskii, "*Lef ili blef?*" (Lef or Bluff?), *Izvestiia*, February 25, 1927, p. 5. Future references to this one-page text will not be noted separately.

44. A. Zavedeev, "Veshch' i ideia," *Zhurnal dlia zhenshchin* no. 12 (1925): 9. Future references to this one-page text will not be noted separately. The magazine had been started in 1914 as competition for the successful *Zhurnal dlia khoziaek* (Housewives' Magazine), which had been started in 1913.

45. This poster is cataloged under the heading P2.XI.3 in the Department of Graphics, Russian State Library, Moscow. It is 107 x 72 cm., and was published in Leningrad in an edition of 20,000.

46. Another article in *Magazine for Women* in 1925, entitled "How to Shop," takes a similarly Constructivist tone to Zavedeev, advising women to organize a system to tackle the problems of shopping because it takes time and effort to find the right *veshch'*. The author suggests, among other things, making specific shopping lists, mapping a route, and wearing comfortable shoes. This brief article reveals that the assumption at the time was that women do most of the shopping, most people working in stores are women, women are responsible for all housework and meal preparation, and there are long lines in every store. For coping psychologically with long waits in line, she suggests using the time to look around and learn useful techniques from observing the shopping habits of others. See V. Levenets, "Kak nuzhno pokupat'," *Zhurnal dlia zhenshchin* no. 9 (1925): 9.

47. For the full text of the newspaper, reproduced only in English translation, see Drevina, Rodchenko, and Lavrentiev, eds., *Ornament and Textile Design*.

48. Leah Dickerman refers to the bottle as an "alcoholic superhero"; see Dickerman, "The Propagandizing of Things," p. 71.

49. This reading is in keeping with Freud's insistence on the inherent reversibility of the sexual instincts; see "Instincts and Their Vicissitudes."

50. Tugendkhol'd calls Rodchenko's club "dry and hard" and complains that the chairs are uncomfortable to sit in. See Tugendkhol'd, "Stil' 1925 goda," p. 65, n. 2. Dickerman discusses the discomfort of the club furniture; see "The Propagandizing of Things," p. 75. The reconstruction of the club produced by the Henry Art Gallery of the University of Washington, Seattle, which I saw at the exhibition "Art into Life" at the Walker Art Gallery in Minneapolis in 1990, confirmed Tugendkhol'd's criticism of the chairs: they were very uncomfortable, no matter the size and shape of the individual sitter.

51. These designs for workers' club furniture made under Rodchenko's direction at the Moscow Proletkul't workshop were published in the journal *Rabochii klub* (Workers' Club); they are illustrated in Khan-Magomedov, *Konstruktivizm*, pp. 350–351.

52. See the magazine *Rabochii klub* and such short books on the topic as *Pochemu vzroslyi rabochii ne idet v klub?* (Why Doesn't the Adult Worker Go to the Club?) (Moscow: Proletkul't, 1926); *Iskusstvo v rabochem klube* (Art in the Workers' Club) (Moscow: Vserossiiskii proletkul't, 1924); and *Zhenshchina i byt* (The Woman and Everyday Life) (Moscow: Proletkul't, 1926).

53. Polonskii responded to these remarks with particular indignation in his article in *Izvestiia*, challenging their veracity and taking them as an affront to the proletarian integrity of the Parisian workers: "Workers play football and dance in cafes—this is in 1925!—when there was a wave of workers' strikes against the war in Morocco!"

54. In the workers' club, the multifunctional, collapsible object works with the human body, but it had taken a different form in earlier Constructivist stage design. Stepanova's sets for Meyerhold's biomechanical staging of the play *The Death of Tarelkin* in 1922, for example, included transformable objects that demanded an acrobatic response from actors.

55. Rodchenko was not alone in his preoccupation with club cleanliness. Valerian Pletnev, president of the Federal Council of Proletkul't and an expert on workers' clubs, worried about the dirt and excrement he found in the typical Moscow workers' club with the same energy as Rodchenko in Paris: "Dirt, smoke, soot, peeling walls. . . . The buffet, in which you will always find cloudy tea resembling castor oil, and always in a dirty glass. . . . All of this on a dirty counter, with dirty chairs . . . from the toilet comes a breeze of poisonous air for breathing, the floors are full of holes." See V. F. Pletnev, *Rabochii klub: printsipy i metody raboty* (Moscow: Vserossiiskii proletkul't, 1923), p. 7.

56. Walter Benjamin, *The Arcades Project*, p. 396 (K3a,2), translation modified according to Buck-Morss, *The Dialectics of Seeing*, p. 123.

57. This article is published as an appendix in the *Moscow Diary*, pp. 123–124.

58. Buck-Morss, *The Dialectics of Seeing*, p. 275.

59. N. Neznamov, "Na parizhskoi vystavke," *Rabochii klub* no. 8–9 (1925): 82.

CHAPTER SIX

1. I cited a significantly different version of this section of the same text in chapter 4; the source was Rodchenko, "Rabota s Maiakovskim," in V. A. Rodchenko, ed., *A. M. Rodchenko*, p. 67. I take this citation from the version of the manuscript "Rabota s Maiakovskim" preserved in the Manuscript Department of the State Mayakovsky Museum, Moscow, p. 41.

2. Rodchenko, "Rabota s Maiakovskim," State Mayakovsky Museum, Moscow, p. 41.

3. Lissitzky is perhaps the most famous and highly regarded modernist artist of Russian Constructivism; his work has not formed a part of this project until now because during the

central years on which this study has focused, 1923–1925, he was working primarily abroad. In his autobiography, Lissitzky famously announced the importance he attached to his design work: "1926. My most important work as an artist begins: the creation of exhibitions." See El Lissitzky, "Autobiography," in *El Lissitzky* (Cologne: Galerie Gmurzynska, 1976), p. 89.

4. The play was not published in its entirety during Tret'iakov's lifetime. He published two scenes as "Khochu rebenka!" in *Novyi Lef* no. 3 (1927): 3–11, but the entire play (the first variant) was not published until 1988. See Tret'iakov, "Khochu rebenka," *Sovremennaia dramaturgiia* no. 2 (1988): 209–237. Future references to the play will be cited parenthetically in the text as "KhR," with page numbers from this publication given. The circumstances of the censors' decision to grant permission to Meyerhold to mount the play as a "discussion piece" are detailed in the commentary following the publication of the play in *Sovremennaia dramaturgiia*, pp. 238–243. An English translation of the play has appeared as Sergei Mikhailovich Tretyakov, *I Want a Baby*, trans. Stephen Holland, ed. Robert Leach (Birmingham: University of Birmingham, 1995).

5. S. M. Tret'iakov, "Chto pishut dramaturgi," *Rabis* no. 11 (1929): 11, cited in A. Fevral'skii, "S. M. Tret'iakov v teatre Meierkhol'da," in S. Tret'iakov, *Slyshish', Moskva?!—Protivogazy—Rychi, Kitai! (P'esy, stat'i, vospominaniia)* (Moscow: Iskusstvo, 1966), p. 204.

6. The script remains available only in a blurry carbon copy in the archives of Glaviskusstvo in the Russian State Archive of Literature and Art (RGALI). See RGALI, f. 645, op. 1, ed. kh. 536, pp. 28–55, which includes a two-page introduction to the script by Tret'iakov, and the handwritten comments of the censor, who did not approve it for production. The narrative of the script is essentially identical to that of the play, though the play's extensive dialogue is replaced, in the silent film, by terse intertitles augmented by vivid images and montage sequences. Tret'iakov had planned the film to be directed by Abram Room, who had directed the highly successful film *Tret'ia Meshchanskaia* (known in English as *Bed and Sofa*) in 1927. Future references to the script will be cited parenthetically in the body of the text as "KhR-S." The citation here is from p. 35.

7. See Groys, *The Total Art of Stalinism*, and my discussion of it in chapter 1.

8. In the "negative" model of eugenics, unfit men would be forcibly sterilized; this was practiced around this time in several states in the United States, originally in Indiana, but not in the USSR. On the history of eugenics in Russia, see Mark B. Adams, "Eugenics as Social Medicine in Revolutionary Russia," in *Health and Society in Revolutionary Russia*, ed. Susan Gross Solomon and John F. Hutchinson (Bloomington: Indiana University Press, 1990), pp. 200–223. For a more detailed analysis of eugenics in relation to the *novyi byt* and to Tret'iakov's *I Want a Child!*, see Christina Kiaer, "Delivered from Capitalism: Nostalgia, Alienation, and the Future of Reproduction in Tret'iakov's *I Want a Child!*," in Kiaer and Naiman, eds., *Everyday Life in Early Soviet Russia*, pp. 183–216.

9. Dr. Bernatskii, "Chto nuzhno znat', vybiraia muzha i zhenu" (What You Need to Know in Choosing a Husband or a Wife), *Gigiena i zdorov'e rabochei i krest'ianskoi sem'i* no. 15 (1928): 2.

10. Dr. Bernatskii, "Chto nuzhno znat', vybiraia muzha i zhenu (Okonchanie)," *Gigiena i zdorov'e rabochei i krest'ianskoi sem'i* no. 16 (1928): 6.

11. This androgynous female figure quickly faded from view in the return to more "normalized" gender roles during NEP, only to reappear again briefly in the wave of industrial enthusiasm of the first Five-Year Plan. The paradigmatic example of the Bolshevik ideal of the unfeminine Communist woman from the civil war years is the eponymous heroine of Aleksandra Kollontai's novella "Vasilisa Malygina," published in 1923 in her collection *Liubov' pchel trudovykh* (The Love of Worker Bees), and reprinted as *Svobodnaia Liubov'* (Free Love) (Riga: Stock, 1925). See Eric Naiman's reading of the novella in these terms in *Sex in Public*, chap. 6.

12. The rape itself formed a brief scene earlier in the play, entitled "Hooligans," before this reference to it in the scene in the doctor's office. Tret'iakov is referring to an immediately contemporary event: the gang rape by a group of twenty-six young men, some of them Komsomol members, of a young peasant woman in Chubarov Alley in Leningrad in August 1926. This disturbing rape received extensive press attention as an example of hooliganism among Soviet youth. Although it may seem unlikely that Tret'iakov would have added a whole new scene to his play within two weeks of its completion just to respond to this media event—the rape was first reported on September 12, and he signed a contract with Meyerhold to produce the play on September 28—this is precisely the kind of documentary attention to current events to which Tret'iakov was committed as a writer; the rape scene does not involve any of the main characters, nor is it organically connected to other scenes. Eric Naiman has analyzed the press accorded the Chubarov rape as an aspect of Party efforts to exercise greater control over the private lives of youth; see *Sex in Public*, ch. 7.

13. Sergei Tret'iakov, "Otkuda i kuda?," p. 201.

14. Ibid., p. 202.

15. Kollontai, "Dorogu Krylatomu Erosu!," p. 123.

16. Boris Arvatov, "Segodniashnie zadachi iskusstva v promyshlennosti," p. 86.

17. In early September, an editorial article appeared about the popularity of such contests abroad, especially in England and the United States: "Konkursy grudnykh detei," *Gigiena i zdorov'e rabochei i krest'ianskoi sem'i* no. 17 (1926): 9. Two weeks later, the magazine's own contest was announced, and an entry blank was included in the magazine; see the first-page editorial "K konkursu zdorovykh detei," *Gigiena i zdorov'e rabochei i krest'ianskoi sem'i* no. 18 (1926): 1.

18. El Lissitzky, "Der Innen-Aufbau des Theaters Meyerhold-Moskau für Tretjakows 'Ich will ein Kind,'" in *Das Neue Frankfurt* 4, no. 10 (1930): 226, translated and cited in Peter Nisbet, ed. *El Lissitzky, 1890–1941: Catalogue for an Exhibition of Selected Works from North American Collections, the Sprengel Museum Hanover, and the Staatliche Galerie Moritzburg Halle* (Cambridge, Mass.: Harvard University Art Museums, 1987), p. 40. Lissitzky signed a contract with Meyerhold's theater on March 28, 1929 to complete the stage set for *I Want a Child!* by April 10. See the Russian State Archive of Literature and Art (RGALI), f. 2361, ed. kh. 60, and Nisbet, *El Lissitzky*, p. 52, n. 102.

19. Jean-François Lyotard, "Espace Plastique et Espace Politique," in his *Dérive à Partir de Marx et Freud* (Paris: Union Générale d'Éditions, 1973), p. 303. I take the translation of this passage from Yve-Alain Bois, "El Lissitzky: Radical Reversibility," *Art in America* (April 1988): 169. Bois quotes Lyotard's reading to exemplify the image's nonfigural, anti-instrumental way of generating meaning, without remarking on the almost pictographic nature of the poster's figuration of sexual penetration. In another passage not cited by Bois, Lyotard's language equates the circle with femininity in the terms of contemporary French psychoanalytic discourse; the circle is "by nature a closed and fixed figure" and "is the figure of madness, the figure of death, which lacks the reference of its center" (Lyotard, "Espace Plastique," p. 297, my translation).

20. Naiman, *Sex in Public*, p. 114.

21. Naiman writes that "Meierkhol'd understood the theatrical, scripted character of the contemporary debate on sex, but he was disturbed by its (at least, apparent) lack of control from above"—hence his desire to mount the play as a controlled script that retained the appearance of an open discussion. See Naiman, *Sex in Public*, pp. 112–114.

22. El Lissitzky, "Blokada Rossii konchaetsia," pp. 74–75.

23. Quoted in Fevral'skii, "S. M. Tret'iakov v teatre Meierkhol'da," p. 204, translated in Naiman, *Sex in Public*, pp. 110–111.

24. Paul Wood, "The Politics of the Avant-Garde," p. 1.

BIBLIOGRAPHY

PRIMARY SOURCES: ARCHIVAL AND MUSEUM COLLECTIONS CITED

Central State Archive of Film and Photographic Documents, St. Petersburg

Central State Archive of Moscow Oblast' (TsGAMO), Moscow

Rodchenko–Stepanova Archive, Moscow

Russian Ethnographic Museum, St. Petersburg

Russian State Archive of Literature and Art (RGALI), Moscow

Russian State Library, Department of Graphics, Moscow

State Mayakovsky Museum, Moscow

PRIMARY SOURCES: PUBLISHED MATERIALS CITED

Aksenov, I. A. "Posmertnaia vystavka L. S. Popovoi." *Zhizn' iskusstva* no. 5 (February 3, 1925): 4–5.

Al'manakh proletkul'ta. Moscow: Proletkul't, 1925.

L'Art Décoratif et Industriel de l'U.R.S.S. Moscow: 1925.

Arvatov, Boris. "Byt i kul'tura veshchi (k postanovke voprosa)." In *Al'manakh proletkul'ta,* 75–82. Moscow: Proletkul't, 1925.

———. "Grazhd. Akhmatova i Tov. Kollontai." *Molodaia gvardiia* no. 4–5 (1923): 147–151.

———. "Iskusstvo i kachestvo promyshlennoi produktsii." *Sovetskoe iskusstvo* no. 7 (1925): 39–43.

———. *Iskusstvo i klassy.* Moscow-Petrograd: Gosudarstvennoe izdatel'stvo, 1923.

———. "Iskusstvo i proizvodstvo." *Gorn* no. 2 (7) (1922): 103–108.

———. *Iskusstvo i proizvodstvo. Sbornik statei.* Moscow: Proletkul't, 1926.

———. "Reaktsiia v zhivopisi." *Sovetskoe iskusstvo* no. 4–5 (1925): 70–74.

———. "Segodniashnie zadachi iskusstva v promyshlennosti." *Sovetskoe iskusstvo* no. 1 (1926): 83–89.

———. "Utopia ili nauka?" *Lef* no. 4 (1924): 16–21.

Bernatskii, Dr. "Chto nuzhno znat', vybiraia muzha i zhenu." *Gigiena i zdorov'e rabochei i krest'ianskoi sem'i* no. 15 (1928): 2–3.

———. "Chto nuzhno znat', vybiraia muzha i zhenu (Okonchanie)." *Gigiena i zdorov'e rabochei i krest'ianskoi sem'i* no. 16 (1928): 6.

Beskin, O. "Otvet napravo—zapros nalevo." *Sovetskoe iskusstvo* no. 6 (1925): 6–16.

Bizet, Georges. *Carmen.* Trans. Nell and John Moody. Opera Guide. London: John Calder, 1982.

Blanche, Jacques-Emile. "L'Exposition internationale de l'Art decoratif moderne" *Les Nouvelles Litteraires* no. 140 (June 20, 1925): 1, 6.

Brik, Osip. *Estrada pered stolikami (v poiskakh novoi estradi).* Moscow-Leningrad: Teakinopechat', 1927.

———. "Iskusstvo ob"iavliat'." *Zhurnalist* no. 6 (1923): 26–28.

———. "Kakaia nam nuzhna reklama." *Zhurnalist* no. 10 (1924): 61–62.

———. "Ot kartiny k sitsu." *Lef* no. 2 (1924): 34.

———. "V proizvodstvo!" *Lef* no. 1 (1923): 105–108.

Chuzhak, N. "Iskusstvo byta." *Sovetskoe iskusstvo* no. 4–5 (1925): 3–12.

———. "K zadacham dnia." *Lef* no. 2 (1923): 145–152.

Dal', Vladimir. *Tolkovyi slovar' zhivogo velikorusskogo iazyka,* vol. 1. 1863–1866. Reprint, Moscow: Russkii iazyk, 1978.

Iskusstvo v proizvodstve. Moscow: IZO Narkompros, 1921.

Iskusstvo v rabochem klube. Moscow: Vserossiiskii proletkul't, 1924.

"K konkursu zdorovykh detei." *Gigiena i zdorov'e rabochei i krest'ianskoi sem'i* no. 18 (1926): 1.

Kollontai, Aleksandra. "Dorogu krylatomu Erosu! (Pis'mo k trudiashcheisia molodezhi)." *Molodaia gvardiia* no. 3 (1923): 111–124.

———. "Vasilisa Malygina." In her *Liubov' pchel trudovykh*. 1923. Reprinted as *Svobodnaia liubov'*. Riga: Stock, 1925.

"Konkursy grudnykh detei." *Gigiena i zdorov'e rabochei i krest'ianskoi sem'i* no. 17 (1926): 9.

Krasnov, V. *Kratkie svedeniia o rabote Mossel'proma s oktiabria 1923g. po aprel' 1924g.* Moscow: 1925.

Kushner, Boris. "Organizatory proizvodstva." *Lef* no. 3 (1923): 97–103.

Levenets, V. "Kak nuzhno pokupat'." *Zhurnal dlia zhenshchin* no. 9 (1925): 9.

Lissitzky, El, and Ilya Ehrenburg. "Blokada Rossii konchaetsia," *Veshch'* no. 1–2 (March–April 1922): 1–4.

Maiakovskii, Vladimir. "Agitatsiia i reklama." *Tovarishch Terentii* no. 14 (June 10, 1923). Reprinted in *Polnoe sobranie sochinenii*, vol. 12, 57–58. Moscow: Gosudarstvennoe izdatel'stvo Khudozhestvennoi literatury, 1959.

———. "Pro Eto." *Lef* no. 1 (1923): 65–103.

———. "V tarifno-normirovochnyi otdel sektsii izobrazitel'nogo iskusstva moskovskogo gubernskogo soiuza rabotnikov iskusstva [1924]." In *Polnoe sobranie sochinenii*, vol. 13, 209. Moscow: Gosudarstvennoe izdatel'stvo Khudozhestvennoi literatury, 1961.

Malevich, Kazimir. "Konstruktivnaia zhivopis' russkikh khudozhnikov i konstruktivizm." *Nova generatsiia* (Kharkhov) no. 8 (1929): 47–54. Reprinted in *Kazimir Malevich: Sobranie sochinenii v piati tomakh*, vol. 2, 198–202, ed. A. C. Shatskikh and G. L. Demosfenova. Moscow: Gileia, 1998.

Miklashevskii, Konstantin. *Gipertrofiia iskusstva.* Petrograd: 1924.

"Modnaia khronika." *Zhurnal dlia Khoziaek* no. 1 (1922): 3.

Mossel'prom v 1924–25 godu. Moscow: Moskovskoe Ob"edinenie Predpriiatii po pererabotke produktov sel'sko-khoziaistvennoi promyshlennosti "Mossel'prom," 1925.

Mourey, Gabriel. "L'Exposition des Arts Décoratifs et Industriels de 1925: Les tendances generales." *L'amour de l'art* no. 8 (1925): 285.

Neznamov, N. "Na parizhskoi vystavke." *Rabochii klub* no. 8–9 (1925): 81–82.

"Novyi byt." *Krasnaia panorama* no. 23 (1924): 17.

Oppel', V. "Chto takoe vnutrenniaia sekretsiia?" *Gigiena i zdorov'e rabochei i krest'ianskoi sem'i* no. 6 (1928): 8–9.

"Pamiati L. S. Popovoi." *Lef* no. 2 (1924): 4.

Pel'she, Robert. "O nekotorykh oshibkakh 'Lefovtsev'." *Sovetskoe iskusstvo* no. 4–5 (1925): 13–22.

Pletnev, V. F. *Rabochii klub: printsipy i metody raboty.* Moscow: Vserossiiskii proletkul't, 1923.

Pochemu vzroslyi rabochii ne idet v klub? Moscow: Proletkul't, 1926.

Polonskii, Viacheslav. "Lef ili blef?" *Izvestiia*, February 25, 1927: 5.

Rodchenko, Aleksandr. *Experiments for the Future: Diaries, Essays, Letters, and Other Writings.* Ed. and with a preface by Alexander N. Lavrentiev, trans. and annotated by Jamey Gambrell, with an introduction by John E. Bowlt. New York: The Museum of Modern Art, 2005.

———. *Opyty dlia budushchego: dnevniki, stat'i, pis'ma, zapiski.* Moscow: Grant', 1996.

———. "Rodchenko v Parizhe. Iz pisem domoi." *Novyi Lef* no. 2 (1927): 9–21.

Rodchenko, Varvara A., ed. *A. M. Rodchenko: Stat'i, vospominaniia, avtobiograficheskie zapiski, pis'ma.* Moscow: Sovetskii khudozhnik, 1982.

Shevchenko, Aleksandr. *Neo-primitivizm. Ego teoriia. Ego vozmozhnosti. Ego dostizheniia.* Moscow: 1913.

Stepanova, Varvara. *Chelovek ne mozhet zhit' bez chuda: pis'ma, poeticheskie opyty, zapiski khudozhnitsy*. Ed. V. A. Rodchenko and A. N. Lavrent'ev with N. C. Lavrent'ev. Moscow: Sfera, 1994.

———. "Kostium segodniashnego dnia—prozodezhda." *Lef* no. 2 (1923): 65–68.

Teknika i iskusstvo shveinoi promyshlennosti no. 2. 1925.

"Transcript of the Discussion of Comrade Stepanova's Paper 'On Constructivism,'" December 22, 1921, private archive. In *Art into Life: Russian Constructivism, 1914–1932*, 74–79. Trans. James West. New York: Rizzoli, 1990.

Tret'iakov, Sergei. *I Want a Baby*. Trans. Stephen Holland, ed. Robert Leach. Studies in Drama and Dance. Birmingham: University of Birmingham, 1995.

———. "Khochu rebenka!" *Novyi Lef* no. 3 (1927): 3–11.

———. "Khochu rebenka." *Sovremennaia dramaturgiia* no. 2 (1988): 209–237.

———. "LEF i NEP." *Lef* no. 2 (1923): 70–78.

———. "Otkuda i kuda?" *Lef* no. 1 (1923): 192–203.

———. *Slyshish', Moskva?!—Protivogazy—Rychi, Kitai! (P'esy, stat'i, vospominaniia)*. Moscow: Iskusstvo, 1966.

Trotskii, L. *Literatura i revoliutsiia*. 1923. Reprint, Moscow: Izdatel'stvo politicheskoi literatury, 1991.

———. *Voprosy byta*. Moscow: Krasnaia nov', 1923.

Trotsky, Leon. *Problems of Everyday Life and Other Writings on Culture and Science*. New York: Monad Press, 1973.

Tugendkhol'd, Iakov. "L'Element national dans l'art de l'URSS." In *L'Art Décoratif et Industriel de l'U.R.S.S.* Moscow: 1925.

———. "Pamiati L. Popovoi." *Khudozhnik i zritel'* vol. 6, no. 7 (1924): 76–77.

———. "Stil' 1925 goda. (Mezhdunarodnaia vystavka v Parizhe.)" *Pechat' i revoliutsiia* no. 7 (1925): 29–66.

Vaillat, Leandre. "A l'Exposition de 1925: U.R.S.S." *Le Temps* (June 5, 1925): 3.

Zavedeev, A. "Veshch' i ideia." *Zhurnal dlia zhenshchin* no. 12 (1925): 9.

Zhenshchina i byt. Kabinet klubnogo rabotnika moskovskogo proletkul'ta. Moscow: Proletkul't, 1926.

SECONDARY SOURCES CITED

Adams, Mark B. "Eugenics as Social Medicine in Revolutionary Russia." In *Health and Society in Revolutionary Russia*, 200–223, ed. Susan Gross Solomon and John F. Hutchinson. Bloomington: Indiana University Press, 1990.

Adaskina, Natalia L. "Constructivist Fabrics and Dress Design." *Journal of Decorative and Propaganda Arts* 5 (summer 1987): 144–159.

Akademiia Nauk SSSR, Institut Russkogo Iazyka. *Slovar' sovremennogo russkogo literaturnogo iazyka*, vol. 2. Moscow-Leningrad: Izdatel'stvo Akademii nauk SSSR, 1951.

Althusser, Louis. *Lenin and Philosophy*. Trans. Ben Brewster. New York: Monthly Review Press, 1971.

Anikst, Mikhail, ed., and Elena Chernevich. *Soviet Commercial Design of the Twenties*. Trans. Catherine Cooke. New York: Abbeville Press, 1987.

Aronov, V. R. "Firmennyi stil' Mossel'proma v sovetskoi Rossii 20-30-kh godov." In *Stranitsy istorii otechestvennogo dizaina*, 91–108. Tekhnicheskaia estetika, vol. 59. Moscow: VNIITE, 1989.

Art into Life: Russian Constructivism, 1914–1932. New York: Rizzoli, 1990.

Ball, Alan M. *Russia's Last Capitalists: The Nepmen, 1921–29*. Berkeley: University of California Press, 1987.

Baudrillard, Jean. *For a Critique of the Political Economy of the Sign*. Trans. Charles Levin. St. Louis: Telos Press, 1981.

Benjamin, Walter. *The Arcades Project*. Trans. Howard Eiland and Kevin McLaughlin.

Cambridge, Mass.: Belknap Press of Harvard University Press, 1999.

———. "Moscow." In *Reflections*, 97–130, trans. Edmund Jephcott, ed. Peter Demetz. New York: Schocken Books, 1978.

———. "One-Way Street." In *Reflections*, 61–94, trans. Edmund Jephcott, ed. Peter Demetz. New York: Schocken Books, 1978.

———. *Walter Benjamin: Moscow Diary*. Trans. Richard Sieburth. Cambridge, Mass.: Harvard University Press, 1986.

———. "The Work of Art in the Age of Mechanical Reproduction." In *Illuminations*, 217–251, trans. Harry Zohn, ed. and with an introduction by Hannah Arendt. New York: Schocken Books, 1978.

Bernstein, Frances Lee. "'What Everyone Should Know about Sex': Gender, Sexual Enlightenment, and the Politics of Health in Revolutionary Russia, 1918–1931." Ph.D. dissertation, Columbia University, 1997.

Blanchot, Maurice. "Everyday Speech." *Yale French Studies* 73 (1987): 12–20.

Bois, Yve-Alain. "El Lissitzky: Radical Reversibility." *Art in America* (April 1988): 161–181.

Bowlt, John E. "A Brazen Can-Can in the Temple of Art: The Russian Avant-Garde and Popular Culture." In *Modern Art and Popular Culture: Readings in High and Low*, 134–158, ed. Kirk Varnedoe and Adam Gopnik. New York: Abrams, 1990.

———, ed. *Russian Art of the Avant-Garde: Theory and Criticism, 1902–1934*. The Documents of Modern Art. New York: The Viking Press, 1976.

Bowlt, John E., and Matthew Drutt, eds. *Amazons of the Russian Avant-Garde*. New York: The Solomon R. Guggenheim Foundation, 2000.

Boym, Svetlana. *Common Places: Mythologies of Everyday Life in Russia*. Cambridge, Mass.: Harvard University Press, 1994.

Brown, Edward J. *Mayakovsky: A Poet in the Revolution*. Princeton: Princeton University Press, 1973. Reprint, New York: Paragon House, 1988.

Buchli, Victor. *An Archaeology of Socialism*. Oxford: Berg, 1999.

Buchloh, Benjamin. "From *Faktura* to Factography." *October* 30 (1984): 83–119.

Buck-Morss, Susan. "Aesthetics and Anaesthetics." *October* 62 (fall 1992): 3–41.

———. *The Dialectics of Seeing: Walter Benjamin and the Arcades Project*. Cambridge, Mass.: MIT Press, 1989.

———. *Dreamworld and Catastrophe: The Passing of Mass Utopia in East and West*. Cambridge, Mass.: MIT Press, 2000.

Bürger, Peter. *Theory of the Avant-Garde*. Trans. Michael Shaw. Theory and History of Literature, ed. Wlad Godzich and Jochen Schulte-Sasse, vol. 4. Minneapolis: University of Minnesota Press, 1984.

Butler, Judith. *Bodies that Matter: On the Discursive Limits of "Sex."* New York: Routledge, 1993.

Carr, Edward Hallett. *A History of Soviet Russia: The Interregnum 1923–1924*. London: Macmillan, 1954.

Chernyshevsky, Nikolai. *What Is to Be Done?* Trans. Michael R. Katz, annotated by William G. Wagner. Ithaca, N.Y.: Cornell University Press, 1989.

Chicago, Judy. *Through the Flower: My Struggle as a Woman Artist*. Garden City, N.Y.: Anchor Books, 1977.

Clements, Barbara Evans. *Bolshevik Feminist: The Life of Aleksandra Kollontai*. Bloomington: Indiana University Press, 1979.

Cooke, Catherine. *Russian Avant-Garde Theories of Art, Architecture, and the City*. London: Academy Editions, 1995.

Costume Revolution: Textiles, Clothing, and Costume of the Soviet Union in the Twenties. Trans. Elizabeth Dafinone, from the Italian. London: Trefoil, 1989.

Cox, Randi. "'NEP without Nepmen!': Soviet Advertising and the Transition to Socialism." In Christina Kiaer and Eric Naiman, eds., *Everyday Life in Early Soviet Russia: Taking the Revolution Inside*, 119–152. Bloomington: Indiana University Press, 2005.

Delphy, Christine. *Close to Home: A Materialist Analysis of Women's Oppression.* Trans. Diana Leonard. Amherst: University of Massachusetts Press, 1984.

Demosfenova, G. L., and A. C. Shatskikh, eds. *Kazimir Malevich: Sobranie sochinenii v piati tomakh*, vol. 2. Moscow: Gileia, 1998.

Design 1920s: German Design and the Bauhaus, 1925–32; Modernism in the Decorative Arts, Paris, 1910–30. Prepared for the course team by Tim Benton, Charlotte Benton, and Aaron Scharf. Milton Keynes, England: Open University Press, 1975.

Dickerman, Leah. "The Propagandizing of Things." In *Aleksandr Rodchenko*, 62–99, ed. Magdalena Dabrowski, Leah Dickerman, and Peter Galassi. New York: The Museum of Modern Art, 1998.

———, ed. *Building the Collective: Soviet Graphic Design, 1917–1937.* New York: Princeton Architectural Press, 1996.

Drevina, Katerina, Varvara Rodchenko, and Alexander Lavrentiev, eds. *Ornament and Textile Design.* Moscow: Manege Gallery, 1990.

Dunham, Vera S. *In Stalin's Time: Middle Class Values in Soviet Fiction.* Studies of the Harriman Institute. Durham: Duke University Press, 1990.

Dyogot, Ekaterina. "Creative Women, Creative Men, and Paradigms of Creativity: Why Have There Been Great Women Artists?" In *Amazons of the Avant-Garde*, 109–127, ed. John Bowlt and Matthew Drutt. New York: Solomon R. Guggenheim Foundation, 2000.

Eagleton, Terry. *The Ideology of the Aesthetic.* Cambridge: Basil Blackwell, 1990.

El' Lisitskii, 1890–1941. Moscow: Gosudarstvennaia Tret'iakovskaia galeria, 1991.

El Lissitzky. Cologne: Galerie Gmurzynska, 1976.

Etkind, Aleksandr. *Eros nevozmozhnogo: istoriia psikhoanaliza v Rossii.* St. Petersburg: Meduza, 1994.

Etkind, Alexander. *Eros of the Impossible: The History of Psychoanalysis in Russia.* Trans. Noah and Maria Rubins. Boulder: Westview Press, 1997.

Farnsworth, Beatrice. *Aleksandra Kollontai: Socialism, Feminism, and the Bolshevik Revolution.* Stanford: Stanford University Press, 1980.

Fer, Briony. "The Language of Construction." In *Realism, Rationalism, Surrealism: Art between the Wars*, 87–169, ed. Briony Fer, David Batchelor, and Paul Wood. Modern Art: Practices and Debates, Open University, vol. 3. New Haven and London: Yale University Press, 1993.

———. "What's in a Line? Gender and Modernity." *Oxford Art Journal* 13, no. 1 (1990): 77–88.

Foster, Hal. *Compulsive Beauty.* Cambridge, Mass.: MIT Press, 1993.

———. "Who's Afraid of the Neo-Avant-Garde?" In his *The Return of the Real: The Avant-Garde at the End of the Century*, 1–34. October Books. Cambridge, Mass.: MIT Press, 1996.

Foucault, Michel. *Discipline and Punish: The Birth of the Prison.* Trans. Alan Sheridan. New York: Vintage, 1979.

Freud, Sigmund. "Character and Anal Erotism [1908]." In *Character and Culture*, 27–33, ed. Philip Rieff. New York: Collier Books, 1963.

———. "Instincts and Their Vicissitudes [1915]." In *General Psychological Theory: Papers on Metapsychology*, 83–103, ed. Philip Rieff. New York: Collier Books, 1963.

———. "On the Transformation of Instincts

with Special Reference to Anal Erotism [1917]." In *Character and Culture*, 202–209, ed. Philip Rieff. New York: Collier Books, 1963.

———. "The "Uncanny" [1919]." In *Studies in Parapsychology*, 19–60, ed. Philip Rieff. New York: Collier Books, 1963.

Gassner, Hubertus. "The Constructivists: Modernism on the Way to Modernization." In *The Great Utopia: The Russian and Soviet Avant-Garde, 1915–1932*, 298–319. New York: Guggenheim Museum, 1992.

Goldman, Wendy Z. *Women, the State, and Revolution: Soviet Family Policy and Social Life, 1917–36*. Cambridge: Cambridge University Press, 1993.

Gough, Maria. "*Faktura*: The Making of the Russian Avant-Garde." *Res* 36 (1999): 32–59.

———. "In the Laboratory of Constructivism: Karl Ioganson's Cold Structures." *October* 84 (spring 1998): 90–117.

———. "Switched On: Notes on Radio, Automata, and the Bright Red Star." In *Building the Collective: Soviet Graphic Design, 1917–1937*, 39–55, ed. Leah Dickerman. New York: Princeton Architectural Press, 1996.

The Great Utopia: The Russian and Soviet Avant-Garde, 1915–1932. New York: Guggenheim Museum, 1992.

Greenberg, Clement. *The Collected Essays and Criticism*, 4 vols. Ed. John O'Brian. Chicago: University of Chicago Press, 1986–1993.

Groys, Boris. *The Total Art of Stalinism: Avant-Garde, Aesthetic Dictatorship, and Beyond*. Trans. Charles Rougle. Princeton: Princeton University Press, 1992.

Harten, Jürgen, and Anatolii Strigalev. *Vladimir Tatlin Retrospektive*. Cologne: DuMont Buchverlag, 1992.

Hutchings, Stephen C. "Photographic Eye as Poetic I: Maiakovskii's and Rodchenko's *Pro Eto* Project (1923)." *History of Photography* 24, no. 4 (winter 2000): 300–308.

Iakobson, Roman. "O pokolenii, rastrativshem svoikh poetov." In *Smert' Vladimira Maiakovskogo*, 8–34. The Hague: Mouton, 1975.

Ingemanson, Birgitta. "The Political Function of Domestic Objects in the Fiction of Aleksandra Kollontai." *Slavic Review* 48, no. 1 (1989): 71–82.

Jakobson, Roman. "On a Generation That Squandered Its Poets." In *Roman Jakobson: My Futurist Years*, 209–245, trans. Stephen Rudy and ed. Bengt Jangfeldt and Stephen Rudy. New York: Marsilio, 1992.

Jangfeldt, Bengt, ed. *Love Is the Heart of Everything: Correspondence between Vladimir Mayakovsky and Lili Brik, 1915–1930*. Edinburgh: Polygon, 1986.

Katanian, Vasilii. *Maiakovskii: Khronika zhizni i deiatel'nosti*, fifth ed. Moscow: Sovetskii pisatel', 1985.

Khan-Magomedov, Selim. O. *INKhUK i ranii konstruktivizm*. Moscow: Architectura, 1994.

———. *Konstantin Mel'nikov*. Moscow: Stroiizdat, 1990.

———. *Konstruktivizm: kontseptsiia formoobrazovaniia*. Moscow: Stroiizdat, 2003.

———. *Pionery sovetskogo dizaina*. Moscow: Galart, 1995.

———. *Rodchenko: The Complete Work*. Trans. Huw Evans, from the Italian. Cambridge, Mass.: MIT Press, 1987.

Kiaer, Christina. "Boris Arvatov's Socialist Objects." *October* 81 (1997): 105–118.

———. "Delivered from Capitalism: Nostalgia, Alienation, and the Future of Reproduction in Tret'iakov's *I Want a Child!*" In Christina Kiaer and Eric Naiman, eds., *Everyday Life in Early Soviet Russia: Taking the Revolution Inside*, 183–216. Bloomington: Indiana University Press, 2005.

———, trans. Boris Arvatov. "Everyday Life and the Culture of the Thing (Toward the

Formulation of the Question)." *October* 81 (summer 1997): 119–128.

Kiaer, Christina, and Eric Naiman, eds. *Everyday Life in Early Soviet Russia: Taking the Revolution Inside.* Bloomington: Indiana University Press, 2005.

Klein, Melanie. "Some Theoretical Conclusions Regarding the Emotional Life of the Infant." In *Developments in Psychoanalysis*, 198–236, ed. Joan Riviere. New York: Da Capo Press, 1983.

Klein, Richard. *Cigarettes Are Sublime.* Durham: Duke University Press, 1993.

Krauss, Rosalind. *The Originality of the Avant-Garde and Other Modernist Myths.* Cambridge, Mass.: MIT Press, 1985.

Lajer-Burcharth, Ewa. "Pompadour's Touch: Difference in Representation." *Representations* 73 (winter 2001): 54–88.

Lavrent'ev, A. N. "Poeziia graficheskogo dizaina v tvorchestve Varvary Stepanovoi." *Tekhnicheskaia estetika* 12 (1978): 22–26.

Lavrentiev, Alexander. *Varvara Stepanova: The Complete Work.* Trans. Wendy Salmond. Cambridge, Mass.: MIT Press, 1988.

———, and Yuri V. Nasarov. *Russian Design: Tradition and Experiment, 1920–1990.* Trans. Flora Fischer, from the German. London: Academy Editions, 1995.

Lebina, Natalia B., and Mikhail V. Shkarovskii. *Prostitutsiia v Peterburge.* Moscow: Progress-Akademiia, 1994.

Lenin, Vladimir. *What Is to Be Done?* Trans. S.V. Utechin and Patricia Utechin; ed., with an introduction and notes, by S.V. Utechin. Oxford: Clarendon Press, 1963.

Lodder, Christina. *Russian Constructivism.* New Haven: Yale University Press, 1983.

———. "The VKhUTEMAS and the Bauhaus." In *The Avant-Garde Frontier: Russia Meets the West, 1910–1930*, 196–237, ed. Gail Harrison Roman and Virginia Hagelstein Marquardt. Gainesville: University Press of Florida, 1992.

Lyotard, Jean-François. "Espace Plastique et Espace Politique." In his *Dérive à Partir de Marx et Freud*, 276–304. Paris: Union Générale d'Éditions, 1973.

Maiakovskii, Vladimir. *Pro Eto.* Facsimile edition of original publication of the poem with English and German translations. Introduction by Aleksandr Lavrent'ev. Berlin: Ars Nicolai, 1994.

Margolin, Victor. *The Struggle for Utopia: Rodchenko, Lissitzky, Moholy-Nagy: 1917–1946.* Chicago: University of Chicago Press, 1997.

Marx, Karl. *Capital*, vol. I. Trans. Ben Fowkes. New York: Vintage, 1977.

———. "Concerning Feuerbach." In *Early Writings*, 421–423, trans. Rodney Livingstone and Gregor Benton. London: Penguin, 1974.

———. *Grundrisse: Foundations of the Critique of Political Economy (Rough Draft).* Trans. Martin Nicolaus. Middlesex: Penguin, 1973.

Matich, Olga. "Remaking the Bed: Utopia in Daily Life." In *Laboratory of Dreams: The Russian Avant-Garde and Cultural Experiment*, 59–78, ed. John Bowlt and Olga Matich. Stanford: Stanford University Press, 1996.

Matsa, Ivan. *Sovetskoe iskusstvo za 15 let: materialy i dokumentatsiia.* Moscow and Leningrad: Ogiz-Izogiz, 1933.

Minh-ha, Trinh T. *Woman, Native, Other: Writing, Postcoloniality, and Feminism.* Bloomington: Indiana University Press, 1989.

Mitchell, W. J. T. *Iconology: Image, Text, Ideology.* Chicago and London: Chicago University Press, 1986.

Mulvey, Laura. "Some Thoughts on Theories of Fetishism in the Context of Contemporary Culture." *October* 65 (1993): 3–20.

Naiman, Eric. *Sex in Public: The Incarnation of Soviet Ideology.* Princeton: Princeton University Press, 1997.

Neil, Jonathan. "Advertising Diction: Russian Constructivist Cigarette Advertising during the New Economic Policy (NEP)."

Unpublished paper. Columbia University, Department of Art History and Archaeology, 1997.

Nisbet, Peter, ed. *El Lissitzky, 1890–1941: Catalogue for an Exhibition of Selected Works from North American Collections, the Sprengel Museum Hanover, and the Staatliche Galerie Moritzburg Halle.* Cambridge, Mass.: Harvard University Art Museums, 1987.

Noever, Peter, ed. *Rodchenko–Stepanova: Budushchee—edinstvennaia nasha tsel'.* Munich: Prestel Verlag, 1991.

Ockman, Joan, ed. *Architecture, Criticism, Ideology.* Princeton: Princeton Architectural Press, 1985.

Peirce, C. S. *Collected Papers of Charles Peirce.* Ed. Charles Hartshorne and Paul Weiss. Cambridge, Mass.: Harvard University Press, 1931–1958.

Pietz, William. "The Problem of the Fetish, pt. 1." *Res* 9 (spring 1985): 5–17.

Plekhanov, Georgii. *The Development of the Monist View of History, Selected Philosophical Works,* vol. 1. Trans. Andrew Rothstein. Moscow: Progress, 1974.

Pollock, Griselda. *Differencing the Canon: Feminist Desire and the Writing of Art's Histories.* London and New York: Routledge, 1999.

Punin, Nikolai. *O Tatline.* Ed. I. N. Punina and V. I. Rakitin. Moscow: Literaturnoe-khudozhestvennoe agenstvo "RA," 1994.

Rodchenko, Aleksandr, and Varvara Stepanova. "Letters to and from Paris (1925)." Trans. Galina Varese with Mike Weaver and Galin Tihanov. *History of Photography* 24, no. 4 (winter 2000): 317–332.

Roman, Gail Harrison. "Tatlin's Tower: Revolutionary Symbol and Aesthetic." In *The Avant-Garde Frontier: Russia Meets the West, 1910–1930,* 45–64, ed. Gail Harrison Roman and Virginia Hagelstein Marquardt. Gainesville: University Press of Florida, 1992.

Russian Women of the Avant-Garde, 1910–1930: Exhibition, December 1979–March 1980. Cologne: Die Galerie, 1979.

Rybchenkov, Boris. "Rasskazy B. F. Rybchenkova." In *Prostranstvo kartiny: Sbornik statei,* 293–298, ed. Natalia Tamruchi. Moscow: Sovetskii khudozhnik, 1989.

Sarabianov, Dmitri V., and Natalia L. Adaskina. *Popova.* Trans. Marian Schwartz. New York: Henry N. Abrams, 1990.

Schick, Christine. "LEF and the West: Constructivism and Dada in Rodchenko's *Pro Eto.*" Unpublished paper. University of California, Berkeley, Department of History of Art, 2000.

Sharp, Jane. *Russian Modernism between East and West: Natal'ia Goncharova and the Moscow Avant-Garde, 1905–1914.* Cambridge: Cambridge University Press, 2005.

Shklovsky, Victor. *Mayakovsky and His Circle.* Trans. and ed. Lily Feiler. New York: Dodd, Mead, 1972.

Sidorina, Elena. *Skvoz' ves' dvadtsatyi vek: khudozhestvenno-proektnye kontseptsii russkogo avangarda.* Moscow: Russkii mir, 1994.

Starr, S. Frederick. *K. Mel'nikov: Le Pavillon Sovietique.* Paris: L'Equerre, 1981.

———. *Melnikov: Solo Architect in a Mass Society.* Princeton: Princeton University Press, 1978.

———. *Red and Hot: The Fate of Jazz in the Soviet Union, 1917–1980.* New York: Oxford University Press, 1983.

Stephan, Halina. *"Lef" and the Left Front of the Arts.* Slavistische Beitrage, vol. 142. Munich: Sagner, 1981.

Stites, Richard. *The Women's Liberation Movement in Russia: Feminism, Nihilism, and Bolshevism, 1860–1930.* Princeton: Princeton University Press, 1978.

Strigalev, Anatoli, and Jürgen Harten. *Vladimir Tatlin Retrospketive.* Cologne: DuMont Buchverlas, 1992.

Strizhenova, Tatiana. *Soviet Costume and Textiles,*

1917–1945. Trans. Era Mozolkova. Moscow, Paris, Verona: Flammarion, 1991.

Tafuri, Manfredo. "U.S.S.R.–Berlin, 1922: From Populism to 'Constructivist International.'" In *Architecture, Criticism, Ideology*, 121–181, ed. Joan Ockman. Princeton: Princeton Architectural Press, 1985.

Tamruchi, Natalia, ed. *Prostranstvo kartiny: Sbornik statei*. Moscow: Sovetskii khudozhnik, 1989.

Toh, Shauna. "Mayakovsky's Interface with *Byt*." Unpublished paper. Columbia University, Department of Art History and Archaeology, 1997.

Tupitsyn, Margarita, with contributions by Matthew Drutt and Ulrich Pohlmann. *El Lissitzky: Beyond the "Abstract Cabinet": Photography, Design, Collaboration*. New Haven and London: Yale University Press, 1999.

Valiuzhenich, Anatolii, ed. *Osip Maksimovich Brik: Materialy k biografii*. Akmola, Kazakhstan: Niva, 1993.

Wagner, Anne. *Three Artists (Three Women): Modernism and the Art of Hesse, Krasner, and O'Keeffe*. Berkeley: University of California Press, 1996.

Wiener, Jon. *Come Together: John Lennon in His Time*. Urbana and Chicago: University of Illinois Press, 1984.

Williams, Beryl. "Kollontai and After: Women in the Russian Revolution." In *Women, State, and Revolution: Essays on Power and Gender in Europe since 1789*, 60–70, ed. Siân Reynolds. Brighton, Sussex: Wheatsheaf, 1986.

Winnicott, D. W. "Transitional Objects and Transitional Phenomena: A Study of the First Not-Me Possession." *Yearbook of Psychoanalysis* 10 (1954): 64–80.

Wood, Elizabeth A. *The Baba and the Comrade: Gender and Politics in Revolutionary Russia*. Bloomington: Indiana University Press, 1997.

Wood, Paul. "Art and Politics in a Workers' State." *Art History* 8, no. 1 (1985): 105–124.

———. "The Politics of the Avant-Garde." In *The Great Utopia: The Russian and Soviet Avant-Garde, 1915–1932*, 1–24. New York: Guggenheim Museum, 1992.

Yablonskaya, M. N. *Women Artists of Russia's New Age, 1900–1935*. London: Thames and Hudson, 1990.

Zalambani, Maria. "L'art dans la production. Le débat sur le productivisme en Russie soviétique pendant les années vingt." *Annales: Histoire, Sciences Sociales* 52, no. 1 (1997): 41–61.

———. "Boris Arvatov, théoricien du productivisme." *Cahiers du monde russe* 40 no. 3 (1999): 415–446.

Zhadova, Larissa Alekseevna, ed. *Tatlin*. New York: Rizzoli, 1988.

———. "Tatlin—proektirovshchik material'noi kul'tury." *Sovetskoe dekorativnoe iskusstvo* 77/78 (1980): 204–234.

INDEX

Page numbers in italics indicate images.